'We can all be very grateful ... to ... Martin Stannard's thorough investigation of [Spark's] life. He never loses his affection for [her] or his admiration for her books ... fascinating on the religious journey'
A. N. Wilson, *Reader's Digest* Books of the Month

'Stannard is particularly interesting on Spark's early, unredeemed years ... a gifted biographer with a fine turn of phrase' *Independent*

'A brilliant work of scholarship and a testament to its author's graft'
New Statesman

'Compelling on the novels themselves' *Guardian*

'A biography to be savoured by the initiate, bringing out her complexities and idiosyncrasies' Ian Rankin, *Scotsman*

'This long, detailed and thoroughly researched biography unpicks professorially the correspondences between Muriel's experience and her fiction' *Literary Review*

'The time is right for a Spark revival ... An authority on Waugh and Greene, Stannard is well-placed to exploit his exclusive access to archives and interviewees ... he is perceptive on her novels' *Economist*

'Stannard has skilfully woven the novels into the chronology and context of her life. His technique involves considerable insight' *Country Life*

'In his abundant researches, Prof Stannard alerts today's reader to just how real and perfected this great writer's achievement was' *Irish Times*

'Exceptionally well written and lively ... we must believe that The Divine Spark herself has inspired the author ... Stannard has really analysed the roots of Spark's conversion and of her belief with perception and intelligence' Robin Baird-Smith (Muriel Spark's publisher), *Tablet*

'An intriguing and sympathetic portrait of a woman who was much more passionate than she led people to believe' *Scotland on Sunday*

'[A] riveting account, but more importantly makes the reader eager to discover her novels, just as a good literary biography should'
Waterstone's Books Quarterly

'It was Martin Stannard's engrossing new biography *Muriel Spark* that sent me back to her stories'
Helen Simpson, Best Books of the Year, *Granta*

'A warts and all picture of this endlessly beguiling author ... he is particularly good on the early years before Spark became a bestselling novelist and celebrity, and he does not shy away from the foibles that made her a difficult personality' *Sunday Herald*

Martin Stannard is Professor of Modern English Literature at the University of Leicester. He is a Fellow of the Royal Society of Literature and author of an acclaimed two-volume biography of Evelyn Waugh.

MURIEL SPARK

The Biography

MARTIN STANNARD

PHOENIX

A PHOENIX PAPERBACK

First published in Great Britain in 2009
by Weidenfeld & Nicolson
This paperback edition published in 2010
by Phoenix,
an imprint of Orion Books Ltd,
Orion House, 5 Upper St Martin's Lane,
London WC2H 9EA

An Hachette UK company

1 3 5 7 9 10 8 6 4 2

A CIP catalogue record for this book
is available from the British Library.

ISBN 978-0-7538-2749-9

Typeset by Input Data Services Ltd, Bridgwater, Somerset

Printed and bound in Great Britain by
CPI Mackays, Chatham, Kent

Permission from Muriel Spark's estate to quote from
unpublished material is gratefully acknowledged
© Copyright Administration 2009.

Permission to quote from Muriel Spark's published works
is also gratefully acknowledged.

Permission to quote from unpublished material by Howard Sergeant
is gratefully acknowledged © Estate of Howard Sergeant 2009.

The Orion Publishing Group's policy is to use papers
that are natural, renewable and recyclable products and
made from wood grown in sustainable forests. The logging
and manufacturing processes are expected to conform to
the environmental regulations of the country of origin.

www.orionbooks.co.uk

CONTENTS

List of Illustrations   ix

Acknowledgements   xi

Preface: The Cake Be Damned   xv

1   Night and Day: 1962–1918   1

2   Home and Away: 1918–1937   19

3   Out of Africa: 1937–1945   45

4   Finding a Voice: 1945–1949   74

5   Kensington: 1949–1951   99

6   Sacramental: 1951–1954   124

7   Conversion: 1954–1957   152

8   Acquiring Lorgnettes: 1957–1959   178

9   Exposure: 1959–1960   204

10   Transfiguration: 1960–1962   232

11   Time / Life: 1962–1963   264

12   Amours de Voyage: 1963–1965   291

13   Looking Round: 1965–1968   318

14   In the Driver's Seat: 1968–1970   344

15   Lucrezia Borgia in Trousers: 1971–1974   372

16   The Realm of Mythology: 1974–1979   400

17   Goodbye, Goodbye, Goodbye, Good*bye*: 1979–1982   427

18 A Speck in the Distance: 1982–1988   453

19 Settling the Bill: 1988–1992   479

20 Dark Music: 1992–2006   506

Epilogue   533
Note on References   537
Endnotes   539
Select Bibliography   585
Index   601

ILLUSTRATIONS

Section One

Adelaide Uezzell (Estate of Muriel Spark)

Tom Uezzell with Cissy (Estate of Muriel Spark)

Louis Camberg (Brian Godfrey)

Henrietta Camberg (Brian Godfrey)

Watford shop (Estate of Muriel Spark)

Philip and Alice Uezzell (Estate of Phyllis Batchelor)

Cambergs during the First World War (Estate of Phyllis Batchelor)

James Gillespie's Girls' School, Junior Class, 1930 (Estate of Frances Cowell)

Muriel aged 10 (Estate of Muriel Spark)

Muriel being crowned 'Queen of Poetry', 1932 (National Library of Scotland)

Philip Camberg (Estate of Philip Camberg)

Bernard and Sarah Camberg (Estate of Philip Camberg)

Muriel in 1940 (National Library of Scotland)

Muriel with Robin in Africa (National Library of Scotland)

Muriel in 1948 (Estate of Howard Sergeant)

Howard and Jean Sergeant (Estate of Howard Sergeant)

Poetry reading (Keystone)

Muriel with Derek Stanford (Estate of Iris Birtwistle)

Muriel's despatch book (National Library of Scotland / Estate of Muriel Spark)

St Jude's Cottage (Martin Stannard)

Edwina and Alan Barnsley in 1958 (Edwina Barnsley)

Muriel with Tiny Lazzari (Estate of Muriel Spark)

Christine Brooke-Rose (Ida Kar / National Portrait Gallery)

Alan Maclean (National Library of Scotland)

Muriel in her Camberwell attic (Frank Monaco, Rex Features)

Elizabeth Rosenberg, June and Neville Braybrooke, 1953 (Francis King)

Muriel outside the Macmillan offices, 1961 (Mark Gerson)

Section Two

Muriel in the Knopf offices, New York (Harding Lemay)

Evelyn Waugh, 1960 (Rex Features)

Graham Greene, 1974 (Rex Features)

Rayner Heppenstall

Brendan Gill (Nancy Crampton)

Howard Moss (Nancy Crampton)

William Shawn (*New Yorker* magazine)

Shirley Hazzard (Alfred Knopf)

Beaux Arts Hotel, New York (Shirley Hazzard / Estate of Muriel Spark)

Muriel with Ivan von Auw (Harold Ober Associates)

Blanche Knopf (Alfred Knopf)

Muriel at Keats's grave (photo by Eugene Walter, property of George Nicholson)

Muriel in 1970 (Jerry Bauer)

Eugene Walter (Michelangelo Durazzo)

George Armstrong

Brian de Breffny (George Mott)

Dario Ambrosiani and Zev (Estate of Dario Ambrosiani)

Muriel in India (George Mott)

Muriel and Penelope Jardine, *c.* 1979 (Estate of Frank Tuohy)

Muriel in February 2002 (Ulf Andersen, Getty Images)

While every effort has been made to trace copyright holders, if any have inadvertently been overlooked the publishers will be happy to acknowledge them in future editions.

ACKNOWLEDGEMENTS

Over the decade it took to research and write this book, hundreds of people have generously helped me to trace witnesses, archives, publications, and to secure permissions. As there is no space to name them all, I must begin by apologising to all those not mentioned below.

First on my list must come Dame Muriel Spark herself without whose consent, encouragement and active assistance I could have done nothing. She patiently answered my questions, offered interviews, and engaged in a huge correspondence. The terms of the legal agreement between us were extraordinarily generous, granting me exclusive rights as her biographer, extensive free quotation from her published work and an unspecified amount from her unpublished writings, including letters. She demanded no veto beyond the right to withdraw the imprimatur of 'authorised biography'. She even extended the time-limit on the agreement to allow me as much space as I needed to complete the work properly, and used up a great deal of her own time helping me to revise the first draft. Penelope Jardine, Dame Muriel's companion, has been equally kind, putting me up (and putting up with me) at their home in Tuscany, extending this invitation to my family, and, again, answering many tedious enquiries. Both women suffered the biografiend with benevolent fortitude and good humour.

Next come those others whose support has kept me going. For financial assistance I thank the Arts Council for a Writer's Award; the British Academy for two grants: one to start and one to complete the work; the Harry Ransom Humanities Research Center for an Andrew Mellon Research Fellowship; the Leverhulme Trust for a Research Fellowship; the Society of Authors for an Author's Foundation Award; the University of Leicester for granting me three study-leaves; and Weidenfeld & Nicolson and Norton for their advances. My editors, Ion Trewin then Ben Buchan then Bea Hemming at Weidenfeld, Mary Cunnane then Amy Cherry at Norton, have been exemplary, as has my agent, Araminta

Whitley. For assistance with typing and for research I must thank Catherine Burgass, Lauren James, Rory Waterman and Claire Watson; for similar work and for so much more, Angie Kendall and Sylvia Ouditt. Alex Moseley and Sandy Pearson reformatted the text, Jane Birkett copy-edited it and Douglas Matthews compiled the index. Throughout, I have had secretarial help from Leicester University's Department of English, and unflagging support – financial, intellectual and moral – from the department in general, especially Nick Everett, Richard Foulkes, Bill Myers, Vincent Newey, Julian North, Emma Parker, Mark Rawlinson, Felicity Rosslyn, Joanne Shattock, Philip Shaw, Victoria Stewart, Elaine Treharne and Greg Walker. Other scholars who have offered invaluable advice include David Bradshaw, Bryan Cheyette, Kelvin Everest, Peter Keating, Sir Frank Kermode, Rick Rylance, Valerie Shaw, Patricia Waugh and Nigel Wood. My greatest resource, however, has been my family: my partner, Sharon Ouditt, my children, Zuleika and Leo, my brother and sister, John and Josephine, and my cousin, Charlotte Hart, all of whom have endured my passion for Muriel Spark with grace and love.

For lengthy formal interviews (those who also loaned letters or other documentation are marked '*') I thank the following: Gillon Aitken, Paul Allen*, the late Dario Ambrosiani*, the late George Armstrong, Robin Baird-Smith, Edwina Barnsley*, the late Phyllis Batchelor*, John Bayliss, the late Iris Birtwistle*, Georges Borchardt, the late June and Neville Braybrooke*, Christine Brooke-Rose*, the late Philip Camberg*, Pamela Carrigan*, the late Tristram Cary*, Igor de Chroustchoff*, Prof. Morton Cohen*, the late Frances Cowell, the late Lionel Daiches, Kathleen Farrell, Hugh Fleetwood, the late Christopher Fry, the late Brendan Gill, Peter Ginna, Brian Godfrey, Robert Greacen, Prof. Janet Groth*, Don Gualtiero Mazzeschi, the late Sir John Heath-Stubbs, Robert Henderson, the late Isabelle Holland, Joseph Kanon, Peter Kemp, William Koshland, Peter (Harding) Lemay, Joseph McCrindle, Harry McDowell, Charles McGrath, John McGreal, O. Carm., the late Alan Maclean*, Robin Maclean, Elizabeth Malcolm, the late William Maxwell, Peter Mayer, Ved Mehta, the late James Michie, George Mott*, George Nicholson*, Ned O'Gorman, Peter Owen, the late Jerzy

Peterkiewicz, Peter Prescott, Phyllis Price, Elizabeth Rosenberg*, Margaret Sachs, Sam Sacks, Faith Sale, the late Nora Sayre, the late Jean Sergeant*, the late Father Brocard Sewell*, Jeffrey Smart, the late Clare M. Smith*, Corlies M. Smith, the late Derek Stanford*, Shirley Hazzard Steegmuller*, Saul Steinberg, the late Hon. Guy Strutt*, Raleigh Trevelyan, the late Frank Tuohy*, Diane M. Uezzell, the late Roger Uezzell, Tom Wallace, the late Eugene Walter, the late Auberon Waugh*, William Weaver, Vicki Weissman, Joan Winterkorn, Alan D. Williams, Jon Wynne-Tyson*, and Robert and Linda Yeatman.

Other letters and / or documentation / information / advice were supplied by: Audrey Adaway, Simonetta Berbeglia, Bernard Bergonzi, Muriel Berman, BBC Written Archives Centre (Mike Websell), David Camberg, Duncan Cloud, Peter Conradi, Constable Publishers (Carol O'Brien), Father Kit Cunningham, David Daiches, University of Delaware Library, Special Collections (L. Rebecca Johnson Melvin and Anita Wellner), Mark Downie, Sally Festing, Colin Finlayson, Mark Gerson, Prof. Neil Grill, the late John Guest, Harold Ober Associates, the Harry Ransom Humanities Research Center of the University of Texas at Austin (Cliff Farrington, Cathy Henderson, Thomas F. Staley), Father J. D. P. Hare, Heriot-Watt University (Brian D. Kelvin), Kenneth Hillier, Rupert Hodson, Bruce Hunter, Michael Joseph, Betty Kane, Lauinger Library Special Collections, Georgetown University, Washington DC (Michael North, Nicholas Scheetz), Mark Le Fanu, Michael Lister, the McFarlin Library, Special Collections, University of Tulsa (Kay Calkins, Lori N. Curtis, Sidney Huttner), Jean Macpherson, *The Month* (Tim Noble, SJ), the National Library of Scotland (Robin Smith), Aubrey Newman, Paul Newman, Josephine O'Brien, the *Observer* (Molloy Woodcraft), Norman Page, Princeton University Libraries (Alice V. Clark, Margaret M. Sherry, Dr Don Skemer), Flora Rich, The Robert Woodruff Library for Advanced Studies, Emory University, Atlanta, Georgia, St Michael's College, Vermont (Michelle McCaffrey), Wilfred Sheed, Rosemary Sheed Middleton, Susan Sheehan, Ian Shein, the late Richard Swift, University of Victoria Library Special Collection, Victoria BC (Howard E. Gerwing, Chris Petter), the late John Updike, Washington University in St Louis Library, Special Collections (Alison Carrick), Angela Williams.

In addition to those above who have allowed the use of copyright material, thanks are also due to the following for copyright permission: Judith Attfield, Arthur Batchelor, Sister Reingard Berger, OP, Anita Brookner, Richard Copsey, O. Carm., J. P. Donleavy, Margaret Drabble, Donald Fraser Foord, Lindy Foord, Holly Gill, David Higham Associates, Macmillan Publishers, Victoria Orr Ewing, The Peggy Ramsay Foundation, Peters, Fraser & Dunlop Group Ltd., Isobel Poole, Rogers, Coleridge & White Ltd., Julia M. Rowlandson, Martin Shipperlee, OSB, Emma Tennant, and A. N. Wilson.

The Cake Be Damned

With Graham Greene and Evelyn Waugh, Muriel Spark completed a grand triumvirate of Catholic-convert novelists. After Greene's death in 1991, she was often described as 'the greatest living British writer', and both her predecessors were awed by her talent. She was something of a monument in the literary establishment yet, like Greene, was also subversive of institutions, an exile and an enigma. For four decades, since the *New Yorker* devoted an entire issue to *The Prime of Miss Jean Brodie* in 1961, she was a celebrity on both sides of the Atlantic – but a quiet celebrity. Although she could count W. H. Auden, Iris Murdoch, John Updike and Tennessee Williams among her fans, her readers rarely found her on a TV chat show or even on the radio. In interviews her various public images remained polished and impenetrable. Her writing was both popular and experimental, the opposite of confessional. So when her autobiography, *Curriculum Vitae*, was announced in 1992 it became a literary 'event' and an immediate best-seller. Jacqueline Kennedy Onassis, then an editor at Doubleday, offered $100,000 for world rights and was disappointed not to get them. Garbo speaks? Here, reviewers hoped, the real Muriel Spark would finally stand up.

She did – and she did not. Among journalists, her reputation was that of recluse: a mysterious figure whose biographical file was anorexic. Thus she entered the realm of mythology as a high priestess of English letters, intangible. This, though, represented only a half-truth – about the woman who would appear for the press or, when writing, disappear from an otherwise active social life. She disliked public speaking, always deflected attempts to discuss her private life. A writer needs fame for survival and she suffered limited publicity ventures. But fame also brought interference from an army of time-wasters, from betrayals: the sale of her letters, the leaking of stories. She fought back when people dared to discuss her, rather than her work, as a public property. It was, she insisted, *her* life, and she was determined to control it.

Obsession with factual accuracy was characteristic. 'Details fascinate me. I love to pile up details. They create an atmosphere.'[1] Yet the details of her childhood were obscure. She remembered them in her auto-biography, rather as Greene did in A *Sort of Life*, as colours, tastes, smells, epiphanies, but without his wilful fabulation. She recalled the aroma of baking bread, explained the variety of loaves, how many pennies constituted a shilling, how to make a good pot of tea: a bread-and-butter existence. Her parents and brother loom in and out of the narrative like ghosts. We learn little of people's appearance or of their working lives. A young American couple, Professor and Mrs Rule, 'stayed with us for a time'[2] – we are not told in what capacity – then returned to the States. Mrs Rule taught Muriel to read. Of the constant callers, 'the immense list of characters who peopled our lives, and who largely ignored me',[3] the more exotic are itemised; some, heard of only by report, given a brief history. Those who failed to attract her attention had 'no colour, no taste, no smell'.[4]

Slowly, abstractly, an image resolves into half-focus of a clever, red-haired Scottish girl acutely aware of social distinction, well-behaved, overweight, with an eye for the fantastic and the grotesque, an ear for the invigorating non sequitur. We learn something of her mother's family in Watford, near London, almost nothing of her father's in her home city, Edinburgh. Her father she remembered as a kindly, dapper man who blew smoke-rings from his cigarette, made shadow-rabbits on the wall, and once stopped her crying by wiping imaginary tears from her dolls' eyes. If she were late home, he would dress up in a ghost-sheet and pretend to be frightening. Her mother was characterised as nervous, superstitious, showy. She was English and embarrassed Muriel by her accent and over-dressing: 'decidedly out of place amongst the northern worthies who came to collect my friends.'[5] Her father, on the other hand, 'wore the same sort of clothes as the other fathers and spoke as they did, about the same things. He was an engineer. I still have the contract of his seven-year apprenticeship signed, in schoolboy calligraphy, "Bertie Camberg".'[6]

Most reviewers were enchanted yet simultaneously frustrated. 'As an account of a writer's formation,' Anita Brookner remarked, '*Curriculum Vitae* is clearly disappointing.'[7] Jenny Turner, in an otherwise glorious eulogy, thought that it did not represent anything 'very frank and sustained'.[8] Victoria Glendinning hit the nail squarely: 'One cannot tell from this book which people, if any, she loved with passion.'[9] But that, as Turner implied, was not the point. 'Although it skates over many things about which eager beavers may want to know more: Muriel's disastrous teenage marriage [...]; her twenties in Rhodesia [...]; her son from that marriage [...] none of this is anybody's business but Spark's own.'[10] The title was precise. A CV is a public account of one's career, suggesting continuous progress. The function of this book was not self-examination but to set the record straight. There is no suffering or embarrassment here, no complaint. Like a ministerial statement, it reveals only as much information as is necessary for correction and discreetly clouds the rest with neutral facts. It does not lie. It does not invent. Its *faux naïf* tone is deceptively ingenious but never deceptive. Excerpts were first published in the *New Yorker*. Introducing Muriel's reading from the book, Charles McGrath mentioned that the magazine's scrupulous fact-checking department had scoured the text for inaccuracies. None was found.[11]

Curriculum Vitae, however, is a much subtler book than this might suggest. The details it withholds – notably of her religious conversion – are as implicitly important as those unveiled. Absence defines presence. She reviews her early life both with the eyes of a child, open to the wonder of childhood, its blinkered vision, its egotism, and with the sharp detachment of the mature writer. It is a Proustian narrative. The child and the woman are strangers to each other, yet are halves of the same personality. Given that she restricts herself to writing only about that which she can document or verify by living witnesses, she restrains her inventive power and acknowledges a distinction between autobiography and fiction. 'Truth,' she states, '[...] especially in a work of non-fiction [...] is to be cherished.'[12] At the same time, though, no one acquainted with her fiction can ignore its persistent suggestion that there are as many kinds of truth as there are observers in a world where evil and stupidity are ubiquitous. A structural irony thus develops between what can be known through observation and documentation, and what is true: reality.

I asked her once about the relation between fact and fiction in her writing. 'Three of my novels', she replied, 'are very much *nouveaux romans*. [...] I rather liked [Robbe-Grillet]'s idea of the novel [... that] you leave out "he felt" [...] – no thoughts or feelings. You're just observing, that's all. A sighter. You're only seeing what people do. You read between the lines what they think [...]. We've got no right whatsoever to say [...] what they're thinking, feeling, because you don't know. [...] It really gives you another dimension because people fill it in.' I remarked that her novels accumulated a mass of circumstantial detail but, unlike similar details in realist writing, they told us little of the characters' motivations. 'Details are important,' she replied, 'to give a tone of authenticity.' 'But is authenticity the same thing as truth?' 'No. It's just that it's plausible.'[13]

Similar principles apply to *Curriculum Vitae*. She had, of course, strong feelings about those who peopled her first thirty-nine years but, examining herself as a stranger, and with limited data, refused to guarantee the authenticity of her or anyone else's feelings and thus largely omitted them. Her readers must fill those in. All she could offer was the authenticity of facts while simultaneously hinting that 'reality' for her lay elsewhere, somehow connected to these data but in a fashion about which she considered it inappropriate to speculate in non-fiction. When she did wish to speculate, the only legitimate field for this was fiction. Her fiction is her life reconstructed, sometimes with versions of herself as heroine: an extended exercise in self-justification. Literary composition to her was not merely a profession, it was a compulsion. She would have done it had she been starving. She did it for years when she *was* nearly starving. If we want to see this side of her – the passionate artist concealed in her autobiography, the woman consumed by a controlled fury with those who obstructed her work or tried to talk her down, the celebrator of female strength, style and subversive wit, the mystic and the sibyl – we must turn to novels like *The Comforters* (1957), *Robinson* (1958), *The Mandelbaum Gate* (1965), *Loitering with Intent* (1981) and *A Far Cry from Kensington* (1988). Two short stories, 'The First Year of My Life'[14] and 'The Gentile Jewesses'[15] (see Chapter 1) are also important to any account of her origins.

In 'The First Year of My Life', she imagines her infant consciousness. The tale is partly a fantasy:

> You will shortly be hearing of that new school of psychology [...] which [...] has established that all of the young of the human species are born omniscient. Babies, in their waking hours, know everything that is going on everywhere in the world; they can tune in on any conversation they choose, switch on to any scene. We have all experienced this power. It is only after the first year that it is brainwashed out of us [...].[16]

Here we have a typically unnerving and powerful comic invention (she was a 'magic realist' long before Angela Carter) that is also a metaphor for artistic vision. She often spoke of 'tuning in' to voices. Babies, she thought, had a strange wisdom in those eyes that followed one round the room. Autobiographical and historical 'facts' are welded on to these mysteries and the result is an abstract account of the formation of her mind. The dark side of Edinburgh is revealed, the macabre relish for truth which separated her from her polite environment. 'I was born', she writes, 'on the first day of the second month of the last year of the First World War [...]. Testimony abounds that during the first year of my life I never smiled.'[17] The story is about how she came to smile, not with joy but with sardonic glee.

'My autobiography [...] started in the very worst year that the world had ever seen so far.'[18] The historical backdrop is the 1918 German

Spring Offensive, conscripted soldiers leapfrogging corpses to be gassed, machine-gunned or simply to drown in mud, while Field Marshal Foch ('the old swine') declaimed: '*Tout le monde à la bataille!*'[19] The baby listens in to this, to pious nationalism in the House of Commons, and to the dominant literary figures of the day. All fail her. D. H. Lawrence ('Dreary old creeping Jesus') is preoccupied with the wish to be a fox; Conrad and Shaw are telling people to shut up; 'Virginia Woolf yawned and reached for her diary.'[20] At home the baby bangs her spoon irritably upon her high chair while her six-year-old brother struts with a toy rifle singing 'The Grand Old Duke of York'. She is surrounded by women, 'my mother or some other hoverer',[21] dressed in British black, who have somehow mislaid their husbands. They crowd and cluck, bounce her, trying to elicit a smile but she is 'not amused'.[22] Her mother's brother enters briefly, coughing, poison-gassed from the trenches, brass buttons gleaming, only to return to the conflict. Two verses structure the narrative as leit motifs: 'The Grand Old Duke of York' and 'I Have a Rendezvous with Death'. The first is the silliest song she has heard, epitomising the charade of the war; the second undercuts it, situating the whole sequence of events *sub specie aeternitatis.*

We see the world here through a consciousness discordant with every-thing. Her home is a trap; 'those black-dressed people, females of the species to which I appeared to belong',[23] offer not sisterly collusion but cloying sentimentality; and, as for the men, her father is absent, her brother a fool, and the 'strongest men on all fronts were dead before I was born'.[24] Most important in this equation, it seems, is the slaughter of the poets, and the irrelevance of the literary establishment. 'Generally, I preferred the Western Front where one got the true state of affairs. It was essential to know the worst, blood and explosions and all, for one had to be prepared [...].'[25]

During her first birthday party, beyond the Armistice, she still scowls. Her mother is 'obviously upset'. There is a gathering of opinionated folk for the occasion. A stout gentleman 'with his backside to the fire' approvingly quotes Asquith: '"All things have become new. In this great cleansing and purging it has been the privilege of our country to play her part ..."' 'That', she says, 'did it. I broke into a decided smile, and everyone noticed it [...].'[26] At that moment her brother had blown out the candle on her cake. This is assumed to be the cause of her sudden gaiety. But the narrator leaves us in no doubt: 'The cake be damned. Since that time I have grown to smile quite naturally like any other [...] house-trained person, but when I really mean a smile, deeply felt from the core, then [...] it comes in response to the words uttered in the House of Commons [...] by the distinguished, the immaculately dressed and the late Mr Asquith.'[27]

On first reading, *Curriculum Vitae* and 'The First Year of My Life' appear to offer conflicting accounts of Muriel's roots. They are, rather, companion pieces. Each suggests a different aspect of a personality in conflict. The first recounts the surface detail of facts and families, of struggle and success; the second, the time-space of the imagination and the spirit. That word 'time-space' was Muriel's invention (an inversion of Einstein's term), often used in her letters to describe the nebulous mental universe of the artist, half in, half out of the material world. *Curriculum Vitae* reports generously on her childhood sense of belonging and coherence, the origins of self-discipline and analytical thought in the city of David Hume. The short story echoes those, then unconscious, repressed irritations which ultimately necessitated her escape and confirmed her artistic nature. Oddly, it is the baby who suggests the mature consciousness. The infant is a Tiresias figure, 'bedridden and toothless'[28] who, like some ancient seer, appears to have foresuffered all. The girl in *Curriculum Vitae* has lost this wisdom – but by implication, only temporarily. The hard road she walked to recover it is behind her. Documents could recapture these troubles but not decently (or legally) during the lifetime of so many of the protagonists.

Throughout her life as a professional writer, Muriel harboured these documents. Her personal archive performed several functions. It was a record of business transactions, a research tool, a form of coded diary. For over fifty years, no one but her secretaries was allowed access to these files. Then, after completing *Curriculum Vitae*, she sold them to the National Library of Scotland. A decade before this, she had sold most of her literary manuscripts to the University of Tulsa.[29] But the NLS transaction was something quite different. She withheld very little. Shortly afterwards, she came to an arrangement with a biographer (me), demanding no favours, no flattery, no veto. Her agent suggested that she take a cut of the advance. She refused. She did not wish to be involved in the process beyond the terms of the agreement.

The Edinburgh archive is extraordinary. One's initial reaction might echo Brookner's: 'As an account of a writer's formation [it] is clearly disappointing.' There are no soul-searching diaries. The thousands of letters are mainly fan mail, business correspondence, chatty scrawls from her mother, emotive literary criticism from her lover, the poet Derek Stanford; they concern social and travel arrangements, odd glimpses of those (often humble) figures who constituted her circle of friends. Letters from the grander literati – Greene, Murdoch, Updike, Waugh, Williams et al. – are amiable, admiring, but brief and essentially formal because she knew none of them intimately. Perhaps a quarter of this tonnage of paper constitutes ephemera: bills for everything from groceries to hairdressing; Post Office books, bank statements, cheque stubs; greetings telegrams, shopping and party lists, Christmas cards. She hoarded everything. In *Loitering with Intent*, Fleur Talbot does the same thing: 'Why did I keep these letters? Why? They are all neatly bundled up in thin folders, tied with pink tape, 1949, 1950, 1951 and on and on. I was trained to be a secretary; maybe I felt that letters ought to be filed, and I'm sure I thought they would be interesting one day. In fact, they aren't very interesting in themselves.'[30]

Although the novel supplies no answer to Fleur's question, the Edinburgh papers suggest several responses. Writing was principally a vocation to Muriel but it was also a business. The very ordinariness of these documents reminds us of both her long apprenticeship and of the hard bargaining this had taught her. They stress the impoverished and un-literary nature of her origins and, for the fourth decade, provide details of her clothes, diet, and rent. From doctors' and pharmacists' bills, we learn of stoically played-down illnesses and operations. These details reveal the grit around which grew the pearls of her fiction: rows with publishers and lovers; vindictive poets; a burnt dress. Nothing was wasted. And it says something when one discovers a Fortnum & Mason receipt for a small, expensive pot of jam during a period of her direst penury. Like Fleur, she would not be deflected and, surmounting all obstacles, went on her way rejoicing.

The archive represents the fabric of her daily life. Like everyone else's material existence, it is clotted with tedium and discretion. Her own contributions tend to be carbon copies of business letters. Diaries were for appointments, not self-reflection. Just twice the mask cracks, releasing bottled and preserved anger: once with an intrusive Italian landlady, once with someone who physically assaulted her. Usually the persona is that of the tough working woman: industrious, ambitious, and with a fierce eye for detail. What is lacking here, of course, is her personal correspondence. This was often handwritten out of courtesy. She kept few copies. When the two are matched, a complex personality emerges which constantly flies by the nets of material considerations. And here, at last, we recognise the voice of so many of her female characters: the simple, complicated wisdom, sharply funny at the expense of hypocrisy.

Ultimately, there is no simple answer to Fleur's question. Rather, a variety of often contradictory impulses suggest themselves. And from behind these, something else emerges: the sense of a woman alone in the world amid comfortless strangers, isolated yet invigorated by her artistic vision. When in 1954 she suffered alarming hallucinations, she fought her own way out of the crisis. She was a survivor, a phoenix rising from the ashes of past lives, and this resilience was attractive. She made many friends, often among the young. But her life was also littered with disputes because she refused to concede to anyone the power to intimidate or correct her. A sense of threats resisted hangs over these papers. Most importantly, perhaps, her archive was the ultimate defence against misappropriation and betrayal. Enemies would lie at their peril: she had the records.

The penultimate chapter of this book explains how I fell into her life – not that I ever became part of it. Why this intensely private person should have invited someone to write her biography remains mysterious. She had grown bored with the research involved in writing her own account. Perhaps she simply wanted someone to finish the job. Was this a way of putting her literary house in order, leaving her remaining years free for creation? *Curriculum Vitae* closes with the publication of her first novel. To continue might have involved too intimate a discussion of the relationship between her life and her work. And that relationship, she insisted, was fundamental. It would be my task to discover it. Neither of us hesitated for long but from the outset we both agreed that any arrangement would have to guarantee my independence. How, I wondered, should I conduct this relationship while remaining objective? Although she was quickly very friendly, signing her letters 'Best love', it was difficult at first to avoid the sense of being someone called in by the headmistress to write the history of her school. She saw the answer immediately. On my first visit to her Italian home, she led me to a huge dining-room table piled end to end and half a metre deep with files: the archive soon to be transported to Edinburgh. 'I think you might find it interesting. It's the story of a writer's struggle. Treat me', she said, waving a hand towards her records, 'as though I were dead.'

In some respects, she always treated herself as though she were dead, or in a play or a dream, and this distance generated her pleasure in the world, beat back its terrors. Humour became a defensive weapon, although she knew the terrors well enough, the sense of falling and of threat. The experience of hallucination was both terrifying and fascinating. It toughened her. The brevity of life lent it vigour and simultaneously emphasised its absurdity. As a young woman, half in, half out of the Edinburgh Jewish community; as the colonial wife under the yoke of her husband's violence and white Rhodesia's racism; as the divorced, impoverished poet in post-war London or the novelist at first rewarded with plaudits rather than plunder, she was both seasoned to disappointment and remorselessly hopeful. And so she remained, closing the stage door on each performance, entering the next, expectantly. She liked to get up when she chose and to do something with every day. She woke to a kind of innocence. The tone of her writing is witty and knowing but its meanings are unstable, spiked with sceptical *joie de vivre*. Human beings are ridiculous. At the same time, however, their pantomime efforts to take themselves seriously render them sympathetic. The voices of her fiction are often trapped, in communities and language communities, alienated, locked into the madness. They exist, as their author had, on borderlines, displaced persons. A powerful sense of the unknown permeates everything, the consciousness of exile and of the transcendental. We witness not so much scenes as scenarios, plausible rather than true, insubstantial. From one angle they are amusing, from another, the stuff of nightmares. Quite early, I found that I was writing several lives, and that while some presented an image of coolly impervious self-assurance, others described a woman who had suffered dreadfully. But she sought no one's pity, would never construct herself as a victim. Public displays of emotion embarrassed her. Anyone who tried to embarrass her was turned into a public display.

Finding a title for this book, therefore, proved difficult. Each attempt seemed either too dull for so vivacious a character or too restrictive. For a while I toyed with *The Nine Lives of Muriel Spark*, hoping this might suggest her multiplicity, her feline quality and affinity with the cat's graceful independence, her capacity to reinvent herself, to melt into shadows or to come out spitting when threatened. The 'nine lives' would refer simply to nine places – Edinburgh, Southern Rhodesia, Milton Bryan, Kensington, Aylesford, Camberwell, New York, Rome, Tuscany – in which the major scenes of her life's changes took place. But no, this would be to define her artificially. In intermediary periods she lived several of these lives simultaneously. During any one day she could flick on and off between various personae. And of course she was not just the cat, the knowing, mysterious solitary, she was also gregarious and vulnerable, the artist who preferred to inhabit a cloud of unknowing when writing, a woman perfectly at home discussing Bingo with her landlady. She was a scholar, a mother, a daughter, a businesswoman, streetwise and strict, the gentle and affectionate supporter of those who did not threaten. She was Cinderella and St Monica. She broke all the rules, the mistress of constant surprise. She liked to astonish and to entertain, refused to be whatever anyone wanted her to be, always reserved the right to change her mind, to walk out to new life.

It was no good, trying to sum her up. Ultimately I settled on the simplest of options – *Muriel Spark: The Biography* – although even her name was a cipher. 'Spark' was her divorced husband's name, an anglicised Lithuanian-Jewish patronymic. She kept it, not out of respect for him but for her son. (It was important in those days for a schoolboy to have the same name as his mother.) And what should I call her in this book? 'Dame Muriel' would be formal and correct but sounded inappropriately frosty. 'Spark' would be the normal address. But as we had been writing to each other for ten years on first-name terms, this seemed rude. At the risk of appearing over-familiar, I decided to describe her simply as 'Muriel'. This does not signify that she counted me as a friend.

CHAPTER 1

Night and Day

1962–1918

Muriel Sarah Camberg arrived in the middle of the night (3 a.m., 1 February 1918) and immediately became her parents' princess. Later in life, she would occasionally amuse herself with the fantasy that she was a real princess, kidnapped by gypsies (her parents). She saw her life as a Cinderella story – and Rossini's *La Cenerentola* was not one of her favourite operas for nothing. How she had emerged from that family intrigued her. She was born in a small rented flat at 160 Bruntsfield Place, in the Morningside district of Edinburgh. Her brother, Philip, had made his appearance in the middle of the day five and a half years earlier,[1] in another flat, down the hill and round the corner at 55 Viewforth. He welcomed his new sister guardedly. As they grew up together this emotional distance increased. And they remained night and day to each other for the rest of their lives, uncomplementary (and sometimes uncomplimentary) opposites. 'My brother', she remarked to me, 'is like a Chekhov short story. When you meet him you'll know what I mean.'

During April 1962, with the great success of *The Prime of Miss Jean Brodie* behind her and life as a celebrity ahead, she began to reflect on all this. She was back in Edinburgh, attending her father's deathbed in the Royal Infirmary. What was she doing in the elegant North British Hotel when her mother, brother and son were gathered in the family home? By hitching her legs up on to the window-sill of her room she could prop herself on one side or the other. The broad sash was lifted, opening, to the left, on the craggy outcrop of Arthur's Seat, to the right on Princes Street Gardens, just coming into bloom in cold spring sunshine. Above everything loured the castle, erupting between the Old Town and the New. This brutal caesura, dividing the tangle of ancient closes from the rational elegance of eighteenth-century town planning, seemed to her somehow symbolic. There was a link, as yet still an abstraction, between the topography of Edinburgh and the topography of her mind. Most people in her circumstances would have been saturated in melancholy. But Muriel was not like most people. Her response to the world was rarely one of self-pity. She was an artist, a channel through which impressions could flow, a cold medium. At moments like this, when she could feel an image crystallising, the thrill of creation isolated her from the injuries of the terrestrial world and she would give herself up to the process, never knowing where it might lead. On this occasion she felt 'an inpouring of love'[2] for her native city: its style, its tricks of speech, its provincial puritanism and cosmopolitan hauteur. It was the city itself rather than her family that had nurtured her as an artist.

She belonged nowhere, was determined to belong nowhere and to no one. 'It was Edinburgh', she wrote, 'that bred within me the condition of exiledom: and what have I been doing since then but moving from exile into exile?' This was not a lament. Exile for her, as for James Joyce, was the natural condition of the artist. 'It has ceased', she wrote, 'to be a fate, it has become a calling.'[3] Edinburgh was her Dublin, redolent of escaped impositions yet bred in the bone of her art. It was the locus of conflicting memories: of those who had tried to impose guilt for the audacity of claiming independence, of the solid pleasures of a well-regulated, prelapsarian life. Her father, Bernard (Barney) Camberg, was a Jew; her mother, Sarah (Cissy) Camberg (née Uezzell), a woman of eclectic religious tastes, had been brought up as a Christian but, probably to please him, had married him in a synagogue. It was a liberal-minded, happy-go-lucky family. Having married out, Barney maintained an unswerving devotion to his wife and daughter. There were others, Muriel felt, who had betrayed her. And as she looked out over the city she realised that this unexpected welling-up of affection 'was psychologically connected with my love for my father and with the exiled sensation of occupying a hotel room [...] meant for strangers'.[4] Now that he was dying, she would soon, metaphorically speaking, be homeless. She had cast herself out as a young woman and had never wished to return. Nevertheless, Edinburgh was the home which had made her independence possible, and, for her, all the positive qualities of 'home' centred on her father.

The day of his death – 21 April 1962 – was for Muriel something of an epiphany, and the necessary metaphor centring on the castle began to take shape. 'To have a great primitive black crag rising up in the middle of populated streets of commerce, stately squares and winding closes', she wrote, 'is like the statement of an unmitigated fact preceded by "nevertheless".' The speech habit, she now remembered, which had always fascinated her when listening to her teachers or to the murmuring tight-lipped women in musquash coats taking tea at MacVitties, was that 'word of final justification', 'nevertheless':

> [...] my whole education, in and out of school, seemed even then to pivot around this word. [...] I approve of the ceremonious accumulation of weather forecasts and barometer-readings that pronounce for a fine day, before letting rip on the statement: 'Nevertheless, it's raining.' I find that much of my literary composition is based on the nevertheless idea. I act upon it. It was on the nevertheless principle that I turned Catholic.[5]

Edinburgh had taught her this, epitomised paradox. It was a grand European city; nevertheless, it was provincial. It was her home, had given her a strong civic pride; nevertheless, she was, in terms of class and her father's religion, an alien. It had instilled in her a fundamental feminism and exactness of mind; nevertheless, she was not a 'political' feminist and she was, first, last, and always, a poet. Human beings could organise themselves into complex and comfortably self-justifying structures: towns, families, languages, systems of manners and authority; nevertheless, in the midst of everything and usually ignored reared the savage 'unmitigated fact' of death. This ultimate point of reference, of departure, had fascinated her since adolescence. She had always been a 'watcher', an outsider, silently recording the antics of anyone who swam into her gaze. Now the sustaining fiction of her childhood – the supportive family – had died with her father. And although she could look out on the city with the nostalgia of one who was grateful to have known a place where she had once felt safe, she knew that the last shadow of its unqualified love had faded. From that point, she was on her own, and she began to make arrangements to live abroad. It was the hinge of her life, the point at which the second half of her existence began to rewrite the first.

*

Bruntsfield Place today is much the same as it was during Muriel's childhood: a city street, a ribbon of commerce servicing the residential areas near by. Respectable grey stone tenements rise three floors above a string of small shops. Between these shops, at regular intervals, the heavy staircase doors are tight-shut against strangers. A pile of surnames details the occupants. In 1918, visitors stood between Miss Morrison's confectionery and Lauders' Shoes to pull a brass knob which, through an elaborate connection of wires, rang the bell. It tinkled frequently in the Cambergs' first-floor flat, and Muriel listened for it eagerly. Then someone would go out on to the landing, pull a lever to open the street door, and shout down enquiry and welcome. The district was like a village within the city, Mrs Camberg one of its 'characters'. These regular callers brought a welcome gust of the outside world with them when dropping in on her for a chin-wag over a cup of tea, something to eat, possibly a full meal. No one left that house hungry or without the latest neighbourhood gossip.

Beyond the front door, the main bedroom was immediately to the left, at one end of a central corridor and, next to it, the sitting room, a parlour kept conspicuously tidy with a sofa, a piano, an ornate over-mantel and the bay window. Off this room was a windowless bed-closet. These rooms overlooked the street, with its rattling electric trams, and the more elegant terrace of Bruntsfield Gardens. At the other end of the corridor were the small back bedroom, the bathroom, the coal cellar and the kitchen, which also had a bed-recess. Lodgers (who included

Professor and Mrs Rule) usually occupied the main bedroom, occasionally the sitting room. Most of the life of the house took place in the kitchen. Muriel's parents usually slept in the boxroom off it. When her maternal grandmother, Adelaide Uezzell, moved in during 1927, Muriel gave up her back bedroom and for six years slept on a sofa in the kitchen. It was there that Cissy held court.

This large room looked out on to a back green enclosed in a square by the tenements of Bruntsfield Place, Bruntsfield Avenue, Viewforth and Montpellier. As usual in Edinburgh, the grassy space was shared by them all as a place to hang out washing or as a safe area for children to play. To the left of the kitchen window stood a gas oven and, on the left-hand wall, a cast-iron cooking range, remnant of Edwardian days. Over this hung a grim photograph of some Jewish patriarch whose identity Muriel never discovered. Its only interest for her was that it suddenly fell and smashed on the evening before her maternal grandfather's, Tom Uezzell's, death.[6] The most important item stood in the centre of the room: an eight-seater table which often groaned with food like an inexhaustible smorgasbord.

Cissy was twenty-nine when Muriel was born, Barney thirty-two. In terms of economic classification they were working-class but they had risen somewhat in the social scale by moving up the hill from Viewforth. Morningside was the province of the professional classes and their new situation brought with it the strain of keeping up appearances. Bruntsfield Place was comfortably petit-bourgeois. Few of its residents were working-class. Fewer still were Jewish. Muriel's brother felt this sense of alienation intensely: the embarrassment of having to take in lodgers, the whiff of anti-Semitism. As a lad, Barney had run away to sea but been quickly tracked down and returned. Then he had completed an apprenticeship as a motor-car engineer, although he never earned his living doing this.[7] Jobs were scarce. Both parents were anxious about financial security and keen to provide for their children's advancement. So Barney took skilled factory work at the North British Rubber Company and remained with the firm, as a fitter and mechanical engineer, until he retired at the age of seventy.

It was tough work. On lathes and drilling machines he would shape the heavy castings for a motor-car tyre known as 'The Clincher'. Each day he would be out of the house early in his overalls to walk a mile down Viewforth to the huge brick building at Castle Mills. In fine weather he would see the Firth of Forth glittering in the distance. In winter he would frequently arrive soaked and frozen for his eight-hour shift. Often it was longer. Whenever there was overtime, he took it. Each night he would return as black as soot, sometimes bearing large boxes from the factory to bust up for firewood, then bathe, change into suit, tie and well-brushed shoes for the evening's alternative life. This might be work or play. They could not exist on his wages, not, at least, if they were to maintain some sense of style – and Barney and Cissy enjoyed clothes, dancing and a drink. He smoked ten Players a day and sported a homburg. She was, Philip remembered, 'a real hat woman. She had to go out looking like a millionairess even if she only had two pennies in her pocket.' Always well-dressed, she had the bearing of the late Queen Mother. Both parents were determined to send their children to fee-paying schools. So, throughout Muriel's early childhood, they took in lodgers and Barney would occasionally disappear into the gloaming to arrange some small-scale, tax-free deals in second-hand furniture. He acted as an agent. Someone would want something. He would find out how to get it and take commission. Tired as he was, he enjoyed his trading. He often thought of establishing his own firm, and this dream reflected a persistent anxiety. 'My father's family did not think too highly of him', Philip recalled, 'for the simple reason that he was just a working engineer. [...] The rest of the family were in business and if you're not in business, according to them, you're nobody.'

One senses that Barney was a frustrated man: resilient, droll, industrious, yet taciturn and lacking the real fierceness of ambition. When he mentioned the idea of opening a shop, Cissy would dissuade him. Think of the outlay ... Think of the risk ... Once, Professor Rule offered him a much better job in America. But Barney was anxious about uprooting the children and, anyway, Cissy, constitutionally nervous, would not take the chance. When living in their first flat in Viewforth, she had suffered a breakdown after disturbing an intruder, and she never allowed anyone to forget it. From that point, she drank every day to steady herself: small quantities of 'port wine' at first; later, a bottle of Madeira a day. If she were going on a journey, she would always take her silver flask. She was never drunk but she liked being queenly. Alcohol released her vivacity and transformed inhibitions into eccentric self-confidence. Barney, it seems, ignored her habit, happy to reclaim a handsome wife who could laugh and go out on the town with him. He was a protective, courtly husband. Occasionally he would lament that, had it not been for her, he might have been a greater success. But this was, more than anything, a family joke. Marrying Sarah, and defending her, had signalled a cooling of relations with his own people. She was also working-class, Gentile, and a Sassenach to boot. Philip had only the faintest knowledge of his paternal grandparents, Muriel none – Barney never talked about them – and neither knew much more of their father's siblings. The family extended rather to Watford and to Cissy's parents and brothers.

There was little time or money for holidays. On sunny weekends or bank holidays, the Cambergs might board a tram for the nearby beaches of Portobello. These were Philip and Muriel's only bucket-and-spade excursions with their parents. She had warm memories of being carried back, contented in her father's arms, along the last, gaslit stretch of pavement. But for Barney's free fortnight, usually during late summer, they would head south. 'I used to put all the chairs together in the hallway like a train weeks before we went,' Philip recalled:

Such a build-up of excitement until […] we got a cab down to the Caley [Caledonian] Station. Mother would make sandwiches for the trip – eggs and cress and sometimes ham and fruit and of course her bottle of wine. The most amazing thing was, before the train started to go Mother would be giving our sandwiches to any other people in the carriage, so that by the time we got to Carstairs, all the food was gone.[8]

Reckless hospitality was Cissy's most endearing characteristic. As fast as anything came in, it went out. Slender means, she determined, need not constrain magnanimity, and thus the financial pinch was eased by gusto and style. The Cambergs were a short family – short of cash, short in stature, small figures in the rarefied class-structure of Edinburgh – but they walked tall, and in Watford enjoyed a certain cachet among their country cousins.

Watford in the twenties was a tranquil market town encircled by fields, not, as now, by motorways and the seamless brick infill of Greater London. The city was a train ride away through farmland. Many Watford folk knew their wild flowers; agricultural life still ebbed and flowed in seasonal rhythm. This is the Watford the Camberg children visited. At first they all stayed with Cissy's parents, Adelaide and Tom Uezzell, sleeping in one tiny bedroom above their shop-of-all-sorts at 288 High Street. Across the road, in a tumbledown row of cottages, lived one of their rare customers, an ancient, inquisitive woman: Mrs Longnose to Tom. The marketplace was a stroll away where farmers still clicked and whistled their cattle into pens, and stalls were heaped with fruit and vegetables. Philip remembered a thunderstorm which so terrified the pigs that they broke loose and stampeded, squealing past the house. But the town was already changing. He also remembered an accident in which a lorry knocked down a young girl and terribly injured her. Barney carried her into the house, distressed, the blood soaking his jacket. Behind No. 288 ran the Bushey Arches, a viaduct carrying the new electric railway. The cottages opposite were demolished to make way for a sour-smelling gasometer. Although its rural traditions continued, Watford had already provided substantial acreages for the capital's printing industry – and work for Muriel's male cousins.

In retrospect, it seems appropriate that Muriel should have spent so many contented hours of her childhood in close proximity to hot type. But in those days she knew nothing of it. She flew box kites with Philip, played among her grandfather's chickens and rabbits in the back garden, went on picnics to Croxley Green, Hemel Hempstead, St Albans. One precious day would be set aside for an excursion to London. Her absorbing interest, however, was the Dickensian atmosphere of the shop itself.

While Philip was train-spotting, she would be pattering about Adelaide's skirts, watching, listening. She was always listening.

Muriel's experience of similar establishments in Edinburgh was quite different. Miss Morrison's side of the confectionery counter had been built up to lend an air of authority. She ran a tight shop. Any child attempting purchases without parental supervision would be closely questioned as to the source of the cash. The Uezzells' way of doing business was to provide a ramshackle assortment of goods: sweets, penny packets of tea and of arrowroot biscuits, mineral waters, ginger beer, lemon squash. On the counter, beneath a fly-blown glass cover, sat an ancient cake laced with 'telegraph wires' of crystallised sugar. Fruit and vegetables crowded the large, open front window. Odd groups of children (unsupervised) wandered in, as did the local geriatrics, an occasional policeman and, of course, the family. Three doors down, at No. 282, Cissy's brother Phil, Alice and their six children[9] lived in equally cramped conditions, until they moved to No. 292, and eventually to a larger place in the suburbs.

Uncle Phil was a railwayman turned tailor, his sideboard crammed with precious thread and fabrics. Alice had been a professional cook for gentlemen's clubs in London. They were of the skilled working class, providing service for the gentry. Their children were brought up with strong discipline but, in comparison with Philip and Muriel, ran free. All went out to work at fourteen, the three boys entering 'the print'. While deeply respectful of their parents, they saw themselves as belonging to a more adventurous generation. Roger Uezzell's first job was to carry printers' proofs to London three times a day by train, and he used his season ticket regularly in the evenings to escape to the city's entertainments. 'I liked me London,' he said with a wry smile in interview, but as to Muriel, whom he had known quite well during their childhood, he was utterly baffled by what she had become, had never read her work.[10] Printing may have been her male cousins' trade but writing was not important to this family. They were simple folk, lively and warm. Describing their father, Phyllis and Roger remembered 'a dead gentleman',[11] strict but genial, always laughing, often at himself, close to his sister and, like her, generous, affectionate, sentimental.

Uncle Phil and Cissy must often have talked of their brother, Harry. He is the wraith-like figure who appears briefly with his brass buttons gleaming in Muriel's 'The First Year of My Life'. Gassed in the First World War, Harry had returned to marry Bessie, a silly creature in family lore, and to live in Edinburgh where Barney had found him a job at the rubber factory. By her Harry had a son and daughter before dying in their infancy of a tubercular throat. Bessie had revisited Watford briefly, then disappeared to the South-West. Uncle Phil begged her never to part with the children, to come to him if ever she needed help. She promised. Later it emerged that she had placed them in separate orphanages. The ghosts of those lost children still haunted the Uezzell clan in the 1990s. 'It broke Dad's heart,' Phyllis remarked – and the anecdote says much about the determination to maintain family unity which Phil and Cissy shared. Both were loyal to their curious parents.

Adelaide and Tom were an odd couple. She was tiny, brisk, smart-tongued, and with a face fit to terrify those of nervous constitution. But she had her softer side – for those she liked. As a single woman, she had been in service, possibly with Lady de Rothschild's household.[12] When married, she marched with the Watford Suffragettes. Exploring the shop one day, Muriel discovered handbills wrapping dusty bundles of candles: 'Votes for Women!' 'Why do you Oppress Women!'[13] Adelaide filled her granddaughter's head with stories, acted them out and rapidly became a heroine to the girl: 'I see her in the vanguard, leading the women in her dance of triumph.'[14]

That 'dance of triumph' typifies the joyful victory of Muriel's fictional heroines over their oppressors, men and women alike. Adelaide was a mystery, a fabulist, a valkyrie. Almost nothing is known of her background. No birth record can be traced. She told Muriel that her father was a quack doctor; on her death certificate he is cited as Philip Hyams, shoemaker. He was, she said, Jewish, her mother Gentile. Within the family she 'boasted of her Jewish blood because it made her so clever'.[15] But, having known poverty and discrimination, she was pragmatic where money was concerned and said nothing of her Jewish heritage to her customers. Apparently, she laid the foundation stone of the local Methodist church (now demolished) and attended it regularly. When Muriel asked her about her religion, the old lady described herself as a 'Gentile Jewess', and the phrase struck home. It was also, Muriel felt, an apt description of her mother and of herself. Adelaide had fallen in love with Tom, six years her junior, hunted him down and won him. It was a story repeated by Barney and Cissy – and Muriel admired this passion, snapping its fingers at convention. Two generations along the line, she was intrigued by her Jewish roots. The experience of growing up in a family of diverse origins was integral to her vision of the world.

Adelaide appears to have been raised in Bethnal Green, then an impoverished quarter of East London, and was possibly the child of immigrant parents. They were a poor but respectable family who seem to have followed the Jewish observances of the father. The Tom who had courted her was an affable fellow, six feet two inches, handsome and bearded in the style of the young Joseph Conrad. A Watford man with the local drawl, he came from a line of grim churchgoers mostly holed up in Vicarage Road. They were displeased by the match. She was a rough diamond from a 'mixed marriage', and had a sister in Edinburgh who had married the son of a Jewish minister. Tom's father, John Uezzell, was a prosperous master baker with impeccable Anglican credentials. Nevertheless, there was an urgent matter to be resolved, for Adelaide was several months' pregnant when Tom married her at St Bartholomew's Parish Church, Bethnal Green, on 3 January 1886. He was twenty-five, she thirty-one.

His own family, it seems, Tom found unendurably tedious. Piety had never been his strong suit. Sacked from the Metropolitan Police for drunkenness, he spent the remainder of his days comfortably idling between the pub and his garden. 'He doesn't work,' Adelaide growled. 'I keep him.' Tom would accept the obloquy, shrug his shoulders and amble off to tend his chickens. On her death certificate he is described as a 'gardener', on Cissy's as a 'baker'. He was neither, except in an amateur capacity. He did nothing and did it perfectly. Each morning he would rise early and bring his guests tea in bed. Most children adored him and feared his wife. To Muriel and Philip, both were 'characters', amusingly at odds with the mundane. A no-nonsense exotic, Adelaide dressed in severe Victorian black: ankle-length skirts with multiple petticoats. Occasionally she would hoik up her dress for the children to display a bag, heavy with coins, suspended from a tape round her waist. This was her 'purse', the symbol of her independence. She ran the shop, ruled the roost, was effectively head of that branch of the family. She also preferred the Cambergs to the Uezzells and made no secret of it. It was Tom who used to slip bars of chocolate into the pockets of Roger and Phyllis. Adelaide did the same for Muriel.

Inevitably this favouritism bred small resentments among the Uezzell children. The shop was tiny. One walked straight off the pavement into it, and through the back to a parlour and kitchen. A rickety staircase led to two bedrooms. It was a tight fit for six people. So when Uncle Phil and his brood moved to their larger house a couple of miles away, Philip stayed with them while Muriel remained with her parents at the shop. Philip contentedly mucked in with his cousins (and was still visiting them in Watford during the 1990s); Muriel was kept at a distance. 'He [Philip] really enjoyed himself,' Phyllis recalled. 'The girl was never allowed to play or do anything. It was holding daddy's hand and "Pet, no. No, Pet." He'd got her hand and would never let her go. I never remember her dressed in anything but kilt and oatmeal jumper. We had to do what *they* said, according to grandmother. Grandfather was different. He was like we were. He was for us. But grandmother, no.' There was, Phyllis felt, a class difference between the Edinburgh and the Watford children. 'Aunt Ciss [...] she was always a lady. [...] She had *two* children, if you understand me. My mother had six and had to look after six.' This, however, was a reflection on Adelaide rather than on her daughter. Everyone loved Aunt Ciss. Roger was devoted to her. It was Barney, Phyllis felt, who was aloof.

Adelaide never welcomed Uncle Phil's children. She was an appalling cook and there was always the danger that she might offer food. Hilda and Phyllis were sent to visit during the Christmas of 1926. It was a long, cold walk. No buses were running. Hilda was twelve years old, Phyllis

nearly fourteen. They didn't want to go. Adelaide's consistent spite-
fulness towards their mother and her unfavourable comparisons
between them and 'little Philly and little Muriel' were deterrents enough.
But Tom was ill. 'Hello grandmother,' said Phyllis on the doorstep.
'Dad's asked us to come and ask, "How is grandfather?"' 'You can go
back and tell him,' Adelaide snapped, 'if he was dying I wouldn't send
for him.' Then she softened. 'I suppose you'd better come in.' Thick
slices of indigestible Christmas pudding, clotted with flour-and-water
paste, were cut: 'There you are. Eat it.'

Unfortunately, Tom *was* dying and lasted only until 28 December.
Adelaide took in a young couple as lodgers, quarrelled with them, then
fell down the stairs, fracturing her shoulder. When she came out of
hospital, Uncle Phil offered her a home, the shop was boarded up, and
that concluded the Cambergs' Watford holidays. Adelaide's sharpness
towards the Uezzells was temporarily blunted by dependency. She gave
Alice one of her gold sovereigns, modified her behaviour towards the
children. Before long, however, she had registered her discontent
strongly enough for Barney and Cissy to come down, take the old lady
back to Edinburgh, and install her in Muriel's bedroom. Muriel was
then about nine. She didn't mind in the least. It never occurred to her
to mind. The Cambergs' duty, they all agreed, was to close ranks and to
make Adelaide's last years as comfortable as possible. Cissy was a devoted
daughter and, from Muriel's point of view, this addition to their household was a positive benefit. At last she had this delightful eccentric at
close quarters. On many evenings Muriel would sit at a small table in
the back bedroom while her parents were out dancing or at the cinema,
completing her homework, writing poems or letters, listening to the
radio and making desultory conversation with her grandmother. Everything about this rebarbative septuagenarian fascinated her: clothes,
jewellery, sovereigns, tricks of speech, even her slow death.

Adelaide's removal generated some heat on the Edinburgh / Watford
axis. There was the complex and largely unarticulated issue of how well
or ill Uncle Phil's clan had cared for her. The Cambergs' assumption of
this responsibility was welcomed; the implicit accusation of neglect was

not. The shop's effects were probably distributed at this point. According
to Phyllis, Barney angered his brother-in-law by briskly staking claims:
'"I want this. I'd like that." And my grandfather's gold watch and chain,
he took it as well. Everything of any value, he wanted. So my father said,
"Oh well, all right Barney. If you want it all, you can have it."' On the
piano stood a pair of hideous pink Victorian vases with crystal tears
which tinkled when brushed. Barney added them to his list and left Phil
to see to the packing and carriage. Phil, never one to start an argument,
agreed to everything and satisfied himself with the quiet revenge of
dispatching it all cash-on-delivery.

This was the Uezzell version. But Barney, of course, would have been
under instructions from Adelaide to ensure that all her valuables went
with her. They were her only resource beyond the coins swinging among
her petticoats. When she died, she would will everything (as Muriel
herself did) to those who took best care of her. Adelaide was a caustic,
practical woman, not in the least fearful of causing offence, and she
must have known that Cissy and Phil were far too close to permit open
warfare in the holy citadel of The Family.

There had been a regular traffic of relations from Watford to Edinburgh for decades and, despite the debacle, it continued. In the early
days, Adelaide and Tom would come to stay, separately, it seems, so
that someone could mind the shop. Tom would shamble up from the
Caledonian Station like Dick Whittington, his few possessions tied in a
piece of cloth on a stick across his shoulder. His wife's visits were more
regal. She probably came to help Cissy immediately after the birth of
the children. (On one famous occasion, baby Muriel's screaming had
become intolerable. Her grandmother had pleaded for someone to shut
that child up. Five-year-old Philip, eager to help, had pressed a fur muff[16]
over Muriel's face and Adelaide had arrived only just in time to save the
girl for literature.) Uncle Phil would often be at 160 Bruntsfield Place
for New Year. From the 1940s until Cissy's death, his children came up
regularly for Scottish holidays. Muriel, however, felt that something had
irrevocably changed since Adelaide had moved in. The event represented
a stage in her developing self-consciousness, as her father's death did

later, from which there was no retreat. After that, if her parents or brother travelled to Watford, she stayed at home. Insofar as she had ever shared interests with the Uezzell children, those interests were now dead – and, anyway, she actively preferred the company of her grandmother. This quiet but determined separation, and the gravitation towards those much older than herself, became a feature of Muriel's existence. For this shyly self-possessed young woman already had literary ambitions. Dreamily in love with the idea of the artistic life, and scenting her vocation, she craved mentors: not only those who could provide formal education but also, and more importantly, vivid figures who could teach her to 'know the worst' and to laugh in its face.

Adelaide was just such a figure. When she arrived she was about seventy-three: shaky but still active and mentally alert. For the last three years of her stay she was mostly bedridden, crippled by two strokes a year apart. Muriel helped Cissy to nurse her, learning the techniques of feeding and heavy lifting. Adelaide was paralysed down one side, her speech scrambled by aphasia. Many children would have found this distressing or tedious. Not Muriel.

> Before her stroke I had noticed how her memory worked. It came in snatches, vignettes. I was beginning to practise memories myself. When my grandmother talked of her sister, Kitty, gloating over her because she had finer clothes, I would egg on my grandmother: 'And then what did you say?' 'I just walked out of the room and I said, "Goodbye, Rotten Row".'[17]

The phrase amused Muriel. Its light-hearted contempt well describes her own reaction to insult. Adelaide somehow empowered her – and could make her laugh. The two things were connected.

When poleaxed by cerebral haemorrhage Adelaide was in one sense diminished. Muriel recalled a terrible day when the old lady had panicked, misunderstanding the family's preparations to take her to the seaside for an attempt to place her in a home. 'We were all full of consternation that [she] should imagine that we could treat her so badly. It made me realise how vulnerable the aged are.'[18] Nevertheless, for

Muriel, the phenomenon of aphasia and the imminence of death were fascinating. Adelaide called Philip the 'dressing-table' and Gillespie's School 'laryngitis'. Muriel conducted elementary verbal experiments and discovered that there were no symbolic connections. That sense of the gap between words and meaning also became fundamental to her as an artist – as did this first brush with mortality: 'I think my experiences in minding and watching my grandmother formed a starting-point for my future novel, *Memento Mori* [1959], in which the characters are all elderly people.'[19] She might also have mentioned a string of affectionate portraits of eccentric old ladies, abused by the fools who surround them and loved by the heroine: Louisa Jepp in *The Comforters* (1957), Charmian Piper in *Memento Mori*, Lady Edwina in *Loitering with Intent* (1981). Grandmother Uezzell (she was always 'grandmother', never 'granny') became for Muriel an abstract image of the female artist: isolated, considered by the 'sane', male-dominated world to be dangerously unhinged, yet simultaneously released from Mr Asquith's liberal nonsense into a new, infinitely flexible, discourse between the imagination and the material world. That world would always try to silence women. Adelaide taught Muriel to speak out, to walk out, to savour the delicious swerve of the non sequitur, verbal and mental. It was strength. Like Fleur Talbot in *Loitering with Intent*, she believed that 'weakness of character [...] is no more to be despised than is physical weakness. We are not all born heroes and athletes. At the same time it is elementary wisdom always to fear weaknesses, including one's own; the reactions of the weak, when touched off, can be horrible and sudden.'[20] Grandmother Uezzell, wife of a charming but weak man, taught her this, too.

When Adelaide was dying, on 10 August 1933, Muriel was called in:

It was about 9 p.m. The doctor had just left. I had put my hair in curlers. For some reason I felt that this would be unseemly at a death-bed, so I took out the curlers and combed my hair before I went in. My grandmother was unconscious. There was a strange sound. My father said softly, 'It's the death rattle.' Something was happening in my grandmother's throat. Her eyes were closed. The rattle stopped. She gave a great sigh and died.[21]

That is all: no maundering eulogy. The facts of death are baldly stated. When Muriel remembered her, she remembered her spirited defiance, 'above all her sardonic, humorous and robust remarks when privately discussing certain of her neighbours with my mother',[22] and her fabulous 'blue silk brocade going-away dress'.[23]

Muriel had dubbed this garment 'Bluebell' because Adelaide, in a brief moment of escape, had worn it to a fancy-dress party at Watford Church Union. She had gone as 'A Bluebell', hat and basket decked with fabric flowers, and for once in her life had won a prize.

> Of course, I tried it on, and although it was far too big, I swept around in it, thinking of all the parts I could take in period plays. Alas, after the death of my grandmother [...] I succumbed to the current fashion and, with my mother's approval, cut up the bluebell gown to make cushion covers. They looked wonderful, but the dress itself should never have been touched. It glowed with its deep and heavy brocaded blueness. It was sewn by hand, with a minutely stitched lining.[24]

Although no interpretation is offered, this apparently innocuous passage is pregnant with association when one knows of the importance of this woman and of the word 'Bluebell' in Muriel's life. These are Proustian touchstones of memory. The dress is presented as a work of art whose intricate structure she was too young to appreciate. Yet she is obliquely sensible of its aesthetic force. It shimmers darkly in a dark world, gathering meaning in retrospect as an image of the power of art, attached in Muriel's mind to the power of untrammelled womanhood, both of which are threatened by conventional femininity. One might even see her mother as implicated in this destruction. She *should* have known better. Instead, cushion covers were allowed to triumph over the single, coherent, artistic object. Simultaneously, there is also pathos here: the image of the dress as a talisman in Adelaide's otherwise mundane existence, a symbol of what might have been, of her rare entries into the fantastic. The dress is the non sequitur of Adelaide's life.

The word 'Bluebell' held magic for Muriel. Years later, when she was struggling to bring her first novel into being, she gave her precious half-Persian cat this name and wrote a poem, 'Bluebell among the Sables'. In this, 'Bluebell, my beautiful', a green-eyed sprite, attacks the furs of an elegant but dull lady visitor, 'Shaking their kindly tails between her teeth.' The visitor is horrified, Muriel amused: 'No need for alarm; / Those dead pelts can't cause Bluebell any harm.'[25] The poem renders a moment of vision: the live cat invigorating the inert furs. But there is more to it than this. Bluebell, surely, represents the artistic spirit, the feline spark confronting the mundane, the merely fashionable. The cat is Muriel. Muriel is the cat, smiling with sardonic joy.

None of these interpretations, of course, is exclusively 'right'. Many more would be possible. Muriel always wrote like this: leaving voids for the reader to fill. But there is a recurrent strand in the pattern of her life and work: that the energy of creation was her oxygen rather than the desire to be liked or even to be 'happy'. 'I preferred to be interested as I was', Fleur Talbot remarks, 'than happy as I might be.'

> I wasn't sure that I so much wanted to be happy, but I knew I had to follow my nature. [...] What is truth? [...] When people say that nothing happens in their lives I believe them. But you must understand that everything happens to an artist; time is always redeemed, nothing is lost and wonders never cease.[26]

The penalty of this joy, and its source, was alienation. Somewhere, clouded among the trophies of her girlhood in Edinburgh, lay the roots of that rootlessness which she finally came to ponder as her father lay dying in 1962.

CHAPTER 2

Home and Away

1918–1937

No. 160 Bruntsfield Place was a small, crowded flat but, by the standards of the Watford folk, imposing with its high corniced ceilings and heavy Edwardian furniture. It was important to Cissy not only to make visitors comfortable but also to put on a show. In later years Roger Uezzell gained the impression that his aunt never went shopping and had everything 'sent up' by local tradesmen. Phyllis remembered her in the 1960s tucking bills behind the mantelpiece clock with the words 'God will take care of them.' (God, in this case, was Muriel.) Like her mother, like Muriel, Cissy avoided cooking whenever possible, always had a cleaning lady, and worked on the principle that if one neglected housework it somehow 'got done'.

Cissy sailed through life like a ramshackle galleon. In her youth she had given professional piano lessons and would regularly perform a double-act with Barney in the sitting room, gaily tinkling the ivories to his baritone renditions of 'Forever and Forever', 'Because (God Made Thee Mine)', 'Roaming in the Gloaming'. They were an unpretentious couple but, at the same time, proud and nervous. Philip remembered his mother's disappointment. She had married in the expectation of escaping the working class and, although they lived their public lives as though they had, somehow they hadn't. She didn't blame Barney. She was, after all, the one who refused risks. Nevertheless, she lived with a debilitating sense of anticlimax never quite counterbalanced by her *joie de vivre*. Her perpetual hospitality sprang confusingly from a genuine delight in entertaining and from neurosis – the terror of being left alone in the house.

Cissy was constantly 'getting about', as she put it. She was attractive to men and enjoyed this power. A string of chaste flirtations with trades-men spiced her day. As Muriel became conscious of her surroundings, a pattern of these visits structured her life: to Howden's for bread, to the Maypole Dairy Company, to the Drysdale Cake and Candy Store. The names held magic for her, as did the mysterious operations of commerce: the girl in crisp white overalls, smacking butter into shape; the floury baker. Her brother was rarely part of this pattern, had no clear sense of their life together which, it seems, was minimal. He remembered her as a very private person and himself as solitary. Although for nineteen years Muriel and Philip inhabited the same house, from the outset they had rarely communed.

'My mother was largely to blame for that', he recalled, 'because she dressed [Muriel] up. She made her feel like she was a lady at a young age [...] the finest clothes that we could afford: fur coat. Nothing was good enough for Muriel. [...] I didn't resent it [...] because I felt, well, girls come before boys.'[1] Barney had a hot temper. Occasionally he would thrash Philip (never Muriel) with a razor-strop. But if Barney was sometimes loud, Cissy was dominant, and in this matriarchy Philip kept a low profile. Short-sighted and physically awkward, he struggled at school, was sensitive to insult, and saw his home as a haven from external threats: 'Most young children [...] have friends who visit back and forward. But in the environment that we were brought up in we didn't have anybody like that. Strangely enough. [...]. You see, we were con-sidered Jewish people and most of the other Jewish people were at the other end of Edinburgh [...] where the doctors and dentists and the better class [lived] ... We were probably the only Jewish family in that whole area [...] and you can feel it [...]. You can feel it like you can feel the rain coming on. [...] We didn't go to church on Sunday and most people do.'[2] For many years Philip's only friend was Billy Wright on the top floor of their staircase. Billy was the son of Mary, whose depressed husband was an alcoholic who regularly assaulted her.

Philip's memories, then, although of a happy childhood ('In our family', he remarked rather unconvincingly, 'we were all number one') are coloured by embarrassments. Class, religion, physical appearance and academic competition all tortured him. And to add to this confusion, his sister appeared immune to their threats. When speaking in interview about their lodgers, he mumbled apologetically as though referring to a stain on the family's honour. You have to remember, he insisted, that times were hard. People had to do many things they would otherwise ... Then an anecdote would surface, related with a wry smile. When he was ten or eleven, their paying guests were the alcoholic minister of a local church and his wife. One Saturday evening he returned drunk, abused Barney as a 'dirty greasy Jew', and threw a punch at his head. Barney ducked. The minister's hand smashed into the wall. He retired to the front bedroom, groaning and nursing his bleeding knuckles. For the rest of the night, he and his spouse could be heard raging at each other. In the morning Barney threw them out.

Muriel was then about five years old. She had no memory of the incident. As the older child of more desperate times, Philip had a stronger sense of the family's struggle. But this had as much to do with the different temperaments of brother and sister as it did with social conditions. She was always impatient with him. Where he was introverted and dogged, she was sharp-witted and someone to whom learning came easily. Where he collected facts, she lived through the imagination, eagerly garnering splinters of the exotic. He was a sentimentalist; she was detached. He had the dogmatic, analytical frame of mind that eventually enabled him to become a research chemist and engineer. Muriel's parents did not only receive news of their daughter's glorious progress. In 1962 Cissy sent her a cutting from an American paper: 'Philip Camberg [...] is working with the Californian firm designing and building the Saturn S-11 booster to be used to launch the Apollo spacecraft on its journey to the Moon [...].'[3] (In fact, he was employed by Boeing as Lead Engineer on the Minuteman missile programme – which could not easily be advertised.) Above the article, a spry, clear-eyed forty-eight-year-old Philip gazes out, a far cry from the shambling adolescent of his Edinburgh days.

What, then, did Muriel and Philip have in common? As children, both were shy, self-conscious, industrious, ambitious. Both relished the skills of concise writing (Philip always enjoyed constructing his reports). Sibling competition seems to have underpinned the relationship. The essential difference, perhaps, was that where he was a problem solver, she was a problem creator. Where he made cut-out toys for her and crystal-set radios, she wrote poems and revelled in paradox. She kept records; he eliminated them, preferred to forget. He had kept no letters or family photographs. 'Problems' for Philip were something to be rationally erased. For Muriel, they became the lifeblood of her aesthetic and theological contemplation. He was conventional, she subversive. In retrospect, she inevitably comes off better from any comparison because he was a normal, screwed-up, intelligent professional and she had genius. But her gambling on that creativity lasted for over a decade before it paid off, years during which her more stolid brother opted for a secure career path after failing with his own business. A certain amount of resentment, on both sides, leaks out from all this. Muriel's love was reserved for those with unqualified faith in her talent.

Philip and Muriel went to the same school, although the five and a half years that separated them rendered their experience of the place utterly different. James Gillespie's was founded in 1803 as a small operation: sixty-five boys and one master. As it developed, it began to admit girls. In 1908 the Edinburgh School Board took over the management and Gillespie's moved to Bruntsfield Links. It was this co-educational establishment that Philip attended. Only during Muriel's time did it separate itself from the boys' school and, taking a step up, become James Gillespie's High School for Girls. Philip left at fourteen before the separation, when Muriel was eight, to work for the North British Rubber Company. Barney had found him a job ('white collar', rather than blue) as apprentice work's chemist, determined that his children should do better than he had. Even if it meant starting at the bottom (Philip was at first the dogsbody laddie sweeping up sawdust in the chemical laboratory, making tea, running errands), it was a career leading away from the noise and grime of the shop-floor.

Philip persevered. Having performed dismally at school, he trudged on, taking and retaking his matriculation, failing it both in Edinburgh and London. Then he discovered the less rigorous Senior Certificate of the College of Preceptors, passed it after many more hours of private coaching, began evening classes at Heriot-Watt College, and eventually achieved a respectable HND.[4] He was nothing if not tenacious. During the evenings, the atmosphere of the family flat was often one of hushed study, broken only by dance-band music on the radio and the clatter of trams.

Education, as in so many Scottish households, was seen as the key to unlock future prosperity. Despite Barney's low wages, the Cambergs insisted on sending their children to a fee-paying school. ('They didn't want us to go to rough schools,' Muriel commented in a tone of gentle approbation.[5]) Although the fees were modest, and at the age of fourteen Muriel won a scholarship, it was at first this extra burden that necessitated the lodgers and Barney's trading. Cissy brought in nothing beyond feckless expenditure and friends requiring tea. But somehow they managed. In the easy-come-easy-go domestic economy of that overcrowded household there was always enough food, clothing, good company, and a little cash to spare. There were, however, no books – or none at least of the sort Muriel began to crave. Her mother read women's magazines and romantic novels; her father concentrated mainly on the racing pages of the newspaper. Neither had the faintest interest in literature. In fact, both had only achieved a moderate level of literacy.

*

Gillespie's was not one of Edinburgh's glamorous schools. In the second rank behind Daniel Stewart's, Heriot's, and Fettes, in the 1930s it was the equivalent of a small local grammar school. Serious-minded, respectable, disciplined, and keen to develop its new status, it nevertheless did not send flocks of girls to university. The Sixth Form was small. Many pupils, like Muriel, left after matriculation to train as secretaries. Typing and shorthand were part of the curriculum for the less academic classes. The pupils came from a wide range of religious backgrounds. 'The official religion of [...] Gillespie's', Muriel wrote, '[...] was Presbyterian of the Church of Scotland; [...] later [...] expanded to include Episcopalian doctrines. But in my day Tolerance was decidedly the prevailing religion, always with a puritanical slant.'[6] Several girls came from 'mixed' marriages: Catholic / Protestant, Jewish / Christian. There were Indians and Muriel remembered Jews in most classes.

Edinburgh was then, as now, cosmopolitan. For all its stern façade, its political traditions were egalitarian. Muriel always shared a Scottish sympathy for the dispossessed. Her paternal grandparents, Louis and Henrietta Camberg, were Russian Jews. Louis had married Hadi (née Reibman, later known as 'Hannah', then 'Henrietta') in Kowno, Russia, on 15 August 1871. Two of Barney's sisters, Esther and Annie, were born in Russia. Beatrice, the third of eleven, was the first to be born in Edinburgh. Louis, who described himself alternately as a 'jeweller' and as a 'hawker of jewellery', was probably a 'traveller' rather than an established tradesman. 'Selling', as Muriel's brother pointed out, 'was the name of the game' for Jewish immigrants.[7] For many years they lived in cheap districts. Only Beattie and Jacob were born at the same address.[8] Neither parent could speak English when the family arrived and on the birth certificates of Barney and Rebecca (the ninth and tenth, 1885, 1888) Henrietta was still signing with an 'X'. Perhaps she never became fluent. Registration of the last child, Gertrude, was completed by her sister Annie, some twenty years her senior.

Barney's family, then, like Adelaide's, knew all about deprivation, and to add to their troubles, his baby sister, Rebecca, had died aged seventeen months from some appalling accident with scalding water. He was then nearly four and remained haunted by the event. It was one of the few pieces of information about his early life which he passed down. No details. Just the event, the pain of it. Another lost child. His parents' addresses possibly tell their own story. Edinburgh was then a staging post for European Jewish immigrants, and the city's welcome was not always offered by individual landlords. Frequently, refugees, having paid to sail to America, were simply dumped on Leith docks. Anti-Semitism in the city was common. Oswald Mosley addressed a rally outside the Usher Hall in June 1934, and Muriel recalled with distaste Blackshirts strutting round its streets during the 1930s. To be Jewish, without a steady job, and with a large family, would not have eased Louis's search for accommodation. In *The Prime of Miss Jean Brodie*, Muriel described 'the reeking network of slums which the Old Town constituted in those years. The Canongate, The Grassmarket, The Lawnmarket, were names which betokened a misty region of crime and desperation [...].'[9] Unknown to her then, these were the districts where Barney's older siblings grew up.[10]

In their last years, Louis and Henrietta Camberg lived just round the corner from Bruntsfield Place in Viewforth Square. Barney, a loyal son, visited regularly, and it may be that his mother was alone there for some time while her husband was still alive for, having had heart problems for six and a half years, he died in Edinburgh's Royal Asylum suffering from senile dementia. Both died aged sixty-seven, he in 1917,[11] she in 1920.[12] Muriel, two years old in 1920, naturally had no memory of either. Philip could only recall an ancient woman with very long hair. But it is noticeable in such a close family that these grandparents were not more talked about in Bruntsfield Place. Cissy rarely visited her parents-in-law, and when Barney signed his father's death certificate, describing him as a 'commercial traveller', he perhaps wondered why being 'just an ordinary working engineer' should condemn him as a failure. His parents were Orthodox. Doubtless they urged him to put in more regular appearances at the synagogue. And then there was the question of Cissy's Christian background, the fact that she had never converted, and her drinking. But his first loyalty was to her and to his children. If that isolated him from his own clan, so be it. Philip remembered his Camberg uncles and aunts as notoriously thin-skinned: 'If you said the wrong word they would stay away [...] very easily offended. Touchy. [...] My father was always falling out with Rae, sometimes with Esther [...]'[13] – and Barney was equally sensitive to insult, real or imagined. It was a family trait shared by both Philip and Muriel.

Muriel, however, found Rae (Rachel) and Esther, Barney's older sisters, delightful, and both were influential figures. Esther married Isador Goldfar, a Turkish-Jewish tobacco merchant by whom she had four sons. All entered business or the professions.[14] Philip recalled a fond, hospitable aunt who never lost her rumbustious sense of humour. Muriel retained an image of Isador as charmingly exotic. When they began to prosper, they were never pretentious. But Barney's ears always pricked at any suggestion that he might have done better. The families met, for whatever reason, only occasionally.

Rae was perhaps less of a threat. Like Barney, she had 'married out' – to Stuart Marwick, a master mariner turned tobacconist. It was Uncle Stuart who taught Philip to make his crystal set. He also provided Barney's younger sister, Gertie, with employment as a cigarette maker in one of his kiosks[15] by Newington Station. In the mid-1920s, Gertie stayed with Muriel's family, sleeping in the bed-closet off the sitting room, leaving each morning for work. Muriel never knew what she did. Barney and Philip found her vivacious but difficult: 'a little flirt [...]. She was all right. She used to sulk a lot. A very moody person.'[16] Muriel's opinion of her was quite different. She relished the company of her young aunt (only twenty-three when Muriel was born), and had fond memories of her practising the Charleston with Cissy on the kitchen linoleum. '[Gertie] went out with boyfriends, dressed in a short-skirted navy blue outfit and a cherry-red hat that hugged her bobbed hair. She regarded most of her boyfriends as objects of amusement, regaling us, on her return, with pointed, merry anecdotes.'[17]

Gertie, like Adelaide, provided Muriel with a female exemplar. 'We often laughed at others in our house,' Muriel noted, 'and I picked up the craft of being polite while people were present and laughing later [...].'[18] The appeal of these women centred on their sardonic mockery, particularly of men. Cissy had once asked her mother how one kept men happy. 'You have to feed 'em both ends,' she replied.[19] Muriel admired the attention both paid to clothing, was attracted simultaneously to the old woman's grim reserve and to her aunt's sceptical gaiety. She grew up, and remained, intrigued by the extraordinary rituals and penalties of courtship but, like Adelaide and Gertie, had little interest in offering sustenance at either end. 'Feeding' men, acting the cook and courtesan, was impossible for her.

Gertie never found a husband in Edinburgh. Ultimately she accepted an arranged marriage in Australia to a man she did not know and was never seen in Scotland again. Muriel missed her. Once, when her parents were out at Musselburgh Races, Gertie had whisked her off to the Lyceum music hall. Florrie Forde, a fantastical sex-bomb in 'a one-piece suit resembling the modern body-tights, all gold-bronze spangles,'[20] reclined on the stage and sang 'Dream Daddy'. Sir Frank Kermode, the critic and later a friend of Muriel's, recalls in his autobiography seeing Florrie Forde on his native Isle of Man: '[She] came year after year for a generation, fat, loud, rich, fantastically overdressed, but certainly in touch and offering the audience a hugely magnified image of their own Cockaignes. It's said that when a man threw a banana at her she caught it, ate it, and invited him to come back afterwards and get his skin back.'[21] On being told where Gertie had taken their little girl, Barney and Cissy fell about laughing. But this surreal, unfocused image of female power cut permanently into Muriel's imagination: 'Other people on the stage came and went, especially men in evening dress, but Florrie in her spangles dominated the enormous house.'[22]

Relations with the rest of Barney's family were more formal: 'Esther [...] was a practising [...] Jew and my mother was always anxious to hide from [her] evidence of ham, bacon, pork sausages or any other unholy delicacy [...].'[23] Cissy's sitting room was a monument to religious eclecticism: she lit the Sabbath candles on Friday nights; on one table stood a 'Buddah on a lotus leaf [...] on another a horrible replica of the Venus de Milo. One way and another all the gods [were] served in [her] household.'[24] She muddled along between faiths, attending the synagogue on Yom Kippur as Barney's wife, carrying in her handbag a locket containing an image of Christ. Good and bad luck figured in her sense of the supernatural. She would not wear green. Crossed knives and cracked glass were to be avoided. She would slip down to the street to chant: 'New moon, new moon, be good to me. Bring me presents, one, two, three', and, staring up, turn a sixpence in her purse. As a child, Muriel accepted this pagan Christian Judaism as a quite normal, indeed stimulating, aspect of Edinburgh's tolerance and her mother's eccentricity. Esther's orthodoxy brought with it a certain (amusing) strain. But, as usual, there was a 'nevertheless'. Esther 'took a keen interest in my reading and writing, and I loved her for that.'[25] In the summer of 1923, with her new maroon blazer and her Nelson's Infant Primer, Muriel was eager to start her formal education.

*

Gillespie's took children between the ages of five and eighteen: Infants, Juniors, Intermediate, Senior. The imposing building, 1904 muted Scottish baronial, presented a granite face to the world but harboured its charges tenderly. Muriel remembered its classrooms as light and airy, always decorated with flowers. On one side its high windows stared out to vast northern skies and the seagulls swooping over the Links; on the other to the four-storey tenements of Marchmont. School was a ten-minute walk from the Cambergs' flat: up Bruntsfield Place and then diagonally across the Links through an avenue of trees. Throughout Muriel's Infant and Junior years, Cissy would accompany her each morning; each afternoon, pick her up. It was only during her last two years in the Juniors, when Muriel came under the influence of a charismatic teacher, that she developed a sense of amusement about Cissy. The school was far from snobbish. It did, however, teach its girls discrimination, offering an environment in which female intelligence could flourish.

Muriel's teachers were strict but, literally and metaphorically, 'always tending plants'.[26] The timeless vitality of *The Prime of Miss Jean Brodie* derives at least partly from its affectionate portrait of Gillespie's as the Marcia Blaine School. Miss Brodie herself bears a strong resemblance to the woman in whose class Muriel sat awestruck as a dumpy eleven- and twelve-year-old: Christina Kay. That 'character in search of an author, whose classroom walls were adorned with reproductions of early and Renaissance paintings [...] entered my imagination immediately. I started to write about her even then.'[27] Brodie's famous remark that her girls were the 'crème de la crème' was also Miss Kay's. '[She] realized',

Muriel noted, 'that our parents' interest in our welfare was only mar-ginally cultural.'[28] In her autobiography, Muriel conscientiously refused to complain about this lack because she did not feel disadvantaged. But when Miss Kay veered off in the middle of a sentence to discuss Corot's touch of red or the Latin root of 'to educate', Muriel discovered in herself the artist and the intellectual craving sustenance which could not be provided at home.

Like Philip, she appears not to have had a wide circle of friends. Her chum until she was nine years old, Daphne Porter, died. Thereafter, Muriel was closest to the girl with whom she shared a desk until they matriculated: Frances Niven. Both were interested in imaginative writing, particularly poetry. Both were selected by Miss Kay, like sur-rogate children, for special treatment. The 'Brodie set' was six, the Kay set just two. Frances was an only child: timorous, over-protected, gentle, bright, eager to be led into Muriel's vibrant imaginative world. The Nivens lived in a mid-Victorian town house near Robert Louis Ste-venson's birthplace, already a museum, in Howard Place,[29] and the literary associations thrilled Muriel. In the basement they played witches. 'Hallowe'en was celebrated by a roaring fire in the handsome old fireplace of a room which must once have been a large kitchen or servants' hall.'[30] It was all rather different from the cramped accom-modation in Bruntsfield Place, and from the age of eleven, Muriel's home and her intellectual life were at odds. She visited Frances every week. Frances rarely visited her. Muriel went off with Frances for summer holidays at her grandmother's home in Crail, a seaside town in Fife. After school they would write letters to each other, to be exchanged the next day. At weekends they would explore the Botanical Gardens near Frances's house where, beneath an ancient tree, they buried a jointly written story.

At her own expense Miss Kay drip-fed Muriel and Frances with Edinburgh's cultural life, and her effect on both was fundamental. Florrie Forde, the Charleston and the form at Musselburgh races were quite another world. Miss Kay took the girls to see Pavlova's last per-formance at the Empire Theatre, to contemporary poetic drama, to concerts, even to films. In class she was a magnetic performer with her dark eyes, olive skin and her passion for education, the sense of being European rather than Scottish. Education was not for her a matter of pouring information into empty vessels but of drawing out her girls' native talents.

Muriel and Frances went with Miss Kay to hear John Masefield, recently elected Poet Laureate, read parts of 'Dauber' to a huge and appreciative audience. It was an experience which nurtured an appreciation of narrative poetry and sowed the seeds for Muriel's book on Masefield twenty years later. Another pupil was so impressed by Miss Kay's passion for all things Italian that she wondered whether their schoolmistress might have had Italian forebears:

> I have never seen the Colosseum, the catacombs, the Sistine Chapel [...] but through Miss Kay I feel I know them quite well. Interspersed with the Italian masters and the French Impressionists of the 19th century and the Dutch School (Rembrandt's portraits in particular) and literature and poetry and interior decorating (I moved all the ornaments on our sitting-room mantelpiece to form a more pleasing 'line') we still had such an excellent grounding in the traditional three Rs [...]. With Miss Kay I *liked* mental arithmetic and long division and multiplication sums, and those spelling lists, and found grammar thoroughly enjoyable [...].[31]

So did Muriel. She, too, became an Italophile and went to live there in 1967. She, too, developed a sharp mind for grammar (although not for figures). Muriel was once asked if Miss Brodie's admiration for Mussolini reflected her own feelings at the time. 'Women, particularly single women', she replied, 'adore a strong man, a liberator. There were many in those days who admired Hitler. I guess you could say [...] that Mussolini was a *big* bad man and Hitler a *little* bad man. But we didn't know that then. Remember, the story is set in 1930.'[32] She never thought of Miss Brodie as a fascist.

It was more the style than the content of this teaching which excited and empowered Muriel: Miss Kay's mental habit of proceeding by 'dazzling non-sequiturs' rather than by logical progression. Behind everything lay the primacy of colour: 'She loved colours. She taught us to be aware of them. [...] To her, colour *was* form'.[33] Despite Miss Kay's naïve interest in Mussolini, she was profoundly anti-nationalist. They were taught (by the school's ethos, not just by Miss Kay) to *listen* to what was so easy to sing, 'not to be carried away by crowd emotions, not to be fools'.[34] This was a priceless gift, part of which, for Muriel at least, was a nascent scepticism about all systems of power and their potential for corrupting free will. Miss Kay taught her to reject the politics of victimhood, the tetchy, apologetic embarrassment of her brother.

For all this, however, perhaps because of this, her teacher's spirit is reincarnated in Jean Brodie as ambiguously beneficial. The loyalty she demands of her pupils becomes an imposition. While aspiring to release her 'set' from the shackles of petit-bourgeois convention, she unconsciously claps on the even tighter irons of emotional dependency. She lays her pupils open to danger, does not let them 'know the worst', particularly about 'strong men'. She cultivates not independent spirits but slaves. She is, in fact, another version of that recurrently sinister figure in Muriel's fiction: the incubus. Brodie is not Kay, but Kay transfigured. The 'Muriel-figure', Sandy, is not Muriel but a metaphor for Muriel's adult consciousness evaluating her adolescent infatuation. Shirley Hazzard once asked large-eyed Muriel why Sandy Stranger (clearly, she thought, a self-portrait) had been given small eyes. She used to have small eyes, Muriel replied, but they had enlarged with knowledge.[35] Sandy betrays Brodie, becomes a nun and writes about 'The Transfiguration of the Commonplace'. So did Muriel – in her way.

When the novel was adapted for television, Muriel noted that, although this serial was 'closer [than the Maggie Smith film] to my own personal concept of what the times and place and woman were like', Geraldine McEwan possessed physical characteristics rather different from Brodie's: 'I've always thought of [her] as being more voluptuous in her build, but that's OK.'[36] Edinburgh was greyer in her memory than the coloured film, opalescent: 'Auld Reekie' with its smoke-caked buildings capable of suddenly transforming into the ethereal structures of the Athens of the North by the effect of northern light. Nevertheless she was perpetually intrigued to see how any adaptation would fill the spaces she had left. She rarely drew from life. It is rather the differences between her characters and their 'originals' which is telling, particularly in the case of Kay / Brodie.

At first sight there appears to be little enough glamour in either. Miss Kay had a stocky, middle-aged figure with thick legs, cropped hair with a fringe and a heavyish black moustache. Miss Brodie shares her brown eyes and hair, her olive complexion, but her physical appearance is amorphous and varies according to the vision of those she enchants. Miss Kay may have borrowed her reproductions from the 'dishy' art master, Arthur Couling, but she no more fell in love with him than did any of the girls. Although she wore well-cut tweeds with small flirtatious touches – a cloche hat, a flower in the buttonhole – she was distinctly neither a *femme fatale* nor a revolutionary subverting the school's conventions. In July 1936, a year after Muriel had left, a sad note appeared in the school magazine. Miss Kay ran the Former Pupils' Gymnastic Club. For the last year it had met on Tuesday evenings for physical jerks, folk dancing and games. Old girls wore school uniform. Not surprisingly, attendance had been poor and the club was threatened with extinction.[37]

The huge influence of Miss Kay, then, had little to do with physical beauty or iconoclasm. She was a devout Christian. Under her wing, Muriel flourished in Scripture studies. Yet her teacher lingered in Muriel's memory as a figure of fantasy who strangely concentrated the political and sexual forces surging round her in the Edinburgh of 1929–30:

> Did Miss Kay have a sweetheart in her life? I think she did, long before our time. [. . .] She was of the generation of clever, academically trained women who had lost their sweethearts in the 1914–1918 war. There had been a terrible carnage. There were no men to go round. Until we ourselves grew up there was a veritable generation of spinsters. At any rate, Miss Kay told us how wonderful it had been to waltz in those long full skirts. I sensed romance, sex.[38]

In an autobiography which ruthlessly omits undocumented speculation, Muriel allows herself this one indulgence. The 'Great War' and subsequent Depression touched her life only marginally through the death of her Uncle Harry and the fearful exhibitions of poverty apparent everywhere in the streets. As we can see from 'The First Year of My Life', however, the effect of the war on her was not marginal. It represented a fundamental schism in British society, and Muriel both approved of its disruption of a complacent patriarchy and lamented the death of romance. Discussing a photograph of Harry (in uniform) standing by her parents, she broke from her cool commentary, touched by the picture: 'Aren't they sweet. Wartime.'[39] Before that point lay comforting illusions about marriage; after it lay sex. Before it, men like her father protected women; after it, a girl of slender means had to look out for herself. It had, she knew, always been a rough world and she wanted nothing more than the chance to look out for herself. But for years the illusion of romance, of marriage, clouded her judgement of men. She was, as she admitted, a bad picker.

*

Teachers in the Junior School covered the entire curriculum in their own rooms and thus had a captive audience. In the Senior School, girls were streamed according to ability and moved from class to class between subject specialists. Two of these – Alison Foster and Anna Munroe – were also influential. The first taught English, the second, Classics, Muriel's two best subjects. Alison Foster edited the school magazine and promoted Muriel's verse there. Anna Munroe was equally enthusiastic. Yet somehow Muriel could discover in neither the glamour which attached to Miss Kay. Why? She was fond of both 'but conscious of outgrowing them especially as a person-of-the-world. M. thinks their experiences of men were limited, whereas she liked the boys, or at least the idea of them.'[40] Alison Foster kept in touch for many years, writing long letters about her nervous breakdown, offering a friendship Muriel could not reciprocate. Anna Munroe 'was thin with hair coiled over her ears. Very old-fashioned.'[41] Both were kindly, dedicated teachers, but there was something spinsterish, provincial, introverted about them.

Brodie is, as much as anything, a book about female adolescence. It opens with a striking image:

> The boys, as they talked to the girls from Marcia Blaine School, stood on the far side of their bicycles holding the handlebars, which established a protective fence of bicycle between the sexes, and the impression that at any moment the boys were likely to be away.[42]

Misses Foster and Munroe perhaps approved of such protective fences. Muriel wanted to vault them. On the other side lay 'romance, sex', the excitements of the real world.

That this 'real world' also held misfortune only increased Muriel's desire to enter it as the proper habitat for the artist. 'I don't know', she wrote, 'at what point before I went to school I became aware of poor men or women, sometimes accompanied by children, singing for pennies in the back green':

> [...] I looked out at them with tears. Usually my mother wrapped up a penny in a piece of newspaper and threw it out [...]. [...] This was part of the distress following the First World War. The men who had returned could not find work and the social services were inadequate. I once saw a child of about seven selling newspapers at Toll Cross on a winter night, without so much as a vest underneath the thin jacket of his coat. He was barefoot.[43]

During the Depression the 'shivery possibility of a revolution'[44] hung in the air. 'To grow from childhood into adolescence,' she noted, 'and live as a teenager in the 1930s of Edinburgh, was to be aware of social nervousness.'[45] One might add that, although she was largely untroubled by it, and never considered herself part of the tight-knit Jewish community, this nervousness was particularly felt by the city's Jews in a period of open anti-Semitism. Fostered in the tolerant atmosphere of Gillespie's, she learned the arts of sitting quietly and not showing off.

As an infant Muriel was shy, as an adolescent inclined to be fat. Like her brother, she was self-conscious about her physical appearance, intrigued by the awkward opposite sex. At home, males remained something of a mystery and this seems to have been how she preferred it. It was, she said, 'an absolute gypsy household. [...] There was always a shuffling around' of sleeping arrangements depending on whether they were poor enough to need lodgers. 'We managed the division of the sexes quite well. [I]t was a terribly modest life [...]. We never discussed sex. We should have, perhaps, but we never did.'[46] Philip's comment on this was that 'In those early days sex was not really an issue at all. The issue was having enough money to live, to eat, to clothe ourselves.'[47] Even so, as a schoolgirl and a young woman, Muriel did not wish to be associated with the 'failure' of spinsterdom. Sexual power was an important aspect of the vitality of that 'real world' she was determined to enter. She craved escape from her adolescent frame as much as from the restrictions of poverty. But it was perhaps the idea of men rather than the intrusive fumblings of flesh-and-blood males that she desired. On one occasion, she told Derek Stanford, her brother had pulled her on to his knees and rubbed himself against her. This was just horseplay but it was unpleasant and she did not forget, or forgive, such things. She hungered rather for that gracious world mythologised by Miss Kay's pre-war memories, wanted to be a poet and the war had killed the poets.

Under these circumstances, allegiances proved confusing. Muriel had an excellent analytical mind, prospering almost as well at school in Science as she did in English and Classics. Her attraction to her father was based not only on his kindness, tenacity and charm but also on the fact that he 'had an engineer's thinking'.[48] That systematic attention to detail remained important to her. *Curriculum Vitae* reveals her as a woman who enjoys exploring and explaining systems, even if it is only the practical details of how she helped her mother to sit Adelaide up in bed to get her on and off the commode. Muriel's dolls were not surrogate babies but actors subject to her direction. Later in life she often astonished publishers and agents by pointing out blunders in contractual detail. Like Clovis in *Not to Disturb* (1971), she always read the small print.

At the same time, however, there was that other, contradictory, and more important side to Muriel's nature: the artist who sought order through imaginative transformation. This became, and remained, the essence of her being and was, at this time only obscurely, linked with spiritual life. 'I had no specific religion', she remarked, 'but at the same time I had a strong religious feeling.'[49] When she was about nine she had 'a kind of religious experience':

> I saw a road-workman knocked down or hit by a tram-car. He ran from the spot with his arms spread out and fell beside the pavement. I saw this from a place where I was playing with some other children from school. We were all speedily ushered out of the way [...]. My father could find nothing about it in the evening paper. But the image of the workman with arms outspread stayed in my mind for a long time. I fancied he had gone to Heaven [...] in his workman's cap and overalls. I thought he liked me. I spoke to nobody about him.[50]

This 'strangeness' about Muriel was often remarked on by those who knew her. Some described it as a kind of 'second sight'. They noticed the coincidence of her presence at serious accidents, the composure with which she dealt with them. Her Catholic friends believed her prayers to be particularly efficacious. Evelyn Waugh told his children to protect her because she was a saint. Shirley Hazzard always remembered 'Muriel with the X-ray eyes' and believed that somehow things happened, odd things, when she was around. Muriel herself mocked all this. Nevertheless, the notion of the artist's 'second sight' and of its relation to religious experience was with her from childhood:

> There were times when [...] I was aware of a definite 'something beyond myself'. This sensation especially took hold of me when I was writing; I was convinced that sometimes I had access to knowledge that I couldn't possibly have gained through normal channels [...]. When I was young [...] the confidence that arose from my sense of receiving 'given' knowledge and ideas constituted my religion.[51]

It was this confidence, to open herself up as a conduit for voices, that Miss Kay gave her.

Muriel, however, did not distinguish herself academically at Gillespie's until she was fourteen and had left Miss Kay behind. In 1932, the year before Adelaide died, Muriel suddenly appears in the end-of-year rankings for Form 1B: second in English, second in Latin, third in Mathematics, second in Science. She never excelled in the other subjects of this basic curriculum: French, Art, Physical Training and Dressmaking. Only as an adult did she find it easy to attempt a modern foreign language; her drawing was clumsy; PT was tedious; the dresses pupils were instructed to make were irredeemably charmless. But she was industrious and keen, sat in the front row, trudged eagerly through the snow to extracurricular Greek at eight in the morning. In 1933 she did well again in English, Latin and Science, both she and Frances were promoted to the 'A' stream, and Muriel's bursary relieved her parents of fees for the following year.[52] Thereafter, no mention is made of her performance in the school magazine, other than to note that, with seventy-one others, she gained her Day School Certificate (Higher) in 1934.[53] She stayed on for a couple of terms, vaguely planning to go to university because her teachers begged her to, then gave it up and left.

'I was studious,' she comments, 'but I liked my own form of studies, picking and choosing books in the public library.'[54] With the rest of her family's tickets she could borrow a weekly armful of volumes, and in these she lived: Wordsworth, Browning, Tennyson, Swinburne; and, for more modern reading: Blunden, Brooke, de la Mare, Yeats, Alice Meynell, Bridges and Masefield: 'I was a passionate admirer of Masefield's narrative verse, especially *The Dauber* and *Reynard the Fox*.'[55] Among the novels she read were *Jane Eyre, Cranford*, and, with less enthusiasm, *The Mill on the Floss*. During her last year at school she was happily devouring *The Seven Pillars of Wisdom*. It was a random selection, rather conservative. The huge influence of T. S. Eliot, Proust, Baudelaire, Beerbohm, Waugh and Ivy Compton-Burnett came later as she progressed steadily towards her own literary experiments. During her adolescence it was the Romantic and the Gothic which offered escape from Edinburgh's grey walls.

Her fame at Gillespie's, then, rested not on her examination performance but on her poetry. Although there is scant mention of the former in the school magazine, scarcely a year passes without some reference to the latter. It was rare to publish more than one contribution by a pupil in the same issue. Alison Foster, however, thought the poems of twelve-year-old Muriel 'so much out of the ordinary' that she included five.[56] Three – 'The Sea', 'The Winding of the Horn' and 'The Victims' – agonise over the relationship between hunter and hunted. The other two – 'The Stars' and 'The Land of Poetry' – suggest a mind divided between rational relativism and the mystical. Both seek distance from nature red in tooth and claw, and all these subjects were to remain important to Muriel's artistic vision. 'The Land of Poetry' was the ultimate haven.

Muriel's verse was modest in its intellectual scope, sentimental about animals, certainly not precocious like Evelyn Waugh's schoolboy writings. Its most striking aspect is its tight control of form. In 1931 a selection of poems from Edinburgh school magazines was issued as a book, *The Door of Youth*, in which Muriel's work figured prominently.[57] The following year she won an Edinburgh schools' competition to mark the centenary of Sir Walter Scott's death for which she was publicly crowned and made to feel like 'the Dairy Queen of Dumfries'.[58] Sixty-one years later the photograph still made her shiver: 'I was totally fat at that time [...] pudgy.'[59] But there were compensations: the prize of books; the acknowledgement of her talent; the sense that others sympathised with her indignity.[60] She often judged her friends by their empathy with her embarrassment. Visiting Muriel's class in the Senior School, Miss Kay held up the awful photograph: 'You can see the sensitivity in that line of Muriel's arm.' To Miss Kay, her former pupil was not the public image, the stocky adolescent in a cheap chiffon dress. She was a poet and should be treated with respect. Muriel was not fooled by Miss Kay's generosity. The sensitivity in the line of her arm she saw as 'an involuntary shudder'.[61] The significant factor was the public act of faith.

With this support, then, Muriel's poetry continued to flourish. In 1934 she came first in the school's Intermediate Section of the Sir Walter Scott and Burns Club prizes. But it was all very 'Scottish'. At sixteen she was already sensing the limitations of her horizons. The last of her poems for Gillespie's magazine, 'Dust', echoes Yeats's 'The Scholars'. Vivid life is opposed to dreary study, and in this opposition Muriel knew where she stood. 'Dust' was addressed to an anonymous dead academic, also, perhaps, to all her teachers except Miss Kay as a kind of valediction:

> Poppies laugh while they are young,
> Wild and bright and burning,
> You were dusty all your days
> With your books and learning.
> Poppies grin upon your grave,
> Your dusty soul is gone.
> Crumbles the rest to dust and dust
> Under that cold stone.[62]

At sixteen Muriel was very much 'wild and bright and burning'. She had done well, much better than her brother. But this was a point, the first of many in her life, at which the crude materiality of circumstance was forced upon her. To continue to study for university was not an option. Her parents could not afford it; her family simply did not offer a cultural background which could envisage such an enterprise: girls were educated, worked, and then got married. Muriel once remarked that the only thing she regretted was not having had a university education. In her early days as a professional writer this had left her vulnerable to patronage from gentlemen poets and publishers – or so they thought. On the other hand, 'I would have liked to have gone to a university but merely in order to obtain a degree, and that only for the uncertain purpose of getting a better job.'[63] Jobs for Muriel were always a means to another end: to support her career as a writer. In reality, she wanted out, had wearied of school and, necessity being the mother of convention, she half-embraced it. She wanted money, clothes, independence. By the time she matriculated she was in no doubt that she was an artist and that 'in order to write about life as I intended to do, [...] I had first to live. [...] [T]he essentials of literature were, to me, outside of literature; they were elsewhere, out in the world.'[64] The dutiful earnestness of the female students at Edinburgh University did not appeal. That was death. Art was life.

*

In the meantime she had to do something with her life. She had grown up, like Philip, influenced by Barney's industry and self-reliance. So, while Philip worked all day at the rubber factory and laboured his way through night school, Muriel enrolled at Heriot-Watt College for a rudimentary course in business English. Always intrigued by literary concision, she took a course in précis-writing and regarded it as completing her 'education in English prose. [...] The idea of a more scientific [...] approach to English, in contrast to the broad, humane, poetry-loving approach of Gillespie's, appealed to me [...]. I find "managerial" speech unpretentious, direct, quite expressive enough.'[65] Next, she took an unpaid job teaching English, Arithmetic and Nature Studies at a small private school in return for tuition in shorthand and typing from the school secretary. It was an odd establishment with junior boys and senior girls. The boys were preparing for public school, the girls to be 'finished' on the Continent. For a while Muriel was amused by the genteel atmosphere but as soon as she had acquired the necessary skills, she resigned and went to work in the office of William Small & Sons, an exclusive women's department store on Princes Street.

Small's was then one of Edinburgh's leading emporia, distinguished by its service. Whatever the hour, a 'shop-walker' dressed in morning coat, top hat and striped trousers would greet his ladies at the door, make polite enquiries of madam, and call over the relevant assistant. It was a scenario later parodied in its decline by the British sitcom *Are You Being Served?*. In Edinburgh of 1936 the whole display was in deadly earnest and Muriel relished 'this perpetual ballet of refinement',[66] 'the mixed atmosphere of luxury, real elegance and silliness'.[67] Here, at last, she was touching a microcosm with its own manners and absurdities, and she listened eagerly, her mind whirring as it always did, like a tape-recorder. She worked as a secretary for Mr Small himself, an ancient, courtly Scot with a grand piano in his room, was invited to help him choose fabrics, taken to the counting-house where four women crouched over sloping desks, dipping pens and ruling lines. Miss Ritchie, the middle-aged chief accountant, 'was by far the most sexy. In fact, she was rather vulgar and told dirty jokes. For that alone, I fairly despised her, and was merely astonished at the abnegation of all femininity in the other three.'[68]

The comment is interesting. *Curriculum Vitae* mischievously invites feminist attack. Muriel was as typically provocative on sexual politics as she was on any other issue. Miss Kay might have bred a band of 'incipient feminists' but feminism for Muriel began and ended with the claim for economic equality. Once that was achieved, she required no favours. She made no apology for loving designer dresses, jewellery, poise, charm. Elegance in clothes, as in writing, was for her the perfect control of aesthetic expression; it was rhythm, style. Decorous behaviour between men and women was the stately minuet of civilised life. Both for her were social arrangements which allowed women to keep their distance. No woman could have defended female independence more fiercely. Yet that word 'sexy' recurs as a positive term in her autobiography. What does it mean? Certainly it does not suggest titillation. That would be merely vulgar – and dangerous. Women who degrade themselves thus in her fiction court their own destruction. The word seems rather to evoke a sense of those women (and men) who enjoy the power of their sexuality as an art form, as performance. Many have wondered if Muriel had lesbian tendencies. So far as she knew, she had none. Lesbians tended to worry her. All the evidence points to her having been a red-blooded heterosexual young woman. Nevertheless, she was a curious mixture of aspirant *femme du monde* and naïf, and that love of courtly display led her into difficulties. She looked for protection and did not find it. She liked older men and found most of them married. Worst of all, she was often attracted to gay or bisexual men and did not discover their sexuality until it was too late. She learned to present herself as 'sexy' and developed a charm which drew men like flies. But it was a mask. It offered the power, not to seduce, but to wrong-foot the seducer.

The essential distinction here is that between the artist Fleur Talbot and the tedious Beryl Tims in *Loitering with Intent*. Fleur maintains a sardonic distance from men and women alike and refuses to be called her lover's 'mistress', a term 'which [. . .] had quite different connotations from those proper to my independent liaison [. . .]'.[69] This liaison is with a married man. Fleur is a Catholic. Nevertheless, she is pragmatic about the affair: if the wife does not like it, she can leave her husband; if the lover feels guilty, he can leave Fleur. Either way, it is none of her business. She has extracted herself from any emotional contract and, like Muriel in many of her relationships, refuses to take responsibility for how anyone else might feel about her. When Fleur's lover does leave her, her principal emotion is relief. Beryl panders to men and represents a despicable type: the simpering English Rose. Female sentimentality about men surrounds Fleur and she wrecks it with remorseless logic. When Beryl says, '"Men like to see a bit of jewellery on a girl"', Fleur's response is pointed: 'It was always a question of what men liked [. . .]. The second week of my job she asked me if I was going to get married. "No. I write poetry. I want to write. Marriage would interfere."'[70] This was the Muriel Muriel became, in 1949, the year of the novel's main setting after she had become Secretary of the Poetry Society and lost both the job and her married lover, Howard Sergeant. Or, rather, it was the Muriel she was still struggling to become – for she never accepted that her vocation was incompatible with marriage.

*

In 1936, aged eighteen and eager for romance, she greeted her uncertain future cheerfully. While the Spanish Civil War was raging, Europe hurtling towards another global conflict against the backdrop of the Depression, life at 160 Bruntsfield Place had never been merrier. Muriel took pride in her secretarial efficiency, doubled her salary over the year from three to six pounds a month, and with the staff discount could buy a small selection of smart clothes and make-up for herself and her mother. She lost weight, wore lipstick, put her hair up and went out dancing. She could even afford to contribute a little to household expenses. With both children at work, Barney and Cissy now had no need of lodgers, and every Sunday evening provided a generous supper for American medical students Philip had met through Jewish social clubs.[71]

At this stage Muriel and Philip were closer than they had ever been, or were ever to be again. He took her out. At twenty-three, and still without a girlfriend, he was happy to have his sister in attendance. It was she who introduced him to girls and, indirectly, to his future wife, Sophie. After leaving Gillespie's, Muriel lost contact with Frances Niven and returned to the protected environment of home, half in, half out of the Jewish community, where Philip was definitely *in* it. Miriam Levenson became one of Muriel's closer companions, and through Miriam, Philip met Sophie who had been born in Poland, the daughter of a Jewish refugee family.

Muriel ran a string of boyfriends, escorts rather than lovers, to take her out and there was always Philip when none was available. So long as she brought her suitors home, no objections were raised. 'I was just a kid,' she remarked, 'I never slept with anyone before I got married because no one anyway ever asked me. You didn't. There wouldn't have been anywhere to go. I wasn't in that way of life. They came round to meet your parents. That sort of thing. Sit and look at each other. Drink tea. Eat fruit.'[72] The Overseas Club on Princes Street was considered a select establishment. Philip and Muriel attended its dances regularly. One night she met a man there who changed her life.

Small and nervous, Sydney Oswald Spark was a lapsed Jew, thirteen years her senior. Very little was known about his family. Like Barney's parents, Sydney had been born in Lithuania. His father apparently wandered the Borders, hawking whatever he could, gaining a reputation as 'Meshugah [Mad] Spark'.[73] Barney was suspicious, Cissy prepared to be generous. Sydney seemed a kindly fellow, intelligent and besotted with Muriel. His mother and sister had settled respectably in Edinburgh. And 'Solly' (as he was known) had done well for himself. He had an MA from Edinburgh University, was a mathematics teacher and considered himself an intellectual. So did Muriel. It seemed to be a meeting of minds in the romantic atmosphere of the constitutional crisis. Muriel and Solly listened to Edward VIII's abdication speech on the radio together. She was nineteen, he thirty-two. She enjoyed being the object of an older man's infatuation. He seemed restless and interesting, planning to emigrate to teach in Africa. Muriel was attracted to this exotic prospect and to his apparent lack of machismo. She had no intention of becoming a housewife. He promised servants to leave her free to concentrate on her poetry. Above all, she wanted to escape from Edinburgh and its claustrophobic social microcosm. She needed room to breathe. Solly was, like her, an unbeliever. He said he felt lonely. He brought her flowers. She felt sorry for him. And so, after a year of chaste courting and chatting about books, they became engaged and he left for Southern Rhodesia (now Zimbabwe).

Shortly after, on 13 August 1937, she was aboard the *Windsor Castle* with her third-class ticket, diamond ring and trunk, waving goodbye to her family as the ship slid from Southampton docks. Her parents, brother, and Uncle Joe Shapiro had travelled down with her. On the train home they had dissolved into tears, never expecting to see her again. And although she did return, divorced, in 1944, in a sense their fear was well-founded. For they never did see again the Muriel they had known. She had left as little more than a schoolgirl. She returned a woman, herself a mother, formidable, self-possessed and immune to emotional blackmail. Africa taught her many things.

CHAPTER 3

Out of Africa

1937–1945

Muriel Spark may have been raised in Edinburgh but she grew up in Africa. There, she said, 'for the first time [...] life and death came very close together.'[1] The ease with which sanity could fracture, the surreal sensory effects of the climate, the atmosphere of unreality, of prejudice and violence, left her isolated and, almost immediately, wanting to return home. In *Heart of Darkness*, Conrad described Kurtz's impulse as 'the fascination of the abomination'. Muriel also saw something of that. But for her the horror was the complacent racism and cruelty of the white settlers. She loved Africa's wildness. As to marriage, she soon realised that she had made a terrible mistake.

These formative experiences are briefly sketched in *Curriculum Vitae*[2] and elaborated in a series of brilliant short stories and a radio play, 'The Dry River Bed'. The stories – 'The Seraph and the Zambesi', 'The Portobello Road', 'The Curtain Blown by the Breeze', 'Bang-bang You're Dead', 'The Pawnbroker's Wife' and 'The Go-Away Bird' – were written in the 1950s and 1960s. A long time passed before she turned to prose fiction; had to pass, perhaps, before she could assimilate the revelations of her six years in the Tropics and six months in South Africa. When she did begin to write about them in 'The Seraph ...' (1951), she drew directly on those banked-up feelings, and revealed that Africa had provided something like a spiritual experience which placed personal sorrows in perspective.

None of these stories is reportage; the characters are types rather than portraits and supernatural creatures stalk the terrestrial world. Chronological time collapses into flashbacks which threaten the reality of the narrative present. 'I observed them [the British colonials]', Muriel remarked, 'although I didn't write about them at the time.' When asked who in her life was a Chakata (the white farmer in 'The Go-Away Bird'), she replied: 'There was a local white chieftain in Fort Victoria and I think he owned the Fort Victoria Hotel where I had to stay. [...] Freaks like that. I knew it.' Raw material. Stored images. Quoting Wordsworth, she described the artistic process as 'emotion recollected in tranquillity'. How did she feel when writing about these people? 'Completely cold, and yet completely hot about my characters. I didn't care what they ... I didn't know them intimately.'[3]

Collectively, these stories present a fragmented, abstract auto-biography: a coherent symbolic exploration of Muriel's state of mind between 1937 and 1944. Each focuses on a young, acute white female and confronts her with forces threatening conformity or obliteration. Violence flickers like lightning in the stormy life of the colony, and as these heroines catch 'wafts of the savage territory beyond the absurd drawing-room'[4] they realise that 'There was something in the air of the place that affected the men [...] with an overturn of discrimination.'[5] Spark's women seek instead the development of discrimination, the power to come to terms with their sexuality and intelligence, to stand outside obsession; cold observers, even of themselves. Daphne's 'Oh, I see' in 'The Go-Away Bird' steadily increases its significance in proportion to her maturity. The expression begins as anodyne naivety and ends as resonant wisdom. She sees – right through. With each new attempt to invade her integrity, Sybil in 'Bang-bang You're Dead' develops the arts of sceptical withdrawal until she is entirely, and contentedly, alone. 'One learns', the narrator remarks, 'to accept oneself.' So did Muriel. But this acceptance carried the price of exclusion: '"[...] Am I a woman or an intellectual monster?"' Sybil calmly asks herself. 'She was so accustomed to this question [...] that it needed no answer.'[6]

Muriel was nineteen, attractive, sharp-witted and eager for experience. For a while she tried to play the wife but her husband was seriously disturbed. Sybil's self-accusation is typical of the voices, particularly female voices, her heroines see as ranged against them. They say that there is something wrong with them, something adrift in their sex-lives, that they should either marry or enter a convent. '"I don't see why [...]," Sybil retorts, "I should fit into a tidy category."'[7] Neither did Muriel, and if these stories reflect anything of her mental development, that journey to freedom was painful.

One of the issues plaguing Sybil may well have tortured Muriel: 'Other women do not wish to be married to a Mind. Yet I do, [...] and I should not have married. In fact I am not the marrying type.'[8] Engagement to Ossie had represented engagement to a 'Mind'. Or so Muriel had thought. Neither of them was 'trousseau-minded'.[9] Both had Jewish forebears; she was agnostic, he an atheist. He was 'smallish, thirty-three at the time. Curly sort of hair. Glasses. Not bad looking. Not good looking.'[10] His main attraction was his intelligence. Volatile and well-informed, he appeared spirited, seemed to know what he was doing. His brother, Louis, ran a store in Southern Rhodesia. They visited him once but Muriel disliked the man: 'He was [...] stupid, ignorant [...], rather different from my husband.'[11]

Sydney / Solly / Ossie had a three-year teaching contract. Muriel had entered into the arrangement on that basis: that their emigrant life would be temporary. On the boat out, she had flirted recklessly for the fortnight with a young South African. At Cape Town, his parents had invited her to stay and marry him. But no: although she was rather in love with the man, one could not behave like that. A Thomas Cook representative met her with flowers, put her on the train, and she was married to Solly in Salisbury Register Office on 3 September 1937, a matter of days after arriving. The wedding would have taken place sooner, had they not met an unexpected obstacle. She was a minor. Where was her father's written consent? Frantic cables to him and to the High Sheriff of Edinburgh secured it. Only then would the magistrate proceed.

There was something bohemian about all this which appealed to Muriel. Their first destination was Fort Victoria (Masvingo), then a one-horse town where Ossie was teaching, near the famous Zimbabwe ruins. She had arrived in the spring of the Southern Hemisphere. It was hot. Flowers blazed in the veldt; the local Africans tended their rows of maize, the Europeans their tobacco plantations, rolling hundreds of miles down twin strips of tarmac in ancient Ford V8s to visit neighbours. The space, the light, the heat, the cacophony of insects and languages were at first pleasantly surreal. And for the whites, there was also the seductiveness of power.

Muriel and Ossie lived in a hotel. She had nothing to do but write her poetry, and in this respect her situation was ideal. But town life was lethargic, and from the beginning she would escape to the ruins to explore this astonishing site of Bantu antiquity. One approached it then through thick surrounding bush and a narrow clearing, to burst upon the floor of a valley criss-crossed with a maze of eight-foot stone walls. In its haunting atmosphere she could slip free of the English life of Fort Victoria, with its calling cards and chit-chat, into the perspective of eternity.

The chemist's wife, the doctor's wife, the schoolmasters' wives: all left cards. Muriel politely acknowledged them. The implicit suggestion was that they (the whites, and particularly the white women) should stick together. Muriel 'had no calling cards and didn't intend to have any. Actually, I felt too young and too intelligent for all that formal married-woman business.'[12] She quickly discovered that there was no one to talk to. The blacks she found strikingly handsome, the veldt exotic and magnificently untamed. Yet in the midst of this romantic landscape, the town whites huddled in a makeshift Barsetshire. It wasn't why she had come. Perhaps it might have worked out if her husband had been what he had at first appeared. But he wasn't. Her Edinburgh friends had been amazed that she had married him. He was known to be moody, awkward, an oddball. At the time these had seemed positive qualities to her. She soon learned otherwise.

In 1937 Southern Rhodesia was barely fifty years old. The vast territory of the Colony was populated by 55,000 whites and about one and a half million blacks. The number of whites was more or less static; the number of blacks increasing fast. From the outset it seemed obvious to Muriel that 'the white people out there were very impermanent. One could see that it wouldn't last. *They* didn't know that. They carried on as though everything would go on for ever, and I knew it wouldn't.'[13] The stench of corruption was immediately in her nostrils. She was fascinated by the black Africans. Ossie was a thoroughgoing colonist and later a disciple of Cecil Rhodes. 'He accepted [the Africans] as an inferior race. Some-body to run around, black his boots. He had no principles whatsoever.'[14] And in this he was not unusual. The conversation among the more vulgar whites was thick with sneering stories about 'fixing' uppity blacks, and they lodged in Muriel's imagination. It was thought amusing that when an African on a bicycle had refused to move off the tarmac to allow a white driver to pass, the man had simply been run over. One of these tales Muriel preserved in 'The Curtain Blown by the Breeze'. A black boy had been caught watching a white woman breast-feeding. Her husband shot him dead. There were many 'shooting affairs', not least because there were three white men to each white woman. It was a gun culture and Ossie in his feeble and distracted fashion was infected by its machismo. He bought a 'baby Browning' revolver 'which he liked to fire off in corridors and courtyards'.[15]

One of the many things Ossie had failed to tell Muriel about himself was that he had been seeing a psychiatrist before their marriage, and that his desire to work in Africa had been prompted less by a sense of adventure than by the fact that he could not hold down a job in a British school. When she asked him why he had withheld this information, he replied that, had he been honest, she wouldn't have married him. He was quarrelsome, had lost a series of posts. Within weeks of their arrival in Fort Victoria, he was in trouble again with the education authorities and she was pregnant. He proposed that she have an abortion. She refused. During her pregnancy, he was shifted from school to school, becoming increasingly depressed.

The baby was born on 9 July 1938, at the Lady Rodney Nursing Home, Bulawayo, after a labour which lasted from Thursday evening to Saturday afternoon. Although she was devoted to her son Robin, an oasis of innocence in an otherwise arid life, her milk dried up and she could not feed him for long. Post-natal depression set in immediately and lasted for months. Ossie was sinking. Late in life she commented on their wedding night: 'An awful mess. Awful. Such a botch-up.'[16] Sexual relations had ceased with the birth, probably long before, and never resumed. When he tried bullying, she withdrew further into chilly distance. He beat her up. That was it. Any remnants of her original affection disintegrated with those blows. In their quadrangle hotels, she and Robin had one room, her husband another next door. They were effectively separated.

After two years of this, seriously frightened of Ossie, Muriel hid his revolver, feeling that he was quite capable of shooting her. One of the more amazing coincidences in her life was the discovery that an old friend from Gillespie's, Nita McEwan, was staying in the same hotel. Nita, also red-haired, was known at school as Muriel's double. One night Muriel heard a disturbance and an explosion. The next morning she discovered that Nita's husband had shot and killed her and himself. It seemed like an omen. Ossie raved, smashed things, was later bound over to keep the peace. Subsiding into self-pity, he would plead with her to give the marriage another chance. She was immune to this suggestion. Oddly, when he got drunk, he was least threatening, 'just giggled himself to sleep'.[17] She had a newborn baby, was just twenty-one and financially dependent on her husband. War had broken out; all civilian transport home was stopped. She had to be cautious and the best way of being so was to try to help him. On one occasion they visited the Victoria Falls in the hope that it might relieve his depression. It didn't, but it proved a formative moment for her.

When Muriel's African life began to shape itself into the metaphors of those short stories, she felt 'a compulsion to describe the Zambesi River and the approach to the falls through the mysterious Rain Forest as a mystical experience'.[18] The massive river plunged three hundred and fifty-five feet into a chasm of churning foam. Its spray dropped in silent, continuous light rain for miles around. Dressed in oilskins, she and Ossie had trekked through the forest, unable to hear or see anything extraordinary at first. Then she heard the voice of what she later called 'the seraphic river':

> *Musioa-tunya* – the smoke that thunders – is the name given to the falls by the local tribes. Amid this great roar, one looks up, one looks down, and from side to side: no more sky, no more forest – everywhere is a mighty cascade of water.[19]

Her commentary on its significance is telling:

> [...] I knew my married life was over. Strangely, the experience [...] gave me courage to endure the difficult years to come. The falls became to me a symbol of spiritual strength. I had no settled religion, but I recognized the experience [...] as spiritual in kind. [...] [It made] for the reasonable contemplation of our humanity, and a sense of the proportions in which we should think.[20]

The falls became in her imagination a giant non sequitur, another, 'nevertheless', their vertiginous beauty catapulting the mind into the sublime. In 'The Seraph . . .', she 'expressed, symbolically, how the aridity of the white people there had affected [her]'.[21] 'It was', the narrator remarks, 'like a convalescence after fever, that frail rain after the heat.'[22]

This decision, to be 'against dryness' as an act of will, permeates the African stories. Negative images of desiccation, the dust-devil (whirlwind), the dry river-bed, the women's prematurely aged skins – are associated with violence and mental collapse. It is a landscape of a neurosis from which the observing consciousness must separate itself or go mad: 'A storm in the Colony was such that before it broke the whole place was spasmodic, like an exposed nerve [...].'[23] Muriel's wise young women observe the loveless sex, the boorish men shooting off pistols and opinions, the gabbling wives, the sitting on the stoep watching the lightning through torn mosquito wire – but maintain their distance. Most of the colonials drank too much. Muriel stayed off the liquor and for years did not touch alcohol. It was a dangerous place of snakes and leopards, a place where material corruption was omnipresent: rapid burials because of the heat, ants creeping into the sugar bowls, locusts. As each night fell, the chorus of insects and tom-toms recalled the fragility of white control, and Muriel gave nothing away in her dealings with other Europeans. 'I didn't like these women,' she wrote. 'They were very sure of themselves as women.'[24] She was alone and had to grow up fast. So, like Sybil in 'Bang-bang You're Dead', she 'learnt those arts of leading a double life and listening to people ambiguously, which enabled her to mix without losing identity, and to listen without boredom.'[25]

The escape route was art and a sense of identity as an artist. Throughout her time in Rhodesia she wrote poetry and read voraciously. Odd copies of *Penguin New Writing*, of T. S. Eliot's and Ivy Compton-Burnett's work trickled through to this cultural desert but mainly she plundered the Bible and Shakespeare. Like Sybil, she was 'precocious, her brain was like a blade'.[26] Part of Ossie's irritation must surely have derived from the realisation that he had married a woman he had hoped to patronise but who was infinitely more intelligent and tougher than he. Muriel's sharpness allowed distance and protection. Seeing this charade as material to be observed, stored, drawn on, neutralised its horror by allowing her to control it aesthetically. She was frightened only by Ossie, not by Africa. Indeed, those first two years taught her something which was to become characteristic of her mature literary voice: the ability to think in two directions simultaneously.

In 'Bang-bang You're Dead' this double life is rendered by a brilliantly simple device. Muriel's resemblance to Nita McEwan was the seed of this story: how easily Muriel might have been the victim, the narrow borderline between order and chaos, life and death. Sybil is back in England watching the home movies of her African existence with a group of bourgeois friends. Their banal commentary is spliced with flashbacks into the reality of Sybil's experience which ends in murder. She should have been the victim but her jealous lover mistakenly shot her lookalike neighbour. Intercut are Sybil's own psychological crises which focus particularly on her sexuality:

For some years she had been thinking she was not much inclined towards sex. [...] Can it be, she thought, that I have a suppressed tendency towards women? [...] She surveyed, with a stony inward eye, all the women she had known [...]. No, really, she thought; neither men nor women. It is a not caring for sexual relations. It is not merely a lack of pleasure in sex, it is dislike of the excitement. And it is not merely dislike, it is worse, it is boredom.

She felt a lonely emotion near to guilt. The three love affairs [...] were an attempt, thought Sybil, to do the normal thing. Perhaps I may try again. Perhaps, if I should meet the right man ... But at the idea 'right man' she felt a sense of intolerable desolation and could not stop shivering.[27]

Was this autobiographical? If it was, it was not so much about Muriel's feelings in Africa as about how she came to feel after two men she had wanted to marry had failed her. Derek Stanford, one of those men, certainly recognised her here and was moved and troubled by the story. It might, at least, answer the question about whether she was, or was not, gay. Muriel, it seems, had thoroughly interrogated herself about this and had dismissed the notion of a 'suppressed tendency'. It was her art, not her sexuality, which estranged her. God and Scotland might somehow have omitted sentimentality and the agonies of sexual desire when they created Muriel Camberg but she had received something much more valuable in return: immense willpower, distance, wit and vision, without which she could not have become the great comic artist of the macabre that she did. Being an artist necessitated this double life, but it wasn't the artist who was split or her character-observers, it was the 'normal' world itself.

Sybil's perspective presents a maturity Muriel was yet to achieve in 1939. But she was already beginning to think like her. Life ticked past as a structureless shadow-play; reality and dream were indistinguishable; the cold eye of the artist could alone make arrangements which suggested, but did not dictate, meaning. Somehow these two halves of her mind had to be synchronised in a manageable existence, and this question quickly crystallised into an imperative. She had to free herself from Ossie, get home and earn her living as a writer. 'One day', he had said to her, 'this will all appear to you as a bad dream.'[28] That was exactly her intention. Then the declaration of war, on their second wedding anniversary, had trapped her in Africa. No civilian passage to Europe would be available in the foreseeable future. Like Sybil, she was 'caught [...] under the lioness'.[29] But Muriel was not to be deflected. Ossie joined the Army and from that moment they were on the road to divorce.

*

The chronology of her next two years is uncertain. Documentation is scarce. Muriel was unusually vague about the period. It was indeed like a bad dream. She was caring for Robin, seeking work and a divorce. Among their many moves, the 'family' had set up home longest in Gwelo, a comfortable small town six hundred feet above sea level which Muriel preferred to the larger cities because blacks and whites could mix more comfortably. Nevertheless, if she was to find work, she had to move to a city. She and Robin appear to have gone first to Bulawayo, leaving Ossie in his Gwelo military camp. By 1939 she had begun her literary career in earnest, submitting articles and poems to local magazines, winning a First Class Award for Poetry at the Rhodesian Eisteddfod Society, reading her material on the radio. But, pleasing as these successes were, they were no kind of living. Her first recorded paid employment in Africa was as a temporary typist with an insurance company, c. October 1940–March 1941. Her next was as a shorthand typist and secretary for a 'Brokers, Commission and Insurance Agents' where she met the glamorous owner, Basil Frost, c. July–December 1941; her third was as a stenographer, April–August 1942. All these are evidenced by testimonials recommending her as bright and conscientious. Whatever she did, she did well. Ossie was a millstone and was clearly determined to make their separation difficult. She could, however, sense some relief from the mental torture she had suffered between 1937 and 1939, for she was now controlling her own destiny. The testimonials register a gradual rise in status, a willingness to take any kind of work and to learn the ropes. Through sheer industry she made herself highly prized and raised her stock job by job.

With Basil Frost she had a 'very romantic affair'.[30] He was captivated by her and she strongly attracted to him. Twenty years her senior, he was wealthy, married, cosmopolitan. He 'spent a lot of time gazing at me over the desk, telling me how young and fresh I was, and explaining how these facts affected him. The truth was that neither May [a friend] nor I was ready for love affairs; there was a cloud of sadness over both our lives. We felt a predominant concern for our toddlers, and very isolated from home.'[31] Nevertheless, she slept with him, and the tone of wry amusement about his passion is typical. She enjoyed appearing attractive to men: it was their problem if they fell for it. Being paid court to was for Muriel one of life's great pleasures, and in 1941, Frost's ardour did much to repair her damaged self-esteem.

'May' was May Heygate with whom Muriel shared a flat in Bulawayo. A Classics graduate from Bristol University, Heygate also had a husband in the Army and a daughter of similar age to Robin. She worked as a receptionist for Dr Shankman, an eye specialist, and it was through him that they had met. Both women were eking out an existence in bedsits, so they struck up a friendship and pooled resources. Servants were cheap. A cook, Moses, and a nanny, Esther, oiled the wheels. Monday to Friday, Muriel and Heygate would be at work. Their weekends would follow a steady routine: taking the children for picnics or going to the cinema. On rare evenings they might hit the town. It was a more regular, and certainly a more vital existence than Muriel had known for two years. She was able to write and think in her few free hours.

The separation, however, crushed Ossie. When all hope of rec-onciliation had evaporated, he became fanatically possessive; he 'stalked' her, jealous of her new friends. Muriel was once invited to join a party at the Midnight Club in the Grand Hotel, Bulawayo. When she was dancing with Dr Shankman, Ossie burst in and began punching him. Ejected on that occasion, Ossie, like the jungle, never seemed far away. 'This sort of harassment', she remarked, 'made me hesitate to go around with my friends. It isolated me considerably.'[32] It was, though, more than a question of social embarrassment. Muriel became convinced that her husband was a psychopath. In rages he had threatened to kill her. Her health was not strong. She had already succumbed to a near-fatal bout of septicaemia and the constant nervous strain lowered her resistance to influenza. Her doctor, Rose Sugarman, a confidante, advised her that her life was in danger.

*

The first item on the solicitor's account relating to Muriel's divorce is dated December 1939. Another, 'Our fee re. Shankman', appears to be dated 1 October 1942. Dr Shankman's evidence was clearly important but, in itself, insufficient to secure Muriel's freedom under Roman Dutch law. 'The very mention of mental instability or cruelty in either of the partners', she commented, 'was enough to ruin the case; these factors were grounds for legal separation, but not for divorce. The grounds for divorce were infidelity (especially on the woman's part) and desertion. I chose desertion. My husband would not desert me, so I deserted him.'[33] It was a wearisome process. As the hotel incident indicated, Ossie was not easily deserted. The divorce was not made final until March 1943.

The crucial, appalling, problem facing Muriel during this period was how both to escape from her husband and to keep her son. Ossie's behaviour ruined the possibility of any normal life in Africa. In order to support Robin she had to work but there was little chance of making a career in letters anywhere but London. 'Life in the Colony', she wrote, 'was eating my heart away [...].'[34] Before anything else could be organised, she had to get out – not just out of one city and into another where Ossie might intrude at any moment, but out of Africa altogether. 'I wanted the reality of home, even though it meant the bombs of war.'[35] The divorce court's lack of interest in Ossie's mental condition meant that, astonishingly, they would award custody to him. There was, in any case, a complete embargo on transporting children to the UK. It was a quandary to which there appeared to be only one desperate solution: if she could settle Robin safely, she would escape without him. Wartime parents at home were regularly separated from their evacuee children. Well, she would evacuate herself. Her only hope, she thought, was to return to England, explain her case from there, and pray that after the war the British authorities would see sense and return Robin to her. The dangers were obvious – that he might feel abandoned (he was only four years old), left in the care of strangers and his curious father; that she might be killed on the passage home; that England might lose the war and the separation become permanent – but she faced those dangers bravely. She had not the slightest concern about appearing the guilty party if, in the long term, there was a future for her and Robin. The first step was to place him as a boarder in a convent school in Gwelo. Then, during the autumn of 1942 she moved alone to 8 Fountain Court, Salisbury (Southern Rhodesia), to await the completion of the divorce and to plan that future.

It was a period of freedom before inevitable hardship. Huge Air Force camps had sprung up all over the country to train crew whose life expectancy was a matter of months. A febrile air of *joie de vivre* abounded: parties, dances, hosts of dashing young fellows eager to enjoy themselves while they could. In this atmosphere Muriel could breathe, and she wrote about it in 'The Go-Away Bird'. Her heroine, Daphne, 'met dozens of young fighter pilots with their Battle of Britain D.F.C.s. She was in love with them collectively. They were England.'[36] Two images of England obsess her: '"Queen Anne house", "Kensington", "Chelsea"' and '"Soho", "poet", "attic", "artist"'.[37] Muriel's future was to contain both worlds – a polite, well-regulated life invigorated by bohemianism – and somehow the stylish sangfroid of the RAF's young bloods compounded both. She attended their social gatherings and rather fell in love with one of them, a young flight lieutenant, Arthur Foggo. Their few weeks together ended when he was drafted. Melancholy again, she had seen him off from Salisbury station on 4 October, 1942. Two days later he wired indiscreetly: 'Leaving immediately will write you as soon as I arrive.'[38] He never did arrive. That night his ship was torpedoed outside Cape Town.

Given what had happened to Foggo's ship, and the fact that this was quite normal, her next step was distinctly courageous. Travel from country to country was difficult, even within Africa. In order to obtain a permit, she went to a magistrate (oddly, the same one who had conducted her marriage) and said that she wished to go to Cape Town to study literature and drama. It was a ruse. She travelled to Cape Town but she 'simply didn't go back. I put my name down for a passage to England with a shipping line.'[39] That was in the autumn of 1943. Languishing in a lodging house at Sea Point, Cape of Good Hope, she was in this respect like the heroine of the only story she wrote about that time, 'The Pawnbroker's Wife'. Her father wired her money, having also dug into his savings to fund her divorce. She took casual jobs to survive. The city seemed generally depressing, as 'empty of intellectual life'[40] as Southern Rhodesia. Nevertheless, she found some.

At a dinner party with her doctor, she met Marie Bonaparte (Princess Marie of Greece). The conversation turned to 'poetry, symbolism, Freud'.[41] The Princess was charmingly eccentric and, most important, a writer. As exiled royalty and a former pupil of Freud, a certain glamour hung about her. Muriel was immediately attracted to her 'bright, dyed red hair, and shrewd eyes sunken into an elderly face'.[42] The family, heavily protected by the police, lived in a small villa, the top floor of which was occupied by Princess Frederica of Greece and her boisterous son, now ex-King Constantine. Over twenty years later, when Queen Frederica, she and Constantine were to become Muriel's friends in Rome. In Cape Town, Muriel's social situation was rather different but not her self-confidence. Unable to entertain guests in her bedsit, she would visit Marie regularly to talk poetry and psychology. 'Sometimes the family would need the drawing room. Then I would go to her bedroom, and it was funny to see the things on the mantelpiece: silver-framed pictures of royalty and then a tin of Bemax. These trappings of exile.'[43]

More non sequiturs. Exile and literature were the common ground of this friendship, and it was somehow typical of Muriel, as a penniless twenty-six-year-old of humble origins, with only secretarial jobs and a ruined marriage to a demented schoolmaster behind her, that she managed to carry it off without the slightest social hesitation. (Princess Frederica was, by all accounts, very 'royal' indeed.) Immune to nervous class-consciousness, Muriel impressed everyone by her sheer vivacity and weight of intellect. She was just here and now and vital, to be taken on her own terms or not at all. Neither Edinburgh nor Rhodesia had 'created' her, neither explained her. Neither was home. She was free, and joyfully so. For if these places had taught her anything, it was the suffocation of belonging. A central autobiographical image in the African stories is the go-away bird, so called because its song echoes 'Go-away, go-away'. 'I was', Muriel remarked, 'really, myself, a "Go-away Bird".'[44] She had cut herself loose to contemplate the exquisite doubleness of life. On the beautiful South African coast, bathers tumbled and laughed in the surf. Nevertheless, the same waters were a memento mori: 'At Sea Point [...] there was everywhere the sight of rejoicing, there was the sound of hilarity, and the sea washed up each day one or two bodies of servicemen in all kinds of uniform.'[45]

In February 1944 she finally obtained a berth with thirty other women on a troopship zigzagging its way between U-boats via the Azores to Liverpool. At night the women were stacked four-deep in bunk beds and instructed to remain fully dressed in case of a German attack. The possibility of sinking was with them at every moment. By way of a joke, dark trousers were recommended to deflect the attention of sharks. Throughout, they clutched life-belts and chatted. But danger was the last thing on Muriel's mind. She was satisfied finally to be engaged with the reality of war. Colonial Africa had represented, among other things, a sense of disconnection from the real. Muriel always wanted to be where the action was and, as she said in 'The First Year of My Life', she 'preferred the Western Front where one got the true state of affairs [...] one had to be prepared [...].'[46] In her tight berth she read Eliot's *The Dry Salvages*, contentedly anticipating life as an artist. And by March, a year after her divorce, she was home and free. It was a dour evening, all lights extinguished by blackout, and she was transcendently happy.

*

Muriel returned to Edinburgh but only for a few weeks. She had been away six and a half years, had given birth to a son her parents had never seen, had suffered terribly in exotic places. It is difficult to imagine Cissy not encouraging Muriel to unpack her troubles during long hours round the kitchen table. But Muriel was quite different now from the nineteen-year-old they remembered. She was cautious, critical, entirely self-reliant. Her mother's questions met with brief, non-committal responses. There was a gap between her cool independence and Cissy's cloying sentimentality. Muriel paid her dues, told them not to worry, and boarded a train for London where she knew no one. There she stayed briefly at the Euston Station Hotel, found a cheap room at the Helena Club on the Bayswater Road, and went to sign on at the Department of Employment.

As usual, she had a book with her. She said she was trained as a secretary, would do anything. The woman taking her details noticed the novel, asked what it was. It was by Ivy Compton-Burnett, at that stage one of Muriel's passions, and, as it turned out, a favourite of her interviewer. A literary discussion followed, after which the woman exchanged the cards she had extracted for another set. Muriel, she said, could do better than humdrum tasks. How would she like to work for the Foreign Office? Within another few days, she was entering Sefton Delmer's room, perched at the top of the BBC headquarters in Bush House.

*

On her first night in London all hell had let loose: incendiary bombs, fire wardens bellowing, most of the hotel guests scuttling to the basement. Muriel had stayed in bed. This was the life she had waited for, one sort of reality. And to be in Bush House was another. Delmer, formerly Berlin correspondent of the *Daily Express*, had travelled round Germany with Hitler's entourage and knew Goering, Goebels, Hess and Himmler; he was friendly with Martha Huysmans, the Belgian Prime Minister's daughter, Prince Bernhard of the Netherlands, Dick Crossman, Bruce Lockhart, Ian Fleming and Hugh Carleton Greene. When Muriel met Delmer he had charge of Allied 'Black Propaganda' and had just moved to his white eyrie under the roof of Bush House, '[a]s though to symbolise the TOP secrecy of my work for "Overlord"'.[47] His regular 'hush-hush' callers were European officers in resistance groups. The base of his operation, 'CHQ', was Woburn Abbey, acting as a nerve-centre for propaganda radio broadcasts from the neighbouring village of Milton Bryan. During her brief interview, Muriel began to feel that she was at last at the heart of something significant. She signed the Official Secrets Act and, after three anxious weeks while her security vetting was completed, was able to tell the girl with whom she shared a table at the Helena Club, that she had secured a job with the Foreign Office. No details, of course, could be revealed. Even so, the mere mention of the FO was a badge of success. '"You must have tons of influence,"' the girl remarked. 'I replied that I had no influence at all, just luck.'[48]

From 7 May to 2 October 1944, Muriel lived happily between Milton Bryan and London, officially employed in the Newsroom of the Political Intelligence Department as 'Duty Secretary'. Four days a fortnight she could escape to town, and three weeks after starting the job she wrote home:

> Dear Mum,
>
>   I am so thrilled about the news of Phil's baby. I am sure it has brought me luck with Sonny [Robin], and that I shall have my baby here soon. Won't it be grand?
>
>   Please wire Sol [Ossie] 'Will welcome you and Sonny with pleasure' or something like that. If only Sonny comes, he will at least be over here, and S.O.S. poor devil can get a job. I don't wish him any harm. I can help with Sonny, and I am sure he will be a source of great pleasure to you. He is a little darling – so affectionate and loveable. I enclose 10/- for the cable. I am not badly off for cash, but have not much over after Income Tax and board etc. are paid. At least I am independent which I have not been for many years [. . .].[49]

'S.O.S. was her wry name for Ossie (Sydney Oswald Spark). Her brother's first child, David, had been born on 28 May 1944, while Phil was working as a Technical Assistant at the Royal Ordinance Factory in Kirkby, Lancashire. Muriel was earning £4 17s 6d a week. The letter suggests a mixture of contentment, and perpetual unease about Robin. She wants her mother to welcome Ossie so that everything possible should be done to get the boy home. There was always the danger that Ossie might have another relapse and use the child as a weapon of revenge. Indeed, this is just what happened.

Despite her new freedom, Muriel's life was far from untroubled. She wrote regularly to Ossie, trying to raise his spirits, and to the Mother Superior at the Gwelo school for bulletins on Robin. But letters often took two months to arrive and correspondence was persistently out of date. By this stage he was a day-boy and had lived (on paper, at least) with his father for a year. This routine was then disrupted. Ossie lost his military job at the Gwelo Drill Hall and placed his son as a full boarder again at the convent. Ossie's nerves were now thoroughly shattered, not least by the news, broken to him by the headmistress, of Muriel's departure for England. He had hoped that when his ex-wife returned from South Africa to Rhodesia, she might care for Robin during this mental breakdown. Now he felt isolated and impotent. How Robin felt, we can only guess.

Ossie's illness was characterised by an inability to act, to respond to anything beyond the terrors of his disintegrating ego. Guilt and self-justification battled it out hopelessly. When Muriel told him that his sister, Becky, had been committed to a mental home after raving and soliciting in the streets of Edinburgh (Barney and Cissy, after being threatened with a knife by her in 1938, had sorted out that crisis, too), Ossie's only response was that he was surprised but that he could see nothing clearly. He had tried to do his duty by his son and wife but had failed. Life overwhelmed him. Robin, he reported, was on holiday and staying with some friends who ran a fruit shop.[50] And if this was worrying, worse was to come. Three months later Ossie was corresponding from the Nervous Disorders Hospital in Bulawayo, more than a hundred miles away from their son, in a state of total collapse. He had already been there for over six weeks and had endured an unsuccessful course of ECT which had revealed spinal arthritis.[51] All Muriel could do was to wait and try to ensure her independence in readiness for Robin's return.

Her appointment at Milton Bryan was probably the result of Delmer's expanding his staff in preparation for Operation Overlord. Just one month after she had started, on 6 June 1944, the balloon went up, the ramps came down, and thousands of Allied soldiers spilled on to the Normandy beaches. By 23 August, Paris was liberated. Most of south-eastern England hummed with vehicles and aeroplanes; trains were thronged with soldiers of multiple nationalities. Then London was assaulted by a new terror: 'doodlebugs' (V-ls), followed by the much more powerful V-2 rockets. Muriel, it seems, was in her element, sympathising with Delmer's sense of shame about the permanent 'tube dwellers' during the earlier Blitz 'absenting themselves from their work-shops while they lay on their mattresses in the Underground, publicly copulating on the platforms, and blocking up the stations for those who had to go to work'.[52] Yet her time at 'M.B.' was a strangely 'nevertheless' existence against the backdrop of D-Day.

Amid the cacophony, life in that pocket of rural England was tranquil. German prisoners of war assisting with the broadcasts lived in seven houses in Apsley Guire. They were bussed in daily through the check-points in the high wire fence around the compound, having picked up on the way any of the secretarial staff or other workers staying near by. Muriel was one of those who joined the bus and returned after midnight. The young women were encouraged to take the POWs for walks in their off-duty hours. Muriel worked mainly during the afternoons and at night. She remembered delightful mornings rambling the countryside with a German farm-hand[53] and a monocled Austrian Count. It was a fine spring and summer. The lanes were empty, signposts removed. She admired the courage of her prisoner-friends, sympathised with their sense of alienation, amused herself with the bafflement of the locals at the appearance of these obvious foreigners. On other mornings, while waiting to start work, she would write poetry. Afloat in this strange world of air, light and coded signals she was content. It suited her to be incognito.

Muriel's job was to receive messages, type them and to pass them on. Delmer's task was the production of entertaining German-language broadcasts, most of which comprised accurate, up-to-the-minute news and commentary enlivened by dance-band music. Inserted into the documentary content, however, would be slivers of misinformation designed to rot the morale of Hitler's troops. The whole enterprise, of course, relied for its credibility on offering apparently bona fide programmes from behind enemy lines. By the time Muriel had joined the outfit, its operations were highly sophisticated in an attempt to combat the 'jammers'. After years of struggle with Whitehall, Delmer had finally gained access to 'Aspidistra', the powerful Crowborough transmitter in Sussex. When any German station went off the air to avoid acting as a beacon for incoming bombers, Aspidistra would switch to its frequency with an undetectable transition, thus giving the impression of a continuous German programme. In 1944, this was a revolutionary technical achievement requiring split-second timing.

Delmer was in his early forties, seventeen and a half stone, bearded, pop-eyed, and pushy. An Oxford graduate, he was nevertheless a tough journalist of the yellow press who prided himself on being a man of the people presenting vivid, sharply focused coverage, the 'human angle'. The BBC's 'white' propaganda, scrupulously telling only the truth, infuriated him. His own colourful gang played high-stakes poker with fascism:

> For a more weirdly assorted group it would have been hard to find anywhere in Britain at the time. German refugees, German prisoners, Balkan beauties, Italians, Hungarians, Romanians, Bulgarians, British girl secretaries, British and American editors and executives, all jostled each other in the passages of M.B. talking their different languages and their assorted varieties of English. Each of them dressed as the fancy took him or her.[54]

Muriel delighted in this cosmopolitan tumult no less than he. Delmer charged about coordinating the seeming chaos while insisting on absolute efficiency. Lives were at stake. The operation was serious, exhausting, tightly organised, yet driven by the delight of subjecting the pompous rationalists across the Channel to an endless stream of practical jokes. (One of these suggested that the Generals' unsuccessful attempt to assassinate Hitler had, at least, blown his trousers off.) It was the department of dirty tricks, extending into all types of forgery: ration cards, passports, postage stamps – with the staff perpetually duping each other 'in the best "black" manner'.[55]

M.B. contained studios, a record library, intelligence files and newspaper and radio newsrooms. Muriel worked in Delmer's small office adjacent to the rackety radio newsroom, and in another office used a green-painted 'scrambler' telephone, taking down the processed reports of recently returned aircrews. Experts would rapidly interpret the information, examine photographs through stereoscopic viewers, and using maps and local knowledge, reconstruct this distant damage with the immediacy of a street-by-street eye-witness account. Detail lent plausibility; plausibility disguised lies. In Delmer's life, Muriel was an anonymous secretary, forgotten in his autobiography. But another aspect of her job was to maintain contact with the Foreign Office in London, and her communications with the FO were quite different.

The voice which came down the line from London belonged to Colin Methven. Official exchanges soon became informal, and they arranged to meet. Methven, a gentleman of independent means, also had extensive experience of Central Africa and a child from whom he was separated by war. (His daughter, Deirdre, had been evacuated to Canada.) Twice divorced, in late middle age, he was an elegant, handsome fellow in need of company and with adequate loose cash to give a girl a good time. Methven took Muriel to dinner at the Savoy, the Ritz, the Café Royal, Prunier's, her first taste of the best London restaurants; often they would go on to the theatre. Back at the compound the atmosphere among the grander women could be prickly. Marcelle Quennell, the separated wife of the author and critic Peter Quennell, had a sharp sense of her social distinction. Muriel had secured a room of her own at their billet in the Old Rectory. Such accommodation, Marcelle stated, should be the privilege of those, like her, who were over thirty. 'I don't know how you can exist in England without a private income,' she once declared. Muriel was simply amazed: 'I had never met anyone like her. I knew she was unbalanced.'[56] In London with Colin she could be a lady with none of this nonsense.

Muriel was not seeking an affair and Methven was too much of a gentleman to suggest one. It was enough to have this vivacious aspirant writer on his arm, and to be of service to her. He was of the courtly variety of older man with whom Muriel always felt safe, a father-figure rather than a beau. She certainly brightened his life and he released in her affection which she had thought permanently crippled by Ossie.

> I had always been aware of 'gaining experience' for some future literary work. No experience, I felt, was to be overlooked, even that of my darkest hours in Africa. But about the time I met Colin [...], I felt the need to 'give experience' [...] to give pleasure through my writings [...] that would be an 'experience' to the reader.[57]

This is a telling aside in her autobiography. Sexual passion is replaced by aesthetic passion; the desire to communicate is artistic rather than physical, with a reader rather than with a lover. Actual lovers, as she was to discover, would only spoil the purity of this passion. Methven, who returned her chastely to the Helena Club, acted as a catalyst, allowing her to relax into her vocation. And the club itself was crucial to this process.

'Charming' was one of Muriel's favourite adjectives. She had a 'charming friendship' with Methven; the Helena Club was 'absolutely charming'.[58] Both protected her and nourished her self-confidence. The club comprised three elegant houses knocked into one at 82 Lancaster Gate. Founded thirty years earlier by Princess Christian, it was little changed in 1944: a respectable establishment to which parents could entrust their daughters. In the high-ceilinged sitting room a portrait of Queen Mary (commemorating her 1932 visit) cast a stern eye over the young ladies as they gossiped, read magazines, played the piano or canasta. The French windows of the music room opened on to a wide terrace and the garden. Men were admitted only to the downstairs part. Ping-pong and dancing lessons, evenings in with cocoa, watching the pennies, girls camped on the stairs chatting through the wall-telephones with boyfriends or family were rather more the norm than bohemian nights on the town. It was a safe and smart place for 'secretaries, models and civil servants', like a 'boarding school or one of the women's services' but without their severity. 'Girls do not stay here', one post-war journalist remarked, 'if they prefer independence and a measure of hardship to comfort, security and lights out by midnight.'[59] On various occasions over the next four years, Muriel attempted the rigours of bedsit life, always to return to the haven of Lancaster Gate. It was another 'nevertheless' environment with its girls'-school atmosphere, warden, regulations and lights-out times, while the noticeboard happily advertised lifts to the 400 Club, 'lights out' only applied to the public rooms, and all the young women had latch-keys to return as late as they liked.[60]

The club was arranged on three floors, with a laundry in the basement. A massive green front door presented an implacable face to the world, its brass shining brightly. Beyond, were the public rooms: the warden's chintzy office, the sitting room, dining room, games room, music room. A broad, carpeted staircase led to first- and second-floor dormitories. Some of these had four beds. Others crushed in twelve, six on each side, separated only by the width of identical dressing tables. Curtains ran the length of these rooms, along the foot of the beds, as in a hospital ward. When full – and it was always full – the place held more than one hundred and twenty women. On the top floor were the most expensive single rooms: 'Park Lane' to the members. Muriel had one of these at the back of the house. The club's front windows looked out over the grass and fountains of Kensington Gardens. Setting off from there, Muriel had Hyde Park to her left, Kensington to her right. It was a splendid situation for £1 12s 6d a week, including two meals a day. For a decade, until she moved south to Camberwell in 1954, she usually lived within a square mile of this place: Vicarage Gate and the Old Brompton Road; the Kensington of Ezra Pound and Roy Campbell rather than the Bloomsbury of Virginia Woolf. She had discovered a point of reference, her stamping ground. Much of her fiction returns to these streets and to the women who, like her, inhabited the borderland between the smart set and bohemia.

The Helena Club had many attractions for Muriel: it was a community of working women (no students were admitted); it had an air of elegance, was cheap and well regulated. You did not have to cook. Maids cleaned the rooms and changed the sheets. It was convivial, alive with chatter and because of the historical moment at which Muriel discovered it, egalitarian. Everyone was poor. Food was scarce and the members handed over their ration books, to be supplied with substantial plain fare. 'But we thought nothing about food [...]. Everybody's lot was equal, and lives were being lost everywhere.'[61] Again, the proximity of death, and the common cause, clarified values.

Although Muriel worked only six months at Milton Bryan, its effect, like that of the Helena Club, was profound. The compound and POWs feature significantly in her New York novel, *The Hothouse by the East River* (1973). The club becomes the May of Teck Club in *The Girls of Slender Means* (1963). Both are transformations but both clearly draw on intense experience. The operations of the compound in *Hothouse* suggest male neurosis and self-deceit, where *The Girls* offers both a gentle retrospect and a vision of savagery which reviews this as an illusion, or, at least, as a temporary truth.

In *Hothouse*, the heroine, Elsa, walks like Dante 'along the edge of the wood'[62] with her fellow exiles, the POWs. She does what Muriel did in Milton Bryan and in one conversation, a supposedly brilliant superior, Miles Bunting, patronises her: 'I think you're out of your element.' 'I think you're out of your mind,' she replies. 'Our war effort here is extremely valuable,' retorts Bunting. 'Valuable to yourselves,' she says. 'No, to the country [...]. We have means of testing the results. There are things you don't know a thing about.' The next paragraph is equally pointed:

> She has said the place is ridiculous. Deep in the heart of it, she is nevertheless deprived of any insight into its doing. It is the policy of the little organization to tell the workers only what they need to know to perform their individual functions.[63]

Delmer prided himself on checking the effectiveness of his ruses and was convinced that black propaganda was a major influence on the

Allied victory. He was a dynamic, amusing figure. But he was also an egomaniac. Her job, Muriel remarked, was 'wonderfully interesting'.[64] And so it was. But a sense of threat also hangs over her fictional reconstruction.

Milton Bryan was a kind of super-university, crammed with Oxbridge graduates like Dick Crossman who delighted in parading their intellectual dexterity. Marcelle Quennell was an expert linguist. Delmer, and everyone else in a position of power, spoke fluent German. Muriel, like Elsa, did not. The only people with whom she talked at length were the Germans: brave, melancholy eccentrics, a gypsy band of 'traitors' communicating in a foreign tongue. In *Hothouse*, because Elsa does not know their language, even they 'underestimate her wits'.[65] Muriel denied any link between Elsa's sense of being patronised and her own experience. She was, she said, employed as a secretary and treated accordingly. She did not care to complain. But it is difficult to believe that she would not have been irritated by such treatment. When journalists and interviewers later made the mistake of believing her to have been in an executive position, she never corrected them. Like her brother, she felt intellectual competition keenly.

More importantly, though, the effect of the war on Muriel was to project her into a fantastic world which became an image of the instability of literal truth. Bunting's and Delmer's notions of proof and significance were relative and unproveable. The war was both temporary and actual. Whatever might appear true during the war might not be true after it. Both states could be both true and untrue. There was for her something invigorating about this, like dreaming and waking simultaneously, which could only find expression in poetic symbolism. The object of Delmer's unit was to confuse truth and lies in the service of a greater truth. His instruction – 'Accuracy first. [...] We must never lie by accident [...] only deliberately'[66] – and his emphasis on scrupulous research to produce a plausible narrative, also describes an aspect of Muriel's working practice as a novelist.

London in 1944 presented her with a literal vision of the surreal, brilliantly depicted in *The Girls of Slender Means*. Wrecked buildings took on the appearance

> of ancient castles until, at a closer view, the wallpapers of various quite normal rooms would be visible, room above room, exposed, as on a stage, with one wall missing; sometimes a lavatory chain would dangle over nothing from a fourth- or fifth-floor ceiling; most of all the staircases survived, like a new art-form, leading up and up to an unspecified destination that made unusual demands on the mind's eye.[67]

The observing consciousness here is coolly fascinated rather than appalled. The meaning of that word 'normal' begins to wobble. As the narrator remarks, 'There was absolutely no point in feeling depressed about the scene, it would have been like feeling depressed about the Grand Canyon [...].' London lies in ruins; thousands die each day on the battlefields of Europe and Asia. Nevertheless, in the May of Teck Club, a building unhinged by nearby explosions but still standing, its occupants have never been happier: 'few people alive at the time were more delightful, more ingenious, more movingly lovely, and, as it might happen, more savage, than the girls of slender means.'[68]

That stylish tonal shift – 'and, as it might happen, more savage' – suggests moral condemnation. Almost certainly this is not the case. One of the more disturbing aspects of Muriel's mature writing is its amorality. The barbarism of human behaviour intrigues her as the varieties of cancer might a surgeon. And, like an honest surgeon, she refuses her readers the luxury of dismissing anxiety by pretending that they are normal and the disease abnormal. In her Catholic vision we are all implicated in what Cardinal Newman described as an 'aboriginal calamity': the Fall of Man. But even before she had become a Christian, this sense of ubiquitous corruption was at the centre of her thinking. Understanding the proximity of death, the brevity of life, the absurdity of humanist rationalism, was, she felt, the first stage in saving one's sanity. Africa had begun to teach her this; wartime England emphasised it. She was young. One of her great subjects is the celebration of the resilience of youth. Yet she was also old – in experience – a woman among girls at the Helena Club. She felt different from most people. She saw things they didn't, could think in two directions simultaneously.

Despite her bright public exterior, despite her efficiency, her love of life, her invigorating presence; despite her jaunts with boyfriends and rambles with prisoners, she was essentially solitary. What she liked best was the supporting structure of a communal life which left her alone to think and to write. She did not crave intimacy. In *Hothouse*, Elsa confronts authoritarian women who insist, as Marcelle Quennell did, that 'girls under thirty have to share a room'. '"I need a room to myself,"' Elsa says. '"I won't share. [...] It wouldn't be comfortable for the other girl. I see things. [...] I am really a bit uncanny. I have supernatural communications."'[69] Muriel was no spiritualist. She never had a 'psychic' experience. As an artist, however, she always considered herself a visionary. She kept herself apart, half in, half out of others' daily lives. A psychiatrist might say that her disastrous marriage had made her fearful of commitment. But her temperamental alienation ran much deeper than this.

*

Over the next eighteen months, until Robin's return, she had a series of temporary jobs: with the Office of War Information (another Foreign Office post) in the Strand, where she was paid in US dollars; with the East India Tea Company in Lombard Street; with the American Red Cross in Edinburgh. Employment was scarce. She worked for the Tea Company throughout Christmas 1944 rather than take a holiday. Her tax returns reveal that, until 12 March 1945, she was unemployed for less than a month. From March she was back in London again and, for the first time in her life, trying to earn her living as a writer. In October, Ossie had written to wish her luck with her 'book', no trace of which survives.

Throughout those months an erratic trickle of letters arrived from Gwelo. Ossie was wading deeper into depression. He felt jittery, his mind wouldn't work; his papers and belongings were strewn about the country. The National War Fund might provide his and Sonny's fare home but he could not get the application organised. Muriel advised him to pull himself together, yet even his intelligence failed him. He was fearful of saying the wrong thing, of performing the tiniest action.[70] Trying to come to terms with the divorce threatened the last shreds of his self-esteem. When Muriel's mother wrote to invite him to stay with them, his gratitude was touching: he did not, he believed, deserve such consideration, acknowledged that he had been selfish. He felt completely isolated.[71] That Christmas, he stayed away from Robin, sensing that his presence upset the boy, and Robin spent his holidays like an orphan on the convent farm. 'I dare say you miss Sonny very much,' the Mother Superior wrote to Muriel, 'but you mustn't worry about him. He has everything he needs and we see to his clothing.'[72]

That letter took three and a half months to reach Muriel and she did, of course, worry. Ossie's desperate epistles contained pleas that, as the stronger party, she should rescue him: come out to Africa and shepherd the two of them home. During July 1945 a stranger wrote to explain that she had been caring for Robin during his holidays because his father appeared incapable of doing so. Robin was cheerful and easily pleased but this lady had two children of her own and her concern was naturally also for herself. As things stood, neither parent seemed able to relieve her of this responsibility – so the authorities took charge.

A probation officer arranged Robin's passage in the care of an RAF family, and the plan was to send Ossie back with him. Muriel's correspondent, Rotha Sanson, thought Ossie would never be fit to travel. He had been in bed for a month, unshaven, malnourished. But, after six weeks of this abjection, at the last moment he rallied just enough to allow Mr Riddle (Robin's escort) to make every arrangement for both. Mrs Sanson's advice to Muriel was adamant: 'refuse to allow him to go and stay with your parents & just go to bed & make everyone support and look after him – it will be his ruin. [...] I know [...] you feel sorry for Mr Spark but [...] [y]ou will be happier staying free now you are on your own. He is terribly exhausting [...]. Anyone attempting to live with him would be driven quite mad [...].'[73]

Ossie and Robin set sail on 9 September 1945, Ossie under medical escort, his son in the charge of the Riddles. Mrs Sanson had written on that day to inform Muriel of this but the ship arrived before the letter. The only details she had received, courtesy of Rhodesia House, concerned Robin's arrival. As she stood on Liverpool docks watching the ship berth, she was expecting only her son.

CHAPTER 4

Finding a Voice

1945–1949

'I am so delighted to hear that Sonny has arrived on the Mersey *(vide* 9 PM news),' Colin Methven wrote. 'I can picture your excitement – and his.' Excitement for both son and mother, however, was not undiluted. Seven years old, Robin was small for his age, nervous, and in the company of strangers. He had not seen his father during the voyage, must already have been half-aware that something was adrift with that parent, and was about to meet a mother he had not seen for two years. From Muriel's perspective, much as she longed to see the boy, she had no means of supporting him.

During her three-month Red Cross job in Edinburgh, Muriel had lived with her parents for the last extended time, and in March 1945 had returned gratefully to London to start her literary career in earnest. She was writing a surrealist verse play about Mary Queen of Scots. Methven, her closest ally, had lent her books. From Edinburgh she had sent him cakes and tulips. In London, he had lent her his Mayfair flat. His daughter, Deirdre, had returned from evacuation in Canada, and Muriel and this wild fifteen-year-old had discovered an immediate rapport. Muriel had been with Methven for VE and VJ days, scenes of public rejoicing which she was to reconstruct in *The Girls of Slender Means*. But his heart was failing. He soon retired, taking Deirdre with him to live with his sister in remotest Scotland, and by July Muriel was alone again and back in the Helena Club. His departure had been a serious loss. He was her confidant. Now there was no one in London to whom she could turn for counsel, and her existence as an artist was in danger of termination scarcely before it had begun. Throughout her life, Robin was, unconsciously at first, then very consciously, associated in her mind with obstruction and her disastrous marriage. So when the ship docked on 23 September 1945, the thrill of reunion was tempered by concern for their future together. As soon as she crossed the gangplank, trouble erupted.

The first shock was to learn that Ossie was also on board. Muriel did not meet her ex-husband on this occasion, but he ruined this feast as he had ruined all others:

> [The immigration officials] handed Robin over and they asked me if I would take on the father as well. I said, 'No. I'm divorced. I've no means of support apart from . . .' I didn't say very much because Robin was there and not of an age to understand. [. . .] Then Ossie had a brainstorm when they were questioning him and they said to me: 'Well, my dear, if he hadn't had this brainstorm we would have had a problem. But now we don't have a problem.'[2]

Leaving Ossie in Liverpool, she returned with Robin to Edinburgh. The 'problem', however, would not go away. It concerned custody and was to torment her for years.

Ossie turned up in Edinburgh, a hopeless case. Muriel stayed for a few weeks to see Robin through the transition. He was withdrawn but resilient. This was his first meeting with his grandparents and all went well on that front. He settled in and was enrolled at Gillespie's. Muriel then headed for London to try to earn some money, while Cissy and Barney also took Ossie in. That arrangement lasted about a week. He wouldn't get up, so Cissy put him in a hotel. He had a disability pension. Money presented no immediate difficulty for him. But 'he told the hotel girl he could jump out of the window if he wanted so they brought an ambulance and took him off to the bin.'[3] In the meantime, Muriel corresponded urgently with Rhodesia House.

Their first letter held out more than hope. The trouble at Liverpool, they said, had resulted from 'lack of information sent forward from

Rhodesia'.[4] As soon as they had a medical report on Mr Spark they would contact Salisbury. During October Muriel had undergone an appendectomy and, as usual, was looking on the bright side: at least she was losing weight. She had travelled to Leeds for the wedding of her cousin, Edgar Jackson.[5] Then Rhodesia House wrote again, enclosing a cable from Salisbury stating that she had been awarded only temporary custody. If Ossie were sufficiently recovered, the original judgement of the Rhodesian court should apply.[6] Impasse. Muriel battled on with the authorities, took elocution (poetry reading) lessons, came down with bronchitis.

All this time she was writing poetry, sometimes about Robin and Africa, getting to know the *Poetry Quarterly* group with Charles Wrey Gardiner as its editor and focus. She joined the Poetry Society, entered and won competitions in its *Poetry Review*, and by March 1946 had published 'Three Thoughts in Africa' in its *Poetry of To-day* supplement.[7] One of the first people to whom she sent copies of her work was Methven, a man baffled by contemporary art but a bluff and enthusiastic supporter of Muriel's cause. Her poem, he said, made him homesick for Africa, 'with its barbaric sunsets and the hot steamy midnights. [...] Your "Frantic a Child Ran" opens up a big subject concerning the psychology of intensely imaginative people who confess to crimes which they never committed.'[8] Later in the year she opened other large questions with 'Poem for a Pianist' and 'They Sigh for Old Dreams'. The first dealt with the inability of the artist to comfort her audience, the second with lives withered by frustration.[9]

This was not great poetry, as Muriel was the first to recognise when she omitted both lyrics from her *Collected Poems 1*.[10] She was still finding her voice, writing against the sub-Georgian jingling which dominated the *Poetry Review*, writing out of the tradition of Auden rather than of Bridges, picking up on the newly revived interest in 1890s' exoticism. 'They Sigh for Old Dreams' gently abuses self-deception and elevates the dream above rational analysis. The symbol of the Persian Caravan, the final image of the fulfilment of desire, is clouded by the world's analysis and 'infinite regret'. Such winsome longing – something on which her mother's imagination fed – was sentimental to Muriel. If there was a Persian Caravan swaying into Baghdad, she was determined to be aboard it.

Muriel was never to be the victim of the 'pram-in-the-hall' syndrome described in Cyril Connolly's *Enemies of Promise* (1938). Her 'pram', her domestic responsibilities, were to remain in someone else's hall. Fetters were to be relinquished if they impeded the progress of art, and if that meant divorcing oneself from 'that eternal chemistry of family/and family affairs'[11] then so be it. Her immediate aims were to establish herself as a writer and to set up home with Robin. She had no doubt as to what took priority in this equation. There was, she felt, no choice, even though she plunged herself into poverty and went against the received wisdom of Edinburgh. Robin was safe. He could stay where he was for the time being. She was also, she convinced herself, interested in satisfying her parents' desire to have Robin with them: Robin loved Cissy and his presence rejuvenated her. Muriel felt that she had to take her chances, for his sake and for her own. But there was, perhaps, another unacknowledged factor: that she could no longer accommodate a child's emotional needs, that Robin reminded her too sharply of that terrible African life. He was part of the 'bad dream' from which she was waking. Driven by her vocation, she would not be driven by anyone or anything else, and had no intention of spending the rest of her life sighing for what might have been.

This dynamism, glittering from a witty, irreverent and beautiful young woman, soon secured her friends. Muriel was a breath of Caledonian air in the stale closes of the metropolitan poetry circuit. Amid the rows and the politicking of this new bohemia recently released from war, she seemed both oddly proper and glamorous, placable yet capable of delivering a conversational killer punch if threatened. And given that the majority of these people were men who saw themselves as passionate eccentrics, Muriel had an additional asset. She was, to use her word, 'sexy' – and she enjoyed that power. Poets old and young, but particularly old, were given to drooling into their beer about this fabulous creature, apparently on the loose. Muriel, smiling, courteous, and not a little teasing, kept her distance – which of course rendered her all the more seductive.

Beneath that elegant exterior, however, there was caution. Marriage had seriously damaged her trust. Men and sex were associated with violence and threat. She enjoyed the company of men but was, and remained, unwilling to abandon herself to anyone. And, as at Milton Bryan, there was also the difficulty of intellectual competition. Many of the poets with whom she now mixed were university graduates, apparently at ease discussing Freud, anarchism and philosophy from Plato to Wittgenstein. Muriel had left school at seventeen and for nearly seven years had lived in the cultural wasteland of Southern Rhodesia. Although she soon saw through the verbal exhibitionism of her new male friends, there was something attractive about it. It was a shadow of the analytical strength she yearned to develop, but she needed first to impress them with her own literary personality – and she was not entirely confident that she could do this. Derek Stanford, who was to become a grade-A bête noire in her life, described his own thinking as 'indubitably grade B'.[12] But even with him her uncertainty at first led her to play down her acuity. In the past, she wrote to him in 1949, she had always been confident that when her mind could not seduce, her body could. He was better than her, she felt, at the exchange of ideas.[13] She was ambitious, biding her time, learning by osmosis. She listened, read voraciously, took notes, took advice, became an utterly charming auto-didact not uncritically intoxicated by these thin spirits.

*

The slow journey from misplaced deference began in 1947 with her appointment as General Secretary of the Poetry Society and editor of its magazine, the *Poetry Review*. For two years she had been making her presence felt in the Society, both as a new creative voice and as a mind disciplined by good business practice. When the post felt vacant, she applied and was appointed, not unopposed, but with a clear majority. Under its previous 'Director', the Chevalier Galloway Kyle, the Society had maintained a supreme reputation for mediocrity. Kyle continued to live in the top-floor-front at 33 Portman Square, the Society's London headquarters, and it was agreed that this flat, or another in the same building, would be made available for Muriel. She planned to bring Robin down from Edinburgh to share it with her. Everything for once appeared to be going right: £30 a month, a steady job with influence in the literary community, and the promise of cheap accommodation. The chance to transform the Society, and particularly the *Review*, into something vital presented itself as an invigorating challenge. She was in high spirits.

No one, however, was more aware than Muriel of the struggle that lay ahead. Wrey Gardiner, soon to become one of her closer friends, had published a volume of autobiography the year before in which he spoke of 'still suffering' in his youth 'from the miasmic mellifluence of the Poetry Society [...] its would-be authors bumbling in the metres of yesteryear. [...] So serious. So intense. Leading nowhere [...].'[14] Gardiner had abandoned all this by setting up Grey Walls Press and by founding *Poetry Quarterly* in 1939. The following year Cyril Connolly had established *Horizon*. These magazines, Tambimuttu's *Poetry London* and Howard Sergeant's *Outposts*, dominated the post-war poetry scene in England. In addition to publishing the best of the younger British poets – G. S. Fraser, Nicholas Moore, W. S. Graham, James Kirkup, David Gascoyne, Alex Comfort, Dannie Abse, Mervyn Peake, John Heath-Stubbs, Ian Hamilton Finlay, Michael Hamburger – Gardiner also took work from Stephen Spender, and had the audacity to print verses by foreigners: Apollinaire, Pasternak, Cocteau, Verlaine. If the atmosphere of *Poetry Quarterly* was that of a cosmopolitan, male-dominated Soho pub, the atmosphere of *Poetry Review* was that of a Browning tea: a comfortable mutual admiration society with educational aspirations. As Secretary, Muriel had responsibility for schools' examinations in verse-speaking, for poetry competitions, Brains Trusts, lunch-hour poetry readings. She also had to take on a gaggle of half-baked *littérateurs*, often businessmen and ancient gentlefolk, whose tacit suspicions of this apparently flighty young woman (she was just twenty-nine) needed delicate handling.

Nevertheless, it was a breakthrough. If she could turn the Society and the *Review* round, she could establish herself. And the job also gave her excellent administrative experience. As she said in her CV nearly two years later when the whole arrangement had blown up in her face: 'I handled all stages of [*Poetry Review*], from the acceptance of material to the final make-up [...]. The entire control of the staff of the Society was in my hands. I have a good knowledge of sub-editing, advertising, publicity etc. and can take shorthand notes and type very quickly. I am especially experienced in committee work.'[15] Muriel had no objections to the disciplinary side of poetry – the sonnet-writing competitions, the verse-speaking, and she used the Brains Trusts to draw in some of Gardiner's circle. Before long the content of the *Review* began to resemble that of *Poetry Quarterly*. She raised the cover price and advertising rates, began to pay contributors. Usually she would work late into the night and return alone to the Helena Club. It quickly became clear that she was both ferociously industrious and a woman of acute business acumen. She was also, at first, politic, and deferential to the old guard.

Three men in particular looked troublesome: Kyle himself, Robert Armstrong and William Kean Seymour. As the founder and 'Honorary Director' of the Poetry Society, Kyle (1875–1967) was untouchable. Since 1909 he had run the whole show. In fact, he was little short of a crook who went under two names. During 1918, exposed by the Society of Authors, he had foolishly attempted a retaliatory legal suit, and lost, the judge expressing stern 'disapproval of [his publishing] firm's way of doing business',[16] but had somehow managed to ride out this storm as Director of the Poetry Society. When Muriel succeeded him in 1947 after nearly forty years, she inherited a business organisation aimed at amateurs and one that was seen, despite its apparently democratic structure, as Kyle's intellectual property. Only old age had bundled him into retirement. One of her jobs was to raise a fund for this venerated fraud, and two of its early contributors were Armstrong and Seymour.

Muriel's method of dealing with the elderly figures who resented her authority was to use her charm. It is doubtful whether she could have admired Seymour's verse. But she was not above political praise. Seymour was the magazine's senior reviewer, a Society elder, well known as a conservative London bookman with friends in many courts. He had probably voted against her election, having made clear to her that he had himself coveted the editorship. She had to tread gingerly across the live coals of his potential antagonism but, since she conscientiously sought his advice, his chilliness began to thaw. During August 1947 she was sitting alone in the office, busy and happy, having just completed the first number of the *Review* for which she had had sole responsibility, and exchanging slightly flirtatious postal pleasantries with him. He had sent her a poem and she had reciprocated with her 'The Bells at Bray'.[17]

In July, Muriel had taken her first holiday for years, a week in a hotel at Bray in Berkshire. She still travelled to town each day but was at least able to enjoy the long, peaceful evenings and to write a little. There she had relaxed and formulated her strategy. 'I plan to break down the lamentable reputation the "Review" has for being tradition-bound,' she had informed Seymour, 'also I want to cut out the awful letters of appreciation which appear in its pages along with similar twitterings.' Seymour's collected poems had formed part of her luggage and she wrote to praise them.[18] Sending 'The Bells at Bray', an unequivoval and passionate statement of chaste vocation, had marked a warming of their relations. He told her of his holidays. She kept him informed about literary London and was soon addressing him as a friend. Ignoring the poem's refrain of sexual denial, however, he seems to have interpreted it as a disguised invitation. At any rate, he was infatuated.

Seymour was not alone in this. Various poetic gentlemen in, or beyond, middle life were invigorated by her presence. Most restrained themselves, supported her reforms and encouraged her writing. For these courtiers, she reserved her respect. They were in the Methven mould: father-figures promoting this daughter of the muses: intelligent, scholarly fellows – a senior civil servant, a diplomat, a barrister, a brigadier – most of whom took her out to dinner and the theatre. All were married – and this suited her perfectly. Her first six months of office were spent circling gaily among these gentlemen and many intelligent and interesting women, working twelve-hour days, and trying to maintain the delicate balance between the diehards and the reformers. Apart from anything else, she had to learn the job. During 1946, she had acted as a researcher and editorial assistant for *Argentor*, the journal of the National Jewellers' Association. For this glossy 'art publication' she had written articles of which she remained proud. But the *Poetry Review* post was quite different in scope. Here, all responsibility lay on her shoulders and she needed advice. Those who offered false counsel and plotted against her, entered her private bestiary: Robert Armstrong; the Chairman, H. W. Harding; Seymour; Marie Stopes, the proponent of birth control. Muriel later lamented that Stopes's mother had not been better informed on the subject.

*

One of Muriel's closer friends was Arnold Vincent Bowen, an ebullient Welsh eccentric whose work she admired, and who counted John Cowper Powys among his acquaintance. Muriel submitted her work to Bowen and took his criticism seriously. Trips to London allowed him to escape his cosy provincial life in Liverpool and to enter an alternative identity as metropolitan artist. One of these visits she described to Seymour:

> Arnold Vincent Bowen and some of his lovely disreputable friends have just left this office where they have been making noisy pronouncements about Realism in poetry. Realism to them usually means a dustbin but Vincent and I know that every fantastic image is real.
>
> On Friday A.V.B. took me to the Wheatsheaf which is a poet's pub and the first I have been to. Wide-eyed with awe I breathed the same air as the picturesque Tambimuttu upon whose shoulder rested the blonde hand of a slimmer and later Byron. Everyone seemed to be posturing in the Greek style. [...] I went with funny Sir Eugen Millington-Drake to see the International Ballet do Swanlake [*sic*] on Saturday afternoon. This Ballet Company annoys me by making visible what should exist in the imagination of the audience if the dancing were expressive. [...] After the ballet I went to Vincent's party at his temporary flat where there were yet more poets. Howard Sergeant was the only name I recognized since he is one of my contributors [...]. We played a game in which someone

picks a poem title out of a hat and everyone has fifteen minutes in which to write a poem upon it; the results were surprisingly good.[19]

The younger poets she was now meeting rejected both the social realism of early Auden, and the 'Apocalyptic' school of Henry Treece, feeling their way towards a new engagement with anarchism and surrealism. 'Neo-Romanticism' was emerging with one foot in European surrealism and the other in the English tradition of Wordsworth. The tone of her description here is intellectually intimate. It shares her experience, as though introducing Seymour to a tumultuous world as foreign to him as to her. And indeed it was foreign to both. In 1947, she was unsophisticated, sexually inexperienced, and wrote in traditional form, while the remark 'every fantastic image is real' hints at the direction her writing was soon to take.

The night of Bowen's party, 20 September 1947, dates a crucial moment in Muriel's development. At that stage she was not on the Executive of the Council, having first been appointed acting editor of *Poetry Review*. Field Marshal the Earl Wavell was President, H. W. Harding Chairman and Treasurer. But she wasted no time. What she didn't mention to Seymour was that she had not only met Howard Sergeant and been strongly attracted to him; she had also enlisted his support to alter the *Review* in ways bound to antagonise fossils like Seymour. In fact, according to Sergeant's diary, 'there is a belief that Harding will be thrown out if he does not resign. [...] I can hardly believe that Muriel has the backing of the whole committee, as she seems to think.'[20] Indeed not, especially as 'Harding wanted [her] to edit the magazine as he [wished], and that she should go to bed with him.'[21] As she refused both kind offers, trouble was clearly imminent. Harding soon resigned under pressure, there was an enquiry at which Wavell refused to stay to hear Muriel's evidence or the Committee's findings, and the Field Marshal later wrote to everyone stating that, as it was usual for both parties in such disputes to leave office, 'unless [she was] given notice within three months, he would himself resign [...].'[22] Sergeant, whom Muriel was encouraging to become Treasurer, felt distinctly nervous. Wavell's threat represented a serious assault on Muriel's editorship. And there was another anxiety. 'Afraid that she is getting rather keen on me from a personal angle,' Sergeant noted. 'Dangerous. Must watch this relationship.'[23] Nevertheless, within a month of their first meeting, they were having an affair, soon an open secret. This, more than anything, became the focus for the resentments of those Poetry Society enemies eager to bring her down.

Around this time, Muriel was invited to dinner by Seymour. His wife, the novelist Rosalind Wade, treated her with 'eloquent coldness' and the following day's events explained why. Seymour turned up to apologise for Rosalind's rudeness:

> He said he had been unable to sleep at nights and had spent those nights walking up and down some corridor or gallery, because he had been thinking of me. He had told his wife all about it.
>
>   I told him he had better inform her that his feelings for me were not reciprocated and that he was putting me in a false position. But this seemed to please him. I got him out of the office and wrote a letter to his wife telling her plainly that I didn't want her husband and that I already had a boyfriend [...].[24]

Harassment from this 'banker and amateur literary man of sixty' was intolerable. He was 'a born mediocrity'[25] in Muriel's eyes and was treated as such when his presumption became intrusive. No one, least of all Sergeant, would have accused her of tact in this matter.

Sergeant was nearly four years older than Muriel: tall, bespectacled, an itinerant Civil Service accountant for the Ministry of Supply and a blunt Yorkshire Methodist who promoted provincial poetry. 'One big attraction of Howard', she wrote, 'was that he danced so beautifully. [...] Another attraction was that he was fairly manly.'[26] That 'fairly' is sharp. The relationship, at first passionate, soon degenerated into routine rows. It ended with a letter from him which she never forgave. *Curriculum Vitae* is dismissive of his 'street-corner attitude. I thought it petty, low. [...] I really could not like that man.'[27] We only have Sergeant's half of the correspondence and his diaries but these make it plain that he was insanely in love with her, bewitched and simultaneously terrified by this loss of control. Her hair, her eyelashes, her soft Scottish brogue, her low-cut dresses, her boots – all enslaved him. 'Today is the 20th,' he wrote in October 1947. 'Exactly a month ago you walked into a room and my life with such gaiety and charm.'[28]

Sergeant, however, had a problem: his wife and daughter, Dorothy and Deirdre, living in Blackpool. It is difficult to judge just how 'married' he was. His job took him all over the country. When he was working in London, where he rented a bedsit, Muriel and he saw each other regularly. But he was often away and if the affair had its recurrent arguments, it also suffered from a chain of agonising separations on station platforms. Both partners craved continuity. After they became lovers he spent most of his free evenings with her, often at the Poetry Society, busy with his own editorial work, helping with hers, or meeting at their special place, the Cumberland Hotel. The impression he conveyed to Muriel was that his marriage was ruined. She had assumed him to be free. The nature of his profession had presumably acted for some years as cover for irregular appearances in Blackpool. He had enough excuses to avoid confronting Dorothy. Muriel, it seems, was not the first 'other woman'. But she was, for more than a year, *the* woman: the boon companion, the enchantress for whom his romantic spirit had always ached. And Muriel reciprocated. When he tried to end it, it was she who offered a truce and regenerated his passion. She did not want to lose him. She wanted marriage.

'The suddenness of our love is bound to raise some doubts in both of us,' he wrote:

[...] I find it difficult to believe that such a wonderful person as yourself can ever love me. [...] You, too, have your doubts. I know – I've felt them when we've been together. [...] Drag the doubts into the light and let's [...] analyse them together. [...] I can see your eyes now shining with that infinite tenderness which melts me completely.[29]

These themes became the leitmotifs of his letters: sexual attraction dazzled then rendered him panic-stricken. Unlike Gardiner, Sergeant was not of the whimsical, lose-your-manuscript editorial school but a man who guarded himself against passion by orderly systems. There was much of this in Muriel, too. Always irritated by business inefficiency, she was adamant that the lazy practices of the Poetry Society be disciplined. As two editors, two artists, two people with children and bad marriages, they seemed ideally suited. The most important thing in any relationship for Muriel at this time was the opportunity for intense literary discussion. Sergeant certainly provided this, applauded her work and her editorial ambitions. Like Bowen, he sent lists of names and addresses, offered close analysis of her verse, wrote her love poems. Both lived and breathed poetry. Poetry, for Sergeant, had 'almost the effect of an orgasm',[30] and Muriel's poetry and person were at one in supplying this effect.

Those 'doubts', however, never evaporated. In fact, Muriel and Sergeant were radically unsuited. Although he admired her independence and found it sexually stimulating, it unmanned him. His desire was only for the placable side of his lover, his banter a form of light-hearted patronage which irked her. He wanted those limpid eyes eternally staring up at him, was moved by the lock of hair falling over one eye, wished to reach out and tousle that pretty little head, was most sympathetic to her melancholy when he could interpret it as her craving for him. At first he appears to have seen himself as an unhappy combination of desperado and quiet master. Muriel preferred to characterise him as a cowardly puritan. His attraction for her was that he seemed strong, protective. He was the 'senior partner' by virtue of his greater reputation, but he had discovered in her someone with whom he had not the faintest idea how to deal: a free and powerful woman. By mid-November the Committee passed a vote of confidence in her, and Wavell, who was simply notified of the result, resigned. Sergeant had thought that she could not possibly win against such opposition. 'I become more & more astonished', he noted, 'at Muriel's capabilities.' After supper in Queensway, they had walked back together through Hyde Park to the Helena Club: contented, ankle-deep in autumn leaves. 'Muriel was wearing a very provocative dress which showed the first delicate curve of her breasts. Looked really lovely. I was glad that she had recovered her spirits and was in good form.'[31]

The affair, however, left Muriel in a vulnerable position. Throughout its early stages, the battle for Robin's custody rumbled on and antagonism towards her editorial policy never diminished. She couldn't afford a scandal which might present her as an unsuitable mother or editor. Financial insecurity was a constant threat. She was living in one room on £7 10s 0d. a week. After tax, National Insurance and rent, she was left with about three pounds, some of which she sent to Edinburgh. As General Secretary she had to maintain a smart appearance for the office. At her own expense, she had to take taxis back to the Helena Club when working late, often till two or three in the morning. There were bills she couldn't pay without borrowing money.

That bitter winter of 1947/8, Muriel's closest friend at the club was Pamela Flood, an elegant young woman who modelled designer hats. Mrs Carrigan, as she became, had no memory of Muriel's lamenting her troubles about Ossie, Sergeant or the Poetry Society. She met Sergeant but could not remember doing so, perhaps, because more often than not he would leave Muriel at the door with both in ill-temper. Instead, Mrs Carrigan recalled odd, joyful excursions to the cinema, and padding along the corridor to Muriel's (larger) room after dinner and huddling round a shilling-in-the-slot electric fire to listen to her reading her poems. Muriel, it seems, kept her life in watertight compartments. Having established her career, she was impatient to drive straight ahead, make a home for her son, write books. At every turn, however, she was frustrated, confronted by people who wanted to construct her as arrogant, disloyal, flirtatious, and it is clear from Sergeant's and from Methven's letters that, as these external pressures mounted, she suffered terribly. For it was to them that she turned in her distress. The sourest taste was left by Sergeant, damning her himself as arrogant, disloyal, flirtatious. Ultimately, there was nothing to choose between his dreadful letter and those from Seymour and Stopes.

*

In early November 1947, Sergeant at last went to Blackpool for a council of war with Dorothy. He had written to her, explaining how his life had changed. This had made her ill. On the cold morning of his arrival, she stood there shivering, hysterical in a dressing gown, the infant Deirdre in the background. Sergeant refused to speak in front of his daughter. Dorothy pressed him. Had he slept with Muriel Spark? If he had, she would forgive him. Was he in love with Muriel Spark? He took Deirdre to school and then returned to answer the questions:

> For your sake I emphasized that the situation had been developing over a number of years, how totally incompatible we (Dorothy and me) were [...]. Recriminations followed [...] – I was very selfish, had [...] never given her a chance. You were a very evil woman, planning to find a husband at her expense, and must be very loose in morals: you had a mother & father – she was entirely alone in the world. How could I leave her to bring up Deirdre by herself? [...] I was deserting Deirdre to be a father to Robin. [...] [S]he will fight you to the end. [...] It has not occurred to her yet to strike at you through the Poetry Society; but if she contacts the Bowens, they may suggest it.[32]

'For your sake'? His opening sentence suggests that the question of divorce had never arisen openly; that the situation had not been developing for years. Muriel nevertheless accepted the situation. She wanted this man. 'As you remark,' he continued, 'the present position is no different from that we had foreseen.'[33]

This emotional maelstrom boiled with neuroses: Dorothy's terror of desertion, Sergeant's hesitation, Muriel's stressful poverty and the threat of Dorothy's 'striking' at her through the Society. Not least among these anxieties was the damage this business might wreak on the children. 'You once said to me', Sergeant added, 'that if our relationship threatened to cut you off from Robin, then you would break the relationship.'[34] Copying this passage in the notes for her autobiography, Muriel commented: 'Well, it did!'[35] All that, however, was still eighteen months hence. During their separations she wrote to him several times a week. They often telephoned each other. One letter enclosed a poem expressing

her love for him, later published as 'Standing in Dusk'.[36] Sergeant was
flattered but nervous. Her decisiveness confronted his caution, her chilly
resolution rebuked his passion: 'I saw you in the train after I left you
(you were not aware) and you looked so perfectly calm and content;
and I was tormented. In fact, all the time I have known you I have
swung backwards and forwards, like a pendulum, between torment and
delight.'[37]

Muriel calmly proposed various ways ahead: that he should break
communication with his home for six months; that she should change
her name to Sergeant by deed-poll; that they should set up together in
a flat. The first idea was unacceptable: his only news of Deirdre came
through telephone conversations with her and in Dorothy's letters. 'As
for taking the flat now,' he continued,

> I do not think it advisable. We should not attempt anything until your
> 'probationary period' [...] at the Poetry Society has expired. [...] Take
> the flat at the Poetry Society. By the end of December, the position should
> be clearer. [...] Do be very careful what you say to people down there
> (particularly Seymour). I think that you trust them far too much and
> forget that your male friends will not really be so willing to help you as
> they were when you were ... 'unattached'.[38]

By the end of December the position *was* clearer – or rather, more
clearly miserable for Muriel. She had dashed to Edinburgh to respond
to Ossie's attempts to resume custody of Robin. He was also suing her
for the balance of what he claimed were unpaid costs awarded against
her in the Rhodesian divorce (£34 12s 0d – a huge sum for her, impossible
to raise). The Inland Revenue withdrew the Child Allowance since Ossie
was now stating that he was both Robin's legal guardian and his sole
supporter. Methven had lent a large quantity of household items, kept
in store since his departure from London, for her to set up house in the
Portman Square flat. But by Christmas the Society was still doing
nothing to make it available. Muriel knew from Sergeant's warning letter
that her enemies were closing ranks. The last thing they wanted was to
see her installed as a permanent fixture. During December there was a

mass resignation from the Council. Methven's packing cases cluttered her office like a symbol of frustration and betrayal.

The relationship with Sergeant, barely two months old, did nothing to alleviate this sense of ubiquitous attack. In mid-November he had visited Edinburgh, taking a room at the Caledonian Hotel, and was as usual baffled by his lover:

> Muriel arrived just as I was coming down the stairs – she wore her fur coat & a new brown hat with a net. [...] Muriel's mother met us for lunch [... ,] a small, shrewd woman with a tiny mouth. Her eyes are dark. Imagine that she was weighing me up. After lunch we went to the flat at 160 Bruntsfield Place [...]. Robin and I got on well – I spent about an hour rigging [his toy] ship for him – Mr Camberg is dull but goodhearted. He had little to say but hung around awkwardly offering me cigarettes and drinks. It was very interesting to see Muriel in her home circle. It was obvious that she felt out of place and that the family irritated her. Even Robin got on her nerves & she showed little patience – this, I gather, is the result of a conflict in her mind. Mrs Camberg has, quite naturally, taken Muriel's place as a mother to Robin who looks upon Muriel as someone who visits him occasionally & gives him presents. Robin is frequently rude & unpleasant to Muriel, but that again is a psychological effect. Muriel analyses the situation but does not resolve the conflict because that would mean more responsibility and [...] she prefers [...] being financially responsible but having no other ties. At the same time there is a resentment both to Robin and Mrs Camberg. There seems little maternal feeling in Muriel – but she may have been suppressing.[39]

Against this tense background, their discussions had continued – hopelessly – for two more days. He felt she regretted having introduced him to her family. Then back in London, Weston Ramsey, someone Muriel had considered a friend on the Poetry Society Council, had released a defamatory account of the recent events to the *Evening Standard*, followed quickly by another 'Wavell-hand-out'[40] in the *Daily Telegraph*. When Sergeant returned home, his daughter had insisted on listening to the Royal Wedding radio broadcast and his wife had burst into tears, refusing to divorce him.

It was a terrible period for both parties. From Sergeant's point of view, Muriel neurotically veered from rage to reconciliation. From hers, he shilly-shallied, careless of her feelings. Both felt used by the other, professionally and emotionally. He was terrified of being pushed into something for which he was unprepared – and on 8 December wrote to say that they must part. She rang him, 'torn between fury [...] and tears', 'terribly distressed', at first making 'cutting remarks' and then becoming so 'calm and philosophical' that he found her '[a]lmost magnificent' and could not leave her. Although she failed to understand the depth of his affection for his daughter, Muriel agreed not to press for divorce and that they could not yet live together.[41] He accepted her terms, then three days later encountered her in the company of Peter Ustinov, Director of the Arts Theatre: 'As soon as we were introduced it was obvious that Peter was greatly taken by Muriel and she certainly gave him all her charm. It might have been deliberate. [...] Muriel basked in it all and it was very obvious how much she enjoys the luxurious life.' When they returned to Portman Square, believing that she had deliberately started an argument, he suggested again that they should part, and walked off. 'She chased after me [...] and caught up with me at the bus stop [...] very soft and tender – how she can change! – but I was quite adamant. I took her home in a taxi & left immediately.'[42] And so it went on. Muriel's 1947 Christmas was spent in London, Sergeant's in Blackpool. When she travelled to Edinburgh to meet up with him for Hogmanay, they danced the night away at the North British Hotel: 'Muriel lovely in her evening gown [...] in white with large red & green floral pattern, crinoline effect. She wore no jewellery round her neck. Very very gay and exciting.'[43] But there was, inevitably, another Cinderella moment. After waiting an hour for a taxi, they were forced to take the bus in all their finery back to her parents' flat.

Robin, now nine years old, continued to live with her parents in baffled expectation of a future with his mother. Muriel was making every effort to effect this but had first to secure her job and to settle the dispute with Ossie. He was now insisting on access. Her solicitors informed her that although it would be difficult for him to enforce the Rhodesian custody order, Robin would have to visit him, starting in the New Year. Ossie's lawyers were pugnacious: '[...] our client informs us that after the divorce was granted, the boy was in his custody in Gwelo for a period of a year, during which time Mrs Spark visited the boy on two occasions. This is hardly consistent with the suggestion that notwithstanding the terms of the Order, Mrs Spark was to have custody.'[44] The statement, Muriel insisted, was a lie deriving from the sick imaginings of her ex-husband and, ignoring the threats, she returned to London, determined to be officiously polite to Seymour until her authority at the Society was better established.

It never was. Government paper restrictions forced her to abbreviate contributions. Seymour took this, and her editorial suggestions, as personal affronts. When Muriel rejected one of his reviews and passed the book on to Sergeant, Seymour implicitly accused her of taking editorial direction from her lover. This was too much. Muriel was furious.[45] Seymour backed off. Perhaps she hoped that, having stood her ground, and with a new tranche of Council members, her troubles might recede. She was making arrangements for Robin to board at a preparatory school in Reigate, a few miles south of London (Methven had offered a cheque for the first term's fees). Ossie had apparently disgraced himself. Although he had worked satisfactorily as a temporary teacher of mathematics since early 1947, he had now been suspended, accused of assaulting a pupil with a leather strap. Weals had been found on the boy's face, legs, arms and back. If Ossie's grounds for custody were that he had reclaimed his senses, that claim now seemed frail.

Meanwhile, the younger poets had come to regard Muriel as guardian of their cause. They dropped in at Portman Square, wrote her love lyrics. Everything for a while was progressing smoothly. She had also acquired an admirer in Derek Stanford, with whom she could share her work and whose first volume of verses, *Music for Statues*, she vigorously promoted. This sense of purpose and achievement, however, soon collapsed. Ossie was acquitted of inflicting excessive punishment. Seymour had retreated only to lick his wounds and, under this stress, her five-month affair with Sergeant degenerated into mutual recrimination. In January 1948, he had insisted that they break off sexual relations until he had resolved matters with Dorothy. 'I have been trying to build up a picture of you as the intellectual in exile,' he wrote while reading through Muriel's work. 'Didn't you try hard to be worldly-wise and mature? Unfortunately you have left out all the love poems – which are the most interesting from my point of view – and I see you as you were then. [...] Oh, the years in Africa that take away the innocence of us all.'[46]

He was beginning to irritate her with his glib sympathy. She was having a bad time, had been forced to auction some of her property and, to economise, had stopped going to the hairdresser. He seemed to think this funny. And when she told him that Weston Ramsey was machinating to get Seymour on the Council, Sergeant's only response was: 'Still, you are a capable person and will be able to look after yourself.'[47] He was leaving her to the wolves, didn't trust her not to cause trouble and threaten his own literary ambitions. The love-talk echoed hollowly now. Towards the end of February he was claiming an 'unbalanced state' in which he spent nights patrolling the Liverpool river-front in 'emotional slavery to the idea of [her]'. He was, he said, 'terribly depressed and lonely, but have regained a little of my self-sufficiency. Your own calm and detached manner on the phone has been of some assistance in this respect.'[48]

More direct criticism soon followed:

What provoked me to act in that irrational manner? Your own taunts. [...] You rouse in me such a fury and resentment as no other person could possibly do. And yet at the same time as my bitterness, I am perfectly aware that I am so much in love with you that I should lose my anger were you to speak to me in your tender voice. [...] I feel unjustly treated, and knowing myself, my impulse is to 'run away'. [...] Darling, however you analyse your own behaviour (for instance as part of your methods for getting things done), for me your behaviour with others seems to be a complete lack of duty towards me.[49]

Sergeant's self-justification left her dry-eyed. His tendency to adopt authority as amateur psychoanalyst bored her. He was, she thought, simply jealous. He wanted to possess her but was unwilling to commit himself to marriage. She felt restricted. His attempts at objective commentary struck her only as a litany of suppressed abuse. Fearful of confrontation, he was sidling up to the long goodbye.

For Sergeant, the root of the difficulty was her 'methods': flirting with other men 'as a means of achieving certain ends'.[50] Derek Stanford, his friend, was also clearly enamoured of her. At that time, February 1948, she had written a poem for Stanford, 'On Music for Statues', which Sergeant not unreasonably construed as an expression of love, although it was more about her relationship to the Poetry Society generally. Staring out through the eye holes of the life-in-death mask of her job, offering her 'alabaster smile', she began to feel that Sergeant was of a piece with the Society's chummy self-regard. His jealousy and desire to shift blame, his fear of female freedom – all cast him in her eyes as tediously provincial.

More sinister, however, was the threat of the Kyle crowd's plans for her literary execution. Muriel had struggled to be polite to Seymour, my-dear-Williaming him through gritted teeth. On 13 May 1948 he had called to return review copies and they had gone out for tea. The chit-chat had seemed amiable enough. Then, shortly afterwards, an extraordinary letter arrived. In case there was any misunderstanding, Seymour explained, he wished to state that:

> I am not any ally of yours in this dispute [...] which is already splitting the Society into two bitterly opposed factions; [...] I supported and shall continue to support the demand for a full enquiry [into] the 'retirement' of Mr Kyle, [and] the resignation of Earl Wavell, Sir Ronald Storrs, Sir Charles Tennyson [...] and others. As I listened to the debate I prayed that you would take one of two courses: either to welcome the proposed enquiry or to resign.[51]

This was it. At last all pretence was abandoned. War was declared.

The Annual General Meeting to which Seymour was referring had taken place two days earlier. He was not known as 'Schemer Seymour' for nothing and Muriel, expecting trouble, had come prepared. A sustained and calculated assault on her authority had been launched by him and by Marie Stopes, at the heart of which lay their rage over those resignations. Stopes had demanded a poll on the question of an enquiry and a postal ballot had been arranged. Muriel doubtless irritated her enemies by setting the deadline just twelve days after the meeting but she wanted to clear the air quickly. As a result, of 2,486 papers sent out, scarcely five hundred were returned, the large majority opposing an enquiry. She thought she had won.

At the time of Seymour's letter, of course, neither he nor she knew how the ballot would turn out but the uncertainty of her position merely charged her courage. Her reply was a masterpiece of controlled derision. When it came to epistolary confrontation, Muriel's letters were heat-seeking missiles. His accusations, she said, disgusted her. If Seymour persisted in this calumny, she would sue him for libel. In future, he was instructed, he would address her as 'Mrs Spark', call only by appointment, and resist distracting her assistants.[52] Seymour replied by return, restating his position, rebutting all charges, and saying that her threat of legal proceedings 'was all of a piece with the rest of the arrogant nonsense in your letter. [...] You have always had a strange complex about your "importance".'[53]

Battle lines were drawn. As soon as the ballot result was declared, Stopes began investigating Muriel's marital history. Muriel telephoned and reprimanded her. Stopes wrote back, addressing her as 'Madam'. As a Vice-President, she insisted, she was entitled to conduct these investigations, demanding to know whether Muriel's husband had divorced her,[54] and littering her name with degrees and fellowships. 'Madam,' Muriel replied, 'I have received your outrageously impudent letter [...]. My private affairs are no concern of yours and your malicious interest in them seems [...] most unwholesome. [...] [Y]our attitude fills me with contempt.'[55] Clearly, Kyle's supporters would try anything to eject her. Christmas ('Toby') Humphreys, a barrister and prominent Buddhist, was at least one member of the Council on whose loyalty she could count. He had selected her poems as competition winners and supported her election. She was his 'Sparklet', and she turned to him for legal advice, to Methven for uncritical moral support, and to Stanford for aesthetic discussion. But it was a loveless existence, with the prospect of marriage to Sergeant rapidly diminishing.

'How sad is your letter this morning,' Sergeant wrote:

> I feel furious that these little people at the Poetry Society should upset you in this way, but I realise that it is mainly due to the attack of depression, which I know will pass. [...] It reminds me very forcibly of the many plots in the time of Elizabeth [...] you would have made an excellent Elizabethan queen; and I should have enjoyed leading piratical expeditions in between writing sonnets to my beloved Sovereign.[56]

Even so, by the summer it had become clear that if she were to be a sovereign, she would have to be Mary Queen of Scots rather than Elizabeth. She was being forced out. All she could do was to make her expulsion difficult, and to lay her own plans to found a counterblast magazine.

Throughout that summer of 1948, Muriel was often unhappy. The Reigate school kept writing to ask whether Robin *would* be coming. Eventually, she had to relinquish this idea when Ossie refused to agree to the boy's moving so far from Edinburgh but Robin was often at the centre of her thoughts. 'I believe [his] problems will be cleared', Sergeant wrote, 'as soon as you can arrange to have him with you. The transition from living in Africa to living in Edinburgh was [...] tremendous [...], but he weathered it. [...] I do know how you must feel about him and that it must almost break your heart at times.' 'What can I do or say to make you happier?' Sergeant asked.

> In other circumstances you would turn to me, as your lover, for comfort and assurance, but you give the impression that I am the cause of your depression. [...] It is a terrible thing to hear you, of all people, say that life hasn't meaning and that your only pleasures were simulated ones.[57]

Their intimacy, disintegrating again, perversely fed off its own misery. 'There is already a great divide between us,' he wrote,

> and, of late, I have not had the slightest idea of what is going on in your mind. Yesterday you implied that there was no purpose and no joy for you in our love (though, later, you tried to bind me closer to you). On Sunday you were sweeter to me than you have been for some time. [...] Are you tired of me? [...] Don't you really feel that it would be best to part? Isn't that what you want and are afraid to say?[58]

For ten more ghastly months they dragged on in this fashion, during which time she finally lost her job.

*

Muriel left the Poetry Society on 29 November 1948, choosing to be sacked rather than to resign in order to force them to provide three months' severance pay. John Gawsworth, friend of Wrey Gardiner and Stanford, took over as editor of the *Review*, Lord David Cecil as Chairman. In her last days as editor, she and Sergeant spent long evenings secretly typing out the Society's mailing list for the alternative magazine they planned to found. The atmosphere surrounding her departure was acrimonious. Insulting statements were issued (by Seymour, she believed) to the *Daily Express*.[59]

All lies, damned lies. But Muriel did not rise to the calumny. Instead she took practical measures, arranged for Methven's tea chests to be returned to storage, left the Helena Club and went temporarily to live with Toby Humphreys and his wife in Marlborough Place. Sergeant helped her move in. Several members resigned with her from the Society – among them, Sergeant, Stanford, John Bayliss, Herbert Palmer – and gathered for a reading at Humphreys' house in a show of solidarity. A photograph taken of the event was released to the press, Stanford and Sergeant prominently displayed, Muriel obscured in the background. There was talk of setting up an alternative society, 'Poetry in Exile', based in the home of the ancient Sir George Cockerill. In the event, however, this resistance was short-lived. Markets for poetry were scarce and Gawsworth was soon printing the work of Bayliss and Palmer.

A week before the publicity photograph, Sir George had resigned through illness from the founding group, and the editorial board[60] of the proposed magazine wound it up, leaving Muriel to develop it alone.

At first, Muriel had a new post as Organising Secretary to the British Institute of Political Research which planned to take over *Whitehall News* and to instal her as editor at £10 a week. Hearing of her new security, Sergeant posted a letter abandoning her. She rang him. They went for dinner in a Chinese restaurant. But this discussion was as futile as all their others. Just a fortnight later she lost this job, too, and, although she soon found work on another magazine, *European Affairs*, that long-cherished hope of reunion with her son was again deferred and her relationship with Sergeant in ruins. Muriel simply closed the door on the cacophony, looked ahead, and set about founding her new publication. By mid-January 1949 she had moved into a 'flat' at 1 Vicarage Gate, off Church Street, Kensington, near Kensington Palace and Gardens, just a stroll across the park from the Helena Club. It was a dowdy bed-sitting room she could ill afford – but it was freedom. It was also a 'good address', important for her new role as editor. Her time would come: of that she was perfectly confident.

CHAPTER 5

Kensington

The affair between Muriel and Sergeant was over. Nevertheless, in keeping with the *danse macabre* their relationship had become, they had found themselves drawing closer again during and immediately after the Poetry Society upheaval. She rang him regularly and assisted him with *Outposts*. He helped her move from the Humphreys' to Vicarage Gate and was part of her new editorial board. In Muriel's jaundiced memory he hung on, leering and gloating, envious of her being at home with the Humphreys where he was received with chilly good manners. At the time, although half-despising him, she needed and encouraged his support and, while he thought her manipulative, he remained infatuated. It was an emotional disaster area for both, made worse by the need to work together on the new magazine. She wanted to call it *Poetry Exile*. Sergeant and Humphreys advised against this, preferring her alternative: *Poetry Forum*. Eventually it became *Forum: Stories and Poems*. Sir George Cockerill and Mrs William Vestley put up the money, and the first issue came out during the summer of 1949. By then it was already a dead baby. Only one other number appeared, co-edited with Derek Stanford.

Throughout the winter of 1948/9 Muriel and Stanford had gravitated, flirtatiously but chastely, towards each other. Although sexually inexperienced, he was more engagingly eccentric than Sergeant and had something of the dandy about him. Where Howard wore suits, Derek sported checked shirts, a bow tie, lurid socks and a canary-coloured waistcoat. Howard danced well and cultivated an air of manly confidence. Derek was physically awkward, bald and short. His attempts at sangfroid were often spiked with misjudged aggression but he was a popular character among his numerous male acquaintances in the penumbra of literary London. Most of those who now emerged as Muriel's supporters – Gardiner, Bayliss, Palmer and Waller – had first been Stanford's friends. He acted as confidant in her confused emotional life. With him, she felt, she was under no pressure. Where she found Howard intrusive, always advising, warning, assuming possession, Stanford listened, admired, and appeared to claim no territory. He left her alone which was how, she discovered, she preferred to be: not deserted to fend for herself but supported and free.

At the beginning of the relationship with Sergeant, careless of scandal, she had published 'Letter to Howard', a passionate love lyric likening its subject to the wildness of Africa.[1] Another poem, 'He is Like Africa', again compares her subject to the Zambesi and the Niagara Falls.[2] Both lyrics were part of a sequence, including 'Song of the Divided Lover', and Muriel was very much the divided lover at this time. When the imaginative impulse of her work was charged by love or hate, it moved restlessly back to Africa. In love, Africa was light, space, freedom, exotic and mysterious, its savage power offering glimpses of the transcendental. Images of strange energies erupt: the moon, the leopard, muffled drums; above all, the rush of the Zambesi, that 'seraphic river', towards the thundering falls, the epitome of ecstasy, the very thrust of creation. In hate, Africa was figured as the Dark Continent, confronting the farcical attempts of mankind to impose control; it was the dust devil, the wasteland, a reminder of essential corruption and alienation, the meaninglessness of the purely material. Any association of Sergeant with invigorating wildness, however, was sadly misplaced. In those days, he was the committed Christian, she the questioning philosopher; he the one who would return to his bedsit after their rows to restore equanimity with prayer and Bible study, while she could find no spiritual home in his stony Methodism. She had looked to him for strength and permanence, to discover only a timorous beastie cautious of his reputation.

She frightened him and, just four months later, he wrote finally to crush what remained of their love.

From the beginning of her new life in Vicarage Gate, Muriel had sought full-time employment. On St Valentine's Day of 1949 she had begun as personal assistant to Pearson Horder, a publicity consultant. Five and a half days a week she worked in the office, writing speeches for industrialists. Her literary life, now largely confined to evenings and Sundays, was nevertheless energetic. She joined the Society of Authors, maintained an extensive correspondence, often to lay the foundations of *Forum*, wrote poetry whenever she could in the pauses between money-earning essays and reviews. But trying to do all this in her few free hours inevitably bred frustration.

A letter to Stanford in the last week before she was bound upon the wheel of commerce, offers a glimpse of the life she sought. She sent him a poem for criticism, reported on her reading (Eliot's essays) and writing (a piece on Eliot's drama for *Women's Review*). The tone is light-hearted: 'Have you ever wanted to become a Catholic? I would if I could find Faith. I shall set out on a pilgrimage, I think, turning over small stones and leaves, climbing rare mountains in Tibet and making odd enquiries in public libraries, searching for Faith.'[3] Everything was fun – while she felt free and creative. Then some insult at work (her boss had suggested that a trip to the country with him might expedite a rise in salary) threatened her financial stability. Still confiding in Sergeant, she received guardedly affectionate responses. 'Darling,' he wrote:

I don't know – you do strange things to me. It was so nice to talk to you [on the telephone] the other evening: didn't we get our money's worth?

I am writing this before going to bed, so you will know that I'm thinking of you. Indeed, it is difficult to do otherwise.

And you needn't think that you're going to put your trade-mark on me: I can see that it's time I took you in hand. You're getting too uppish these days.

Don't worry about the job, Sweet, I just can't imagine anyone being so crude & vulgar as to make such a suggestion, but don't let it get you down. Start looking for another job.[4]

When she most needed him, Sergeant offered no protection. She replied in terms that must have slapped his face. There was another monumental row,[5] to which his response was formal and furious, addressed not to 'Darling' but to 'My Dear Muriel':

> I agree that your attitude is intolerable. As usual you take things out of their context, distort circumstances, and fail to see how the things you complain of are usually a reaction to some unpleasantness of your own. [...] I have never resented your editing the Poetry Review [...]. You like [...] to sit back and dream of the past glory. The truth is [...] that you were so terribly arrogant & conceited about it all [...]. In no sense have you ever showed any loyalty. Indeed your one concern has always been your own self and everything & everyone else had to take second place. [...] [Y]our sole conception of [love] is selfish [...].[6]

Curriculum Vitae stresses the absurd provincialism of his regarding *Poetry Review* as 'past glory'. Her contemporary reaction was again to regard insult as opportunity for release. Stanford was now her chief literary comrade. On the morning that she received Sergeant's letter, 22 April 1949, she called on a publisher, Lindsay Drummond, proposing to edit the complete works of Anne Brontë, with an introduction to the novels by Stanford and to the poems by herself.[7] A new phase of furious book-making was opening in her life.

One letter captures exactly her volatile existence. On 20 May Muriel was sitting in Horder's office at 10 a.m., expecting him to arrive that afternoon, 'sucking a piece of cotton wool which I sometimes do for comfort', and writing to Stanford. Trying to compose a poem, she found that she could not because inspiration had been killed by secretarial tasks. A kind of amnesia gripped her, grief for the dead poem, the sense of wage-slavery. But she was glad, at least, to have Stanford as an ally. To him she could explain her occasional despair and she knew he would listen, encourage. Sergeant had condemned her as an arrogant coquette.

Stanford, she thought, saw through this to the vulnerable creature beneath. She felt a sense of a collaborative future with him.[8]

When at the end of May she lost her job at Horder's, she tried again to set up as an independent writer. *Forum* was due out in June. It included work by Roy Campbell, Alec Craig, John Waller, Herbert Palmer, Kathleen Raine, Wrey Gardiner, Elizabeth Berridge, Robert Greacen, Iris Birtwistle, Hugo Manning – a modest but respectable list drawn mostly from friends. Birtwistle, a warm and eccentric Catholic convert, was a 'deb' with artistic ambitions (poetry, painting, photography) who had lent Muriel a typewriter and whose vocation was to support struggling artists. Over the next four years she, Muriel and Stanford became friends. Manning, who worked all night on a Reuters desk to leave himself free for poetry during the day, was another kindred spirit: a lapsed Jew turned spiritualist, ebullient and generous. Muriel produced an affectionate portrait of him in *Loitering with Intent* (1981) as Solly Mendelsohn, 'a man of huge bulk with a great Semitic head, a sculptor's joy' and (indirectly) of herself as Fleur Talbot, the heroine.[9] When an enquiry arrived in 1995, asking if Fleur's love for Solly was Muriel's for Hugo, her street-slang annotation[10] made it clear that the question was ridiculous. There was, however, affection.

In her novel, Mendelsohn during his last illness sends Fleur those two autobiographies so important to Muriel's sense of artistic identity: Cardinal Newman's *Apologia Pro Vita Sua* and Benvenuto Cellini's *La Vita*. Manning sent neither but rather collections of his verse which Muriel cherished. Associating his fictional alter ego with such crucial influences was a tender touch and a form of obituary. When *Loitering* appeared, Manning was dead. She had not seen him for twenty years. Yet somehow he still epitomised the positive side of her existence in the late 1940s and early 1950s. She was grindingly poor, with scarcely enough to eat; nevertheless she was exultant to be 'an artist and a woman in the twentieth century'.[11] *Loitering* sketches the interior of her Vicarage Gate room:

> a gas ring for cooking, a bed for sitting and sleeping on, an orange box
> for food stores and plates, a table for eating and writing on, a wash basin

for washing at, two chairs for sitting on or [...] hanging washing on, a corner cupboard for clothes, walls to hold shelves of books and a floor on which one stepped over more books, set in piles.[12]

The table was a folding card table; the bed, single: everything temporary, functional, convential in its austerity – and dominated by books, books, books.

It was this cluttered space that Stanford would visit before returning to his permanent home, his parents' house in the suburbs of London (Hounslow). He had a part-time job at the Baldur Bookshop on Richmond Hill. Like Muriel, he was working his passage, furiously composing poems and articles, scanning the horizon for new markets, nagging editors, cultivating useful friendships. Both had left school after matriculation, had not gone to university, saw their destiny as artists and intellectuals. Both felt vulnerable beneath their public images. In *Loitering* Muriel writes Sergeant / Stanford out of her life in the form of the repulsive Leslie (no surname), a married boyfriend who annoys her 'in the extreme by small wants of courtesy. [...]. He was ambivalent about my writings, in that he often liked what I wrote but disliked my thoughts of being a published writer.'[13] This was Sergeant. Lesley's inaccuracy, inefficiency, selfishness; his 'proprietary way'[14] with her food, writing paper, reputation, reflect how she came to regard Stanford. In retrospect, the first was a bully, the second a sponge. The novel is in part the story of how Fleur rids herself of these deadly influences and releases her own talent. At the time, however, Muriel was far more tolerant of Stanford. Indeed, she loved him, and the relationship lasted, in one form or another, for five years, during which they regarded each other as a brother- and sister-in-arms on the battlefield of English letters.

They eventually became lovers during the summer of 1949, on St Swithin's Eve. After that they appeared to their friends to be cohabiting, and conducted most of their social and literary life together. They wrote together (books, poems, translations), edited the final issue of *Forum* together, approached publishers as a unit, visited friends as a couple, regularly shared domestic space. Yet as they wrote, so they lived: in separate compartments. The domestic space was always Muriel's. It is true that Stanford visited and stayed overnight, that they let the landlady of her next room, in the Old Brompton Road, believe that they were married, and developed elaborate fictions to keep up this pretence. It is not true, however, that they lived together. Those London bedsits were Muriel's, her island. She paid the rent.

Their extensive correspondence bears witness not only to the intensity of their early feelings for each other but also to the amount of time they spent apart. From the very beginning, there are apologies from both for a certain coolness with the other. In June 1949, for instance, Muriel had just begun a biography of all the Brontës, including the parents, and felt like a 'pregnant tigress' about it.[15] Lindsay Drummond was to have published it alongside the edition of Anne Brontë's works. Muriel and Stanford had moved fast on both projects. Just eleven days after Drummond's letter expressing interest in the Anne Brontë volume, they had posted their Introductions, and in the course of preparing her final draft, Muriel had received a commission for the biography. There was no contract – just a cheque for fifty pounds and encouragement. But throughout their joint work, Muriel and Stanford had difficulty negotiating territory. Both craved intellectual intimacy yet both were loners. Addressing him as her beloved prince, she assured him that she would never betray him; that the affection she felt was uniquely wonderful in her life.[16] He called her his 'most adorable half-sister Sarah': 'Believe me, darling, [...] I rest secure in [...] my sense of your gifts: that the unique & urgent talent is there, even if the publisher looks the other way.'[17] 'I am your well-wisher,' she wrote, 'and your intimate too, and although you don't need encouragement I will give it nevertheless.'[18] His confidence fuelled her indomitable creative energy. The difficulty was that where his mind was vague, hers was precise. Where she saw the shape of any book immediately and was impatient for completion, he dithered. Her letters are evocative, sharply etched; his meander through clouds of verbiage.

Before long, though, both her books collapsed. Another firm was already reprinting Anne Brontë. Muriel discovered Oxford University

Press announcing a new life of the four Brontës. Fearful of competition, Drummond sent ten pounds as consolation and cancelled. Muriel then switched to Bransten, an American publisher Stanford had found. When this approach failed, she proposed to Wrey Gardiner that she reconstruct the wreckage as an edition of Brontë letters for Grey Walls Press. Nothing came of this (although she eventually sold it to the publisher Peter Nevill), nor of her ideas for an edition of Jane Austen's letters and two books on Dorothy Wordsworth. Letters to Bransten tell a typical story of wasted effort, frustration, attempts to get him to change his mind.[19] It did no good. The biography was abandoned. But one last project still smouldered. Alan Wingate had accepted a proposal for a centenary volume on Wordsworth.

Despite poverty and disappointment, despite aggravation from Solly Spark in Edinburgh and the continuing uncertainty surrounding Robin, Muriel pressed ahead. In July she had woken one morning and immediately written to Stanford to say how much she loved him. All the sourness of previous experiences seemed to evaporate under his influence. She had never, she said, been happier – because she was *writing* and he facilitated that work.[20] In turn, he appears to have been pleasantly astounded to be so cherished, uncertain how to deal with it:

> In the past, because I never approved of what I loved, I would often behave with sadistic nastiness [...]. But in moments of doing this, I did not suffer, as I suffered the other night with you. In the past I really wanted to mock. It was torture the other night when I did it.[21]

He had, he said, a masochistic tendency, a desire to prolong and relish depression, 'to be relieved of all my inbred miserliness'. Intimacy was new to him and he wanted to 'have you well-acquainted with all the tortuous thoroughfares of my make-up':

> That is, the feminine strata of my nature – which needs & desires a high sense of pleasure from being made love to at certain times whilst remaining almost passive in return. I wanted, in other words [...] to be

partly ravished by you. [. . .]. On the whole, perhaps, I like an equal collaboration.[22]

Perhaps. All this appears as a postscript to an enthusiastic love letter, praising the 'ritualistic air' of their Sundays together, spent in 'delightful loafing'; thanking her for holding a 'midnight vigil in the Churchyard that has been so friendly to us, and to which we have carried our grief'. It is written on *Forum*'s headed writing paper. Under 'Editor: Muriel Spark', he has added '& Derek Stanford'.[23] That heading was soon reprinted with Stanford's name alongside hers.[24] Joint publication was a form of literary wedlock – one of the worst mistakes she ever made.

Stanford was bright. He had just completed an essay on Herbert Read's poetry, much appreciated by its subject. In addition to *Music for Statues*, he had produced a critical book, *The Freedom of Poetry* (1948, a study of ten modern poets), and a monograph on David Gascoigne. A respected poet, Stanford could turn out an article on anything literary within the week. At thirty-one, three months younger than Muriel, he was fired by the energy of gate-crashing the British literary establishment, advocating anarchism and surrealism, putting himself about, cultivating his eccentricities. He felt a particular affinity with the writers of the 1890s and had developed the speech habit of dropping the final 'g' from his words. Neville Braybrooke and his wife, June, then also aspirant artists, close friends of Muriel, recalled Stanford's once saying: 'I was thinkin' of askin' you, sir, your opinion of Mr Beardsley.' He drank beer with a dash of Benedictine in imitation of Dowson's circle. He even drank in their pubs, would take people on tours of their haunts. With one foot in late-nineteenth-century decadence and the other in post-war scepticism, he was, like Muriel, culturally and intellectually divided. But where she woke to innocence, he woke to recrimination.

The world, Stanford felt, had dealt unfairly with him. His notebooks from the 1940s (now in Texas) record his conversations with Bayliss, James Kirkup, John Heath-Stubbs, Gardiner. There are lists of obscure words to check for future use, of books to read in order to keep up-to-date. They are the diaries of an autodidact, an egomaniac of an undangerous, passionate variety. He emerges as an amateur philosopher who generalises about 'Romanticism' or 'The English Mind' in a form of ceaseless, self-torturing enquiry. Adrift on his own rhetoric, he sees himself as a bohemian man-of-the-world, womaniser, drinker, unjustly sidelined as hack critic. In later life he made several attempts at an autobiography: the garnerings, as he saw it, of an important voice which would one day be heard. And in the meantime he talked to himself or to anyone who would listen, turned up hours late to his job in the bookshop, proud of his penury in the cause of the noble calling; dismissive, as was Muriel, of time-servers; time-serving himself with his tongue in his cheek. But Stanford was neither womaniser nor drinker. His self-portraits reflect an image of what he thought he ought to be (much more like Wrey Gardiner) rather than what he was. Many were fond of him: of his passion for poetry, of his gentleness. If his friends arranged to meet him in a pub, they would expect him to lose his way. He was, and remained, a troubled man. But he was also a man nervously eager for life – and that was attractive.

Some of Muriel's more elegant female friends thought Stanford a strange partner for her. June Braybrooke (the novelist 'Isobel English') remembered enduring him for Muriel's sake. Birtwistle felt much the same, while regarding him more sympathetically. There was no mistaking, she thought, his innate kindness, his total dedication to Muriel. Neville agreed: Stanford, he accepted, could be irritating but he was essentially amiable. Once, when the Braybrookes and Muriel were meeting him off a train, Neville had casually remarked: 'Here comes little Derek.' 'Not so much of the little,' Muriel corrected him.

*

In the early 1950s Muriel and Stanford fought their cause together. He had his bookshop job. She worked as editorial assistant for *Women's Review*,[25] then for *European Affairs*. The second and final issue of *Forum* (undated) probably appeared, much delayed, in early 1950, the manuscript of its editorial[26] revealing an expansive draft by Stanford, cut and sharpened by Muriel. It was a provocative little magazine but if its collapse was a disappointment, it was also a relief. The business side of it was sucking them into swamplands of correspondence while the magazine itself was plainly not selling, with barely eighty subscribers compared with the *Poetry Review*'s two thousand. The *Review* under Gawsworth had a more serious competitor, *Nine*, edited by Peter Russell, pro-Pound and anti-Neo-Romanticism, which was openly to attack Stanford's scholarship. There was, then, to be no alternative group with Muriel at its head, no public self-justification in the field of editorship. Instead, she gave her mind to producing her own books, and that last editorial reflects the issues with which she and Stanford felt engaged: psychoanalytic criticism and, as artists, the need to balance the 'Romantic' and 'classical attitudes'.[27] Muriel's powerful critical mind, however, had yet to find common ground with her tumultuous imagination. Her criticism and her poetry tended to occupy separate rooms, and when *Tribute to Wordsworth*[28] appeared in the spring of 1950, the same dichotomy was evident.

Tribute was a book of two halves. Stanford contributed an introductory essay to a selection of Wordsworth's nineteenth-century critics. Muriel discussed his twentieth-century biographers and critics. (Herbert Read, Stanford's new-found supporter, provided a Foreword to give the volume the *imprimatur* of an established literary figure.) Stanford's piece acts as an Introduction to the volume, adopting an air of easy learning, while Muriel's wrestles with the history of recent debate. What interests her is its uncertainty of approach since Legouis's 1922 revelation of Wordsworth's affair with Annette Vallon, and de Selincourt's variorum edition of *The Prelude*. The latter had demonstrated that Wordsworth was trying to write Vallon out of his life. Muriel discusses 'the two main opposing groups of younger critics [...] known as neo-romantic and neo-classical' and concentrates on the issue of Vallon, Wordsworth's desertion of her and their child, and the question of how critics deal with (or choose to ignore) this intensely personal matter.[29]

In the light of her own history with Robin, this question was always in danger of becoming subjective. After converting to Catholicism in

1954, Muriel regarded psychoanalysis as an absurd humanist delusion. At this stage, though, she was clearly interested in it,[30] believing that Wordsworth was a poet 'to whom the application of psychological treatment is supremely justified',[31] and keen to analyse his verse in terms of erotic suppression. Opposed to this, the voice of T. S. Eliot acted as a corrective, insisting that such interpretations had led to 'fantastic excesses and aberrant criticism'.[32] The fundamental issue here was the origin of inspiration, a subject which was to intrigue Muriel for the rest of her life. Yet the tension between 'classical' (or 'neo-classical') authorial control, and the fluidity of the Romantic (or Neo-Romantic) imagination, remains unresolved. 'George Fraser', she remarked to Birtwistle, 'once described me as an "agitated classic" which I have been pondering upon ever since. Herbert Palmer says I'm just plain "difficult". But then we can't all be Phoebes.' ('Phoebe' was Phoebe Hesketh, a poet whose work Muriel despised as sentimental.) Birtwistle's self-description – 'primitive romantic'[33] – seems to have appealed to Muriel as a term which might also define her own work.

The erotic element was rarely absent from Muriel's verse; writing itself was akin to an erotic act. Stanford had at first resolved a double repression in her, allowing these two forms of supercharged emotion to combine where before they had been exclusive. Throughout her Wordsworth essay an exiled female voice politely confronts male colonisation of the subject. These irritating fellows stated what was, and what was not, of 'first-rate' importance while lacking any idea of how an artist thought. She and Stanford, on the other hand, saw themselves first as artists rather than as critics, and also as equal partners. Nine months earlier she had explained her feelings about this: how her creative mind worked, travelling from the material to the metaphysical and back again along a chain of Proustian connections, and how she saw Stanford as integral to the process. He had sent her a pink carnation which sat in her multi-purpose bathroom glass and she had felt slightly, inexplicably, sick. The flower seemed to come alive, to make her feel romantic. Associations with Pavlova's tutu, her tyrannical artistic perfectionism, rose up (after that trip to the Empire Theatre paid for by

Miss Kay,[34] Muriel and Frances Cowell had felt nauseous) and made an obscure but definite link to the present and to her love for Stanford. Most men, she said, 'do not like to see women as an island and attempt to land and set their flag on it'. In the past she had wasted her creative time, defending her island against Ossie's and Sergeant's possessiveness. Stanford seemed to release her from this by helping to build protective walls within which she could work. The female artist is characterised as solitary, exotic, and industrious within her stockade.[35]

Muriel and Stanford both drew energy from this stimulating combination of erotic and aesthetic desire. But where she saw him as a guest on her island, he saw himself as co-tenant waiting to take over the lease. He left her alone, it seems, because he was anxious about entering an adult relationship which might infringe his own freedom to be erratic. If she made arrangements for them as a couple, he became quarrelsome. Muriel and Stanford's mother exchanged Christmas presents but they never met. Their letters express bafflement at Derek's secretiveness. In London, Muriel introduced him to her parents, and to Robin. Cissy liked him (a 'character', she said), anticipating marriage as a resolution of her daughter's rootless existence. When Cissy proposed a second visit, however, Muriel insisted she would be away. She wanted her intimacy with her lover to be exclusive, their secrets hidden. Stanford, on the other hand, was indiscreet. He was in the habit of discussing her with his male cronies, Sergeant included. Her initial response to his fear of being controlled was sympathetic. This was, after all, how she had felt with Sergeant. When Stanford offered her a ring (if she went out and bought it), she declined this half-cock engagement. But to confuse matters further, her sexuality, conditioned by the period and by Edinburgh propriety, led her still to seek a strong man, 'mind' rather than machismo, and to give that mind room to pontificate. Each paid elaborate court to the other.[36] The whole arrangement, however, was based on a misconception: that Stanford was free of patronage. What ultimately divided them was religion – but this was a symptom rather than a cause of their incompatibility.

*

Few signs of these difficulties emerged until 1954. Eighteen months after the affair had begun, in January 1951, she was still writing to him affectionately. Their life together, she said, had taken her pleasantly by surprise. In the past, the lives she had hoped for had either failed to happen or become distasteful.[37] By this stage their prospects had improved. Muriel had moved to a larger room in the Old Brompton Road, at 8 Sussex Mansions. Thanks to her driving industry they had edited two books together: *Tribute to Wordsworth* and *My Best Mary: Selected Letters of Mary Shelley*. Stanford had written a monograph on the playwright Christopher Fry, and she had edited *The Brontë Letters*, completed a biography of Mary Shelley (*Child of Light: A Reassessment of Mary Wollstonecraft Shelley*) and was working on a book about John Masefield. Their literary 'marriage', however, was already under strain. Signing *My Best Mary* in 1995, she did so 'wishing the other contributor wasn't there. It was a harrowing "collaboration".'

Muriel's work rate was phenomenal. Stanford was easily distracted. She had great difficulty in bringing him to the point in discussion, and even greater difficulty in actually getting him to *do* anything. Since he was her lover, she suppressed these irritations and encouraged him to greater efforts. Blind faith in each other's talents was a vital ingredient in those penurious days. Although it was becoming clear to Muriel that she worked better alone, she enjoyed the idea of comradeship. *Tribute*, however, had scarcely flickered in the London press, included as it was in reviews of other Wordsworth centenary volumes (among which was one by Sergeant who had, Muriel said, admitted to lifting the idea to spite her), and none of the other books was yet published. In the tax year 1950/51, Muriel earned just £31 from writing: *My Best Mary* and *The Brontë Letters* did not appear until 1953 and 1954 respectively. Impatience with Stanford's indolence perhaps seemed slightly less harrowing than the multiple tortures exacted by the shoestring publishers with whom they then dealt. But this irritation was a seed which grew. In 1949 they *had* been equal partners. Indeed, Stanford's reputation was, if anything, better established. By 1951, Muriel had the lead.

Stanford's attitude to this, conscious or unconscious, appears in an unpublished and unfinished *roman à clef*, written six years later, 'Good-bye Bohemia: An Idyll'. As a fictional impression of how he saw Muriel, it is revealing, and rereading it after half a century he 'felt even more of a silly bugger than he had taken himself to be'.[38] 'Good-bye . . . ' presents a mocking portrait of its hero, Charles (i.e. Stanford). His lover, Susan, is plainly Muriel. One section describes Susan's accompanying Charles to 'Wytton' (later 'Wotton') to visit the writer Martin Day, on whom Charles is writing a book. This is also transparently autobiographical. Muriel and Stanford visited Christopher Fry at Shipton-under-Wychwood in early June 1950.

Having secured £150 from the Royal Literary Fund, Stanford was for once in the money. He and Muriel set off jauntily on a bus from Vicarage Gate to Paddington to take the train to Oxford and then Shipton in the Cotswolds. It was hot. Fry met the train and drove them first to the Shaven Crown, an inn at which he had booked them a room, then on to his cottage where they met his wife. The 'novel' records visits to Martin (Fry), Charles's struggles to make his ideas understood, and the way in which this encounter changes the visitors' lives. Dissatisfied now with their cramped accommodation in Kensington (i.e., 1 Vicarage Gate), they move to a larger bedsit, a fourth-floor room looking out towards Lots Power Station (i.e. 8 Sussex Mansions). Throughout, Susan is regarded as an accessory. He 'thought, felt and believed', Muriel commented on reading the story in 1997, 'that any women [...] were his inferiors. I became convinced of this, to my amazement.'[39]

Fry's account[40] bears this out. A generous and mild-mannered man, he had known poverty and obscurity himself, although he was now a huge success, an intimate of T. S. Eliot, with *Venus Observed* succeeding *The Lady's not for Burning* on the West End stage.[41] He was happy to assist aspirant writers. But he hardly knew Stanford and had not seen him for more than five years. Stanford had apparently presumed on their slight wartime acquaintance and had even then been an irritant, having passed on one of Fry's poems, inaccurately transcribed and without permission, to a London editor. Fry recalled not wishing to talk about his work in Stanford's pseudo-philosophical fashion; Muriel remembered agonising embarrassment 'as it dawned on me how much Derek was pushing himself on a famous man. I kept rather quiet [...].'[42] To Fry, Muriel was the interesting one. Yet Stanford never introduced her as someone with an independent literary career. In the story Susan is cluttered by the paraphernalia of femininity, 'a demure pigeon (indignant no doubt, at the privileges of men)', capable only of 'pointless comments'. Her function in the narrative is to act as support for Charles's greater talent and as a guarantee of his virility. Ultimately, we are asked to see him as neither a 'detestable old fraud' nor as benign, but as a genial, 'argumentative sod', distinctly in charge of the relationship. Stanford's self-image, then, appears confused. In retrospect Muriel believed he might have been gay, that she was his 'cover-woman'. He denied this. The fact of the matter appears to have been that he was simply unable to deal with Muriel's strength. The image of his bohemianism promoted in his *Inside the Forties*[43] as a Roy Campbellish rough-and-tumble belligerent, careless of convention, was a denial of his neuroses. Actually, he was rather timid, often teetering on the verge of hypochondria and nervous breakdown.

*

As in Stanford's story, Muriel moved into her new place within a fortnight of the Shipton visit. Sussex Mansions was a brick-built block on the Old Brompton Road, Kensington, where she rented a room in the flat of Mr and Mrs Andipatan, a Mauritian couple. Since Christmas, she had worked three days a week as an editorial assistant and secretary to Peter Nevill, the publisher of Stanford's Fry book, whose premises were just over the road. It was a hand-to-mouth existence, made worse by her confusion as to how to interpret her lover's behaviour:

> I shared my rations with him. [...] He left his ration card with his mother, so that he got sumptuous extra meals while I starved. [...] Where money was concerned he was a frightful scrounger. As soon as I had any he was very much in evidence. [...] No marriage with him would have lasted. I found him convenient as a literary partner up to the time I did a selection of Mary Shelley's letters with him. After that he was just a drag.[44]

Such sour memories compressed time a little. The completion of her *Child of Light* in September 1950 was the real turning point in this relationship. That summer they were still close.

During August she had taken a holiday with her family in Morecambe and wrote to Stanford, longing for his attentions, and to return to her 'own spiritual household'.[45] Alienation from her family was now complete. Muriel was thirty-two, Robin twelve. Stanford was her London life, her adult and creative life, Morecambe the apotheosis of drabness: a semi-detached house in which she shared a room with her mother, her father sharing his with Robin; soggy food and worse conversation, day trips to the Lake District and intrusive enquiries. In this mood she could see her companionship with Stanford as freedom.[46]

The gap between that sense of a 'spiritual household' with Stanford and his reduction to 'just a drag' is partly explained by the subject on which she was working. *Child of Light* is a remarkable book – the first serious attempt to reclaim Mary Shelley's writings and influence from her more famous husband's shadow. The author of *Frankenstein* now needs no defence. Her mother, Mary Wollstonecraft, is a monumental presence in the history of feminism;[47] her father, William Godwin, a leading theorist of Libertarianism, was a thinker revered by Shelley, Wordsworth and Coleridge.[48] But in 1950, this talented family and their works were popularly remembered as historical curiosities, while the reputation of Shelley himself laboured under Matthew Arnold's description of him as a 'beautiful and ineffectual angel'.

Muriel's is very much a post-war book, rereading Mary Shelley in the light of modernism, the Holocaust, Hiroshima. It sees her writing as uncannily predictive of contemporary angst:

'I neither pretend to protect nor govern a hospital,' says Ryland, the Protector [in Mary Shelley's *The Last Man* (1826)], '– such will England become.' It was a universal hospital and finally a universal morgue that Mary envisaged, before the French Symbolists had cried in their several ways, '*Cette vie est un hôpital,*' to be echoed by Rilke and T. S. Eliot; and before the possibility of the world's entire devastation was only a bomb's-throw away.[49]

These were Muriel's more recent influences – Verlaine, Rilke, Eliot. She shared their (and Yeats's) sense of imminent apocalypse, of inhabiting a moribund culture of degraded heroic ideals. But they were masculine voices and she also needed feminine ones. Mary Shelley, speaking out of 'her own experience of solitude, from the personal landscape of devastation she felt around her',[50] somehow provided a style of existence for the female artist against which Muriel might define herself. Mary's death-day (1 February) was Muriel's birthday; both shared the same initials, their married names being their writing names. Throughout *Child of Light*, it is impossible to escape a sense of personal association between author and subject. And in clarifying her vocation and her form of feminism, Muriel inevitably confronted the miserable realisation of how far her relationship with Stanford fell short of that between Mary and Shelley.

The book's general line of defence is to rebut the then dismissive characterisation of Mary as a dull and depressive companion for Shelley. Muriel cleans off this sludge of sexist varnish and restores a portrait of a woman of intellect, 'practical, staunch, rational and broad-minded',[51] courageous in the face of poverty, public abuse, her beloved father's insensitivity, the deaths of most of her children, and, of course, of Shelley himself. Above all, we see the artist, always observing, always reading, always talking, and talking to herself in her journals. Many of the interpolations recall Muriel's own struggles: 'Nothing is so detrimental to the behaviour of a family as financial worry'; 'No one is independent of material things'. One finds echoes of her letters to Stanford: '[W]e feel warmly towards those who can offer a meaning for our suffering and ignominy.' The word 'integration' recurs. Great lovers like Mary and Shelley are seen to create for each other the means of integration with the material world and to support each other's vocation. Mary Wollstonecraft in Muriel's story never achieves this coherence, either with Godwin or through her work. Both parents are characterised as chilly rationalists, 'drained of passion'. Their daughter's masterpiece, *Frank-enstein, or the Modern Prometheus* (1818), is represented as an analogue of this dichotomy between reason and passion, another version of that mid-twentieth-century impasse tangling Muriel's mind – classical or neo-classical versus Neo-Romantic or surrealist: 'The influential cur-rents of these two minds – Godwin representing the scientific empiri-cism of the previous century, and Coleridge, the nineteenth century's imaginative reaction – met in Mary's first novel.'[52]

They were also to meet in Muriel's first novel, *The Comforters* (1957), and her analysis of *Frankenstein*'s technique as 'the first of a new and hybrid fictional species'[53] identifies Mary Shelley as the originator of a kind of female Gothic surrealism of which Muriel herself was to become the high priestess. It is not that she thinks highly of Mary's fiction beyond *Frankenstein* and *The Last Man* (and even in these finds *longueurs* and implausible links). But this Child of Light had discovered a plain style in which realism and fantasy could cohabit: a voice, a variety of themes (the doppelgänger, the relationship between hunter and hunted, the imbalance of reason and imagination), and the ability to write across fictional genres which would help Muriel to discover her distinctive voice.

In describing the Godwin / Shelley entourage, then, Muriel offers an oblique reflection of the landscape of her own mind. Shelley writes to Mary much as Muriel had to Stanford: '"I never before felt the integrity of my nature [...] and learned to consider myself as an whole accurately united – rather than as an assemblage of inconsistent and discordant portions."' In Mary, 'Shelley found for the first time combined erotic and intellectual elements', just as Stanford had discovered this in Muriel. Mary, she insists, 'was a woman with a mind'.[54] Mary's flight into exile from the orthodox world, content in the company of her race of artists, is enthusiastically endorsed. But Muriel's book is not only about these 'romantic' early days. It is equally concerned with Mary's struggle, after Shelley's death, to support her one surviving child and to earn her living by her pen. *Child of Light* is a study of female depression and resilience, fiercely defensive of its subject's mental health. When a critic condemns

Mary for 'abject begging' in proposing '[t]heme after theme [...] for books which she felt she could write',[55] Muriel springs to her defence:

> Mr Jones is immoderate because Mary was not begging. She was an author who had enjoyed considerable success, who had faith in her own powers, and who was offering a publisher the commodity in which publishers deal. Many an author before Mary, and many a one after her, has plagued a good publisher no less [...].[56]

There is a distinctly personal ring to this.

Among Muriel's many book proposals was one on 'the intellectual and social emancipation of women during the 19th century' – and she wanted 'Resistance' in the title.[57] Further ideas were for a volume on contemporary women's poetry (Edith Sitwell, Lilian Bowes-Lyon, Kathleen Raine) and another on 'Women Novelists of the Nineteenth Century'.[58] The range and concentration of Muriel's reading here, and the revelation of a vigorous, idiosyncratic feminism, are striking. She likes Alice Meynell's work because it 'did not see the assertion of the female as necessarily attendant upon the decline of the male, nor did she claim female dominance at the cost of womanhood'.[59] Muriel had turned herself into an authority on nineteenth-century women's writing, determined to explain a form of female subversion, a 'cold war', which she admired. But her 1950s feminism was closer to that of the 1990s than to that of the 1790s (or even of the 1960s). It is the feminism of intellectual and economic partnership in which women are free to indulge in all the conventional manifestations of 'femininity'. *Child of Light* is essentially the story of someone 'finding her own inward reservoir of inner certitude',[60] and writing her biography performed the same general function for Muriel, separating her from Stanford's influence. Most importantly, it was the first book she had written alone and it was plainly better than anything he had achieved.

*

Muriel never rested. Soon after *Child of Light* was completed in September 1950, she gave her first radio broadcast: a Third Programme talk on Mary Shelley.[61] In November she contacted John Masefield, who agreed to her writing a book on his work, and as Stanford's stock began proportionately to fall, she bolstered his self-esteem. Fry's letters to him steadily chilled. The poet and biographer Robert Gittings had attacked the Fry book as presumptuous. 'To return (as I can't resist doing) to Derek again,' she wrote to Gittings, 'any element of "harm" in his work is in fact mildly operative against himself. [...] [I]f I am wrong, you must put it down to my partiality for him.'[62] For to return (as she couldn't help doing) to Stanford was to return to the place where she had first found her voice as a writer of books, and she dared not confront the idea that this had little to do with him; that the voice of her mature poetry, of *Child of Light* and of *Masefield*, was writing him and his parboiled intellectualism out of her life.

Muriel's dealings with Masefield were noticeably more professional than Stanford's with Fry. Before accepting the contract, she sought her subject's approval. When she visited him on 6 December, she travelled alone. Her whole approach was modest and courteous.[63] She had, she said, long admired his work.[64] Masefield might have seemed a strange choice for her. He was seriously out of fashion, an old man in a dry season for narrative verse, and it is true that there was an element of pragmatism in her decision. As usual, she had a practical eye on the market. *Tribute* and *Child of Light* had both been produced to coincide with their subject's centenaries, and Masefield's status as Poet Laureate guaranteed publicity for any book on him. But her enthusiasm for his work was genuine. Somehow he had become an influence, ever since, as a schoolgirl, she had been taken by Miss Kay to hear him read. Her letters to him develop the critical attitude of those *Forum* editorials: the revival of narrative verse, the Romantic / classical conflict, the uneasy balance of 'the imaginative and the logical, the fantastic and the factual'. '[T]he questions absorb my mind constantly', she wrote, 'of how the creative mind gets into focus, what distinguishes one type of poem from another, and what makes the miracle of a poem [...].'[65]

In early 1951, then, Muriel had two writing lives: her own work (criticism, biography, poetry) and her bread-and-butter book-making projects with Stanford. Wrey Gardiner, appointed as literary editor of the *Daily Mirror*'s *Public Opinion* magazine in 1950, passed on reviews and essay work to them both. By this stage she had also published in the *TLS*, the *Spectator*, the *World Review*, the *Fortnightly*, the *New English Weekly* and the *New English Review*. But her literary status remained insecure. When *Child of Light* appeared, Tower Bridge Publications, the ramshackle outfit to whom she was contracted, did little to sell the book. Two years later they still had seven hundred copies in stock and remaindered most of them. She continued to work three days a week at Nevill's and had returned under duress for one day at Pearson Horder's. Before this, she appears to have taken some awful job on a women's magazine. 'Re my day at Horder,' she wrote to Stanford:

> I did an article for him which seared into my inner heart – all about good will in the factories – for some man who was knighted for his factory [...]. I'm to be paid as 'expenses' i.e. no tax. [...] I must write a satire on these industrial knights as soon as I get a little more horrible insight. On the whole, as it is work which I can vent *hate* upon, it is better than being at 'Model' which was simply a corrosive bore. At least hate starts the juices working. [...] Gastons have turned down both your books so I was foiled of my gain. (Have you considered the difference [...] between 'gain' and 'profit'? The word 'gain' was much used in Victorian times by the impoverished gentility to deprecate those who were 'clever' enough to make a profit – Charlotte Brontë's friend, Ellen Nussey, was pleased that Charlotte made a profit from her books, but said her publishers were too eager 'for gain'.)[66]

Here, at last, the voice of the mature Muriel struggles free. The tone of her letters to Stanford has changed, has become more confidently brisk. She is busy, needs him less. The poems she wrote with him were cluttered with word-spinning alliteration, attempts at comic-vulgar sur-realism. When she wrote alone, a quite different literary personality emerged: spare and stringent. Where the joint poems[67] were effusive, sceptical celebrations of nature or love, often little better than Georgian verse in modern dress, her own work was tightly controlled by con-ventional forms and imbued with a macabre sense of loss.

One of these, 'Edinburgh Villanelle', puzzled her in later life when she had warm memories of Edinburgh. What did it mean when she said that the 'Heart of Midlothian' was 'never mine'?[68] Her early letters supply the answer. In these she feels spiritually discomfited when visiting her family, and the poem surely dramatises her alienation in (and from) that city:

> These eyes that saw the saturnine
> Glance in my back, refused the null
> Heart of Midlothian, never mine.[69]

Edinburgh, she felt, was 'hostile' to her artistic vision, and 'Verlaine Villanelle', on the facing page in her *Collected Poems I*, offers a contrast between that alienation and the joy of creation in London:

> Like poor Verlaine, whom God defend,
> I see the sky above the roof,
> And write my book till summer's end.[70]

*

It was 1951, Festival of Britain year. Muriel seems not to have joined the crowds thronging the South Bank to visit the Skylon and the new Festival Hall. Instead, she was buried in creation. The book she was writing that summer was *Masefield*. But in between, while staring out from her Kensington table across the rooftops, she was hard at work on her poetic *magnum opus*. For some months she had been trying unsuccessfully to place a volume of verse, *Flower into Animal*, with various publishers. By June she had completed a long narrative poem and sent it with others to Howard Sergeant. 'The Ballad of the Fanfarlo', she explained, was her most important poem, drawing attention to the main character, Samuel Cramer. By way of preface she quoted from Baudelaire's story, 'The Fanfarlo': '"Samuel Cramer, who used to sign himself by the name of Manuela de Monteverde, or some such romantic folly [...] is the contradictory product of a pale German and a brown Chilean woman."' Muriel had, she said, borrowed the characters rather than the story,[71] but it seems that in doing so she had translated them into the psychodrama of her own mind. In Baudelaire's tale (introduced to her, ironically, by Stanford), she had finally discovered the image of the artist towards which she had been straining for a decade.

One wonders what Sergeant made of her long, obscure analysis. He replied politely, saying he was fascinated by the poem but had not yet found time to give it his full attention. He did not publish it. Indeed, no one wanted 'The Ballad of the Fanfarlo' until Erica Marx printed it in a booklet for her Hand and Flower Press in 1952. In the light of Muriel's history so far, however, and of her sudden emergence in 1957 as a major postmodern novelist, this letter and the poem reveal themselves as crucial documents.[72]

In the poem, Cramer sees himself as an outsider, 'racially different', beyond time and history, a prophetic figure, the product, as was Muriel, of North and South. The Fanfarlo is 'sexy', a former dancer (hints of Pavlova), past her first youth but pure rhythm and inspiration, Cramer's lover and muse, an extravagant product of the Romantic mind but also a flesh-and-blood woman. Both are exiles, exotics, in a world where rational humanism attempts to reduce the artist to nothingness. Cramer circumvents this assault by being intangible, by being, in a sense, both himself and the Fanfarlo, himself and his nom de plume. He is motiveless, untrappable and, like Muriel, inhabits several identities: the artist and the flesh-and-blood woman, the rationalist and the romantic. Were these an expression of her divided self still hungering for integration? It is certainly possible. For ultimately the poem glorifies neither Cramer nor his art but, implicitly, God. Birtwistle had been supplying Muriel with theological books and in her letter to Sergeant she quotes from the Catechism, an early record of her drift towards Christianity as the only resolution of her intellectual impasse. Disaffection, or the renunciation of the corporeal, was symbolised for her by death which required a dark and blind faith.[73]

*

During that autumn she noticed an advertisement for a Christmas story competition in the *Observer*. She still had no aspirations to be a writer of prose fiction. But the prize was £250 and she was poor. She thought she might as well have a go, wrote it quickly, scrounged some typing paper from a local shop, posted her entry, and forgot all about it. Two months later she answered the telephone, anxious that it might be a dentist dunning her for unpaid bills, and heard the voice of Philip Toynbee, the newspaper's literary editor. She had won the competition, beating off nearly seven thousand other entries. Suddenly she was famous. In the small hours of the morning of publication, 23 December, David Astor, the editor, banged on her door to deliver the first copy himself. On Christmas Day she was feasting with Stanford, toasting her good fortune with liqueurs supplied by Birtwistle. 'Do you like my "Seraph"?' she wrote. 'A very Catholic one, Derek says.'[74] On 2 January she was lunching with Astor and the *Observer* staff at the Waldorf Astoria. There was an open invitation to submit material to the paper. She became one of its reviewers. The telephone rang incessantly with congratulations from friends and from other editors seeking her work. The story was 'The Seraph and the Zambesi'. Its central characters were Samuel Cramer and the Fanfarlo.

CHAPTER 6

Sacramental

'The Seraph and the Zambesi' was a glass of postmodern champagne among the musty realism of the other entries. It was sparkling, fresh, possibly the first example by a British author of what became known as magical realism. Inevitably, some conservative *Observer* readers were outraged. 'It is certainly astonishing', one wrote in, 'to find a reputable newspaper awarding a prize to such a preposterous thing.'[1] But the judges – David Astor, Terence Kilmartin and Philip Toynbee, all to become loyal supporters of Muriel's talent over the next five difficult years – held fast. They were certain that they had discovered a unique voice. And they were right.

Why then did those ghosts from Baudelaire – Samuel Cramer, Monteverde, and the Fanfarlo – so haunt her at this time? They appear not only in 'The Ballad of the Fanfarlo' and 'The Seraph' but also in a long narrative poem, 'The Nativity', where they figure alongside a trio of swearing shepherds and a choir of angels. Mankind in 'The Nativity' is merely a 'mess of meat and bone', 'no one' without redemption into a spiritual sphere of being. Human discourse has degenerated into egocentric squabbling. As the final section of the poem suggests, however, everyone is also unique and 'known to no man'. There is beauty and sanctity in this uniqueness which paradoxically brings with it the painful isolation of being human. The Seraphim here discuss profound questions. Their dances signify 'the resolution of discrepancy'. Ultimately – and these are the final lines –

'Uncommon men become
Common to men in Christ's face,
Mediator of angels and of men.'[2]

This was Muriel's first overtly religious work but it is, like 'The Ballad of the Fanfarlo', obscure, surreal, the product of a chaotic imagination torn between scepticism and engagement with theology. 'The Seraph' is her first religious story, a kind of metaphysical prose poem. Yet here a witty lucidity has replaced the earlier confused debates. Something had happened in between to clarify her mind.

In 'The Ballad' Cramer is a sympathetic figure, an artist tempted by, and resisting, three ghosts: Monteverde, his artistic self; the Fanfarlo, his lover; and Death, renunciation. In 'The Seraph' he is more obviously the fraud of Baudelaire's original. 'The Ballad' was the summation of her poetic life, deeply personal, written by someone teetering on the brink of religious faith but who had not yet made that leap. Cramer there is 'a divided being fitting into no category' – someone rather like Muriel at that stage. Ghoulish, bandaged figures rise up in a 'hellish dormitory' and offer him various ways of accommodating himself to the material world. All, apart from the scholar, describe themselves as being 'No Man'. His battle with these accusing voices, his struggle for self-justification as a 'feverish poet', was surely also Muriel's, and her letter to Sergeant makes plain part of her intention. Rationalism and humanism attempt to render Cramer 'No Man' in a 'mechanised, totalitarian age'.[3] The poem dramatises his resistance.

'No Man' in Muriel's writing is uniformly negative: an absence or reduction of human potential. Such matters had interested her since witnessing racism in Africa but particularly since the biography of Mary Shelley. The threat is always of collapse into that state of non-being which is the focus of tormenting questions. What constitutes mankind's uniqueness? Does this uniqueness imply isolation? Is the individual merely a 'mess of meat and bone', a nothing amid nothingness? Is the artist a monstrous egoist? What is the source of artistic inspiration and how might it be linked to spirituality? In a 1951 notebook she wrote a

'Meditation on Disaffection', and there, as in 'The Ballad', we see a mind calmly in turmoil. Inspired by the magnificence of creation, struggling to create nothingness as the positive space inhabited by the exile, she keeps bumping into potential horrors: spiritlessness, meaninglessness, darkness, isolation, silence. Like Cramer, she resists them with ingenious linguistic twists. There is no self-pity in her meditation. Absence here defines presence, an idea that was to become important to her theological development. Love is self-loss. Itemising problems arising from this position she lists faith, hope and charity – the greatest of which was charity.[4]

As an artist Muriel craved isolation, silence, self-loss. Like Graham Greene, she was uncomfortable with institutions, would maintain no loyalty which might impede creation. From childhood she had sensed her separateness. Since returning from Africa she had felt awkward in Edinburgh and had effectively orphaned herself from her family. Although her letters to Stanford continue to express love and belief in their 'spiritual household', his invasion of her 'island' was becoming ever more palpable. Love might be self-loss but in this case it appeared to require loss of artistic self. 'Disaffection' in theological terms means 'renunciation', and she was coming to realise that this characterised her native state of mind as the go-away bird. Cramer in 'The Ballad' was in a sense her old self, incapable of religious faith. In 'The Seraph' she has distanced herself from him and he has, in effect, become Stanford.

'The Seraph and the Zambesi' thus marks a transition. The chirpy Seraph introduces a new, fourth dimension. It is an anti-rationalist tale whose 'plot' is at once simple and fantastic. The narrator opens by wrecking plausibility. Cramer is introduced as 'half poet, half journalist', who was said to be 'going strong in Paris early in the nineteenth century' and was still going strong in 1946, the date of the narrative present. Instead of a realist 'character' we have a figure from another fiction who is one hundred and fifty years old and who looks forty-two. Then, with disconcerting rapidity, we move from this into a 'plausible' realist section, and finally into the realm of metaphysics.

Cramer owns a petrol pump near the Zambesi and has 'some spare rooms where he put up visitors to the Falls [...]. I was sent to him because it was Christmas week and there was no room in the hotel.' Immediately, then, there are suggestions that 'The Seraph' will be a parallel Nativity story. The narrator is introduced to five others drinking highballs on the stoep. Among these is Mannie (Monteverde) and Fanny (the Fanfarlo), now a blowsy dancing teacher. Cramer has given up writing. '"Life[...]"', he says, '"is the important thing."'[5] He has, nevertheless, written a Nativity Masque, ludicrously casting Fanny as the Virgin and himself in the starring role as First Seraph. The whole tone of the narrative is suddenly lighter than that of the poetry, rippling with crisp, implicit mockery which makes the ironies easier to read. Some of it resembles Evelyn Waugh's early work, *Vile Bodies* in particular, when we discover the 'troupe of angels', false beards, and the physical absurdity of Cramer's appearance:

> He had on a toga-like garment made up of several thicknesses of mosquito-net, but not thick enough to hide his white shorts underneath. He had put on his make-up early and this was melting on his face [...].[6]

Everything dissolves in the heat: noises, voices, the human will.

Into this tropical wasteland bursts a blazing Seraph. 'This was a living body,' the narrator insists:

> The most noticeable thing was its constancy; it seemed not to conform to the law of perspective [...] altogether unlike other forms of life, it had a completed look. No part was undergoing a process; the outline lacked the signs of confusion and ferment which are commonly the sign of living things, and this was also the principle of its beauty.[7]

In this transcendental context Cramer is revealed as egotistical, belligerent. His immediate reaction is to attempt to dismiss the Seraph who tells him peaceably to 'get off the stage and stop your noise'. Cramer insists that this is his 'show'. 'Since when?' asks the Seraph:

> 'Right from the start,' Cramer breathed at him.

'Well, it's been mine from the Beginning,' said the Seraph, 'and the Beginning began first.'[8]

It is a confrontation between the material and the spiritual. Later, the narrator accompanies Cramer and the Fanfarlo to the Falls, Cramer absurdly intent upon catching the angel:

Just then, by the glare of our headlights I saw the Seraph again, going at about seventy miles an hour and skimming the tarmac strips with two of his six wings in swift motion, two folded over his face, and two covering his feet.

'That's him!' said Cramer. 'We'll get him yet.'[9]

But of course the Seraph is impalpable. The final passage is similar to that section from *Curriculum Vitae* describing Muriel's and Ossie's visit to the Falls as a quasi-religious experience. In the story, the spray from the Falls 'was like a convalescence after fever':

Then I noticed that along the whole mile of the waterfall's crest the spray was rising higher than usual. This I took to be steam from the Seraph's heat. I was right, for presently, by the mute flashes of summer lightning we watched him ride the Zambesi away from us, among the rocks that look like crocodiles and the crocodiles that look like rocks.[10]

Crocodiles and rocks. The apparently substantial moves beneath our feet, and in that final image we glimpse Muriel's mature literary imagination operating on the 'nevertheless principle'. What is true in one context is not true in another.

Only one thing is established: the limitation of Cramer's conceptual powers. And given the history of Cramer/Fanfarlo/ Monteverde in Muriel's writing, the Seraph suggests the fire of artistic creation, the unadulterated muse which Cramer has betrayed, and which Muriel will not. The vision of the Seraph riding the Zambesi takes place at midnight on Christmas Eve, at the very point of Christ's birth. It is a surreal Nativity story, but it is also about her own rebirth. For she, too, was on the point of a variety of nativities: the births of faith, hope and charity; the birth of her unique voice as a writer, of a new life in which all the 'discrepancies' of the past would be resolved. There is a sense of relief about the story, of release from 'fever'. Through this, and the pervasive association of the Seraph with purging fire and water, there is even a suggestion of baptism.

That bitter struggle to find meaning in the visible universe alone, and to make sense of the 'classical / Romantic' arguments about the artist's relation to it, was almost over. The narrator of 'The Seraph' relaxes into absurdity and enjoys it as a satirical tool. She is careful about her writing but not about the world. The world fascinates her but she is somehow detatched from it, as though listening to voices through a wall or watching the figures act out their pantomime behind plate glass. The ghastly objects of investigation no longer have the capacity to hurt. They have become comic. The power relation between narrator and subject has changed. The author is now coolly 'knowing', invulnerable, playing with these characters. Someone once put it to Muriel that she did not much like the people she wrote about. 'Oh no,' she replied, 'I love them all; when I'm writing about them I love them most intensely, like a cat loves a bird. You know cats do love birds; they love to fondle them.'[11]

*

John Masefield, completed in February 1952, was the last book Muriel wrote as an agnostic. In January, just after her *Observer* success, she had contacted Father Ambrose Agius, a Benedictine monk and poet she had known from the Poetry Society, enquiring about predestination and free will.[12] During March, a visit to Edinburgh had been typically provocative, Cissy irritating her with advice and the desire to show her daughter off among the Bruntsfield Place gossips.[13] Muriel's amused discontent had soon deepened to fury. Feeling suffocated, and alienated from Robin, she buried herself in reading Proust's *À La Recherche du Temps Perdu*, trying to obliterate her own present time, as anxious about her landlady Mrs Andipatan's inquisitiveness as she was about her mother's. She felt compelled to keep her movements secret from both,[14] uneasy about the evasiveness of her double life.

Robin had always presented Muriel with difficulties. Although she refused to feel guilty about leaving him in the care of her parents, she was protective of the boy and of his image of her. At thirteen he was still small and shy, rather isolated at school and academically slow. She wanted the best for him, sought to defend him from the influence of his father, worried about his progress. In her role as distant organiser and protector, she was content to be doing her duty but as she was moving towards Christianity, Robin had aligned himself with Judaism. On 13 January 1952, he had celebrated his bar mitzvah. Delighted for him to have something in which to believe, Muriel had paid for it with £50 from her *Observer* prize. Knowing that Ossie would be there, she had not attended.

John Masefield offers a priceless insight into her intellectual life at this moment of transition. Only three of his long poems are analysed in detail: 'The Everlasting Mercy', 'Dauber' and 'Reynard the Fox'. Critical of Masefield's over-production, she was also surprisingly abrasive about his work, even about parts of the three poems she wished to rescue as original. A scene in 'The Everlasting Mercy' is described as 'irredeemably bad, if not nauseating'. 'Dauber', she states, contains 'positively bad verse, really unconsciously comical'. An air of mild irritation permeates the argument – 'Masefield simply cannot depict women even in fun' [15] – and she uses his work, as she used all her reading, as a point of departure and self-definition.

'His imagination,' she writes, '– that is really our subject'. In Masefield she discovers another wanderer, driven by 'the unconscious motive of preserving himself as an artist'. Her Memorandum Book records her visit to him on 6 December 1950 as a delightful day. 'When I told him I sometimes take a part-time job he said, "All experience is good for an artist." I felt flattered – about the "artist" bit.' It was a statement she treasured as a defence against melancholy and, as we have seen, echoed in *Loitering with Intent*. Masefield regarded depression as he regarded bad weather. It would pass, the muse would resume her song. Muriel admired this stoical self-belief. His remark, 'I knew, then, that life is very brief, and that the use of life is to discover the law of one's being, and to follow that law, at whatever cost, to the utmost' also resonated.

At the outset, then, she had for her subject a kindred spirit: gracious, isolated, widely read, driven by vocation, one of the race of artist-exiles to whom she felt attached. Like her, Masefield sought 'philosophical formulation', found the 'rational-humanist position' unsatisfactory, sensed 'that this world is a shadow of another world'. But she found his thinking limited, stuck fast in 'Platonic idealism'[16] at the point from which she was eager to press forward.

Muriel approved of the 'entirely concrete', factual surface of Masefield's work. His search for an impersonal voice, 'as if trying to speak through a hum of other voices which, none the less, he felt the need to listen to',[17] echoes her own aesthetic dilemma. And her concentration on those three narrative poems has a distinctly autobiographical ring. 'The Everlasting Mercy' deals with conversion; 'Dauber' with the artist's attempt to preserve a sense of vocation when assaulted by philistinism; 'Reynard the Fox' with the theme (as in her schoolgirl poems) of hunter and hunted:

> the *moral vision* of the poet, which appears in all his stories, is not lacking
> here. This moral vision may be described as a profound sense and love
> of uniqueness in all the visible world.[18]

Here we are back to the paradoxes of 'The Nativity', 'The Ballad' and 'The Seraph': to ubiquitous 'uncommonness', to isolation and vocation, to the 'glory of created things'. But where for Muriel these formed one half of an unresolved meditation on disaffection, Masefield was content to settle for pagan celebration of diversity. In arguing this out, she offers interesting asides on conversion. What was at stake here was the nature of that voice which calls unbidden and which creates order out of chaos:

> [...] the moment of illumination which every artist experiences at times,
> a kinship with that primitive order of religious revelation [...]. That is
> the paradox of inspiration – the incredible and the impossible are felt to
> be present and therefore (for what is more actual than what we feel?) are
> credible and possible. If such an experience, a mystical revelation, is
> 'unutterable', if the inspiration itself cannot be conveyed, the work of art

which is its flower will probably spring where the seed is sown. The poem will have an organic connection with its physical origin, and the pattern of events and their movement at the visionary instant will be translated symbolically until in the end the work itself becomes the real thing and the events the symbols of it.[19]

This is an extraordinary statement for a British writer in 1952 – almost a little manifesto of postmodernism. (The word 'unutterable' is footnoted with a reference to Wittgenstein's 'what can be revealed cannot be uttered'.) But it was also a theological statement about the seeds of faith and the sacramental sense of the Christian writer.

*

Muriel was entering a period of massive mental reorganisation. *The Fanfarlo and Other Verse*[20] had just been published when, on 26 July 1952, she went to see an Anglican priest, the vicar of St Augustine's in Queen's Gate Terrace, Kensington. Increasingly, she had felt the need to attend a church and Stanford had sometimes accompanied her, sitting awkwardly behind a pillar at the back. He was a residual Anglican but refused to be confirmed. Public worship embarrassed him. St Augustine's was not the nearest church, being a fifteen-minute walk from her room in the Old Brompton Road, but it was the nearest Anglo-Catholic establishment. She needed advice so the vicar put her in touch with Father Wells who lent her a couple of books and, eventually, on 10 October, they sat down together for an hour. He gave her, she recorded, sound counsel about a difficulty she was encountering with a third party.[21] A week later, she wrote to tell Wells that she planned to be baptised as an Anglican by Clifford Rhodes.[22]

This third party was, of course, Stanford. Rhodes, the erratic editor of the *Church of England Newspaper*, was a friend of them both and an ordained clergyman. He often channelled work their way. A belligerent modern churchman (*not* an Anglo-Catholic), he was given to firing off editorial cannonades aimed impartially at the Pope or the Archbishop of Canterbury. His principal concern was to drag the Church of England out of abstraction, to make it a force confronting social problems.

Inhabiting both the literary and ecclesiastical worlds, Rhodes could understand the plight in which Muriel and Stanford found themselves. Put simply, she wished to become a Christian while Stanford still hovered on the brink, and Christian teaching forbade sexual intercourse without marriage. It was a price she was willing to pay for spiritual equanimity and, on 7 November 1952, Rhodes baptised her.

Stanford was there or thereabouts and acted as one of her sponsors. This symbolic act took place in the church of St Bride, off Fleet Street, after which they set off in high spirits for one of their regular jaunts to St Albans.[23] For years they had taken country walks there, exploring the Roman ramparts, visiting the Abbey, dropping in on the ancient poet and friend of Masefield, Herbert Palmer. St Albans had been the scene of many a delightful escape from London. A copse had become their secret bower, referred to with a sacramental sense of place as their Sacred Wood. They had made love there, written poems. The impression Stanford conveys in *Inside the Forties* is of a light-hearted spree, but it is doubtful whether he was as contented as he makes out. She was forcing his hand.

A more accurate record of his feelings is contained in his private 'gutch book'. This describes a scene a few months earlier, in the late summer of 1952:

Muriel presented me with the denouement of her inner condition on Tuesday evening. She told me that she desired us to live in chastity together, as she had come to see our physical love as sin, a state of fornication. I argued with her for some time, because I believed that her discovery had not come from the wells of her spirit [...] but was the opinion she had borrowed from the Anglican priest who had been advising her. I thought this because, right up to the last, she had not been able to admit his statement that our intercourse was sin to be correct. However, I realised, after a while, that if the opinion had, first of all, come from external authority, it now represented to her an inner spiritual truth. I could not concede her right to be right, but her sense of it I had, naturally, to respect.[24]

According to this account, they had dined with Iris Birtwistle that night in the 'vaulted jazz-filled parlours of the Pheasantry Club'. This 'hardly provided a vicinity in which we could both dwell upon this new condition. But there was nothing for it but a mask of unconcern.' Birtwistle drove them back, 'and before getting into our separate celibate beds, [we] chatted about the evening's trivia like any old pair of true conjugal parties. To the new partitioning of our flesh, we did not refer; though we acted upon it.'[25] This was 'disaffection' in practice – and it was tough.

Muriel was plagued by discordant emotions: her anxieties about marriage to Stanford confronted her sense of spiritual release; celibacy cleared her mind yet appeared to condemn her to solitude. It all compounded a terrible sense of things running out of control in her life. Had she gained or lost?[26] St Mary Abbots, mentioned in passing in a tender letter on this subject to Stanford, was off Church Street, Kensington. The church had particular associations for them. Its graveyard had been her garden in Vicarage Gate days. Muriel and Stanford had once lain on their backs in the grass there and composed a joint verse. There she had sat happily alone among the tombstones with notebook, pencil, sandwiches and cigarettes, puzzling out her own poems. It is in this churchyard that she sets the opening scene of *Loitering with Intent*, on 30 June 1950: a turning point in the heroine's life, bang in the middle of the twentieth century.

Loitering celebrates Fleur Talbot's release into independence as an artist. In many respects it is an affectionate self-portrait – but of a self now largely a memory to both narrator and author. Fleur is a poet and Catholic convert who becomes a successful novelist. Those who try to claw her back into mundanity are spared no mockery. Yet the rich comedy of this work again lies in its ambiguities, for it is also a swansong. In escaping her poverty, Fleur is also bidding farewell to her youth and to the pleasurable insecurities of bohemianism. The narrative is not, of course, *literally* autobiographical. Fleur never suffers the panic that occasionally gripped Muriel. The time-scheme is much contracted. What happens to Fleur in a matter of months took seven years for her creator and led in and out of terrifying hallucinations. *Loitering* nevertheless precisely conveys the atmosphere of Muriel's mental life between 1949 and 1954: the sense of waiting to be born.

In 1952 that possible future still contained Stanford. Two days after her baptism, she sent him her views. She wished, she said, to marry him but would prefer to wait until he could consent to religious vows. She was anxious not to cause pain to her parents, and particularly to Robin. None of them would understand that she and Stanford now lived together celibately. Perhaps they could have a civil marriage? Perhaps she should move out? The thought of separation appalled her.[27] This eight-page letter was followed by an eight-page postscript, emphasising brighter moments: 'The House of the Famous Poet' accepted by *Norseman*;[28] an article in *World Review*;[29] reviews in the pipeline for the *Observer*. Her *Brontë Letters* seemed to have found a home with Peter Nevill.[30] *Masefield* and their edition of Mary Shelley's letters[31] were due out next year. She was no longer panicking about her play. All that it needed was time, for it was 'being composed in Time-Eternal'.[32]

'Time-Eternal', however, was the focus of her difficulties: that metaphysical realm which now began to enclose her was loosening her grasp on matters terrestrial. And, in the meantime, there was Christmas in Edinburgh to negotiate. More duties, more polite evasions. No reference is made in her letters to Robin's or her parents' reaction to her baptism – and for good reason. She was withholding this information until the Stanford situation resolved itself.[33] She wished to be scrupulous in her moral dealings but found herself enmeshed in compromise. Truth to God fitted ill with truth to those who loved her. Ambiguities stretched her between the secular and the sacred, and the Church, now her only haven, threatened conformity: 'If we were constant beings by nature, like angels, it would be easier. But we are flux, mere flux. No, not "mere" flux – necessary, right & proper flux.'[34]

She did not despair. She was resilient, industrious and dutiful. It was just that these native strengths produced competing loyalties. 'No man', she wrote in *Masefield*, 'can serve two masters'[35] and it was the attempt to do this which created the strain. The will of God and human will were at odds. It was, she believed, the will of God that she should be a Christian and a writer. Human will tugged her back towards rationalism, sensualism, a life littered with obligations. And there was a further complication. In her art and her life she demanded acknowledgement while receiving little in either sphere. She was not breaking through as a major poet and Stanford was hesitant about marriage. No one was better aware than she of her tendency to press matters towards immediate resolution[36] but the future looked bleakly solitary. She was horrified by the thought of isolation in a bedsit, comforted only by her immaculate conscience.[37] Nevertheless, this is precisely what happened.

*

Four months after Muriel had completed *Masefield*, the publisher Peter Owen had revived a project for a 'life and works' of Emily Brontë. Again, Muriel was to write the biographical section, Stanford the critical. But she still saw herself primarily as a poet and critic. The *Observer* prize money, she had announced, would buy time to complete a verse play. She had been at work on this – a satirical drama, *The Cocktail's not for Drinking*, parodying T. S. Eliot and Fry – during 1951 and kept it simmering for another two years. By 1953 it had reached proof stage and was on the point of publication when the press (Roebuck) went bankrupt. This was a typical story of frustration. When *The Fanfarlo and Other Verse* appeared five months after 'The Seraph', it sank almost unnoticed and sales were negligible. What she considered her most important poem, then, fell on stony ground, and her verse play was stillborn.

Christmas in Edinburgh had, as usual, been a time of mixed emotions for Muriel. The city had been frosted and slippery, her family too warm for comfort and privacy. But back in London in January 1953 her optimism revived. Books long submerged in the offices of impecunious publishers began to bob to the surface. Peter Nevill had agreed to take her *Brontë Letters* and Wrey Gardiner's Grey Walls Press finally produced her *Selected Poems of Emily Brontë*.[38] By early April, Wingate's had *My Best Mary* on the bookstalls and Muriel had written five more short stories: 'The Pearly Shadow', 'Ladies and Gentlemen', 'The Pawnbroker's

Wife', 'The Quest for Lavishes Ghast' and 'Harper and Wilton'. *Masefield* was due out in June. Three books in six months: the ball was rolling at last. True, there was little income, the advances being long since spent and the print runs small. But her name now appeared more frequently in the literary pages and, with this impetus, in March 1953 she reached a final decision about Stanford. She moved out of Sussex Mansions and took a room at 1 Queen's Gate Terrace, close to St Augustine's. It was only a few streets away from the Old Brompton Road, but it might as well have been America. During April she was confirmed and took her first communion in this church.

Muriel's new life at least allowed her to shed some of the deception. She wrote immediately to Stanford's mother and the old lady replied, puzzled by her son:

> When Derek first started staying away from home I was naturally upset for I instinctively realised something was amiss [...] he never enlightened me as to the true state of affairs.
>
> However it was with pleasure I learnt that you love Derek dearly & [...] I do hope that eventually the tide will turn in your favour & that you will be able to marry [...].[39]

Stanford was obviously wounded by Muriel's departure. An unpublished lyric of his survives, 'Poem in Separation',[40] full of sad, coded messages for her. Where she was fulfilled, he felt rejected – and for a man with such a shaky sense of self, this was devastation. But he should, perhaps, have seen their parting as inevitable. Almost two years earlier, during July 1951, just after she had been trying to explain to Sergeant the themes of disaffection and faith in 'The Ballad of the Fanfarlo', she had published another, quite different and intimate poem, 'Chrysalis'. This described how she and Stanford had, one London winter, placed a chrysalis in a matchbox and 'in cold spring' been at first puzzled to discover a butterfly in their room. The reader is invited to celebrate release, transformation. Muriel, or Muriel's spirit, is figured as 'the pretty creature' emerging from the hard 'broken shell', 'whispering about the curtain' – and then out of the window, away from the 'small violence'.[41] It was a poem suggesting conversion and escape, oddly predictive of the conversion and escape that had now changed her life for ever. If he was surprised by this turn of events, it seems that she was not.

Muriel's Introduction to *Selected Poems of Emily Brontë* also hinted at personal associations. She could sympathise more easily with this tortured woman than with Masefield. Reading the various critical images of Emily – 'as mystic, as poet of Christianity, as heretic, as heathen, as intellectual thinker, as psychical hermaphrodite, [...]' – Muriel seems obliquely to be noting the misdefinitions from which she had herself suffered. Swinburne, she says, got it right when he located in Emily 'a dark unconscious instinct as of primitive nature-worship [...].' Emily's 'passion' is stressed, 'her sense of exile from her natural home', and her 'obvious misanthropy'. She is 'a mystic of passion', or more specifically in Arthur Symons's words, '"the paradox of passion without sensuousness"', a phrase which might well describe Muriel. The voice of the Border ballads is identified, and Emily's 'acute auditory sensibility'.[42] Consciously or unconsciously, Muriel seems to have been talking as much about herself as about her subject.

The Brontës had struck deeply into her imagination during adolescence. This group of tough-minded northern exiles, women with a polite face for the world and a pagan one for their art, pragmatic, dedicated, a law unto themselves in the kingdom of the imagination, offered a tempting model for the female artist. But if there were similarities, there were also differences, certainly from the woman Muriel was to become. In the late 1940s and early 1950s she could not conceal her irritation with Charlotte, 'the spokeswoman of the tribe',[43] and her matronage of Emily and Anne. Muriel defended Anne against Charlotte's capacity to ignore her 'sense of structure, emotional conflict and an obsessional will to write'. In Anne's 'Three Guides' she sees a tormented mind reflected in the poem's conflict between its three spirits: of Earth, Pride, and of Faith. There was a link here for Muriel between Anne's work and her life, a tangle of desires: for 'the conventional life', for 'spiritual and artistic freedom', and for 'a State of Grace',[44] and a correspondence emerges between these 'Three Guides' and Cramer's three tempters. The Fanfarlo could be read as the Spirit of the Earth, Monteverde as the Spirit of Pride, Death as (or requiring) the Spirit of Faith. When Muriel wrote that poem, these spirits remained in conflict, still awaiting the resolution of faith. Now she had it – but a painful road still lay ahead for this pilgrim. In 1953, Muriel was working on a life of Anne, a book on Job and one on T. S. Eliot. None was completed. No trace of them survives. All were washed away in a tsunami of change as the life she had known disintegrated and re-formed itself in different patterns.

*

The move to Queen's Gate Terrace was to a tiny, sparsely furnished room. She bought a kettle, a chest of drawers, a Catholic prayer book, and thirteen volumes of Newman. At nine o'clock each night the ghostly clip-clop of a riding school passed beneath her window. She wrote a poem about it, 'My Kingdom for a Horse', describing the 'white-coated riders, white-sided / Beasts blanketed against the cold and skyless / And groundless general benightment.' If the poem is an accurate record of her feelings, she chose this room, arbitrarily, because of this 'white presentment'. An image of bleak, 'hemmed-in' renunciation is presented:

> Because
>
> Of this I came to stay, small as it was.
> Smaller still by daylight; much crockery
> Had to go; many books were abandoned; so too,
> A hoard of smooth planks, they had to go.

> It is not altogether a mockery.[45]

From these cramped quarters, she continued her correspondence with Father Agius and began serious browsing in Roman Catholic teaching. Money was perilously tight. While working part-time at Peter Nevill's, she rented a study on his premises across the street from her previous flat in the Old Brompton Road. Stanford, it seems, still used that place but nothing had been said to Mrs Andipatan of Muriel's departure. He picked up her mail and was in regular contact. They still went out together. She saw her removal not as a final break but as a breathing space. If he could follow her into the Church, they could reunite. And meanwhile it was business as usual with their collaborative work.

They had, for instance, that contract with Nevill for a joint life and work of Emily Brontë. Simultaneously, they both had independent projects. Stanford was writing a monograph on Dylan Thomas; both were producing poems, stories, essays, reviews. As the year wore on, however, these prospects dwindled as rejections poured in. Despite the apparent success of those three books in one year, Muriel was perpetually nagged by a sense of slavery to the incompetence of others. While linked to Stanford, she was embroiled in a form of amateur scholarship fruitlessly trying to impress the London literati. Her markets were still largely his: low-key outlets for stories and poems, a stable of shoestring publishers for books: Tower Bridge, Wingate, Peter Nevill, Falcon Press, Peregrine Press, Grey Walls Press. Of these, the last three formed part of a small conglomerate operating out of offices in Crown Passage, an alley between King Street and Pall Mall, near Piccadilly. It was a good address but not much more. Captain Peter Baker, MC, MP, Chairman of the group, was soon to be arrested and imprisoned for fraud. And, living as she did by her pen, day-to-day, the strain steadily mounted. One person to whom she and Stanford had always turned for companionship in such times was Charles Wrey Gardiner. As an icon of Muriel's Kensington time, his rise and fall personify what she had once found attractive and had now outgrown.

Gardiner often held court in Crown Passage, where Muriel and Stanford would visit him and tour the pubs. With his cosmopolitan background (Africa, Paris in the twenties), and his large, seventeenth-century house (Grey Walls) in Billericay, Essex, he was a stylish, easy-going bohemian in a grey suit, given to heavy drinking and girls in the afternoon. As editor of *Poetry Quarterly* and founder of Grey Walls Press, he had offered a major channel for 'Neo-Romantic' and surrealist British verse. It was he who gave Stanford his first chance, and Muriel also owed him a considerable debt. In 1951 she had published a 'Birthday Acrostic' celebrating his fiftieth – and his distraction.[46] By 1953, however, Gardiner's life was a catastrophe rather than the mess it had always been.

Thanks to his remorseless infidelity, he and Cynthia (his second wife) had separated many times. At fifty-two he was still chasing girls, attending strip clubs and staring down the front of Muriel's low-cut dresses. Melancholic and effusive by turns, asthmatic and suffering from eczema, he dreamed of the warm south, of his youth, his lost lovers. The Billericay house was gone. His doting mother was gone. This literary gentleman now earned his living as a landlord and spent much of his time collecting rents, complaints and laundry. Even his leases were running out, portending a final economic smash in 1958. There is something about Gardiner's autobiographies (four of them)[47] which is both sharply observed and maudlin, repetitious. Yet he loved poetry, and Muriel and Stanford loved him for that. He was, like them, first, last and always a poet, walled in by books, perpetually reading, scribbling verses and diaries deep into the night, waiting for some redemptive miracle: inspiration, love, a windfall to pay the bills littering his Sheraton card-table. Over the years he had been steadily selling his antiques. Ultimately, even that table had to go to supply alimony. Fond as Muriel was of him, he came to represent everything she was determined to avoid.

Nineteen fifty-three marked the onset of Gardiner's decline for it was then that his favourite child, *Poetry Quarterly*, finally died after thirteen years. *PQ*, as it was known, and Grey Walls Press were brother and sister, both promoting Neo-Romanticism. When Baker bought out Grey Walls and incorporated it with Falcon Press, he had installed Paul Scott as accountant and Roland Gant as publicity manager. It was probably in Crown Court that Muriel first encountered Scott. Gant, translator of Verlaine, later became a senior figure at Heinemann. Poets ran the house for poets (even Baker knocked out doggerel) and Gardiner's staff on *PQ* – Nicholas Moore, Frederic Marneau and Sean Jeanette[48] – were all known to Muriel amid the tumult of post-war literary London. It was a strong team. Gardiner had the top floor and he brought with him a substantial list of authors. Financial backing for the operation was guaranteed by Baker's father, Reginald, the cinema magnate of Ealing Studios.

The only problem was Baker himself. As the biographer Hilary Spurling explains, it was Scott who found himself at the pointed end of Baker's sharp dealing[49] and he sensibly left to join a literary agency – Pearn, Pollinger & Higham – before 1954 when Baker was in the dock of the Old Bailey and sent down for seven years. Muriel's last contract with his firm – for a reprint of Mary Shelley's *The Last Man* with a preface by her – predictably came to nothing. The text was set towards the end of 1953 but Peregrine experienced difficulty in getting Muriel to respond. She was in serious trouble herself, a religious crisis, and by the time it was resolved, Peregrine, Grey Walls, *PQ* and all the other imprints of Baker and Gardiner had been cast into oblivion.

In 'A Mug's Game', an unpublished autobiography, Stanford noted that the disappearance of *Poetry Quarterly* was 'like the loss of a friend. It was an indication that the sands of Neo-Romanticism were now running feebly through the glass.'[50] Insofar as he and his fellows had represented a group opposed to Auden's, their claims died with the flagship publication. This Kensington mafia with Gardiner as their naughty uncle, Alex Comfort as their theoretician, and Herbert Read as their philosopher, had been the network to which Stanford had introduced Muriel: John Waller in Cheniston Gardens with John Heath-Stubbs as his tenant; the anarchist George Woodcock; Robert Greacen and his wife, Patricia Hutchens; Roy Campbell 'with his stick and war-wound limp. This bevy of poets was not a school, but pubbed and clubbed together for drinking purposes and party going.'[51] That was in the late forties, when Muriel and Stanford had just become lovers. By 1953 it was a far different story.

Reviewing the situation in May of that year, Stanford felt 'burdened with dismay' at his 'many unkindnesses' to Muriel, signing himself stiffly as 'Derek S.'[52] A month later he was more buoyant but remained melancholy:

Dear Chunder Puff,

I am wearing the shirt I bought four years ago, upon the afternoon of which day we sat pulling cherries 'neath a tree in the Park. You were going to the dentist's later, the sky was clear, and the mood of all things pleasant.

In the evening we went to Ted Toeman's, stopping to booze at several bars upon our way. Then we went back to Vicarage Gate together, and made love in all fullness for the first time.

You were wearing black that midnight, and looked very white and radiant in it. A long time ago now.[53]

A long time indeed: St Swithin's Eve of 1949 with many rainy days to follow. She had taken her first Anglo-Catholic communion on Maundy Thursday. By mid-June she had completed her section of *Emily*. Anglo-Catholicism was not to Stanford's taste. His section of *Emily* was late. From this point, Muriel's drift towards the Roman Church isolated him, and in their professional life he lagged behind.

*

That summer saw Muriel establishing a new circle of supporters: June and Neville Braybrooke, Father Agius, Rosamund Batchelor, Frank Sheed and Maisie Ward, Jerzy Peterkiewicz and Christine Brooke-Rose. All were Catholics or sympathetic to Catholicism, and although Stanford sauntered along as Muriel's partner, it was clear to him that this was now *her* world in which he was the guest.

What Muriel needed was intelligent and sympathetic company. This she found in Frank Sheed, when Iris Birtwistle introduced her to him. An Australian, Sheed was not only a senior Catholic figure as Director of the publishers Sheed & Ward but also a good listener. Immediately impressed by her writing and thinking, he commissioned the book on Job. That relieved the financial pressure and she approached him to enquire about canon law relating to her former marriage and a possible marriage to Stanford.

The investigation centred on the 'Pauline Privilege', Sheed decorously referring to the respective parties only algebraically: 'A' (Ossie) and 'B'

(Muriel). Using this curious form, like a mathematician explaining a theorem, Muriel related her sad story: of Ossie's paranoia, violence and hospitalisation; of how she had left him and how he had divorced her for desertion. She had been told that she could not remarry,[54] that if she were to become a Catholic she might have to remain celibate and to lose Stanford for ever, not only as a husband but also as a father to Robin. Sheed thought not. His canonist, 'the best in England', told him that the case could be dealt with under the Pauline Privilege rules, 'and the marriage will be dissolved on the second marriage of B. The insanity of A is an obstacle, since he will not presumably be able to respond to the interrogations [...]. The diocesan curia which takes the case will be able to deal with this obstacle, though it may mean that more time will be required before the matter is settled.'[55]

With this news, she revived. 'I had a hunch', Father Agius wrote, [...] that you would not be satisfied to be "driftwood" always.' He was, of course, delighted that she was 'absorbing great gusts of Catholic teaching', guessing 'that when you have assimilated all you can, you will want the rest of the story & the true "cosmopolitan" feeling which makes one at home all over the world.'[56] This wise counsellor sensibly left her to proceed at her own pace. As a poet, he understood the artist; as a much-posted Maltese monk, he shared the consciousness of exile. It was she who eventually had to press for a 'conference' with him. In the meantime, she read voraciously: through those thirteen volumes of Newman, in the Gospels (particularly Matthew), in the Old Testament (particularly Job), in the Apocrypha (The Wisdom of Solomon), and through books requested for review.

In the light of Muriel's religious transformation, her critical writing from this period appears strikingly personal. Sheed passed on a poem recently published by him: Michael Mason's *The Legacy*. She shot off to the Edinburgh Festival aboard the Flying Scotsman as correspondent for the *Church of England Newspaper* to review, among other things, the first run of T. S. Eliot's *The Confidential Clerk*. She also produced a front-page essay on Proust and, elsewhere, discussed the work of Karl Heim, a Lutheran theologian. All these pieces touch on the same theme: the move from agnosticism to belief as a 'fearful journey into faith' for what she calls the 'post-rationalist generation'.[57] It was that generation which had bred Neo-Romanticism. Having outgrown its contradictions, she felt she was coming spiritually to life as Stanford and his cronies remained mired in anarchism. Although she did not realise it at the time, that journey to Edinburgh was a Victoria Falls in her life, beyond which all was utterly transformed.

*

During her first week, Muriel exhausted herself haring from show to show, 'between officialdom and fringedom', and was further depressed by her mother's and son's complaints that they were neglected in favour of her smart friends. Cissy's desire to show Muriel off to the neighbours left her daughter feeling like a creature in the zoo. They rubbed along[58] but there was simply no time to explain that it was just a job, that she was there to *work*. Each morning Muriel would disappear, thanking God that the radio was broken and she was at least spared *Music While You Work*. Sunday found her in the Cathedral Church of St Mary, an island of sanity amid artistic chaos, listening contentedly to a sermon 'on the theme of Failure, its existence in the Church from the earliest times, when facing that which is obdurate and conventional'.[59]

Muriel's second article for the *Church of England Newspaper* dealt exclusively with *The Confidential Clerk*. Immediately the play became an obsession. 'It has,' she wrote,

> to do with faithfulness and idolatry, security and rootlessness, vague desires and precise fulfilments, parents and children, art and craft, success and failure.[60]

It had, in short, to do with all the theological, aesthetic and domestic paradoxes that were pulling her apart. Moreover, she detected in it an allusion to the Book of Wisdom and her title, 'The Wisdom of T. S. Eliot', reflected this directly.

Muriel's analysis was acute, so good that Eliot himself was astonished. It struck him 'as one of the two or three most intelligent reviews I had read. It seemed to me remarkable that anyone who could only have seen the play once, and certainly not have read it, should have grasped so much of its intention.'[61] Her critique concerned wisdom and vocation; her pieces on Mason and Heim dealt with the problems of 'Truth' and the claims of science; the Proust article developed the sacramental conception of matter and of Time. Taken together, these three reviews suggest a complex system of belief in which the artist and the priest (or prophet) fulfil similar, and reciprocal, functions. And at the root of all this lay the idea of vocation.

The Confidential Clerk is centrally concerned with vocation, religious and artistic. Muriel saw its Greek origins, its dark echoes of the Old Testament. She read it as a didactic and explicitly Christian work, giving:

> renewed life to some points of Christian teaching which seem irrelevant
> to the modern world, such as our calling to a specific station in life, the
> need of parents for the security of children as much as the other way
> around, our need for roots in God.[62]

This seems to have been the key for Muriel to unlock her anxieties. She was thirty-five. Her life was chaotic and, as the years ticked past, a gap was opening between the claims of the material world and those of the spiritual. *The Confidential Clerk* addressed this directly. 'I would call [it] a Catholic play,' she wrote, 'meaning that it presents situations which are wholly true, and are everywhere and always true.'[63] This was the appeal of the Roman Church. But, for her, 'Truth' remained a problem: literal truth which had its 'own dear beauty',[64] the attractions of rationalist scepticism, as opposed to anagogical or mystical / symbolic / artistic truth.

The 'problem of Truth' is dealt with in her review of *The Legacy*. Here the clergy is seen to be mistaken in equating 'the conscientious unbeliever' with 'the gross materialist'. She admires the honesty of the 'modern intellectual agnostic', is drawn to Mason's distinction between:

> that widely-held notion of 'Christian resignation' and the actual experi-
> ence of surrender (or what is theologically termed 'disaffection'). This

surrender is shown as an act of will, not a reluctant consent forced upon an exhausted spirit.[65]

For Muriel, Mason's distinction was fundamental. Surrender did not come easily to her. Her will was indomitable. Surrender as an act of will resolved that difficulty – but not that of defining God's existence.

For this she turned to Heim, a theologian unwilling to ignore science. He believed that the Church could learn from the agnostic who

takes life as he finds it, and is content to observe the phenomena of life without the need of positing even so remote a concept as a First Cause. [...] [Heim] traces [this approach's] source in a *scientific* world-view. The top levels of scientific thought have perforce relinquished the Cause principle, and are devoted entirely to Effect.[66]

This concentration on effect rather than cause foreshadows a significant aspect of Muriel's technique as a novelist, and she had already touched on the idea in a 1951 poem, 'Elementary', which opens with the shimmering image of the speaker displaced in a wet, dark street:

> Was it myself? If so I found
> An odd capacity for vision.
> Capacity, I understand
> Is limited by fixed precision,
>
> Being a measure of displacement:
> The void exists as bulk defined it,
> The cat subsiding down a basement
> Leaves a catlessness behind it.[67]

The relation between absence and presence was at the heart of the matter. Was God absent or present in the world? Did His apparent absence somehow define His presence? Central to Heim's scheme was the idea of evidencing presence through absence: God, subsiding into the basement of European thought, has left a God-shaped hole behind Him which is not a void but a space filled with the sense of His immanence:

[...] science has now reached a point at which it is necessary for practical purposes to presuppose a perpetually unknowable factor; before it can pursue its aims of discovering the unknown, physical science needs must acknowledge a factor which it is incapable of knowing. This is supported by abundant quotation from authoritative scientific sources, and Dr Heim, in St Paul's fashion, locates the unknown God in the vacant 'unknowable' of the scientific world.[68]

One last conflict between the material and the spiritual remained. In her essay on Proust, Muriel criticised the kind of contemporary Christian writing which assumes 'a dualistic attitude towards matter and spirit':

[Matter and spirit] are seen too much in moral conflict, where spirit triumphs by virtue of disembodiment. This is really an amoral conception of spirit. For [...] a representation of life which [...] escapes the tendency to equate matter with evil, and for an acceptance of that deep irony in which we are presented with the most unlikely people, places and things as repositories of invisible grace, we have to turn to a most unlikely source – Marcel Proust.[69]

Proust was not a Christian. He was, she stresses, an agnostic hedonist: neurotic, egotistical, exotic, a hypochondriac, a 'sexual pervert'. Yet she recommends him to the Christian reader of the *Church of England Newspaper*. Why? Because, despite his lack of 'a moral sense' and a faith, he 'writes always with the insight of a gifted religious and the fidelity of one devoted to a spiritual cause'.

This paradox is ingeniously explained through an analysis of Proust's fictional presentation of Time. There are, Muriel suggests, two fundamentally opposed conceptions of Time: 'hierarchical' and 'evolutionary'. Since the seventeenth century, she argues, the European consciousness has lost the 'hierarchical' sense which is 'sacramental' and intrinsic to the Christian imagination. This has been replaced by the 'evolutionary' mindset: 'one form replacing or usurping another eternally as in the temporal laws of change'. In the evolutionary notion of time, anything that perishes ceases to exist. In the sacramental notion, absence constitutes presence through 'the vast structure of recollection'. She gives a simple example of Proust's literary technique: 'Most of us will recognise the experience. Suddenly the taste, smell or texture of something evokes the past in a [...] meaningful way. Proust uses this sensation as a point of contemplation', seeing his men and women as '"monsters immersed in Time" [...]'. He 'satirizes them in the flesh, by the same method that he exalts their essence, under that "aspect of eternity which is also the aspect of art".'[70] So, seeing life *sub specie aeternitatis*, Proust, like the Christian mystics, insists upon the synchronic nature of Time. History is not, as Millais amusingly put it, 'one damn thing after another', but eternally 'present'. It is a Blakean notion, 'the eternal Now', developed by Eliot in *Four Quartets*, and by thinkers like Bergson and Jung. But how *exactly* is Proust's pagan art to be rescued as a subject for Christian contemplation?

The answer for Muriel lay in that word 'sacramental', stressed throughout. The 'sacramental view of life [...] is nothing more than a balanced regard for matter and spirit'. Muriel therefore felt that she could illuminate Proust's notion of 'remembrance' with the writings of a seventeenth-century Anglican divine:

> The nature of a Sacrament is to be the representative of a substance, the sign of a covenant, the seal of a purchase, the figure of a body, the witness of our faith, the earnest of our hope, the presence of things distant, the sight of things absent, the taste of things inconceivable, and the knowledge of things that are past knowledge.[71]

The ultimate sacrament, then, was Christ himself, embodied in the eucharist. And, to the artist, any tiny, apparently insignificant item or event, like the taste of Proust's madeleine cake, can perform this function, transfiguring the commonplace into time eternal, just as the priest translates the bread and wine into the actual body and blood of Christ.

At last, it seems, Muriel had resolved the dichotomies of 'The Ballad of the Fanfarlo': the oppositions between body and spirit, between the claims of the material world and those of vocation. Her letters battle this out, resisting the theology which insisted upon immateriality. If Heaven was a 'place', as she believed, rather than a 'state', it followed that nowhere on earth was a 'true place', and this explained the common feeling of belonging elsewhere.[72] No contradiction now existed in her mind between artistic and spiritual vocation. Both derived from the consciousness of exile. Both required an act of faith, of renunciation, disaffection. The dualism which condemned matter as evil (and from which she had suffered) was discredited. Matter and spirit were held in balance by a sense of the sacramental.

*

Muriel spent Christmas of 1953 with Roy Foster, her Anglican vicar at St Augustine's. It was another turning point. Letters began to arrive – from the Braybrookes, from Birtwistle and her mother, from her old English teacher, Alison Foster. Most offered congratulations. The new year had inaugurated Muriel's formal instruction at Ealing Priory under Father Agius and she was received into the Roman Catholic Church on 1 May 1954. 'I was so pleased to hear you were so happy,' he wrote, 'you looked radiant.'[73]

Happiness and radiance, however, had scarcely characterised her previous six months. In October she had left Queen's Gate Terrace and moved back into Sussex Mansions, to a smaller, cheaper room. Stanford now rarely visited. She no longer worked there but in her study at Peter Owen's premises nearby. Eliot's play tormented her and she went to see it again in London. Somehow it now spoke to her even more directly. Perhaps this all started arbitrarily because an offstage character is called 'Muriel' and some of the family names resemble those of Muriel's forebears: B. Kagan is 'Barney', 'Mrs Guzzard' echoes 'Mrs Uezzell'. Whatever the reason, she began to research Eliot's work meticulously and signed another contract with Sheed & Ward for a book on him, only to find herself unable to write it, or her *Emily* or the *Job*. For some months she had been innocently popping Dexedrine, then readily available from chemist shops to assist dieting. It seemed an ideal drug to get her through this difficult time: she economised on food, lost weight, and her wits were sharpened for those long working nights: three books to write, reviews, poems, letters, and reading, reading, reading. Theological and aesthetic ideas jangled around the anxieties about Stanford, her family and, not least, the attempt to live on a tiny and erratic income.

Then, shortly after she began instruction, around 15–20 January 1954, something went badly wrong. Her friends noticed the trouble before she did: T. S. Eliot, she insisted, was sending her threatening messages. His play was full of them. Some were in the theatre programme. Obsessively she began to seek them out, covering sheet after sheet of paper with anagrams and cryptographic experiments.

CHAPTER 7

Conversion

1954–1957

'So far as I am able to describe my condition,' Muriel wrote in May 1954, 'now that I am recovered, of course it seems to me rather absurd, but it was very real at the time. It was due to overwork and insufficient rest; I am a literary critic and had been working very hard on a book [...]. Briefly, the trouble was that I began to imagine secret codes in everything I read, even in the press.'[1] This letter was to the Ministry of National Insurance which had disallowed her claim for National Health benefit. Muriel was, and remained, exact with money. Whatever else she denied herself, she had always paid her stamps and property insurance premiums. This pragmatism, however, had dissolved. Half the stamps for 1953 were missing and by mid-January 1954 so also was half her mind. But she did not panic, simply tried to battle her own way out of the nightmare, wrote nothing and lived off loans.

Two other people, one from her past and one from her future, were simultaneously enduring similar torments: Alison Foster and Evelyn Waugh. Foster, Muriel's former English teacher, had had a nervous breakdown and withdrawn to a clinic. By late 1953, still fragile, she had resumed part-time teaching. Muriel wrote to her, on the very brink of her own breakdown, offering support, explaining her 'recent religious crisis and its solution'. This solution (Roman Catholicism) was closed to the Presbyterian Miss Foster. None the less, she was touched by Muriel's display of loyalty: 'Repudiate you, my dear? No. I think my feeling is almost envy of you for having found the answer, even at the cost of what must have been a very painful sacrifice in the matter of personal relationships.'[2]

Muriel had begun seeing Dr Lieber, a general practitioner, in December 1953. During her crisis, he treated her for 'anxiety neurosis'.[3] The physiological cause of the hallucinations was straightforward. She was suffering, as Waugh was in early 1954, from drug poisoning. Dexedrine, now known as 'speed', is an 'upper'. When she stopped taking it, the delusions slowly evaporated. Malnutrition had added to her troubles. She began to eat better and, after three months, the months of her Catholic instruction, returned to her normal vigour. Frank Sheed advised her to concentrate on her Job book and to put aside the one on T. S. Eliot. She took yeast tablets, slept better and, although her decoding continued through April, by then she could regard the phenomenon as an intellectual curiosity and was planning another visit to *The Confidential Clerk* to investigate its mysteries further.[4]

Was Sheed's advice an attempt to deflect Muriel from her Eliot obsession? Most of the friends who saw her through this terrible period – Stanford, Jerzy Peterkiewicz, Christine Brooke-Rose, June and Neville Braybrooke – had come up against the same thing. Muriel insisted that Eliot was the Braybrookes' window cleaner, that he was prying into their papers. She asked Neville if he had received any letters from him. He had a few. Muriel asked to see one. 'She had some extraordinary method of a code [...] taking [...] maybe the ninth letter [...]. "Have you ever had any trouble with Dannie Abse?" [...] "No. I've met him and I quite like him." [...]. "Well," Muriel replied, "there's a message in this letter which says Danny Abse is out to get you."' Another, she said, secreted in the programme note on Eliot's play, had threatened her.[5] To her, it was like metaphysical black propaganda; to her friends it looked more like persecution mania.

Peterkiewicz and Brooke-Rose were told of messages in Faber blurbs.[6] 'We loved her very much during that period,' Peterkiewicz remarked, '... seeing the struggle. It was really like watching someone using spiritual crossword puzzles: pedantry plus ingenuity. It emerged in such a way that you wanted to believe it [...] it was part of that fantasy world we had built for ourselves for the sheer pleasure of it. Now I think that perhaps the pedantic ingenuity / fantasy, being on the border of madness, [...] is something that the poets have to possess ... and sometimes it possesses them. [...] The text [of the play] kept her mind somehow together ... This was another part of her mind ... the sense of structure. [...] [There was] the idea of prying, of being watched.' How did they deal with this? 'I think one had to be a good witness. To ask questions and yet not to be in any way crude or insensitive.'

Similar cases of dextro-amphetamine poisoning are well documented. The small yellow pills Muriel took were widely used as a stimulant (much as caffeine is today) and as an appetite suppressant when the addictive potential of such drugs was not understood. It was only later in the 1950s that amphetamine use (and abuse) began to be associated with symptoms resembling those of schizophrenia, the most prominent being paranoid delusions, i.e. strongly held beliefs, based on little or no evidence, that the individual is being spied upon and generally persecuted, either by a group (the state, a cult, etc.) or by an individual. Symptoms could also include auditory and / or visual hallucinations.[7]

Muriel's delusions fit this scenario exactly. They were visual rather than auditory, and the detection of codes in Eliot's writing presents a classic case of amphetamine poisoning. Words jumped about on the page, rearranging themselves into frightening anagrams. The word 'veil', for example, became 'evil'. Dr Lieber later prescribed Largactil (one trade name for chlorpromazine or CPZ) which was introduced around this time to treat schizophrenia. Muriel thought, and had doubtless been told, that it was a mild drug. In fact, it wasn't. We now know that CPZ would also be an effective treatment for amphetamine psychosis and, although this knowledge was not available at the time, far-sighted clinicians could have used the drug for this purpose, given the similarity of the symptoms. Clearly, Dr Lieber, although no specialist, was either far-sighted or lucky in his choice of this new remedy. Withdrawal from the use of Dexedrine frequently causes depressions and, over the next year, Muriel suffered them. But Largactil, the support of her friends and of her Catholic counsellor, Father O'Malley, above all, perhaps, her fearless self-belief, effected a steady recovery.

Muriel was fortunate in her friends: all writers, all intelligent and sympathetic to visionary experience. That 'fantasy world' involved angels. In 1963 Peterkiewicz wrote a novel about angels.[8] A trickle of laughter always ran through his East European accent. Sensitive, handsome, a Polish exile and cradle Catholic alive with metaphysical speculation, he was utterly charming to Muriel. He and Brooke-Rose had first met her after her success with 'The Seraph', probably in early 1952 when Brooke-Rose, twenty-nine years old, was a research student and Peterkiewicz an ill-paid teacher of Polish. They were, as Brooke-Rose put it, 'just poor people living in lodgings, on the make, full of ideas'.[9] For fifteen years from 1946 they shared a cheap, rent-controlled room in Chelsea with a bathroom on the landing, while cheerfully battling to establish their literary reputations. Peterkiewicz, in fact, had already become a celebrated poet in pre-war Poland, his fame there a casualty of communism. But he determined to start again, and by 1953 had published a novel,[10] while Brooke-Rose had set her own course towards becoming a novelist and critic. Both were psychological exiles belonging to several cultures, a dash of the exotic flickering in the background of their disrupted early lives.

As Muriel inhaled the volatile air of her new Catholic friendships, Brooke-Rose, feeling some religious pressure from both Peterkiewicz and her mother (who had become a nun after being widowed), was wrestling with doubt. They were all discussing Simone Weil, whose work had just been published in English, and appreciating her 'passionate commitment and refusal to join'.[11] Ultimately Brooke-Rose remained unpersuaded, indifferent to the whole issue, but for some years she enjoyed tortuous theological debates with Muriel who was intensely *funny* about religion, always cracking irreverent jokes. Both loved talking in multiple registers. No subject was sacrosanct. Muriel's 'breakdown', Brooke-Rose thought, was not a breakdown as such: Muriel didn't collapse. It was rather an attack of paranoia. Usually she handled it with verve, fascinated, invigorated, even when it touched on delicate issues.

One of Muriel's 'messages', which Brooke-Rose remembered but Muriel did not, said: 'Dirty Yid.'[12]

Peterkiewicz's and Brooke-Rose's introduction to Muriel had been through Rosamund Batchelor; Batchelor's was engineered by Frank Sheed. Birtwistle and the Braybrookes loved Sheed, too, and much of the good in Muriel's life at this time can be traced back to him. Batchelor, who worked for Sheed & Ward, shared a flat in Redcliffe Square, ten minutes down the Old Brompton Road from Muriel's place. They had liked each other immediately. Thereafter, even before her crisis, Muriel was invited to Catholic gatherings. Batchelor was interested in Poland and Russia, had learned and spoke perfect Polish. The conversations over tea and biscuits, Peterkiewicz recalled, were intense and 'very poetic'.[13] Michael Mason, whose *Legacy* Muriel had reviewed, would turn up. It was there that the angel fantasies proliferated amid laughter and companionship. The whole focus of Muriel's life had shifted, enclosed and protected as she now was by the Household of the Faith. Maryvonne Butcher, literary editor of the *Tablet*, wrote warmly as a co-religionist rather than as a businesswoman. Father Caraman, Evelyn Waugh's friend and editor of the *Month*, attended her reception and soon put work her way. 'I somehow felt', Birtwistle wrote, 'that Frank Sheed would be all that was needed to bring you safely Home.'[14] 'Home' was the operative word. Muriel had never felt at home with the Jewish community in Edinburgh. She had never felt at home anywhere until she entered the Catholic Church. The competitive scratchiness of the Poetry Society and Neo-Romantic circles had been replaced by the welcome of an international spiritual family. She became godmother to Birtwistle's elder son, Damien. Sheed's daughter was fond of her, as was June Braybrooke's. The bush telegraph drummed with concern at her condition.

The Braybrookes were an important part of this new network. Neville, seven years Muriel's junior, had known her slightly through the Poetry Society since the late forties. He had fond memories of her 'painted up to the nines' then, taking on the old guard. A poet and critic, he inhabited the same fringes of literary London as she did. He was another charming eccentric, tall and ebullient, boyish, superstitious. And for his part, he was struck by Muriel's knowledge of the Scriptures, of Jung, of Proust, by her refreshing fantasies and strain of racy anecdotes, by her loyalty. This was the Muriel the Braybrookes loved: the woman who stood by June when her father was dying, paid hospital visits with her, encouraged her writing: 'She was absolutely like a tiger in one's defence.'[15] Like Muriel, June was a convert with a child by her ex-husband. As 'Isobel English', she was already producing prose fiction of real talent. She and Muriel read each other's work and Muriel gave her the titles for two later novels: *Four Voices* and *Every Eye*. The latter, from Auden's 'Every eye shall weep alone', was an idea that appealed to the tragic vision of both women.

So the circle opened. Neville had been at school (Ampleforth) with the novelist Francis King. They all knew Kay Dick, the chic lesbian novelist and translator then living with Kathleen Farrell. The stalwart Hugo Manning, who had sent Kierkegaard's *Diaries* to Muriel during 1953, was as supportive of the Braybrookes as he was of her. 'All the nice people', as Muriel put it in *The Girls of Slender Means*, 'were poor.' And Stanford remained an important part of her life. Their friends still regarded them as a couple. It was he who took control when she lost her grasp on the material world: acting as her business manager and secretary, organising a fund for her support, and, perhaps most importantly, writing to Eliot to ask whether any messages in *The Confidential Clerk* were encrypted in Greek. Muriel was sure that they were. 'If there is any code concealed [...],' Eliot replied, 'I shall be interested to know what it is.'[16] Stanford forwarded the letter, trusting that it might set her mind at rest. 'I was full of joy over this,' she wrote in March, 'just what I wanted':

Now I feel released from a very real bondage & can make use of the experience. The real deliverance is the feeling that I can discover things about myself independent of the 'code' – things that I didn't intuitively find among the anagrams but which I hope will come to light in my mind & in fact have already done so. But the awful part was not really knowing what sort of illusions I had to face.[17]

She had, she said, other things to do and would return to the conundra when she had refurbished her Greek and finished *Job*.

A month later she was able to revive her normal practice of laying out worksheets for herself, and one for 30 April–2 May offers some idea of these other things: reviews for the *Observer*, the *Tablet* and the *Church of England Newspaper*; Falcon Press proofs, probably of her ill-fated edition of Mary Shelley's *The Last Man*; seven letters, including one to 'Lady Abbess' and another to Pearson Horder seeking a part-time job; typing a story to send to *Encounter*; work on her Anne Brontë biography; and arranging Hebrew lessons.[18] Part of Muriel's problem was the craving to make every waking moment productive, and the sheer volume of tasks here is interesting, as is the date: not simply because it was a weekend, but because it was perhaps the most important weekend of her life. Amid this furious schedule, on the Saturday, she had travelled to Ealing Priory for her reception into the Church. Neville Braybrooke's twelve-year-old stepdaughter attended and afterwards asked her what she (Victoria) should do 'if she had a vocation to be a nun but didn't want to become one'. Muriel said: '"If your vocation is strong enough it will override everything."' (She spoke with a convert's fervour.)[19] Beyond Muriel's immediate circle, however, she was already irritated by the bland piety of her co-religionists.

Missing Stanford's lively scepticism and addressing him as 'Brother Mine' in a sixteen-page letter, she explained her sense of loss since conversion. She considered herself a loyal Catholic. Nevertheless, she found herself frustrated by others' blind faith,[20] and her refusal to succumb to humourless ecclesiastical authority remained with her for life. On various occasions friends complained that she could not just make up her religion as she went along. But many British Catholics, she explained to Stanford, were over-anxious about betraying their Church and she insisted on distinguishing between doubt and disbelief:

> I am of the type of Catholic who must take recourse to the living waters of the defining mind. And what is the defining mind but the mind that 'doubts well'?[21] There can be no definition without doubt, unless it be an

intuitive definition in which case we must return to doubt in order to verify the intuition. Doubt [...] is not a fixed principle. [...] [It] moves towards one or more objectives, sometimes of a conflicting nature. Disbelief, on the other hand, if it is honest and not confused with doubt, is a fixed principle. [...] Doubt is never fixed, never at rest until it finds truth by *defining*. [...] Catholics are scared stiff of the Holy Ghost, and that's the truth, though the Church teaches far otherwise. It was St Thomas who took the pagans and heretics and infidels as his sources of truth. [...] All the great mystics have understood doubt.[22]

This discussion, of course, impinged not only on her religion but also on her writing. The necessity of doubt, unfixed, capable of incorporating multiple viewpoints, is the essence of the 'nevertheless principle'. The Old Testament God the Father had always presented her with a problem. God the Son required selfless charity. As an artist, the Holy Ghost was to her the most important element of the Trinity.

Stanford's replies rarely engaged with these debates. Suffering undiagnosed abdominal pain and intense melancholia, he was, it seems, a wall off which Muriel could bounce ideas. 'My heart is moved', he wrote, 'with a deep and helpless love, [...] for love is preserved by dying to what it was in order to be born into a new condition.' While her 'beauty' had 'appeared hitherto as enchantment', it now seemed 'a glory. I understand, in a fresh fashion, Yeats' *Easter* line: "A terrible beauty is born".'[23] 'Helpless' says much – and 'terrible'. While Muriel was hailing him as an ally, he stood bemused, watching her drift out to sea: not drowning but waving goodbye. He did not attend her reception. After promising to be at her confirmation on 30 May, he reneged. They now met more rarely, perhaps once a week, less if he were ill. Sometimes he would stay the night but celibacy clearly distressed him. In truth, he could not cope with her independence, physical or spiritual. It depleted him. Approaching forty and still living with his parents, he was sliding into a mid-life crisis as Muriel disappeared over the horizon.

This disappearance occurred in three stages. That mysterious entry in her worksheet, 'Lady Abbess', explains the first, for, just two months after her reception, Muriel was thinking of becoming a nun. During July 1954 she stayed for a week at The Hermitage, a guest house attached to Stanbrook Abbey in Worcestershire. The routine of prayer and study attracted her, as did the isolation in a community of intelligent women. Stanford received enthusiastic letters detailing her discussions. She borrowed a shelf-full of Job books and investigated other orders but preferred the Benedictine whose vows were Stability, Conversion of Life and Obedience, rather than Poverty, Chastity and Obedience.[24] Commitment to poverty and chastity held only limited appeal. Independence involved financial independence and control over the distribution of her resources. Either way, there was the problem of obedience which was simply impossible for her.

From Stanbrook she sent Robin a cheque for his sixteenth birthday. He also presented a difficulty. If she were to take the veil, she wanted first to be assured of his security. Who, for instance, would care for the boy should Cissy die before he came of age? Muriel left it to Providence but trying to juggle the urgent requirement to work with the need for rest left her at best agitated and at worst spiralling downwards into depression. Stanbrook was her holiday during those months of part-time clerking for her publisher, Peter Nevill. But no sooner had she returned than Nevill's called in the receiver and her income was lost again, including that from her books under their imprint.

Peter Owen, a partner at Nevill's firm, set up independently and commissioned Muriel to edit a volume of Jane Austen's letters. This provided fifty badly needed pounds but also more pressure. It was Owen who had contracted *Emily Brontë* and the Anne Brontë biography. The former had been late; the latter had fallen into a black hole and, like the *Job* and the *Eliot*, had progressed no further than notes. So alarmed was she by the stalling of *Anne* that she had co-opted Stanford again, only to set it aside and concentrate on *Job*. She loved the latter, she explained to him, and one had to write with love. To do anything else would be a kind of death. But now three contracted books were deferred, and the fourth not begun. The thought of repaying these spent advances horrified her. Only one thing seemed clear: 'that I'm paralysed as a writer unless I write according to this queer dictatorial sense I have.'[25] Towards the end of September, the receivers ordered the tenants of Nevill's premises to quit by Christmas. Even her workroom was taken from her.

All this, it seems, led to another collapse. During September 1955 Stanford completed the forms for her appeal to the National Insurance tribunal, and attended on her behalf. She was, he said, 'too ill to compose a letter' but had signed it,[26] referring the tribunal to the letter quoted at the opening of this chapter. This gave 'some indication of the incapacitating nature of her ailment of which the present trouble is a more serious recrudescence'. Most weeks she visited Father O'Malley, described in the appeal as a 'lay psychoanalyst'.[27] Dr Lieber sent her a certificate, enquiring whether she was taking the iron tablets and eating properly: 'but you must be patient as the trouble you have does take a little time.'[28] Patience was never her strong suit.

*

In early October 1954 Muriel left London for the Kent countryside. This inaugurated the second stage of her disentanglement from Stanford, and was financed by the 'plight fund' he had organised: writing to anyone with money who knew her work, and introducing it to those who did not. David Astor had already sent £100. Later, Graham Greene and A. J. Cronin contributed. The basis on which this money was supplied was that Muriel, a gifted writer, was suffering nervous collapse and needed to convalesce. She was at a Carmelite establishment, The Friars at Aylesford Priory, a retreat which welcomed troubled Catholic artists. Father O'Malley had probably arranged this. After staying briefly in the guest house, she moved to a cottage in the grounds of nearby Allington Castle, also owned by the Carmelites. There she remained until mid-1955, by which time she had completed five chapters of what was to become her first novel, *The Comforters*. The house was originally called 'Red Cottage'. Muriel renamed it, with droll scepticism, 'St Jude's Cottage' after the patron of lost causes.

At the guest house she had lived simply, with the total support which had attracted her to Stanbrook. Bed and board were four guineas a week. Two pounds' spending money supplied typing paper, cigarettes, stockings and, once she was settled, regular trips to London to see Father O'Malley and Stanford. Aylesford offered tranquillity structured by religious observance but also a life which had not isolated itself from the material world. The priest with whom she had closest contact was Father Brocard Sewell, a worldly fellow who ran a press and founded a literary journal, the *Aylesford Review* (1955–68). Later he started the *Antigonish Review.* Both were well regarded as 'little magazines'. He also had, Neville Braybrooke thought, 'a real vocation to get on with very tarty girls and remain a very religious man at the same time'.[29] When the Profumo / Stephen Ward scandal broke in 1963, Sewell offered house-room to the glamorous prostitutes involved. Inevitably, he fell foul of the Church authorities. While Muriel was there, work was furiously in train, converting the vast Tudor interiors of the castle into manageable spaces as a retreat house and conference centre, reconstructing the Priory as a Marian shrine capable of accommodating three thousand annual pilgrims. A crypt was built to house the skull of St Simon Stock.[30] There were torchlight processions; trade was brisk.

Like Sewell, Muriel came to find something about all this uncomfortable. Edwina Barnsley recalled standing with her above the shrine's foundations. 'All these people hanging about, waiting for *miracles*,' Muriel muttered crossly. Father Brocard remembered her as an instantly attractive presence: gregarious outside her working time – then limited to three hours daily on doctor's orders. But the communal life of The Friars was too intrusive – and expensive – for her. Within a month she had discovered her cottage and organised the removal of her effects from Sussex Mansions. This was the real parting of the ways from Stanford. At the time she was grateful for his offer to clear her flat, although even this led to acrimony. Greene's film-production company agreed to pay her £120 in six-monthly instalments in return for a non-existent script and, with a rent of just £1 a week, her fund stretched ahead as a living wage for more than a year. She lived humbly on a rough diet of eggs, baked beans and white sliced bread. The house itself was tiny: semi-detached, red-brick Victorian, two up, two down, no electricity. One of the maids slept upstairs. Muriel had the two downstairs rooms, one of which also served as a kitchen.

Muriel made friends easily and at the centre of her new group were the Barnsleys. Alan and Edwina ('Dina') Barnsley lived in Maidstone, the nearest town, where he was a GP and the prison doctor. His real vocation, however, was writing. When Muriel met him he was completing his first (highly praised) novel, *In the Time of Greenbloom* (1956) under the nom de plume 'Gabriel Fielding'. Muriel was frequently with the Barnsleys for long weekends. Both were Catholics and engaging eccentrics: tall, effusive, welcoming. Dina, 'a very sweet woman'[31] with two sons, seemed perpetually pregnant and offered Muriel another surrogate family. Alan, frequently infatuated with other women, was soon half in love with Muriel. But all three managed to avoid embarrassment by treating his bewitchment as a joke – until a final row blew the whole thing apart in 1961. An elderly neighbour, Miss Martin ('Martie'), provided Muriel with her dearest companion: the Persian kitten she named 'Bluebell', and for the first time in many years, Muriel was happy. One winter morning she wrote to Stanford from her bed: books and papers piled about her as she struggled to compose a *Tablet* review; hot-water bottle, Bluebell perched upon the window-sill watching birds in the snow. Peace. She had waited a long time for this moment.[32]

Stanford ran Muriel's business affairs and both had signed up with a young literary agent, John Smith of Christy & Moore, just before her confirmation in May. That took care of the correspondence. To Smith she had submitted nine of her short stories and he was (unsuccessfully) investigating the American magazine market. Independently, she sent these to the publisher Macmillan in October. Tony Strachan, a friend from Grey Walls days, was now working for the firm and had recommended their fiction editor, Alan Maclean. This was the breakthrough. Stanford had also sent some of her stories to Graham Greene who found them 'extremely alive and interesting'.[33] When Muriel wrote at the end of January to enquire whether readers' reports had arrived, emboldened by Greene's support, she added: 'As I think you know, my earlier plan to make these the basis of a book of short stories has developed into the writing of a novel [...] it is taking shape quite nicely'[34] – and asked them to commission it.

Maclean replied by return. His job as a young editor was to seek out new talent. Yes, he said, they were certainly interested in her work, including the novel. How much did she want? She asked for £100, and got it. Half was to be paid immediately, the remainder in June. She trusted that this was non-returnable, should Macmillan ultimately refuse the book. Maclean hesitated at this, but in such playful fashion that she must have known they would become friends. It was not a 'commission' as such, he said, but an option: 'In the mournful event that we do not want to publish [...], we shall lock you up in a tiny room on the top floor here and feed you on old catalogues. Seriously, if that does not happen we shall naturally hope to get our money back [...].'[35] She promised half the novel by the summer to avoid 'a sinister fate in your top-floor lock-up',[36] applied to have electricity connected to her cottage, and settled down in the snow to work on nothing but fiction.

*

Evelyn Waugh coped with his illness by writing it up as *The Ordeal of Gilbert Pinfold* (1957).[37] Muriel was doing much the same thing with *The Comforters*. The story centres on Caroline Rose, a young Catholic convert who, on religious grounds, has stopped sleeping with her lover, Laurence Manders, suffers a nervous breakdown, and retires to a retreat house. She is a literary critic who has written a treatise on the Novel and is now writing a novel herself. At the retreat Caroline encounters Mrs Hogg, a devout, interfering Catholic whom she finds morally and physically repulsive. Hogg, devoid of self-enquiry, is a woman of blind faith: fleshy, dogmatic, an enemy of the individual. She exists only as a member of her group of co-religionists. When she is alone, she 'disappears'. Humourless, she thus becomes the butt of the novel's comedy. (The first working title was *The Loving of Mrs Hogg*.) In a parallel plot we are introduced to Laurence's grandmother, Louisa Jepp. *The Comforters* opens with him going through her bedroom drawers, trying to deduce how the things he finds add up to the story of her life. Throughout, he fruitlessly attempts to relate the effects of her actions to imagined causes. Superficially, she is a respectable old lady with a circle of male admirers. In fact, she is running a gang of smugglers and her air of dizzy inconsequence masks a form of omniscience. She is tough, independent, sharply witty at others' expense, an older version, as it were, of Caroline and of Muriel. Caroline suffers delusions, appearing to herself as a character in the novel we are reading. A typewriter taps in her head, speaking the narrative of her life, predicting it. Torn between the spiritual and the material worlds, she goes mad – and can only reunite the two halves of her psyche in fiction. This was precisely Muriel's dilemma.

Although the autobiographical element is diffused, the essence of Caroline's breakdown was the essence of Muriel's. In *The Comforters*, neither Caroline nor the reader knows whether she is inside or outside the text. Is she the narrator or a character in someone else's (Muriel's? God's?) story? It was this inability to distinguish inside from outside, fact from fiction, which was at once terrifying and stimulating to both Waugh and Muriel, and writing this novel was integral to her recovery. She enjoyed the work. It clarified her situation. But it took all of her huge resilience to return to the edge from which she had retreated, while the very charity on which she depended produced strain. When Sheed sent her another $100 in March, she accepted it gratefully but remained anxious. Theoretically, this was a further advance on the *Job* book which she had now also put aside on Father O'Malley's advice. Even writing a short piece on the subject had rendered her melancholy.[38]

That article was a long, carefully argued review of Jung's *Answer to Job*,[39] a book which she found whimsical in its theology and careless as literary analysis. And, given that Father O'Malley was a Jungian, this perhaps also marked a separation from him. 'As theology,' she wrote, '[Jung's book] is far too anthropomorphic to be satisfying [...].' The supernatural, rejected by Jung, was to her, as to Waugh, the real. Theology, she insists, 'has to do with objective reality', and 'We cannot tell [from Jung] whether God and the unconscious are two different entities.' He ignores the epilogue in which God restores Job's fortunes. But 'if [he] wants the prologue (and his whole theory hangs upon it) he must have the epilogue, no less than his hero Job had apparently to suffer his reward.'[40]

The notion of Job's *suffering* his reward (just as she was suffering her conversion) is crucial to her reading. To the humanist, like Jung, or Louis de Bernières in his 1998 interpretation, God appears in this story as a megalomaniac. De Bernières sees Job as unjustly persecuted – all he asks is a straight talk with a crazed oligarch – while God seems a 'frivolous trickster [...] who even botches up the reparations [...]' and Job emerges as 'a very modern figure [...], one who asserts his individuality and integrity in the face of conventional wisdom. He is [...] a classic existentialist hero.'[41] Muriel agreed with much of this. The idea of God pontificating from a whirlwind she always found comic, and the Book of Job intrigued her for the rest of her life. She wrote a novel, *The Only Problem* (1984), focusing on it. For Job asks the most important question for those seeking faith: how God's supposed bene-volence can be squared with ubiquitous suffering.

Muriel responds to this by suggesting that the problem lay not with God but with our construction of Him in the human image:

> At the point where human reason cannot reconcile the fact of evil with the goodness of God, an anthropomorphic conception of God breaks down. Is this not the main point of the Book of Job? [...] Read aright, the epilogue is not merely a conventional happy ending; it represents something beyond the reach of discourse which Job, for all he was an upright man, really had to come to terms with in order to gain his peace.[42]

Integral to this wisdom was the interpretation of God's 'reparations'. In Muriel's view, He did not 'botch' them but calculated them very carefully indeed with a kind of grim humour. De Bernières complains that Job's slaughtered kinsfolk were not restored: there was no justice for them. Instead, a new family was created. Muriel's imagination, however, was not struck by this but by the names of Job's later daughters: Jemima, Kezia and Karenhappuch, which translate as 'Turtle Dove', 'Cassia' (a perfume) and 'Box of Eye-Paint'. 'Can we really imagine', she asks, 'our hero enjoying his actual reward?'[43] For her, Job's wisdom depends upon his reading the irony of his 'happy ending'.

A year after her period of delusions (March 1955) she wrote to Frank Sheed, certain of her recovery and willing that recovery through faith. Periodically she would reflect upon the phenomenon objectively. At those times she felt gloriously released. At others, she remained horrified.[44] Muriel empathised entirely with Job's predicament. He, too, was endangered by a form of breakdown which he resisted. He spoke her darkest fears: of failing to fulfil her vocation (artistic and spiritual), of subsiding into resentment, of finding in exile not the exhilaration of freedom but isolation and irrelevance. Although she regarded Sheed as a fellow exile with a strong sacramental feeling about his roots in Australia, her own sense of a homeland was more complex. Somehow she did not feel rooted in Scotland. Rather she had a passion to visit the Holy Land, not contemporary Israel so much as the land of her Jewish ancestors.[45] When she did get there, in 1961, it was to attend the Eichmann trial, a profoundly distressing experience.

*

Muriel was determined to conceal her hallucinations from Robin and her parents. Stanford was sworn to secrecy on the subject. He was, however, in an awkward position. Their erotic relationship had died and had reverted to friendship. They had been heading for final separation when she had become ill. To his credit, he had responded generously. Her suffering, he said, was his, and he did much to relieve it. But something fundamental had changed, for he could no longer speak frankly to her. As the person with whom everyone else dealt when enquiring after Muriel, he maintained a separate discourse with them, the basis of which was that Muriel's illness was more serious than she realised. But she battled on with *The Comforters*, exactly on schedule. By the end of May 1955, she planned to begin typing and revising.[46] 'M's book is going very brightly,' Alan Barnsley informed Stanford, 'and she herself is well above pathological introspection.' She was, he said, 'a small scarlet bundle of anguish and smiles', 'wonderful company'.[47]

Barnsley's enthusiasm for her work was important. When the first five chapters were typed, he pronounced them excellent. His own *Green-bloom* was a Proustian revisiting of adolescent sexuality, pathological introspection his stock in trade. He would read out sections for hours at a stretch. A hyperactive egomaniac and fantasist, he was an acquired taste. The Braybrookes found him vain and theatrical. Women, in particular, thought him difficult. Words burst from him in unfordable torrents, his literary power strangely compromised by emotional immaturity. A man tortured by calf love, his innocence and energy attracted Muriel at first. 'We had an argument this morning about [Herbert Read's] The Green Child [...],' she wrote to Stanford. 'He has no logic, Alan.' But this also signalled a fundamental incompatibility. When the Barnsleys discovered a poem by Read in the *Listener*, they condemned it. Muriel thought it a 'remarkable piece. "I believe in my unbelief" [...] I think that belief in unbelief, in Read's sense, is not sterile.'[48] These questions never left her. Indeed, they were fundamental to *The Comforters*. Revising her own Chapter 3, she explained that 'everyone falls under suspicion from everyone else [...] throughout the story [...], everyone is suspected [...] of being other than they are. Human judgement is fallible – that's the accepted viewpoint.'[49]

Muriel sent her five chapters to Maclean in June 1955 under a new title: *Holiday of Obligation*. He replied quickly, enclosing the second £50, concerned that Caroline's 'voices' should not 'dominate the whole' narrative,[50] and immediately commissioned a short story for the *Winter's Tales* series he had started. That was another £50. Muriel agreed that she might have 'overdone' the voices: '[They] are essential to the story but only as a contributory factor'[51] – a diplomatic concession for she still had no contract, and only got one four months after submitting the complete text.

The story commission excited her. She needed a break, and the working notes for her first novel reveal why. The manuscript is a tangle of revisions, quite unlike the clean notebooks of later work. Here we see a mind in pyrotechnic display, translating the debates of her journalism into fiction. The book at this stage represented a defence of Caroline's withdrawal. She hates Mrs Hogg but must learn charity enough to love her. Mrs Hogg obeys authority; Caroline resists it. How can this be squared with the dogma of the Church? Originally, Caroline was to have given her life to save Mrs Hogg. Ultimately she does not. (Christian charity did not extend *that* far.) A distinction is established between human time and God's time, human plots and God's plot, which was implicitly to structure all Muriel's writings. Caroline may be determined to command her destiny but the tapping typewriter suggests that observation alters the observed. Much of Muriel's work plays with this relationship between an observing consciousness and 'reality': 'Observed, observer,' she had noted in a 1952 poem, 'we must always be / one or the other, and neither is sufficient.'[52] She created fictions about creating fictions in which spying or voyeurism figure. In this case she was writing a novel to see if she could write a novel about an expert on the novel who has become a novelist – and its title regularly changed. Next it became *Characters in a Novel*, then *Types and Shadows*, then *Shadow Play*, until finally settling as *The Comforters*. 'This', she told Maclean, 'pins down my main theme.'[53]

The theme of her *Winter's Tales* story, however, remained obscure. But she had the first sentence: '"One day in my young youth at high summer, lolling with my lovely companions against a haystack, I found a needle"'[54] – and with the exception of 'against' for 'upon', this became, and has remained, the opening line of one of the twentieth century's finest short fictions, 'The Portobello Road'. Later, she often worked like this. A sentence would form, a title, and a network of metaphors would crystallise around it. No plan; no argument – and definitely no change of title. The shape of a narrative would grow round a verbal construct like a pearl round grit. Writing to Stanford, she was jubilant. Inspiration, she felt, was dependent upon the Holy Ghost and, although three days later confidence failed her again, she felt that with encouragement she would find 'the secret heart of [her] story'.[55] It was as though it already existed, waiting for her discovery, and she wrote it in a week. It was the first to draw directly on her African experience, the first to use the device of a 'ghost narrator'.

*

'The Portobello Road', like much of Muriel's fiction, operates on two time-schemes, and 'Needle', the heroine, is clearly an extension of Muriel's personality. The opening image is of youthful innocence: a vivacious group of friends on a haystack, frozen in a photograph carried about, increasingly battered, through the terrestrial time of the narrative. The otherwise anonymous Needle is named after this moment when, in the midst of their 'merciless hacking-hecking laughter', she pricks her thumb like the Sleeping Beauty. The blood signals mortality and prefigures Needle's murder by one of these friends, counterpointing the photographic image of the quartet: 'each reflecting fearlessly in the face of George's camera the glory of the world, as if it would never pass'.[56] She is dead in this world but alive in another, in time eternal. Finding the needle in the haystack registers her visionary power.

Needle is a writer, a Scot, and a Catholic, 'secure in [her] difference from the rest'. Like Muriel, during her life she 'was a drifter, nothing organised. It was difficult for my friends to follow the logic of my life.' Indeed, her life annoys people in pedestrian jobs and marriages. Needle, they insist, is 'lucky'. Only she knows 'the bitter side of [her] fortune', the sense of falling short as an artist: 'Sometimes, in my impotence and need I secreted a venom which infected all my life for days on end and which spurted out indiscriminately on [...] anyone who crossed my path.'[57] Muriel was surely writing from the heart here, although the 'venom' was largely repressed at this stage, turned in on herself. Needle is cooler and more confident than was the Muriel who invented her in 1955 but perhaps she became Needle through the act of creating her: the tough Scot of fierce theology, immune to sentimentality and the bullying which tries to blackmail her out of her visionary dream. Needle became the prototype for a chain of mocking females in their prime. She is the van-courier of truth, the proverbial daughter of time. She terrifies the sinner who is the only person able to see her. Her intervention is a process, like Job's, of self-justification. She was murdered by a friend because she would not lie. Now she returns to punish, to play with her aggressor like a cat with a bird. George, the culprit, suggests predatory masculinity: 'I saw the red full lines of his mouth and the white slit of his teeth last thing on earth.'[58] He kills her, in another haystack, by stuffing straw into her mouth. But she will not be silenced. She testifies against him.

'The Portobello Road', however, is much more than a fantasy of female retribution. It is a theological meditation: on disaffection, on human and divine time, on justice and conscience, on the collision between 'the glory of the world' and its corruption. It is the eternal story of a fallen world. The title locates the place where Needle 'appears' to George: a street market in North Kensington. It is the site of something everlasting and of something transitory. She recalls the 'pleasurable spread of objects', like the Woolworth's displays which had excited her as a child, as they had excited Muriel.[59] But Needle now sees things *sub specie aeternitatis*. The stalls lay out human history from Georgian spoons to rayon vests, the wreckage of 'breakable homes'.[60] It is the transitoriness which is permanent, as is the inability of the secular mind to perceive this. In its way this is hilarious – and simultaneously tragic. The fact of death, everywhere apparent among this glittering rubble of human aspiration, is perpetually forgotten. Needle arrives as a memento mori with the laughter of the gods on her lips: 'He looked as if he would murder me,' she remarks of George, 'and he did.'[61]

*

With 'The Portobello Road', Muriel had found her mature voice, had cured herself of the babel in her head. In her collections of stories, she always placed 'Portobello' at the front, as though to acknowledge it as the first perfect fruit of her imagination. For with it she had crossed her final bridge. There were no more relapses, the novel sped ahead to completion just four months later and, in the meantime, she had moved out of her cottage and back to London, this time far away from Stanford to a house in Camberwell. This was the third and final stage of her disentanglement from him. It was here, at 13 Baldwin Crescent, that she finished *The Comforters*. Here she wrote, in quick succession, *Robinson* (1958), *Memento Mori* (1959), *The Ballad of Peckham Rye* (1960), and *The Bachelors* (1960) – all brilliantly original works which stormed the literary citadels. Usually, she had one book finished while another was in proof and a third being launched. Macmillan could hardly keep up.

Muriel left Allington Castle in August 1955, grateful for its respite, impatient to be gone. After eight months the haven of her cottage had become a prison. The retreat was provincial – full of prying eyes, too cosy. She longed to reconnect herself to the normality – and anonymity – of the metropolis. The decision to go was made in July, shortly after she completed 'Portobello'. Father O'Malley had a niece, Teresa Walshe, who lodged with a Catholic landlady. It was one of the best introductions Muriel ever received. 'Tiny' Lazzari was a vivacious, chirruping Irish widow with a Cork accent, small of stature, big of heart. No. 13 Baldwin Crescent was her own house. She lived on the ground floor, her son, his wife and their two children on the first. The third was for tenants, including Teresa. Muriel occupied a pair of cramped attic rooms adjacent to a kitchen, and looked out over the back garden. On the same floor there was a spare room which Robin might use (although he rarely did). A new Catholic church was just round the corner.

Baldwin Crescent was a quiet street behind the thundering traffic of Camberwell New Road. Turning left down this, Muriel could catch a bus to central London or walk to the Oval Tube station in ten minutes; turning right, she soon reached the shops, Camberwell Green, and, further on, Peckham Rye. It was a rackety district. In 1955 the Catholic congregation predominantly comprised Irish immigrants where now it is predominantly Afro-Caribbean. Otherwise, the area is much the same today: tumultuous, largely working-class, spliced with some tranquil rows of yellow-brick houses like Baldwin Crescent, left over from Victorian and Edwardian prosperity. To live there was to live in two worlds. Muriel could sit in silence at her desk, staring at the patch of lawn, or walk down the road and turn a corner into the noise. She loved it, and stayed there for eleven years, gradually colonising more of the house. This was her British base when she went to work in New York during 1962, and remained her London home until she left for Rome in 1966. When she became famous, Evelyn Waugh advised her to move to a better address. It was, she knew, good advice – which she ignored.

After *The Comforters* was typed in November, she threw a party in

Camberwell (the first of many) but money remained tight and, with Macmillan's still wavering in February 1956, she was seeking a full-time post while urging Maclean to send contract and cheque. She wanted, she told him, to start her new novel (eventually restricted to a short story), *The Go-Away Bird*, in early March. He replied saying that he knew what a 'crashing bore' it was to 'have to wait for a final decision'[62] but a senior colleague was looking it over. And so it continued. Muriel was trying to live on the remains of her 'plight fund', small commissions, and £2 a week Sickness Benefit. It was deep winter with final-demand electricity bills to pay. She had to do something quickly and, on 27 February, began work with Peter Owen: three days a week as editorial assistant. 'The decor [...] would amuse you,' she wrote to a friend [...]. 'It is like a scene from a play of the thirties. Bare boards, up-turned packing cases of wood and cardboard for working purposes, old bits of sheaves of tattered manuscripts. Peter, who is quite nice really, rushes in and out at a pace. Sometimes bits of the set collapse.'[63] She must have felt like a ghost returning home. The firm was at 50 Old Brompton Road, the same place where she had worked for Nevill's and had hired a workroom, just across the street from her old flat in Sussex Mansions. At 5.30 p.m., though, instead of walking up the road to Stanford she now boarded a bus for Camberwell and Mrs Lazzari.

Owen quickly realised that he had a valuable asset in Muriel: industrious, meticulous and with keen literary acumen. She reorganised his office: 'The best bloody secretary I ever had,' he once remarked. Years later, he was still using the card index file she had set up. Later still she drew on some of her memories of this office for Nancy's memories in *A Far Cry From Kensington* (1988). Whatever Muriel did, she did well, and no experience was wasted. She acted as an adviser, guiding Owen to foreign literature: Cocteau, Hesse. Often she would be up half the night composing her next novel – *Robinson*, as it turned out – or reading for, and writing, reviews before coming into work in the morning. Occasionally exhaustion would overwhelm her,[64] but rarely for long. She was a woman driven.

Shortly after receiving her contract for *The Comforters* during March

1956, she had met Maclean for the first time in Macmillan's oak-panelled offices in St Martin's Street. His room, full of stuffed birds, had horrified her. He, however, had not. Maclean was thirty-one, ex-Foreign Office, elegant, public-school educated (Stowe), drolly self-effacing: a willowy gentleman with impeccable charm. Rather impressive – and attractive. He was also something of an unwilling celebrity, being the son of a prominent member of the Liberal Party and brother of the infamous spy. Alan had lost his Foreign Office post in America when Donald Maclean had suddenly disappeared with Guy Burgess in the 'Missing Diplomats' furore of 1951. Burgess and Maclean had popped up in Moscow just a month before Muriel met Alan. They didn't talk about it, although the entire Western world was humming with the news. Muriel never asked personal questions and deflected enquiries about her own life. Discretion was both protection and simple good manners. Reputations, good or ill, were irrelevant. She took people as she found them, in the present tense, and was focused on the matter in hand – in this case whether Macmillan would publish her stories and commission another novel. 'You know my position,' she wrote afterwards, 'I can't do much creative writing unless I have an advance on royalties first.'[65] One looks in vain in Muriel's early letters for engagement with public events. During the 1950s, the Coronation, the ascent of Everest, general elections, spy scandals, the Suez Crisis, the Hungarian uprising – all appear to have passed her by as shadow play. Her chief interest in Harold Macmillan, Chancellor of the Exchequer in 1955 and Prime Minister in 1957, was that he was the (absent) head of her publishing firm.

Unfortunately, Maclean could do little for her. They had, he said, to wait and see how *The Comforters* went. Muriel thus entered into her penultimate joint project with Stanford, a selection of Cardinal Newman's letters to be published by Peter Owen. At the time, this must have seemed a wise decision. Just two months later, Maclean refused her stories.

*

When Father Caraman wrote asking for a contribution to his series *Saints and Ourselves*, Muriel chose a sympathetic figure: St Monica, the mother of St Augustine. Like Mary Shelley and Muriel, she had lived two adult lives: one as a married woman, one beyond marriage when her true vocation emerged. St Monica was gifted with the 'virtues of patience, modesty and tact' but 'became a sort of holy terror, [...] above tact'. Muriel was drawn to her subject as someone both 'highly civilised' and 'deeply primitive', with the attraction of fierceness, of the exotic, 'like one of those inspired resolute women of the Old Testament', 'a saint to be contemplated rather than copied': 'no wretched Dido' but 'a sort of Diotima figure' in a 'country-house symposium'. She was 'wise, oracular Monica', who had 'advanced ahead of herself into eternity', not 'the lachrymose type of woman in the ordinary sense, on the contrary [...] good and tough'.[66]

Muriel often contemplated such women. Adelaide Uezzell, her grandmother, had been the first. In her agnostic phase she had written a poem, 'Magdalen',[67] and the figure of the prone Magdalene, washing and drying Christ's feet with her tears and hair, also appears in an earlier verse, 'You, Dreamer'.[68] Here Mary is presented as peacemaker, in the conventional guise of female abjection but which to Muriel was a highly erotic gesture. In 'Magdalen' (post-Sergeant), she is a more positive female principle, an image of acute, tormented consciousness embattled by 'dissuasive' voices, who rises up and eats men like air. Above all, perhaps, she is the sinner, the fallen woman persecuted by convention but beloved of Christ. Muriel was always on the side of the sinner.

Muriel did not imitate Adelaide, Monica or Mary Magdalene but she drew strength from their resilience and there was something of her in them all. In *The Comforters*, Louisa Jepp was a similar figure: a laughing stock to her materialist nephew; in 'reality', the reality she creates, a gang leader with diamonds in her bread. It had been stressful for Muriel to combat the dissuasive voices before the justification of her talent. From all sides there had come echoes of doubt, particularly from men, who thought she took herself too seriously; angry voices, voices quietly corrective, conventional, self-satisfied, like Job's comforters or Samuel Cramer's tempters. We hear one of them in a 1965 poem, 'Note by the Wayside',[69] where the narrator confronts the accusation of having placed career before kindness, and there is an enabling bitterness in the riposte: 'But are you so very clever and so very nice?' Wise oracular Muriel was about to be born.

*

Barnsley sent proofs of *The Comforters* to Evelyn Waugh; someone (Stanford?) sent them to Greene. Both came up trumps. 'The first half,' Waugh replied, 'up to the motor accident, is brilliant. The second half rather diffuse. The mechanics of the hallucinations are well managed. These particularly interested me as I am myself engaged on a similar subject. Mrs Spark no doubt wants a phrase to quote on the wrapper and advertisements. She can report me as saying: "brilliantly original and fascinating."'[70] Greene, when prompted by Stanford, offered: 'one of the few really original first novels one has read for many years.'[71] With these recommendations press attention was assured. An American publisher, Lippincott, offered an advance of over £200, and with money in her pocket at last Muriel set aside *The Go-Away Bird* and began *Robinson* in January 1957. Publication day for *The Comforters* was 7 February, less than a week after her thirty-ninth birthday, less than a month after Harold Macmillan had succeeded Anthony Eden as Prime Minister and the very day Bill Hayley and the Comets were about to take Britain by storm with their first UK concert. Out with the old. As Muriel approached middle life, she was rejuvenated as a blazing new talent in the literary firmament.

The previous November, Maclean, tying up loose ends, had asked her for a 'biographical note'. When it arrived he had promised to use it 'in some form or another'.[72] Doubtless there was a wry smile on his face. Like Owen, he had begun to discover the holy tenor beneath that placable exterior. Once the contract was signed, she had established the ground rules. He was not, she said, to alter the punctuation which was intentionally unorthodox. He should leave in those passages deleted on the grounds of 'mild indecency'. She had added a couple of pages by way of 'envoi'.[73] All this was expressed with exquisite tact, ostensibly leaving decisions to him. But there was no mistaking the adamantine will of an artist who knew exactly what she was doing and who would fight as furiously as St Monica to see her offspring properly launched. Her self-portrait read:

> Born in ice cave of southern Tyrol year 609 B.C. of centaur stock, mother descended Venus. Muriel Spark rose from the waves as is well known. Demands fabulous fees.[74]

CHAPTER 8

Acquiring Lorgnettes

1957–1959

The Comforters was dedicated to the Barnsleys and Alan was convinced it would make Muriel's fortune. She was more circumspect. It might, she thought, make her *name* but Macmillan, having sat on the book for nearly a year, were clearly uncertain. Advertising consisted of a low-key announcement in a flyer, omitting Waugh's plum quotation already printed on the dust jacket. Later she saw such lapses as typical of the firm's incompetence. Barnsley and Stanford had secured the Waugh and Greene 'puffs'. Macmillan's exertions were scarcely perceptible. In early 1957, however, she was in no position to complain. The reviews changed all that.

Just a fortnight before publication she was still seeking full-time work. Paul Allen, a young Irish ex-schoolmaster and aspirant writer, had become a friend. When he resigned from the *London Mystery Magazine* she applied (unsuccessfully) for his editorial post. 'I am known', she wrote, 'predominantly as a mystery writer'[1] – which was both true and untrue. Muriel was predominantly known as a poet and critic who wrote short stories. Some of these had supernatural elements. None was of the hoot-and-moonlight variety which formed the magazine's stock-in-trade. Nevertheless, she was, and remained, both a writer of mysteries and a mysterious writer.

Inevitably *The Comforters* met with some bafflement. The book was certainly weird: a 'Pirandello-puzzle of identities'[2] in the words of the *TLS*. And as if this were not enough, there were also the questions of the book's engagement with Catholic 'mysteries', of its whimsical feline humour, flickering between gaiety and acerbity. For a couple of hacks this was simply intolerable.[3] The British Catholic press largely ignored it.[4] In the vast majority of reviews, however, Muriel's brainchild met with huge acclaim. Most of the 'quality' broadsheets lauded it, as did *Time & Tide* and the *TLS*. Coverage was excellent for a first novel, and best of the bunch was the *Spectator*'s full-page eulogy from Waugh.

'It so happens', Waugh wrote, 'that *The Comforters* came to me just as I had finished a story on a similar theme and I was struck by how much more ambitious was Miss Spark's essay and how much better she had accomplished it.'[5] This was generous, given Waugh's anxieties about his failing powers. The novel delighted him: 'complicated, subtle and [...] intensely interesting [...]. [A]t a time when "experimental" writing has quite justly fallen into disrepute, her book is highly exhilarating.'

> The first theme is the mechanics of story-telling, the second a case-history of insanity. [...] The interest is in the relation between author and character. [...] The area of Caroline's mind which is composing the novel becomes separated from the area which is participating in it, so that, hallucinated, she believes that she is observant of, observed by, and in some degree under the control of, an unknown second person. In fact she is in the relation to herself of a fictitious character to a story-teller.[6]

Muriel, Greene and Waugh were all exiles, looking to the Church for a home (or at least a hotel). But in one particular (apart from the fact that she was a woman), she was radically different from both her supporters: they were products of the Oxford-educated bourgeoisie. She had fought her way into their intellectual company through sheer force of talent, and lived precariously in two attic rooms at a weekly rent of £2 10s 0d. She was also half-Jewish. The consciousness of exile was to her not the 1950s angst typical of post-war writers but an inbred cultural dynamic. Cultural dislocation was not a mournful condition. She nurtured it, walking out of one existence, closing the door, and into another: Edinburgh, Southern Rhodesia, Milton Bryan, Kensington, Aylesford,

Camberwell, New York, Rome, Tuscany. In each of her nine lives, she was the cat who walked alone. So here she was, in February 1957, at the beginning of her sixth new life, finally liberated at the age of thirty-nine: acknowledged, justified, her mind boiling with books. Her next four novels, transfiguring four of her past lives, were already written in her head. She resigned from Peter Owen and set up as an independent author again. This time, she determined, there was to be no turning back.

*

Things now began to happen fast. Macmillan contracted for *Robinson* and the short stories they had previously rejected. Rayner Heppenstall wrote from the BBC. They had met once, he believed, in Hugo Manning's company. Indeed they had and, although it was almost nine years earlier, he remembered her. Muriel had arrived with Sergeant, who recorded the party in his diary with a typical mixture of infatuation and resentment. Muriel, he thought, in her floral dress and Paris red coat, perfectly made-up and keen in conversation, was the most stunning woman in the room. When he had briefly left it, however, Heppenstall had taken his place and they had spent the rest of the evening as an awkward trio, Sergeant droning on about regional writing while Muriel fell asleep with her head on the fireplace.[7] A long time ago. 'I see your name so frequently nowadays', Heppenstall wrote, 'and wondered whether you were predisposed [...] to writing in a dramatical form for broadcasting.'[8] She was, set to work immediately on a radio play, 'The Party through the Wall',[9] and instructed Macmillan to despatch a copy of *The Comforters* to the BBC for possible adaptation. On 28 March, she received her first letter from Rachel MacKenzie of the *New Yorker*. The publishers Hamish Hamilton, MacKenzie said, had spoken highly of 'The Portobello Road'. Would she care to submit something similar? *Harper's Bazaar* followed suit in June. Offers of review work poured in. By the end of June, Macmillan were announcing an urgent reprint of *The Comforters*, and *Robinson*, begun in January, was finished by July. Amid this furore of activity, Muriel also wrote half a dozen reviews, another story ('The Black Madonna'), visited Edinburgh and the Barnsleys, had her play broadcast and, on 28 August, Lippincott's edition of *The Comforters* appeared to an excellent reception in America. Almost as a sideline, her and Stanford's edition of Newman's letters[10] came out and was widely praised.

Stanford still haunted Muriel's life. They were in contact over the Newman book and even planned another joint volume of his sermons. Both had left their agent, John Smith, and signed up with Paul Scott at Pearn, Pollinger & Higham. Stanford had had some success himself when his *Fénelon's Spiritual Letters* appeared just after *The Comforters*. But he was finding the whole arrangement with Muriel increasingly awkward as she accelerated into the literary stratosphere. During January 1957, he had begun 'Good-bye Bohemia' (discussed in Chapter 5), racing to complete it before Muriel's first novel was published. It was all about Muriel, a companion piece to *The Comforters* from the point of view, as it were, of Laurence Manders (who also loses his lover to the Church). The impression Stanford created on the poet John Bayliss was of a man in top form. In fact, as 'Good-bye Bohemia' collapsed, its author began to collapse with it, and his review of *The Comforters* is revealing. 'The novel', he wrote, 'is concerned with the problem of human communicability [...].' Ultimately, he cannot *like* Caroline. She is 'clever' but 'tormented' and 'lacks direct appeal and wholeness. In creating her so, the author has been faithful to an image of the type of woman whose search for integrity causes herself and others distress.' [11] It must have been difficult for Muriel not to read this as his comment on her.

She had written to Stanford in 1953 on departing to live alone, trying to raise his spirits. Their friendship, she said, was important, more successful than their attempt at an erotic relationship.[12] Four years later he was still sulking and, although they remained close, they were no longer intimate. Stanford now formed part of her loosely associated group of 'bachelors' – Paul Allen, Igor de Chroustchoff, Brian Parker, Hugh Maguire, Leonard Hill, Geoffrey Tickell[13] and Hugo Manning – with whom she socialised in the few hours she allowed herself away from her desk. It was a complicated situation for Stanford. He craved a lover to repair his self-confidence. Needing a clean break, he was unable to make one, his loyalty to Muriel confused by pragmatic basking in her reflected glory. She introduced him to Heppenstall who then mocked him to his face. To Wrey Gardiner, however, who recorded this period in his autobiography, they appeared an enviable couple:

> David Starcross and Moira come in for the evening and we drink odd quarter-bottles of whisky [...]. As always they warm me to the possibility of some kind of life. They are both indefatigably writing and publishing, getting more and more successful. [...] Moira is one of the few people I know who will speak to the point, who will say the thing she thinks in the language we are all afraid to use. She would drink with me but David (of whom she is nauseatingly fond) prefers coffee.[14]

The truth was far more messy.

Muriel didn't comment on Stanford's opinion of *The Comforters*. If his coolness suggested that he was trying to establish distance between them, that suited her well enough. In any case, his piece had appeared late, in August, simultaneously with the American reviews. The *New York Herald Tribune*, *New Yorker* and *New York Times Book Review* all loved the novel, as did the American Catholic press. Rachel MacKenzie thrust it in the direction of discriminating readers. John van Druten, a dramatist with a huge reputation in America, had written to Muriel congratulating her and they began corresponding. Ivan von Auw, of Harold Ober Associates, one of the most powerful New York agents and later a close friend, began dealing with Muriel's work in the States. During July she had written 'The Go-Away Bird' to complete her collection of stories. With *Robinson* finished, she had two new books ready within six months of publishing *The Comforters*, and her reputation was rocketing. Nevertheless, in both her professional and her family life, there were constant assaults on her equanimity.

During that summer, Muriel had a serious row with Stanford while writing 'The Go-Away Bird'. He asked to see it. A stiff and dutiful letter returned explaining that Father O'Malley had advised her not to reply. But she sent the story and, as she wrote to Stanford, so she warmed. The previous day, she reported, Alan Maclean had taken her to visit Edith Sitwell, holding court at the Sesame Club. Each evening at six, iced gin and grapefruit juice were dispensed to disciples. Dame Edith, then in her seventies, had presided, queenly in gold tunic and jewels. Muriel was impressed. The great Dame's hauteur, her reckless mixture of idiom, her sharp, salacious stories, all conveyed female power. Here was another of those women of the Old Testament, 'good and tough' like St Monica, glamorously eccentric.

Maclean, she wrote, saw her clearly: a generous-hearted egotist, a complicated and fascinating woman.[15] But that balance between the egotism of vocation and the maintenance of human warmth was proving difficult for Muriel. The previous Sunday, she told Stanford, she had suffered an unpleasant experience in her Camberwell church. Next to her, a foul-smelling man had fidgeted and brushed against her while she was trying to pray. When they had sat up before the Sanctus she had noticed that he was exposing himself. After this, Dame Edith had come as a breath of fresh air.

Flashers and detractors had much the same effect on Muriel: they violated her privacy and dignity and, in so doing, increased her resistance. It was important to her to be 'respectable', both socially and intellectually. She would not be abused or embarrassed. Yet for someone so acutely aware of corruption, there was a strange (and attractive) innocence about her. She gave, and expected, support and protection. Rational criticism she could take, indeed encouraged. Where she drew the line was with her publishers and agents whom she (not unreasonably) expected to be on her side.

'I do hope I did not depress you too much the other day', Paul Scott wrote, 'when I told you of my slight reservation about that particular aspect of ROBINSON.'[16] Scott's reaction to her crucial second novel festered in her mind for decades. This was the first work for which, as her agent, he was to negotiate terms with Macmillan. Already a published novelist himself – later hugely famous for his *Raj Quartet* sequence, on which *The Jewel in the Crown* television series was based, and *Staying On* – Scott was a man with a similar background to Muriel's: many working-class relations (including a dominant mother); a close, proud family, pleasantly eccentric; education at a small private school his parents could ill afford. Like Muriel, he had emerged alert to social discrimination and with indomitable personal industry bred from a horror of financial embarrassment. Both were driven by their muse. In many respects they were ideally suited and, indeed, became firm friends over the next few years. But this was a bad start. Scott had disguised his origins so well that he appeared to her as disdainful.

Forty years later she wrote up that encounter – which had taken place earlier on the same day as the meeting with Dame Edith:

[W]hen he read *Robinson* (if, in fact, he did read it) he wasn't at all impressed. He asked me to come and see him about it. My clothes were old-fashioned but my best. He sat there pontifically with my manuscript in front of him [. . .] and wondered, after all, what was this novel about. A man and a girl on an island? It was, in fact, about a lot more than that. As he spoke, Paul flicked the typescript of my novel across the desk towards me with a contemptuous gesture of his third finger and thumb. I fairly loathed him for that. I said: 'Don't represent me if you don't want to.' 'Oh,' he condescended, 'I'll see what I can do.'[17]

'Pontifically', 'contemptuous', 'condescended': the weary assumption of superiority, the egregious smile. Scott was certainly a charmer but he had picked the wrong woman on whom to exercise his languor.

She left his office fuming. 'The very thought of his *touching* my typescript now offended my guts.' But it was to be a classic 'nevertheless' sequence: Dame Edith 'brought a totally new dimension to my day. She [. . .] had no doubt whatsoever of what the artist in literature was about. High priests and priestesses: that's what we all were.' This was more like it. Arrogant? Yes: controlled, self-defining hauteur. And why not? This grand figure of English letters was not too proud to say how much she admired *The Comforters'* 'mysterious qualities'. Her arrogance was reserved for the philistines. When Muriel told the story of her treatment at Scott's hands, Dame Edith had the answer. '"My dear," she said, "you must acquire a pair of lorgnettes, make an occasion to see that man again, focus the glasses on him and sit looking at him through them as if he were an insect. Just look and look.'"[18]

*

Exhausted from six months' continuous writing, Muriel went to Edinburgh for a rest, only to discover more anxiety. Aged nineteen, Robin had completed his schooling and faced the prospect of immediate call-up for National Service. Muriel wrote to Stanford about a flood of resentment she detected in her son, directed against herself and her mother, attributing this to the morbid influence of the boy's father. But she did not react.[19] Barney, she wrote, was 'marvellous – takes no part in the transactions, simply reads the paper', and Muriel, too, abstracted herself. Work kept her steady. Although outraged by Robin's behaviour towards Cissy, she could not admire the woman's idolatry of her men: '[S]he takes these things so badly – makes the great mistake of putting all her hopes on Robin or (as previously) my brother. She has a powerful loving nature, very sacrificial, and simply lays herself on the altar. Fortunately, she can treat me as more of a friend because she does not dote upon me quite so much as on the male progeny.'[20] As someone who cherished the company of intelligent women, it saddened Muriel to discover only twittering inconsequence in Cissy. She was the classic female victim, ubiquitous in Muriel's fiction, courting her own immolation. Where Muriel responded to Robin simply by informing him that he was a pain in the neck, Cissy wept and proclaimed that all the citizens of Edinburgh would rise up to defend her. It was a curious spectacle.

Since Sergeant's departure, Stanford was the only friend who knew her family. Muriel could ask him to write to Robin and to her mother, to lift and share that burden. Robin would stick a carnation in his buttonhole in imitation of him. She appreciated his defence of the boy as sensitive and highly strung. 'Please give Derek our fond love', Cissy had written in July, 'he is so sweet [. . .] Of course while you have dear dependable Derek you are indeed alright.'[21] With impeccable ineptitude, she still believed that Stanford and her daughter were 'together' more than four years after their separation, and Muriel did nothing to disabuse her. It was a private matter. Shortly after this, Muriel and Stanford had

had their row and had ceased seeing each other altogether. His letters to her in Edinburgh, however, appear to have healed the wound. Hers progress from 'My Dear Derek' to playful endearments; his from 'My Dear Muriel' to 'Dear Best Dingbat'. He signed himself 'Bobby Boulter' and 'Peter Pussboots'. It was a game they had always played.

So it was that they entered the last lap of their difficult companionship. They renewed their occasional trips to St Albans. As Newman's sermons were already in print, they produced a synopsis for another volume, *Newman by his Contemporaries*, and took a £100 advance each from Macmillan. As a smack on the wrist to Scott, Muriel withdrew her short fiction from his agency, dealt with the bigger magazines directly, and left the smaller fry to Stanford. Autumn had begun badly and she was pleased to reclaim his support.

When Scott passed on the first two chapters of *Memento Mori*, Maclean thought them 'enchanting' – but refused an advance until half the book was written. Muriel was incensed. They were proposing the same deal for *Memento Mori* as they had for *The Comforters*: 'and so I decided, never again. No decent writer would do it.'[22] Damn them, she thought: it was humiliating. If they couldn't do better than this, Scott must find her another publisher. He replied with airy patronage, calling her in again, explaining as though to a child that 'life isn't really as simple as that.'[23] And indeed there was no alternative. She was forced to accept the terms, and a seething irritation with Macmillan took root. The margins of her letter from Scott are inked with furious doodles: cross-hatched, black enclosed spaces.

Muriel put her novel aside and took as much reviewing as she could get. She did not repine, and Lynn Carrick of Lippincott soon wrote to say how wonderful he thought those opening chapters. Certainly she must stay on their list and he would arrange a contract through von Auw. As American sales of *The Comforters* had only been modest (1,500 copies), this was generous, and she appreciated his enthusiasm. Scott was negotiating a small Lippincott advance on *Robinson* and a larger one on *Memento Mori*.[24] Macmillan then promised to publish *Robinson* and the short stories in the new year (summer and autumn). Although in the short term she remained penniless, her future as a novelist seemed secure. During the tax year 1957/8 she earned just £108. Stories old and new were posted off in relays. She counted them all out and she counted them all back: 'Rejections are coming in fast,' she reported, '3 in 2 days.' But this letter to Stanford was gaily optimistic. They had just been for a campfire picnic to their St Albans copse, and were planning another excursion the following weekend. She enclosed a copy of 'The Black Madonna' for him to forward to Greene, hoping for the best.[25] With the Lippincott news, the clouds had lifted and she was on her way again, rejoicing.

*

Robinson was published on 26 June 1958, when she was in the middle of her final contretemps with Stanford. Corrected proofs had been returned in February, just after her fortieth birthday. Sometimes she liked it,[26] sometimes she did not.[27] So much in it was the translation of images which had welled up unbidden. It touched on her own transition from agnosticism to Christianity, her hallucinations, female empowerment, isolation and community. In those days she knew little of Dante or of opera[28] yet the book was operatic in its melodrama, circling restlessly round that Dantean theme of entering the tenebrous wood of middle life, echoing Rossini's *La Cenerentola* which she had seen and loved during that traumatic 1953 visit to the Edinburgh Festival.

The plot is simple enough: January Marlow, Tom Wells and Jimmie Waterford are the survivors of a plane crash on an island. Robinson, who owns the eponymous island, nurses them back to health, and halfway through, disappears, presumed murdered from a trail of blood and clothes leading to the 'Furnace', a ghastly volcanic pit. Towards the end he returns. No explanation or motivation is offered for his hoax. At first, January is furious with him because he had left her in the company of two possible killers and Robinson's distraught adopted son, Miguel. During Robinson's absence, Wells attempts to bully her into signing a document saying Robinson has committed suicide and, when she refuses, steals her journal and tries to murder her. With Robinson's 'resurrection', order is restored and rescue arrives. A year later, January reads that the island has sunk and that he has removed himself to another place of exile. Round this narrative is the frame of her past and future life – her sisters, Julia and Agnes, her two brothers-in-law – Curly Lonsdale (a vulgar bookmaker), Ian Brodie (a sadomasochistic cradle Catholic) – and her son, Brian.

It is a puzzling story: a sequence of apparently unrelated vignettes spliced with excerpts from the heroine's journal. Although it looks like a realist novel, it plainly is not. January scrutinises the 'facts' but the facts will not explain the reality. She constantly changes her interpretation of data, laying out lists of events and possible motivations for the protagonists' actions and reactions, but the link between intention and action, cause and effect, collapses. It is the arbitrary nature of Robinson's disappearance which troubles January most. *Robinson* is a 'mystery story' but it is more a story about the sense of mystery in the material world, about the shortcomings of the rational mind, than a puzzle with answers. The reality of life on the island when she thinks Robinson has been murdered is quite different from the reality when she knows he has not.

This, of course, was an issue at the centre of Muriel's thinking. It was the problem presented by Job: 'At the point where human reason cannot reconcile the fact of evil with the goodness of God, an anthropomorphic conception of God breaks down.'[29] Robinson might well be construed as a God-figure, in whose absence chaos reigns. He is unknowable. One of the transitions January undergoes is to learn to appreciate him. At first he appears to her as an inflexible control freak. Later she sees his reserve as positive and discovers similar characteristics in herself: the desire not so much to 'preserve distance [...] as to prevent intimacy'. 'I like', she says, 'to be in a position to choose, I like to be in control of my relationships with people.' So did Robinson (so did Muriel) – and his refusal to subject himself to January's attempts to sum him up ultimately becomes a virtue. Both suffer a 'fear of over-familiarity'.[30] His island divides into what is known and cultivable, and what is mysterious and fearful. The narrative voice itself is divided between that of the artist and that of the rational Catholic opposed to paganism. What joins them is the sense of mystery in the Catholic faith epitomised by the heroine's rosary (a visual leitmotif Muriel was keen to emphasise on the dust jacket where the cross of the rosary doubles as the wrecked plane). The symbolism, she felt, might only be clear to Catholics but she liked the idea.[31] January Marlow, like Caroline Rose and Muriel, is a Catholic convert and a writer struggling to transform an old life into a new one. The dating of January's stay on the island, from plane crash to rescue, corresponds almost exactly with the period between Muriel's emergence from breakdown and her visit to Stanbrook Abbey: 10 May–8 August 1954.

Muriel shared many of January's characteristics. When her heroine says: 'A woman in my position can easily let herself in for ridicule',[32] one hears the voice of Muriel's letters. There was the time when her crazed next-door neighbour had followed her down Camberwell New Road screaming that Muriel was a scarlet woman. Muriel seemed to think herself prone to such insults.[33] There was the flasher. There was always the Tom Wells syndrome. As an attractive woman, she was plagued by men, particularly married men, who misread her gaiety as sexual invitation. And then there were those disapproving voices haunting her life and her reciprocal desire to double-bluff, to lay false trails for the self-righteously nosy. Like Muriel's, January's creative mind is Proustian: 'some word or thing, almost a [sic] sacramental, touches my memory, and then the past comes walking over me as we say an angel is walking over our grave, and I stand in the past as in the beam of a searchlight.'[34] It is precisely this exiting from 'real time' which leaves both character and author feeling vulnerable when confronted by materialist philistines. The sense of threat which permeates the novel is not simply the threat of rape or murder, of physical intimidation. More subtly it is the threat of appropriation by those compromising the freedom to reinvent oneself. Muriel and her heroine both have grandmothers from Hertfordshire and adult sons from a brief marriage; both are poet-critics with a sharp tongue for the insolent; both are devoted to a Persian cat called 'Bluebell', both suffer from mood-swings and fear guns. There is even a reference to a bogus fortune-teller: 'Muriel The Marvel with her

X-ray eyes. *Can read your very soul.* Scores of satisfied clients ...' – and to a 'Brother Derek'.[35]

So private a person was Muriel, however, that the connections between author and subject seemed oblique, even to those who knew her well. Some of the personal references no one but Stanford could have recognised. Only he knew that Muriel had endured moments during her breakdown when she could not stop crying, just as January weeps uncontrollably on seeing the wreck of the aeroplane. He discussed the novel at length in letters. As the rejected lover, he saw its subject as the death of romance, epitomised by the sinking of the island. The plane crash and subsequent terror also seem to symbolise January's spiritual transformation, drawing on Muriel's state of mind after her Catholic instruction and her delusions: the point at which all that had been known became strange, the point of transition between the natural and the supernatural. And, like most of Muriel's fiction, *Robinson* investigates female identity, the island here recalling that 1949 letter in which she spoke of herself as an island which men tried to colonise.[36] All of these themes seem to intertwine: the death of romance, the acceptance of faith and the emancipation of her voice as a free woman.

Behind everything, perhaps, lay the 'only question'. Few writers better describe the bleakness of the human condition, the collapse of anthropomorphic notions of God. Yet no writer was more sensitive to the thrilling mystery of consciousness, to the intersection of the supernatural with the natural world, red in tooth and claw. And across that gap, between hope and despair, sparks the electricity of faith and of mystery: 'mystery' in the religious sense, and 'mystique' in the Proustian sense of the strange sacramental aura of otherwise perfectly ordinary things and words. Robinson the island is both substantial and insubstantial, a place of transitions like Prospero's territory in *The Tempest*. 'In a sense', January concludes, 'I had already come to think of the island as a place of the mind. [...] It is now, indeed, an apocryphal island. It may be a trick of the mind to sink one's past fear and exasperation in the waters of memory; it may be a truth of the mind.'[37] *Robinson* is another novel about conversion. Going about her business in the King's

Road, 'sipping [her] espresso', 'feeling not old exactly, but fussy and adult', the memory of the island flashes up and 'immediately all things are possible'.[38] These are the last words, echoing Gabriel's last words to Mary after the Annunciation: 'with God nothing shall be impossible' (Luke 1:37). It was an important statement for Muriel.

*

Macmillan launched the novel quietly with a half-page advertisement in the *Bookseller.*[39] It was generally well received, most reviewers agreeing that the characterisation and dialogue were sharp. Notices divided, however, according to their patience or otherwise with its symbolism. The *TLS*'s opening shot – 'a finely written, suggestive, and irritating book' – might summarise the attitude of the impatient: 'Is some kind of symbolism really intended? Or allegory? Or, more simply, what is she really getting at?'[40] This (predominantly male) approach found Muriel's imagination vivid but undisciplined. Others were equally baffled but content to relish originality. The *Daily Mail, Spectator, Time & Tide* and *New Statesman* all applauded. Honor Tracy gave the book long and serious treatment in the *Listener.* The Catholic press praised it. Penelope Mortimer recommended it to *Sunday Times* readers as 'pungently written, amusing and adult'.[41] But perhaps Muriel's chief triumph was to capture another major critical voice, John Davenport, chief fiction reviewer of the *Observer.* Davenport, like Tracy, discovered not only a graceful artist but also a 'resourceful and original mind'. And he isolated one of the novel's central ideas: that life '"is based on blackmail". Herein may lie the clue to Miss Spark's odd morality play.'[42]

For those seeking only escapism *Robinson* was vaunted as a gripping desert-island mystery. For those in search of weightier material, it was noted for its scholarship and dark comedy:[43] 'There is a lot of fear in the book; there's a strange sense of evil. Miss Spark has [...] the gift of being able to [...] cut through time: so that her writing becomes like a piece of memory, blurred yet real, and a long way from the conventional novelist's picture postcard.'[44] Somehow she had again performed that most difficult literary high-wire act: to be reviewed as a novelist suitable for the public library and as a powerful voice of the avant-garde.

Anthony Bloomfield set *Robinson* above Beckett's *Murphy* in a *Books & Bookman* piece delighting in experimental writing. She was, he said, 'an author of as interesting and individual a talent as has revealed itself for a long while'.[45]

Muriel expected her publishers to capitalise on all this. They did nothing. There had not even been a 'launch party'. All such techniques were seen as vulgar salesmanship: the best-seller, Macmillan thought, should sell itself. It was more dignified to allow an author's reputation to acquire its own momentum. Frank Tuohy, Maclean's friend since their schooldays at Stowe, and soon to be Muriel's, was another talented young writer impatient with Macmillan's approach: no promotion, little cherishing of, or gambling on, talent. It was, he said, a 'gentleman and players' firm.[46] The Macmillans were the gentlemen; the players were the writers: oddballs politely refused entry to the pavilion. Writers, the gentlemen assumed, should be grateful for the honour of the imprint and should certainly not reveal their vulgarity by requesting a living wage. That, at least, was how Muriel felt she was treated. And she had an additional problem with her editor. Maclean was charming but something was clearly wrong with him. During the previous October, she had been informed that he would be temporarily unavailable because he was entering hospital for a week. In fact, he was entering Dr John Dent's clinic for large injections of apomorphine as a cure for alcoholism. Beneath that jolly exterior, he was a depressive. His brother's defection had wounded him badly. For some time he had begun drinking first thing in the morning.

In his brave and self-effacing autobiography, Maclean tells the whole story, recording an early conversation with Dent:

'Do you get through the day without falling over?'

'Yes, I have a job which I do quite well.'

'You mean you think you do it quite well.'

'Well, I haven't got the sack yet.'

'Not yet. What do you do after your waking-up drink?'

'Look for my clothes.'

'D'you remember where you've been the night before?'
'Sometimes.'[47]

Like most alcoholics, he thought no one had noticed. Muriel had, and was at first sympathetic. She was instinctively supportive of those with a fragile nervous constitution. But this empathy had led her into disastrous relationships with Solly Spark and Stanford. Having no protection from the world but her own talent, she came to see Maclean's blunders as imperilling her livelihood. After a major row in 1960, he was replaced as her editor. This seemed to make it easier for them to be friends, and they remained close for over thirty years – until, on Muriel's recommendation, he was interviewed for Stephen Schiff's 1993 *New Yorker* profile of her. Schiff asked him about her hallucinations. 'She was', Maclean declared, 'really quite batty. [. . .] When she was doing the *Observer* crossword, she believed that the answers to the clues were messages mocking her. And she thought I was one of "them" – "them" being the people who were planting the clues. For a long time afterwards, when she was under pressure she would react very badly. She would feel that people and things were against her.'[48] For Muriel, this was the final insult and Maclean joined Stanford in her menagerie of bêtes noires, the unforgivables.

The reviewer who described *Robinson* as full of 'fear' was surely right, but one should add that it is fear confronted and overcome. Again, a central female figure is threatened – by Tom Wells's violence and insolence, by Robinson's authority, by the agonies of isolation generally – and she finds the strength to live alone once all those who surround her have become strangers. Muriel's suspicion of betrayal remained with her for life. Nearly all those friends from her earlier lives became strangers.

*

Rayner Heppenstall was not Muriel's sexual type but she was attracted to him as a serious artist. His novel *Blaze of Noon* had just appeared in paperback and, an acute and encouraging editor, he ran the BBC's slot for radio drama. Treating her as an intellectual equal, he would tear into any subject regardless of offence. All this she relished: the liberal mind at work. She and he had much in common and, since he was married, she thought there was small danger of untoward incidents. Everything came to a head, however, on 31 May 1958 when she invited him to lunch at Baldwin Crescent. He had arrived bearing a bottle of gin, knocked back most of it, and attempted to seduce her. Robinson had suddenly become Tom Wells. It was an intensely embarrassing situation, compromising their professional relationship.[49] She was anxious that Mrs Lazzari might have heard the commotion. To raise her spirits Muriel went straight out and bought an expensive dress, only to discover that the shopgirls had swindled her.

When she wrote to Stanford about all this, he laughed it off. As 'a softly softly boy myself', he said, 'I am sorry Rayner made such a full attempt.' He wasn't mocking her, he insisted, but he found the spectacle amusing because 'Rayner is partly interested in you (with an eye to everything amorous doing), you are interested in Rayner (with an eye to anything doing in radio). So, in a sense, you are both, in part, of course, only – using each other.'[50] She received this letter having just returned from a tooth extraction. While waiting, she had sat in a café trying to boil down Stanford's tangled story, 'The Dug-Out'. His facetiousness did not go down well – but she did not fling it back in his face. Yes, she accepted, there was a sense in which he was half right about her and Heppenstall half using each other. Nevertheless, his behaviour was unacceptable: 'All I know is 1) I don't like violence & I don't like insults, and 2) my work is jolly good and normally I don't think of using people to promote it [...]. 3) There are interesting sides to Rayner besides his "uses", but he is a self-iconoclast in that he destroys his own virtues underneath your eyes.'[51] Stanford, she knew, had troubles of his own: still suffering stomach pains, quietly breaking down. He had taken Muriel's advice and begun seeing Father O'Malley, was arranging to attend a psychiatrist at the Middlesex Hospital. There was the general sense of his entering the dark wood with nothing much achieved. What she did not know, however, was that he had, at last, found another woman.

Just as he had with Muriel and 'Good-bye Bohemia', Stanford

attempted an autobiographical novel about his new love in which she appears as leading lady.[52] During January 1958 a young American had come in late to his contemporary poetry class at the City Literary Institute. Dark-haired, poised and pretty, she had made an impact. Stanford had recognised her immediately. He and Muriel had met her at a party at the Braybrookes' house in Hampstead. She was related to John Rosenberg, and the Rosenbergs were a regular part of their social circle. Elizabeth Rosenberg, under Neville's influence, had become a Catholic. John, a New York Jew by birth, was an Anglophile agnostic, novelist, reviewer, script reader and publisher who later became a distinguished TV drama producer. Muriel promoted his novel *The Desperate Art* in her letters to van Druten. And they shared many acquaintances: Brooke-Rose and Peterkiewicz, Scott, Maclean, Kay Dick, and Terry Kilmartin of the *Observer*. The Rosenbergs had attended Muriel's parties at Baldwin Crescent. So when Stanford asked his student to stay behind after that class and invited her out, he must have known that gossip would spread. To Muriel he said nothing, terrified of her reaction.

Elizabeth Rosenberg recalled the situation clearly.[53] Stanford had appeared odd to her: dandyish, ostentatious, aping the manners of the upper classes, an inappropriate partner for Muriel. The young woman had lodged with the Rosenbergs for a few months. Stanford took her out every week – and she dated other men, too, without telling him. Although she came from a well-to-do New York family, was beautiful and superficially self-confident, she had led a sheltered life. In London, after leaving the Rosenbergs and taking a flat on her own, she apparently decided to let loose a little. Stanford's attention flattered her because he appeared to be a prominent writer, on easy terms with Christopher Fry. For his part, Stanford found her refreshingly frank and sexy. Then it began to get serious.

From January to May 1958, Muriel and Stanford had been sharing their troubles by post. She had been poleaxed by 'flu, throat and ear trouble, and an abscess on the gum which had finally sent her to that dentist. As usual, she had not taken to her bed, had even managed in

April to resume *Memento Mori* and to write a chapter in a week. But she was clearly low. Why didn't he ring?[54] Was he ill? What was his news? There was an extended bus strike, forcing her to take the claustrophobic Tube for visits to central London. Alan Barnsley had been scampering around bad-mouthing her and a row had blown up over this. She was anxious about *Robinson*'s future. Under the circumstances, Stanford's support was a resource, albeit a slender one. '[W]hen travelling abroad alone,' January remarks in *Robinson*, 'it is wise and actually discreet to take up with one well-chosen man on the journey. Otherwise, one is likely to be approached by numerous chance pesterers all along the line.'[55] Muriel also acted on this advice. The burden of Stanford's frustrated desire had fallen away and he could now fill the useful role of escort, keeping other men at bay. He had, she believed, accepted this – and indeed he had. He supplied her with a 'fool', licensed to say things she would not take from others, and a foil to other 'pesterers'. In return, she spoke freely to him, commented on his work and generally propped him up. Her recent enquiries, however, had met with silence.

Suddenly, in mid-May, he sent Muriel a shocking letter. If she were thinking of going to the Rosenbergs on Thursday, he wrote, she should know that he was 'extremely attached' to the young American. 'I tell you this, because I would not have people take advantage of you by trying to tell you something which they think you may not know.' He wasn't, he added, sure how much the Rosenbergs knew – but of course they knew everything. Stanford, also due to attend, had cancelled:

I have been an imperfect friend to you [. . .] but many times have spoken & acted to maintain your name. [. . .] Between us, you know, there loomed always the shadow of dear old Holy Mother Church [. . .]. I want, at the moment, to be rather alone.[56]

The letter was shocking, not because it revealed a lover, but because it placed Muriel in a false position. But if this was his attempt to terminate his role as escort, it failed. Muriel replied politely, saying she had 'no possessive feelings'[57] and the postal friendship resumed. He continued to act as agent for her short pieces. She remembered him at Mass, proposed more jaunts, and missed him.[58] The whole question of the new woman was dropped – although she did not go away. Not yet, at least.

A lot was not being said here. Stanford and Muriel were, of course, in part using each other. His lover told Elizabeth that Muriel was so jealous, she had set spies on her and Stanford, a nonsense possibly deriving from his neurotic imaginings. Perhaps Stanford was trying to provoke a row to clear space for his new relationship. Perhaps his lover had insisted ... Faced with Muriel's implacable loyalty, however, he was confounded. A secretive creature, Stanford was constitutionally incapable of saying anything straight. He still cared for and admired her but he had no future as her partner. And there was this beautiful young woman, apparently infatuated and doubtless irritated by Muriel's inexplicable hold over him. Muriel had no desire to become embroiled in this fiasco. Stanford's amatory adventures were entirely his business and she refused to be cast as an unrecognisable character in someone else's melodrama. All she required was honesty. The difficulty was that, in public, they still presented themselves as a couple.

Wherever Muriel looked among her friends, domestic and professional complications sapped creative power. Psychosis, religious mania, alcoholism and a train of prams in the hall seemed to greet her at every turn. Scott and Barnsley both had difficult marriages, children and full-time jobs. John Rosenberg was trapped in the drudgery of script-reading and report-writing for MGM who rarely bought anything,[59] Wrey Gardiner was a picturesque wreck, Stanford cracking up, and Heppenstall self-destructive. Iris Birtwistle, once a productive poet, now had three babies and had become the guardian of a twenty-year-old depressive. Muriel had assisted with the latter, escorting her to and from the Maudsley psychiatric hospital. It was another distressing case. The young woman, Muriel reported, seemed perfectly sane to her, indeed bright. It was just that she had been shoved about:[60] an assessment that was both far-sighted and inaccurate. The woman *had been* psychotic, spending hours screwed in a ball on the floor, screaming. Soon, however, she developed into someone remarkable. Her name was

Jini Lash. She became a novelist, painter, sculptor, and the mother of the famous Fiennes clan: Ralph, Joseph, Martha, Sophie and Marcus.

*

That summer Muriel completed *Memento Mori* about a month after *Robinson*'s publication, and corrected proofs of *The Go-Away Bird and Other Stories*. She expected to start on the Newman book with Stanford in September. *Memento Mori*, she instructed Scott, should be published in a much bigger way and suggestions for constructional changes would be unwelcome. She was withdrawing from dangerous intimacies. Increasingly, she saw virtue in simple good manners and reserve. Barnsley and Heppenstall, both married, sought a closeness to her she could not reciprocate.[61] She visited Heppenstall, then kept her distance. He took rejection badly: 'I am empty, miserable, anxious and unwell. [...] How hostile you have been lately. Do you turn on people when they betray weakness? For this started before I showed disappointment with "Memento Mori". You *have* a cold, arrogant, spiteful, rather mad side [...] but of course you have other sides too, and I love you very much. Are you coming here?'[62] No, she was not. Heppenstall was on holiday with his wife in Suffolk. The nun and the tigress were precariously balanced in Muriel's nature. The two sides of her psyche, the Catholic and the sceptic, the respectable lady rising in fury to defend her reputation and the bohemian artist, were often at odds. Self-defence was an instinct.

To Stanford alone she could speak of such things in her jolly, slangy letters. Praising 'The Go-Away Bird', he had warned her against avoiding 'the pain of being human'[63] and she took the point. Entering ancient minds in her novel had been a humbling experience. Teresa Walshe (her fellow tenant at Baldwin Crescent, a nurse), Maclean and Barnsley had provided details of geriatric wards. 'They fascinate and terrify me,' she wrote to Scott. 'I visualise myself one day occupying a bed as Granny Spark.'[64] It was not that she did not feel the pain of being human, it was just that in order to cope with it in her work she transformed it into comedy.[65] Some things, however, were simply not funny – and the death of her cat was one of them.

Bluebell was put down in mid-August after six weeks of distress. Although Muriel thought it 'plain silly', she had 'a sort of mystique'⁶⁶ about her. Bluebell had been her closest companion since the bleaker days at Aylesford Priory, insinuating herself among Muriel's papers, sitting on her shoulders as she wrote, watching birds from the window. Muriel understood cats. She wrote reviews of cat books, 'Cats are Arche-types. I myself, if I did not already have a religion would certainly worship the Cat [...]. Insofar as cats are inscrutable, unobliging and swift to pounce, they are undoubtedly godlike. [...] Sensible cat books are devoted to praising the cat for its catness [...].'⁶⁷ In the human world, Muriel's 'catness' could appear threatening to those who wished to possess her. When she spoke of Bluebell, it was not as of a pet but as of an equal or doppelgänger.

'My perfect cat', she wrote some years later, 'was a late Persian called Bluebell; she was delicate in health and of small dimensions; she had no rival for wit and understanding; she glowed before rain with a blue unearthly light; she was a gifted clairvoyante, [...] leaped for joy at good news: she would sit on my notebooks if what I had written therein was all right [...] I have never seen her equal for catness, charm and radiance.'⁶⁸ This was love. Yet the letters describing Bluebell's death are utterly unsentimental. Close attention is paid to raw detail: to the stink from the pus in the ear, the last twitching of the paws, the glazed eyes.⁶⁹

Simultaneously, Stanford also died from her life. At the very point when they were due to begin their Newman book, he went missing. Scott couldn't find him. Muriel had (not without ironical affection) dedicated *The Go-Away Bird and Other Stories* to him and by mid-September was holed up in Aylesford again making a start on her fourth novel, *The Ballad of Peckham Rye*. A letter from her mother suggests Stanford's final betrayal. 'You came to Edinburgh so bright and happy,' Cissy wrote, 'it was a pity you were upset. I know it takes a while to feel oneself again.'⁷⁰ During August, Stanford had visited the Cambergs while covering the Festival⁷¹ and had, it seems, mentioned Muriel's hallucinations. When she disappeared to Aylesford, Stanford (obviously avoiding her) came into town to see Scott, and wrote explaining that he could not cope with his half of their book. Seeing Muriel made him ill: 'the last time we met I was laid up with dreadful agony, continual vomiting & all the trimmings.' Perhaps sensing the imperfect nature of the compliment, he stressed his 'long affection' for her. Muriel was not convinced (on the envelope she scribbled something uncomplimentary).[72]

Michael Swan was at Aylesford and Muriel took him out. This elegant, talented writer had cut his throat. It was, she informed Stanford, a heart-rending spectacle. Scratching odd words on a slate, Swan tried to explain himself. Muriel did her best to inspire him with her resilience. He told her his brain was 85 per cent impaired; she told him to concentrate on the 15 per cent that still functioned. His agony was to her a ghastly (and religious) mystery. Swan scribbled 'Despair' on his slate. The only time she saw him smile was when she remarked that no one understood anyone else.[73] At this he shook his hands above his head. All anyone could do was to pray but, as Muriel guessed, nothing could retrieve his desire to live. (His next suicide attempt was successful.) She was moved, so moved that the encounter revived her sympathy for Stanford's delicate mental health. The tone of her letter is conciliatory, gently supportive.

Echoes of malicious gossip, however, persisted. Stanford, far from leaving her life, continued to capitalise on her fame by planning an article on her and Barnsley. Barnsley called on Heppenstall who wrote to Muriel about this 'curious and, it seems, elaborately calculated visit':

> [. . .] My interest in the conversation was that of trying to find out whether you were heading for another breakdown. From a number of obser- vations and indeed from your statements about yourself, this had begun to seem a real and worrying possibility. Any attempts to raise a giggle at your expense were Barnsley's. He was, for instance, very droll about your parties [. . .] the nastiest little creature it has ever been my misfortune to meet. [. . .] I think you are fascinated by evil. I am not. [. . .] I think, too, that you like human relationships to be complicated. I don't.[74]

She then contacted Barnsley who admitted betraying her 'a little' to tease out Heppenstall's venom.[75] She would not have her private life discussed by these men. Barnsley, she insisted, knew nothing of it: he, like Heppenstall, was an hysteric.[76]

Muriel's patience with the whole pack of them was exhausted and that long-stifled resentment over Stanford's behaviour in Edinburgh finally exploded. How *could* he have revealed her breakdown to her parents? It was, she felt, unforgivable to divulge such a secret. She tried to forget it, saying she would attribute it to his illness. But she couldn't. As this long letter wore on, it chilled. Barnsley had told her about something else Stanford had kept hidden: that he planned to marry his lover. Stony congratulations were offered: how delightful it was to learn that he had enough money to support a wife: '– it must give you a sense of achievement. I do wish you had told me of this sooner. Of course it is no business of mine. But I am always interested in your welfare.' 'Best wishes once more,' she concluded. 'I'm dining with the Rosenbergs on Monday and perhaps they will tell me all about your news.' The next sentence is savage, translated from blessing to damnation by the under-lining of a single word: 'You can't do better than [her].'[77]

*

The Go-Away Bird and Other Stories received an excellent press over the next two months alongside *The Stories of Colette* and Kay Dick's *Solitaire*, Muriel's work usually coming off best.[78] With the Third Programme dramatisation of *The Comforters* on 17 December, *Memento Mori* due in March, and *The Ballad of Peckham Rye* already under way, she was securely launched. She bought a diamond ring, had a few hundred pounds in the bank, took out insurance on her manuscripts, and by late February had completed *The Ballad* before *Memento Mori* hit the bookstalls. Here, at last, was her triumph. She was a 'name', had power. It was, nevertheless, a time of mixed sensations. As she told Stanford, 'being so occupied keeps me like a country without a history, which is supposed to be O.K.'.[79] It wasn't, though. Not entirely. For she had no family or lover with whom to travel this new road. The more famous she became, the less she felt she could trust her friends to be discreet. She could settle into no satisfactory relationship with Robin ('either irritated beyond endurance or falling over myself to make up to him'[80]) or with her parents. She was about to post Stanford to the outer circles of hell while still wanting an exclusive relationship, love, with a man, still half-wanting to be married at a time when the most important person in her life was her landlady. She had crowds of acquaintances. Nevertheless, she was forty and alone.

On 9 March 1959, Stanford entered hospital for a gallstones operation. Ten days earlier they had bumped into one another in a London street. As he was still hiding from her, he was covered in confusion. Having accepted a six months' deferment on the *Newman*, he had written nothing. He burbled; she listened, amused by his discomfiture. It is doubtful whether he told her that his lover had returned to America and that the plan was for him to follow, and to marry her. (He never went and soon married someone else.) Muriel's elegance appears further to have disconcerted him. 'How swagger you looked yesterday:' he wrote, deploying his worst 1890s charm, 'a most taking ensemble of effects!' – and went on to detail his imminent surgery.[81] They had parted on amicable terms – for the last time.

Muriel's reply was sharply sympathetic. For Stanford's mental health, she knew, he had to cure himself of morbid self-dramatisation (he was fearful of death on the surgeon's table). But released from moral obligation, she was content to assist him towards recovery with a playful boot up the pants. The tone of her letter is that of a character she had yet to create: Miss Brodie. Confidently dictatorial, self-consciously extreme, it instructs a lukewarm Anglican on the minutiae of Catholic teaching, while all the time whispering between the lines (between the teeth): 'I see through you.' 'If it is gall stones they are taking out', she wrote:

get them to keep them for you in a jam jar [...]. It is a moot point whether such stones and appendices [...] are counted as part of one's natural body at the Resurrection. [...] There is also the question of first teeth & the extracted second teeth. Do we rise again with two sets? So hang on to your stones, in case. Also warn them against removing any other fittings while the mood is on them.[82]

Stanford, she felt, had been a stone, an appendix in her life, constantly hindering. Recently, he had produced little but pain and embarrassment. The letter says two things simultaneously: 'Get well soon' and 'Get lost.'

CHAPTER 9

Exposure

1959–1960

Memento Mori remains one of the great novels of the 1950s: perfectly constructed, hilarious, tragic, wise, absurd. Easily accessible to the general reader, it offers wonderful stretches of farce and perhaps the most moving depiction of old age in British fiction. At its heart, and close to Muriel's heart, is the ancient Charmian Colston, another of Muriel's self-projections. She is not a self-portrait but Muriel was perhaps imagining through her the kind of future she might have endured had she married Sergeant or Stanford. Parallels between how Muriel came to see these men and her son, and how the novel depicts Charmian's husband and son, are difficult to avoid, yet when Muriel was writing the novel she was on amicable terms with both Stanford and Robin.

Recently she had invited Robin to London and toured him about her literary friends for a weekend. 'He looks very sweet in his [National Service] uniform,' she informed Stanford, 'and has some amusing army stories to tell. He doesn't mind it more than most.'[1] Everyone who met them together remembered her pride in her son. Now that he was an adult and was away from Edinburgh's provincialism, she hoped he might become a friend. *The Ballad of Peckham Rye* was dedicated to him 'with love'. In the summer of 1960, just before it was published, she took him to Nice for a week. Stanford, however, recalled an earlier occasion when she had asked him to place the kitchen knife outside on the window-sill before one of Robin's visits, and the Nice trip had been disastrous.

Writing *Memento Mori*, it was as though she knew what would inevitably happen, not because she was psychic but because she had a kind of death wish on all close relationships, a fear of exposure that led her to preserve distance and prevent intimacy. Boundlessly forgiving of human failure in general, she was boundlessly unforgiving of it when she saw it as obstructing her vocation.

Charmian is eighty-five: gentle, stylish, clever, another version of Caroline Rose or January sixty years down the line. As a celebrated Edwardian novelist she conquered the literary world and, although her reputation has declined, it is now reviving, much to the irritation of her husband, Godfrey. Their son, Eric, is fifty-six, neurotic, idle, and a failure. Trying to outdo his mother, he has just published his second novel but cannot compete. His whole identity, like his father's, is negative, defining itself through resentment of Charmian's talents and charm. Although she has had a stroke, has 'grasp of neither logic nor chronology'[2] and suffers from aphasia, perpetually calling Mrs Anthony (her housekeeper) 'Taylor', she remains a more engagingly intelligent human being than Eric.

Jean Taylor, Charmian's companion and maid for decades, had become accustomed to the smart life at her mistress's side. It had been a kind of marriage. Now crippled by arthritis, Jean lies in the Maud Long Medical Ward '(aged people, female)'[3] with eleven others, waiting for the end. A 'woman practised in restraint',[4] Jean finds her self-control here tested to the limit. Her previous social identity demolished, she must accustom herself to being part of this crazy Greek chorus and to being called 'Granny'. In all, they are twelve, like the disciples. The narrative is punctuated by their deaths and by the demise of the elderly Kensington gentlefolk beyond the hospital who each receive anonymous telephone calls saying 'Remember you must die.' Only the Catholics – Charmian, Jean Taylor, Granny Barnacle, Guy Leet – and Henry and Emmeline Mortimer, accept the message fearlessly. Most of the others misunderstand it and continue to behave with the competitive malice which has characterised their lives. At the still point of this Websterian nightmare we find the wisdom of Charmian and Jean. The relationship between them is the book's moral focus, made all the more poignant because they are never again allowed to meet.

Both are strong women surrounded by those who try to infantalise them. Both resist. Dignified, intensely private people, they suffer more from the 'lacerating familiarity'[5] of their minders than from their physical and mental damage. Both are Catholic converts and the Catholic contemplation of death is a defining principle, providing distance from an otherwise meaningless existence. Catholicism, as Granny Barnacle says, is a hard religion, but it allows laughter and celebration. Muriel was no proselytiser; she did not think of herself as a Catholic when writing, or write 'Catholic novels'. Nevertheless, Catholicism was now her natural frame of mind; it had released her from babel. The terror at the heart of her mature fiction is the opposite of this release: the horror of being rendered voiceless, anonymous, a prey to the power of strangers.

It is the immolation of identity that Charmian and Jean resist, and in order to do this they must betray misplaced trust – a theme repeated in *The Prime of Miss Jean Brodie*. Charmian leaves Godfrey; Jean reveals the long-held secret of Charmian's affair with the poet Guy Leet to protect her from blackmail. As with Caroline Rose and January Marlow, the freedom they claim is the liberty not to be ensnared in others' plots. Old age here is like wartime. The over-seventies exist in a corpse-strewn battlefield and as such, paradoxically, and despite their infirmities, see things more clearly. The law of gravity drags them down. Life, whatever one's class or comforts, becomes primitive. In this sense, it is a book about human vulnerability, a book of death, a remorseless stare into the chasm of what it is like to be *sans* everything. Periodically, otherwise strong characters break down and weep silently. But something else is also going on: the interplay between fact and fiction, truth and reality.

One soon detects, for instance, the instability of the narrative voice, sometimes suggesting external authority but in a tone of quizzical amusement, and sometimes the mental landscape and linguistic register of whatever character is being described. In fact, 'objective' narrative interventions are rare: we often switch sharply from vignette to vignette (each mainly in dialogue, as in Waugh's early writing) as though walking into the middle of a play, turning a radio dial, or tuning in successively to bugged rooms. When the narrator does speak directly to us, as at the beginning of Chapter 5, it is more likely to be unnerving than reassuring, full of swerving non sequiturs.

Towards the end we discover that there is no rational explanation for the telephone voices. They could represent any number of things. The idea of an untraceable, ever-expanding gang of malicious callers (male and female) is absurd. Are they, then, the projections of the listeners' minds? Alec Warner, a gerontologist, believes the phenomenon results from mass hysteria. This is possible. More weight, however, attaches to the interpretation of two other rational figures, Jean Taylor and Henry Mortimer: that the voices are those of Death itself. A metaphysical dimension thus emerges, and ultimately this becomes a literary question. The voices are a metaphor, parading themselves as metaphor, resisting deductive reasoning, and we are back in the realm of a reflexive, self-conscious postmodernism. The art of fiction, Charmian informs us, is 'very like the practice of deception'.[6]

In a cancelled preface to *The Prime of Miss Jean Brodie*,[7] and in several later interviews, Muriel repeated this idea. Fiction was not true and, although it offered an image of the truth, the fact remained that it was not fact. Matter was fact and she admired the Catholic Church for addressing the question of matter.[8] For Muriel, all these issues were interrelated: style, religious faith, and the relation of fiction to fact. There are facts but in themselves they relate merely to dead matter. One of these facts is that our bodies shall themselves become dead matter. Understanding is interpretation. Interpretation requires the fictionalising process to relate the elements of dead matter. This process must not be infected by sentimentality or the desire to instruct. *Memento Mori* is full of characters who reject matter. It ends with a quiet rebuke for them, a cold menu of mortal ailments, parodying the realist writer's closure, picking up Newman's 'What were they sick, what did they die, of?',[9] and it is related by Alec who has by this time himself suffered a stroke: 'Lettie Colston [...] comminuted fractures of the skull; Godfrey Colston, hypostatic pneumonia; Charmian Colston, uraemia; Jean

Taylor, myocardial degeneration [...].'[10] Nothing further need be said. The medical terms drape each corpse, masking it by reducing it to data. But it will not be masked in Muriel's work. For this novel focuses on a paradox. As Muriel put it in an interview with Venetia Murray: 'The prospect of death is what gives life the whole of its piquancy. Life would be so much more pointless if there were no feeling that it must end.'[11]

'Gautier wrote "I am a man for whom the visible world exists." That makes him an existentialist,' Muriel noted in 1997. 'There was a philosophical question "Do we exist?" going round. The answer is scientifically unprovable. In my *Memento Mori* Alec Warner asks Jean Taylor that question. The couple are out for a walk, passing a graveyard. She answers that the gravestones are proof that we do. Death proves life.'[12] The ingenuity of Muriel's deployment of 'Remember you must die' lies in the fact that none of the foolish characters believes it. To them it is simply a threat. Thus a parodic detective story unrolls in which the police seek the identity of the caller – or callers, for each person hears a different voice. As readers, we are sucked into this 'plot', desiring resolution, attempting to connect action with intention through a logical sequence of cause and effect leading us to the culprit. But it leads nowhere – except to return us to the unpalatable fact of our own mortality. One rises from this novel, as Peter Quennell wrote of Waugh's *A Handful of Dust*, 'as from a reading of one of the sterner and more uncompromising Fathers, convinced that human life is a chaos of inclinations and appetites, and that few appetites are strong enough to be worth gratifying.'[13]

Mrs Pettigrew, Charmian's rapacious third housekeeper, would have made a fine concentration-camp guard. Godfrey's eroticism has come down to a fishy stare at Mrs Pettigrew's stocking-tops. He can only enjoy his wife's company when she is discomfited, and a macabre link emerges in Muriel's work between violence and sex, between the need to hurt others and the desire for self-definition. There are so many deaths apart from that of the body: of sexual passion, of confidence, of reputation, records, identity. Yet this is a joyful novel. In Philip Larkin's poem 'The Old Fools' he asks of the aged, 'Why aren't they screaming?' In *Memento*

Mori, Muriel's grannies *are* screaming. They rise up against Sister Burstead, do not go gentle into that good night. The narrative champions Newman's doctrine of 'final perseverance'.[14] When Charmian makes a small mental recovery, this is 'in part, due to an effortful will to resist Mrs Pettigrew's bullying'.[15] Just as death gives life its piquancy, oppression breeds the power to subvert it. The evil in the world defines its goodness, lends strength to the subversive.

*

Memento Mori was a huge critical success in Britain. The young V. S. Naipaul described it in the *New Statesman* as 'brilliant, startling and original'; Greene and Waugh again provided plaudits for the dust jacket. 'This funny and macabre book', Greene wrote, 'has delighted me as much as any novel that I have read since the war.' Waugh thought it a 'Brilliant and singularly gruesome achievement' and commentators in the *Sunday Times, Listener, Queen* and *Observer* agreed: 'In *Memento Mori*, half Poe, half Powell, Miss Spark has established total rule over her inhabitants.' Her talent was described as 'quite exceptional', Elizabeth Jane Howard proclaimed that 'she has an original mind, writes beautiful English, and has an ear for dialogue sharper than almost anyone [...] excepting Henry Green.' 'This Death's Jest Book', John Davenport believed, 'will become a treasured possession for everybody past jiving age.'[16]

A month later, however, American reviews were again disappointing: another 'mixed bag', despite high praise from the *New Yorker*. Lippincott's Lynn Carrick was convinced of the book's quality, but while it had hovered briefly in the best-seller list in the UK, sales in the United States were again low. He had needed all his urbanity to persuade his board to contract immediately for *The Ballad of Peckham Rye* and *The Go-Away Bird and Other Stories*. The American ball was rolling but only slowly, and the reward was reputation among the discriminating rather than riches. Lippincott's advertisements always plugged the *New York Times*'s notice of *The Comforters*: 'Trend-watchers are advised to note the name of Muriel Spark. Before long they may be able to boast that they read her when ...'[17] They were still waiting.

Under the circumstances, Scott felt he could not reward Carrick's loyalty by pressing for higher terms. Macmillan were a different matter. They had only contracted for *Memento Mori* after its completion and Maclean had incurred Muriel's wrath by suggesting a rewrite of the opening paragraph. Although the row had been brief, a pattern was emerging. Sales were robust; they had the most talked-of novel of the season – and Macmillan's response, she felt, was to splash out on minuscule publicity. True, they had advertised in the *Bookseller* forecasting that this would be her 'breakthrough' novel. They had also arranged a book signing at Fortnum & Mason's with amusing display cards bordered in black. But that was the extent of their efforts, other than to recommend the interview with Venetia Murray who described Muriel as 'Plumpish, fair-haired and forty-ish [. . .] a little like Hermione Baddeley [. . .] with a jolly, motherly, buff-suited appearance.'[18] After that, Muriel had demanded close control of her public image, and had anticipated with relish Scott's squeezing Macmillan's gentlemanly pips until they squeaked.[19] This he duly did. The royalty rate was driven up and the advance doubled for *Ballad*.

Although she was forty-one and now established, Muriel was an innocent in the role of celebrity. At Fortnum's one reporter had noticed that, despite the 'macabre theme of her novel, Miss Spark turned out to be a bright and cheerful character who, when she was not signing copies [. . .], was helpfully wrapping Easter cards for customers who mistook her for an assistant.'[20] On the one hand, all this publicity business seemed absurdly removed from holy poverty and vocation. On the other, she needed fame to earn a decent living. It had been a long, hard road. Arrived at her destination, she wished to enjoy its comforts, and in that interview an intriguingly volatile personality emerges, by turns ascetic and sybaritic, shy and bold.

There is the artist-philosopher insisting that 'People don't think about death in time [. . .] or appreciate it' as a defining principle. She recommends the convent training of children to consider their mortality each night as 'an excellent thing'. There is the hedonist fantasising about buying Robin a sports car, 'a very noisy red one', and herself a wardrobe of Parisian clothes. There is the humble writer who lives in Camberwell, likes talking to her landlady and hates 'Europe'. Then, with equal suddenness, she becomes the woman of the world. She hates Europe and its 'scenery', she says, because, after Africa, 'you find all those lush meadows and mountains [...] terribly fake and artificial.' She preferred housing estates in the Home Counties. If she were to travel, she would go to South America and Mexico. The problem with Europe was the languages. How did she feel about writing? Well ... she loathed graphomania, spent only a few hours of her day on her novels. If she made money she would give up writing for a year or more. Did she have a 'message'? No. She wrote, she said, like 'an observer from another planet'.[21]

Murray describes this 'extraordinary' personality as 'egregious' – an unfortunate epithet given that it can mean either 'distinguished' or 'gross, flagrant'. Beneath the veneer of praise, Muriel detected venom. To describe her as 'plumpish [...] and forty-ish', 'jolly' and 'motherly' seemed spiteful. The general tone is of amused patronage, of a desire to play up her dottiness to play down her talent: 'There has been a tendency to review her fiction as if it were terribly highbrow', runs the byline, 'resulting in lower sales than she deserves. In fact her stories are quite straightforward [...].' One is left with the impression of a dizzy girl-ishness, as though there were something inappropriately coy about the whole performance.

This was Muriel's first major interview. She had chatted unwisely, as she might have with a friend, spinning fantastic responses for comic effect. Her experience of housing estates in the Home Counties was limited to Watford; she had never been to 'Europe'. Although she restricted her creative hours, many others were consumed by research and the mental preparation to write, by reviews, personal and business letters. She was industrious; writing was her business. Everything she had said was in its way true. It was true that she loathed 'scenery' and was sure she would dislike picture-postcard Europe. She certainly had a horror of the graphomania epitomised by Stanford (later lampooned as the *pisseur de copie* in *Loitering with Intent*). She had no 'message' in the sense of the Angry-Young-Man or social-conscience novels of her contemporaries. Nothing could be plainer, however, than the 'message' of *Memento Mori:* 'Remember you must die' – and in truth she was nearly killing herself writing two books a year in search of that break-through.

The American critics might have been waiting, but Muriel was not. That May, Macmillan struck a deal with Penguin. By early June she was on holiday with Robin and Father Brocard in Wales[22] to start her next novel, *The Bachelors*, and the first translation contracts had begun rolling in: Denmark, Sweden, Germany – all wanted her work. *Queen* and *Vogue* commissioned stories. She wrote another radio drama, *The Dry River Bed* and by August had finally got to Continental Europe. 'You would love S. Karnten,' Muriel wrote to Paul Allen in August 1959, 'huge Gothic mountains and yet the people are so gentle.'[23] She was in southern Austria, on the border of Yugoslavia, with Christine Brooke-Rose and Jerzy Peterkiewicz. Scarcely five months since the break with Stanford, her life had been transformed. Without exerting herself unduly she completed four chapters of *The Bachelors* and two short stories during her five weeks abroad. In the mountains she felt free – for a while at least.

*

Being an island, a country without a history, was perfect for composition but Muriel missed her London bachelors.[24] With one triumphant novel behind her, her mind ablaze with another, she sat in Austria and was almost, but not quite, happy. Her friends had invited her because she had seemed depressed and, while she appreciated their support, she did not wish to be regarded as someone who needed it. Brooke-Rose and Peterkiewicz were in Austria to work. They had made similar cheap excursions to Europe for some years to provide creative space. Brooke-Rose was deep in a novel about her hated father (former monk, thief and fornicator), *The Dear Deceit* (1960), and Peterkiewicz was writing a play. Much as Muriel valued the invitation, however, there was something uncomfortable about being a single woman in the company of lovers.

She spoke no German when she arrived: Brooke-Rose and Peter-kiewicz were both fluent. It would have been easy to have pottered in their wake but Muriel had no intention of playing the spinster goose-berry. Instead, she immediately set about mastering enough of the language to roam where she liked.[25] In good weather, the mountains glittered; in bad, the cloud shut down the view. The road from Vienna ran past the guest house and occasionally brought climbers and walkers. Few stopped. Small clutches of bronzed young campers braved the icy water, but there was little else for tourists to do. When the rain blew in from Yugoslavia, the locals joked (repeatedly) about Tito sending it over. As a lake resort, Ferlach was distinctly low-key: precisely right for a group of artists in search of silence.

In this changeable climate they wrote well and relished each other's company. At the end of the holiday, however, Peterkiewicz would have to return to his lectureship at London University's School of Slavonic Studies, and although Brooke-Rose had now established a powerful reputation with her 1958 critical book *A Grammar of Metaphor*, three novels, two prizes, and regular journalism, she had abandoned the search for an academic job and her literary income remained precarious. Muriel's situation was different. Better paid and comfortably freelance, in a state of near-permanent euphoria at her new freedom, she thought she might appear frivolous to her companions. In fact, she did not. All three worked separately, often in cafés, and would meet for meals. Brooke-Rose's and Peterkiewicz's routine had always been to remain largely silent over dinner, reflecting on the day's work in preparation for reading it to each other later. Muriel preferred to talk, often about her agents, contracts and earnings. She seemed to demand attention, which Peterkiewicz supplied. But that was all right. That was Muriel, and they loved her. There was always an endearing enthusiasm about her, a kind of knowing innocence. On one occasion at their first *Gasthaus*, the two women were working together at a wooden table. Muriel read out a passage which Christine considered ungrammatical, and said so 'with a smile, never thinking she'd object. She said, to my astonishment and also admiration: "If I write it, it's grammatical."'[26]

Muriel had her own discourse, which another tiny incident seems to point up. Brooke-Rose and Peterkiewicz had met her off the plane at Klagenfurt Airport, and they had boarded the local bus. In high spirits at the reunion, they were soon motoring through the countryside. Beyond the windows reared the Austrian Alps. Christine invited Muriel to comment, expecting her to be pleased. 'It's just like Wales,' came the reply – and they all laughed. To Christine, it was just another of Muriel's delightfully unexpected remarks. Although privately she thought it verged on bad manners in a guest and always remembered it as oddly naive, she wasn't in the least offended. Even so, the phrase lingered in the imaginations of both women. Muriel detected reservation and found it amusing that anyone should think her comparison inappropriate. She really *did* see Austria as Wales writ large,[27] didn't care for 'scenery', and almost immediately put the dialogue into a short story she wrote there, 'A Member of the Family'.[28]

In this story, Austria acts as a backdrop to the first meeting of two women who might be read as refracted versions of Muriel and Brooke-Rose. Muriel took random memories – the landscape, the sense of slight disapproval, the comparison with Wales – and connected them. Many of her heroines image not how she saw herself but how she saw others as observing her. The 'Muriel figure' here, Trudy, is a silly creature, the 'Brooke-Rose figure', Gwen, a knowing schoolmistress impatient with her friend's frivolity. Both are approaching thirty but Trudy, determinedly the more girlish, knocks seven years off her age when introduced to an eligible man. Trudy, like Muriel, is interested in men; Gwen is a caustic bluestocking spinster. The eligible man is Richard, a fellow teacher at Gwen's school, who has supposedly turned up by coincidence. Gwen seems to know him well (he kisses her on the cheek) and his mother even better. Trudy and he begin an affair and continue it at home. Here Muriel draws on another set of experiences – with Stanford. Richard will never introduce Trudy to his mother; he is charming but secretive, avoids the subject of marriage. Eventually he invites her to his home and she discovers that she is one of many lovers or ex-lovers

Adelaide Uezzell (née Hyams),
Muriel's maternal grandmother

Muriel's maternal grandfather,
Tom Uezzell, with her mother,
Sarah (Cissy)

Muriel's paternal grandparents, Louis and Henrietta Camberg

The Watford shop of all sorts

Cissy's brother, Philip, and his wife, Alice: Muriel's Watford aunt and uncle

Cissy, Philip and Bernard (Barney) Camberg, with Harry, Cissy's brother (in uniform), during the First World War

James Gillespie's Girls' School, Junior Class, 1930: Muriel is 3rd row, 2nd from right; Frances Niven (Cowell), 3rd row, 3rd from right; Miss Christina Kay, centre

CROWN FOR YOUNG POETESS

Muriel Camberg, of James Gillespie's Girls' School, being crowned at the Ideal Home Exhibition in Edinburgh. She won the silver crown presented by the Heather Club for the best poem commemorating the death of Sir Walter Scott.

Muriel aged ten aboard her fairy cycle: 'It was £3. [My father] had to earn that money. Almost a week's pay. He had to save it for me.'

Muriel being crowned as 'Queen of Poetry' in 1932 by the actress Esther Ralston, and being made to feel 'like the Dairy Queen of Dumfries'

Philip Camberg, Muriel's brother

Cissy and Barney Camberg,
Muriel's parents, 1940s

Muriel in 1940

Muriel with her son, Robin, in
Africa, early 1940s

May 1948: the picture Muriel gave
to Howard Sergeant

Howard Sergeant and his second wife, Jean,
early 1950s

Muriel with Derek Stanford, early 1950s

Photograph released to the press of 1948
poetry reading at Christmas Humphreys'
house, supporting Muriel after she was
sacked from the Poetry Society. *Left to right*:
Howard Sergeant, Derek Patmore, Muriel
Spark (obscured), Derek Stanford

Muriel's despatch book, October–November 1951, recording her first great literary success: winning the *Observer* Christmas short-story competition

Right: St Jude's Cottage in the grounds of Allington Castle, Kent, where Muriel began her first novel, *The Comforters*

Left: Edwina and Alan Barnsley (the novelist 'Gabriel Fielding')

Muriel and 'Tiny' Lazzari, her landlady, in the garden at 13 Baldwin Crescent, Camberwell, Muriel's London home from 1954 to 1965

Christine Brooke-Rose, late 1950s

Above right: Alan Maclean, Muriel's editor at Macmillan, 1954–80, and brother of the spy Donald Maclean

Right: Muriel in her Camberwell attic

Below, left to right: Elizabeth Rosenberg, June and Neville Braybrooke – all friends of Muriel's

Muriel leaving the Macmillan St Martin's Street offices, London, 1961

(including Gwen) who regularly take tea with his mother as 'members of the family'.

It is all beautifully ambiguous. Richard could be a Bluebeard, gay or bisexual, a combination of all three, or simply someone who will not marry. The tale celebrates ambiguity. Trudy is mocked for her naïveté, yet is more attractive than Gwen whose 'maddening imperturbable eyes' turn upon her friend 'as if to say, you are the unjust and I'm the just'.[29] Again we are back with the Sparkian paradox: the conflict between the analytical and the associative mind. Gwen 'knows' more than Trudy but lacks her capacity to reinvent herself. When Trudy decides she is twenty-one, she *is* twenty-one. There is a fragment of Muriel's psyche in both characters: the tough and sceptical woman and the sociable 'girl' (she often referred to herself as a girl at this time) who loved her accessories and delighted in paralysing people with charm. Indeed, after that Murray interview, Muriel had decided to rejuvenate herself. Photographs of her over the next decade appear to reveal her steadily increasing youth. Unlike Trudy, however, she did not do this to catch men but to maintain her independence, to escape the judgemental eye, and for the sheer pleasure of perfect form. It was a magnificent mask, a game, a defence. It was fun. It was her public image. If language was power, so too was beauty. As the artist at home, she would slop about in jumpers. When she left the safety of Mrs Lazzari's house or invited guests to it, she dressed to kill.

The other story completed in Austria was 'The Ormolu Clock'.[30] This, 'The Dark Glasses'[31] (written just before she left London) and 'The Curtain Blown by the Breeze'[32] (written on her return) form a trilogy. All deal with voyeurism. In the first, the topography of the lake town takes more abstract form as Muriel's imagination becomes attracted to familiar symbols: the narrow path leading up to the mountain, to the border. In this case, the path also separates the guest house in which the narrator is staying from the Hotel Stroh and, as the tale progresses, becomes the dividing line between success and failure, female and male, the observed and the observer, the just and the unjust. The bare bones of the narrative are simple enough and, indeed, were autobiographical.

Just a few feet from Muriel's window, across the path, a fat old man sat with field glasses and stared into her bedroom.[33] Nine days later, when the party had moved down the frontier to Seelach and all three had completed their work, Muriel wrote to Paul Allen again. Sitting on a café terrace beneath huge trees, facing an ancient Slovene church and graveyard, she was in benign mood. Graveyards always enlivened her. Allen had written ahead, so a letter was waiting for her on arrival. He was sending his autobiographical articles, then being published in the *Guardian*. This sense of integration with another's vocation was important to her.

After six ghastly months in 'publicity' with Taylor Woodrow (Muriel had drawn on his experience to flesh out Dougal Douglas's job in *The Ballad of Peckham Rye*), Allen had returned to schoolmastering. Muriel encouraged him in every aspect of his life: as an Irishman living in England; as a Catholic; as a creative 'personality'; as a teacher. In all his roles, she assured him, 'The more spirit you give out, the more you retain [...]. [...] You must wear your grand new clothes as a sign of your confidence [...].' She is grateful for his kind words, self-effacing, anxious that the new rewards for her writing might contaminate the purity of her vision. Although she was famous and Allen almost unknown, although they rarely met and he was a decade her junior, there was no hint of patronage. Rather, she found relief in being able to tap her own humility, to speak frankly. For a few months, Allen and his friends occupied the vacuum left by Stanford. 'A Member of the Family' she described as 'a little story for Vogue'. 'The Ormolu Clock' she thought rather better: it was, she informed Allen, about Frau Antonitsch's 'mighty character', and her confrontation with the peeping Tom. 'She is (in my story, I mean, for I have greatly enlarged her) an ambitious pagan, or perhaps not quite pagan – more like one of those terrifying women of the Old Testament – Judith, Miriam, Esther.'[34]

When Peterkiewicz had passed on Muriel's complaint, the voyeur (who was not the landlord) disappeared. In Muriel's story he becomes the landlord, and she transforms his correction into a subtler, crueller, revenge. The Muriel figure disappears to be replaced by the ferocious

Frau Chef who says nothing but places a valuable ormolu clock on the ledge above her window. Her competitor's trade has diminished in the face of her remorseless enterprise. To raise cash, he has been forced to sell this clock to her. Placing it outside, precariously balanced, conveys humiliating messages: 'You have no power over me. I shall be the victor. This clock, which you prized, is as nothing to me. You are a fool and now all the world can see it.' On reflection, Muriel thought that the clock echoed the head of Holofernes. It is another tale of female strength, linking us to all those 'good and tough' ladies throughout her writing. And it was a significant factor in her own empowerment because the *New Yorker*, having turned down all the other work she had sent, bought this story, inaugurating a long and fruitful association with the magazine.

Frau Chef outstares her voyeur. In an extraordinary scene, she sits (as Muriel did not) hour after hour facing the man with the binoculars trained upon her. 'The Dark Glasses' and 'The Curtain Blown by the Breeze' play variations on this theme. Both take as a motif an image of a membranous borderline between inside and outside, between vulnerability and power. In the first, there are two such borderlines: the dark glasses which conceal the narrator's eyes, and the rain-flooded window through which, as a girl, she had seen into the guilty secret of her interlocutor's life. In the second (Muriel's last African tale, developed from the shocking story she had heard in Southern Rhodesia), there is the fluttering curtain at an open window. The person outside, a twelve-year-old black boy, innocently watches a white woman suckling her child and is murdered for this impertinence by her husband. Ultimately the husband returns from jail to stare through the same window before murdering his wife and her admirer. Both of these strange, bleak tales focus on female violation. Their worlds are emptied of strong, protective men. Instead, we witness communities of women to whom their erratic males are little more than drones.

*

Judgement, watching and being watched, the sense of vulnerability to the gaze of strangers and the need to resist this – all were much on

Muriel's mind at this time. Post-Stanford, that sense of exposure seems to have intensified and with it, an equal and opposite reaction set in: the determination never again to allow anyone the power to embarrass her. With no man in her life now, she was alone with her bachelors, and joyfully so. But she would not be English-spinsterish. She would control the situation, reinvent herself. Now that she was in the driver's seat, she would drive.

Back in England, she left Macmillan and her agent in no doubt about this and storms with both firms began to rumble. In November she had caught Higham's out in sloppy accounting. The *New Yorker* breakthrough she had instigated herself by sending 'The Ormolu Clock' direct to Rachel MacKenzie. When it was accepted, she waited a month and then asked Higham's to return all the short stories they had unsuccessfully been trying to market. David Higham she considered 'an old wooffie behind moustaches'.[35] Her only reason for staying with the firm was to deal with Paul Scott – and he was due to retire at the end of March 1960 to take his chances as a full-time writer. Since April 1959 he had only been a part-time agent, her daily business passed on to Sheila Watson. As Muriel told Scott, her market value was steadily rising[36] and she felt she was not receiving enough attention to catch the tide of her growing reputation.

'I like purple passages in my life,' Muriel remarked in 1970. 'I like drama. But not in my writing. I think it's bad manners to inflict a lot of emotional involvement on the reader – much nicer to make them laugh and to keep it short.'[37] This gap between the life and the work registered a certain tension. Her talent fulfilled, she had never been happier but the protection of that talent made her cautious of 'emotional involvement' in her life. Suspicious of familiarity, she nevertheless sought human warmth like one dying of hypothermia. In order to write she still had to wake to innocence – as she had as a girl. That detachment was integral to her vision. If she woke to fury or anxiety, the day was wasted. Her pen was a key to an alternative reality from which the imperfect form of her own existence could be excluded. In this universe she was God, omnipotent, and, while there, she wanted not to be disturbed. Nothing irritated her more than people wasting her time. At the end of each novel, she felt depressed, compulsively filling the vacancy created with a new birth. Home was wherever the artistic spirit was stimulated, and it was often best stimulated by the company of strangers. Yet she was fearful of strangers. She needed her landlady, her bachelors, her married friends by whom she was always cherished, always 'in the right'. When she tried to extend this network to include interviewers, publishers and agents, however, she found their conviviality and encouragement hollow. Nineteen sixty was a year of many 'purple passages', many separations.

Sympathetic to artists' neuroses, and particularly to the self-doubt and persecution mania bred by neglect, Muriel would always breathe life into the embers of vocation. Rayner Heppenstall dedicated *The Greater Infortune* (1960): 'To Muriel Spark: reviver of faint hearts', and this was how Paul Allen, the Braybrookes, Brooke-Rose, Peterkiewicz and Scott regarded her during this period. Her success was an example of what could be achieved by the doctrine of 'final perseverance' but that success also revived old anxieties: the sense of the fragility of reputation, the carelessness with which this precious commodity was handled by third parties, the exposure to competitive defamation and gossip-mongering. If she felt threatened on any of these fronts, the generous, supportive Muriel could instantly transform into the tigress grande dame. Between 1959 and 1960 her trade as a writer increased enormously. Ideally, she would have preferred to have left the business side of things to the professionals. But she had spent so long looking after herself, was so practised a hand at accounting, office management, self-promotion and the chasing of editors that she was preternaturally alert to slovenliness. In the event of a disagreement, the natural tendency of Higham and Maclean was towards diplomatic fudge. No blame was apportioned, apologies for apparent blunders would be balanced by the author's understandable failure to grasp ... Writers were usually so much in thrall to their masters that they would back off. Not Muriel. She knew what they should be doing and she knew when they were not doing it.

No one understood better than Maclean what a valuable property Muriel could soon become. He also liked her immensely. Into his isolated and damaged life she injected the hard drug of *joie de vivre*. He was a gifted publisher with a genuine enthusiasm for good writing. And beneath that glamorous frivolity lurked a reticent sensibility, integrity, and a resilience which had brought him through a series of private tragedies. As a Christian, he was active in charitable work with ex-convicts. All this Muriel liked. Yet whenever he felt relaxed and convivial, the commercial side of the relationship would rise up and smack him down in her estimation. Given his own anxieties, Muriel's intolerance of the slightest professional laxity must have been stressful. Although as a talent scout he (and his assistant, Tony Strachan) had done brilliantly to land this big fish, she was perpetually in danger of wriggling off the bank. She had already written him a letter which could only be described as a sound spanking. She was, she insisted, neither foolish nor weak. If he did not do better, she would find another publisher.[38] Macmillans, who disliked being pulled around like this by authors, left him with a small budget to placate her as best he could. And, it seems, he did try harder.

After the Murray interview, however, such free publicity was clearly going to be difficult. Muriel had insisted that she never again be exposed to aggressive 'personality' analysis. He guaranteed that in future a third person from the firm would always be present. New photographs were commissioned. Maclean went with her to see Tony Godwin to arrange the Penguin deal on *The Ballad of Peckham Rye* and to discuss a possible Book Society recommendation. In January 1960, a full-page advertisement appeared in the *Bookseller*. Critics from the *Evening Standard* and the *Daily Express* trailed out to Camberwell to discuss the novel and it was prominently displayed in Foyles window. The *Standard* and *Express* pieces, both eulogies, appeared on publication day: 3 March 1960. Maclean, nevertheless, held his breath.

He need not have worried. The reception was triumphant. *Memento Mori*, George Millar of the *Express* remarked, 'was – and remains – a big literary success. But its tinge of mysticism, its acid flavour perhaps put off the wider reading public. That should not be so with this Peckham one, which deals with lusty, dancing, fighting youth [...] a novel purged of dead matter, a "big" novel packed, squirming and growling, into 202 small pages.'[39] Storm Jameson thought it

> remarkable [...], with the vividness and wild poetry of the ballads and something of their almost innocent savagery. The story [is] witty, inventive, often brilliantly funny, [and it is] less simple than it looks [...]. The illusion of the speaking voice, so difficult to bring off, runs through dialogue and narrative alike: Miss Spark's ear is as acute and subtle as her mind.[40]

Stevie Smith, whose *Not Waving but Drowning* Muriel had reviewed favourably in 1957, was at last able to pay her respects: 'Muriel Spark has a real genius for being gruesome and hilarious in practical circumstances, gay in city graveyards, gothic in factories. [...] But this hero-scourge, Dougal Douglas? Who is he? Well, he is Eulenspiegel, if you like, or he is the Goethian Mephistopheles, the spirit who denies and disturbs.'[41]

The Ballad of Peckham Rye, Muriel's fourth novel in three years, focuses on Dougal Douglas. A deformed Scot with one shoulder higher than the other and two bumps on his head, he is a shapeshifter, an attractive, manipulative flirt with second sight who dances throughout, alone and in company, delighting in the embarrassment he causes. He has been employed as an 'Arts man' in a small Peckham factory making nylon textiles, to create a sense of community and combat absenteeism. Instead, he divides everyone, tempting them with freedom and advising that they take days off. He does no work himself other than to unearth his colleagues' secrets and to create fictions. He is a moral philosopher. To all intents and purposes he is a metaphor for the novelist, Dougal with the X-ray eyes. Indeed, in the positive effects he has, he is Muriel transfigured; he revives faint hearts but will never give his heart, sees things others don't. He is a man of vision, wickedly perceptive and dangerous to the mundane.

Ballad opens with a prolepsis, an hilarious scene in which Humphrey

Place is kneeling at the altar. When asked if he will take the awful Dixie Dean as his lawful wedded wife, he replies: '"No, [...] to be quite frank I won't."'[42] Everyone blames Dougal for this and it is true that he has put the words into Humphrey's head. But the facts of the narrative are constantly blurred, gossip about Dougal echoing round Peckham in various forms, just as he presents himself in whatever guise he thinks will be effective to elicit confidences. Everyone but him is anxious about being watched. Throughout he is ghosting the autobiography of an ageing music hall star, Maria Cheeseman, inventing it all from local stories, and periodically making telephone calls to his sick ex-girlfriend whom he cannot bear to be with because his 'fatal flaw' is that he cannot bear illness. Ultimately he escapes, like a recusant, through a tunnel constructed by nuns centuries earlier, becomes a monk, is thrown out of his monastery (like Brooke-Rose's father), and ends as a successful writer.

The book is an extraordinary comic tour de force, by far Muriel's funniest work and the closest to Waugh's style of black comedy that she ever came, brilliantly subtle in its use of orchestrated dialogue. But it is many different kinds of novel simultaneously. In part, it is that satire she had promised herself to write when labouring in 'publicity' for Pearson Horder, lampooning the discourse of enlightened industry, of personnel-speak and union legislation. In part, it is a parody of the working-class novel, of the British obsession with class and the culture of victimhood. It is her take on the Americanised rock-and-roll generation of youth clubs, glass fights and tyre slashing set against the backdrop of Harold Macmillan's newly prosperous common people (Humphrey is a refrigerator engineer) but really set in Time Eternal. For there is, as usual, a metaphysical register. Several reviews pondered the cultural history of Muriel's anti-hero. Was Dougal merely an 'engaging picaresque charlatan'[43] or Satan incarnate?

This confusion was, of course, productive in one respect because it kept readers buying. Less than a fortnight after publication, *Ballad* was No. 5 in the *Evening Standard*'s list of London's best-sellers. It was also, and for the first time, critically productive. Reviewers were beginning to tune in to Muriel's voice and to debate it. Christopher Derrick detected a satire on the humanist assumption that education can provide a 'developed personality and the comfy integrated society'.[44] And so it is – in part. The *TLS* saw it as 'a vividly lyrical morality tale, haunted throughout by a menace-tainted gaiety [...] many souls are lost and consequently saved: no grace can be experienced until sin is understood is in effect her core of faith.'[45] It is this, too. Others found the treatment of the working class snobbish, Phyllis Young amusingly accusing Muriel of writing about people with whom she had had no contact.[46] This is scarcely surprising: *Ballad* was published at the height of the vogue for working-class writing and reviewed alongside Dennis Potter's *The Glittering Coffin* and David Storey's *This Sporting Life*. No one realised, of course, that, in terms of her origins, Muriel was as much a 'working-class writer' as any of them, nor did she wish anyone to read her in this fashion. Her art did not feed off a sense of social injustice, guilt or anger. To write with a political agenda was anathema but the problem faced by the politicised reviewers of 1960 was how to read postmodern writing before 'postmodernism' had been invented as a concept.

Ballad appeared in America during August 1960 and, at last, American notices began to reflect Muriel's London reputation. The *New Yorker*, *Time* magazine, the *New York Times*, the *San Francisco Chronicle* and *Commonweal* all loved the book. Only the *New York Times Book Review* was dismissive, and then by way of clumsy compliment. Puzzling over the anti-hero again, it likened him to Thomas Mann's Felix Krull, only to deny Dougal such 'subtle implications': 'Miss Spark is not protesting against anything, or championing anything either. [...] Britain has a new entry in the light-comedy, family-style class.'[47] This trivialising assessment, however, was more than outweighed by Robert Phelps's piece in the *New York Herald Tribune*:

What [she] has devised is an unponderous way to put matters like Good and Evil and Death and Revelation back into a novel which also deals with contemporary British life. The people and the *mises-en-scène* [...] are the same ones depicted by the Angry-Young-Men brigade: managers and clerks, pubs and rooming houses [...] – but the meaning goes far beyond jockeying for room at the top.

Essentially, her fantasy amounts to an inspired, though controlled use of the non sequitur. Much of Dougal's character as a not-quite-human being is purveyed by his habit of saying unrelated things in a series, or changing the subject without reason or warning; and the narrative tone itself can be unpredictable, intently [sic] naturalistic one minute, and slightly hallucinated the next. I am reminded, especially in the opening chapters, of Rayner Heppenstall's *Saturnine*, a 1943 novel which has been recently reprinted as *The Greater Infortune* and which remains one of the most inventive pieces of prose narrative in English Literature.[48]

The reference to Heppenstall here is interesting, and strangely inapposite despite his novel's dedication to Muriel, for it was at precisely this moment that her relationship with him collapsed.

*

She had thought about writing to the Heppenstalls from Austria but had restricted herself to a postcard. Heppenstall, she believed, was something of an irreligious mystic but that definition seemed tautologous. Her opinion of him varied. Sometimes he seemed amusing, sometimes so negative and self-destructive as to be positively depressing.[49] She had said nothing more of his attempt on her virtue. But even without this, their friendship would have been difficult. Passionate and bullying, he did not care for the direction her radio drama was taking. When the musical version of *Ballad* was arranged, Christopher Holme, infinitely more encouraging, had taken over production. Another 'ear-piece', *The Danger Zone*, had been submitted and ignored. Muriel, businesslike as ever, sent a formal note to remind Heppenstall that the play had been revised at his request and had been with him for over five weeks.[50] He replied, dismissive of her presumption to call him to order. Such confrontations, not only with him, but also with Maclean and Higham, were settling into an irritating pattern of people wasting her time.

Maclean and his superior at Macmillan, Rache Lovat Dickson, were about to decamp to New York on other business in the run-up to the publication of *The Bachelors*. The only people who understood Muriel's needs, it seemed, were Mrs Lazzari and Paul Scott – but Scott had now retired and was busy with the proofs of his own novel, *The Chinese Love Pavilion*. Perhaps the absence of Maclean and Dickson, she remarked with grim humour, would benefit the novel's sales. She was keeping out of Maclean's way, unable to bear his apologies. When he rang, Mrs Lazzari would say that Muriel was out; with Scott, at least, she could feel cherished and unthreatened. The trouble over *Robinson*, if not forgotten, had been buried. She had written an enthusiastic 'puff' for his book and was touched by his promise to do the same for *The Bachelors*. Now that he was a fellow artist rather than a businessman, they inhabited the same universe and she could encourage him unreservedly. Her letters from this period reveal a buoyant, amusing personality: caustic, passionate, loyal, vulnerable, skittish, self-effacing, resilient, conveying both modesty and strength, the excitement of success and its silliness.[51]

During another row with Maclean, he had said she was crazy and she had rebuked his impudence.[52] Three months later, in September 1960, Heppenstall wrote to say that he had passed on the script of *The Danger Zone* to Christopher Holme 'For no other reason than that I dislike [it] intensely. [...] Before the peculiar episode of the "formal note", I had for some weeks been decided that I could [no longer ...] be your friend and your producer at the BBC.' Ridding himself of this script, he said, had produced intense relief. 'You have not telephoned (a source of worry, at one time, that you would, so that the sound of the telephone frequently provoked the fear that it might be you).' Asking for written acknowledgement, he accused her of being 'the world's worst letter-writer out of, I have always thought, some kind of feeling that you ought to be paid for anything you wrote'. In conclusion, he hoped that, with business suspended, she might come to visit them again and chatter away as she used to do. 'It is so nice', he added, 'to feel one's heart open.'[53]

If the tone was intended to be abrasively amicable, it failed. More insolence. Many writers receiving such a letter might have screwed it up, taken a taxi to Ladbroke Terrace, and stuffed it back through Heppenstall's letter box. But Muriel didn't. She filed it neatly for posterity and maintained diplomatic relations for a couple more years. Holme, already busy with the musical version of *Ballad*, had employed Joyce Cary's son, Tristram, to compose the score for Muriel's lyrics (sometimes she used to sing them down the telephone to him), and the result was another success which, in revised form, won the Prix d'Italia. Muriel's response to Heppenstall was to send a collection of her radio plays and stories to Macmillan in November. They accepted it immediately, Lovat Dickson placing *The Danger Zone* at the front as the strongest of the dramas – and there it stayed, to be met with excellent reviews the following year. Heppenstall was a loss. She was fond of him. He was, she thought, one of the cleverest men she had met. But she was thankful to have escaped his neurosis. It was a period for clearing the decks.

The previous August more old rigging had been shipped overboard when she had finally decided she could bear David Higham no longer, and wrote to tell him she was changing agents. She had returned from Nice during July, depressed by Robin's company, to discover that Higham had negotiated absurdly low advances from Penguin for her first two novels when the others had fetched more than four times as much. Surely some mistake? At first she had contacted Maclean. She was, she said, thinking of moving back to John Smith of Christy & Moore – 'no *power* stuff at all' – and thus much preferred to the 'old Woofie'. She disliked changes in her business life, but Higham's seemed incapable of relieving her of the additional work her writing was generating. What did Maclean think? Her friendship with him had been equally tricky, and with what she regarded as Higham's perpetual misrepresentation of her to her publisher, she foresaw herself and Maclean heading for inevitable smash-up.[54]

Maclean's reply avoided any commentary on the Penguin deal (he must, after all, have agreed to it) but said he had heard good things of John Smith. The latter remark was in a scribbled postscript. It was his habit to use this form, or the telephone, for 'personal' matters which would not appear on the filed carbon – a habit which came to infuriate Muriel. While she felt it necessary to be as exact as he and Higham were vague, they seem to have felt that she was constantly interfering with delicate negotiations. Maclean, however, intensely aware that she *was* clearing the decks, could afford to say nothing which might condemn his firm (and possibly his job) to the jetsam. Four days earlier, she had written to him, preparing the ground. Storm Jameson, she said, had made contact, trying to engineer a meeting with her friend, Blanche Knopf. Between the lines there was more than a hint that Lippincott (and Macmillan) needed to maintain enthusiasm for her work, that other publishers wanted her. Several warning signals had flashed out. Maclean had proposed new publicity photographs for the launch of *The Bachelors* in October. Muriel had agreed but had insisted that the choice of pictures be hers alone. Macmillan's previous attempt, posing her amid silhouettes, looking down on Peckham from a cloud, she regarded as a vulgar gimmick and she would have no more of this.[55] Her tone was amusing but strict.

With Higham, she was simply strict. After her brief note explaining her decision to leave, he had rung her – something, she thought, he was usually too busy to do. She was mistaken, he said. He *had* discussed the Penguin deal with her. This she refused to accept. He was in error and refusing to acknowledge it. He said she was always changing her mind. She agreed. But this was hopeless. 'I hope I always respect a man's pride', she wrote to Scott, '– but vanity in a purely business relationship comes hard to respect; one needs a more personal and loving relationship to make it easy to take another's vanity and display one's own.' She had become fearful of telephoning Higham because he thought he knew best and, in her view, always moved the goalposts of the argument. She found it insulting.[56] So that was that. John Smith, young, vigorous and dedicated to Muriel's greater glory, came as a huge relief and it was under his aegis that her career boomed. The only disadvantage of the new arrangement was that she lost the services of Higham's American counterpart, Ivan von Auw of Harold Ober Associates. She soon put that right, too. Publishers and agents began to realise that once Muriel had made up her mind about something, she was implacable.

*

In all these dealings Scott, despite his 'retirement', was generously acting as intermediary. *The Chinese Love Pavilion* was to be published in late September, *The Bachelors* on 13 October. 'We are coming out more or less together,' he wrote to her:

> Ours will be the best books of the Autumn. We shall drip with mink, diamonds (you) Italian silk suits and sharkskin bathing trunks (me). [...] I think I'm probably a teddy boy at heart. I lust after Italianate short jackets and tapering trousers. [...] Dear Muriel, I am a stinker. I failed to hear your talk about the House of Macneice.[57] By the way, don't all those chaps look old? Did you see that shaking picture of Auden and Day Louis [*sic*]? Those Angry Young Men of the Thirties. The Dog Beneath the Skin now has rheumy eyes and an uncontrollable tremour [*sic*] in the hind legs. We are gay young things by comparison.[58]

This was what she wanted to hear. Onward, Muriel, onward! During March 1960 she had outlined her future plans to J. W. M. Thomson of the *Evening Standard*:

> 'I hope to make a long trip this year to the Holy Land ... Israel.' As a Catholic with a Jewish father, the terms came interchangeably to her. 'That is the theme I want to tackle one day in a novel – the half-Jew. So far I think of myself as having written only minor novels. Perhaps that would be a "big" theme. So many half-Jews deny their Jewishness, and that shuts a door on something valuable, on the great spiritual stamina of the Jews.'[59]

This theme became the spine of *The Mandelbaum Gate* (1965) but, by July, she had changed her mind about the order of events. The excursion to Israel and the half-Jewish novel were deferred, to be replaced by another project: a study of schoolgirls growing up in Edinburgh during the 1930s.[60]

Muriel's public image was still in transition. Both of her *Ballad* interviewers discovered an enigmatic figure: a 'middle aged lady in Camberwell with a son aged 22 [and] with something dreamy, almost couldn't-care-less apparent in her attitude, standing at the doors of fame.'[61] 'This is a fascinating moment in the life of Muriel Spark,' the *Standard* noted, 'a moment when the world, having been blankly indifferent for years, suddenly begins to applaud and reward her' – a comment which was both inaccurate and, in its way, true. She had been applauded for more than three years. Since 1957 she had made a reasonable, if unglamorous, living from writing. Reputation, however, was gauged by the popular papers in terms of sales and riches. 'I was frankly surprised to find her still living in an unsophisticated [...] corner of London. The house is one of those tall, prim properties where Camberwell has tried to be a bit above itself. [She] lives on the top floor. Her room has a single, off-centre window with a prospect of back gardens. Was she not enticed by some more chic (and expensive) address, I wondered, now that the daily problem of being hard up had disappeared? She said she wasn't, she found life quiet and peaceful in Camberwell. And after so many years of being poor, this business of being successful and prosperous still looks rather flimsy and insubstantial.'

Muriel sat there with her cigarette, 'small, plainly and darkly dressed, good-looking with a hint of tension.' The interviewer detected 'a certain irony' in what she told him: 'I've never had any money, so I've never been able to travel. I've never even been to Paris, or anywhere like that. I've only been to the Continent once [...]. All my friends seem to have been everywhere. It seems strange. All the little working girls of Peckham I wrote about take their foreign holidays quite naturally [...].' She was not complaining, she said. She had made her own life.[62] Implicit in this self-portrait, however, was a public rebuke to Macmillan. Her interviewer's 'surprise' at her humble circumstances touched a sensitive spot. Here she was, to all the world a celebrity bringing glory to her publishers while they continued to pay her little more than a secretary's wage. It was the publishers who could afford cars and pensions. Nineteen sixty was the first year in which she had made serious money, thanks mainly to her own efforts. With *The Bachelors*, Penguin, and foreign rights advances she had employed a firm of elegant Gray's Inn accountants. Ken Annikin was seeking film rights on *Ballad*. Donald Albery commissioned a stage play for his New Theatre. But did Macmillan strenuously seek to *sell* her books? They did not. With every novel her fury mounted.

The Edinburgh schoolgirls became Miss Brodie's 'set'. *The Prime of Miss Jean Brodie* made Muriel's fortune and a large sum for Macmillan. But, in fact, they almost lost it, its writing delayed by a catastrophic row. During August, John Smith had taken her to the firm to discuss Penguin's terms and the hardback launch. She had emerged satisfied, informing Smith that he could pass on to Maclean her sense of pleasure in the deal.[63] Soon, however, everything changed when Macmillan appeared to have reneged on a verbal agreement of a first printing of 10,000, and by November the gloves were off. If her earlier reprimand of Maclean had been a spanking, the letter she now wrote was a knuckle-duster job, openly accusing him of lying. She was exhausted, she informed him, by his evasions. If he wanted any more of her novels, he had better start an energetic campaign for *The Bachelors* to rescue the current disaster.[64] She did not trust him, had somehow gained the impression that he thought she wrote too fast. Smith was asked to explain that she refused to decelerate to match the steady C. P. Snow.[65] Her mind, she insisted, was a tumult of books, but Macmillan seemed content to leave her marooned in an attic. They basked in her fame while paying her meanly. It was cramping.[66] They had betrayed her. She was tired of explaining to interviewers the disparity between reputation and riches, and disabusing others of the idea that her publishers had done well for her. The reverse, she stressed, was the case. She had done well for *them*.[67]

It was a tirade, whistling through the bonhomie of St Martin's Street, pinning Maclean to the wall and giving him no opportunity to deal with the matter privately. She wanted her complaint to be a matter of public record, demanded an official reply. So he had to take it 'upstairs'. It was, as it was intended to be, profoundly embarrassing. Had he been less well regarded (he was to spend twenty years with the firm and to retire as Director of General Books), it might have signalled the end of his career. And for him, this was not only a professional matter but also a personal one. He was shocked. Up to this point, he had considered himself to be Muriel's friend.

CHAPTER 10

Transfiguration

1960–1962

Muriel's letter marked a watershed in her relations with Macmillan. Four days later she reflected upon it, amused at her indiscretion. The accumulation of small blows, she thought, had been the real impetus[1] – but she regretted not one word. Macmillan had assured her of prominent publicity. Associated Television had made *The Bachelors* its November 'choice'. Bookshops should have been crammed with copies but that cautious first printing had left their display cases empty. She had been promised a *Sunday Times* splash vaunting only her work and John Wain's. Instead, her novel was jammed into a general announcement of current titles.

Reviews had been excellent. Paul Scott declared that she had 'done more outstanding work in a short space of time than any living writer',[2] the *TLS* offered five and a half column inches of undiluted praise, *Time & Tide* described *The Bachelors* as 'a great novel' and, when it appeared in America a few months later, John Updike devoted a subtle *New Yorker* piece to an overview of her work. 'Mrs Spark', he wrote, 'is one of the few writers of the language on either side of the Atlantic with enough resources, daring and stamina to be altering, as well as feeding, the fiction machine. [...] [D]etachment is the genius of her fiction.'

The use by a serious author of fun-house plots, full of trap-doors, apparitions and smartly clicking secret panels, may strike American readers as incongruous. [...] But in the last analysis human experience is mired in solipsism to which America's strenuous confessional [fictional] exercises are faithful, and authors who rise above the accidents of autobiography are at the mercy of the accidents of knowledgeability. Mrs Spark knows a great deal. [...] Her God seems neither the dreadful *deus absconditus* of Pascal and Greene nor the sunny *lux mundi* who illumines the broad optimism of Aquinas and Chesterton. As in a photograph of an eclipse, a corona of heresy and anxiety surrounds a perfectly blank, black disc.[3]

British reviewers regarded her as a phenomenon demanding wide and serious attention, and her outburst is perhaps best understood in the context of a letter from Evelyn Waugh:

> How do you do it? I am dazzled by *The Bachelors*. Most novelists find there is one kind of book they can write [...]. You seem to have an inexhaustible source. *Bachelors* is the cleverest & most elegant of all your clever & elegant books. I have no idea how wide your success has been up to date. I suspect that you are still the sort of writer whom people rejoice to introduce to their friends; *Bachelors* shall take you clear through that phase into full fame. May you enjoy it.[4]

Why the hell, she wanted to know, were Macmillan incapable of capitalising on all of this?

Macmillan, on the other hand, had believed themselves to be doing splendidly: two full-page pre-publication advertisements in the *Bookseller* and, on 13 October, Muriel's first launch party at their oak-panelled premises. Cocktails, laughter, the Scotts, the Heppenstalls, Walter Allen, Peterkiewicz and Brooke-Rose (the novel was dedicated to them), Tristram Cary, Maurice Macmillan, the press, and on the house, Mark Gerson, the celebrated literary photographer, to provide a permanent record. Six days earlier, the musical version of *Ballad* had been broadcast to more fine reviews. The day before the party Muriel had broadcast a talk on her 'nightmare-figure',[5] Heathcliff, for *Woman's Hour*.[6] Radio interviews were lined up; her radio play *The Danger Zone* was scheduled for February. She was seemingly always on the airwaves and in the newspapers. Macmillan had almost doubled her advance for *The Bach-*

elors. The argument over first printing had been resolved with the promise of an immediate second printing of 3,000 which soon sold out. What was she complaining about? Her letter, they thought, was offensive. They had acted impeccably and she was defaming them for making her fortune. But the problem for Muriel was simple: they were not making her fortune, *she* was; and fond as she was of Maclean, she thought her business was unsafe in his hands. Paradoxically, she wanted belief in her skill and vision to be quite separate from considerations of the market place while simultaneously feeling that success in the marketplace was the only reliable register of her publishers' enthusiasm.

Aspects of this conundrum emerged in *The Bachelors*, which dramatises the clash between true and false vocation. In bedsit London, its lonely men confront their isolation. At various stages, couples dance stage-front to discuss an essential question which still troubled Muriel: 'to be or not to be' constructed as 'to marry or not to marry'. Her work often focuses on an 'artist-figure', and here we have two, a positive and a negative version. Ronald Bridges is not a creator like Caroline Rose or Charmian Colston. He is a Catholic, a graphologist and an epileptic but, nevertheless, a man with a vocation: to be a first-class epileptic. Patrick Seton is a medium, a crook, a homicidal maniac, and the parallel between his trances and Ronald's fits runs throughout. The latter's seizures have debarred him from vocations he would have preferred: the Civil Service and the priesthood. They have also excluded him from marriage and he has become, like Seton, a kind of secular priest. Other bachelors come to Ronald, as Muriel's friends came to her, to confess their troubles and seek advice. Women gravitate towards Patrick, whom they see as 'poetic', in search of spiritual consolation.

At first, this parallel appears to offer a satiric opposition between the 'truth' of Ronald's religion and the absurdity of Patrick's fraudulence. It is Ronald who struggles against untruth and betrayal, who catechises his friends with the question, 'Do you want to get married at all?' (They always answer, 'No.') Patrick, on the other hand, is a sinister hypocrite who describes his crime as an 'unfortunate occurrence'. Ronald uses language exactly; Patrick's speech is awash with cliché and euphemism.

But no sooner have we settled on this interpretation of authentic versus fake than it is undermined. Ronald, eventually, does lie. The price of his faith is manic-depression. He loathes other Catholics. Periodically his 'mind's ear' plays back conversations to him as a psychodrama of jabbering demons. Conversely, Patrick is more at peace with the world. Doubtless he would have faked trances had this proved profitable. In this one instance, however, it would seem that he is genuine. Ronald himself acknowledges it. Both men are 'possessed'; both are 'mediums' tormented by voices; both are, in their fashion, artists.

Several reviews picked up on part of this, assuming Muriel's primary subject to be 'demonic possession' (for 'Seton' read 'Satan'). 'By the end of the book [. . .]', Penelope Gilliatt wrote, 'Ronald has somehow been changed by Seton and absorbed something of this devil's likeness.' The ancients, she notes, saw epilepsy as 'a diabolical visitation, and [Spark] rather leans to the same view: satanic possession is a recurring theme in [her] canon.'[7] To leave it at that, however, would be reductive. The novel reminds us that epilepsy, the falling sickness, was also regarded as a holy condition. Certainly Muriel was fascinated by the problem of evil, and few writers better convey the nauseous terror of the uncanny (Seton's 'I creep' would vie with the best of Stephen King or Polanski). But, in fact, like Graham Greene, she was impatient with the medieval notion of an interventionist Devil. She followed Aquinas's teaching: that evil was absence of good.

For both Greene and Muriel, 'evil' was a state of mind, a lack. Their own depressions were a form of 'possession' requiring exorcism through creation, and, paradoxically, this compulsion to expel their torment into the realm of art was intensely exciting. It transformed an otherwise grey world into one of vivid colour. Both needed to hate in order to deflect the temptations of self-hatred. Muriel, one suspects, felt a deep affinity with Ronald's disease:

It was at these moments of rejection that the obsessive images of his early epileptic years bore down upon him and he felt himself to be, not the amiable johnnie he had by then, for the sake of sheer goodwill and protection from the world, affected to be – but as one possessed by a demon, judged by the probing inquisitors of life an unsatisfactory clinic-rat which failed to respond to the right drug. In the course of time this experience sharpened his wits, and privately looking round at his world of acquaintances, he became, at certain tense moments, a truth-machine, under which his friends took on the aspect of demon-hypocrites. But being a reasonable man, he allowed these moods to pass [...].[8]

The sudden attack on Maclean suggests a similar scenario. Muriel's vision was both a blessing and a torment. To see as clearly as this was to be rendered an oddity, like a child speaking plainly among adults; it was to be constantly threatened by 'probing inquisitors' seeking to lobotomise the vital and extraordinary. It was a dangerous gift. The artist, she accepted, was in one sense 'possessed' by her vision but must never *be* possessed by anyone or anything obstructing this vision. Above all, she must not be possessed by insanity. Great art always walked close to that borderline but the great artist always knew her way back.[9] Nothing of value, she believed, derived from the vision of madness.

The Bachelors is Muriel's 'autumnal' novel. The male characters are either approaching middle age or already there. The chronological setting, October–November 1959, passes through Hallowe'en and All Souls' Day. And in this respect it was a screen upon which Muriel's own night-thoughts were projected, displaced and translated. For what lay behind that row with Macmillan was a range of anxieties concerning her identity not just as a writer but as a social being and a Christian soul. *The Bachelors* could equally be read as a novel about middle age, marriage, celibacy, sexuality, vocation, existential angst, responsibilities, possessiveness, jealousy, the relativity (and banality) of good and evil, original sin, the distinction between brain and mind or between fact and fiction, the struggle against contempt and accidie. That phrase 'fraudulent conversion' sounds throughout, linking them all, while her creative mind was beginning to pull her back towards her half-Jewish origins. Ultimately, perhaps, it is, like all her novels, about trans-figuration.

*

A 1960 radio talk, 'How I Became a Novelist', was reprinted that December to publicise *The Bachelors*. The article was capped by a photograph from the launch party: Muriel, cocktail glass in one hand, evening bag in the other, smartly turned out and smiling, chatting with an eager (and obviously attracted) Walter Allen. She had edited the text and selected the photograph. As an exercise in the creation and control of a public image, it was a triumph. Dialogue, she stressed, was essential to her art. 'Also ever since I can remember I've had the habit of going over conversations which I have overheard, or in which I have taken part, recasting them in neater form.' The 'really good, appropriate answer' often only came to one later. She presented herself as an enigma. No mention is made of Ossie, her divorce, son or parents. Her crisis and convalescence are touched on, but left vague. There is no hint of her passionate sense of vocation. Quite the reverse: 'I soon found that novel-writing was the easiest thing I had ever done. [. . .] But because it came so easily, in fact, I was in some doubt about its value.'[10]

The self-portrait here, of one strangely gifted, bemused by her talents and success, offers an aspect of the truth: how she felt when relaxed, how she wanted to feel, disencumbered of mistrust. She presents a Venetian mask, perfected over the years to come, which screens her frustrations. She admits to exhaustion on the completion of a work, to life seeming 'unbearable for a week or two', but then immediately adds that 'the actual writing is more like play than work.' She rarely rewrote, she insisted: '[. . .] I really like to finish with it, because so many other ideas come to me.'[11]

This article, innocuous in 1960, proved contentious in 1961. Priming *The Prime of Miss Jean Brodie*, Macmillan sent 'How I Became a Novelist' to *Books & Bookmen* as a press release. Since Muriel had written it, they felt on safe ground. The editor, William G. Smith, obligingly put her picture on the cover and updated the text. She was delighted by his support, she said, but was 'passionate about principle & justice'.[12] No one was allowed to touch a punctuation mark unless she had approved the change. Had he approached her or her agent, it might have been different. As things stood, *he must pay* a small sum: not to her but to a charity (her local church's organ fund). He refused. She threatened to sue for more than double the suggested donation, plus costs. He paid.

Muriel was prepared to antagonise anyone who breached her own strict code of 'principle & justice'. Since the encounter with Venetia Murray she had discouraged interviews, and Macmillan's urging her to accept press invitations served only to irritate. It was *their* job, she insisted, to market books. Every day wasted on 'publicity' was time lost to creation. She was, and remained, notoriously difficult to contact by telephone. When a few reporters managed to struggle past Mrs Lazzari, Muriel felt obliged to dress the part, provide drinks and food. Public appearances were even more costly. She saw herself as subsidising Macmillan's miserly sales strategy, indeed organising it for them, and disliked appearing on television and radio. 'Probing' was the crucial word. She would talk about her books but not about her life. Interviewers were instructed as to no-go areas: her ex-husband, her son, her parents. Privacy became an obsession. And at the root of this hatred of the 'personality' game, lay other elementary propositions. Her private life was the stimulus for her art. She refused to squander her raw material to slake the public thirst for 'colour pieces'. Her art was external to herself, a transfiguration of the personal. She wanted her past to remain a mystery until she chose imaginatively to re-enter it. This was holy territory, as was her domestic space, and its protection led to further accusations of snootiness, to a terminal row with Alan Barnsley, to continual spats with Macmillan and her family. Ultimately, it contributed to her leaving the country.

At the end of October 1960 she had been benignly disposed towards Macmillan. *The Bachelors* had sold 10,000. She was temperate, even joyful, for it was the scheduled moment to abandon business and to return to *Brodie*.[13] Three months had passed since she had set the novel aside and although little of it was on paper, much of it was spooling in her head. Once *The Bachelors* had been published, she had gone on retreat (at home), all communications shut down, with the intention of completing the novel in eight weeks. A fortnight later she had discovered

Maclean's 'betrayal', accused him of lying and delivered her ultimatum. She composed symphonically, refrains of speech patterns interlocking like music. *Brodie*, she agreed with a critic, was Mozartian. It was essential to get the whole thing out, as a piece, quickly. And now the very people whose job it was to protect her talent were, she thought, distracting her with their incompetence, delaying creation for two further months while new battle lines were drawn. Macmillan, to say the least, were puzzled.

*

Her letter certainly had an effect. Maclean was immediately replaced as Muriel's editor by Rache Lovat Dickson, and if the latter contemplated an immediate riposte, he bit back the temptation. A year was to pass before he spoke up, rehearsing the argument with point-by-point rebuttal from the files. At the time, in late 1960, although angered by her assault on his colleague, he was placatory. *The Bachelors* was selling briskly. She was, Dickson assured her, an important writer whom Macmillan wished to cherish. He had discussed the matter with Maurice Macmillan and had arrived at some ideas. Could they drive out to discuss these tomorrow with her and John Smith?[14]

This was a wise move. The previous day Muriel had written to Scott saying that she would leave Macmillan because they suffered from the fixed idea that her books would never sell widely.[15] When Dickson's eulogy arrived, however, she paused. Could victory over the gentlemen at last be in sight? The result of her letter, she informed Scott, 'is that the directors offered to come & see me in my attic in their Daimlers & Jaguars'.[16] Instead, she went to see them with John Smith. If new terms were to be struck, they would be struck in businesslike fashion on business premises.

First, however, she went out and bought a Paris model dress for twenty-eight guineas. Entering the office in style was important. She asked to take her coat off so they could see the dress. Dickson began by saying that a third printing of *The Bachelors* was in hand. Then they offered an annual salary and the promise either to buy her a house (repayment from royalties) or to arrange an endowment insurance policy which would mature in fifteen years. Altogether a good day's work. Macmillan advanced another hefty sum on *The Bachelors* and promised to boost advertising providing she give them an option (first refusal on the next book). It was difficult to invest in an author, Dickson explained, if her loyalty were not guaranteed. She had never met him before and was impressed. He, at least, was a writer (his autobiography was about to appear), and an exile (a Canadian). She decided to give him his chance. Her sense of the firm's class-bound patronage still rankled[17] but with her immediate future secure, her bleak mood lifted. After *Brodie* she wanted a rest, perhaps a year off, to think about her magnum opus, that 'half-Jewish' novel. Before it, she had to collect her radio drama and uncollected stories for *Voices at Play*, to sketch a full-length play (*Doctors of Philosophy*), to write a stage version of *Ballad* and to collaborate with Holmes on an edited version of the radio adaptation as an entry for the Italia Prize. All this, including *Brodie*, was to be completed within three months.

Muriel sensed the possibility of a radical change in the direction of her career – towards the theatre – and while at first she began to look out for small houses, she soon decided against Macmillan's offer and owning property. Mrs Lazzari as friend and gatekeeper was a crucial figure in her life. So Muriel opted instead for colonising the next floor down at Baldwin Crescent, spending some of her money on furniture and redecoration, and investing the rest. Leaving the attic was a symbolic act. Another new life was beginning, and an elegant apartment (like the Paris model dress) an essential accessory. *The Bachelors* was her own 'Good-bye Bohemia', a farewell to the rackety bedsit world she had inhabited since the war. In his review, the young David Lodge noted a central theme: 'how recognising that one is no longer "single" but a "bachelor" can create many problems for the individual'.[18] Muriel had accepted this distinction years before. She cared for her bachelors (Paul Allen makes a brief appearance as the lovable Matthew Finch) but she had tired of living as they did with other people's curtains.

The flat and the dress were both part of this shift away from feeling rootless and indebted. She was creating a home, as it were, from scratch.[19]

Indeed, the concept of 'home' was new to her adult life. It did not last but the imposition of aesthetic order on her furnishings and clothes was a corollary to artistic control. She became an odd sort of dandy, disguised by turns as bohemian, gentlewoman, media star, recluse. She never forgot her parents' struggle, never lost a deep, instinctive sympathy for the poor. But there was nothing romantic, she felt, about poverty. In *The Bachelors* the worst bore is a class bore, Ewart Thornton, who boasts to a society hostess of 'his deepest pride':

> She listened to him wonderingly as he told her of the real miner's cottage of his birth [...]. 'Latham Street Council School; Traherne Grammar School; Sheffield Red Brick [...].'
>
> 'Were you ever in trouble with the police?' Isobel said, looking round in the hope that someone was listening.
>
> Ewart looked gravely at a vase of flowers [...] 'No, to be quite honest, no. But I recall being chased by a policeman. With some boys in some rough game. Yes, definitely chased down a back-street.' He took out his snuff-box and looked vexed. 'I was definitely underprivileged by birth,' he said, 'though not delinquent.'[20]

Muriel would have no truck with such inverted snobbery. Thornton's diatribe was the sort of thing interviewers sought. She pulled down the shutters. So far as she was concerned, her own working-class origins had nothing whatsoever to do with her literary imagination. 'My aim', she explained later, 'is to present the supernatural as a part of a natural history.'[21]

For Muriel, there was an urgent personal question relating to this large issue. Where did she come from? She revered so much in Jewish culture: its resilience, its humour, its strong sensual women, its sense of the interpenetration of the material and the spiritual. And yet she had become a Christian. Her self-questioning touched delicate matters after the Holocaust, matters she wanted only to investigate with the full power of an undistracted mind. It would take her back, as her writing always did, to the 'danger zone', to the frontier of absurdity. But this time, she knew, the expedition would be more than usually perilous.

*

Muriel already had a mental sketch of her 'half-Jewish' novel: an auto-biographical opening chapter, 'The Gentile Jewesses', describing her relationship with Adelaide, her grandmother, to be followed by the story of a different woman on the borderline between Judaic and Christian civilisations. It would be another extended metaphor for that sense of alienation and self-translation which had always fuelled her fiction but this time she would be digging deeper into her unconscious racial memory. In order to do this properly she needed to travel to Israel. She wished to visit Mount Tabor, the site of Christ's transfiguration and, in the Old Testament, of Deborah the warrior poet mustering her troops for the defeat of Sisera. This was where Christ had cast out the evil spirit from an epileptic child and uttered those words so precious to Muriel and repeated by Barbara Vaughan in *The Mandelbaum Gate*: 'With God all things are possible.' In the novel Barbara sits on Mount Tabor gazing towards the Dead Sea and her estranged lover, revaluing her past. Her conversation with Saul Ephraim, an amiable lecturer in archaeology, seems significant in a chapter entitled 'Barbara Vaughan's Identity'. Christianity, he points out, is a Gentile faith. 'Not essentially,' Barbara replies. 'After all, it started off as a new ordering of the Jewish religion.' 'Well,' he says, 'it's changed a lot since then.' 'Only accidentally. It's still a new order of an older firm.'[22] This was, perhaps, one unconscious object of Muriel's quest: the unification of the split culture of her childhood. But all she knew was that, like so many others then, she wanted to get to that country: to 'the Holy Land', to 'Israel', to 'occupied Palestine', whatever the Christians, the Jews, or the Arabs wished to call it. Somehow that was, or might be, 'home'.

Another row exploded with Macmillan just before her departure. Dickson offered to facilitate Muriel's Israel trip, and feeling supported at last, she revealed vulnerability. Her difficulties, she explained, were not financial but she was fearful of travelling alone, anxious about moving around such a dangerous country.[23] She did not wish to go in a Catholic or Israeli group because each would see it through the eyes of its own prejudice.[24] This was of no use to a Catholic Gentile Jewess. Her new novel with its autobiographical opening, she informed Dickson, touched her directly. She was in search of symbols, particularly of her grandmother's origins. It was not simply Israel that she wanted to see and to feel: it was the Holy Land in all its complexity.[25] She needed to go soon, she said. Would he please rack his brains?

Dickson must have thought that his troubles with Muriel were over. During June 1961 he had invited her to a meeting. All sales, publicity and editorial staff involved with the launch of *Brodie* were present, with the object of involving her directly in the process from the outset to avoid any possibility of further misunderstanding. She had left contented. Options were granted, advances and percentages again increased. Her letters to him were warm. She so wanted him, she said, to share her enthusiasm for her work in progress. And he did. Few publishers could have been more encouraging. The firm's connections were instantly deployed to answer her enquiries. Maclean wrote to Foreign Office chums in Tel Aviv and Amman; Maurice Macmillan approached the British Ambassadors to Israel and Jordan. It all seemed to be comfortably in hand.

In fact, Muriel was quietly seething. Dickson had made a fundamental mistake. Everything hinged on his reading of her requests for assistance. It was, she insisted, a journey essential to her next novel. It was work, not a holiday, for them as much as for her. When their response to this was to offer a further advance, she suddenly shifted ground. She did not see, she said, why she should have to borrow money from them, and accused Macmillan of consistently embarrassing her in this fashion by forcing her to wrangle over rights and small sums. In future, she said, they would have to do the wrangling. Her difficulties, she added, were not only personal and logistical but also financial. The implications seemed plain: they should have *known* this; she was furious with them.[26]

Dickson was stunned. At a stroke, all his diplomatic efforts were nullified and she was threatening to leave them again. He had, he replied, been assured by both Muriel and her agent that money was *not* the problem. However, if it was, Macmillan were willing to do anything necessary, financial or otherwise. He suggested that her letter must have been written while she was suffering from anxiety about making this journey.[27] It was a daring riposte. But Dickson, she accepted, had a point. She was under strain. The mistake he had made was to read her letters literally. She had trusted him to understand her unwillingness to ask him openly to arrange the trip. Perhaps that was unfair. A few days later, Dickson himself drove her to London Airport to wave her cheerily through passport control. It was a sunny morning and she was in convivial mood again.

*

That summer, Muriel climbed Mount Tabor, seemingly suspended between heaven and earth, and saw the Holy Land laid out before her. The Sea of Galilee sparkled bluely in the heat haze some twenty miles to the north-east, Nazareth lay ten miles west, Jerusalem a hundred miles south. Having flown into Lydda on 25 June she had been driven up through the hills to Jerusalem where she had spent five days attending the trial of Adolf Eichmann for the *Observer*. Then she had motored north to Capernaeum where Christ had walked upon the water, Cana where he had changed water into wine, Nazareth where he had spent his youth. These were holy places of spiritual intoxication but material reality was forever jogging her elbow.

On Mount Carmel her guide had crashed the car into a market barrow and she had been taken to her hotel in a police van. Moving on to Tel Aviv for four Mediterranean days she would lie still at night when the radios had stopped, listening to the waves, thinking back to Eichmann and to David's golden city: its muezzins calling to Allah across the old and new sectors at three in the morning, its sandstone glittering as the sun rose at five. All this she related breathlessly in the first half of a long letter to John Smith.[28] The second half was a precise sequence of business instructions. Everything in the Holy Land seemed divided, like Jerusalem, like her letter, and yet intrinsically whole as the site of Christ's healing mission. On 6 July she went with her two visas through the Mandelbaum Gate to Jordan, then on to Bethlehem and the other shrines debarred from the Jews; on across the blazing plains of Sodom and Gomorrah to Amman, the capital, which, like Tel Aviv, had sprung almost from nowhere in the last twenty years. A million or more Arab refugees had spilled out of the former Palestine since the creation of the State of Israel in 1948. Millions more Jews had poured into Israel in the wake of the Second World War. The world's eyes were on Eichmann in his glass booth. It was a region ripe for war, volatile with sects and spies, and, to Muriel, dangerous, magical. A place of transfigurations. When she flew home via Rome and Antibes she had been away just four weeks. She came back distraught, having undergone a transfiguration of her own. Since her return, she informed June Braybrooke, she had been terribly depressed, sleeping a lot, crying, unable to locate the reason for this.[29]

This depression perhaps derived from overwork and the perennial sense of threat. Even before leaving, she was suffering from 'nervous exhaustion'.[30] Dr Lieber had prescribed pills and ordered rest. But something else seems to have happened to her in Israel, something abstractly investigated in *The Mandelbaum Gate*. Ultimately she had made her own arrangements through a travel agency. To travel alone was to confront her vulnerability and to overcome it. Nevertheless, she knew that her desire to roam independently and to pass from Israel to Jordan would appear equally suspicious to the authorities of both countries. She also knew that once she had passed through the Mandelbaum Gate, she could not re-enter Israel and would have to find her way home from Jordan. Fear of Israeli spies ran high. Like Barbara Vaughan, Muriel was advised not to mention her Jewish origins, and the Gate became a symbol of transition, a point of no return. Beginning this trip with Eichmann cannot have been easy. In retrospect, Muriel put down her sadness on return to the experience of that trial. Echoes of anti-Semitism were part of her oral tradition. Dispossession ran in the blood. Although she had no memory of any of this affecting her directly or being discussed in her family until Hitler came to power, she did recall the Edinburgh Blackshirts, and loathed Father Brocard Sewell's flirtation with Oswald Mosley's politics. The West's shifty unwillingness to use the term 'anti-Semitism' was soon to infuriate her at a congress of Jewish writers in Paris. The narrator of 'The First Year of My Life', sickened by euphemism, prefers 'the Western Front' with all its horrors to the Liberal platitudes of Asquith, and for anyone with Jewish relations, Eichmann *was* the Western Front.

Muriel placed distance between herself and the proceedings by concentrating upon them as an absurdist drama. Writing to Smith, she apologised for her convoluted sentences, a habit, she joked, contracted from the diction of Eichmann and his counsel.[31] Evil was as much evasion as malice. It was also, here, a form of class-bound myopia. Eichmann's deference to the bench while patronising his lawyer sickened her.[32] But there was perhaps another nagging sensation which she was supposed *not* to feel: that there was something pernicious in this desire to crush so pathetic an object of hatred, a self-righteousness she had always resisted, encapsulated in the phrase 'the letter killeth'. Having just completed *Brodie*, the issues of fascism, Calvinism, transfiguration and the relative nature of 'betrayal' still rang in her head. Eichmann had betrayed humane values. But the trial itself rendered her incapable of discussing it.[33] As a result of their barbaric treatment, some of the Israelis, Muriel thought, seemed to have lost that amiable sensuality and sense of self-mockery she so loved in Jews elsewhere. Instinctively, she always resisted what she took to be a culture of victimhood in politics or sexual relations. There was a simplicity in Arab houses, an openness to metaphysical experience. The Jews seemed more interested in material culture. It was all profoundly disturbing. The subject was so complex that it could only be dealt with in a novel.

'I had a map of all the ancient sites,' she remembered, 'and I had [...] difficulty with [an Israeli] guide who wanted to take me to the modern sites and show me the cement factories [...]. I thought that was nice, too, but I really wanted to see where Gaza was, where Cana was.'[34] Her letters home fizz with excitement and irritation. It was this fellow, a recent Polish immigrant, who had crashed the car. Loaded into a black Maria, 'with all the population wagging their fingers at me', she had been driven to her hotel where she lit a cigarette to relieve the shock. More finger-wagging and jabbering about breaking the proscriptions of the Sabbath. Later, in the Jewish quarter of Jerusalem, she had been upbraided in the street for wearing a sleeveless dress and the experience clearly distressed her.[35]

At the same time, however, she was transported by intense religious and aesthetic experience. 'I felt it could be a spiritual place of origin, especially lyrically. It's the place of the Psalms. [...] I had always been attracted by David the poet.' Of the three tribes of Israel, her father belonged to the elite: the Cohens, the Khans, the Kings. 'We're supposed to be descended from David ... which of course we're not ... it's all a mish-mash.' Despite being a 'poor working man', her father 'had to go first in the synagogue. He made nothing about it. He couldn't [have cared] less about this sort of thing.'[36] Nevertheless, there was this biblical connection linking her creative mind to Jerusalem. There were also associations with her grandmother and those heroines of the Old Testament. Above all, there was the extraordinary experience of walking in Christ's footsteps.

Much of this went into *The Mandelbaum Gate:* the guide, the heckling, the cement factories, muezzins, the tumult of feelings. The novel can be read as an accurate travelogue spliced with the invented adventure of Barbara's disappearance although, in a sense, Muriel soon also 'disappeared' for shortly afterwards she was to be transfigured into her new life as international celebrity. Barbara's experience of travel was close to Muriel's: 'There seemed no difficulty about the miracles, here on the spot. They seemed to be [...] factual, considered from this standpoint.' Doubt, however, defines faith. Barbara is on Mount Tabor. The priest explains that its church marks the place of Christ's Transfiguration. 'Only probably, said Barbara's mind; there's a rival claim for Mount Hermon [...].' But the details, the facts, are ultimately irrelevant. 'Wherever it did take place, she thought, I believe it did take place all right. Transfigured, and in a radiant time of metamorphosis, [Christ] was seen white and dazzling, to converse with Moses and Elias.'[37]

For Muriel, the Transfiguration was fundamental to Christianity, the junction of the divine and the human, of the spiritual and the material, of Old and New Testaments. And transfiguration was also the essence of art, the translation of fact into fiction or 'vision'. Sandy Stranger in

Brodie becomes Sister Helena of the Transfiguration. Her famous treatise, 'The Transfiguration of the Commonplace', examines the psychology of moral perception. And this title equally describes Muriel's writing with its constant slippage between natural and supernatural. A sense of wonder and horror coexist. The ordinary becomes strange, the strange ordinary, an effect enhanced in *Brodie* by a narrative structure which became a hallmark of her mature style: beginning at the end and diving backwards and forwards through time. There is, as in all her work, a sense of déjà vu, of double time and split identity.

Miss Brodie, we quickly learn, was in many respects foolish, a born fascist, an egomaniac irresponsibly displacing her frustrated passions on to her pupils. She encourages the fifteen-year-old Rose Stanley to have an affair with the art master. She mistakenly sends Joyce Emily Hammond to a futile death in the Spanish Civil War. Realising this, Sandy betrays her mentor. Yet the authorities, the Calvinist pleasure-crushers, eager for this betrayal, are worse fascists with their smug team spirit. It is a confrontation between their sepulchral chill and Brodie's heat. She is in many respects a great figure, a unique individual, a creator of souls despite herself. 'Where there is no vision,' she declares, 'the people perish.'[38] Discovering her weakness is a shock to Sandy, a fall from grace, but this knowledge leads to wisdom, to Catholicism, to her treatise. Although Miss Brodie fails in her attempt to mould her charges in her own image, another transfiguration takes place which would have been impossible without her as the catalyst:

> Sandy felt warmly towards [her] at those times when she saw how she was misled in her idea of Rose. It was then that Miss Brodie looked beautiful and fragile, just as dark heavy Edinburgh itself could suddenly be changed into a floating city when the light was a special pearly white [...]. In the same way Miss Brodie's masterful features became clear and sweet to Sandy when viewed in the curious light of the woman's folly [...].[39]

The imagery of white light here evokes the biblical scene on Mount Tabor. But Sandy is not Christ, only his bride. She is a 'stranger', an alien in the world of conventional men and women, not unlike her author.

*

While Muriel was abroad, *Voices at Play* had been published to good reviews. *Brodie*, she knew, was excellent and due to appear that autumn. Better still, John Smith soon sold it to the *New Yorker* which was to devote its entire October issue to a version edited down to 40,000 words. Her fame was bush-fire on both sides of the Atlantic. Plans were made for her to travel to New York in January 1962 for *Brodie*'s American hardback launch. Everyone wanted her. Nevertheless . . .

In Rome, stopping over on her return from Israel, she had met the flamboyantly gay Eugene Walter. An American writer and actor on the fringes of Fellini's saturnalia, and formerly secretary of Princess Caetani, Walter had corresponded with Muriel when the Princess's *Botteghe Oscura* had published 'The Portobello Road', and since then kept distantly in touch. She had spent only two days in the Holy City but the visit had lit a fuse. Getting off the plane, she had dropped her sunglasses and was pleasantly surprised by the concern of the ground staff. It was a tiny incident but it made the place seem welcoming. 'It stuck in my mind', she remarked, 'that I liked Italy very much. It was a place where I wasn't known. I could write in peace and get away from family and the literary world.'[40] Then she had travelled to Antibes (Juan-les-Pins), where the Braybrookes were sharing a villa with friends.[41] Muriel put up in an hotel. Neville Braybrooke recalled being sent there to collect her passport, with the caution, half joke, half serious, that he should not open it to see her real age. It was an enjoyable break but, as she remarked afterwards, she found 'holidays rather hard work'.[42]

Brodie reached back to the root of her consciousness when it had been bounded by Edinburgh and Miss Kay. Sandy speaks of her mother as Muriel did of Cissy in *Curriculum Vitae*, with wry humour rather than resentment: as an embarrassment, as flashy and over-protective. Muriel had returned to Bruntsfield Place in December 1960 to write the novel in just four weeks while tuned in to Edinburgh diction. Within a fortnight it had been typed, corrected and submitted. She had given her parents some money and they had left her alone with the silence she needed. The back bedroom – first hers, then her grandmother's, then hers again – was the cave of echoes she had sought. But it was occupied by Robin, so she had taken over the front one, above the racket of the street. Barney, now retired, spent most of his afternoons watching televised horse racing. Robin worked in a jeweller's shop, manoeuvring between his grandparents' flat and his father's. Cissy's instinct was still to chatter and to show her daughter off, overtures discouraged by Muriel and particularly so on this occasion. 'They had no idea, none of them, what it meant to be an artist, a writer. They didn't appreciate that side of my work: the artistic process. No idea whatsoever.'[43] If the atmosphere, superficially convivial, was somewhat strained, Muriel remained unconcerned. Her family loved her and were proud to have her as their guest. She had returned with her well-cut clothes to blanket herself again in the voices of provincialism. It was a pragmatic decision, necessary for her work.

Betrayal, partly the theme of *Brodie*, dogged Muriel's thoughts. It seemed to her that each break for freedom, for the liberty to write and to live her own life, engendered accusations from one group or another. Her new London friends, bright young acolytes like Auberon Waugh and Gillon Aitken, knew her only as a success. To them she was a powerful figure, talented and confident. These charming, well-bred escorts, twenty years her junior, rejuvenated her in a way friends of her own generation could not. They took her out to the best restaurants and to the theatre. Muriel had always been a magnet for those seeking advice, and she had enjoyed playing the sage. Kay Dick wrote to confess her lesbian adultery; June Braybrooke to explain problems with her ex-husband and mother; poor reviews had plunged Christine Brooke-Rose into melancholy; Paul Scott, depressive and alcoholic, his marriage a wreck, had half-heartedly tried to kill himself. But they were like the troop of visitors to Sandy Stranger's cell, and Muriel had no wish to be a nun with answers.

Ultimately she refused Macmillan's financial package (annual salary, endowment mortgage) for two reasons: she was advised that she could do better by negotiating from contract to contract, and she was fearful of her family's intrusiveness. 'When I should have bought property', she later reflected, 'was then but I simply couldn't because I didn't know what my family's [...] demands were going to be. I really felt, too, that if I had a house [...] I'd never get my family off my nut. They'd [...] regard it as money in the bank for them. They'd expect me [...] to raise money on it, or to rent rooms or to do something for them.'[44] 'They' here referred mainly to her mother. Her father was not a problem. Muriel was happy to accept limited liability. For years she had been sending them money, currently a monthly cheque. In addition, she had offered to pay the household expenses, by which she meant bills for gas, electricity, television hire. These were sent to her accountant who deducted the sums from her earnings. Then she discovered that *all* bills, down to shoe repairs, were arriving. As her family's sole support, she felt exploited. Robin was twenty-three, a grown man with a full-time job. Why, she wondered, did he not leave home and set up independently? She would write to friends about it, by turns cross and considerate, still hoping to rescue him from Edinburgh. *Brodie* was abstractly about how she rescued herself from it – with the help of Miss Kay.

Sandy, like Muriel, was haunted by a spirit of repression in the city. Something shrouded its glories, wagging its finger. Its monolithic blackened buildings issued grim warnings. In their shadow, all efforts to be original or to escape were foredoomed. Perhaps it was only during the writing of her novel that Muriel identified what had driven her out. It was John Knox and Calvin. Muriel even came to see Edinburgh's tight-knit Jewish community as, in its own peculiar way, Calvinist. For Sandy, Calvinism was the unacknowledged 'other' that she had to discover in order to reject it and to define herself. It is everything that the headmistress personifies and Miss Brodie opposes: chilly team spirit, information as truth, education as indoctrination, patronage, fear of the unusual and the desire to crush it into conformity.

Miss Brodie's swarthy Roman profile turns itself towards Europe, colour, light and air. She teaches her girls to think for themselves, to cultivate the Gioconda's composure. Her non sequiturs dart past analytical logic towards poetry, drama, opera, the expansive gesture, metaphor. She has the artistic temperament. Her girls are her vocation. Education is a leading out, not a putting in. To put in is to intrude. She is another of those Sparkian heroines who dismiss their enemies, 'flattening their scorn beneath the chariot wheels of her superiority',[45] head up, up. Her bony opponents stalk past her in the corridors, 'saying "Good morning" with predestination in their smiles',[46] inquisitive rather than questioning.

We laugh at these Calvinists as Miss Brodie teaches her girls to laugh at them. And yet (here comes the trademark Sparkian rug-pull), ultimately there is little to choose between Miss Brodie and the Calvinist head-mistress, or between either and the Fascists conquering Europe in the background. One of Miss Brodie's dictatorial statements reads: 'Art and Religion first; then Philosophy, lastly Science. That is the order of the great subjects of life, that's their order of importance.' In the manuscript, this is followed by a deletion which explains Sandy's rejection of this dogmatism, and then her girlish acceptance of it as the easier route, an expression of her devotion to her teacher.[47] This conversion of the honest 'No' into the fraudulent 'Yes' was very much Muriel's subject, and the source of her own inability to maintain loyalty to those who, she considered, had betrayed her trust. As Sandy says later: 'It's only possible to betray where loyalty is due.'[48] And in a novel where love produces only misplaced loyalty and loyalty is due only to God, love and truth are fatefully opposed. A 'creeping vision of disorder'[49] plagues Sandy until she is liberated by 'betrayal' and condemns her mentor: 'She thinks she is Providence, thought Sandy, she thinks she is the God of Calvin, she sees the beginning and the end. And Sandy thought, too, the woman is an unconscious Lesbian.'[50]

The Bachelors, Muriel remarked, started from a fascination with the collision between spirit and matter: 'I had this feeling that the two did have a connection in that the confirmed bachelor is rather a Manichaean person ... very good and evil, spirit there and matter there, and [...] that confirmed bachelors had this all-spirit or all-material thing which culminated in – this is all very metaphysical – that kind of hysteria, or suppressed hysteria, like epilepsy.'[51] 'Suppressed hysteria' equally describes the atmosphere of *Brodie*: the girls making their way through sexual discovery, Miss Brodie's (and Teddy Lloyd's) emotional displacement, authoritarian repression, the rise of Hitler and Mussolini. The appalling treatment of Mary MacGregor as scapegoat for everyone's malice is a subtle reminder of the hysterical racism of the Holocaust. If *The Bachelors* centred on the neurosis of single men, *Brodie* concerned the neurosis of single women.

*

Publication of *Brodie* in the UK was deferred to allow the *New Yorker* a free run on 14 October 1961. Muriel was the first British woman to receive their 'entire issue' accolade. Suddenly, from having cult status and modest American sales, she had 430,000 readers and the imprimatur of the glossiest arbiter of American literary taste. Lippincott produced enthusiastic publicity, reminding readers that earlier in the year Muriel and they had been awarded the Thomas More Association Medal for 'the most distinguished contribution to Catholic publishing in 1960'. Would this furore affect British sales? Unfortunately not.

British reviews were generally good but a surprising number were either baffled or unimpressed. Given the brilliance and durability of *Brodie*, the obtuseness of the British literary establishment in this case was astonishing. Anthony Burgess thought it thin and humourless.[52] Bamber Gascoigne found the characters' motives unconvincing.[53] *The Times* dismissed it as 'a bundle of contradictions and not much else besides'.[54] Francis King carped about Muriel's word selection, and prompted a sharp exchange of letters in *Time & Tide* by suggesting that she was shrewdly promoting her public image. Her first reaction to this was an epistolary Exocet which John Smith persuaded her to redraft, much to Lovat Dickson's relief.[55] 'I live a secluded life in an unfashionable suburb', the final version read. 'I rarely mix in literary circles. I have no famous friends. If it is not well known that I discourage the personal probings of reporters and interviewers, and that my agents and publishers have been requested to do so on my behalf, it ought to be.'[56] All he was trying to suggest, King explained, was that 'Mrs Spark might perhaps be [...] publishing too much in an understandable eagerness to consolidate her position.'[57] Even her admirer on the *Observer*, John Davenport, was disappointed by the book: over-simplified, in his view, full of evasions and repetitions. He couldn't see the point of it. A leitmotif emerges in this sort of notice: that she was writing too quickly. 'Miss Spark recently admitted to guilt because her novels came too easily to her,' Arthur Calder-Marshall remarked. 'In this case she has some reason for feeling it.'[58]

There remained, of course, a host of admirers. Evelyn Waugh was still dazzled, enthusiastically waving her banner. As usual, she had sent him a copy. 'All the book delightful,' he replied. 'The letter pp. 95–96 genius.'[59] (This was Sandy's and Jenny's composition, imagining Miss Brodie's correspondence with Gordon Lowther – 'Allow me, in conclusion, to congratulate you warmly upon your sexual intercourse, as well as your singing' – one of the few sections primly cut from the *New Yorker* version.[60]) Muriel had invited Waugh to the publication party at Macmillan's on 10 October and, although he had declined on the grounds of deafness, senility and distance, he had sent in his stead a copy of his last novel, *Unconditional Surrender*, just out, dedicated 'For Muriel Spark in her prime from Evelyn Waugh in his decline.' He had praised *Voices at Play* in the *Spectator*.[61] This time, unfortunately, he reviewed only the American edition of *Brodie* four months later and his jubilant endorsement[62] could not be used to rebut those who agreed with Burgess. Of her other supporters, Brian Aldiss,[63] Peter Green ('I doubt if there is a more original or more morally aware novelist writing in English today'),[64] Malcolm Muggeridge,[65] Norman Shrapnel,[66] W. J. Igoe[67] – few struggled beyond generalised eulogy. Only Christopher Derrick and David Lodge wrestled with the novel's implications – and, although their pieces appeared in major Catholic papers, these were of relatively small circulation.[68] The *TLS* saw it as an 'entertainment' in the style of Greene's, lightweight and stylish: 'One may argue that Mrs Spark is at her best in avoiding bulky themes, but if her admirers are right in thinking *Memento Mori*, the most serious of her books, by far the best, it will not be long before she must tackle material tougher than the vaguely symbolic portrait of a memorable eccentric lady of the 1930s.'[69] This was a common lament and one which Muriel was trying to address with *The Mandelbaum Gate*. It was time, she felt, to give her talent free rein in a big novel. Trouble, however, lay ahead. Insulted by a joke Dickson had made over a luncheon to celebrate *Brodie*, and amid her dispute with Francis King, she wrote without warning to cancel the option clause in her contract, refusing to debate the matter.[70]

This was a facer for Dickson. Muriel's suggestion, he explained to John Smith, was unacceptable. She then typed an eight-page, single-spaced letter venting the banked-up frustrations of five years. Advertising for *Brodie*, she said, had been pitiful. During that June meeting they had *promised* a major campaign – and, again, failed to deliver. She spoke passionately about vocation and discrimination. She could recall no other Macmillan author who had abjured marriage to place art before financial security. Creation, she insisted, involved sacrifice. Despite her statements in interview, her fiction did not come easily to her. Macmillan's behaviour left her feeling nervous and unprotected. Would they have called Pamela Snow into St Martin's Street to be confronted by five Macmillan executives to discuss her sales and advertising? That June meeting, it seems, kept replaying itself in her head: 'Leaving aside what was agreed or not agreed, the whole thing was a damned insolence.'[71] For Dickson, this throwaway first clause was precisely the difficulty. Even allowing for her expressions of affection for him and for Maclean, even acknowledging that mistakes had been made, he could not 'leave aside' a signed contract. The time had come, he decided, to respond forcefully.

He took a week to think about it, meticulously examining the files. He was, he said, fond of her, too, and admired her writing hugely. Nevertheless, the charges she laid against the firm and its other authors were false. John Wain, Walter Macken and Pamela Hansford Johnson (Pamela Snow) had all endured sacrifices and poverty to write. As for the June meeting, it had come about because Muriel had behaved with appalling rudeness to Maclean, after which it had been impossible for him to continue as her editor. When Dickson had taken over, he had ensured that she should meet and talk with everyone involved with her work. To characterise that meeting as 'damned insolence' was both offensive and self-contradictory.[72] Letters ran back and forth. Slowly the temperature cooled. She remained grateful, she said, to Macmillan for giving her a start, agreed that individually they were honest enough. It was just that trust had collapsed. As she pursued the debate, she wrote not as a termagant but as a member of a family disabled by loyalty and unable to explain why she must leave. Exasperation and weariness dog the sentences. It was a correspondence (or lack of it) between her spirit and Dickson's matter, hopelessly at odds. Macmillan, she said, just didn't *understand* her work.

With this argument still raging, she broke communication and fled London for Aylesford Priory. Only John Smith could contact her, and then only by letter. In a quiet room above the monastery workshops she completed the third and final act of *Doctors of Philosophy*. Somehow she cut her knee badly and Barnsley, who was a GP in nearby Maidstone, had been summoned to bandage it. Ignoring the pain, she kept writing. Unusually, she needed to redraft. This new genre tested her. Smith came down for a weekend in early December to find her in good spirits, glad to have finished the play, anticipating America. But *Doctors* required further revision and she wanted it done before the New Year. Her family saw little of her that Christmas. Although she was with them in Edinburgh, she was again mostly holed up in a bedroom. Late on Christmas Eve she emerged, job done, drank her sherry, ate her turkey, pulled her cracker and left, whisking Robin off for a few days in London. It was her last Christmas with her father.

*

On 12 January 1962 Muriel touched down in New York to find that city ready for her in a way that London was not. Lippincott had booked her into the Algonquin, arranged parties, press interviews, dinners and a trip to their Philadelphia headquarters. *Brodie* was published on the 17th to a crescendo of adulation. To celebrate, Lippincott threw a cocktail party at the St Regis Hotel where Updike, W. H. Auden and Lionel

Trilling paid homage amid the *crème de la crème* of literary journalists. The *New Yorker* treated her more royally still. The next day she was lunching at Le Pavillon with the magazine's legendary editor, William Shawn, and Rachel MacKenzie. This, at last, was celebrity and a form of redemption. Muriel was delighted and grateful. Even Dickson had flown over, ostensibly on general business but really to junket with her and to guard his prize author. Hilary Rubinstein of Gollancz was not alone in making contact with a view to publishing Muriel's books. Tom Maschler of Cape was, as ever, dogging her footsteps. Among *New Yorker* writers she quickly made friends with Shirley Hazzard, Dwight Macdonald and the blind Indian writer, Ved Mehta. Her Lippincott editor, Corlies ('Cork') Smith was young but one of the best. At Muriel's request, MacKenzie took her to the hit shows of the moment, the titles of which – *How to Succeed in Business Without Really Trying* and *A Funny Thing Happened on the Way to the Forum* – perhaps seemed ironically amusing. For she had been battling for over twenty years for this success and a funny thing had happened to Muriel on the way to New York. A photograph of her there reveals an astonishing transformation. She looks twenty years younger than she had in pictures taken by Mark Gerson just five months earlier. Her face is narrower, her eyes larger and more luminous. A translucence has emerged from the earlier square-set face, the homeliness of Gerson's shots replaced by a modest, yet knowing, exoticism. She had become a star, not merely in name but in her whole appearance.

Cork Smith, tall and droll, squired Muriel round the city, fascinated by his companion. She seemed ageless, 'bird-like', a tiny dynamo of a woman, elegantly dressed but unpretentious. He and his wife had taken her to dinner on the night before publication. Around ten o'clock, in a cab returning to the Algonquin, she had asked when the morning papers appeared. 'They should be out now.' 'Why don't we pick them up?' He paused, anxious that she might be disappointed. It was considered a great coup to be reviewed on publication day by the *New York Times* or *Herald Tribune* and, given the half-million distribution of the *New Yorker*, he feared that the novel might be too well-known for immediate attention. She, however, was 'wonderfully confident'. They were passing Grand Central Station. The cab was stopped. He dashed in and returned. Furious flicking through newsprint in half-darkness. And there were the notices, just as she had predicted: rave reviews in both papers.

On her last day they lunched in an Indian restaurant on Central Park West. She had spent her entire time blazing from appointment to appointment. Was there anything, he asked, that *she* wished to do? As a matter of fact, she said, there was. She wanted to see Mother Cabrini, the first American saint. See? Smith looked puzzled. His knowledge of Catholicism was, as he put it, 'certainly negligible'. On this point, however, he felt secure. 'Muriel,' he said, 'I think she's dead.' 'Of course she's dead,' came the reply, 'but I believe she's been stuffed and one can view her.' He found a telephone and rang the archdiocese. The saint was to be found at the tip of Manhattan Island. So they jumped into a cab and went.

In a modern, pretty chapel they discovered Mother Cabrini stretched out in a glass case. The only visible 'flesh' was that of the hands and face, not flesh at all, as they learned, but leather masking and wax. Beneath this and the habit was a complete skeleton. Muriel was excited, as indeed was he. She took out her rosary and prayed. The place hummed with high-school kids, priests and nuns. One nun was quietly crying. It was, for both Cork and Muriel, a moving experience. Leaving the place, she seemed to glow. 'You'll see now,' she said as they returned to the cab, 'something wonderful will happen because it always does when you visit a saint.' About a week later she rang him from England. 'Has anything wonderful happened?' No, he said, but nothing terrible either. She was excited again. Something had happened to her: an unexpected bonus from the *New Yorker*.

Muriel returned jubilant. At 30,000 feet above the Atlantic she suddenly came to a decision: no more business – for her at least. When Dickson made contact again there was no hint of his earlier stuffiness. How delightful, he said, were their encounters in New York. How right she had been to make the journey at that point in her career. Having seen the esteem in which she was held in America, he took her more seriously. But there was also genuine affection here. He was, it seems, half in love with her, and as the task of resolving the option problem had been passed upstairs to Maurice Macmillan, Dickson could relax again.

Maurice juggled his chalice gingerly. She seemed, he wrote, to have no confidence in the firm and 'so little regard for our point of view' that he wondered whether her demands were 'meant to be refused. If you really cannot bear to deal with us it would be more straightforward to say so rather than to push us to breaking point.' She wanted to reserve paperback rights. She requested increasingly high advances that were not earned back. She refused options while expecting special treatment. He was not, he said, willing to succumb to threats and was 'deeply hurt'.[73]

Muriel's response must have been unnerving. She avoided the subject altogether. She was concerned, she said, only with the manipulation of words. And here he was bothering her with business. The tone was affectionate, placatory, girlish, with the buried blade of mockery. Dickson, she said, had reassured her in New York. Now she was puzzled again. Why should Macmillan not pay as much as other publishers? Threatening? No, her agent was merely explaining alternative offers. It was really all Macmillan's fault for provoking these offers by telling everyone that she had a nervous breakdown every time she wrote a book. She had heard this everywhere, even in America. Of course she took no notice 'because I realise that [. . .] Macmillan conceive of authors as failed civil servants [who] have never quite made the F.O. grade'. That was all right, but of course, far from being deterred, other publishers *would* enquire if one was entirely happy where one was. Regarding paperbacks, she hoped there would be some way to accommodate his principled stand. In the meantime, why didn't he come out to Camberwell for a drink?[74]

Ultimately, Macmillan saved face by an absurd form of words – saying that they could not cancel the option clause but would not enforce it – and kept her for another eighteen years.[75] Muriel now looked to America for her living and settled on treating the firm as a club whose subscription she might cancel at will. She went to the races with Maurice and Alan. When Sir Harold Macmillan resigned as Prime Minister in October 1963 and returned to publishing the following January, she came to know him better, and occasionally went to stay at Birch Grove. He admired her writing and although she doubted whether he understood it, she found him easy, witty company. From her point of view, she had simply to relinquish trying to make the firm behave like a commercial concern. It was hopeless. In New York, Ivan von Auw had offered his services again: '*very* professional. *What* a difference between [him and] all these humbugs in England.'[76]

On 22 February 1962 Muriel encountered someone else she came to see as a humbug. Alan Barnsley had just completed a fine novel, *The Birthday King* (1963). Still employed as a doctor, he was tortured by indecision. Should he give up the day job? This was a legitimate anxiety as he now had five children, and he wanted to talk to Muriel about it. In London to meet his publisher, he had brought his wife along, and had rung Baldwin Crescent. Mrs Lazzari had taken the call. Mrs Spark, she said, was at the hairdresser's and was then going out to lunch. Ignoring the hint, they drove out and encountered Muriel just returning to the house. Jovial greetings were crushed. She was furious. Would they mind, please, going away? She was busy. Dazed and angered, they returned to their car while she shut the door on them.

All might have been well had Barnsley not written a letter recounting the incident and cancelling their friendship: 'Good bye. God Bless You. Please never write to me again, but pray for all of us when you can as we will continue to pray for you.'[77] If its object was to elicit guilt or apology, it was sadly misjudged. Muriel was repulsed by the implication that she was too famous for them now. Why could not he, of all people, as a writer, understand the need for solitude? Her day had already been mapped out: discussions with the theatre people backing *Doctors of Philosophy*, followed by a dinner party. She likened the Barnsleys' behaviour to disturbing a surgeon who was at work on a patient. They had ruined her day. She wished him well with the novel, admired his work. She would not, however, be staying with them again because he required too much in return. Enclosed was a brief typescript: 'Notes for the Secretary of Miss Aurora Cavallo, Novelist'.[78]

'Notes for the Secretary [...]' is an hilarious list of possible responses for a writer's gatekeeper: Miss Cavallo is abroad, in the bath, has renounced interviews for Lent, etc. Barnsley, somehow unable to see the funny side of it, interpreted this document as a personal attack and returned it with a sharp note. A few days later he tore into her letter: 'The "surgeon" was not "in the operating theatre" when we called; "he" was round the corner having a shampoo and set [...].' He had, he said, been writing *his* novel when called out to attend to her knee. 'Mrs Lazzari, had she dared, might have told you that on the telephone we said we wouldn't even see you if you were busy. In this event, I told her we'd see her for ten minutes in her sitting-room when I would discuss with her her son's illness about which, at your request, I had that morning consulted my partner [...].' Her 'deliberate rudeness and door-step exhibitionism' was intolerable. *He* had *three* jobs ...[79]

It had all run horribly out of control, a simple misunderstanding escalating into an epistolary brawl. Muriel, incensed by his disrespect, scribbled furious responses all over the letter, readdressed the envelope to him – and then didn't post it. What was the point? It was the end. Seven years of close friendship were finished. His behaviour, she said, was not manly. It was misogynist. Men, she advised, should always treat women courteously. But that mention of Mrs Lazzari's son must have hurt. She had not realised that Barnsley had offered medical advice. 'Bunny', a middle-aged man, was dying of cancer. Ironically, Barnsley had written on New Year's Day remarking on the oddity of fame as 'a cloudy rumour in the minds of others'[80] – and she had agreed. Fame, she thought, was an intriguing subject. It provided money but it had no reality, generating only a vacuous form of self-esteem. It did nothing but obstruct creative work, was bad for the soul. But she needed it. She needed to learn how to manage it. Above all, she decided, she needed to get away.

*

At this moment the worst telephone call of Muriel's life arrived, and she rushed to Edinburgh to be with her dying father. Felled by a stroke,

Barney was in the Royal Infirmary. When he asked why the Rabbi didn't visit, she lied and said he had come while Barney was asleep, privately putting down his non-appearance to the fact that her father was too poor to merit attention. It was the Church of Scotland minister who helped him lay his bets on the horses. Then his condition deteriorated. He became delirious with palatal palsy and any hope of recovery faded. On the night of 21 April 1962 Muriel was jerked from sleep in her hotel room by the telephone bell. A nurse was speaking. Her father was dead. Half-dazed, she received the news dispassionately and walked to her window. In the darkness the castle loomed, 'as if one might have expected otherwise'.[81]

There was a calmness about Muriel in the face of death. She had been brought into the Church by reading Cardinal Newman. In times of trouble, he was her resource. 'Lately I've been re-reading Newman,' she wrote during another crisis in 1995, '– the Apologia and the Letters. It was good to come across memorable phrases [...], still fresh, such as "Ten thousand difficulties do not make one doubt", and "What do I know of substance or matter? Just as much as the greatest philosophers, and that is nothing at all." What wonderful English prose, how lucid.'[82] In this lucidity she had discovered distance and acceptance: distance from a mess of torturing emotions, acceptance of spiritual and corporeal corruption. On the back of an envelope containing an otherwise jolly letter she had recently scribbled a version of Newman's famous edict: 'We are all implicated in some vast primordial catastrophe.'[83] The concept of original sin coloured her whole view of life, had released her from depression into a relish for human absurdity. But while this detachment allowed her the space to become a great comic artist of the macabre, it had also separated her from the comfort of sentimental intimacies. 'Back home again, having buried the dead,' she wrote to one of her new American friends, the Catholic poet Ned O'Gorman. 'My father's funeral was our first warm day. A man he did not like fell into his grave.' Such coolness might be mistaken for insensitivity. In fact, the reverse was the case. There was no disguising the wound inflicted by this death. 'My father had more affection for me than anyone else, so that is gone out of the world.'[84] 'I loved and miss him very much,' she informed Shirley Hazzard. 'Lots of family problems at the mo but they will dissolve with time.'[85]

Knowing little of the religious requirements, Muriel left arrangements for the Jewish funeral to her brother, Phil. Shortly after the ceremony, however, he had had to return to America. It was then that the full force of the family problems came home to her. Her mother had a saying: 'A son's a son until he gets a wife, but a daughter's a daughter all her life.' Like her father, Muriel had a tidy mind. Her mother's affairs were chaotic. Unnerved, she wanted to become dependent on her vigorous daughter. Muriel was famous. She appeared to be rich. She would sort things out, take over where 'Father' had left off. Not if Muriel could help it.

At first, Muriel had stayed with Cissy and Robin, appalled by what she found. Her mother was drunk, the flat a shambles. Muriel got a bucket and a scrubbing brush, went down on her hands and knees, and scoured the kitchen floor. Robin had helped but was, she thought, distinctly sullen. Periodically he would go off to his father's house. Muriel did the shopping and each day sat by Barney's hospital bed. At that stage, no one knew whether Phil planned to come over from San Francisco. He had been contacted but had confirmed no arrangements. Then Robin apparently sent a wire: 'Come immediately. Spare no expense. Mum will pay' – that, at least, is how Muriel remembered the message. She was enraged, refused to pay. Her brother had an excellent job and had done little to support his parents. Everything, she felt, had fallen on her shoulders and would do in the future. She had no intention of subsidising him.

In the event, Phil had acted independently and was embarrassed by Robin's telegram. But it was a sign of worse to come. Before Phil's arrival, Robin and Muriel had another argument: '"You get out of here," she later recalled him saying. "You've got to go."'[86] Whatever may or may not have been said, that is how she came to be alone in the North British Hotel, sitting in a window seat as she contemplated love, death and exile between visiting hours at the Royal Infirmary. She felt excluded from her childhood home – and shortly afterwards went to live in New York.

CHAPTER 11

Time / Life

1962–1963

After the funeral, Muriel settled her mother's debts and provided a small capital sum. This only complicated matters. Distracted and depressed, Cissy soon ran through the money, drinking heavily, visiting her Watford relations, and attempting (unsuccessfully) to drop in at Camberwell with Robin. But if the expectation now was that Muriel would provide limitless resources, she strangled it at birth. When the second chapter of *The Mandelbaum Gate* stuttered to a halt, she took a harsh decision and for over six months broke contact with her family.

If Cissy telephoned, Mrs Lazzari and John Smith stonewalled: Muriel was always in the bath, out, ill or abroad. Smith offered the slender hope that she might be able to see them during her August visit to Edinburgh as the Scottish representative at the 1962 International Writers' Festival. When she went, however, she stayed with the High Sheriff and lived only the public life of a celebrity. There was no longer, she felt, a home for her in that city. Her accountant, Arthur Warne, was instructed to inform Cissy that she had 'nothing left'. No more bills would be paid until another book was completed: let Philip and Robin take their turn at caring for her. In fact, Muriel had plenty of money. But how long would these reserves last if she could not write? 'I have not done any complete work this year due to family upheavals,' she wrote to Warne, '[and] have had to put aside one novel, and start a lighter one which I can do more quickly. [...] I always had wonderful peace of mind when I was struggling for a living, and was able to write two novels a year!"

The deferred novel was *Mandelbaum*, the 'lighter' one *The Girls of Slender Means*. At the end of July she had disappeared to Aylesford Priory for a fortnight to start it, leaving Smith to research details of rationing in 1945 and to post them on. She had finally decided to leave Macmillan, and Tom Maschler of Cape was expecting to publish *Girls*. Macmillan she considered too coldly officious for the diplomatic handling of Robin and Cissy.[2] Then she had come to Edinburgh for the Writers' Festival where, three months after her father's death and closeted among signings and interviews (one intrepid BBC reporter had caught up with her and Lawrence Durrell in a café; the BBC had broadcast a discussion between her, Norman Mailer and Angus Wilson in which she was almost incoherent), she had managed to avoid the folks at home. Just before this, she had written that painful piece about Edinburgh, death, exile and the 'nevertheless principle'.[3] It was published a week before her arrival in mid-August 1962, almost as a press release for her mother and son. In this short time, barely a month after her correspondence with Maschler, she had changed her mind again and decided to stick with Macmillan.[4] Maclean's mother was dying. He had only recently returned to work after major surgery. Muriel sympathised with his distress and dedicated *Girls* to him. Now that he was no longer her editor, they could resume their friendship. The same thing applied to Lovat Dickson who had now passed her on to the young Robert Yeatman. Macmillan, perhaps, for all the incompetence she detected, was the nearest thing she had to a hotel for her talent. It would do until another establishment offered better terms. And in the meantime she was looking elsewhere: to New York, to Paris, to Rome.

*

Nineteen sixty-two was a frenetic year when her chief literary interest was neither *Mandelbaum* nor *Girls* but her play. *Doctors of Philosophy* had gone into production in June. Peggy Ramsay, the leading theatrical agent, coordinated operations; Donald McWhinnie directed; Michael Codron was to present it first at the revamped New Arts Theatre Club and then in the West End. There was a good cast (including Laurence Hardy, Ursula Howell and Fenella Fielding). Although small, the Arts was famous, along with the Royal Court, for avant-garde drama. It was perhaps dangerous to 'open cold' in London rather than to follow the normal practice of experimenting in the provinces. But it seemed a small gamble. Muriel had a high reputation, particularly as a master of dialogue, and Codron and McWhinnie were delighted to have secured her first stage play. She took their advice, confident of success.

Doctors opened on 1 October, less than a fortnight before she was due to fly back to New York. Neither Cissy nor Robin was invited to the first night. It was to be a glamorous occasion with free tickets only for her London entourage. A fortnight before, she had been in Verona with Tristram Cary and Christopher Holme to receive the Italia Prize for the radio musical version of *Ballad*. Her father's death had marked a Rubicon. Beyond it lay her full translation into international celebrity. If Barnsley whined and Heppenstall bullied, if her family sponged, then so be it. Goodbye Rotten Row. She would reinvent herself on a wider stage – and that first night seemed to go well. The audience applauded heartily. Afterwards Maurice Macmillan threw a champagne supper party with three more of the firm's ambassadors (Maclean, Dickson and Yeatman) in attendance to extinguish any hint of their earlier uncertainty about financing her to write a play. With *Doctors* now scheduled for their 1963 list, everyone was wheeled out to cheer. Unfortunately, with two exceptions, the London critics did not.

Harold Hobson, the solitary supporter of early Pinter, was one of the exceptions: 'It all goes on with the quiet confidence of a proposition in Euclid, only more entertainingly.'[5] T. C. Worsley of the *Financial Times* relished the sharp dialogue and sense of the bizarre.[6] The rest were often harsh. 'The Critics' on the BBC's Third Programme acknowledged amusing lines and situations, then savaged the piece: 'manufactured feyness and clumsy obscurantism'; 'half-converted stereotypes, or unfinished enigmas'. Its wit and intelligence, they thought, failed to disguise a flawed dramatic structure. 'In fact, it's rather a shambles. But it's not a *boring* shambles.'[7]

One member of this panel was supposedly Muriel's friend, albeit a distant one: Pamela Hansford Johnson (Mrs C. P. Snow). Given the *mise en scène* – a household of academics detached from reality – Muriel must have smiled at Johnson's call for a 'play doctor' to knock this drama into shape. *Doctors* took people like Johnson's husband as its point of departure. The Snows, prominent Macmillan authors, were Maclean's 'pals' and assisted his efforts to drag the firm into the twentieth century. But even he had to admit that they could be unconsciously amusing. 'Our trouble', he recalled Pamela once saying, 'is that we've never had time for any fun',[8] and Muriel had already lampooned her writing. In *The Ballad of Peckham Rye*, among Dougal Douglas's notes for his ghosted autobiography of the faded music-hall star is a collection of clichés echoing her voice: 'I thrilled to his touch'; 'As he entered the room a shudder went through my frame'; 'I became the proud owner of a bicycle'; 'I had no eyes for any other man'; 'We were living a lie' etc.[9] Muriel had lifted the entire list from Johnson's novels.

The scholarly or 'intellectual' woman had become something of an archetype in Muriel's imagination since writing *Child of Light*. The sharp-tongued self-confidence of women like Mary Shelley, their depressions, competitive cattiness and awkward relations with men feature regularly in her fiction. Among her friends she recognised this 'academic type' in Christine Brooke-Rose. There was something of her in *Mandelbaum*'s Barbara Vaughan, in Miss Brodie, in Caroline Rose.[10] And, as Muriel admitted, there was also much of herself in these figures. They are equally attractive and repulsive, hot and cold, independent and difficult to love. She felt defensive of their willed isolation. Their intellectualism renders them spinsters, nuns, teachers, scholars, frozen off from the comforting sentimentalities of domestic life. With this, she could sympathise. Their attraction lies in their mockery of subjection, their silliness in their rationalism. *Doctors*, superficially a three-act Wildean social comedy, playfully circles the issues of female vocation and exile.

Doctors takes place in the London house of Catherine Delfont and her husband, Charlie. Catherine, formerly a brilliant scholar, has abandoned her career for marriage and family. Charlie, a leading economist, acts merely as a plot device to enable the discussions between his more interesting wife and two other female characters. Dr Leonora Chase, Catherine's cousin and oldest friend from student days, has remained single and become a Fellow of an Oxford college. Annie, Catherine's other cousin, is something of a Puck in this household, as Muriel often was in the homes of her more conventional friends. Reckless, amusing, exotic, and lacking a PhD, Annie walks about the landing in her knickers, has the audacity to discuss subjects on which she is not an authority, and dresses provocatively to subvert her family's solemn self-assurance. The action progresses through sudden revelations that destroy previous certainty. Leonora has a breakdown centring on her sense of being 'fruitless', childless. The validity of her research is undermined by a new discovery. All such rationalist theories are 'blown to hell'.[11] Leonora, however, is intrigued rather than distressed. 'Reality', she explains to Mrs S., the cockney housekeeper, 'is very alarming at first and then it becomes interesting.'[12] The scenery, she tells Annie, 'is unreliable'.[13] It is as though those who can break role are saved. The damned condemn themselves to one dimension, and this notion emerges as much from the form of the drama as from its content.

Act Two, for instance, opens on a bare stage, pulleys and switches exposed, with the scenery being erected by the characters. Leonora starts shoving the seeming-solid set about. Mrs S. veers across an improbable range of linguistic registers like Pinter's Lenny in *The Homecoming*. There are shades of Beckett when she says, 'You're late, Charlie. I've had to keep the conversation going',[14] echoes of farce and pantomime, and of absurdism generally. When Leonora speaks of her 'definite sense of being observed and listened to by an audience', Annie responds enthusiastically: 'Leonora, this is thrilling. All my life I've had a feeling of being looked at by an audience. That's why I always take care to be suitably dressed.'[15]

In this vein, *Doctors* is postmodern, its characters referring to themselves as characters in a play. But where self-reference in Beckett's work signals fragmentation of the self, here it relates to developing self-consciousness, the liberating acceptance of multiple selves. The neurosis of rationalism (in this play of the academic mind) stems from the hopeless desire to render multiplicity as singularity. Leonora refuses conventional psychotherapy, as Muriel had, because it would reduce her 'to the ranks', and she is not prepared to be thus reduced 'now that I have obtained such an exhilarating glimpse of my dramatic position'. She has realised that she is 'a woman of destiny'.[16] The word 'thrilling' becomes important in contradistinction to 'exciting'. Muriel often used it, too. Despite the play's technical complexity and debates about the nature of reality, it focuses on female identity in middle age: on 'the change', on saving face when one appears erratic. 'Saving face', Leonora says, 'is essentially a dramatic instinct for those who insist on playing dramatic roles.'[17] The crucial question is how best to maintain *joie de vivre* in middle life. And the answer is simple: get up, walk out, change role. Leonora is off to America and is thrilled by the prospect.

*

Muriel flew back to New York on 13 October 1962, equally thrilled and conscious of her 'dramatic position', checked into the Hotel Gladstone and contacted Shirley Hazzard. Although she had planned to spend only a few weeks in America, her stay soon extended to three months with a view to making New York her permanent base. She already had an account with the Chase Manhattan. At the *New Yorker* (which had just published 'The Gentile Jewesses') William Shawn had reserved an office for her. She now looked to America for the bulk of her income and, above all, longed to put the Atlantic between herself and Cissy. On the advice of her *New Yorker* editor, Rachel MacKenzie, she leased a modern furnished apartment in the Beaux Arts Hotel at 310 East 44th Street, and by the 24th had moved in.

An 'apartment hotel', the Beaux Arts had a ground-floor restaurant to send up meals. Muriel's flat was on a corner of the thirteenth floor: small sitting room, bedroom, bathroom and a galley kitchen. It was expensive but perfect for her needs: functional, anodyne and serviced entirely by others. The price included laundry, maid and stationery. She never used the kitchen for cooking. Picture windows framed the UN Building, the East River and spectacular sunsets. From 1 November she had her *New Yorker* room in which to work, also on a corner, on the eighteenth floor. Every day she would travel uptown by taxi and work comfortable office hours: 10.00–4.00. Through that window she could see the scarlet Time / Life sign at Rockefeller Center flashing on and off. 'When it says "Time"', she told Hazzard, 'I write. When it says "Life", I want to go out.'[18] It was there, within the month, that she (almost) finished *Girls*.

Shirley Hazzard, author of *The Transit of Venus* (1980) and *The Great Fire* (2002), is now a leading American novelist. In 1963, however, that career was only just beginning and she was grateful for Muriel's introductions. Visiting London after Muriel's first American trip, Hazzard had been embraced as a sister and invited to a Camberwell party. Already published by Macmillan, she had grown to know and like Rache Lovat Dickson and now, through Muriel, met Alan Maclean, who was to become a lifelong friend. Brooke-Rose was there, and Heppenstall.

Returning to America, Muriel had, as usual, brought with her an air of mystery. Indeed, even Hazzard's account of this aura breeds mystery. She recalled Muriel expressing romantic interest in a man she expected to re-encounter. Nothing had been arranged. Nevertheless, Muriel was certain they would meet. One day the two women were walking up the steps of the Metropolitan Museum to attend a recital by the Budapest String Quartet. At the top a man had come out to smoke a cigarette. 'There he is', Muriel said, and moved ahead. Hazzard watched the couple greet each other affectionately. The man's evident tenderness towards Muriel seemed almost to embarrass him. Then Hazzard realised that she also knew him. He was Lionel Trilling, the eminent Jewish academic and critic. She approached and shook hands before going into the auditorium with Muriel, who was in high spirits. 'It was, of course', Hazzard remarked, 'one of her extraordinary things'[19] – but according to Muriel it was nothing of the sort: no more than a banal encounter with a casual acquaintance. Hazzard, she thought, was 'romancing'. Hazzard was certain she was not. What was going on here?

It was true that Muriel scarcely knew Trilling. He had turned up at the St Regis Hotel launch of *The Prime of Miss Jean Brodie* when she had signed his copy 'For Lionel from Muriel'. They had only met socially in

Paris when she had attended a 1962 conference to discuss the plight of Soviet Jews. Thoroughly engaged with the subject ('it fairly curdles the Jewish part of my blood'[20]), she had admired Trilling's robust attack on anti-Semitism. On this occasion, clearly having forgotten her, he had advised her to read *The Ballad of Peckham Rye* and she had replied: 'I wrote it.' Perhaps, away from his wife, the formidable Diana, he had flirted. If so, nothing had occurred beyond flirtation. No letters passed between them. Nevertheless, she was attracted, sensed something might happen, that she could will it to happen – and her apparent powers of foresight could be unnerving, as Hazzard was to discover.

Towards the end of her stay, on 26 January 1963, Muriel threw a farewell party and presented Hazzard with another of those 'extraordinary things'. Introducing Francis Steegmuller, Muriel said that this was a man Hazzard might marry. Steegmuller was fifty-seven, tall, reserved, witty, but still grieving two years after the death of his wife, the American painter, Beatrice Stein. Hazzard was thirty-two, shy and brilliant. He was a grand figure among *New Yorker* contributors, multilingual, with an international reputation as biographer, translator and critic: one of the last of the gentleman-scholars. His French rendering of 'The Owl and the Pussycat', a recent *jeu d'esprit*, had improbably become a best-seller. Hazzard, Australian by birth, had spent her dislocated youth following her father's postings in the diplomatic service. At the United Nations Secretariat in New York she had spent further years in the metaphorical dungeons, escaping, first, through an assignment to Italy, and subsequently through the *New Yorker* where her first stories had been accepted by William Maxwell. She was still an impoverished apprentice writer. On the face of it, a match with Steegmuller seemed unlikely – rather like the owl and the pussycat, in fact. But they sat in a corner, buried in talk for two hours, and left separately with the intention of meeting again. That December they married and formed one of the great literary partnerships of post-war American letters, broken only by his death in 1994. When they returned from their wedding journey, Muriel sent a picture of her apartment block with the relevant window inked in: 'The Scene of the First Encounter between

Shirley Hazzard and Francis Steegmuller by Muriel Spark. (Her best book ever.)'[21]

Muriel had the power to take people over. Her friends were sometimes apprehensive of becoming a figment of her imagination. As Ved Mehta remarked: 'She'd absolutely conquer you immediately. And then of course she'd move on to someone else.'[22] She was mercurial, forceful, a pyrotechnic conversationalist. If she liked someone, she would home in and slash through social defences. One felt first exposed, then prized, then abandoned. Mehta was in his late twenties, Hazzard in her early thirties, Muriel forty-four. She seemed ageless and unstoppable: ruthlessly funny yet unpretentious. She saw through everything (those X-ray eyes) and yet possessed, almost perversely preserved, a disconcerting candour of response. It was like dealing with St Monica and Cinderella simultaneously, the Cinderella being a trap which St Monica could spring with vengeful alacrity on anyone attempting to patronise her.

Muriel lent passionate sympathy to her young friends' causes. She warmed immediately, for instance, to Ned O'Gorman, the poet introduced to her by Anne Fremantle. To him she could speak openly of the joy of creation and her bouts of melancholy. He treated her as a poet, which she loved, sometimes feeling expelled from the Eden of her original incarnation as an artist, yet stressing that when writing her novels she was an entirely happy displaced person.[23] Her excitement was infectious and endearing, and Hazzard's own *joie de vivre*, nurtured through her continuing visits to Italy, was ignited by this frankness and energy. *Carpe diem.* In New York, Muriel's darker moods were quickly obliterated by an invincible gaiety and her attachment to life's absurdity. Novelty – new faces and places, new pleasures – refreshed her, appeasing, Hazzard thought, a fugitive need for dismissal and change. Observing her friend's light-heartedness then, she characterised her with a line from *Much Ado*: 'A star danced, and under that I was born.'

During Muriel's New York stays, and until Hazzard married, these two saw each other almost daily: dinners, concerts, exhibitions, all drifted on a stream of talk and laughter. They would go to the cinema and cry together unashamedly. Muriel's remarks were particularly apt at skewering their past imperfect relations with men. She enjoyed the company of a platonic friend of Hazzard's, Robert Sonkin, a philologist at City College, struck up an acquaintance with a series of gay young fellows and soft-spoken liberals like Trilling. For Muriel, the (mild) attraction of the former was that they made congenial squires, of the latter that they were gently flirtatious. Neither attempted to 'possess' a woman. Such arrangements made for an amiable social life but the former were useless as lovers and the latter too spiritless to confront her strength of character.

Whether Muriel wished to remarry, or even to have a serious affair, was probably as much a mystery to her as it was to her friends. She was cautious, had been badly damaged by Solly Spark and by her attempts to replace him with Sergeant and Stanford.[24] Nevertheless, she enjoyed the ritual of courtship, and the myth of the strong, sensitive – ideally, solvent – man who might rescue and protect her died hard. Shirley had found one. Why shouldn't *she*? But love left one vulnerable, interfered with work and independence. Muriel had no capacity for worship of the male. She would not serve. And now that she was prosperous and famous, how was one to sift out the fortune-hunters? Only a man both rich and homosexual would be exempt from suspicion. Impasse.

Hazzard recalled one autumn evening in Dwight and Gloria Macdonald's apartment. The Macdonalds often threw these impromptu parties, dispensing plain fare and good talk. The conversation was the attraction: cocktail-fuelled writers balancing plates and firing the night with aphorism. Through these and other hosts Muriel had met W. H. Auden, Stephen Spender, John Updike, Alastair Reid, Robert Lowell, James Baldwin, Herbert Read, William Maxwell, Saul Steinberg, Brendan Gill. And in such sharp company, the city's intellectual elite orbiting the *New Yorker*, she was herself a meteor, confident and unpredictable. On this occasion, Norman Mailer was there, and Trilling and his wife. Muriel returned to the sitting room with her plate of chilli con carne and sat down by Hazzard. Her affection for Trilling, she said, was over. His nervousness when Diana was present had instantly revealed that something was amiss.[25]

The speed with which Muriel repudiated her interest in Trilling suggests a death wish on any potential relationship. She relied on her instincts, backed up by fatalism. If something was meant to happen, it would. Those instincts, however, so finely tuned in other respects, had always been erratic where men were concerned. Trilling, tough as he was intellectually, was anxious to placate Diana and he represented Muriel to her as an embarrassment. 'I believe you know Muriel Spark,' Diana remarked later to Hazzard and Steegmuller. 'She introduced us,' Hazzard replied. 'I'm sorry to hear that,' said Diana. Hazzard rose instantly in her friend's defence: 'I'm not.' Diana smiled: 'We have to go cautiously there. She has a thing about Lionel.'[26] Hazzard said nothing. She had seen Trilling's reaction on the steps of the museum – and then Muriel's over the chilli con carne.

*

The *New Yorker* in 1962 was on West 43rd Street, just across from the Algonquin 'which was everybody's living room'.[27] One of the first staff writers Muriel met was Brendan Gill. Later the magazine's unofficial historian,[28] Gill was then nearly fifty, married with children, and conducting a heated affair with a young woman who wrote (appropriately enough, for the affair was no secret) the 'Talk of the Town' column. He was a lapsed Catholic. While Edmund Wilson was attempting to tear him away from a faith in which he no longer belonged, Muriel tried to reclaim him. Once she gave him a splinter of bone from St Robert Bellarmine. Housed in a gold reliquary, this exquisite piece, Gill thought, would be perfect pinned to the bodice of a dress. (It had, indeed, been pinned to Muriel's own dress in photographs Mark Gerson took of her in Camberwell.) Unsure what to do with the object, Gill kept it in his desk drawer, prevented by 'a childhood fear of blasphemy' from offering it to his lover: 'A saint's bone between a pretty girl's breasts! I wish I had the nerve.'[29] But this, he felt, was typical of Muriel: no proselytising; just the perfectly chosen, disarming present. Whenever she travelled, she always returned bearing exotic gifts for her editors, agents and friends.

Gill was immediately attracted by Muriel's vivacity. He had expected the author of *Memento Mori* and *Brodie* to be melancholy. Instead, he discovered 'a kind of girlish joyousness [...] all open and ready to receive an infinite number of impressions.' The *New Yorker*, from his perspective, was populated by 'very gloomy writers. There was no joy in the corridors. [...] I was always found odd there because I was singing and merry [...].'[30] Under William Shawn the magazine had nurtured the best talent but there was something stiff about it, in Gill's view: for all its merits, this grand institution had become something like a church or an Ivy League college, with its own lore, clergy and faculty. (Hazzard's and Mehta's impression was precisely the opposite.) Those who were 'in', Gill felt, were of the elect. Muriel shook it up. She brightened everything.

Shawn, never 'William', even to his closest associates, had the aura of a sage. Muriel's grandfather had once called Mrs Pankhurst, 'Mrs Spankarse', and the phrase had been used in 'The Gentile Jewesses'. Shawn cut it. Muriel raised no objection. 'Mr Shawn', she noted with respectful amusement, was always pronounced as one word. Editorship was his vocation and his reputation was enhanced by his reserve, his nickname, 'the iron mouse', was appropriate. He was a small man of adamantine will, overwhelmed by his own courtesy. Hazzard remembered him affectionately both as 'neurotic and immensely disciplined', cultivating a 'hushed', private atmosphere, and also as inimitable, irreducible, a central figure of contemporary literary culture.[31] Myth has it that, meticulous to the point of obsession, he once traced a writer to the jungle in order to request permission to alter a comma.

Shawn's phobias were legend. When automatic elevators were installed, he refused to use them, fearful of heights and of being trapped.[32] A little big man, he was principled and devoid of arrogance. Complicated. Unknowable. A grave of confidences. Napoleon and St Francis of Assisi, as Gill put it. An accomplished jazz pianist, Shawn played only at home, or rather, at his two homes. Married with three children, he was devoted to his family while simultaneously running an alternative household with Lillian Ross.[33] The affair lasted for forty years, until his death in 1992, but colleagues never spoke of Lillian to him. If he wished to discuss something, he would not summon but tap lightly on doors, enter for a few barely audible words, and disappear like a benevolent ghost. Anyone less resembling a modern 'executive' it is difficult to imagine – and Muriel loved him. When Tom Wolfe assaulted his reputation in 1965 with a parody profile in the *Herald Tribune*'s Sunday supplement, *New York*, she reared like a cobra: 'MR WOLFE'S STYLE OF PERSONAL ATTACK', she telegrammed from just down the road, 'IS PLAINLY DERIVED FROM SENATOR MACARTHY [*sic*].' [34]

Under Shawn's aegis, Muriel at last found something like a home. Offices were distributed gratis to writers he supported, even a 'drawing account' if necessary. This money, supposedly an advance, was often not earned back. Muriel never took it. The eighteenth floor was a warren of authors (rarely of fiction). Rooms were generally small and bare: metal desk, telephone, an ancient typewriter. Paper and carbons were available on request. No one would intrude. On the other hand, you were not isolated. There was always someone interesting to talk to by the water cooler in the corridor or in the Algonquin over the road. Muriel's office, previously occupied by Joe [A. J.] Liebling (legendary war, food and travel correspondent) was the largest. Next door was Ved Mehta. Keeping steady control over Shawn's generosity was Milton Greenstein, the magazine's avuncular lawyer. Manners and fine writing were promoted. They went the extra mile to nourish talent. How different, Muriel, felt, from Macmillan. 'Hospitality' was the word which sprang first to her mind, then 'liberty of expression', 'encouragement', and 'open friendliness'.[35]

Cosseted in this utopia, she made many friends: Macdonald, Hazzard, Steegmuller, Mehta, Gill and his lover; also Maxwell, Greenstein, Howard Moss (the poetry editor) and his companion, Mark Pagano. All the staff of the fiction department were creative writers, some (Maxwell and Joseph Mitchell in particular) with considerable reputations of their own. They were also, according to Gill, 'self-confessed misfits', insular and neurotic; people who rarely mixed with another social set.[36] This suited Muriel well enough for the 'Time' side of New York. For the 'Life' side, she had other 'sets': introductions made through Ned O'Gorman; through Shirley and Sonkin, who drew Morton Cohen and Richard

Swift into her orbit. 'Mort', later the celebrated biographer of Lewis Carroll, also taught at City College; 'Dick' was another academic, an expert on international law. A youthful, cultivated couple, they were eager to take Muriel about. Everywhere she went, strangers craved her company. It was, in its way, heaven, but for her the border between protection and oppression was always narrow. By the end of November, just one month after occupying her office, she wrote to Shawn saying that she no longer needed it.[37] Something had already gone wrong.

*

Muriel hardly knew Rachel MacKenzie and, finding that their paths now crossed more frequently, disliked what she found. MacKenzie, also Hazzard's editor, was then in her fifties, tall, robust, a minister's daughter with grey hair and glasses: benign, Hazzard thought, and with the smile of the New World.[38] At the magazine, MacKenzie was liked and respected. She edited several major authors including Isaac Bashevis Singer. Some found her convivial, others noted a deepening solemnity. She prided herself on closeness to her writers. Indeed, in Muriel's view, she was a clinger and control freak. After initial friendship, Hazzard had begun to find the woman's attentions excessive but, as a relative newcomer, had said nothing. In the evenings, MacKenzie would telephone with maternal inquiries. If Hazzard were out, MacKenzie wished to know where she had been, making the younger woman feel called upon to account for herself. One day, MacKenzie, who already lived in the neighbourhood, told her that she was moving her apartment 'to be nearer to you'. Enter Muriel, like Annie in the play.

MacKenzie would invite them both to claustrophobic Sunday suppers. 'Muriel,' she would say, 'you must be so tired. Put your feet up.' She would tell Hazzard that she looked exhausted. Returning from one of these evenings, Muriel summarised it: 'Trying to immobilise me.' And then: 'How long have you been putting up with this? She tries to make you a victim.' MacKenzie certainly believed in her own good intentions but, as Hazzard remembered Muriel phrasing it, 'The Unconscious is on top with her; you have to dig down to find the Conscious.'[39]

Both women became convinced that, like Brodie, MacKenzie was (unconsciously) a lesbian.

Muriel listened carefully and recounted her own experiences. 'Just how old are you, Muriel?' MacKenzie had asked. The reply was a cheerful snub: 'I've told so many people so many different dates, I don't even remember myself.' But 'Auntie Rachel', as Muriel called her, seemed immune to rebuff. Later she turned up at the Beaux Arts where she ran her finger along the door. It was merely dust, Muriel remarked. The cleaning in her apartment block was inefficient. 'You'll just have to do it yourself, then, won't you?' From that moment, Muriel would have nothing to do with the woman and told Maxwell that she wished to change editors. Such a demand was unprecedented in that mannerly atmosphere; but Shawn and Greenstein dealt with it. Muriel went to Robert Henderson and Hazzard to Maxwell. 'Old-timers at the *New Yorker*,' Hazzard remarked, 'couldn't understand how anyone could be so harsh. They might have had more imagination. In those days, one didn't speak of being "abused".' Muriel saw it as a necessary severity. Shirley, relieved by her own release, marvelled at her friend's single-mindedness – and at MacKenzie's lack of self-enquiry.[40]

As it turned out, Muriel never relinquished her office, but her offer to do so perhaps also related to two other matters: her decision to leave Lippincott, her American publishers, and her desire to protect her public image. Lynn and Virginia Carrick now lived in London, where he attended to the firm's European business and she was Longman's American 'scout'. Cork Smith had resigned to take a better job at Viking. In the hands of strangers, Muriel felt no loyalty. The managing editor, George Stevens, had invited her in for a welcoming chat. Where did she live? Beaux Arts? 'Ah, now my daughter has a brownstone walk-up on the West side and you'd find that sort of thing much cheaper.' Muriel, less than pleased by this response,[41] was not alone in disliking Stevens's style. Apparently, he alienated other female authors. A perceptive and decent man, he was also patrician. She had not, he noted, earned back her advances. That did it. When she felt attacked by anyone, she informed the publicity director, she responded in kind.[42]

She needed, she explained to Carrick, to find a publisher who understood her. This had nothing to do with him and she trusted their friendship would survive (it did). Nevertheless, there was one thing on which she wished to put him straight: she was not subsidised by the *New Yorker* as some of the Lippincott staff appeared to believe.[43] Any prospective publisher should harbour no doubt about the need to *sell* her books and to provide fat advances. It was a commercial decision of the kind which soon prodded John Smith down the gangplank. Muriel would not be misrepresented. The year 1962 saw a spate of dumpings. Smith's firm, Christy & Moore, was a small outfit, struggling to manage the range of her foreign contracts. Replying to his long letters consumed whole days. It was more efficient to deal direct with von Auw who absorbed all the pressure. When Lippincott attempted to play hardball over contractual obligation he smiled it away. What was the point? What could they achieve? Grudgingly, they let her go, cancelling options. To this day, 'How Lippincott Lost Spark' remains a mystery in its company lore.

Speaking of Lippincott and of Smith, Muriel said much the same thing. She was fond of both, but loyalty to publishers and agents was a luxury which, as a single woman, she could ill afford. Part of the thrill of New York was the poker game being played between publishers to win her custom, with von Auw acting as impassive banker. And the stakes ran high. She was a magnetic field. The publisher Blanche Knopf had taken her out to lunch and offered double any other bid. It was as simple as that. Lippincott were a respectable firm with another recent triumph in Harper Lee's *To Kill a Mockingbird* (1960). But they were not a major literary house like Knopf. Publishing with Knopf increased both status and revenue. They produced beautiful books and marketed them ferociously. How could she refuse? 'I really was in business,' she explained. 'The spirit of the affair, I can provide that in my writings. After that, it's business.'[44]

*

Blanche and Alfred Knopf were commanding New York figures. Tall and droll, Alfred was a connoisseur of food, wine and books; close-fisted in negotiation, liberal of hospitality with those he liked – and he liked Muriel. Blanche was a creature of myth. Nourishing herself daily on one Martini, three shrimps and a stick of asparagus, she weighed scarcely seven stone. Yet this small, fastidious person, seemingly held together by jewellery, was pure granite. Beneath that elegant metropolitan exterior lay the woman who used to ride to hounds. Her quarry was the best new writing. Each year she would tour the world and set up court: at Claridge's in London, at the Ritz in Paris. Largely due to her efforts, Knopf represented a gold standard: Thomas Mann, Wallace Stevens, Sigrid Undset, Ivy Compton-Burnett, Elizabeth Bowen, Freud, Gide, Sartre, de Beauvoir, Camus, Yukio Mishima, Updike. Blanche, rarely deflected, knew what she wanted, and Muriel Spark was a prime target.

'You didn't *apply* to go and see Blanche,' Maclean recalled. 'She never showed the slightest interest in Macmillan or me or anything until Muriel showed up. Then I would be sent for every year [...] for one purpose only [...]: "I still want to publish Muriel Spark. What can you do about it?" And the answer, of course, was that I could do nothing about it. But she got her in the end.'[45] Muriel and Blanche were of a kind. Among the tributes at Blanche's death in June 1966 were two by Harding ('Pete') Lemay and William Koshland, both of whom worked with Muriel at Knopf. Lemay recalled Blanche's 'civilized humour, her grace of spirit'; Koshland her 'dogged persistence', 'feminine allure', 'impulsive penchant for naughtiness' and 'cheerful pessimism'.[46] In Muriel she recognised a kindred spirit.

The Knopfs' marriage was a ruin of such magnificent proportions that preserving it became a work of art. They had separate apartments, convening at either household, at the office, or at their country house at Purchase on Long Island, to welcome (and photograph) authors. They lived through and for the vocation that had brought them together half a century earlier: the passion for books, excellent books finely printed. In later life, Blanche's apartment was a scene of controlled hysteria: French maid and cook screaming at each other in the kitchen, a diminutive poodle, 'Monsieur', bouncing off the furniture and yapping at guests' heels. One evening during the 'great blackout' power failure of November 1965, Maclean and Muriel arrived for a dinner party to discover the place in even greater turmoil.

The cook, Virgie, a woman of substantial girth, in taking Monsieur down the stairs to the sidewalk, had slipped in the icy darkness and fallen on him. Monsieur was not killed but dangerously flattened. Blanche was distraught, Maclean embarrassed, Alfred (who had just turned up) unconcerned and ineffective. Muriel took control. 'She said all the right things [...] in a very sort of cooing, comforting way.'[47] It was an odd scene: two of the toughest women in New York lamenting as though for an injured child. But both possessed the gift of empathy, erratically dispensed. Maclean remembered Fred Winter, the champion jockey and trainer, driving Muriel to Cheltenham Races. Muriel sat beside him. When Winter, shy in close proximity to a famous author, stared silently at the road, Muriel put him at his ease by talking of nothing but horses: 'She instinctively knew how to behave for other people.'[48] She also understood how one could love a dog or a horse more easily than one could another human being.

Blanche's communications with Muriel were finely judged. Her letters and telegrams cooed love, support, enthusiasm, fierce defence. Domestic life may have been anathema but she knew how to make her authors comfortable. Muriel saw little of Alfred and became so infuriated with Lemay (her editor) that Knopf did not keep her long. Blanche, though, she always loved in the quizzical, fascinated fashion of one woman of destiny confronting another. Blanche was a house-trained eagle, her long talons the colour of blood ('my blood', Muriel would joke). But she was, in her way, entirely admirable. Facing pain and death, she ignored them. The woman Muriel met was sixty-six, nearly blind, half-crippled and young in spirit. Muriel relished such resistance wherever she found it.[49] Indeed, she was probably the last author to speak to Blanche, that conversation lingering in the novelist's mind like a scene from Memento Mori. Muriel had gone to East Hampton for a rest, to a hotel overlooking the sea. Knowing that Blanche was ill, she rang to ask if she could manage to be driven out. No, Blanche replied, she couldn't make it. 'I said to her, "Blanche, can you hear the sea?" She said, "No, but I'd like to", so I put the telephone receiver out of the window for her to hear the waves and then she said, "Yes, I heard the sound of the sea." She must have died a few hours later [...].'[50]

Muriel signed up with Knopf in late January 1963. In just four months she had renovated her entire professional life in America as though she had walked into a store wearing a serviceable British outfit and emerged undetectably Fifth Avenue. John Guest, a distant friend from London and literary adviser to Longmans, remembered attending a New York party given for him by the Carricks. 'In the middle of it a strikingly dressed woman rushed up to greet me; [...] I have an impression of white fox furs and diamonds and a very sophisticated hair-do – I just hope she wasn't disappointed by a possibly somewhat wary reception on my part. When she had gone I asked Virginia Carrick who she was. To my amazement (and horror) she said that it was Muriel! I simply didn't recognise her.'[51] Everything had changed. Smith was replaced by von Auw (for American contracts), Lippincott by Knopf, MacKenzie by Henderson. Muriel had sold a revised version of the first chapter of *Mandelbaum* to the *New Yorker* and had nearly completed *Girls*, hoping that the *New Yorker* might take that, too. This period of triumphant success, however, was also one continuously spiked by frustration.

*

'Volatile' scarcely describes Muriel's emotional state over the next three years. New York inspired her, the thought of her family cast her down. In New York she was rejuvenated and at work on *Girls*, one of her finest novels. But she was anxious about it, thought she might have lost some of her public with the reviews of *Doctors of Philosophy*,[52] and it was with her readers that she now felt her closest tie. Although she had left the play (kept on for an extra week) pleasing audiences well enough, Michael Codron exasperated her. When he worked with Joe Orton, *Loot* was continually rewritten both during its first unsuccessful run and later to shape it for a London production. This was how the commercial theatre worked. It was not, however, how Muriel worked. Codron would wake her in the small hours with transatlantic telephone calls, wanted to rewrite and to retitle the play *Charlie Is My Darling*. When he sent his revised Act 2, she stuffed it in a drawer. And there it would stay, she said, until he found a West End theatre. As he could not find one without a revised script, the project soon collapsed. When von Auw arranged for his British counterpart, Edmund Cork of Hughes Massie, to act on her behalf, she took a dislike to him and insisted that von Auw alone should deal with her writing. Dorothy Olding, his business partner, came over to London in the spring of 1963 to find herself refereeing a full-scale dispute with Muriel in the depths, unable to work. Crossing Park Lane on the way to their council of war with Cork, they were almost killed by a runaway ambulance. Strange things did seem to happen when Muriel was around but somehow von Auw kept her steady. Christmas, 'the frightful feast' to her, was often a bad period, promising what it could not deliver, and the Christmas of 1962 had been spent in America, with her up one moment and down the next. London remained her 'Mother-metropolis'.[53] New York thrilled, but its strangeness and hysterical speed left her craving something more slow-paced. Von Auw's present of orchids had hit the spot: 'the most mysteriously lovely objects in the world.' She kept them in the refrigerator at night, intending to use them, one by one, as special decorations. They revived her: 'flourishing in their confidence without any need to be useful creatures [...].'[54]

Von Auw was important to Muriel because she trusted his judgement so completely that he acted as a tranquilliser. If he told her not to worry, her anxieties melted. Writers were his hothouse flowers and, nurturing her confidence, he became her close friend and principal New York escort. When Frank Kermode met her in the States, he thought she had a Russian boyfriend. This was von Auw, not her boyfriend at all but her entirely delightful protector. He was a great cook and party-giver, one of the few agents who read deeply and for pleasure. Small, balding, with close-cropped sandy hair, he behaved in business with a polite ruthlessness towards inaccuracy. His private life was rather more decadent, with his prominent position in the city's gay community and a taste for expensive paintings, but he is remembered more for pragmatism than for reckless generosity. With his partner, Paul Peters, he lived between New York and Long Island (later in apartments in Portugal and Puerto Rico). Morton Cohen, who knew both men well, thought it typical that when Peters died during a Greek holiday, rather than cancelling the trip von Auw placed his lover's corpse in a morgue and finished the cruise before burying him.[55] Muriel, however, loved von Auw. He was one of those rare beings to whom she could reveal her vulnerability.[56] He understood the switchback of an artist's moods.

On the plane back to England Muriel had suddenly burst into tears, overwhelmed by melancholy. Holed up in snowbound Baldwin Crescent with her ancient landlady, Mrs Lazzari, bounding up the stairs to check pipes and roof, she recovered. Anxious letters arrived in Camberwell from Hazzard, detailing her developing relationship with Steegmuller. How should she proceed? Muriel's replies were gentle and modest, sharing her own fear of emotional damage.[57] She had, she admitted, a tendency herself to be attracted to the sensitive, often gay, male rather than to machismo. Always supportive, she stressed the evident love between Hazzard and Steegmuller while never forgetting her friend's vocation: 'All that matters is that you are full of possibilities in life & work. I'm enormously pleased to hear that your novel's going well, it will be a famous one, born of suffering as the best are – but not too much pain – that's fatal.'[58] Von Auw, she said, was 'the only man I've ever had to do with who hasn't tried to push me around' . Hazzard was a soul mate. Nevertheless, it was a relief to be back in a cold climate with Mrs Lazzari, hot-water bottle, and the euphemistic inflexions of British English in her ears: 'The air is sharp, but I can breathe it.'[59]

Writing *Mandelbaum*, Muriel felt peculiarly vulnerable. By her standards, it was taking an inordinate time to squeeze out the chapters and, as she explained to Hazzard, she was suffering the unusual experience of self-doubt – while simultaneously warning that one should 'always *act* with confidence'.[60] This advice was oblique advice to herself: act up, give nothing away, make a stand, save face, refuse to be victimised. Pride was important, a certain haughtiness in the face of threats. Hazzard, she thought, was tough but perhaps too much the lady. She might try swearing at Francis now and again.[61] When MacKenzie had a heart attack in February and Shirley had been teased with guilt, Muriel clarified matters: it was absurd, she believed, to feel in any way responsible.[62] Emotional blackmail was detected. When Hazzard rang MacKenzie's sister to offer sympathy and received a cool response, Muriel was pitiless, wishing she had been granted the opportunity to give the woman a piece of her mind.[63] The whole affair Muriel saw from her distance across the Atlantic as a 'positively Jungian-dream ordeal' from which she and Hazzard had 'emerged unscathed, nay scatheless [...] from now on'.[64]

This correspondence with Hazzard was the last in which Muriel spoke frankly of her own turmoil. She missed her friend, gave her access to the bedside telephone,[65] a number withheld from almost everyone else. The mock-Kensingtonian chit-chat – adding 'ers' to the end of names and verbs – was a private joke, a linguistic infection from the time-space of *Girls* and a signal of intimacy. She rarely spoke like this. The only other people to whom she wrote in this register were von Auw and Maclean. Trying to read Hazzard's anxiety, she read it off against her own.[66] Praying unselfishly for her friend's success in love (which meant her own exclusion as principal confidante), she allowed the situation to feed abstractly into *Mandelbaum*, and particularly into that second chapter, 'Barbara Vaughan's Identity', which was 'long & (for me) rather philosophical, & therefore difficult to shape'.[67]

Mandelbaum was to be Muriel's Great Book and the weight of her ambition oppressed her. As with Evelyn Waugh and *Brideshead Revisited*, this was the point at which she would step forward with her heart, to some extent, on her sleeve and talk about love, divine and carnal. That fear of being hurt was not restricted to her private life. She had tried so many stylistic experiments and succeeded. Suppose this one failed? To fail while making the grand gesture might permanently damage her reputation. The novel discussed no less a subject than the intersection of Judaic and Christian culture. This was dangerous ground. Hence the perpetual defensive self-mockery, describing the work as her 'magnus opium': because it dealt with religion. At the time, she maintained that she was better pleased with a foreword she had written for Father Vincent Blehl's selection of Newman's sermons, 'in which

I let rip against the moralists who want showy morals whereas it is the love of God that counts'.[68] All this went into *Mandelbaum*, too.

The essay acknowledges that Newman was more influential in bringing Muriel to the Church than all the 'authorities'. 'He was out for the psychological penetration of moral character, and he achieved it.'[69] To Charles Kingsley's famous cry, 'What, then, does Dr Newman mean?', she replies simply: 'He meant that God had not been educated at Rugby.'[70] He meant that 'conscientious people of high moral principle may be on the side of evil [...] those who are genuinely pleasing in God's sight, only God knows. The disposition of every soul is a secret matter, not easily discernible.'[71] Ultimately, it is Newman's 'Simplicity of intellect and speech' that she admires, and no one knew better than Muriel how 'Simplicity is the most suspect of qualities; it upsets people a great deal.' Froude's 'He told us what he believed to be true. He did not know where it would carry him' would serve as an epigraph for her own *oeuvre*. She had no sense of direction.

*

That April, Muriel was in Edinburgh, staying with Cissy and Robin for her mother's seventy-fifth birthday. Life seemed drab, *Mandelbaum* dragged. She had taken Mrs Lazzari to Paris for a few days at the end of February. The trip had been for business (Laffont were at last to publish her) and after she and her landlady had plunged into back streets in search of seamstresses, the old woman had sailed back through Customs sporting an extraordinary hat concealing contraband. Both had returned with high morale. In May, they set off again for a fortnight with Tiny's Irish relations in Cork. That, too, was refreshing: country excursions with convivial, unliterary people. Mrs Lazzari was vigorous, devoid of self-pity and passionate in Muriel's defence. All this Muriel loved and needed. Tiny, she admitted, was a better mother to her than Cissy had ever been. But she no longer needed a mother and in Britain the ghosts of her past still haunted her.

On her return to England at the beginning of 1963, Jon Wynne-Tyson had written. Formerly a fringe member of Muriel's London bohemia, he had run Centaur Press since 1954. His tone – the boisterous familiarity of one who had also known 'the Derek / John Bayliss / Robert Greacen gang' for years – was magnificently misjudged. He had, he explained, accepted a volume on her life and work by Derek Stanford, and was 'having all hell' trying to get the book out of him for autumn publication. Would she care to check the typescript for errors? Perhaps they could meet?[72] His letter alarmed Muriel. It was the first she had heard of the book. Autumn publication would coincide with the launch of *Girls* and reviewers would be bound to take note. Stanford, she thought, was a desperate man, a parasite. What would he say? He had been parading himself as an authority on her work in American magazines, had even used her *Observer* pseudonym, 'Evelyn Cavallo', for a piece on Gabriel Fielding (Alan Barnsley). Now this. Would she never be rid of him?

Her reaction astonished Wynne-Tyson. On St Valentine's Day she screamed at him down the telephone, threatening court proceedings.[73] She had, he replied in a letter, accused him of being a 'disreputable publisher' trying to extort money to suppress publication.[74] The charges, he insisted, were absurd. But Muriel did not let it rest, contacting her solicitor, Michael Rubinstein, intending either to drag Wynne-Tyson through the courts or to scare him off. Energised by anger, he remained undeterred. Coincidentally, Rubinstein was also his lawyer, an old friend, and the man found himself acting for both parties in reading the text for libel. Nothing was discovered. *Muriel Spark: A Biographical and Critical Study* was published, as planned, that autumn. Muriel gave her copy to Hazzard, unopened, and always refused to read it. There was a brief battle of letters in the *TLS* – but she need not have bothered. Stanford's book was, as he later admitted, rushed and patchy. Its few notices were obliterated by an avalanche of rave reviews for *Girls*. This, she hoped, would be the last she would hear of him – but it wasn't.

Just four months later a dealer, Lew Feldman, came to see Muriel in Camberwell, pursuing her trunkful of exercise books housed in Mrs Lazzari's garden shed. He said 'he was interested in authors who were "passionately worked over", so I enquired what he meant in frigid tones, but he meant the manuscripts of course.' Refusing his request to remove them for valuation, she turned to Morton Cohen and Dick Swift who were in London that summer, and on their recommendation had a catalogue produced. Cohen thought the collection worth a small fortune, news which Muriel greeted with amused delight as a further advance in her rags-to-riches life.[75] Preliminary enquiries were made for a sale to the University of Texas.[76]

Feldman had mentioned that he had purchased her letters to Stanford which were also heading for Texas unless she chose to buy them. This came as another shock, Stanford's worst betrayal yet, but she displayed no emotion. In her view, a civilised institution would return the letters gratis, i.e. she would not sell her literary manuscripts to Texas unless they did so. The whole matter was left in abeyance for eight months. She was in no hurry.[77] Then, in March 1964, Feldman contacted her again in New York. He had those Stanford letters at his hotel. Would she care to see them? The invitation appeared sinister to her. She went along with von Auw, briefly examined the papers, and laughed. An excellent collection, she declared. She was sure he would have no trouble selling it. No one, she knew, could quote from them without her permission. And she walked out, head up, placed the manuscripts of her novels in her London bank and sat tight. Proposals to sell the collection ran back and forth for over twenty years until a suitable price (offered by the University of Tulsa) was agreed. The letters were sold to Texas and remain there to this day.

Stanford's disloyalty brought her nearer to her family as they closed ranks in her defence – but their support soon generated more suspicion and claustrophobia. The precarious nature of a writer's life, she informed von Auw, at least allowed her the freedom to travel and to choose her friends.[78] Edinburgh, to her 'the city of Calvinism, high teas and loveless alliances',[79] always made her restive in those days. When Cissy found a boyfriend, when Robin started antiques-dealing in his spare time, when they showed signs of independence, Muriel could tolerate them. Their dependency she could suffer. It was their wasting her artistic time that she could not abide.[80] One moment she would be telling Hazzard that her family difficulties seemed under control, the next that they had erupted again.

A single telephone call could change everything: the wrong word, the buried implication. After one such call at nine-thirty in the evening, she brooded on the matter for nearly four hours before letting rip in a letter to Hazzard. Her mother, she thought, wanted to take her down a peg or two for supposedly lording it over the family. Yet Cissy and Robin also appeared to her to request help. He wanted to open an antiques shop. She sent him £25, he returned the cheque (not enough was her interpretation), she sent it again. Round and round they went with Muriel grindingly bored by it all and offended because in her view her closest relations seemed always to wish to put her in the wrong.[81] Presents from her family, Muriel felt, were weighed as to the benefit they might bring the giver, hers to them as a gauge of possible future largesse. Nothing delighted her better than Hazzard's spontaneous gifts,[82] for the presents Muriel enjoyed giving and receiving had no subtext attached. She once sent money to Kay Dick via June Braybrooke, insisting that the source be concealed. Such offerings were anonymous donations to those in need – or useless, like von Auw's orchids, perfectly useless other than to give pleasure. They demanded no gratitude or return but opened 'possibilities' in the receiver. They flew in the face of mundanity, were a statement of faith in the recipient rather than a projection of power from the donor.

*

Muriel's existence snapped on and off between 'Time' and 'Life'. 'There's nothing I can tell the public about my life that can clarify my books,' she informed Harding Lemay, deflecting Knopf's demands for publicity material, 'it's rather the books that clarify my life. I haven't got a message to give to the world, it's the world that gives me messages.'[83] But, so far, *Mandelbaum*, cutting to the bone of her most deeply felt convictions, was not clarifying her life. When Yeatman sent a tribute from *Punch*, the phrase that delighted her was 'princess of moralists'.[84] It was difficult, though, to gain this Olympian distance from material so close to home, and her comment on the 'princess' remark was both a joke at her own expense and contained a seed of truth: that it seemed to endorse her girlhood fantasy of being a real princess who had been kidnapped by gypsies (her parents).[85] She told her readers what she believed to be true without knowing where it would carry her, just as she travelled the world with a deliciously vague sense of destination.[86] Writing earlier books, she had entered this cloud of unknowing and allowed it to crystallise into vision. This had been the very thrill of creation. *Mandelbaum* tested this self-confidence to the limit. One thing, however, was clearer now than ever: that if she were to maintain a head of steam as a novelist, she needed to keep Cissy and Robin in the waiting room. Everything was changing. Even her home with Mrs Lazzari was becoming unnecessary. She needed to be gone.

CHAPTER 12

Amours de Voyage

1963–1965

September 1963 saw Muriel returning to New York in even greater style and earlier than planned. Again, she was on the run, a glamorous vagabond. Rache Lovat Dickson collected her from Baldwin Crescent (she always liked to be 'collected') and drove her to Waterloo. Evelyn Waugh had just congratulated her on *The Girls of Slender Means*, touched that as 'an established colleague', she should continue to send her books. The novel, he thought, demonstrated her 'infinite variety' and reminded him of Henry Green's *Concluding*.[1] Aboard the *Queen Mary* she wrote to the American poet and novelist, Allen Tate, and to his wife, Isabella, who were visiting London. Muriel had fixed them up with the flat of one of her boyfriends, Gillon Aitken, so that Tate could have somewhere quiet to write during the day while Aitken was at work. In return, they had ordered champagne for her on the boat. Only three chapters of *The Mandelbaum Gate* had been written but Muriel was joyful, anticipating restful aimlessness during the voyage and freedom to write among the skyscrapers.

Although Muriel had only recently met the Tates (through Frank Kermode), she was immensely attracted to them. A decade earlier, replying to an article in which Tate had proposed that 'in order to write well, the writer to-day must live virtuously', she had argued that 'if the proposition is true, then I would be a better writer, if more virtuous.'[2] At the time she had periodically been living with Stanford in Sussex Mansions. Shortly after, she had moved out to resolve this issue. But the practice of virtue remained a problem. It bored her. Tristram Cary, composer of the music for *The Ballad of Peckham Rye*, had found himself in a hotel room adjoining Muriel's during the Verona trip to accept the Italia Prize. Being then a randy young man, he had proposed that, if she felt like it, perhaps she might ... Pleased by his suggestion, she nevertheless declined on the grounds that, after her appalling marriage, she preferred to steer clear of men.[3] She apparently slept with none of her London boyfriends, frankly explaining to Aitken that he was the same age as her son. There was a certain amount of kissing after a great deal of drinking, but nothing more.[4] Although she liked picking up young men, she always put them down again fairly quickly. They were delightful accessories and, like most of those she now encountered, swam into her ken and out of it, leaving her emotionally untouched. Her fellow passengers, she reported to the Tates, were 'unbelievably my sort of writing-meat, but really very charming, too'. At the Captain's table she watched and listened, amused and distant. 'Nobody on board has read my books, but they have all met an author who lives near their homes in a cottage. [...] I'm having the time of my life [...]. Dear Allen & dear Isabella, I feel I've known you such a long long time.'[5] But she hadn't and, as it happened, this friendship, like so many others, never developed.

Muriel's cottage days were so far behind her that it was as if they had never existed, and in New York, her mood continued to levitate. Hazzard was in Italy but she wrote to her immediately. The address (the Barclay Hotel), she said, was Top Secret, for her eyes only.[6] It was just a few days before Knopf's and Macmillan's launch of *Girls*. Having escaped the British razzmatazz, she also wished to avoid Blanche's publicity campaign, explaining (again) that her job was not sales promotion.[7] There was other work to do and, perhaps, a romance on hand.

Seven months earlier, while Muriel had been tearing into Wynne-Tyson on St Valentine's Day, a telegram had arrived from America bearing love from one of Howard Moss's friends, Bert Beck. She was fond of Moss (the *New Yorker*'s poetry editor) who that summer had visited England with Beck and the poet Joe McCrindle. Muriel had toured them up and down the Thames and found herself strongly attracted to Beck.[8] In New York she contacted him again. Within three weeks, however, during the *Girls* campaign when her name and photograph were splashed across the American press, the relationship had collapsed. Tall, dark and handsome, he was the stuff of Muriel's nightmares. When he proposed marriage and began sending kitchen utensils, Muriel immediately broke communication and looked to von Auw for protection.[9] Letters arrived from Beck expressing bewilderment and guessing (wrongly) at her reasons for deserting him. The truth reads like one of her fictions.

By this stage Hazzard had returned and Muriel had taken a new lease on her old apartment in the Beaux Arts. Muriel had asked Milton Greenstein to enquire into Beck's background. Hazzard was with her when the report arrived and they had clung to each other in terror. Beck, it said, had criminal connections. The afternoon had been spent feverishly discussing the matter and, that evening, Muriel telephoned Greenstein. He chuckled. Had she not noticed the date? A communication in September dated 1 April? Beck's credentials were impeccable. Muriel cracked a smile (she never held this practical joke against Greenstein) but she would not allow Beck back into her life. The story had taken on such reality that it could not be shaken off. Looking for an excuse to be rid of the man, she had found one and was content to return to business as usual, to her single, and singular, life as a working writer.[10] It was a wise decision. Before long he married another woman. Muriel attended the engagement party.

*

Business as usual was brisk. Again, she was in the swim, pleasantly surprised by the success of *Girls*.[11] Perhaps her ambitions for *Mandelbaum* made the shorter work appear light by comparison. She wondered whether it might seem like a rerun of *The Prime of Miss Jean Brodie*,[12] another work concentrating on the transfiguration of a Catholic convert, on a female community – and there were further similarities. In *Brodie*, Mary MacGregor dies in a hotel fire. In *Girls*, there is also a conflagration in a public building. Muriel's modesty, however, was not to be mistaken for insincerity or laziness. She had been appalled by Macmillan's draft blurb. Trying to target the Smart Lady market, they had read the novel as a light-hearted comedy of manners, ignoring the framing narrative of the telephone calls which altered the perspective and which presented Nicholas Farringdon as the hero.[13] This perspective, of course, was the aspect of eternity, a vision of the world coloured by Nicholas's sense of its corruption and transience.[14] If Macmillan were so obtuse, she thought, perhaps they should simply state that it was a serious book and leave it at that. Refusing to write her own blurbs,[15] she could not complain too loudly. Their final effort, at least, seemed marginally better. The narrative, they said, reminded the reader of eternity 'from time to time'.

Girls opens in the bomb-wrecked London of 1945, one week after Victory in Europe Day, before quickly focusing on the May of Teck Club and its young ladies. It is the 'year of final reckoning', a point of transition between an old world and the new. 'Windows', the narrator remarks, 'were important in that year [...]; they told at a glance whether a house was inhabited or not; [...] they were the main danger-zone between domestic life and the war going on outside [...].' Within a couple of pages we fast-forward eighteen years to the narrative present, 1963, and to Jane Wright telephoning her fellow old girls of the club. Jane now works as a newspaper columnist. A Reuters wire has just come through stating that Nicholas has been martyred on Haiti. Certain that this must be the same Nicholas she remembered introducing to the club, an anarchist poet who later became a Catholic missionary, she asks her friends if they recall him. The narrative then switches back and forth between these calls and the May of Teck Club in 1945. Among the many female characters, three are given particular attention: Jane, 'a fat girl who worked for a publisher and who was considered to be brainy but somewhat below standard, socially, at the May of Teck'; Joanna Childe, a country rector's daughter who is training as an elocution tutor; and Selina Redwood 'who was extremely beautiful'.[16] They are, in a sense, three aspects of Muriel's personality: the intellectual from the wrong side of the tracks, the woman of spiritual conviction, and the elegant metropolitan.

Nicholas is remembered for sleeping with Selina on the roof, access to which is through a tiny bathroom window, and this window becomes a crucial metaphor, ultimately suggesting conversion and salvation, the parable of the camel and the eye of the needle. Other, equally slender, girls squeeze through it to sunbathe. When an unexploded bomb in the garden suddenly detonates and fire creeps up the building, this window is the only means of escape. The bulkier girls are trapped; Selina and her slinky companions survive. The nostalgic element of the novel concentrates on the sharing of food and clothes but Nicholas, on the roof trying to rescue everyone, sees Selina go back in, not to comfort her terrified friends but to save a Schiaparelli taffeta dress. This experience, it seems, is the seed of his religious conversion.

The historical backdrop is lightly sketched but nevertheless complex and ingenious. Clearly, during this brief period something has happened, not only to Nicholas but to the Western world. Three public events structure *Girls*: VE Day (8 May 1945), VJ Day (15 August 1945), and, in between, the general election, held on 5 July, results declared on 26 July. On VE Day the Prime Minister's broadcast was by Winston Churchill; on VJ Day, after Hiroshima and Nagasaki, by Clement Attlee. The explosion and fire at the club occur on 27 July, the day after the general election result which swept Labour to a landslide victory (Muriel herself voted Tory) and inaugurated a period of radical social reform. The atomic age began barely a fortnight later. On 27 July, Attlee led a British delegation back to the Potsdam Conference. Two weeks earlier, Churchill had led this delegation to chart the course of post-war Europe. The 'Big Three' of the Allies – the Americans, the British and the Russians – fell out at the second meeting. Stalin dismissed calls from Truman and Attlee for free elections in Eastern Europe, the iron curtain crashed down and the Cold War started. *Girls*'s double time-focus, however, adds another dimension. Contemporary readers were acutely aware both of how the Cold War had escalated and of the Holocaust (Eichmann). The space race was on; there were riots in American black communities. The glory of the Allies' victory had faded. As Muriel was writing *Girls*, during November 1962, Kennedy and Krushchev had faced off over the Cuban Missile Crisis. Three days after publication, Kennedy was assassinated. It was not that she was writing a novel *about* these shifts in power but that the events became metaphors for mankind's infinite capacity for humanist delusion. They are important because in the perspective of eternity they are absurd and irrelevant.

Kermode remembered meeting Muriel in America the day after the assassination, and assuming she would want to cancel a party he had planned for her. That would be ridiculous, she said. Why stop having pleasure because the President was dead? He was only dead because God wanted him. Kermode rang round and rustled up reluctant friends but the event turned out to be far wilder than it would otherwise have been. She showed 'extraordinary aptitude for those party games [...] where you lift the woman up on four fingers'. The next day she wanted to go to Mass. Kermode sat outside the church in the car. While they were out, Lee Harvey Oswald was shot on TV and Muriel, annoyed at having missed this, insisted on watching the replays, displaying 'a sort of spookish calm'.[17] In *Girls*, the unexploded bomb and the atomic bomb are linked, not by an implicit plea for world peace, but by a vision of the world governed by the inevitability of death. They are images of an eternal truth rather than of an avoidable horror. Those who can confront this, like Nicholas, are in better spiritual health. Those who cannot (all the women except Joanna Childe) are dancing on a volcano. Everything is contextualised by eternity.

Before the fire, Nicholas is bullish, principally concerned with his art and with entering Selina Redwood's affections and underwear (ambitions frequently confused in his mind). On the roof, holding the Schiaparelli dress neatly turned inside out to prevent damage, she asks: 'Is it safe out here?' 'Nowhere is safe,' Nicholas replies:

> Later, reflecting on this lightning scene, he could not trust his memory as to whether he then involuntarily signed himself with the cross. It seemed to him, in recollection, that he did.[18]

Then the firemen's whistle sounds and Nicholas and Selina jump clear. The house collapses – 'went down'[19] – with Joanna chanting the Anglican evening psalter of Day 27 (imploring the Lord for release from captivity) like the nuns in Gerard Manley Hopkins's 'Wreck of the *Deutschland*' which echoes throughout as part of her elocution exercises. Nothing is left of the trapped woman. It is as though she had never existed. In the background, though, and counterbalancing this nihilism, is Nicholas's conversion.

There is a passage from Newman which Muriel thought best described her own conversion: 'When men change their religious opinions really and truly, it is not merely their opinions that they change, but their hearts; and this [...] is a slow work; the changes proceed [...] by fits and starts [...] just as a building might suddenly fall.'[20] On Nicholas's abandoned manuscript there is a note stating that 'a vision of evil may be as effective to conversion as a vision of good.'[21] This 'vision of evil' is, surely, not just of Selina, not just of the murderous sailor he encounters on VJ Day, not just of the slaughter of the innocent, but of the entire world from the Fall to the present day. It is Newman's aboriginal calamity gripping human consciousness, mankind's bottomless capacity for barbarism, the sense of perpetual exile.

*

Reviewers struggled with the metaphysical dimension, but generally *The Girls of Slender Means* received a brilliant press and, by December, it was a best-seller on both sides of the Atlantic. Most read it as a nostalgic period piece, struck by the opening sentence – 'Long ago in 1945 all the nice people in England were poor, allowing for exceptions' – but missing its non sequiturs. Others simply ignored the double time of the setting. The stylistic and chronological complexities were elided into general praise of her lucid prose, her bitter comedy, the tonal accuracy of her dialogue, the evocation of *zeitgeist*. But, as Updike said of *The Bachelors*, although Muriel had all the skills of the realist writer, to describe her work simply in these terms is to sell it short. *Time* magazine was pleasantly baffled by the novel's 'cheerful inhumanity'[22] and wondered whether the author was pulling the reader's leg. Its brevity proved a problem (*The Times* idiotically detected a 'featherweight story-teller' with a weakness for 'lightly tossing in the grim')[23]. Often reviewed alongside Mary McCarthy's *The Group* and David Storey's *Radcliffe*, *Girls* sat strangely by both. Reviewers who preferred social realism talked Muriel's novel down by comparison. Arthur Calder-Marshall described her as 'a great minor writer' and *Radcliffe* as 'a major work of literature'.[24] This apparent lack of 'seriousness', however, did not deter the battery of senior critics who grappled with the book's formal and metaphysical complexity. Kermode, Updike, Simon Raven, John Davenport, and Alan Pryce-Jones all paid homage.

Kermode, who later described *Girls* as 'a little miracle of a book',[25] saw Muriel as 'a remarkable virtuoso in her prime [...] a poet-novelist of formidable power'.[26] Updike likened her 'deliberate clarity' and 'mysteriousness' to Kafka's.[27] Raven saw the classical virtues of restraint and harmony in her prose, arranging the dialogue as in a 'Greek tragedy, to heighten the element of debate'.[28] For Davenport, this sparseness presented 'frightening force'.[29] For the Catholic Julian Jebb, the novel was 'an investigation of the possibility of the abstract force of supernatural evil [...] a technical masterpiece'.[30] Pryce-Jones regarded her work as that of a poet-musician, 'beautifully constructed [...] with Mozartian precision. The world in her eyes is as formal and lively as a ballroom. But it is a ballroom which at any moment may burst into flames.'[31] For them all, the questions at issue were profoundly disturbing. And if we return to that first sentence, we can see moral ambivalence implanted from the outset. The fairy-tale tone belies the brutality of the subsequent story. In 1963, 1945 was not 'long ago', although it might have seemed so during the Cold War; and if 'all' the 'nice' people were poor, how could there be exceptions? That word 'nice' jangles. It is the word these people would have used to describe themselves, rather than Muriel's, and the full complexity of this unstable viewpoint is soon brought home: 'few people alive at the time were more delightful, more ingenious, more movingly lovely, and, as it might happen, more savage, than the girls of slender means.'[32]

That statement offers something of a self-portrait of Muriel in the

1940s and the 1960s. A long-lost friend from Rhodesia, Una Pinder (Una Brighten when Muriel knew her), wrote to her just after *Girls* was completed. Muriel's fame, she said, came as no surprise to her. Pinder had kept every poem, every letter, so certain had she been of Muriel's ability to set her course and maintain it. She had always been spectacular: 'Are brassieres still the most important item in your wardrobe!? Do you still scream for a taxi when you are stony-broke? Do you still, *still* burn your dress on the radiator once a year and use the claim money for your month's food!? Do you still live with Derek what's-his-name & drink that ghastly cheap sherry ??????'[33] No, she did none of these things any more but the dauntless spirit remained and, with Hazzard, the plunges into girlishness.[34]

Muriel was, or had been, a version of all the women in her novel, even the fat one, even Selina. She had slaved in publishers' offices, borrowed dresses, consorted with anarchist poets. But she had also become Nicholas with his terrifying vision. She had so many public images now: the professional writer; the celebrity; the seer; the uptown girl with Hazzard, borrowing Picasso's *Maids of Honour* from Steegmuller for her Beaux Arts apartment, spending large sums on clothes, jewellery and at Elizabeth Arden; the down-home girl with Mrs Lazzari; the mother; the daughter; the wise middle-aged woman with answers to her friends' problems. Only the first of these roles was satisfactory and the purchase of Hazzard's trousseau, Muriel knew, signalled another friend's going-away in more than one sense. It was time to recoup, to complete that *magnus opium*, and to accept her ultimate identity as exile. That Christmas she travelled alone to the Virgin Islands.

*

This sort of trip, switching briefly from Time to Life, became the pattern of Muriel's existence. As well as two long visits to America during 1964, in May she went to Stockholm; in October to Mexico City. The following year saw her in Rome again, an excursion that altered her entire perspective. Previously there had always been hesitations, the sort of anxieties experienced when planning the journey to Israel. Travelling alone, even around New York, was stressful. But she had taught herself to do it, developed strategies of protection. She always took cabs rather than the Subway. If she were to attend a party at Morton and Dick's, she would ask them to pick her up from the Beaux Arts. When the Knopfs invited her to their Long Island home at Purchase, she declined because she rarely went anywhere without von Auw and he was unavailable.[35] Escorted by him, she found her exile tolerable.[36] Wherever she went, she gathered an entourage of dragons, squires and maids of honour to keep the brutishness at bay. But as 1964 drew to a close, even these had begun to irritate her.[37]

The Virgins fixed all that. New York pals had supplied contacts. She stayed in Bluebeard's Castle, a hilltop hotel on the island of St Thomas, and made friends with a delightful Southern belle and her family. John Brinnin, the American poet and Dylan Thomas scholar, escorted her to parties and provided a light flirtation; the Dean of the island's college offered a rent-free apartment for three months where she might hide to write. Tempted by this bolt-hole, she nevertheless refused it as an indulgence. Brinnin, clearly enchanted by her ('nice, and fun, with no side'[38]), soon found that she had 'zeroed in' on him 'with romantic responses to which I cannot properly respond. She's as charming and easy and nice as she can be and, in a way, I'm "crazy" about her. But, O dear, that old problem.'[39] That 'old problem' was that he was gay. Writing to his companion, Bill Read, he tried to describe Muriel's extraordinary presence: the gifted artist and the charming child, delighted by her sudden wealth and bemused by the chain of lawyers, agents and bankers she now needed to mind her interests. She showed him the notebooks containing the first three chapters of *Mandelbaum* and what she had written of the fourth, and asked him to read them. In return, she read his poems and looked up from the text with tears in her eyes. She told him about Mrs Lazzari's and Graham Greene's roles in her 'rags-to-riches career',[40] seemed to pour out her life with a sudden, intense intimacy. After their last night together, 28 December, he was left with the impression 'that she did fall all the way'. She had brought him a gift, 'a little inlaid wood box', and driving back from dinner, 'she in the front seat beside Tram [a male friend of his], I in the back, she clutched my hand all the way and kept putting her waif-like head against it and kissing it. I said goodnight to her alone on her hotel balcony (Tram, sensing the situation, remained behind) and we parted in a sort of shocked sense of recognition. She's an absolute doll, and she's pretty and amusing and rich. If I weren't absolutely entangled with another doll [Read], I'd wind her up and say, Come to daddy.'[41] But as usual with those who believed her to be infatuated with them, he was wrong. Muriel knew herself too well to suppose that she could pursue this relationship or work on an island. She was a city writer on vacation, driven round paradise by day and, after dinner, calypso-dancing in local nightclubs.[42] It was her best holiday, but ten days of it were enough.

The completed chapters of *Mandelbaum* had taken about three months each to write, time enough in the old days for three novels. Chapter 4 had stalled: 'I'm not an author any more', she had written to von Auw before leaving for the Virgins, 'only a contractor. It's 2 a.m. [...] and I feel these things strongly, it's the hour of truth & disillusionment.'[43] Returning to New York on 29 December 1963 she cancelled all invitations, re-entered the time-space of Israel in 1961, and completed that fourth chapter, 'Abdul's Orange Grove', in a fortnight. The book, she hoped, could now be polished off before her return to London in March. In fact, it took another year and, ultimately, she brought it to an abrupt conclusion, dissatisfied and overwhelmed. With short novels she could see the beginning and the end, sense their total rhythm and poetic structure. With *Mandelbaum* it was quite different. It was developing as she wrote it. The research was on a grander scale (Arab grammar, rural and natural history, Israeli culture, the Eichmann trial), and the historical framework, the facts necessary for plausibility, were for the first time only marginally part of her life. On the other hand, the cultural experience of the half-Jewish convert to Christianity was intimately autobiographical. *Mandelbaum* was 'spreading itself, its very theme is to be the defiance of pre-laid plots in life, and it's emotional and I hope explicit'.[44]

Muriel's various social groups now rarely intersected and this suited her perfectly. Von Auw would accompany her to the grander events and take her to jazz clubs. She once admitted to Gillon Aitken that she loved von Auw and had done her best to get him into bed.[45] But that was hopeless. Then there were the *New Yorkers*, Gill and Greenstein, Howard Moss in particular, and from among that crowd, three sharp young women: Sarah Lippincott, Susan Black and Janet Groth. Lippincott and Groth both acted as Muriel's secretaries or helpers; all were fond of her. Lippincott and Black were staff writers; 'Jan', the receptionist on the eighteenth floor, later became a university professor and an authority on Edmund Wilson. Eventually, each went the way of Hazzard (Black marrying Neil Sheehan of *Pentagon Papers* fame) but, for a couple of years, they formed part of Muriel's 43rd Street coterie. Beyond this, Morton and Dick introduced Muriel to a swathe of brilliant academics at City College, Yale and Rutgers. Chums drifting back and forth across the Atlantic included Kermode and Maclean. Harding (Pete) Lemay, in the publicity department at Knopf, acted as a personal assistant to Blanche and Alfred and had also been allocated the largely futile role of Muriel's 'editor'. Almost every evening in her diary was booked.

Muriel dropped in and out of each set: vivacious, affectionate, enjoying her money and celebrity, demanding attention. Manicures, waxes, perms, designer dresses, perfume and jewellery honed the public image. Clothing interested her (she could date photographs by outfit) and provided a defensive screen. She was transforming herself into a work of art. Her wardrobe was a palate. A huge variety of garments would be paraded, from the chic and understated to the garish. Lemay recalled a totally pink outfit (dress, gloves, shoes, handbag, even her hair seemed pink). But filling her life with work and social engagements did not entirely deflect the discomfort of being alone among couples. Hazzard detected a cooling of relations after her marriage. Apart from the struggle with *Mandelbaum*, perhaps because of it, Muriel's health was delicate. She ate little, smoked and sometimes drank more than was good for her. She had low blood pressure and the symptoms of anaemia. Gynaecological problems dogged her, resulting ultimately in a hysterectomy. Worse, though, were the non-specific ailments: the melancholy that occasionally defeated her body and her work plans. When she returned to England in May 1964, it was to have a large cyst removed from her head (eight stitches) and to travel to Stockholm for rehearsals of Ingmar Bergman's production of *Doctors of Philosophy*. The play was a triumph, running to packed houses there and elsewhere in Scandinavia for the rest of the year. She remembered enjoying her visit to the theatre at Drottningholm with its ancient thunder machine. The trip should have been a tonic. Instead, she flew back to London in a state of near-total collapse. In early July, when Maclean and Mrs Lazzari were seeing her off for her fourth journey to the States, even New York's magic was beginning to wane.

*

Mandelbaum was becoming an albatross. Chapter 5 had taken another three months. Chapter 6, 'Jerusalem, My Happy Home', had stretched from April to August. No sooner had she settled to complete it in a borrowed apartment than news came through of an accident. Her mother, shinning up a ladder to hang curtains, had fallen and broken her leg. Feeling pressure to return, Muriel resisted it for she was herself at a critical point in her novel, in her life. She had telephoned the doctor who assured her that Cissy was mending well. So she settled the matter with the help of a childhood friend, Jessie Rosenbloom and her husband, Johnny. She would, she explained to Maclean, be desperate if she had to discontinue composition again. Perhaps he could write to Cissy and cheer her up? And would he contact Robin saying that, should money be needed, Maclean would supply it?[46]

Many publishers might have demurred at this. Maclean, however, had more than a professional friendship with Muriel. He was genuinely fond of her, and she of him. Letters ran frequently between 'Dearest Mu' and 'Dearest Al'. One of the prices of her fame was a certain isolation from frankness. People spoke not to her but to the image she had created of herself, trying to second-guess how she might want them to react. Although usually in conversation she was charming and approachable, if she detected criticism an apparently comfortable exchange could suddenly collapse. On one occasion she had encountered the elderly, paranoid novelist, Maeve Brennan, and engaged in something approaching a stand-up verbal brawl. Maclean, it seems, was one of her precious truth-tellers, and she trusted that her relations with him had now reached a point at which both parties could relax. Macmillan could admit that she was a prize; she could admit that writers were creatures driven only by the freedom to write and liable to scream when impeded.[47]

As each understood, the threat of her letting rip was not conducive to *absolute* frankness. Maclean, nevertheless, loved her in his way and did what he could to shield her from her mother. And he knew, of course, that when he was asked to supply money, this would not be his money or even Macmillan's. It would be Muriel's. Cissy was soon singing along to the church services on the ward and writing to her saying that Maclean was her angel. He sent flowers, rang up, kept Robin sweet. And on the home front, Cissy had her boyfriend, the one-legged local butcher, Bill Christie, who wooed her with roses and fruit during daily visits and would write to Muriel as to a daughter. At first his attentions had been kept secret from Muriel because he was married. Muriel could not have cared less and soon came to like him, found him wise. His presence eased her life.[48]

With her Edinburgh family temporarily under control, her creative spirit revived. Chapter 6 had been finished within days of Cissy's accident, completing 'Part One' of *Mandelbaum*. 'Part Two', she decided, would have to consist of a single chapter, 'The Passionate Pilgrims'. Although it was the final stretch,[49] Muriel felt sad again, a pilgrim herself, dragging bloodied feet towards the Mecca of completion: 100,000 words in which she did not always have confidence. Homesick but rootless, she had decided finally to abandon Baldwin Crescent. She was rarely there; it was expensive. But what to do about Mrs Lazzari? This would have to be a problem deferred. In the meantime, she would 'settle down to being a Rover'.[50]

Her assault on that final chapter lasted barely a month before something went wrong again. Anxiety about the book's reception, or exhaustion, she guessed, had caused this hiatus. Correspondence with Knopf and even with von Auw had turned brisk and irritable. Lemay had antagonised her. Whatever it was, work became impossible and the avuncular Greenstein had advised her to 'hop on a plane just as she was' and to 'buy a nightie at the other end'.[51] So she flew to Mexico.

*

She travelled alone but, as usual, befriended people on the journey and had introductions waiting for her. Through the American Ambassador she met Sam Baskett, a young academic touring the country on a Fulbright Scholarship. At the American Embassy she encountered Adlai Stevenson, who admired her work. Moving easily between high society and Sam's intelligent plainness, she drank, danced, gossiped and gave nothing away. A weekend was spent at Acapulco behind high convent walls with her friends from the flight: 'Very Spanish. It was the Days of the Dead. I was given a traditional sugar skull marked Muriel.' Her host was an arch-reactionary. Elsewhere she delighted in pro-communist Indian-Mexicans. For safety she had chosen the best hotel in Mexico City, Il Presidente, but getting into a taxi and giving this address, she had found herself 'behind a huge set of iron gates surrounded by soldiers as bewildered as I was. The cab driver had taken me to the "President's" palace.' Cultivated bewilderment was Muriel's stock in trade, translating the ordinary into the fantastic, ricocheting from one sensation to the next. Drinking carrot juice, she climbed hundreds of feet to the shrine of the Madonna of Guadeloupe. In the city she admired the revolutionary murals. Spare hours were spent with Baskett who took her to the races. As a holiday, it amused her and she returned refreshed. As a country, Mexico left her uneasy: 'I couldn't enjoy it much because of the poverty. People were living on the rooftops, which I could see from my window.'[52] Back in New York, she worked deep into the small hours trying to complete *Mandelbaum*, most mornings slept in.[53] A fortnight earlier she had prematurely announced the novel's completion. Christmas was obliterated by continuous labour. Finally, in early January 1965, she sat up for fifty-six hours without sleep until the last full stop was in place – and collapsed.

*

During the autumn and winter of 1964/5 Muriel had made two new American friends, Nora Sayre and George Nicholson. Sayre recalled their first meeting. Peter Mayer, then the young head of Avon Books, had acquired some of Muriel's paperback rights and threw a party to celebrate. Enter the guest of honour, tiny and elegant in a black silk dress. Someone kept asking what Scotsmen wore beneath their kilts. Taking no (obvious) offence, Muriel abandoned her tormentor and sat down stylishly on a plate of hors d'oeuvres. As she sprang up, Sayre tried to cover the confusion. 'I'm a great admirer of your books,' she threw out hopelessly. Muriel's eyes brightened. Clearly this was an intelligent young woman.

Sayre worked as a paperback editor for Dell (who also had some of Muriel's rights), and she was a writer. Her father, Joel, had been a *New Yorker* contributor and editor and she had been raised in that club, James Thurber often visiting the house. In 1965 she became the New York correspondent for the *New Statesman*. As they talked, Muriel discovered that this scintillating girl really did know her books well. Muriel had reviewed and admired Christopher Burney's *Solitary Confinement*, an account of his torment as a prisoner of war. When Maclean had first met her, he had been living in the basement of Burney's house. Sayre knew both, remembered Maclean attending parties during his recovery phase bearing string bags full of Bitter Lemon bottles. Sayre was passionate about writing: open, unaffected, avid for talk and ideas. Muriel was taken with her. They began to meet. And when Sayre introduced her to Nicholson, her colleague at Dell, they formed a trio. None of Muriel's grander friends knew them. It was like being young again and (almost) fameless. She could be anonymous with them.

Nicholson, a bisexual lapsed Catholic and children's book editor, had been fanatical about Muriel's writing since *Memento Mori*. He first met her at a party in honour of the novelist J. P. Donleavy, catching her name as 'Mrs Park'. The shock of discovering who she really was left him speechlessly 'adulating all over the place'.[54] Again, Muriel was charmed. When he invited her to lunch the next day, she accepted. This was probably early in 1965 when she had completed *Mandelbaum* and was simultaneously correcting proofs and using them to remodel four free-standing sections for the *New Yorker* before volume publication in the autumn. At her desk she was working full-tilt against tight deadlines, her irritation with Knopf steadily mounting. After office hours, with Nicholson, she was a quite different character. For once, she had more than an escort. He became her first New York boyfriend. Until he married in August 1967, they saw a good deal of each other.

'It was the Catholicism,' he thought, '[...] that linked us.' Nicholson, a great communicator, was a non-communicant, unable either to accept the entire dogma or to pick and choose. Sayre remembered vigorous debates between him and Muriel. She couldn't, he would insist, abide by some of the instruction and ignore the rest. Playing by the rules, however, Muriel found tedious. She had 'such a liberated view of the whole thing. Much more French than English.' And although she was 'far more European in her sensibility'[55] than he, he relished the stimulus. She would lament the loss of Latin as the Church's lingua franca but Vatican II left her more bemused than angry. Writing to Maclean she asked what he, as an Anglo-Catholic, thought about the changes: the priest now facing the congregation, standing for Holy Communion, hymn-singing in English.[56] It might, she hoped, at least mean that she and he could one day attend Mass together. Broadly in favour of the new ecumenicism, she saw it as 'opening the doors'. Although she 'was never practising in the sense of going to Mass on Sundays'[57] so far as Nicholson could see, there was no doubting a primal enthusiasm for her faith. It was, though, *her* faith rather than the Church's dogma. Catholicism was what she made it. Infallibility, as an intellectual position, was fallible. She was writing against all 'pre-laid plots' in *Mandelbaum*. During these discussions Sayre sat silently by. And when Muriel and Nicholson went on, usually in the small hours, to twist or waltz or drink the night away at Roseland, hotel bars or discotheques, Sayre went home. She liked her sleep. Sometimes Muriel and Nicholson would dance. More often they would observe. It was the early days of discotheques, and their thunderous flash of energy was absorbing. Then he would take her back to the Beaux Arts. He never stayed the night.

Nicholson remembers Muriel primarily as a conversationalist: 'vivacious and so ready to laugh, though there were those dark sides. [...]

Always when she spoke there was dramatic effect. It wasn't acerbic and mean-spirited. She was very frank about who she liked and who she disliked. [...] There was a lot of snuggling and warmth. I think she needed a tremendous amount of physical affection and there was no other resource [...] such a funny combination of intense privacy and gregariousness.'[58] For him it was an important experience. Ambiguous about his own sexuality, 'mildly disturbed by it, but not operationally', he found her 'very sexual, very flirtatious, very concerned about clothes'. Yet a distance was preserved, for which he was grateful. It was not an 'affair' but it was a sexual relationship: tactile, unconsummated and tender. Neither wished to invade or possess; both needed, and received, gentleness, a space in which to be human. He was about twenty-seven, she forty-six. They discussed marriage a lot, 'not to one another but what the values of it were'. 'I don't remember meeting anybody', he remarked, 'who I thought was more alone.'[59]

To Nicholson, Muriel could explain her frustrations. She was furious with Stanford for selling her letters, anxious about writing private letters in case others should sell them. Despite her fondness for von Auw, she could become irritated by his disappearance after cocktails. Pete Lemay's visits were always aborted by his dashing back to his wife and children for their evening meal. 'She needed an escort,' Lemay recalled, 'just wanted company.' After work, he would walk over to the Beaux Arts around five-thirty, to find her already several drinks into the evening. She wasn't seeking sex with him but he found himself unable to deal with 'the terrible intrusion into my private life'.[60] A playwright, he also had creative work to do and would retire at ten to get up early for it. When Muriel took to ringing at midnight, he asked her to stop this. No one was permitted to talk to her like that. She had already found him bumptious and interfering, and wrote to von Auw stating that she absolutely refused editorial correction from Lemay or anyone else at Knopf.[61]

This letter was signed 'Yours' rather than 'Love'. For some time she had been trying to remove typographical errors from *Girls* while Lemay stalled. As *Mandelbaum* neared completion she wanted Knopf to contract for other work: *Doctors of Philosophy* (alongside *Voices at Play*) and *Child of Light*. To Muriel, a book was not only a work of art, it was also an investment. She had, she said, invested as much time in *Mandelbaum* as the advance merited. Blanche offered more money but Muriel detected resistance. And her instincts were acute. The firm's internal memos reveal hesitation over *Doctors*. Blanche liked it but such a strange piece, she knew, would never sell. Muriel wanted simultaneous publication with *Mandelbaum*. Knopf thought this a bad idea. A general impression emerges of their feeling blackmailed into printing minor work and that Muriel was her own worst enemy in this respect because it would detract from the magnum opus.

From Muriel's point of view, the Bergman production of *Doctors* was running in three Scandinavian countries simultaneously and there were continual European enquiries about its rights. It was earning quite well. It was *not* a minor work. It meant a lot to her. Moreover, Jay Presson Allen had adapted *The Prime of Miss Jean Brodie* for the stage. Unwilling at first to look at the script, Muriel had eventually found time for it and this was now moving ahead. The *Ballad* musical was to be premiered at the Salzburg Festival. She wished to develop the theatrical side of her career. Now was the time to capitalise and she was disturbed by Knopf's sluggishness. This was the moment in the previous October at which something had snapped and she had escaped to Mexico. But the irritation had not ceased. Knopf agreed to do *Doctors* (not simultaneously), then deferred publication. They refused *Voices at Play* and *Child of Light*. Lemay was hesitant about *Mandelbaum* and kept making suggestions for its improvement. When she submitted her typescript, he had the temerity to point out continuity errors. Muriel summarily dismissed his queries and then dismissed him. Bill Koshland, a wealthy, gay man-about-town, second-in-command of the firm after Alfred and Blanche, took over as her 'editor' and touched nothing.

Muriel's uncertainty about Knopf was unsettling because it coincided with her plans to leave London as her permanent home. Her accountant, Arthur Warne, had been to see Mrs Lazzari to prepare the ground for withdrawal, although Muriel could still not cure herself of homesickness for the relaxing damp chill of England. She could hide in Baldwin Crescent with Mrs Lazzari guarding door and telephone, filling spaces with supportive chatter. Macmillan had contracted immediately for *Child* and agreed to anything she suggested. Muriel was now close not only to Maclean but also to Dickson and Yeatman. Yeatman had a key to her flat to pick up mail. His job as her editor was largely confined to acting as her travel agent. She had attended his wedding with Maclean as escort, become godmother to the couple's first child. Macmillan & Co. had become something of a family for her. On the other hand, the majority of her income and the real celebrity were generated by New York. In England she was comfortably middle-aged. In America she was young and full of potential. Neither identity satisfied. She thought of inviting Mrs Lazzari over to housekeep her apartment – but soon abandoned the idea.

For three years, each time Muriel had returned to the States, a weight had fallen from her shoulders. She could sleep well and work hard in New York.[62] In 1964, however, when Muriel had been living in that borrowed apartment, she had surprised a burglar. She did not panic, simply told him to take what he wanted and to leave. But the experience seems to have inaugurated the collapse of her love affair with the city. Instantly retiring to the chillier security of the Beaux Arts, she stayed there for nine months until *Mandelbaum* was delivered. After that, her trips back and forth across the Atlantic became more like business visits to both countries with a home in neither. Dashing back to England in March 1965 she stayed just a fortnight and, while there, told Kermode that she planned to settle in Paris. In New York she was taking French lessons. Having accepted a post as Writer in Residence at Rutgers University she was in the middle of her six-week stint: six days really, with a handsome fee per seminar and door-to-door transportation in a hired limousine. Blanche, wildly enthusiastic about *Mandelbaum*, promised to ask a huge sum for paperback rights. The *New Yorker* was paying well. If the stage *Brodie* were a success, that would net another small fortune, film rights a larger one. After two feverish years, Muriel was harvesting resources ready for the big fly-off. But she was uncertain where to go.

The restoration of privacy was a driving force. Knopf, von Auw informed her, wanted 'updated biographical material for the jacket'. Out of the question. She refused to allow any reference to her trip to the Holy Land.[63] Arranging to attend the premiere of *Ballad* in Salzburg that summer, she had insisted on travelling at her own expense to avoid any promotional activities,[64] and ultimately never went. Von Auw dispatched flowers. She said that it was hypocritical to send them with one hand and to stab her in the back with the other. He said this was physically impossible.[65] So they patched it up, laughing, and by May, Muriel had completed forms handing over power of attorney to him. She wanted, she said, to hear nothing of ancillary offers of work, unless from the *New Yorker*. He could decide the merits of all translations, reprints and adaptations. Von Auw was startled. Was she sure that she understood the contract? She was, she replied. He would take care of all business affairs, leaving her free to enjoy herself.[66]

She needed a city – an ancient city. Suddenly, in July 1965, she changed her plans again and flew from New York to Rome. The place had lingered in her imagination since that first visit on her return from Israel. She had kept in touch with Eugene Walter. Bright, scatty, and engagingly camp, he was a Southern gentleman living on the fringes of the Roman film world. A writer himself, and a friend of Peterkiewicz and Brooke-Rose, Walter survived rather well by juggling several jobs: translating for Fellini, taking bit-parts in his films, designing stage sets for the theatre and opera, making marionettes and performing shows with them, editing *Transatlantic Review*. In his large top-floor apartment, he entertained assiduously, knew 'everyone'. Manoeuvring enthusiastically around the famous as a cultural entrepreneur, he enjoyed life and loved Muriel. She was his 'witch baby' for whom he would do (almost) anything. 'This lady', he said, 'sparked.'[67]

Muriel spoke no Italian and knew little of the country. Translations of her books had only recently been taken by Mondadori – nothing had yet appeared in print. She wasn't famous in Italy. But this was the point. Here she could hunker down anonymously. Rome was at its high point of fashionable decadence in the broad wake of *La Dolce Vita* (1960),

Hollywood on the Tiber, bands of the rich and beautiful sauntering down the via Veneto, in and out of Freddy's Bar, chased by the paparazzi. Most of that was over but Rome remained a focus for American gay culture, the Italian film industry, and elegant expatriates. More importantly for Muriel, the Eternal City was the centre of her faith, vivid with dispute about Vatican II. There was plenty of Life played out against the memento mori of the Colosseum and the Vatican. One of her first appointments was with both romance and death: Keats's grave in the Protestant Cemetery, an icon of exile for all British literary travellers. Walter photographed her crouched by it, skinny and soulful, eyes cast down, clutching violets.

Muriel stayed in Rome only a week but it was a week that changed her life. Returning to Baldwin Crescent, she found all her pre-laid plans about Paris dissolving. The experience, it seems, had been so intense that it had drained her completely. Delayed reaction from the effort on *Mandelbaum*, trepidation about the book's reception,[68] the nervous exhaustion of deciding on her next place of exile, anxiety about leaving Mrs Lazzari, more family concerns – all, perhaps, contributed to one of her darker periods. Dr Lieber had diagnosed anaemia. She could do only one thing a day. Walter's photograph made her look romantically consumptive and she offered it to Knopf for publicity.[69] This was not a joke at their expense. She sent it. (They rejected.)

Cancelling Salzburg, Muriel settled down to recoup in a freezing British summer. Shivering in winter clothes, trying to warm her thin blood, she attended a chain of specialists and fended off Blanche Knopf's demands for direct communication.[70] After a month of doctors, none could discover anything organically wrong. Anaemia was ruled out. The only cause they could suggest was stress.[71] She bought earrings, clothes and a James Farmer painting to cheer herself up. The races seemed the best cure, plodding about Sandown and Kempton Park with Maclean: rain dripping into her gumboots, functional conversation about form and fetlocks. It felt odd being ill without a definable medical cause. The only thing she could be treated for was inflammation of the fingertips,[72] yet when friends from New York, Roy Grutman and his wife, visited, they found her exhausted.[73] Slowly she recovered. Advance notices of *Mandelbaum* were good, in particular Kermode's long, subtle piece for *Atlantic Monthly*, seeing her as Greene's and Forster's equal.[74] Publication was due in October. Everyone, including herself, was sure that this novel would sell better than any of the others. Like *Memento Mori*, *Mandelbaum* was regarded as another 'breakthrough' book, not least because its heroine seemed her most sympathetic, and because it might translate easily into film.

Bill Koshland, Lemay's replacement at Knopf, rather enjoyed the game in which he had now become a player. 'She was treated as a Queen,' he said, smiling, 'and insisted upon being treated as a Queen. She did not take herself lightly. She wanted attention and attention was paid. She wanted to be entertained, wanted you when she wanted you.' Part of the rush with proofs which had left Muriel so debilitated had resulted from her determination not to break her promise to have the book ready in the firm's 50th anniversary year. Koshland remembered the celebratory dinner at the Astor Hotel: 29 October 1965, Muriel in film-star mode, tremendous décolletage, relishing her role. Some years later he visited her apartment in a Roman palazzo. At one point she began waving a hand, glittering with rings. 'I was supposed to notice, and I did.' Muriel then explained that it was his business to sell enough copies of her novels to provide her with such things. 'I came back to Alf', he remarked wryly, and said, "I think we're on the way out." And we were.'[75]

In 1965, though, Knopf were still trying to juggle the demands of their importunate mistress. *Mandelbaum* was announced as 'without question' their 'most distinguished novel of this third quarter'.[76] In this role, she was, indeed, the princess of moralists. On the town with Nicholson and Sayre, at Rutgers with her students, in Baldwin Crescent with Mrs Lazzari, on the racecourse with Maclean, the glamorous mask was dropped. It was there for business, fun and self-esteem. It was there to empower her, to pump up low blood pressure ready for her return to her desk. And when in that underworld, it was the lives of those 'real' people on which she still drew. Koshland remembered Muriel so joyfully drunk once in London that she had to be carried from the restaurant to a taxi and put to bed in Camberwell. Sam Sachs, one of her Rutgers students, recalled an entirely approachable person.

It was a small class, eight Senior Honours students. Unusually, she held it in the evening. Tea would be prepared, a tray of pastries, red wine. She gave not one damn about the grading system. When Sachs failed to hand in an assignment, he expected a stern reprimand, zero marks. Instead, she was exquisitely polite – 'That's all right, Mr Sachs, because sometimes the creative mind doesn't function on a time-clock basis' – and gave him a B anyway. He was delighted: free Bs. Later, he came to appreciate what she was doing. It was as though she were saying, 'I expect the best from you – even though you may not perform this time, I believe next time you will.' 'She always gave people that positive feeling that they could always do their best. A very, very positive approach to teaching.' And so they did perform for her. None had read her books and she was happy to remain mysterious. Asking them initially to write about themselves, she took a genuine interest in their work. To Sachs, she seemed 'very comfortable with herself and with other people', treating her students like visitors to her home. 'It wasn't a classroom at all ... very, very strange' – and delightful.[77] She suggested that they might consider joining the Vietcong while she stayed home and knitted socks.

Muriel was always easiest with the young or the old. In New York she was close to Hazzard's elderly, difficult mother, Kit. Across the road in Baldwin Crescent lived a London University student, a devoted fan. His landlady knew Mrs Lazzari and one day took him to meet Muriel. She was delighted, invited him over for a party. In pressed flannels and blazer he moved wide-eyed and alcohol-struck round a gathering in her sitting room, pleasantly astonished by the frivolous atmosphere (not at all what he had expected). He never forgot her generosity. His name was Peter Kemp. Later he wrote a book on her[78] and, as chief fiction reviewer for the *Sunday Times*, often provided subtle notices of her work.[79]

At Rutgers, Muriel had been given carte blanche to construct her own course. She called it 'Symposium – Amours de Voyage', starting with Arthur Clough's eponymous poem. Then followed Henry James's *Daisy Miller* and *The American*, E. M. Forster's *A Passage to India* and *A Room With a View*, Sinclair Lewis's *Dodsworth*, Charlotte Brontë's *Villette*, and, finally, Newman's *Apologia Pro Vita Sua*. With the possible exception of *Dodsworth*, all were favourite books, and all dealt with 'abroad'. Her handout and some notes survive, suggesting the drift of discussion. Doubt was the intellectual point of departure throughout: the clash between innocence and experience, the innocent abroad, involvement and detachment, self-discovery and the collapse of sentimentality. Her teaching at Rutgers was never divorced from the issues of technique, point of view, beginnings, middles and ends, proportion. Ostensibly, this was a course on literary criticism but her students soon found it becoming one on creative writing. She concentrated on the rep-resentation of time, on the types of innocence and scepticism in a world where women suffered discrimination.[80]

Did Muriel associate with these images of the female innocent abroad? *Mandelbaum*, after all, centred on such a figure. She was herself a form of the type. Perhaps it was the need to revive this sense of the world's strangeness that was driving her from America. The experience of New York was largely exhausted, becoming repetitious and threat-ening. She found its literary culture invasive. At the same time, however, she was the wise writer, alive to omens and sympathetic to the scepticism of Clough, James and Newman, knowing but with a deliberate naïvety. Like them, she saw before and after. Beginnings, middles and ends had always intrigued her.

In 1961, for instance, Muriel had just finished the proofs of *Brodie* when those of Christine Brooke-Rose's *The Middlemen* arrived, and she had replied with a long and thoughtful letter of criticism. Somehow, she felt, her life was bound up with Brooke-Rose's and Peterkiewicz's, and that this was reflected in the style of her friend's novel. Beginnings, middles and ends were not arranged chronologically but were there nevertheless, unrecognised by the characters, as a kind of hidden destiny. *Middlemen* was to Muriel a satire on those who neglected beginnings and ends in lives obsessed with middles. Their anxieties derived as much from events yet to happen as from events in their past.[81] This was also how Muriel wrote: non-judgementally, just watching her characters, but with a sense of the soul's destiny in a larger story. There was human time and there was God's time. She played with these two spheres of reality: using ghost narrators, revealing endings early to destroy conventional suspense, starting at the end or in the middle, fracturing the plausible surfaces of obsessive detail with sudden discontinuities. When she was writing to Brooke-Rose, she had just emerged from another period of nervous exhaustion[82] and was about to begin 'The Gentile Jewesses'. Her sense of her own destiny – her beginning, middle and end – were intimately connected with this story and went on to be developed in *Mandelbaum*. In the summer of 1965, that gestation had come to full term. It was her book of middle age rather than her middle-aged book, celebrating the vigorous wisdom of the median position. Released from the agonies of youth, not yet tormented by the absurdities of old age, Barbara Vaughan must learn to occupy God's time. Freudianism will not help her or explain Freddy's volte-face at the centre of the narrative.

Muriel's publishers were quietly excited. This was what they had been waiting for: a rattling yarn with a 'big' central character and no stylistic tricksiness. One of those advance notices saw it as 'direct', 'a long naturalistic novel about ordinary people in an ordinary sort of mess.'[83] *Mandelbaum*, it said, was moving, amusing, serious: ideal for the intelligent general reader. Best-sellerdom was predicted. Von Auw, clearly pleased, posted the piece to Muriel. She found it 'a long drink of cold water'.[84] 'What I did with *Mandelbaum*,' she explained much later, 'is really experimental but it doesn't look like that. It looks like one of those straight square books. I did every chapter from a different point of view [...] speaking as from the mind of a different character. So that each chapter [...] was like a short story.'[85] In fact, it was her first experiment with Jamesian technique. Her next four novels – *The Public Image, The Driver's Seat, Not to Disturb* and *The Hothouse by the East River* –

were more avant-garde than ever, indebted to Robbe-Grillet and to the *nouveau roman*.

*

As Muriel sat in England waiting for publication, she knew that she was at another point of transition. The four *New Yorker* sections had been well received. Financially, she had never been more secure. Harold Macmillan, having retired from politics and now back at the helm in St Martin's Street, wrote to say that *Mandelbaum* was not only her best novel but also a great one by any standards. With plenty of loose cash, she now moved easily in these circles and one great and thrilling luxury was planned: the purchase of a racehorse. Maclean dealt with the sale and took a small share, as did Arthur Warne and Maurice Macmillan. The majority of the price, however, was put up by Muriel who also paid for the black and gold colours and training at Fred Winter's stable.

Nothing cheered Muriel more than the thought of this horse. It was called Lifeboat and she bought it from the Queen. In one respect it was like von Auw's orchids: hugely expensive, beautiful and useless. Pure pleasure. In another, it was the public seal on her Cinderella story, like Elizabeth Taylor's diamond. Previously, Muriel had been cautious about reports of her financial success, on the simple grounds that such matters were no one else's business – and particularly not her family's. On this occasion, she allowed Macmillan to release the horse story to the press. In New York for publication that autumn, with power of attorney passed to von Auw, money in the bank, and thoughts of her horse racing in her head, she was reinvigorated and sat down to write to Tiny Lazzari.[86] It was a tender note but it was firm. There was, Muriel said, no alternative. She would soon be vacating Baldwin Crescent. Shortly afterwards she informed Warne and Maclean that she planned to move to Rome. Six months later, she announced that she had become a permanent resident of the USA. Two things had happened in the meantime: a dream and a problem.

CHAPTER 13

Looking Round

1965–1968

The dream was *The Public Image*. Muriel woke one morning in 1966 with a version of the entire book in her head. The problem was income tax, or rather, where and how to pay it. For more than a year these negotiations mangled equanimity. In the first respect she was the artist, unlimited, perching on whichever tree she chose. In the second she now represented a substantial business which was expanding by the minute. Between April and December 1965 she grossed enough to buy a sizeable house. Not that she ever did. When she had money, she spent it. Von Auw once enquired if she would like him to arrange for her earnings to be spread over several years. Somehow the idea seems not to have appealed.

Throughout 1965 she had been planning her next novel. Nora Sayre heard all about it: a *big* New York City book on the scale of *The Mandelbaum Gate*. Muriel already had the title, *The Hothouse by the East River*, and the opening dialogue in which a shoe salesman says, 'They fit like a glove.' She talked of researching 'the draft riots in the Civil War when black men were hung from lamp posts [...]. She had really, *really* gone into it.' It was a surprise, then, when the next three novels bore no resemblance to this and, when *Hothouse* eventually appeared eight years later, that it was so brief. No draft riots. No sense of the city's history. It disappointed some of her American friends. Something, they thought, had 'happened' to Muriel in Italy.

Rumours proliferated. Some suggested that Muriel had abandoned

New York because its Jewish critics had attacked *Mandelbaum;* others that she had fallen out with too many people. There had certainly been rows – with Harding Lemay, Peter Mayer, von Auw, Howard Moss and Roy Grutman – generated by their seeming disrespect, and it was true that there had been four bad American reviews. It was not true that these, or the rows, had driven her out. The worst notice had come from an Englishman, John Gross, in the *New York Review of Books.* Muriel, he thought, had 'lost (or abjured) the inhuman touch which previously gave her caricatures their edge'. The plot was 'elaborate and cumbersome', better suited to a 'lightweight comedy thriller'. Barbara's pilgrimage was 'a pretty ridiculous affair'. Muriel's 'faint air of larkiness' on such a serious subject seemed misjudged: 'one doesn't have to be Leon Uris to feel that her response to the Israeli scene is singularly blank.'[2] The one antagonistic Jewish-American critic, Alfred Kazin, echoed this in seeing *Mandelbaum* as expertly written but 'lifeless, cold, just worked-up. It doesn't exist at all as a work of art. It is just very intelligent.' 'The Holy Land', he insisted, 'is *fierce* – and, God knows, it always was':[3] *not* a fit subject for a comedy of manners. *Time* magazine, formerly Muriel's supporter, kicked equally hard: 'page after page of gentle nattering. [...] For the reader it is deadly.'[4] *Newsweek* was softer but found 'the theme of religious quest and the comedy, both high and low, do not enrich one another to form a transcendent synthesis'. One day, perhaps, Mrs Spark might pull it off; at the moment, the masterpiece was 'just beyond her grasp'.[5]

These, however, represented the sum total of negative responses in the major American papers. All the rest, led by Kermode, offered powerful support. *New Republic, Life,* the *Saturday Review,* the *New York Times* and the *New York Herald Tribune* ran long, serious pieces. And in England, *Mandelbaum's* simultaneous publication met with a roar of approval. Sybille Bedford thought the book 'a triumph, a thumping, joyous blow for the pro-novel'.[6] D. J. Enright found it her 'best, her richest and most solid novel so far'.[7] Norman Shrapnel described it as 'clever, lively, discerning, amusing, above all readable'.[8] *The Times* thought that, by the standards of *Mandelbaum's* beginning and middle, the finale was disappointing: 'but, then, what it is to be able to set such standards'.[9] Only Anthony Burgess, writing anonymously for the *TLS*, had serious reservations. A miniaturist overreaching, he thought, setting up unfavourable comparisons with Rose Macaulay's best-selling *The Towers of Trebizond*. Even here, though, hesitation was spiked with eulogy ('The episode of the sanctuary in the Potter's Field is superbly done'), and for him the ending was the strongest section: 'igniting the dry grass and setting the Holy Land on fire with humour and fantasy'.[10] Four months later *Mandelbaum* won the *Yorkshire Post* Book of the Year award and the James Tait Black Memorial Prize. By any standards, it was a critical success.

Knopf had a bagful of glorious quotations with which to plaster their half-page advertisement in the *New York Times*. Sales were brisk. Five paperback houses were bidding. Movie companies kept von Auw's telephone line hot. Muriel, inured to not pleasing all of the people all of the time, had her own views on her magnum opus and generally kept them to herself. It was, she felt, as good as she could make it without spending the rest of her life on endless rewriting. It was better than most. And, in truth, it never could have been 'finished' at this stage in her career because it was an extended metaphor for her own sense of cultural displacement and division, the story of a half-Jew turned private-judging Catholic. Muriel was only at the mid-point of her own existence in this world. She had no idea how it would end. The novel's conclusion in which Barbara, despite her revelation, marries and settles for the compromises of conventional life was never going to be Muriel's future. George Nicholson once admitted to her that he did not like the book. Neither did she, came the reply, but she simply had to write it.[11]

*

As the reviews flew in, Muriel was arranging to fly out. She wrote to a housing agent, seeking a modernised apartment in old Rome, with a lift, a view, and a doorman,[12] planned to spend three weeks over Christmas scouting for a place. Instead of releasing her imagination, New York's neurosis now left her in a mood of near-permanent volatility. Nicholson remembered her at this stage as full of anger, particularly with Peter Mayer.

On the eve of *Mandelbaum*'s publication, Mayer's Avon paperback of *The Comforters* had been released to capitalise on the brouhaha: unfortunate timing as it turned out. The blurb had advertised 'a witty and mysterious prank'. On reading that final word, Muriel reached for her gun: a *New Yorker* lawyer, Roy Grutman, the man who had visited her in Camberwell during her illness and who counted himself as one of her and Howard Moss's friends. Mayer had neither written nor over-seen the text but he was, he accepted, responsible. If the words were misjudged, he hoped she would accept that they were not insulting. He apologised 'although not defensively'.[13] This was not the kind of apology Muriel tended to accept. Legal proceedings were in train, but 32,000 copies had already been distributed and Mayer could only promise revision of cover copy on any future printing. It was three weeks before she called Grutman off, at considerable cost to herself.

Shortly afterwards Muriel received a strange letter from Grutman. Perhaps Moss had tried to dissuade her from suing Avon. Perhaps he had teased her or she had picked up some gossip. At any rate, she sent him a playfully savage telegram offering to review his latest collection of verse as a 'prank', and then thought better of it, cancelling the message by telephone – too late, it seems.[14] Grutman had rung her on business early on the morning of Tuesday 2 November to find his familiar tone rebuked. She sounded 'terribly cold and strange'.[15]

That evening Moss had telephoned Grutman, disturbed by her tele-gram. According to Moss, Grutman had reported to Muriel 'that Howard had said you were a predatory overreaching woman'. A Jamesian situation, then: A reporting to B that B had reported to C that A had slandered C, resulting in A, B and C all feeling slandered by one or other of the trio. For three days Grutman had tried unsuccessfully to contact her. Finally he had given up and written a letter stating 'emphatically' that she 'had no right to make any such false statement attributing it to me'.[16] Muriel was outraged. In her view, instead of asking her politely how this misunderstanding had occurred, he had defended himself by falsely accusing her. How all this had arisen we can only guess. In itself it is insignificant. But whatever had seeded mistrust, the result was that Muriel instantly excommunicated both men.

Throughout her life this scenario repeated itself, the excommunicated baffled by her accusations. New York she now regarded as a snakepit of gossip and impertinence. Few but her young friends, she felt, respected her confidences. As a celebrity, she had a host of hangers-on inviting her out or themselves in. For those she liked, she flung aside the public image (or hammed it up) and trusted to their silence. She would plunge drunkenly into the night with Nicholson (equally drunk), losing and finding her shoes in the street. She would write smutty verses with Sayre, mocking a boss who had sacked her. She could be reckless, eccentric. Sayre recalled her at a party chucking a lighted cigarette into a closet, believing it to be an open window. As with all stories reporting her attractive wildness, or even her making a mistake, Muriel denied it. But whatever the literal truth, it is surely Sayre's image of Muriel's gaiety and confidence that matters. No friendship was possible for Muriel without frankness. As a public figure, however, she could do or say nothing without the guarantee of discretion. Her immediate reaction to betrayal of trust was first shock, then withdrawal into the grande dame persona, frigidly haughty. As Ved Mehta remarked, 'she went through people like pieces of Kleenex',[17] not because she was cruelly dismissive but because she was hypersensitive to insult. Almost everyone she knew closely – even Maclean, von Auw and Hazzard – at some stage received the brush-off direct, a furious corrective letter, or plain silence. Her correspondence from this period suggests her expectation of betrayal, as though she were eager to detect it in order to relieve herself of the burden of intimacy.

At times like these, Muriel could feel ever greater affinity with her hero, Cardinal Newman. His 'constant misrepresentations from all quarters', baulking his vocation, appeared also to be her lot. 'Hardly anything happened to Newman in a simple manner', she wrote, 'without a fuss'. Yet the fuss, she insisted, was essential. What seemed like 'touchinesss on [his] part was no more than a decent sense of propriety'. Muriel shared his '"mistrust of the reality of material phenomena"' and his periodic collapses into 'semi-nervous illnesses'. 'Two things', she wrote, 'seem to have afflicted [him] during the greater part of his life as a Catholic. One was the sense of persecution, and the other was persecution. [...] His enemies were real enemies, not so much that they nurtured personal animosity towards him but they [...] who saw no further than the present tense, frustrated his farther-sighted intentions.' Visionaries, she felt, were always threatened: 'He was isolated from the world, not by his temperament, but inevitably by his intellectual superiority and originality.'[18] In less sober mood, reviewing a biography of one of Newman's contemporaries, she let rip:

It is true that Newman was difficult to deal with, he was irritable and crotchety. His friends said so. Mr Chapman quotes them liberally enough. What the reader [...] might overlook is that Newman is not within that area of comparison with these tiresome people. They were not all giants together [...]. Irritable! That Newman was irritable, merely, with the humbugs who surrounded him, that he refrained from tipping prussic acid into their tea, is sufficient, in my opinion, to establish the present cause for his canonisation.[19]

That apparently casual remark, 'His friends said so', seems to burn with fury at their betrayal.

*

Muriel was distinctly irritable when preparing to leave New York at the end of November 1965. But she was also expectant, anticipating a new life. She cancelled the lease on the Beaux Arts apartment. Harrods were instructed to clear her Camberwell flat and to sell the contents. All the bric-à-brac her parents had sent was to go, her collection of dolls and teddy bears, her pinkish three-piece suite. The Macleans were given a rocking chair and her valuable Stanley Spencer drawing. Various pieces went to Mrs Lazzari as farewell presents. It was an evacuation of all relics from her previous lives.

Back in London, she set up at the Stafford Hotel in St James's Place, employed a secretary and inaugurated a furious work schedule. The advance for the stage *Brodie* had been paid and Maclean was called in to hand over another substantial sum for *Hothouse* (15 February at 11.00 a.m. had been pencilled into her diary to begin it). In the meantime she was tying loose ends, saving for her future, collecting her poems and essays, clearing decks and trying to simplify her life.[20]

The Italian trip had been deferred. On Christmas Eve she flew to Edinburgh where she stayed in a hotel, visited her family and took her mother to Midnight Mass. Two days later she flew back, just missing her brother who had been posted to England for a year. Time was at a premium. Five days a week she worked. Weekends were for play, for the races. Fred Winter was readying Muriel's horse, Lifeboat, for a first outing. Impatient for this, Muriel's attitude was now one of extreme urgency.[21] She set von Auw the task of tracing her published magazine work. Sarah Lippincott was deputed to search the filing cabinet in Muriel's *New Yorker* office but could find none of the manuscripts supposedly there. The book, Muriel said, might be called *The Personal Touch*. But she was at her most impersonal. When the missing documents had not arrived within three weeks, she cancelled the project.

No one could move fast enough for her. Despite the power of attorney arrangement, almost daily letters, long handwritten screeds, were dispatched from the Stafford with instructions for her agent. She refused to deal with von Auw's Hollywood contact to negotiate movie deals, promoting instead someone she had met at the races. She wrote a children's story, *The Small Telephone*, in a morning and sold it that afternoon to Macmillan, again informing von Auw after the fact. Even a waiter scalding her with boiling coffee could not deflect her. Bandaged and battling on, she had larger business on hand, with her lawyer and the British Embassy, establishing complex arrangements to convert her business visa for the USA into a permanent one, becoming a resident alien. She felt herself to be in transition,[22] was crackling with the energy of this latest development of her destiny.

The plan was to return to New York to eavesdrop on its voices while writing *Hothouse*. She hoped to complete that quickly, take a long summer holiday, and then think again. In the meantime, she had to consider how to manage her escalating income. Having decided to abandon England she needed a country in which she could live, write and avoid double taxation. America, she thought, would do while she was pondering Rome. So she crossed the Atlantic again just after her forty-eighth birthday and set to work. Three months later, on 6 May 1966, *The Prime of Miss Jean Brodie* opened in London and Muriel's take of the weekly receipts began to come in.[23] In later life, after the film, a TV version and many stage revivals worldwide, she would describe the novel (quoting Hardy on *Tess of the D'Urbervilles*) as her milch cow. It generated a small fortune, remains the one Muriel Spark novel known to millions. In the year 2003, the writer, critic and Faber editor Robert McCrum chose it as one of his '100 Greatest Novels of All Time'.[24] All this began here – yet it nearly did not happen and would never have done had not Jay Presson Allen successfully transformed an experimental work into a realist one, cutting the theological dimension and concentrating the story on frustrated love. Muriel had nothing do with the adaptation other than to produce a brief set of notes and a few lines for an alternative ending that was never used.

To the brink of the first night, according to Peggy Ramsay's hilariously melodramatic letters, savage disagreements had beset the production. Vanessa Redgrave (lead role), Peter Wood (director), Donald Albery (producer) and Presson Allen – all, in Ramsay's view, had competing claims. Just a week before the London opening, Allen was rewriting, apparently much to the distress of Redgrave and Wood. In Allen's absence, Wood cut the epilogue for the final private dress rehearsal. On hearing this, Allen returned for the public dress rehearsal that evening when Ramsay recalled a more dramatic scene behind the curtain than in front of it. Backstage, dispute again erupted during the interval, at which point Allen stormed out, promising to injunct in the morning. In her office, a stone's throw from the theatre, Ramsay was telephoning and typing till 2 a.m., desperately trying to keep the show on the road. The next day, with hours to go, Allen's lawyer was glowering across Ramsay's desk, apparently intent upon halting the production. Fortunately, Albery and Wood had backed off at dawn and, the epilogue restored, the first night went ahead. Despite the cast's being exhausted by the strain and Allen's refusal to speak to anyone, it seemed to go well.[25] In fact, it went very well. When Ramsay flew the Sunday reviews to von Auw, it was clear that they had a hit on their hands.

Muriel, of course, was delighted. To Ramsay, she appeared to be the very model of a modern major author, a 'brick', offering 'warm support', refusing to interfere.[26] Ramsay, touched by her letter of thanks, passed it on to the cast and pinned up her cable. Morale was high again. In New York, Muriel had taken a larger apartment at the Beaux Arts across the hall from her old one, and observed events in London with some satisfaction. This was the theatrical breakthrough for which she had waited so long. *Doctors of Philosophy* had at last been published by Knopf to good reviews and Ramsay was interested in relaunching it. She also wished to promote Eleanor Perry's earlier adaptation of *Memento Mori* for the West End. Jack Clayton was angling for its movie rights. Broadway beckoned for *Brodie* and a film version seemed certain. With a permanent US visa and UK tax exemption granted, Muriel had employed an American accountant, Robert Bonagura, to manage her financial affairs. This was the point at which she travelled to East Hampton for a break from *Hothouse* and hung the telephone out of the window for the dying Blanche to hear the sea. Muriel was ready for Rome now, and by late July she was there, installed in the Hotel Raphael.

*

The move placed another vacuum chamber between her and the publicity racket.[27] Tax arrangements in those days meant that she could only visit England for some thirty days a year, an ideal imposition from Muriel's point of view. While she longed to see the play, deferral of that treat was small penance for the near-unbridgeable gap that now existed between herself and the press, her family and any other irritating invader of her creative space. There is some amusing correspondence on this subject. Questionnaires requesting autobiographical information were returned blank as 'intrinsically insolent'. Apart from her 'natural, inborn disinclination to answer personal questions', she saw no reason to hand over, free of charge, slices of that autobiography which she planned one day to write. Publishers, she thought, should rather be required to complete such forms for *her*.[28] During the visa application, she had been asked to produce her Beaux Arts lease. Out of the question. It was with great difficulty that the authorities had prised her passport from her. (She was always nervous if this card of identity, and escape, were out of her possession.) The readjustment of insurance schedules caused one firm to enquire into her future plans. These were, she informed the unfortunate Beryl Probert, no business of the Eagle Star Insurance Company.[29] Members of the free world should resist all such invasions of privacy. From now on, she would be a mystery. She liked it when people did not know where she was. The only address her mother had was c/o the *New Yorker*.

Cissy's letters followed a regular pattern: gratitude for her daughter's latest cheque followed by family and neighbourhood gossip. Much to Muriel's relief, Robin appeared to have settled. He was engaged to a pleasant girl and now working for the Civil Service. Then Phil's arrival in England with Sophie and their two children, David and Vivian, lifted the lid on more antagonisms. Phil, Cissy contended, had changed, driven by Sophie's craving for material gain. He had become tight-fisted, his family racked by rows. When Sophie said she would seek a separation, Cissy had torn into her for ruining her son. Invited to stay (at Letchworth), Cissy had at first refused. Phil made it clear that he had no intention of supporting her. Muriel, he knew, was doing that. Cissy, indeed, shouted it from the hilltops . . . All this was poured into Muriel's ear. How much of it was true, she neither knew nor cared. The subtext of these rambling epistles was drearily familiar: 'Without you, dear Muriel, I should be bankrupt. Please keep the money coming.'

There was little intimacy. Muriel could now rarely find in Cissy the amusing woman she had once known, and again the old lady had struck the wrong note. Muriel quite liked Sophie, loathed these betrayals of confidence, stirring feuds; loathed the implicit demands, the attempts to implicate her in Edinburgh's pearly-grey and loveless alliances. Somehow this strange lady who was her mother always succeeded in irritating. She let it be known that Robin had taken to drawing. Shortly afterwards, he wrote to propose himself as an illustrator for her children's story *The Small Telephone*. Muriel humoured both. She did not discourage him but left it to Maclean to write the inevitable letter. For a short while, she had been able to communicate with Cissy's admirer Bill Christie as a rational intermediary. Now he was dead and Cissy had no one to talk to. Muriel let her talk. Although everyone liked 'the idea of a mother and son partnership', Maclean informed Robin, 'I don't think that it is likely to come off. [...] Very simply, the job is to embellish but not to interfere [...].'[30]

Embellishment without interference: this was the only condition on which Muriel would now admit anyone to her life. The uptown girl was translating into the grandee. She would do what she wanted, when she wanted. Even her friendship with von Auw was about to become difficult when she accused him of mismanagement. She wanted all her money from the London play to be transferred to her New York account. He had kept her fully informed, had been given power of attorney, was supremely competent at dealing with authors' international business. It was a transitional phase, he explained, somewhat wearily.

In Rome, still confident that von Auw would smooth her path and apparently unaware of his mounting irritation, Muriel was having the time of her life. Eugene Walter provided introductions. She had even acquired a boyfriend, a painter, Woody Bassett. And the Raphael was perfect for temporary habitation: expensive, but with none of the bland 'international' ostentation of the larger first-class hotels. (Muriel always shrank from the dead acreages of marble and glass in the foyers of such places.) Outside, the Raphael looked county-town English, its tall windows decked with vine leaves. Inside, the small foyer glowed red and gold with discrete treasures. Behind a polished walnut desk, instead of pigeonholes and racks of keys, stood an illuminated glass cabinet containing china and silver. The emphasis was on luxurious domesticity, on comfort, as though one had entered the modernised home of an ancient family: an antique chest here, a marble statue there; on a blank white pillar, a Renaissance icon of the Virgin. Everywhere, there was something to please the eye. It was quiet with the deep tranquillity of old money. Muriel hired a suite, terrace, and studio. Perhaps most important from her point of view was the immaculate commissionaire who stood between her and the street.

*

She stayed there for nearly three months, looking round. Walking straight ahead through the tiny square and down a cobbled alleyway opposite, she could burst into the hubbub of the Piazza Navona with its Roman-Egyptian obelisk and Bernini fountain. This remained one of her favourite places. Turning left she could be at the Tiber, the Castel Sant'Angelo and St Peter's within minutes. Turning right, she was not much further from the Forum and the Colosseum. Here, in the heart of ancient Rome, she felt immediately comfortable. This city was rooted and mysterious, a fantastic collision of the pagan and the Christian. The 'immediate touch of antiquity on everyday life' appealed. A 'fine 15th-century building' would be decorated with 'today's washing'. Children played in the fountains. 'One comes into the territory of the Republican ages, the Caesars, the emperors or the medieval popes at any turn in the road, at any bus stop.'[31] Rome shrieked of death and agony, and in the mid-1960s, of joyous irreverence towards the impositions of its heritage. It was operatic, childlike, bankrupt, and Muriel gave herself up to its artifice. In the decade that she lived there, all her addresses fell within a square mile of the Raphael. The unfurnished apartment she took in the Piazza di Tor Sanguigna that September was just thirty yards away. When she eventually moved in, she could walk to the hotel for meals and to pick up her mail. It became her dead-letter box. For nearly a year she continued to correspond on Hotel Raphael writing paper, masking her private address from everyone but von Auw.

While she was still in the hotel a photographer had rung, wanting to take pictures. How, she asked von Auw, had he found her? The man, Jerry Bauer, claimed to be a friend of Pete Lemay and of Blanche but Muriel had informed no one at Knopf of her address. Settling to dinner and *Conversations with Goethe*, she had been dragged from Elysium to discuss publicity with a stranger. Would von Auw please inform Knopf. ... This letter, however, was quite different in tone from her earlier one rebuking him for mismanagement. Although his calm assurances had failed to convince her that she had been wrong, she now agreed to differ and was off on the opposite tack, explaining that 'an epoch of beauty & pleasure is important in the life of a writer who intends to give beauty & pleasure back.'[32]

Von Auw was one of the few whose good opinion Muriel still sought. Periodically she would produce spectacular displays of business and legal acumen. Then, finding her spirit crushed by calculation, she would push it all away again into his hands and seek sanctuary from detail. Sometimes she was beating her fists against implicit accusations that she was erratic, sometimes relishing the role of skittish sybarite. When Penguin described the pieces in their 1966 *Voices at Play* as 'playful, feminine, catty', von Auw sent a stiff note: 'Muriel says she may be all of these things, but the stories certainly are not.'[33] She drove her business associates hard, had contractual veto over jacket copy and publicity photographs. American editions had to follow English spelling and all texts had to march in step with her punctuation. Translators had to be male, accounts prompt and accurate.

In all this, the obligation to her was paramount, while responsibility for her own changes of plan was regularly handed to others. Ivan was a friend and was treated as such. Yet with him she more often than not played the wise child to his benevolent paternalism. In her correspondence with him, there seems also to be the ghost of a puritan need for obligation while simultaneously she denied obligation to anyone infringing her liberty. Detesting time-wasters, she found it equally difficult to waste time herself. The epochs of beauty and pleasure for which she worked were spaces between work, all too often cluttered with preparations for more work or the struggle to keep abreast of the multiple transactions she constantly generated. In order to clear these spaces, she knew she would have to be even *more* businesslike, and a regular secretary became essential. Eugene Walter was her first assistant in Italy, copy-editing collections of her poems and stories.

*

Jerry Bauer was an enterprising young photographer who soon managed to get what he wanted. When Muriel secured her apartment, it was unfurnished and being restored. At $113 a month, a fifth of the price of the Beaux Arts place, she could afford to maintain both. There was no rush. Walter helped her with the negotiations as she took her first steps in the Italian language. And Bauer, too, proved helpful. She struck a deal with him: photographs in return for releasing her from a wrangle with a shop which had cheated her.[34] As it turned out, his pictures were good. Bauer had a talent for catching Muriel's haunted glamour and she continued to pose for him for thirty years. More than anyone, he was responsible for the pictorial element of her public image.

By late September 1966 Muriel had her new lease signed and her new status cleared by the authorities. In October, she could return to England, if only for the permitted days. With Maclean she at last saw the play and glimpsed her horse Lifeboat dislodging his rider at the starting post. Then on to New York to complete her novel. Back in her old routine, office hours at the *New Yorker*, the book seemed to go well after its doldrums in Rome but this did not last. *Brodie* threw up a geyser of correspondence. Anna Massey was to replace Redgrave who was leaving the cast to film *Blow-Up* with Antonioni. The Broadway version was being discussed. Twentieth-Century Fox offered a small fortune and Jay Presson Allen, as co-signatory, turned it down. She perpetually set Muriel's teeth on edge but this was not the reason for Muriel spending large sums on dental surgery.

Throughout it all, however, Muriel remained benign, even allowing Howard Sergeant to reprint her poem 'Sin' without fee. All her work plans were in order. *Hothouse* stalling again seemed not to matter. Only the disaster in Aberfan that October, when an unstable slag-heap cascaded down a hillside and buried a Welsh junior school, distressed her. Glued to her radio, she found the story 'shattering' and felt strangely angry about it.[35] Other news from home left her merely amused. Harold Wilson's Labour Government had been re-elected in March, much to the distress of the Macmillans. The country was throbbing with youthful exuberance: Vietnam demonstrations, aristocrats growing their hair and working in shops, Mary Quant receiving the OBE, the Beatles, the Stones, *That Was the Week That Was, Beyond the Fringe*, the bad trips, boutiques and dandies. Everything was changing there and, in her way, Muriel was distantly part of it: eager to try the fashions and dances, naturally irreverent herself. As a novelist she was also part of the booming export industry of British culture. She liked the transitory nature of it all. A year earlier, when Macmillan had moved from their oaken halls to more functional premises in Essex Street, she had applauded this exorcism of unwelcome shades.[36]

She needed something new, something older. Like Yeats, she was sailing to her Byzantium, away from the young in one another's arms, and towards a land in which the aesthetic and the spiritual united. Besides, she was missing her Mr Bassett.[37] He told her that she had nothing to worry about with him – which made her nervous. But he was also trying to illustrate *The Small Telephone* with a view to pleasing her rather than her publishers – and this she found enchanting. A year earlier, Maclean had married his secretary, Robin, who was now expecting their first child. George Nicholson was soon to marry. Even old Alfred Knopf was preparing for his wedding in Mexico. Who would be next? she mused.

When she wrote to Maclean from America on Bonfire Night, however, 5 November 1966, she was in a bad way, scarcely able to sleep. Bassett was still eagerly awaiting her return and promising to help her furnish the apartment. Von Auw was the difficulty. He had refused to continue as her agent. Muriel was stunned, and determined never again to deal with agents.[38] But if she had no agent, who would coordinate her commercial transactions, who shield her from the world? Dealing with current business alone would occupy the rest of her life. Work on *Hothouse* had stopped. All she could think to do was to return to Rome, and that dream, the dream of *The Public Image*, now came to dominate her thoughts. It involved her, Derek Stanford, a baby and a suicide.[39]

'Apart from the personal problems which Ivan was suffering', Muriel noted of von Auw's volte-face, 'there was a serious business problem':

Ober's Film man had undergone a car accident [...]. He was entirely crippled, a young man from West Point, very likeable, but without experience. [...]. I disagreed strongly with one of his decisions regarding my contract with Fox Films for *The Prime of Miss Jean Brodie* [...]. Unable to agree to the clause or clauses in question, I took the matter to my London lawyer, Michael Rubinstein [...], which I had every right to do, since Ivan [...] stood by his Film man's decision. (Incidentally I was convinced that Ober were standing by him for sentimental, not business reasons.) A considerable sum of money was involved. [...] Rubinstein [...] saw my point and fought for it. Eventually Fox Films gave in. They agreed to everything and paid my 'costs' – to completely cover my lawyer's bill. Ivan was furious. Furious.[40]

Within ten days, however, von Auw and Muriel had clarified terms which relieved his office of acting as her secretary, rescinded power of attorney, and allowed him to resume as her agent. All correspondence relating to accounting and bills was to be sent direct to her in Rome. Duplicates were to go to her American accountant. Cheques were to be deposited in her New York account. Personal correspondence and books would be forwarded to Janet Groth at the *New Yorker*.[41] Muriel flew to Rome at the end of November, a happier woman. But the row affected her permanently.

She did not blame von Auw, had seen it coming for nearly a year. She had, she knew, used him as a kind of universal answer to the world's untidy demands and not taken enough responsibility for making her own arrangements. From this point, although she always had agents and friends, she withdrew entirely from dependency, and what had previously been difficult, to love with passion, now became impossible. In Rome, the fractured, lovable Muriel of her youth was buried, and Bassett was the first casualty. They were, it seems, genuinely fond of one another. She had even thought vaguely of marriage. On her return, they remained affectionate for a while but a line was drawn. Marriage to such a young man, she thought, would be undignified. It would compromise her career, open her to gossip. Always haunting her mind there was that dream, a nightmare really, of the penalties of dependency.

Von Auw remained the essential catalyst of Muriel's success until his retirement in 1972. The new arrangements cleared the air. She sent Jan Groth a small monthly fee to sift mail and compose polite refusals. It was Groth who was now charged with looking out financial documents, paying bills, doing odd bits of research. At the *New Yorker*, Muriel also had the dependable Greenstein to offer financial advice. In London there was her accountant, Arthur Warne, although they could never communicate on paper about business affairs. (When she was in England, he did not wish, officially, to know.) In Rome, the Raphael's concierge baulked intruders. Other friends found an elderly maid for her, sweet-tempered, quiet, suitably brisk and illiterate. Her property and papers, however, were uncomfortably dispersed: valuables, files and manuscripts in her London bank; books and paintings in her Beaux Arts apartment; other manuscripts and files in the *New Yorker* office. She seemed to be leaving behind her a global paper-chase, and this dilution of centralised control was enervating. The Italian mail was slow, lost things and regularly went on strike. Resolution of the simplest discussions stretched over weeks. She frequently telephoned and cabled but this was costly, as was the expense of furnishing her Rome apartment and maintaining the Beaux Arts one. *Hothouse* was far from complete; all film companies had refused *Mandelbaum*; the movie deal on *Brodie* was deferred. On the brink of being rich, she was still not quite there. Two or three years of living like this would empty the coffers. Yet she was determined to live like this, whether in Rome or New York she was still undecided.

*

It was another 'nevertheless' period. Professionally, Muriel's stock had never been higher. The New Year's Honours List of 1967 had announced her OBE and this both raised her spirits and somehow seemed absurd: absurd that she should be genuinely delighted by the recognition and that it should come at a time when she was unable to write. Should she, she joked with von Auw, embroider 'OBE' on her nightdress, as Blanche had done with her Légion d'Honneur? Replying to over forty letters of congratulation had kept *Hothouse* on ice. A visit to Buckingham Palace was the last thing she needed, particularly as she had no escort. Preparing for it all would knock another chasm in her schedule and in her small allowance of British days.

Overall, her first shot at Rome had been disappointing. The marble floors of her apartment froze her to the marrow and she had succumbed to recurrent bouts of bronchial 'flu. After three months of this, she finally admitted herself to hospital for a week. Tests and X-rays confirmed that she was in perfect health but, weakened and low-spirited, she returned temporarily to the Raphael for cosseting. A rest, a variation from New York: that was how she viewed Rome at first. No sooner was she out of hospital than she suffered her worst attack in reaction to antibiotics: ulcerated throat and mouth, followed by another week in bed with her entire skeleton aching. While her doctor injected her with anti-flu vaccine and her Chekhovian servant pottered in attendance, Walter, her only visitor, looked in with his homeopathic cures and ESP. He detected voices in the cupboard, a relief to Muriel who had also heard them but was fearful of admitting it lest they make off with her. For the first time since Africa, the idea of her decline and death played on her consciousness. In feverish moments she dreamed that she was composing *Hothouse* faultlessly, only to awaken and find it still stalled.[42]

Anticipating new life, she had discovered debility. Was this an omen? Her confidence was at a low ebb. She had to be assisted when she sat down.[43] Here she was in her Eternal City with a stiff left hip. Her apartment was now set up exactly to her taste with modern furniture from Sweden and Norway.[44] Her address translated as 'Bloody Tower'. Outside her first-floor windows, above the traffic of the small square, the Madonna of the Bloody Tower perhaps seemed an apt icon for this new chapter in her progress. But she was not progressing. *Hothouse* had all but stopped. No more Roman winters for her, she decided. Piazza di Tor Sanguigna would be her summer palace. She craved the cosiness of the Beaux Arts and friends a local telephone call away. Although she never complained, reviewing everything as from a great height with herself as both player and director, there is no mistaking the melancholy of her letters. Sometimes she felt dreadfully alone.[45] Had Rome been a mistake? On her arrival she had given up smoking. Now she started again.

*

In this mood she had flown to England with her new suit for Buckingham Palace. Her first choice of escort had been von Auw. It would, she said, mean so much if he could fly over. They could see the *Brodie* play together.[46] Two days later she wrote again saying she did not know how he could refuse. Maclean would be there, and Bill Koshland. She was feeling depressed, having failed to complete her novel in two years, was on her feet but confined to the house.[47] Between the lines, she was reaching out. It would be embarrassing to attend the ceremony unaccompanied. She was asking him, as a special favour, to drop everything and come. Eventually she cabled: would he please wire a reply urgently. He did. Sadly, he said, he would have to decline.

Turning to her second string, Alan and Robin Maclean, she explained how close she felt to them. Her son, she said, was not invited. She would see him and Cissy in Scotland immediately afterwards. It would be best if they were not muddled up with public events. The Macleans' first child, Daniel, had just been born. Muriel was promising a bamboo cradle and a special present, describing how she loved to watch the rapid eye movement of babies when they were feeding. They seemed imbued with wisdom, chomping rhythmically while noting the slightest noise or movement. She promised to stand and stare.[48]

There was little time for gazing: Monday to buy a hat and practise curtseys; Tuesday to the Palace, on to lunch at the Ritz with the Macleans and Koshland as the guests of Harold Macmillan, on to see Anna Massey in *Brodie;* Wednesday to Edinburgh; Friday, return to London to stay with the Macleans; Sunday, back to Rome. Having endured the winter there she thought she might as well give spring a chance. Before leaving, she had begun a short story based on her dream of Stanford, the baby and the suicide. Jan Groth had been researching lightning for *Hothouse* (a character was to be electrocuted down the telephone wire) and the pieces she sent seem to have galvanised Muriel into developing her novel again. In letters, her handwriting changes from a tight and accurate script to the rapid, looping characters more typical of her when inspired. Her poems and stories were published in London that winter, and compiling these volumes restored her working routine. Being back in production again: that was the main thing.[49] With only two chapters of *Hothouse* complete, these projects kept her ticking over while she was waiting for the big inspiration to kick back in. Then, suddenly, it did.

Probably around early June 1967, she put *Hothouse* aside and began to develop her dream story into *The Public Image*. By 20 August she informed von Auw that it was finished – but it was not. Unusually, she took a week's break before revising and retyping. The first part (dream story) did not fit with the novel which had developed from it, so she completely rewrote the opening section. A month later, the novel was done: 37,000 words of alarming and perfect prose, starker than her previous work, she thought, an 'ethical shocker' with only one plot-line.[50] What was it 'about'? A recent development, in Muriel's view: the maintenance of a public persona, a fiction quite different from the private reality.[51]

The Public Image focuses on Annabel, a British film star living in Italy, who is threatened by the professional jealousy of her husband. The story culminates in his plot against her, when he stages his suicide to cause maximum embarrassment, having distributed compromising letters she has written to be discovered after his death. His object is posthumously to ruin her. A 'friend' collects the letters, ostensibly to protect Annabel, then uses them to blackmail her. The moral problem she faces centres on the choice between career and dignity, between her public and private image. The novel contemplates female celebrity and the ways in which this threatens men – a deeply personal theme. Stanford, after all they had shared together, had sold Muriel's letters.

*

It was a strange summer, her first in blistering heat since Israel. Wearing a flimsy nightshirt, she had sweated over her notebooks into the small hours, shutters closed. When she discovered that her building had a roof terrace and an attic studio, she had rented both. On the terrace she could breathe and take in the Roman roofscape but basking there for a few minutes without dark glasses had burnt her eyelids. *The Public Image* was completed in this studio, away from the sun and the traffic noise. Already she was thinking of leaving for a quieter apartment. Rome, she felt, was in many respects the wrong place for privacy. People from her old life would propose themselves or simply turn up unannounced, assuming her to be on holiday.[52] The city released her operatic side, and she liked that, but she was there, as she was everywhere, to work.

Throughout this period she described Eugene Walter as her 'wicked uncle' and, although later she dismissed him as insignificant, she was clearly fond of him in 1967. Much of her social life in Rome was spent among the homosexual community and Walter gave her the entrée to a group of stylish bohemians on the fringes of the art world. He presented her with nerve-steadying white sapphires, escorted her to concerts, introduced her to the gay party-givers of his circle. Another friend was 'Zev' (Daniel Harris), the American painter and jeweller. But as *The Public Image* suggests, its author was also apprehensive of casual acquaintances pouring through her door. She would go out but she would rarely invite others in. When the central-heating system flooded the building, and workmen and neighbours had bustled through in chorus, she felt invaded. She became godmother to a child from one of these families. Nevertheless she did not encourage familiarity. When her maid began tidying her desk, Muriel asked Walter to find a replacement. On Easter Monday, she had discovered a stray female cat, brought it home and named it Pasquetta. Pasquetta was allowed to sit on Muriel's manuscripts, even to play with them. The maid possessed neither the literacy nor the inclination to read any of the material. Muriel could not explain it but she felt that there was a clear distinction between cats touching papers, and people.[53] She was herself becoming untouchable. For years she was anxious about being spied upon. She had a fetish about pens. If anyone touched the one she was using, she threw it away.

Robert Bonagura, the source of most of her frustration, was soon also discarded. In retrospect, their correspondence is another hilarious collision between the mundane and the imaginative. At the time it drove both towards exasperation. This expensive accountant was very sure of himself, as Muriel wished him to be. In April she had sent him two large packages containing all her financial files. In Rome she had engaged a part-time typist, Faye Podell, a Jewish New Yorker, and between them they had compiled everything necessary for Bonagura's deliberations. His job was to calculate her tax liability. During May 1967, he had written to say that she owed the Inland Revenue Service a large sum and himself ten per cent of this figure. This displeased Muriel, not least because the first bill entailed her contracting for *Hothouse* with Knopf before she was ready to do so: a better price could have been secured once the book was complete, the Broadway *Brodie* and film arrangements tied up. She was not, she reminded him, to be dealt with like a minion.[54] Moreover, she thought his charges excessive. Who was this man? she asked Dorothy Olding. Von Auw had mentioned but not recommended him. He had moved offices, without informing her, to somewhere outside New York. Was he a fraud operating from a bungalow?[55]

Olding reassured her. Muriel paid the tax but only half of Bonagura's bill. This cannot have pleased him. From his point of view, Muriel had still not supplied crucial evidence: the dates of her residence in London, New York and Rome. Fine distinctions were being drawn between the times of her *being* in these cities and official *residence* there. He proposed a comprehensive questionnaire. She said that all the required information was in the files he now held. Let his office staff do it. August found her cramped on the corner of a coffee table scribbling a note to von Auw while Mrs Podell occupied the desk, hammering out the third extensive response to Bonagura's probing. Requesting his scale of fees, Muriel had asked him to provide her with a breakdown – and he nearly did.[56]

The difficulty was that she had still not decided where she wished to be based. In the same August letter she explained that she had not yet settled on Italy because she proposed trying American residence first.[57] Her floating freely round the globe, however, failed to satisfy the tax authorities. Alien status in one country implied residence in another.

All she wished to do was to bury herself in her work and to leave these complications to the professionals. She simply wanted her money to finance her future as an artist and the tax question had to be settled before the *Brodie* bonanza could be paid. But as resolution was impossible until she had decided upon a country of residence, poor Bonagura had a problem. Indeed, there was another very simple question to be settled: *where* was this money to be paid and to whom?

Through von Auw, Muriel was already in touch with his man in Milan, the principal agent for English-speaking writers in Italy, Erich Linder, who was ultimately to provide the answer and in a fashion which surprised everyone. During November 1967 von Auw also found her a Park Avenue lawyer, Alexander Lindey. Bonagura had just estimated Muriel's substantial income for the last year (including Twentieth-Century Fox's down-payment on *Brodie*), and explained that she would owe a large sum in US tax. Given that this immediately wrote off her film money, Muriel's response was chilly. Lindey's task was to settle the residence question and to replace Bonagura with an equally classy accountant. Finding one, however, proved difficult and in the meantime he had to deal with Bonagura. Long, dictatorial letters from Lindey arrived in Rome. Would she please provide ... She would recall that in his earlier correspondence he had asked her to ... It was essential that ... Perhaps she had misunderstood ... Muriel did not care for their tone. She already had alternative plans.

When Lindey was appointed she had dashed to Milan to consult Linder. A few days later she flew to New York for ten days: to sack Bonagura, discuss matters face to face with Lindey, settle arrangements for shipping the contents of her Beaux Arts apartment, and to arrange a sublet for the final two months of her lease. There were distinct disadvantages to living permanently in Italy. Income tax was higher than in the States and there was a strange cost-of-living tax which involved interrogation of her neighbours. (The more bottles of champagne one had delivered, the more the authorities demanded.) Her first impression of Italians had been that they were often untrustworthy and disliked animals. A change of personnel at the Raphael that November had removed her charming concierge and all letters now had to be routed directly to her private address. Nevertheless, her mind was made up. Walter and Mrs Podell could screen her from enquirers, and she set about applying for official residence. The Italian people were now her ideal citizens[58] and American tax-racketeers (accountants) the object of her scorn.

*

During early January 1968 Muriel was impatient for Epiphany, the day on which Italian services woke up again after Christmas. She was often trying to wake people up, often working when others were asleep or on holiday. *Hothouse* was back in production alongside another novel then entitled *The Side Effects*,[59] and *Brodie* had opened in Boston on Christmas Day to rave reviews. With Zoe Caldwell in the lead, the full Broadway premiere on 16 January promised well and they were not disappointed: standing ovations, curtain calls, queues stretching down the street, a jubilant press, sell-out advance booking. The London version had finally closed three months earlier. This would be even better and a splendid platform from which to launch the film.

The Broadway news produced an altogether lighter tone in her correspondence. 'THANKS IVAN YOUR GREAT STOP SNEEZE LOVE', ran one telegram.[60] Earlier in the month she had sent Lindey the fourth account of her mysterious movements, estimating that she had posted some three and a half pounds of documents and over 30,000 words. 'Dealing with the bureaucracy', she remarked wryly to him, 'has become my second career.'[61] To be fair to Bonagura, she said, she had not been clear about her intentions. But her 'physical and rubber-stamp' Roman residence was beyond dispute, and she now intended to base herself in Rome.[62] Lindey drew breath and fruitlessly pestered her for more 'facts' in an attempt to link her 'physical and rubber-stamp existence' with her (and his) sense of reality. Three successive firms of accountants, he said, had declined her business as too complicated. Uninterested in their reasons, she took matters into her own hands.

On 27 January 1968 she wrote four letters – to Milton Greenstein, Jan Groth, Lindey and von Auw – which resolved the confusion at a stroke.

She had, she explained, made progress. Taking herself to the American Embassy one day she had met Robert Chandler, one of their taxation experts. It was simple, he said. She should get all her papers sent over. As she was a prized dollar-earner and celebrity, they would be delighted to help her. Greenstein was asked to clear his safe of her financial documents – receipts, investments, bank books, leases, Lifeboat file, and two Premium Bonds valued at £1 each – and to send them to von Auw. Groth was requested to make any file under her guard available to Greenstein, and to stand by to collect and post should von Auw refuse. Von Auw was tentatively encouraged to undertake the task she had already assigned to him: central organiser of the operation. Finally, Lindey was instructed to send all his materials to von Auw. Included with this letter was a list of her professional expenses covering thirty headings.

Lindey's reply was stiff. Clearly he was unused to being taken off the case in such peremptory fashion and wished to make a few points of his own by way of farewell. It seemed to him unlikely that her entire expenditure on clothing and hairdressing would be allowed. He was also of the opinion that, as a legitimate deduction, upkeep of an unprofitable racehorse ranked rather lower. Was his failure to sign deliberate? Muriel's response (dictated by her but addressed to his secretary by hers) left the whole issue of his possible insult (and hers) exquisitely unresolved. 'Dear Madam,' it ran, 'I wonder if I should show Mrs Spark [your] letter [...]. Could it be that it was forwarded before Mr Lindey had an opportunity to add his corrections or second thoughts?'[63] He heard from Muriel a few more times but only to say she was dissatisfied with his advice. She refused to pay Bonagura's final bill. It was the end of a tedious narrative which she closed gratefully. Chandler, she felt, was a mature professional man like Warne, like von Auw. Between the three of them they would clean up this mess. And she had a further trick up her sleeve. In March, she told von Auw that she was just back from Zurich where she had met with Linder and his partners in the agency, Mr Fitz and Réné de Cochor. Von Auw must have smiled on reading her letter. He knew what was going on. A fourth, unnamed, party was the reason for this meeting. Before long, he was to become the Director of two companies to which all her new copyrights would be assigned.

Muriel's life in March 1968 was very heaven. Spring, for once, had brought good things. It was not only Broadway and Fox that promised riches. An old friend, John Rosenberg of Romulus Films, was hunting *The Public Image* for Paramount, who soon offered a fortune. Jonathan Miller was proposed as director for a film of *The Ballad of Peckham Rye*. She felt secure for the first time in her life. Rome offered 'abroad' just beyond her doorstep, and her doorstep was now guarded by various people, including Penelope Jardine, who she had met at the hairdresser's and with whom, eleven years later, she went to live in Tuscany. Muriel adopted another cat, Spider, from Patricia Highsmith. Now Pasquetta had a companion. And the delightful Mr Chandler had helped in another way on hearing that Muriel wished to leave the Bloody Tower. The Embassy, he said, had a list of places for their special people. By the end of the month she was packing. During April she moved into a shabby but grand apartment[64] with no gas or light bulbs. After a successful meeting with Paramount executives she took Walter and Rosenberg to see it, dark and fabulous, and, in bright green stockings and purple shoes, waltzed with them round the huge *salone*.

CHAPTER 14

In The Driver's Seat

1968–1970

Muriel was never happier than when alone, entering her creative dream.[1] In her new apartment she reserved a cell-like room in which to work. There her mind stalked *Hothouse*, which remained inert, a mouse playing dead. Somehow she could not provoke it into life. The time was not right for it. But absorbing the atmosphere of Palazzo Taverna was pleasure enough. For a couple of months she gave herself up to the practical business of moving in: visiting the American Embassy to buy household goods from a diplomat, arranging her Scandinavian furniture.

Rearing four floors above the narrow Via di Monte Giordano, Palazzo Taverna, as much a castle as a palace, occupied a substantial block in old Rome, a few hundred yards closer to St Peter's than Piazza di Tor Sanguigna. Its huge arched entrance was guarded day and night. Beyond the arch one entered a courtyard garden with ranks of long sash windows and the contemplative order of the Italian Renaissance, silent save for the fountain. Still owned by an aristocratic family, the building seemed to have drifted, unmolested, through history. It enwrapped Muriel, enraptured her. Turning right at the fountain, she would cross the open space to a smaller quadrangle where she could enter her apartment either by a white marble staircase or by the back stairs. She used both, depending on her mood and company. There was the exuberant delight of the palazzo as operatic backdrop, her public image; and there was the reality of her life as a working writer in her study, a small, comfortable room with modern furniture and white bookcases. Her sardonic eye for human vanity remained steady. She never lost a sense of temporary habitation but she never ceased savouring the pleasure of its moment. Palazzo Taverna had magic. 'I'd be there still if I had my way,' she remarked nearly thirty years later.[2]

She liked to inhabit surroundings which connected her to history. To her friends only, and to the occasional interviewer, she would reveal her larkiness, whizzing her cats on a rug about the acres of polished Roman tiles in her *salone*. This huge room had once been Cardinal Orsini's library, the 'upper walls and ceilings [...] painted with classical scenes and Orsini emblems'. In winter the central heating would scarcely touch its chill without help from a fire the size of a small shed. She never lit one, never tried to furnish the whole room. Instead, she created a seating area 'in a remote corner',[3] leaving the rest free for walks or dances. It was good both for fun and for making an entrance. Formal visitors would be greeted at the front door by Maria, a plump maid, and conducted down the length of the *salone* to meet their hostess, perfectly dressed, on click-clacking heels echoing up to the frescos. When Brendan Gill arrived, he was delighted by the spectacle. She seemed so tiny, so brave and confident 'playing house' here.[4]

Inviting von Auw, Muriel assured him there would be no crush (seven rooms, three and a half bathrooms, terrace, maid's room, and use of a huge cellar). The fireplace alone would compare favourably with most habitable spaces in New York. Moreover, it was relatively inexpensive – about the same rent as her Beaux Arts apartment – an item she thought would appeal to his sense of good bargaining. To him, the Macleans and Jan Groth, she was warmly welcoming, encouraging them to share the experience before it evaporated. Others – Bill Koshland, Joe McCrindle, Ned O'Gorman, Gillon Aitken, Jerzy Peterkiewicz and Christine Brooke-Rose – proposed themselves and were greeted politely. All were old friends. They were nevertheless *old* friends. She had closed the door on the lives to which they had belonged, felt no animus towards them but expected no positive pleasure from their company. It was these people, particularly the Americans, who now found her aloof because, although she was charming, she was also cool towards them. Where, they wanted to know, was *their* Muriel: the bohemian poet, the lover, the New York uptown girl who saw through everything?

O'Gorman last met her when he stopped off in Rome on his return from Israel. Muriel arranged (and paid for) an expensive dinner. Jerry Bauer, Eugene Walter and Principessa Margherita Rospigliosi (Secretary to the American Academy) were there. 'I was struck', O'Gorman remarked, 'by how absolutely snooty she had become. I said, "Muriel, dear, you remember when I used to take you round New York City when you didn't know anybody?" And suddenly [...] I was so *fucking* mad at her, I said "*What* is going on here?"'[5] Anyone attempting the 'Come off it' routine was dead. She would not be subject to others' disapproval or to the calling in of social debts. She owed nothing to anyone. Her new life was amusing. If people weren't amused, so be it. They need not return. 'Never apologise, never explain' always appealed to her as a response to those attempting correction. If she made a mistake, she had a rule: never offer more than *one* excuse. As a writer and as a woman of the world, she refused to explain behaviour, her own or anyone else's.[6]

Muriel discovered that, by an extraordinary coincidence, living in the flat above hers was Sir Eugen Millington-Drake, one of her supporters from the Poetry Society. An amateur poet and professional diplomat, he had been Minister to Uruguay when the German battleship *Graf Spee* had been chased into neutral Montevideo. Later he had become a minor celebrity when his character was dramatised as droll and urbane in Powell and Pressburger's 1956 film *The Battle of the River Plate*. Sir Eugen was a man who seemed to have fallen out of his proper century. A grand dinner was planned for 27 May 1968, a fortnight or so after Muriel moved in. Apologising for late notice, he wondered whether she might care to join them at the Majestic Hotel, were there to be cancellations? There were cancellations and Muriel attended. Among her papers she kept two guest lists, from this and a later gathering at the Palazzo, which offer a glimpse of the social world she now inhabited.

Sir Eugen provided not only seating plans but also brief biographies. On the 27th there was to be his son (Teddy Millington-Drake, an unmarried painter who was that day to return from his villa on Patmos) and his daughter, Marie (Duchessa di Carcaci). The family would be joined by the Contessa di Monteluce (wife of a Milanese businessman), the Contessa de Notaristefani (born in Austria; dramatic wartime adventures), Contessa Straneo, Prince Radziwill (educated at Downside; wartime officer in British Army; fifteen years in South Africa), Princess Radziwill (American born; sister of Jackie Kennedy), Mrs Buzzard (debutante in St Petersburg 1913–14 where Sir Eugen had known her), and Mr Ader (American tenant in Palazzo Taverna; businessman trading with South America).[7] On 11 October a similar party included Count Mameli (former Italian Ambassador and once Private Secretary to Mussolini when he was Minister for Foreign Affairs) and Renée de Becker (Madame la Baronne de Becker), another fellow resident.[8]

If these lists read like something from Thackeray or Henry James, the weight of grandeur was somehow lightened by the host's enthusiasm for orchestrating a splendid bash, and by his sense of mischief. Mussolini-fanciers were pitched in among British war heroes. Senior Embassy staff sat alongside junior secretaries. Muriel felt perfectly at home. She watched, she listened to these citizens of the world with their immaculate charm, learned how to throw similar parties. Palazzo Taverna offered another universe, another colony ripe for her novelist's ear, and one starkly different from Eugene Walter's circle. 'At that time,' she wrote, 'I made lifelong friends among the expatriate community [...], mostly British and American, almost all of them anxious to put me on the right track as a newcomer.'[9]

Walter ('enormous in girth of physique and heart') had toured her round his favourite restaurants, spilling out 'all the thousand legends he kept in his head attaching to various monuments':

I recall summer evenings at Galleassi's restaurant in the Piazza Santa Maria in Trastevere, where the golden frieze of the 12th-century church gleamed in its floodlight. On the opposite side of the square is a former cardinal's palace. 'Every night at midnight,' said Eugene [...], 'a hand comes out of that door and pulls in the first living thing that passes.'[10]

All this Muriel had enjoyed but it seems to have left her feeling like a visitor. During her first year she had taken Italian lessons, which relieved her of some of this dependency. She persuaded the *New Yorker* to make her their Rome correspondent, a nominal post but one which provided the press card essential to gain independent entry to public functions. Somehow, though, she remained abstracted, sitting in the public squares outside those cardinal's palaces.

Palazzo Taverna changed all that: 'I moved into an apartment full of history [...] and I radiated out from there.' 'Radiated' hits it exactly. Now she had a centre, a point of departure, and all roads led back to her rather than to Walter. Although often ill and nervous, inside the history of the city at last she felt happier as a writer. One corridor of her flat had a Roman pillar let into the wall. Part of the fun of visiting friends 'was to see what portion of history *their* living space occupied'. Old Rome attracted her because 'there are no exclusive neighbourhoods. Rich and poor live on top of each other.' Embassy protocol was wrecked by the tumult of hierarchies:

> In the first place, Italy is a republic, but of course the Vatican cardinals and ambassadors top the cake. Then there is the Old Aristocracy, whose ancestors were Popes; they stood, up to the early 1970s, very much on ceremony if they deigned to go outside their palace walls at all. The New Aristocracy comprise the hurly-burly of princes and counts who have sprung up since the time of Napoleon [...]. And ex-monarchs usually find their way to Rome, which is another headache for the Embassies. (Fortunately, these were not my problems, for whenever I throw a party, high and low as it may include, I make it a buffet.)[11]

Her palazzo was a microcosm of all this, with the possible exception of deposed royalty. But two more old acquaintances had floated to the surface near by: Queen Frederica and the young King and Queen of Greece.

*

When she moved in, Muriel republished 'The Poet's House' in *Encounter*, the second revision of an early radio broadcast. It tells of a wartime experience. In the summer of 1944 she had been travelling from Edinburgh to London by train. During the long hours of the journey she had befriended a nursemaid who invited her to stay at her employer's house in St John's Wood. Short of money, Muriel had accepted. The girl had said that the man was something in a university and Muriel, imagining a fly-blown professor, had only half-caught his name. Inside, however, she experienced an epiphany.

Muriel's bed was made up in the man's study. She could not resist examining the contents of the room. Already a poet, she was saturated in, rather bedazzled by, the work of Auden, MacNeice, Day Lewis and Spender. Here was a library of modern poetry much to her taste. Taking books down, she read inscription after inscription by their authors and suddenly realised that her friend's employer was Louis MacNeice. This had 'an intense imaginative effect'. Muriel 'went round touching everything. I sat at the poet's desk. I lifted the pencils and smelt them. I wanted to draw virtue out of everything and make it my own.'[12] The experience gave her the determination to make writing her life's vocation. It was not the moment at which she began writing but it was the moment at which she became a writer.

The tone of the essay is the opposite of ostentatious. She stresses her poverty, her fear that the MacNeices might return. She admits to the reader (as she had not in the broadcast) the embarrassment of poking about amongst another's possessions, of using the telephone to ring an agent, casually dropping the address to imply intimacy with the Great Man when asking if the agency would like to see her new book. Of course, there was no book. It was all an elaborate mime. The poem she wrote as a result of this inspiration was 'terrible'. She did not, she said, wish 'to exaggerate the importance in itself of this incident'. But something had happened that she wanted to explain. Next morning she went outside to examine the house again, 'wanting to get my first impressions for a second time. And I saw an absolute purpose in everything.' In Rome she also drew on the experience to revise a short story, 'The House of the Famous Poet', which the *New Yorker* published simultaneously with the *Encounter* piece. And there they sat, side by side: fact and fiction feasting off each other as a kind of statement about how their creator had ended up where she was.

The Public Image is another version of this statement. Drawing obliquely on Muriel's first year in Rome, it also reaches back through her whole history as an artist. When it appeared in the UK in June and in the USA during September 1968, however, the reception was mixed. *Harper's* saw Annabel as a 'caricature of a caricature, though the experience is pleasantly and consistently diverting'.[13] Martin Green dismissed the book as 'standard lady's magazine entertainment', stylised in the 'most trivialising and self-exhibiting sense'.[14] Saul Maloff mocked the blurb ('ethical shocker'): this novel's 'ethical content', he said, 'is both banal and thin-to-vanishing, and the only thing truly shocking about it is that so immensely gifted a writer [...] should have produced so shoddy a scenario for an unwritten novel.'[15] And there were other similar complaints: that it might have made a good short story but, at novella length, was unsatisfying;[16] that it read like the script of an Italian movie;[17] that it lacked compassion. Joyce Carol Oates, a fan of Muriel's earlier work, found the 'arch impersonal style'[18] disappointing. The *New York Times* and the *TLS* were equally unimpressed: too slick, thought the first, overplaying the supposedly shocking;[19] muddled symbolism, said the latter. Was it confessional? 'Much is owed to the circumstances of Muriel Spark's new life as an international star novelist, with a public image of her own to bear.'[20]

Confessional it certainly was not. But this critic had hit on something, for the book was in part a study of a relationship which taxed Muriel: that between identity and fame. In the equally large clutch of glowing notices, this and connected themes left fellow writers dazzled. It was, Rebecca West thought, deliciously slippery. One could never guess how it would end or even how one of its paragraphs might end. Unease was generated:

not because she departs from reality in a search for the sensational, but because she observes reality more exactly [...] and lacks the cowardice which makes us refuse to admit its lack of correspondence with our expectations and desires [...]. This must be one of the few contemporary novels in which contemporary crime is adequately discussed [...] the crime which finds its own satisfaction within itself, which is committed simply to procure the pleasure of witnessing the pain and loss of another.

It was no small achievement, West felt, to project a heroine without qualities as 'morally distinguished'. The book was written with 'a unique competence, a unique grace'.[21]

William Trevor, A. S. Byatt, Anne Fremantle, David Pryce-Jones, Julian Jebb, Auberon Waugh, Elizabeth Berridge and Frank Kermode all agreed that there was serious matter here, an atom bomb in an attaché case. Waugh detected an examination of human dignity and identity, 'an extreme example of the way in which this human identity can be lost'. 'Self-knowledge' here had to be sought 'in private'.[22] Trevor, like many, found that the book socked one in the back of the neck after completion. Only then did one realise that 'the pretty, naughty froth that Mrs Spark has been floating you through rises from a sump of living matter in decay'.[23] Byatt read it as a 'metaphysical study of the effect on a person of being a Personality [...] sparse, subtle and grimly funny'.[24] Fremantle relished this tale 'icily told, as expertly as a butcher dismembers a carcass'.[25] Kermode saw a dark moral fable: 'Rome, the centre of truth, is also a centre of phoneys; Mrs Spark moves from the Jerusalem of her last book to Rome, and makes an act of presence not at St Peter's but along the Via Veneto and in the studios. Dull grey in manner, this novella imitates the mediocrity of its characters. [...] A chill book then: short, strict, very distinguished.'[26]

Poised between these opposing camps was Richard Holmes's assessment in *The Times*, detecting not an act of presence but a disappearing act. Her poem 'Elementary' is quoted ('The cat subsiding down a basement / Leaves a catlessness behind it') and to Holmes, *The Public Image* represented 'the essence of catlessness'. Where, exactly, was the author to be found in this book?

> [Her readers] don't just like her. In enchantment and puzzlement, in disappointment and expectation, they obviously *believe* in her. [...] Mrs Spark attracts partly by her impenetrable composure [...]. It is difficult to forget the picture of her in Derek Stanford's study (1963), at one moment striding round the Hertfordshire countryside under a bottle-green corduroy beret, at the next making very neat, very personal translations of Horace and Catullus. [...]. She has, in fact, flirted with enormous success: flirted with beliefs, flirted with thriller plots, flirted with style, flirted even with the accepted novel form.[27]

Holmes here circles various accusations which had plagued Muriel's literary career – that she was 'fluffy', a lightweight, all froth – but he does so to try to explain his own infatuation. Is this novel and the mind behind it a solid thing or an empty shell? A plot résumé made it sound solid:

> but Mrs Spark disperses everything into a Limbo. Rome is lost in the anonymity of Annabel's unfurnished apartment, room after room of sunlit parquet. Characters are merely touched in [...]. Frederick (seen only in flashback) moves among the glass partitions of an Italian film studio and observes the meaningless gesture of a scriptwriter shattering, soundlessly, an alabaster ashtray. It all recalls the senseless public world of the Eichmann trial (the bullet-proof glass enclosure) glimpsed in *The Mandelbaum Gate*. That atmosphere of 'repetition, boredom, despair, going nowhere for nothing' pervades the present book. [...] Every attitude is a photocopy, a substitute for something else. [...] But she will not endorse the judgement, she remains inconsequent, flippant, to the end.[28]

Her best work, he felt, was brilliant because it was compassionate. 'In *The Public Image* she is content with her own poise, delightful as it is.'[29]

In fact, Muriel was attempting a new kind of writing. She had known Robbe-Grillet's work since her friendship with Brooke-Rose. Only now was she beginning to experiment more obviously with his techniques.

In an interview given to publicise *The Public Image* she cited the living writers she admired: Iris Murdoch, Mailer, Malamud, Bellow, Frank O'Connor. 'Robbe-Grillet – I'll always read Robbe-Grillet. I like his repetitiousness [...] [He] is doing something new in his precision. I believe that he was a sighter – a gunsighter – during the war, where every little millimeter counted. And one does see this in his books: an obsession with exactitude.' What did she think of Beckett? 'I like two plays. I like *Krapp's Last Tape* and *Waiting for Godot*. [...] The other plays bore me. I fall asleep watching them. And the books are just very boring to read. Writing about boredom is no use if the reader won't read.'[30] That term 'sighter' became important to her sense of this new style in which the narrator merely watches, withholding any sense of moral equity. The scene observed merely happens and what is really happening is disguised, refracted by events which can mean several things simultaneously. As one reviewer put it, 'Life, she seems to say, is a matter of selecting one's picture of it – one's preferred deception.'[31]

As a satire on the image-making process the novel is amusing and, if this were all it had to offer, it might indeed seem meagre and derivative. But it isn't. Its scenario is just that: self-consciously a fiction, a stage set for ethical debate. It damages the credibility of conventional gratitude and forgiveness (Muriel was never very good at either). It asks whether talent or virtue unapplied can be said to exist, questions what is good about not being bad. It sees human relations in terms of a Websterian melodrama of deceit and counter-deceit. How does one separate love from dependency? An innate sadism, particularly towards women, characterises sexual behaviour. Does the establishing of an identity, the claiming of territory, involve the demolition of others' identity and privacy? Is identity stable? Is there a distinction between 'personality' and 'character'? Does character itself change with the years? '"What is personality", says Leopardi, Annabel's director, '"but the effect one has on others? Life is all the achievement of an effect. Only the animals remain natural. [...] I see no hypocrisy in living up to what the public thinks of you."'[32] Neither, it seems, did Muriel. *The Public Image* was her version of Beerbohm's 'A Defence of Cosmetics' or Wilde's 'The Decay of Lying'. Billy O'Brien, the blackmailing 'friend', tells Annabel to stop posing. She isn't, she insists. This is her – now. It is like a rerun of Muriel's encounter with O'Gorman. Annabel is not the woman O'Brien used to know. She will not remain the woman she is now. Her public image is separate from her sense of self and 'she did not expect this personal image to last long in the public mind, for she intended to play other parts [...]'.[33]

Annabel is obtuse and, until the end, passive. She has allowed others to construct her image. Muriel was clever and had constructed her own. Currently she was involved in a legal wrangle with Jay Presson Allen and *Brodie*'s Broadway producer, Robert Whitehead, who wanted to publish the adaptation. On Broadway, Zoe Caldwell had won the Best Actress award. The film would soon start shooting in Edinburgh. This was the moment, they felt, to consolidate success. Muriel refused. She had neither worked on nor read the play. If Presson Allen and Whitehead cared to visit her in Rome or to send the text for her revisions, she would give it her immediate attention. Otherwise it was impossible for it to appear with her name on it. Whitehead proclaimed himself and Mrs Allen to be astonished by this response. Both, it seems, were enraged. (Muriel had also rejected von Auw's encouragement to allow UK publication in an anthology: *The Best Plays of 1968*.) Whitehead's letter had more than a tincture of bullying patronage about it: if she were embarrassed by the play's text, he suggested, perhaps she should refuse the income Mrs Allen had provided?[34] She should, in short, feel grateful to Mrs Allen. On the contrary, Muriel believed that Mrs Allen should feel grateful to *her*. But she said nothing, simply passing the letter on to von Auw and describing it as overheated.[35]

There was nothing, then, of Annabel's pallid placidity about her creator. She is, like all Muriel's heroines, a screen upon which her author could project her nightmares and her endless curiosity, an image, perhaps, of what Muriel might have become had she been weaker. '"It's frightening", Annabel remarks, "when people start taking over."'[36] Most of Muriel's fiction deals with resistance to attempted 'takeovers'. *The Public Image* opens with Annabel in her new flat. Ostensibly she is to share it with Frederick, her husband. In reality, she has set up on her own. She has left him:

> Until recently her world of people had been full of mutual assistance on all practical matters, and Frederick and his friends had in any case done the talking. Mostly, now, she had paid professional help for everything necessary to life. It was fate, part of the distance from life that had occurred at the same time as the close-ups on the screen. And she started making her arrangements from that point.[37]

Establishing herself alone in a strange city had been a similar rite of passage for Muriel. She took pride in making her own arrangements with agencies and lawyers. O'Brien's collection of acquaintances, international drifters dabbling in one art form after another, was like Walter's circle: talented, amusing, but skittish. As she said in 'The Poet's House', the difference between wanting to create and creating was the discipline to get down to it. And, like Annabel, in Rome she came to feel serene and confident:

> Her old friends were now very few; her success had suddenly put a distance between her and them, it had created that awkwardness in meeting again [...]. But even her old friends swore [...] that Annabel had always had a tremendous business capacity, had coped with complex problems, faced them, solved them. Even to them, she had become a sort of strong-woman, a sort of tiger at heart.[38]

This, surely, was authentic Muriel. What Annabel achieves in buying her flat, Muriel had achieved in moving to the Eternal City, rearranging her finances and employing secretaries. She had reclaimed professional independence[39] and, at last, put herself in the driver's seat. Her heroine, Edwin Morgan remarked, has 'a particular kind of innocence capable of moral growth',[40] and there was something of that about Muriel, too: not naïveté but that 'waking to innocence' essential to her vision.

Bauer's photographs capture a related phenomenon, also touched on in the novel:

> Annabel was still a little slip of a thing, but her face had changed, as if by action of so many famous cameras, into a mould of her public figuration. She looked aloof and well bred. Her smile had formerly been quick and small, but now it was slow and somewhat formal; nowadays she was vivacious only when the time came, in front of the cameras, to play the tiger.[41]

Muriel performed this illusion in reverse. Her publicity shots reveal the aloof and well-bred expression, eyes askance. She is staring into mirrors, eyes shining upwards. She is holding Spider, lips parted in mirthless laughter. She is seated at an antique table in a long, formal silk dress fastened at the neck with a cameo, the very model of stylish control, always immaculate – red-gold hair in perfect coiffure, nails polished, eyebrows plucked. She could be any age between thirty and fifty. Macmillan irritated her by choosing a rare picture of her smiling. She preferred the cooler ones in profile. Melancholy haunts them all, as though her thoughts are elsewhere and she is suffering this indecent exposure to provide her public with something by which they might imagine her. But she offers only a mask. It is impossible to tell what she might be thinking. In discussing these images one is discussing the art of publicity photography rather than her. Just as Annabel was posed by Leopardi, so Muriel was posed by Jerry Bauer.

*

Muriel was right to be cautious about Knopf. Their in-house reader thought *The Public Image* thin and brittle. All they could hope for, this editor believed, was damage limitation. In fact, the novel was successful on both sides of the Atlantic. Knopf announced a third printing barely two months after first publication. In the UK it remained in or around the top ten for three months. The following spring, 1969, it was one of the selections for the first Booker Prize (Rebecca West and Frank Kermode were among the judges). But if Knopf were surprised, Muriel took it all in her stride. 'From now until April 22,' the *Guardian* announced, 'six authors and six publishers will be gnawing their fingernails [...] .'[42] The prize of £5,000 generated considerable journalistic heat. Muriel peered at the cavalcade through imaginary lorgnettes, her fingernails intact. If, as seemed likely, the sponsors required candidates to attend the London ceremony, she proposed to be ill on that day.[43] She didn't win and she didn't care.

Muriel had already suffered too much publicity. The BBC were in Rome filming her in connection with the Booker nomination. For two days she had been walking them round the catacombs, the backdrop of *The Public Image*.[44] Her correspondents now needed to decode her messages: 'in hospital', 'in the country', 'out of the country', 'going to South America' usually signalling that she wished to remain undisturbed. For years she used her hospital, the Salvator Mundi, as a place in which to disappear. There were, however, many visits for medical reasons. Throughout her early fifties she was in delicate health. A checkup in November 1968 revealed the need for a hysterectomy[45] and she was still convalescing when the *Brodie* film was selected for the 1969 Royal Command Performance. At the time, she kept the nature of her operation private from everyone but von Auw and Penelope Jardine. Visitors were rare. The UK edition of *The Driver's Seat* was dedicated to Dario Ambrosiani who became her escort for more than three years. He looked in, as did her part-time secretary, Margaret Aubrey-Smith. Muriel would dictate business letters from her bed but large-scale transactions now seemed unimportant.[46] She disliked appearing weak, disliked others depositing their weakness on her. Illness was an irritation, a tiresome guest. The Salvator Mundi was somewhere she could screen it. It was also somewhere to hide to work. She finished *The Driver's Seat* and *Not to Disturb* there. In between, she admitted herself for bronchial trouble, an operation on her wisdom teeth, an abscess in her ear and the recurrent low blood pressure – something, she remarked, which always struck when she was working on a novel, particularly towards the end.

To von Auw, she presented herself as a hothouse flower and the clinic as her conservatory. On one occasion she stayed there because her refrigerator had broken down.[47] Perched on an airy hill beyond the city walls, the Salvator Mundi was a modern, anonymous building: plate glass, yellow brick. The rooms were spacious and bare, the nurses nuns. It was a place where the Pope or film stars could recuperate from the strain of maintaining their own public images, a kind of expensive retreat providing rest, routine, a chapel, and a full range of clinical services including plastic surgery. The nuns preferred healthy patients, Muriel noted, because they were less trouble. No intruder got past the front desk. You were safe from the press there. Von Auw, though, was concerned about all these hospital visits. And that consort, what about him? Some thought him a rough diamond. Muriel was sending his children's stories, pressing von Auw to place them. They displayed, she thought, an unusual range of sensibility. Ambrosiani she described as a mature man, educated and subtle. Was she taking on too much? No, she was not. Her next novel, *The Driver's Seat*, was her masterpiece. And although many thought Ambrosiani unsuitable, between 1968 and 1971 he provided an anchorage in reality amid the garish social theatre of Rome. Another was Aubrey-Smith, whose time with Muriel largely coincided with his. Both found her generous, beautiful, funny and engagingly modest. Both, in their way, loved her and liked each other.

*

Ambrosiani recalled meeting Muriel first at a tea party given by Daniel Harris one Sunday afternoon.[48] Harris ('Zev') – a married, flamboyantly homosexual, Jewish painter, sculptor and jeweller – was a skilful artist who, like many of the gay community Muriel now knew, lived by his talent and commissions. In Paris he had known Paul Klee and Pavel Tchelitchew. In Rome he bought a small, broken-down flat and transformed it with coloured glass, ceramics and paintings into an exotic Aladdin's cave. Muriel and Ambrosiani were fond of Harris, and they had another friend in common: George Armstrong, Rome correspondent of the *Guardian* and translator for itinerant New York fashion editors. Armstrong had met Muriel at Eugene Walter's. Jardine had helped her move into Palazzo Taverna with the maid and removal crew, Walter and Muriel having gone on ahead to settle the cats in, and drink wine in the large empty apartment while waiting for the others to arrive. Both men had acted as escorts, although by this stage Muriel and Walter had fallen out, about what he could not recall, after she had verbally electrocuted him down the telephone. Margaret Aubrey-Smith, who worked for him in the mornings and sometimes for her in the afternoons, sensed a chill between the two camps. Armstrong and Ambrosiani had been friends for years, since attending the University of Florence together courtesy of the GI Bill in the 1950s. They had shared apartments there and in Rome but by 1968 were living separately. Armstrong liked Walter; Ambrosiani thought him an affected opportunist, and at first sight found Muriel 'a little bit ... peculiar. She looked as if she had been drinking or something. I didn't take to her at all.'[49] In retrospect, however, he was ashamed of this reaction because shortly afterwards she had been taken to hospital. Fearing that he might have been discourteous and wishing to apologise, he joined Armstrong on a visit to the Salvator Mundi.

What Ambrosiani found there disturbed him. Muriel, he thought, seemed frightened. 'She looked like a caged animal, not sure whether to come out of the cage or not.' A few days later, at her bedside again, he told her that if she did not leave soon, she never would.[50] So he took her home and, apart from one row when she tried to throw him out by the back stairs, saw her almost every day for the next three years. It was with him that she attended the Royal Command Performance, with him that she visited Budapest, Vienna, and Auden at his Austrian house. She would arrive with Ambrosiani for dinners with friends. They went to the opera together. Rumour was rife but there was nothing clandestine about their relationship. Was she having an affair? Was he a fortune hunter? Who the hell *was* he? Would they marry? The answers were simple ('No', 'No', 'a sensitive, protective man', and 'No') but never given. None dared question Muriel, and Ambrosiani was the soul of discretion. They moved mysteriously in a city of mysteries. It was not a sexual relationship but it was an affectionate one. All day she worked and he never disturbed her. In the evenings they would eat together, go out. He gave her companionship in this extraordinary place. She lent him distinction.

Ambrosiani's description of Muriel was tender. He was attracted by her physical appearance: her hair, the texture of her skin, her delicacy and feline grace. To him, she was a shy creature of steely will and astonishing creativity. He typed some of her work and was perpetually amazed (as was Aubrey-Smith) by the absence of correction. But behind Muriel's professional mask, he detected uncertainty. 'I think I came into her life when she was particularly sad about her relationship to her fame. She had fled New York [...] and in Rome she felt a little displaced.' When he came to know Palazzo Taverna, he believed he understood why she had been afraid to leave hospital. He disliked the building; its massive architecture seemed oppressive for this tiny, fragile woman, its social atmosphere 'snooty'. Millington-Drake he found appalling, 'not the type of person she would usually associate with'. He sensed her loneliness and depression there, thought she was taken aback by the huge success of *Brodie* and worn down by the (ultimately futile) film dealings for *The Public Image*. She needed him, he said, as she needed von Auw, to shield her from intrusion 'because she's not really that type of person who can deal with things like that, [...] she's not capable of meeting public challenges.' Listening to a recording of her Blashfield Address to the American Academy of Arts and Letters in 1970, he was struck by its timidity: 'it was almost as if she was afraid to speak, her voice was so small. I think she was overcome by the people who were in the audience [...]. As we became more friendly, her assurance gathered more strength but she was always ... retiring.'[51]

In all this there is an aspect of the truth. Rome had proved unnerving for Muriel during that first year but there is no doubt that she was delighted by her apartment and her fame. In the evenings the residents of Palazzo Taverna would sometimes take the air in the grand courtyard. It was pleasant. The Millington-Drakes had welcomed her and she had always liked them. She liked a lot of people Dario found repulsive. Timid? Incapable of meeting public challenges? Von Auw would have laughed at that. Her fingers compulsively itched for the steering wheel in any financial deal, and Aubrey-Smith found her 'very positive and up-beat [...] never bitchy or complaining'.[52] But she, too, witnessed odd fractures in self-confidence. As she typed sections of the novels, Muriel would enquire what she thought of them, keenly interested in her reaction. On one occasion she suddenly asked, '"Do you think I'm crazy?" She said it as though other people thought she was. And I said, "No, you're the sanest person I know [...]." It was absolutely the way I felt about her because she was the most straightforward person I knew.'53

This hesitancy and bluntness, it seems, attracted Ambrosiani because he was hesitant and straightforward himself. Born and bred in Pennsylvania, the burly son of an Italian immigrant coal miner, he had been just eight years old when his father was killed in a pit accident. Sensitive to social slights, Ambrosiani would sometimes describe himself as 'a football player in beads'. He had little money. He was not an artist. He was fortyish, divorced. For fourteen years he had taught English as a Foreign Language in Rome while taking on other work: as stand-in manager of a shoe shop, as a translator for *Vogue* photographers. Among Muriel's aristocratic acquaintances, he cut no social ice. But he was cultivated, passionate about the arts, and well-read in English and Italian literature (Italian was his first language). A modest and intelligent man, he was uneasy in the surreal beau monde, half wanted to fit, half despised its pretensions. Muriel shared some of this ambivalence but he underestimated both her resilience and her desire to absorb the atmosphere of Rome in its totality, from Contessas fake and real to maids and con men. What Ambrosiani did not know when they first met, indeed never knew, was that she was recovering from that hysterectomy. 'I was feeling pretty bad after the hospital,' Muriel admitted. Walter 'was no form of male companion at all. [...] Dario did do that for me. [...] He was more of a man. He had been married and had a daughter so that gave him an edge on everyone else, whatever his tastes were. At least there was something manly about him.'54 Both shared a sense of exile, of having washed up in the Eternal City, refugees together from unhappier previous lives. But where she relished Rome's display, it rendered him anxious.

As Muriel was the chief success of Ambrosiani's life, he guarded it, and her, carefully. The balance of power was plain for all to see. When she was presented to the Queen Mother at the Royal Command

Performance, he loitered anonymously in the background. When he sent a photograph of her, he tore himself out of it. This self-effacement, though, was not simply an act of modesty. The snapshot was taken at one of Zev's parties. Muriel and he were seated on a sofa and Ambrosiani thought his pose undignified. He was a man concerned with *la bella figura*. An important element of his relationship with Muriel was his regard for her as an aesthetic object. The only claim he made to influence was that he changed her appearance. Look at her picture on *The Public Image*, he said, and compare it with the one on *Not to Disturb*. The first reveals a handsome middle-aged woman in a sleeveless black dress, the second a slimmer, apparently younger one in a full-length gown amid a stage set of antique furniture. 'I did that,' he said.

On this subject alone, his vocabulary became proprietary. She was beautiful when they first met, he said, but out of shape. He made her go to a man's tailor (Carlo Palazzi) to have a trouser suit made. He made her go on a macrobiotic diet with him. She wore wigs and too much make-up. He fixed that. He directed her to the best couturiers and often accompanied her because she was sure she would choose the wrong thing. And, in the end, he was pleased with his work. She had become glamorous. This, it seems, he regarded as the one area in which he could instruct her. But no one instructed Muriel. No one made her do things. Her intense interest in clothes dated from her girlhood. True, she had been debilitated by the operation and gladly took the arm he offered. She also preferred not to shop alone, particularly in Rome where the exploitation of foreigners was commonplace. She was open to advice. She was, however, no mere doll for Dario to dress. It was a makeover rather than a takeover and she was in control of the process.

George Mott, an American photographer who came to know Muriel a little later, was entirely sympathetic to her operatic side: 'because what other reason would you have had for being in Rome in that period except to use it as a setting for the acting out, the living out of an inner fantasy about some kind of social prestige?' Muriel, of course, being a Catholic, did have another reason, but his remarks are interesting nevertheless. It was, he thought, a definite *period*, which collapsed with the oil crisis in 1973 when Rome became just another Western city with economic problems, and the lotus land evaporated. (Muriel, indeed, began to stay away from the city shortly after this, in 1974.) Before, and especially during the late 1960s, it was as though *La Dolce Vita* had become reality. Mastroianni's existential wandering was stylish and appealing. 'Believe me,' Mott insisted, 'for a long time it was like that.' Many people from the real world appeared in the film (Eugene Walter is in the final sequence) 'and a lot of people from the unreal world appear in the Roman aristocracy'. Muriel described Renée de Becker, a neighbour in Palazzo Taverna, as a character from Proust and Mott wondered whether Muriel was experiencing 'a sort of Proustian episode in her life [...] re-evaluating existence in terms of the beau monde. I bought it, too, for a long time. It was fun.'[55] 'That's what Rome was. It was a place where you could absolutely assume any identity you wanted.'[56] The Italian title for *The Driver's Seat* was *Identikit*. Muriel liked it and was becoming increasingly engaged with the questions of identity at the heart of that novel and *The Public Image*: the fictional nature of 'personality', the gap between the public and private image.

*

During June 1969 Muriel went on a three-day trip to Florence with Armstrong and Grace Zaring Stone (the novelist 'Ethel Vance'). A sharp-witted American, then in her eighties, Stone was a character from Henry James: East Coast ruling class, widow of an admiral attached to the Berlin Embassy during the 1930s, when she had known Hitler and his crew. Armstrong had introduced Muriel to her and they became friends. But whereas with Ambrosiani, Muriel could enjoy music and painting at her own pace, with Stone there was high-cultural pressure. As a former President of the writers' organisation PEN, she enjoyed public life and failed to understand why Muriel did not. In Florence, Armstrong and Stone toured the museums while Muriel would usually excuse herself and sit quietly in cafés reading the newspapers. At first, Armstrong thought this odd. It was, after all, Muriel's first visit to the city. Only later did he realise what she was up to.

Muriel's obsessive reading had concentrated on one story. A German woman, garishly dressed, had come to Rome and taken a stroll in the park. There she had been tied up, raped and stabbed to death. To Muriel, the compelling feature of this butchery was that the 'victim' appeared to have provoked it. Here was the germ of her next novel. Moreover, she had discovered a new source of inspiration. Three of her next four books – *The Driver's Seat* (1970), *Not to Disturb* (1971) and *The Abbess of Crewe* (1974) – derived from press reports. The one which did not – *The Hothouse by the East River* (1973) – was arguably the least successful.

Hothouse had been put aside for three years now. Six months earlier, the first two chapters had been typed and appeared to her to be rather strange.[57] She sent them to von Auw, saying that she was in two minds about this weird book and would follow his advice. Because he respected her as an artist, she invited his frankness. In Rome, however, she some- times sensed that she was not taken seriously. Gore Vidal, that focus of cultivated, expatriate life, had crossed her path several times, and she liked him. She did not particularly seek his good opinion. Nevertheless, when she invited him home, she detected criticism. *The Public Image*, she reported him as saying, was implausible; female writers like Carson McCullers (and implicitly, she thought, herself) all went to pieces; her *salone* was inadequately furnished. Apparently, he told her that the *Brodie* film was not progressing well and that Fox were disappointed.[58] Doubtless his remarks were presented in the spirit of cheerful (competitive) badinage but Muriel was irritated by them. And with *Hothouse* dragging its heels so badly, Vidal's comments perhaps touched a nerve.

Was it this unfortunate evening that triggered the muse again? Barely a month later von Auw received another letter. She was just back from a fortnight's holiday at Porto Ercole and was writing a psychological thriller.[59] Soon she was in hospital for thirty days to finish it, have dental surgery, diet and rest. On 22 October she emerged, weighing in at just 105lbs, her slimmest ever, with her slender book complete. Maclean had joked that Macmillan would have to print it on very thick paper but both he and von Auw were convinced they were on to a winner with *The Driver's Seat*. On the 24th the *New Yorker* agreed, as they had with

Brodie, to publish the entire text as a single issue. Failing powers? Mr Vidal could think again.

On Christmas Day 1969 she threw a catered buffet for any of her friends at a loose end. Rich and poor were invited, young and old. It was, she explained to von Auw, a cosmopolitan gathering, at which he would have been warmly welcome. But her repeated invitations to him always failed and, in truth, she had no close friends in Rome beyond Ambrosiani. Admirers, yes; a host of charming casual acquaintances. Muriel gave wonderful parties and was in her element as hostess. But when she closed her door on the last guest, when the maids and caterers had gone, she was alone in her echoing pile. She liked it that way. She had, deliberately, made herself a stranger, while simultaneously building massive defences against the neuroses of isolation. For some years, her only intimate relation to other human beings had been with her readers.

*

Muriel considered *The Driver's Seat* to be her best-written and best-constructed novel, and with good reason for she was at the very height of her powers with this study of alienation. The central character is Lise. We never learn her surname. Her country of origin is located only in the 'North', her destination only in the 'South'. Everything beyond her immediate field of vision is blurred. It is the story of a woman who has lost all human contact and who is seeking not a sense of self but the obliteration of self. She is searching for someone to kill her. Since reading those articles in Florence, Muriel had become intrigued by the extent to which the victims of crime might be complicit. This was the reverse of the scenario in *The Public Image* where crime was arbitrary and sadistic. Here the 'victim' gains strength by controlling, indeed encouraging, the criminal. But there is a link. Both investigate sadomasochistic tendencies and the relationship between choice and destiny. Both act as metaphors for the relationship between the artist and the world.

Lise has lived an orderly life. She is thirty-four, single, renting a service flat, an intelligent, independent woman who speaks four languages. For sixteen years she has worked in an accountants' office. From the outset, however, we realise that something is wrong. The novel opens in a dress shop with her screaming at the salesgirl for offering a lurid, stain-resistant garment. This anger does not arise from Lise's fine aesthetic taste. She *wants* garishness *and* staining. Moving on to a department store, she chooses an outfit suitable only for a harlequin and leaves contented. Throughout, she is laying a trail for the police. She argues with the doorkeeper of her flat, picks up strangers. At the airport she buys a book with a striking cover and holds it up before her wherever she goes, like an 'identification notice carried by a displaced person'.[60]

Each move is calculated. What appears to be deranged behaviour both is, and is not. In one respect it is cold-blooded plotting, and yet hysteria regularly overwhelms Lise with fits of laughing and crying. On the plane she sits next to a young man in a dark business suit who immediately becomes so terrified by her that he changes seat. Another fellow snuggles up, touches her leg. The first chap, he says, was not 'her type'. When they disembark in the 'South' (in a city similar to Rome) he makes a date with her which she has no intention of keeping, but does. The dark-suited man has disappeared. An ailing peer is waiting for his car and she tries unsuccessfully to cadge a lift. No one forgets her. After wandering round another department store and into a riot, Lise hides in a garage, survives two sexual assaults by escaping in her assailants' cars, and finally drives to the park where, as we know from the beginning of the third chapter, she will be found next morning 'dead from multiple stab-wounds, her wrists bound with a silk scarf and her ankles bound with a man's necktie [...]'.[61] She has bought the knife and necktie in preparation, as it were, for the inevitable. Throughout, there is a sense of sexual threat as various men misinterpret her approaches. She examines each one to see if he is 'her type' – not of sexual partner but of murderer.

The book's style makes it doubly unnerving. Conventional suspense is wrecked by the early revelation of Lise's fate. The bulk of the narrative is in the present tense, with occasional interjections of the future perfect to detail the police investigation. There is no past – no account of the past, at least, which is reliable. Lise lies freely to present herself in whatever guise best protects her anonymity. Everything happens before our eyes as it does to Lise, and the narrator refuses to interpret: 'She puts the bunch of keys in her handbag, picks up her paperback book and goes out, locking the door behind her. Who knows her thoughts? Who can tell?' The replaying of dialogue, never *quite* the same on reprise, complicates our sense of time. The repetition of words and phrases – 'my type', 'moving quickly away and away' – invites us to patronise lazy writing and then whips the carpet from beneath our feet. Simple words arrest us. Adjectives are poetically displaced. Lise's boss regards her with 'frightened eyeglasses', she moves 'as if with dreamy feet and legs', she 'drags', not 'draws' attention. Short sentences are interspersed with ones of baroque complexity. Abruptly recovering from feigned panic, Lise speaks quickly 'in a burst of spontaneous composure'.[62]

Much of this had been part of Muriel's unique voice since *The Comforters*. The innovation here was the present tense focalising an obsessive mind. 'Present tense', indeed, describes Lise rather well. The tone shifts from the dominantly icy reportage, as though the action were captured on security cameras, to fairy tale, thriller and theological treatise. It reads in part like the scenario of a film noir, switchbacking through other cinematic genres: romantic comedy, slapstick. There is something of Hitchcock about it, something of Powell and Pressburger, something of Buster Keaton. Much of the dialogue echoes the threat and self-concealment of Pinter's unlocated personae. Readers seeking the comforts of realism are slapped in the face and sent spinning about the narrative's immaculate surface. There are no 'characters' to anchor us. The material details of their lives and appearance are scattered like confetti. The only significant 'fact' is something Lise senses: that Richard, the dark-suited man she met on the plane, is a sex-maniac, 'rehabilitated' but still ripe for temptation.

Lise may speak English, French, Danish and Italian, but we are never told which is her native tongue. Adrift in a sea of discourse, she keeps her functional apartment 'as clean-lined and clear to return to [...] as if it were uninhabited'. Alone on her bed she lies like an effigy on a tomb. And in one sense she is already dead. Anonymous, 'neither good looking nor bad looking', she is a blank page on which the world can write its prejudices. Her identity is no more than the Identikit picture constructed after her death. No one understands Lise. She does not understand herself. There is nothing to understand. Her curious heroism lies in the courage to confront this void and, like Caroline Rose in *The Comforters*, conscientiously to turn herself into a story. Lacking religious faith, Lise has, perhaps, no alternative as an act of will. Again, this novel circles that perennial Sparkian theme, the theme of Job: how absence defines presence. Mrs Fiedke asks Lise how she will recognise 'her type': 'Will you feel a presence? Is that how you will know?' 'Not really a presence,' Lise says, 'The lack of an absence, that's what it is.'[63]

Ultimately, however, Lise is mad, and represents a perverse reversal of how Muriel managed her own existence. Like Muriel, in attempting to wrest control of her life from others, she has successfully written her own scenario and found strangers to act out the supporting roles. But where Muriel sought life and the freedom to create, Lise seeks death and the freedom not to exist. Her instructions to her murderer are precise. He must tie her wrists and ankles. He must stab here and here. No sex before death. He ties her wrists and stabs. Only afterwards does he tie her ankles. In between, against her will and before the knife descends on her throat, he rapes her.

When *The Driver's Seat* appeared in the summer of 1970, the duller reviewers were, perhaps not surprisingly, perplexed: 'A quirky, cranky curio preserved in formaldehyde';[64] 'The whole story is told in 128 pages. It leaves one with rather the feeling, "Is *that* all there was to it?"'[65] Among the British critics, most of the powerful voices – Malcolm Bradbury, A. S. Byatt, Frank Kermode, Arthur Calder-Marshall and Claire Tomalin – showered praise. But there was an astonishingly large collection of neutral or plain bad notices seeing the book, implicitly or explicitly, as 'something of a trial of concentration'.[66] Stanford offered lukewarm patronage, implying that most of his ex-lover's fiction dealt with 'batty' women while trading in 'giggles and sniggers'.[67] Muriel's masterpiece flickered briefly as no. 5 in the UK best-sellers, then disappeared from the list. More disappointing was the fact that, despite the accolade of *New Yorker* publication, Americans could rarely make sense of the novel.

Some notices were warm, several admiring, but the general drift was that this was an incomprehensible narrative with an unsympathetic heroine.[68] Clearly the *New Yorker* effect was not going to be repeated. This was no *Brodie* to appeal to the mass market. Sales were only modest.

*

The New York literati had come out in force for her Blashfield Foundation Address six months earlier, on 26 May 1970. William Maxwell, President of the American Academy of Arts and Letters, had invited her. It was the keynote speech before an invited audience of several hundred in addition to Academy members, after their annual luncheon. Muriel loathed public speaking but she liked Maxwell, admired his fiction and had warm memories of him at the *New Yorker*. The time seemed right for a little decorous publicity. So she accepted on the condition that she could speak on whatever she wished as briefly as she wished and read her text. The result, 'The Desegregation of Art', was startling. In effect, it was a companion piece to her novel.

The artist, she said, was 'a changer of actuality into something else' and because literature 'infiltrates and should fertilise our minds' 'ineffective literature must go'. By 'ineffective' she meant the 'marvellous tradition of socially conscious art', 'the representation of the victim against the oppressor'. The problem with social realism was that it offered surrogate absolution. We rise from it chastened but all the more determined to be an oppressor rather than a victim. It encourages 'the cult of the victim' and, wherever this exists, 'there will be an obliging cult of twenty equivalent victimizers.' No, the 'art of sentiment and emotion' had to go. 'In its place I advocate the arts of satire and ridicule.' It was a moment in history, she insisted, 'when we are surrounded on all sides and oppressed by the absurd'. Sharp, unsentimental intelligence was required to unnerve and paralyse it. The function of art was to give pleasure – 'that element of pleasure which restores the proportions of the human spirit' and 'is the opposite and enemy of boredom and of pain' – but the 'cult of the victim is the cult of pathos, not tragedy'. It was exhausted. We had to recognise 'the ridiculous nature of the reality before us' and mock it. 'We should know ourselves better by now than to be under the illusion that we are essentially aspiring, affectionate and loving creatures.' We possess these qualities, but we are aggressive, too. As for herself, she was a 'sort of writing animal'.[69]

It was a sparkling performance but some in the audience were baffled. Shirley Hazzard was there and recalled some prefatory remarks not in the printed text of the 'We-in-Rome' variety, as though addressing the philistines. The Vietnam conflict was raging, anti-war demonstrations and race riots tearing American cities apart. To use loaded terms like 'segregation' and 'desegregation', to speak with apparent levity of 'gross racial injustices' and to place them in the same category as 'the tyrannies of family life on the individual', to say that 'socially conscious art' cheated the reader in the heyday of Mailer, Miller and Singer was perhaps a trifle reckless of local sensitivities. But it was a brave speech in that literary atmosphere, a decade ahead of its time, pure postmodernism.

*

Muriel had flown back to England for the British publication of *The Driver's Seat*, by which time she had been struggling with *Hothouse* for another eight months. During her American trip that summer she had used her old Beaux Arts apartment to try to recreate the atmosphere, but with little success. Back in Rome she set that novel aside again and began *Not to Disturb*, increasingly impatient with Knopf for not selling more copies of *The Driver's Seat*. It was at this moment that Bill Koshland had visited her at Palazzo Taverna and detected, rightly, that his firm was for the chop. She was angry with Macmillan, too. In the middle of her estrangement from Ambrosiani (the American edition cancelled the dedication to him), she was in volatile mood. Periodically, her health would cause trouble and she would retreat to the Salvator Mundi. Her eyes were beginning to fail: cataracts, later removed. Returning from Zurich in October 1970, she cricked her neck so badly taking hand luggage from a locker that a doctor needed to meet the plane and rush her off for X-rays. It was a bad time made worse by the annoyance of not having her lease renewed. The landlady said that she required the apartment 'for her daughter' – and Muriel knew exactly what that meant. After financing the renovation, she was being evicted so that the owners could relet at an inflated rent. By mid-March 1971 she was gone from Palazzo Taverna, across the river and into the trees, shaking off the Renaissance shade of Cardinal Orsini.

CHAPTER 15

Lucrezia Borgia in Trousers

1971–1974

Muriel's new flat was in the Trastevere district of Rome, on the top floor of a nineteenth-century building overlooking the Tiber. It was another large apartment, not quite so smart an address (Lungotevere Raffaello Sanzio 9) but still 'magnificent', one witness thought, 'clearly the sort of [place] in which you could entertain on a grand scale'.[1] The interior was brightly modern: a kitchen in which she never cooked, two bedrooms and a large sitting room around which she could walk when composing. Every window supplied a spectacular view. To the left, not far away, lay St Peter's. At night she liked to stare out at the floodlit monuments and down at the illuminated bracelet of traffic winding along the river and across the bridges. In Palazzo Taverna she used to joke about genuflecting to the Cardinal's ghost as it descended the chimney. Light and air now replaced these shadows, and other ghosts occupied her mind: a houseman, a secretary and the voices of *Not to Disturb*.

Foreseeing the unforeseen was a major theme of that novel, which had been disturbed by the move. The unexpected, Muriel felt, was often predictable. One had to be prepared, to look lively for one's interests. This was another of her purgative moments. Knopf, she informed von Auw, should not be offered her future work. She wanted considerably more money and Macmillan, too, would need to bid higher. The best guarantee of high sales, she insisted, was a high advance. Only then would a publisher push and advertise. Von Auw dealt with the matter delicately – in his view, Knopf was the best American house for her – but, implacable, she was, again, right. Offers poured in and Viking soon closed the bidding with a lucrative three-book contract.

The genesis of *Not to Disturb* had been a widely reported multiple Italian murder involving a Count, his wife, their mutual lover and voyeurism. Muriel shifted the story to the cooler atmosphere of contemporary Geneva and the narrative focus to the servants, in particular to a major-domo butler she invented called Lister. The novel, her most experimental yet, required total immersion, and its inception five months earlier had coincided with, was perhaps stimulated by, her employing a manservant / housekeeper who had rapidly transformed the domestic organisation of the Palazzo Taverna apartment. Since then, however, the arrangement had collapsed disastrously and the enforced move had wrecked her concentration.

Muriel's secretary, Margaret Aubrey-Smith, was a young and beautiful Englishwoman, daughter of the Military Attaché to the British Embassy in Belgrade. The manservant was, she recalled, 'perfect'.² Small and trim, late thirties, Italian, he was punctual, courteous and, for the most part, invisible. The two women had watched him with amazed delight. Muriel much preferred the new arrangement.³ Neither he nor her maid 'slept in'. They came and went according to Italian hours (8.00 a.m. to lunch) unless they were required for an evening party, and, as Muriel often worked at night, her butler fitted seamlessly into this schedule. She disliked being fussed over by women and, besides, there was something about him which amused her. Taking Aubrey-Smith aside one day, Muriel led her to the bathroom where his frilly underwear had been washed and left to dry.⁴

His transvestism was not the problem. He dressed normally for work. She had no prejudice against the varieties of sexual experience. Homosexuality was ubiquitous in Rome's artistic community. Most of her male friends were gay and, although she was not, she remained indifferent to their tastes. Some apparently used street-boys. She felt sorry for these young men, but there was nothing to be done. Privacy was sacrosanct. As a moralist she was a theologian turning the large, abstract issues of judgement and love this way and that as Lister twists a bowl of flowers 'to better taste'.[5] Her butler did a good job. No further questions were asked. Then, after three months or so, he had disappeared and she had been served with legal papers suing her for unfair dismissal. 'It was a scam,' Aubrey-Smith explained. 'People would get jobs and would do the job perfectly and then would force you to let them go and [...] sue you.'[6]

The case rumbled on through the winter and spring of 1970/71, up to and including the move, throughout the major phase of *Not to Disturb*'s composition. And with this additional strain, Muriel could not face the packing and unpacking. Retiring to the clinic for seventeen days, she had transferred responsibility for the entire operation to Aubrey-Smith. There was minimal furniture but an extensive, precious collection of papers and clothes. During 1970 Muriel had come to a decision about both, inaugurating a grand scheme to assemble all her literary manuscripts in America (to have them valued with a view to sale), and assisting the publicity campaign for *The Driver's Seat* by accepting interviews from the fashion pages. On the very point of leaving Palazzo Taverna, she had entertained Beryl Hartland of the *Daily Telegraph*.

Hartland's article offers a rare glimpse of Muriel 'at home', or rather of her performing an act of being at home. What emerges is a strange collision between the sensual and the ascetic:

> Her bedroom wardrobes bulge with long glamour evening outfits so her day clothes have to take their chance in the kitchen cupboards. [...] 'I write best in little cells,' she says. By comparison, her bedroom is almost frivolously feminine, a pale blue and white world, from the blue carpet and the blue and white painted furniture to the sweeping white lace curtains and the frothy blue night attire, laid out on the bed.[7]

Everything was set like a stage, amid which the poised diva sipped her port and lemon ('doctor's orders'), impulsively leapt to her feet to swirl her cats on a rug and proclaimed, 'If I'd been much smaller I could have joined a circus as a midget.' She loved, she said, to live in Rome, entertained liberally: smallish dinner parties and 'a huge monthly dress-up buffet party when she insists the men wear black ties. [...] "It is all pure Verdi, the Italians can't live without grand opera in their lives, there's a scandal every day and never a dull moment."' Later she changed into a 'flowing green dress' and insisted they 'drink Crème de Menthe to match it'.[8] No mention was made of the imminent move, the black-mailing manservant, the general stress which was, within days, to take her to the hospital. The public image was immaculate. Aubrey-Smith, however, aware that switching houses was frustrating Muriel in more ways than one, sensed high-tension mental electricity fizzing beneath that implacable exterior. The evening dresses were costly designer cre-ations. Muriel, meticulous about everything, was particularly so about her clothes. As with her papers, she expected everything to arrive in pristine condition and in the right order.

Aubrey-Smith took her task seriously. Towards the end she was unpacking six days a week till three in the morning. But Dario Ambro-siani, having recently resurfaced in Muriel's life, would often be waiting in the new flat – and there was something strange in his behaviour. He 'would start talking about Muriel. And there seemed to be a great deal of hostility towards [her]. Well, I just figured, I guess, that their relationship was coming to an end or something. I didn't know what was going on. Dario was visiting Muriel in hospital.' Suddenly he would say things like 'She says she's got better legs than you have' or, 'What do you think about the fact that she's wearing hot pants?' – questions seemingly designed to elicit slander. Picking about among the clothes, he would hold up various dresses. What about this? And this?[9] Muriel, Ambrosiani said, was dissatisfied: the move was taking too long, there was insufficient effort: 'I began to get really depressed. [...] I kept thinking, "Why is Muriel saying this? And why is she angry at me? She never expressed anything negative to me, ever. She's always been gracious and friendly."' When, finally, all was ready, exhausted by this litany of accusation, Aubrey-Smith perhaps reacted over-sensitively, interpreting Muriel's suggestion that they were both 'ready for a change' as a polite form of dismissal. Muriel denied sacking her, indeed vividly remembered still being in hospital when the girl left voluntarily in

March 1971. At any rate, her employment ceased forthwith. Later a mutual friend wrote to inform her that 'someone' had been telling Muriel that her secretary had lost no opportunity to malign her. Suddenly, a light ... Could this have been Ambrosiani? But if he was the Iago, what were his motives? She had no idea. Perhaps, she thought, he was jealous of anyone else enjoying Muriel's trust, and competition for this trust certainly seems to have poisoned the atmosphere of her closer friendships with men. It was an old, old story.

The vacuum left by Ambrosiani had quickly been filled by other courtiers, chief among whom were Count Lanfranco Rasponi and 'Baron' Brian de Breffny. Rasponi, the son of an Italian aristocrat and an American mother, was an expert on opera, wealthy and *soigné*; de Breffny an elegant charmer of obscure origins. Ambrosiani disliked them both. De Breffny he saw as dangerous and cruel, Rasponi as a foppish 'contessa', although always kind to Muriel. There was no choice for Ambrosiani, however, other than to fabricate bonhomie and to accept that, since his return to favour, he was no longer her exclusive companion. All three maintained towards each other a spiked courtesy. And against this theatrical background, Penelope Jardine, with her common sense and sardonic wit, was becoming increasingly important to Muriel's equanimity. In her eighties Muriel published a story, 'A Hundred and Eleven Years Without a Chauffeur',[10] offering an affectionate portrait of the then late de Breffny as 'Damian de Dogherty', a magnificent fake. Ambrosiani, she thought, never understood him. In her way, she was fond of and amused by de Breffny and he was possibly, although extremely intermittently, her last lover. In both their ways, they used each other.

*

Regular European excursions now became the pattern of Muriel's life, starting with a week's trip with Ambrosiani to Vienna and Budapest in September 1971. From Vienna, she telegraphed Wystan Auden offering to visit and the next morning Muriel and Ambrosiani took the train to Kirchstetten. In his tiny Volkswagen, Auden drove them up through the mountains to the cottage he shared with Chester Kallman, who prepared lunch while Muriel and Auden talked. Ambrosiani sat silent unless spoken to. It was an amicable, uncompetitive social occasion: 'mutual admiration'.[11] Muriel had not seen Auden since leaving New York where they had met at parties. Once or twice she had dined at his apartment in St Mark's Place. They did not know each other well. But since his dust-jacket tribute for *The Girls of Slender Means* (stating that she 'knew exactly what she was doing'), he had occupied a special place in her affections.

In 1971, Auden was the pre-eminent figure of British and American letters, a man largely withdrawn from the world. Breezing in, she seems to have raised his spirits. Had he, she asked, written anything interesting lately? As a matter of fact, he replied, he had, only last night. They were seated on something like a bed or a couch. Reaching underneath it, he pulled out a notebook and read the poem. Muriel was enchanted but was all too soon clattering back to Vienna. She never met him again. Two years later he was dead – and she felt the loss as keenly as he had the passing of Yeats and Freud. This meeting was a sacramental moment in her life, cherished for twenty-five years until it found artistic expression. Tom Richards's lament in *Reality and Dreams* (1996) was also hers: 'If Auden were alive he would have come to see me in his shabby clothes. Wystan [...] would scramble under the sofa to bring out his batch of poems to read to me.'[12] His gesture, she felt, was an act of communion. Voices like his were rare, precious. She claimed spiritual affinity with them and, following the dictates of his will, destroyed the letters he had sent her.

After two depressing days in communist Budapest, Muriel and Ambrosiani returned to Rome. Austria, though, had made the trip worthwhile:[13] opera most nights, excellent food and wine, all at Muriel's expense. A year earlier, waiting for *The Driver's Seat* to appear, she had described herself as tranquilly anxious.[14] Home again and with *Not to Disturb* due out in a little over a month, she was anxiously tranquil, usually very happy and perfectly confident of the book's quality but nagged by more invasions of privacy. The novel was to appear, simultaneously with Macmillan's printing, in a limited signed edition for

Observer Books, with a frontispiece by Michael Ayrton depicting a bestiary, and she had agreed to a tie-in *Observer* interview with Philip Toynbee.

Toynbee and the *Observer* had a considerable stake in Muriel's career. The publication of this interview marked the twentieth anniversary of 'The Seraph and the Zambesi', and, as the judge chiefly responsible for selecting it as the competition winner, Toynbee sensed 'the slightly satanic feeling of having called [her] into being'. 'You'd be right,' Muriel agreed, modestly talking down her early critical books as Grub Street productions. As an apprentice novelist, she said, she had felt closer to MacNeice than to writers of prose fiction. In the early 1950s there had been no Robbe-Grillet; Beckett was then almost unknown. She did not produce 'poetical prose': 'God forbid.' Durrell's *Alexandria Quartet* turned her stomach. No, she was aiming rather at compression and 'obliqueness'. Again she was asked which modern novelists she admired. Again Robbe-Grillet topped the list, followed by Angus Wilson and some of Iris Murdoch. Kingsley Amis and John Wain 'have done one thing well and then got stuck in a rut. I can't stand Hemingway.' She thought of herself as the opposite of C. P. Snow and had changed her mind about Mailer: 'quite simply a very bad writer.' Much of her material, she admitted, now came from 'the glossies and the newspapers and film mags'.[15] The remark might have seemed flippant but it was not. These, after all, had been Cocteau's working materials and, more recently, those of postmodern art. She was touching here on that new aspect of her work reflecting the theatricality of Italian journalism.[16]

So far, so good. But then Toynbee's questions took an unpleasant turn. How different she was, he said, 'from the dumpy Bohemian girl I then knew'. With her elegant flat, clothes and social life, with her svelte figure, she seemed to have undergone a 'sensational transformation; though I detect a waifish element in you still.' Toynbee was an experimental novelist himself. Under cover of artistic fellowship, he appeared to be trying to embarrass her and had, moreover, made the mistake of arriving with his wife and rather drunk. The subtext of his questions hinted at hypocrisy. Had she not deserted her old friends now that she was rich?

Muriel battled on, shutters rapidly closing. One of her reasons for leaving England, she explained, 'is that I'd outstripped all my old friends [...]. It was painful to be with them, simply because I felt like a sort of reproach to them – and they to me.'[17] Toynbee wrongly scented blood. Every time she began to talk about something important to her ('I'm not really a Vatican-type Catholic. Far from it'), he reverted to his obsession: 'I notice your Scottish accent comes and goes in a rather odd sort of way.' Muriel rolled out her standard response to close that avenue: she admired the Scots' industry but Edinburgh was stifling. 'How important has it been that you're half Jewish?' 'Alfred Kazin once said about me, "She hasn't got a scrap of talent, and she treats the Jews as if they were Eskimos." I suppose he meant that I don't particularly associate myself with Jewish causes. But I defend them sharply if they're attacked.'[18] At last, her inquisitor got to *Not to Disturb* and the atmosphere lightened a little. Was it not rather like Ivy Compton-Burnett, Henry Green, even Ronald Firbank? Yes, she agreed, it was a departure, begun with *The Driver's Seat*. She was trying to pare away everything superfluous.

The interview took place in early October. Ten days later, after BBC Television had been tracking her to capture 'the writer at work', far from being at work, the writer was distraught.[19] On the 12th she had telephoned von Auw asking him to act as her sole channel of communication with Maclean. As Maclean had arranged the BBC and *Observer* interviews, she held him responsible for their effect on her, and after receiving Toynbee's text, that effect was dramatic. Discovering that Maclean was on holiday in France, she demanded his number and made two sharp calls. Toynbee's passages, she said, referring to the Pope, Queen Frederica and her lower-middle-class origins, must be deleted to spare her mother. He promised that they would be – and they were. On his return, he heard from Terence Kilmartin of the *Observer* that she planned to move to the Bodley Head. 'Naturally,' Maclean informed von Auw, 'after all these years it will be sad to drop her from the list but we

shall continue to cherish the back list [...].' This sent a clear, if diplomatic, signal: like it or not, Macmillan owned the British rights of Mrs
Spark's work to date and they were not about to release them. 'On the
personal side,' he added, 'I am sure that Muriel will feel a great sense of
liberation and I hope you will not think me ungallant if I say that in a
small way her feelings will be reciprocated at this end.'[20]

There seemed no road back from this for Macmillan but calmly von
Auw took control. When he asked her about Bodley Head (news to him)
she said that no such plans had been made. It was hardly the best
preparation for *Not to Disturb*'s UK release but there had been previous
bust-ups which they had overcome. Macmillan had raised their advance
for *Not to Disturb* by over thirty per cent and, despite Maclean's odd
blunders over business details, von Auw usually got what he wanted and
the two men liked each other. On the whole, he thought, Muriel could
do worse. Having been in this position before of acting as counsellor to
both parties in a bad marriage, his response was always the same:
give it time. Muriel's rages abated as quickly as they flared. Interviews,
however, continued to torment her. There was to be another flurry over
the BBC programme, broadcast in Scotland during December. At one
point she had talked about pornography and her dislike of censorship.
The camera had then lingered over *The Letters of Cardinal Newman* on
her bookshelves, suggesting, she thought (the titles were indistinct), a
library of smut – so she refused permission for the documentary to be
shown to the wider British audience.

All these spats oddly boiled down to a defence of the liberal imagination while Muriel herself was acting autocratically, attacking
censorship and simultaneously insisting on it. Dealing with the BBC,
she explained, was 'A bloody nuisance, I hate to be my own censor as it
puts me in a blameable position',[21] and the principles of liberalism had
always taxed her. As an apolitical animal, she would be attached to no
ideological agenda. It mattered little, she thought, which government
presided over anarchy. To some principles, however, she stuck fast.
She never allowed adaptations of her work to be shown to segregated
audiences in South Africa. She was a fierce opponent of anti-Semitism

and racism generally. Intellectually, she was a devil's advocate with an instinctive horror of party lines and moral majorities. 'I don't believe in good and evil so much any more,' she had told George Armstrong in 1970.

> No one makes pacts with the Devil as they did in the Middle Ages. Now there is only absurdity and intelligence. [...] I don't like the politics and the power struggles in the Church, and it is outrageous what is done in the name of Christianity. But it doesn't affect me much. I'm only interested in God. Some of the Church's teachings are very foolish. Why not have women priests? [...] They say birth control is wrong because it is against the natural law. I thought we were supposed to obey the supernatural law, like not going to bed with everyone as the animals do [...].[22]

The problem for both Muriel and her publishers was that she wanted wide readership while refusing to pander to popular taste. Above all, she would not have her work talked down as 'mad'. Anyone intimating mental instability was her enemy for life, as Maclean was to discover. She demanded protection but the persistent sense of threat on which her books fed was the reverse of the sense of guilt and failure in Graham Greene's work. Her recent novels, she wrote to von Auw, were more popular in Italy than her earlier ones. The Italians regarded her as a Kafka in a skirt. She saw herself as Lucrezia Borgia in trousers.[23]

*

Questions of judgement and love lie at the heart of *Not to Disturb*. Superficially, it is another 'crime' story but in its cloudy depths the narrator again swims like an electric eel round paradoxes relating to free will and predestination, the artist's relation to her text, God's to creation. The servants of the Château Klopstock await the inevitable bloody deaths of their masters and prepare to profit from this by appropriating the contents of the house and by selling the story. In addition, Lister, on behalf of his collaborators, has been receiving large, regular payments from the secretary to Baron and Baroness Klopstock, Victor Passarat: for what, we are never told. Neither are we told how Lister and his crew know that murder is imminent, and know with such certainty that they have alerted journalists, written a scenario and arranged for two pornographic film-makers to be on hand. Midway, as often in Muriel's fiction, there is an epistemological crisis. The scenario is not working out and the pre-laid plot is blown to hell. Lister learns that the line of inheritance from which he had hoped to profit is not as he had supposed. But, always expecting the unexpected, like a novelist whose work has got up and walked away with intention, he remodels the script, organising an hilarious wedding to secure the property.

If these mysteries (which keep us reading) remain unresolved, other matters slowly clarify. It becomes plain that Cecil and Cathy Klopstock are sex-obsessed and probably in a triangular relationship with Passarat. The château has witnessed bizarre events. Its servants, gatekeepers to its reality, are forbidden to mention the word 'sex' even though they have happily engaged with their employers in blue-movie performances of fairy tales. Lister is involved in an incestuous relationship with his (younger) aunt, Eleanor. The pregnant maid, Heloise, is certain only of who is *not* the father (among many contenders including other servants). Clovis, the chef and scenario writer, is probably gay. Almost everyone appears either faithless, mad, naïve or of unconventional sexuality. There are hints that the Baroness is a sadist, a lesbian or bisexual. In the attic a Gothic creature, younger brother of Cecil, barks and hurls plates when not sedated by his nurse.

This, then, was *not* realism and when it appeared in the UK during November 1971 (the following March in America) many reviewers struggled. For those who liked fiction to disturb, the tumult of styles and voices was stimulating. Bruce Williams saw Lister as 'today's supervisor, the dog beneath the skin, the god beneath the unorthodox, questing religion'.[24] Frank Kermode, in theoretical mood, spoke admiringly of a 'conceit founded on the proposition that since the end of a fable is known [...] from the beginning of the telling, it follows that the telling of it in a manner which admits this fact will help to explain the nature of fictions, the kind of relation we may expect them to have to truth.' Like others, he noted that Lister, as 'the boss of the tale', has a 'marked literary turn'. *Not to Disturb* is laced with quotations – from Webster,

Omar Khayyám, Marvell, *Hamlet*, James Shirley and Job – all emanating from Lister. It was, Kermode thought, a profoundly literary novel: 'All the essential people in this story, except its victims, are specialists in prepared scenarios and confusions, are armed with tape-recorders and cameras, possess idiosyncratic ways of putting things; they are, that is to say, emblematic of the novelist.'[25]

With *The Driver's Seat*, Claire Tomalin suggested, Muriel had 'moved into an impersonal, international world of airports and tourist cities'. Here she had gone 'a stage further into a vision of hell, where all are pimps, bawds, madmen or corpses [...] monsters dancing with monsters in the borders of a bestiary [...].'[26] 'Muriel Spark's last three novels', A. S. Byatt noted, 'have all played games, mocking and sinister, with life and the mass media. [...] Lister turns the almost unseen protagonists into ghosts. [...] What is being displayed is a kind of part-life that has eaten up real people and events. [...].'[27] Isobel Quigly saw similar productive disjunctions in the 'jumbled nationalities' and dialogue 'producing, as always in Switzerland, tiny misunderstandings and mis-statements and mis-firings; and every mis-placed phrase is quotable [...].' But where Quigly detected only 'the dazzling self-confidence of the best send-ups',[28] Kermode, Tomalin and Byatt all expressed reservations. This was not, they felt, up to Muriel's usual standard. It was a chilling puzzle, but it was remote; it did not quite work.

Less sympathetic reviews followed these lines with a vengeance. Muriel now had her literary antagonists – Robert Nye, Stanford, Francis King – who seem to have waited for each book with prepared impatience. 'Brief, brittle, nasty in an arch sort of way, each new text', Nye wrote, 'appears almost consciously designed to dismay.' *Not to Disturb* was 'life-deploring', incomprehensible.[29] Stanford (a latter-day friend of Nye's) thought the novel unbalanced, affected and thin, a version of French farce seasoned with unhealthy eroticism.[30] King compared it unfavourably with Jean Anouilh. Previously, he said, 'what Mrs Spark has left out has seemed to have as much importance as what she has put in', but 'here the blanks suggest nothing so much as the unpainted areas of a canvas the painter has still to fill.'[31] In this 'wearisome tale' full of 'strained linguistic forms' reminiscent of Michael Arlen, the *TLS* found 'no suspense, no laughs, certainly no serious concern, nothing at all to respond to'.[32] 'There is no trace in this posturing, silly book', Nina Bawden proclaimed, 'of Mrs Spark's wry and exceptional comic talent. The only joke would be if anyone were to take it seriously.'[33] 'Posturing'? In some of these notices, even the good ones, Muriel's own image was haunting interpretation. The novel's focus on publicity, Alexander Walker remarked, appeared to derive from 'Mrs Spark's own well-earned celebrity as an expatriate in Rome, conscious of a public image and aware of the movie company currently preparing to film her last book [...].'[34]

One striking aspect of Muriel's physical transformation was her loss of weight. One striking aspect of her novels was their brevity. 'Mrs Spark's own recent fiction', Jonathan Raban observed, 'has tended to a disconcertingly macrobiotic purity and thinness. [...] She is gradually cutting out the unwholesome messiness of life, in favour of an untainted fiction of theology and the higher criticism.' It was a loss, he felt, and one symptomatic of the skinny pretences of postmodernism. Spark was 'one of the most gifted of all our novelists'. *Not to Disturb* was 'as clever as the jewelled movement of a watch, as serious as an essay in *Mind* or a Jewish tract'. But 'there was hardly any weight to trim away in the first place, and now the needle barely flutters on the scales. [...] It has dieted itself into prim invisibility.'[35]

Was Raban's review an exercise in biography as much as in criticism? Commentators had to make what they could of the scraps of 'personal' information in the public domain. Who *was* she? people wanted to know. What were her opinions? No one could make her out. For Muriel *had* 'dieted herself into [...] invisibility', not prim, not self-regarding, but selfishly selfless. She had no domestic life. For much of the past year she had been without a secretary. She had a public existence and in private she wrote. Domestic life was slowly to return with Penelope Jardine but even that was never divorced from Muriel's public presentation, indeed was integral to it. Muriel Spark, the flesh-and-blood human being, had reduced her 'self' to an unknowable abstraction, not irresponsible but unresponsible, 'scatheless', in the desire to be immaculate, and thus free from the world's attempts to impose guilt. Suffering was at the heart of everything she wrote but suffering considered in the lightning flash of its absurdity. Paradoxically, suffering becomes the manifestation of God's grace rather than the proof of His non-existence. Suffering defines. It is, in Auden's word, 'exact' – if infinitely complex. Without it, pleasure would be indefinable.

Late 1971 was a difficult time for Muriel. In September, another Englishwoman, Barbara Powell, one of her original part-time secretaries in Rome during 1967, offered to help in the evenings or on Saturdays but could spare little time from her full-time job.[36] Lawyers had advised Muriel to pay off her scurrilous manservant, and she had. Ambrosiani still loitered but was increasingly sulky since the appearance of de Breffny and Rasponi. Too many of the London reviews of *Not to Disturb* had been disappointing. Muriel spent most of her days alone, working on *Hothouse* as Christmas advanced upon her. Then the New Year brought bad news: von Auw announced his retirement. Her work was passed to the safe hands of his partner, Dorothy Olding, but by Easter her best agent would be gone. He was even leaving America to set up house in Portugal with Paul Peters.

Ever resilient, Muriel wrote to von Auw expressing love and gratitude, then plunged back into *Hothouse*. Two more visits to the clinic saw it finished by May, just after the indifferent reception of *Not to Disturb* in America. These notices she ignored with equanimity. The novel was selling quite well in England and, with *Hothouse* finally out of the way, a seven-year burden was lifted. Its completion closed a distinct period in her career. In June she paid her first visit to Guy Strutt in London. She had met him through de Breffny. Strutt, a scholarly, homosexual gentleman of independent means, was to become a lifelong friend. On her return, she started *The Takeover*, another experiment but this time not at all like Robbe-Grillet. Yet again, she was setting her house in order. After a stressful nine months, she was back in top form and ready for a holiday in Ireland with de Breffny and George Mott.

*

De Breffny was another character from Proust – or from *Not to Disturb*. Muriel had met him briefly at Queen Frederica's house and, when 'Queen Fred' had immediately taken against him and broken contact, he rang Muriel. He was, he said, a great admirer of her books. Would she come to dinner? Muriel accepted (she had met Rasponi through his telephoning in similar fashion). Why not? De Breffny was clever, immaculately dressed, and lived by his wits. He was also startlingly handsome. No one knew where he came from. An authority on geneal-ogy and architecture, he had turned himself into an author. The function of this holiday was to research a book, *The Houses of Ireland* (1975). De Breffny (with Rosemary ffolliott) was to write the text, Mott to provide the photographs.

From Ambrosiani's point of view, the whole arrangement was sus-picious. 'He liked me more than I liked him and I think the only reason he liked me was because he thought he could get closer to Muriel. [...] He was a man who played both sides of the street. He went after rich women but he also had a boyfriend.'[37] Whether Muriel knew that Mott was the boyfriend is unclear. Mott thought she must have known but chose to ignore it. Whatever the truth, she had few illusions about de Breffny. She just liked him. According to Ambrosiani, the Irish trip was aborted, with Muriel ringing in tears from Cork and asking him to meet her at Rome airport. Muriel had bought a car which de Breffny and Mott had driven on ahead to Ireland. This much seems accurate. But Ambrosiani's account was clearly mangled. He recalled her being away just two days before rushing back. In fact, she stayed for a month, almost as long as planned, driven out by continual rainfall rather than by de Breffny.

They (Muriel) had rented 'Dysert', the house of the elderly Irish novelist, Molly Keane, famous in the 1930s for *Devoted Ladies, Full House* and *Rising Tide*, and later famous again for her comeback masterpiece *Good Behaviour* (1981). 'I had a lot of time to observe Muriel at close hand,' Mott said, 'and we got along very well.' There were difficulties – 'I always found her somewhat enigmatic and very, very subject to mood changes [...] and I could never figure out what caused these changes' –

but he warmed to her. 'Dysert' was perched on a steep cliff overlooking Ardmore Bay in County Waterford, at the very tip of southern Ireland. Fog rolled in across the Atlantic. Muriel emerged from her room one day remarking that in the fog she could be anywhere, in New York, anywhere. She often appeared, like Elsa in *Hothouse*, to be elsewhere and then suddenly to tune back in with an odd comment. Most days she was working on *The Takeover* but there were regular excursions, driving off to dinners and to examine houses and landscapes. She could, he thought, be 'a bit difficult and grand' with some of their Irish friends.

> Often the problem with Muriel was that one had no idea what she wanted [...] and her mood could change so precipitately that you didn't know where you were. [...] She determines the agenda and the scale of intimacy. [...] To me one of the fascinating things [...] was her relationship with the books she was writing, and their topicality for her life. [...] Somehow I think that the character of the German girl [Lise, in *The Driver's Seat*] is one that she identified with [...]. Brian was a very aggressive man, flamboyant, all about action, not much contemplation. I think she found him enormously attractive, even when she saw through his falsehood and illusions.[38]

According to Mott, de Breffny was 'never comfortable with his homosexuality. He always had to keep up the pretence of being straight.'[39] So far as one can gather, he was born Brian Leese in the suburbs of London, at Isleworth, Middlesex. His mother (née Odel) was Irish; her father worked as a porter at the Victoria and Albert Museum. She was Roman Catholic, her husband, de Breffny's father, possibly Jewish (occupation uncertain). De Breffny worshipped his mother who was ambitious for her only child to escape his humble origins – and he duly obliged. At this point, however, the 'facts' dissolve and we enter the mythology of his multiple autobiographies. The only thing of which one can be certain is that he was a compulsive liar, and that he believed his lies. Both Mott and Strutt had affectionate memories of the man but, as the latter commented, 'He was far from honest. He did double-cross me on occasion.'[40]

One story de Breffny told was that at an early age he had converted to Mormonism, attended the University of Utah, and returned to Europe as a missionary. But Paris and the grand names had dazzled him. As a Mormon, he had been trained as a genealogist and, researching his own family, had discovered a link with the Irish O'Rourkes and their Jacobean title. Fortunately it was vacant, or so he said. That was how he became 'Baron de Breffny'. Another version involved his being brought up in France under German occupation and studying in Paris. He also claimed to have worked as a bartender in Mexico City, in a liquor store in Havana, as a lecturer at the University of California, as an interpreter at the United Nations, and as a courier. He assured Muriel that his stepfather was a top dentist in Salt Lake City. Then there are the tales which others told of de Breffny: that his shadowy paterfamilias was a small-time bookie or a London cab-driver; that his change of fortune had derived from a win on the football pools; that as a young man de Breffny had been picked up by a maharaja; that he had been one of Guy Strutt's companions; that he would ask friends to carry wads of banknotes back to Ireland to avoid currency restrictions; that he had altered the record of his birth in Somerset House.

Strutt confirmed some of this. He had travelled with de Breffny to Salt Lake City, talked to his father (stepfather?) on the telephone, was obstructed from any contact with the mother. Strutt knew the barony was 'overwhelmingly bogus' and thought his friend was probably illegitimate. They had first met in London through the Society of Genealogists. Shortly after, Strutt had visited Ischia as de Breffny's guest in a rented villa just down the hillside from the composer William Walton and his wife, Susana. De Breffny had already lived with them for a year. Then Jytsna turned up, daughter of the Maharaja of Burdwan: beautiful, fabulously rich and, in Strutt's view, eccentric. On the slightest acquaintance, de Breffny proposed. The couple were married from Daphne Acton's English country house, Aldenham in Shropshire, the seat of the Acton family and well known to Evelyn Waugh, who was close to Daphne, Strutt's sister. All the money and social prestige, however, even the birth of a daughter, Sita-Maria, could not save this disastrous union.

According to Strutt, Jytsna bolted with another Englishman when Sita was scarcely a year old, leaving de Breffny to bring her up in Rome with the help of a Yorkshire nanny, two Indian servants and, later, a British boarding school.

In Rome, de Breffny lived in an elegant two-floor apartment on Via Frattina, close to the Spanish Steps, supporting himself by writing and by performing genealogical services for the socially ambitious. He was not wealthy but liked to appear so. 'I knew what Brian's finances were,' Mott commented. 'Even the business of the Indian staff – they were quite modestly paid. [...] He spent his money on the things that made him look rich. This was very important to him: *la bella figura*.'[41] He also craved alliance with the aristocracy. Some accepted him, some did not. So there he was in 1972, probably in his mid-forties, with his servants in turbans and flowing white robes, the self-created Baron de Breffny. But melancholy hung about him, too: an inability to laugh at himself or 'to distinguish truth from fiction in his own life'.[42] A sense of exile, a wound, Mott thought, lay somewhere in that mysterious past.

Muriel ignored the malicious gossip about de Breffny, and was instinctively defensive of the self-created against accusations of being 'jumped-up' or fraudulent, as though high birth or old money were some guarantee of moral authenticity. She didn't blame him for liking the aristocracy, or even for pretending to be one of them. In this respect he was a fake but in his powerful presence he was intensely real – and industrious. He produced decent, scholarly books, was a good father (something that always attracted Muriel); he supported himself and maintained an elegant appearance. He was fun. True, he was an adventurer but most interesting people were. And he was more interesting than most: a double or treble personality, acute and creative. Later, he even wrote an amusing novel, *My First Naked Lady* (1981), and went on to found the *Irish Arts Review* in 1984. Like Muriel, he was (or appeared to be) half-Jewish (though he never confirmed this) and divorced with a child. Like her, he relished display as disguise, lived by his talents and had a profound religious sense. He, too, had come from nowhere to this operatic city and refused to explain himself. Whose business was it to judge and condemn?

By November 1972, however, with the proofs of *Hothouse* corrected, Muriel found the exuberance of Rome to be waning. Visconti had commissioned an Italian translation of *The Driver's Seat* from Masolino d'Amico with a view to filming it and, although this had come to nothing, it had been amusing to discuss the business over tea with the legendary director, to give grand parties, live in Palazzo Taverna and Trastevere. But looking out of her window towards St Peter's, she often wondered how its centuries of religious order had resulted in the chaos she saw everywhere. Now a woman could no longer walk Rome's streets alone at night. The place was becoming dirty and violent. Frequently it was strike-bound. The world's outrages seemed slowly to be sapping its fantasy. When a stoned representative of Bantam Books had called, requesting 'grass' instead of a drink, she had been alarmed. And one event, Golda Meir's audience with Pope Paul VI in January 1973, had particularly disturbed her. The international press had covered it, of course, but Muriel detected a darker tale – of the betrayal of the Jews by the Vatican. Telephoning William Shawn, she revived her notional appointment as the *New Yorker*'s correspondent, and proposed a 'letter from Rome'. It would need, Shawn explained, to provide a new angle. Muriel, confident that she had one through her friends,[43] settled down to research a 3,000-word article.

*

One of Muriel's sources was HE Amiel E. Najar, the Israeli Ambassador to Italy, and his wife, Vida, a strikingly beautiful Russian Jewess. This vivacious couple Muriel and Ambrosiani had met through a 'big bear of a man', ostensibly a student of cinematic lighting for the nascent Israeli film industry but 'obviously', in Ambrosiani's view, a Mossad agent.[44] Zev knew him first, then Ambrosiani, then Muriel. They used to gather at an outdoor café in the piazza of Santa Maria in Trastevere. The man had read *Mandelbaum* and was impressed by its grasp of Near East politics. He introduced the Ambassador.

Stylish, imaginative and exotic, the Najars were a prominent couple

Muriel photographed by Harding Lemay, her editor, in Knopf's offices, New York; sent by Muriel to Shirley Hazzard, 4 February 1963

Evelyn Waugh, May 1960. Six months later he wrote to Muriel: 'I am dazzled by *The Bachelors* [. . .] the cleverest & most elegant of all your clever and elegant books.'

Graham Greene, 1974. Greene supported Muriel's career as a fiction writer from 1954 onwards. In 1979 he wrote of *Territorial Rights*: 'It's your best, your very best. I thought you'd never top *Memento Mori*, but you have.'

Rayner Heppenstall, producer of Muriel's early radio plays

Above: Howard Moss, poet and poetry editor of the *New Yorker*

Left: Brendan Gill, a *New Yorker* writer and later its unofficial historian

William Shawn, legendary editor of the *New Yorker*, and much admired by Muriel

The Scene of the First Encounter
between Shirley Hazzard
and Francis Steegmuller
by Muriel Spark.
(Her best
book
ever)

Shirley Hazzard in the 1960s,
Muriel's close friend in New York
Right: Beaux Arts Hotel, New York,
where Muriel rented an apartment.
She sent this card to Shirley
Hazzard

Muriel and her agent, Ivan von Auw   Blanche Knopf

Muriel at Keats's grave, Rome, late 1960s: the photograph was taken by Eugene Walter and sent by Muriel to George Nicholson after she left New York

The public image: Muriel photographed by Jerry Bauer in her Palazzo Taverna apartment, 1970

Eugene Walter, writer, editor, painter, actor, cook and cultural entrepreneur. Muriel's first contact in Rome, he helped her to settle into the city

George Armstrong, Rome correspondent of the *Guardian*

Brian de Breffny

Dario Ambrosiani and 'Zev' (Daniel Harris)

Muriel 'up one moment, down the next', in India, 1973

Muriel and Penelope Jardine, *c.* July 1979

Muriel in 2002, aged eighty-four

whose diplomacy was conducted as much through friendship as through formal channels. On the world stage, nevertheless, Najar was a crucial figure. It was through him that contacts between 'Israel and the Vatican were arranged. In 1964 the Pope had visited Jerusalem when the Wailing Wall was still in Jordanian hands. Since then the 1967 war had left Moshe Dayan's troops occupying huge tracts of Arab land, including Bethlehem and the Church of the Holy Sepulchre. Najar had brokered talks between various Israeli dignitaries and the Pope but relations between the Knesset and the Vatican remained volatile. Only a few weeks had passed since a terrorist attempt on the Israeli Embassy at Bangkok. Arab gunmen fired from Roman rooftops at El Al planes, while the Pope considered it his duty to support the rights of all peoples with claims to the Holy Land, including the Palestinians. Much had changed since Muriel's pilgrimage there in 1961 but when she submitted her article, Shawn rejected it, saying in his usual muffled fashion that the material was already well known. It was not, and this troubled her. She was unused to rejection, but this was not the point. She had something to say about politics for once and was being stifled. When she eventually managed to place a shortened text in the *Tablet*, it offered only a pallid version of the original.

What, then, *was* Muriel's story? In brief, it was that the Vatican had lied. Golda Meir had left her audience with the Pope proclaiming herself grateful and satisfied. She did not say that she had been insulted. She played the game and agreed a press release, hoping for peaceful co-existence. Then another emerged from the Vatican, backtracking. Nothing had changed, it said. The Pope still supported the Palestinians. Meir only learned of this on her return to the Israeli Embassy and 'diplomatically stuck to the negotiated version [...]. "Mrs Meir," asked a journalist, "have you seen or heard about the [new] statement [...]? At least some people are describing it as a diplomatic slap in the face ..."' 'This', Muriel commented, 'was understating the case. People were describing it as a stab in the back, Borgia-style [...].'⁴⁵ That was the first point: betrayal. The second was that the admirably 'sensational rhetoric' of the Italian press had forced the Vatican into 'admitting all the points of the Israeli version'. But there was also another matter for Muriel here: the question of a woman being insulted. Meir was 'the first woman head of government to be received in the Vatican [...] a modern prime minister', and she had been treated 'on the level of the old-time renaissance admonishment of the Jews'. It was incredible to Muriel that the Pope could be 'so far out of touch'.[46]

Meir told her own story later:

> Right at the start I didn't like it at all. Right at the start the Pope told me he found it difficult to understand how the Jewish people, who should conduct themselves mercifully, should react, in their country, so harshly. I can't stand it when they talk like that. I said [...] do you know the first memory of my life? The pogrom in Kiev! When we were merciful, and didn't have a country and were weak, then they took us to the gas chamber.[47]

This also seems to have struck home for Muriel. Her own grandparents were Russian Jews and she never forgot that heritage. Had it not been for their emigration, she once remarked, she would have been a bar of soap. Italian women, she felt, usually began as images of the ethereal and soon found themselves carrying their men's baggage. Italian men seeking to do business with her, and unable to understand her independence, treated her like a widowed female relative in need of their patronage.[48]

*

Hard on the heels of the *New Yorker*'s rejection came the British reviews of *Hothouse*: another 'mixed bag'. Arthur Calder-Marshall and Nina Bawden came back onside with high praise but in pieces so brief as to suggest respectful bafflement. Gabriel Pearson, Derwent May and Mary Ellmann in the *Guardian*, the *Listener* and the *New Statesman* respectively, all loved the book and made more serious attempts at interpretation. As for the rest, there were thin pickings for Macmillan's advertisement. Michael Ratcliffe in *The Times* found this novel 'a desperate evasion', lacking in the faith, hope and charity of Iris Murdoch's recent *The Black Prince*. Julian Symons thought *Hothouse* mildly amusing but self-indulgent whimsy. The *Express* and the *Mail* could not fathom it at all. As 'an intellectual puzzle', the latter stated, 'it doesn't work out.' Two characters from Muriel's earlier incarnation as London bohemian popped up: Kay Dick and Martin Seymour-Smith. Neither was impressed. Dick had been pestering Muriel a year earlier to contribute to her second book of interviews and had been brushed off with a letter from von Auw. 'Mrs Spark does not want to know us any more,' Dick began. 'She has left us all behind.'[49] Auberon Waugh held fire until he had read the other notices. Although he disliked both the 'tense jumping' and the 'heroine, Elsa, whom we are supposed to find sympathetic [and] is, in fact, a totally selfish woman', he recommended the novel as 'enjoyable'. 'Hell', he added, 'is seen as a continuation of life on earth made more noticeably hellish only by the increased asperity of one's relations with one's fellow-damned [...]', ingeniously suggesting that *Hothouse* was not so much concerned with a theological or real hell as with a 'literary hell'.[50]

Literary hell was not something Muriel had been used to suffering for two decades but the New York reviews were, if anything, worse. *Time* condemned her as having 'grown more flatly sombre, shorter in style, wit and patience, like a lonely spinster who has become too preoccupied, too saddened by the world to go through the recurring motions of small talk'.[51] This was the first American notice Muriel received and she dealt with it calmly, cut off from the world by a mail strike and impatient to see the rest. But the general view of the major papers was that this was 'not a successful experiment'.[52] The *New Yorker* ignored it. Updike was silent. The one strong recommendation came from the *New York Times Book Review* which concentrated on the novel's dream-quality.[53] Beyond New York, the critics were kinder. The *Washington Post* delighted in Muriel's 'mastery of the formal components of the novel'.[54] The *Chicago Tribune* gave this 'writer of prodigious skill' careful treatment. Every word, it said, required attention.[55] That, however, was the limit of praise from quotable sources. There was no shortage of enthusiasm from the provincial press but plaudits from the *Sunday Oregonia* or the *Colorado Post* were not the stuff of a blurb-writer's dreams.

Not one reviewer of this book of shades and shadows noticed that *Peter Pan* (the story of a boy who never grows up) is a parodic parallel text.

Hothouse, as its title suggests, is indeed a study of various sorts of hell. It offers an image of Manhattan as a locus of competing neuroses where reality is relative and inaccessible other than through dream, faith or imagination. Muriel's original intention – a portrait of a city with its historical backdrop – had disappeared. Two years earlier, she had rewritten the whole thing in the present tense to bring it into line with the three experimental novels that had interrupted it. We see little more of New York now than the interior of an overheated apartment with occasional glances through its windows, and a shoeshop. And we scarcely *see* them: visual information is minimal. The material world has dissolved into voices, memory and, possibly, glimpses of the future. After all her work on it, Muriel was proud of this book and it must have come as a disappointment to find the critics so obtuse about its subtleties.

The narrative, for instance, is structured into three sections by the repetition of the book's second line: 'She stamps her right foot.'[56] Literally this is Elsa trying on boots in the shop. Metaphorically it presents Elsa in her various manifestations as pettish, insistent, and skittishly subversive. At first we see her as mad and her husband, Paul, as sane. These roles soon reverse. We are introduced to the notion that both have been dead since a doodlebug destroyed their train in 1944 – which may or may not be true. If it is true, then this is a ghost story in which Elsa has to learn that she no longer exists on Earth. If it is not true, both suffer from delusions. Ultimately, more and more characters from their 1944 life (all were on the train) rise up in a dance of death round New York's nightspots and cannot be shaken off. They call out for Elsa and Paul to join them, shades reclaiming shades. As the couple try to escape, Paul says, '"We can always go home",'[57] but when they try, they discover that the apartment building they had apparently left only hours before, is half-demolished. 'Home', then, shifts its meaning. The novel ends with an allusion to an anonymous mystical text: 'She turns to the car, he following her, watching as she moves how she trails her faithful and lithe cloud of unknowing across the pavement.'[58]

The central metaphysical image is Elsa's shadow. It falls the wrong way: towards the evening light. In 1944 it was perfectly adjusted. In 1970s New York it begins in the right place but remains at that angle, ignoring the movement of the sun. The novel cuts briskly from dialogue to dialogue, pausing over surreal vignettes: the recurrent ones of Elsa staring through her window at the nothingness beyond or stamping in the shop; the crash of a tray as the maid breaks down; a slow-motion wrestle while Paul madly attempts to yank off Elsa's shoes and read coded messages on their soles; a telephone conversation between New York and Zurich where Elsa is sleeping with her shoe salesman; an hilarious set piece in which Paul and Elsa inadvertently gatecrash a golden wedding and guests and hosts pretend recognition; finally, the dance of death rising to a crescendo, falling to a long bass note with the image of the wrecked building. It is like reading Dante dramatised by Evelyn Waugh while listening to Stravinsky, a satire often focusing on the absurdity of psychoanalysis. Paul's analyst cites half a page of 'problems': the 'youth problem, the racist problem' etc.[59] To this mind-doctor it is a shopping list of curable disorders. In context it is a litany of mankind's crazed ambitions for a life free of pain and contradiction.

No one, Elsa remarks, mentions the 'death problem', and this evasion is personified by the hysterical city:

> home of the vivisectors of the mind, and of the mentally vivisected still to be reassembled, of those who live intact, habitually wondering about their states of sanity, and home of those whose minds have been dead, bearing the scars of resurrection: [it] heaves outside the consultant's office, agitating all around [Elsa] about her ears.[60]

New York here is a city of glass and money, where hard cash tries to bolt down reality and fails. Its inhabitants come to it trailing clouds of glory, only to forget that God is their home. Its essence is discontinuity. It is 'fractional',[61] a mental clinic, a place of burglary and invasion. Elsa and her friend Poppy (both gleefully parading dubious titles) delight in irritating the rationalists. Both threaten the status quo with style. Just as Muriel had advised Shirley Hazzard, Poppy instructs Elsa to '"Liberate yourself"',[62] to be in thrall to no one. And she does and is not. She will not be 'the problem of Mother'[63] or the madwoman on the fourteenth floor. Like Muriel, she will be the artist of her own life. She is 'a woman of intelligence beyond [Paul's] calculation'[64] and she walks out on his construction of her, head up, up. 'He's looking for the cause,' she says, 'and all I'm giving him are effects. It's lovely.'[65]

A revenge comedy, Hothouse, more than any novel since Mandelbaum, seems to throb with displaced autobiography. It is as though Muriel is watching others watching her and offering through Elsa and Poppy a defence of the female artist. '"No man," Elsa remarks, "can sleep with a woman whose shadow falls wrong and who gets light or something from elsewhere"'[66] One can only speculate on why this book was so difficult to complete. It translates, of course, Muriel's own growing distaste for New York. Only eight years earlier she had said of that city: 'Here everyone understands the word busy. One can concentrate. New York is special; the center. It amuses me and makes me happy.'[67] Now it seemed neurotic, peripheral, and she was intrigued by how quickly she had fallen out of love with the place. But Hothouse reaches much further back through her experience.

She, too, had suffered hallucinations, had been 'the problem of Mother', had ceased to be the young woman of 1944. The chasing shades were in one sense like Kay Dick and Stanford, haunting her reinvention, trying to draw her back, and, like Elsa, she was impatient with those 'tangled with umbrage'. '"Oh how you bore me,"' Elsa spits out at her daughter. '"So bloody literal."' – One of Paul's remarks – '"Today she is bubbling with hilarity, tomorrow she'll be brooding again"' – resembles Mott's description of Muriel, and Poppy's '"One should always conceal one's problems"'[68] was certainly a principle upon which Muriel acted, so much so that she would rarely acknowledge a 'problem' of any sort. There was, after all (before all?), only one problem for her – and that was theological rather than psychological.

*

Hothouse, then, was not going to be a smash hit. So be it. If the critics were literal-minded, Muriel's response was to ignore them. Financially, she was secure. Franco Rossellini had just announced the shooting of *The Driver's Seat* starring Elizabeth Taylor, with Andy Warhol oddly cast as the decaying peer. If 1973 had been a bad year so far – her cat, Spider, had died, her maid had died – Muriel, as usual, looked to the future. She was deep in *The Takeover* and so brimming with invention that this was to be one of her happier times in Rome. When Taylor and Richard Burton hit town amid a hurricane of gossip about his abstinence from booze on pain of losing his wife for ever, Muriel stayed clear. She helped Rossellini rewrite some of the dialogue, then retired to her clinic for most of July and another week in August. She employed an amusing and gentle American, Leo Coleman, as her second houseman, and took a brief holiday at Hotel Pelikano in Porto Ercole while planning a jaunt to India with de Breffny. Throughout that broiling summer she found her imagination teased by events in America[69] which seemed to touch on the themes of *The Public Image*, *Not to Disturb* and *Hothouse*: 'games, mocking and sinister with life and the mass media', this time in a vision of America, liberty, surveillance and power.

Amidst all this, India was entirely delightful: the light, the landscape, the company, the courtesy. Brian's cook, Jaysingh, a Christian, was to return for an arranged marriage and, because he was anxious about the prospect, de Breffny had promised to attend and to lend support. Muriel, Mott, Guy Strutt and de Breffny's elderly godmother, Souny (Comtesse G. de Tonnac-Villeneuve), agreed to join him on a tour of the sub-continent. It was a congenial party with Muriel, as usual in any group of friends, slightly off-centre. Mott took photographs of her, abstracted behind her dark glasses, up one moment, down the next, with her latest coiffure, a massive 'beehive', protected by a headscarf. The wedding was the high point: several hundred guests, a sequence of curries served on leaves, a woman playing hymns on an accordion (the bride was the daughter of a Salvation Army brigadier). The ceremony took place near Trivandrum in the far south, where they stayed in a hotel fizzing with mosquitoes.

Over five weeks they travelled much of the country, from Delhi in the north to Trivandrum: by plane between cities, by hired car to see temples and rock sculptures. They had even flitted to Sri Lanka where, reading a newspaper on the beach, Muriel discovered the seed of another novel. 'The lead story was an indignant report of an [Indian] M.P., summoned in a hurry, attending Parliament without his shirt being buttoned. A downpage item was a tiny paragraph on Watergate. She saw it all in proportion.'[70] Dazzled as she was by India, her mind was often elsewhere. A metaphor had clicked into place. Later they were in Cochin, Mott recalled, 'in a hotel with a magnificent terrace right on the water and there was a sunset that practically ate you up [...]. We were sitting and Muriel was in her room reading *Time* magazine because the Watergate scandal had broken. [...] She was elated. There was this kind of rapture: "I must tell you that I've the most wonderful idea [...]. I shall tell you but you mustn't say."'[71]

Watergate had not 'broken' during their absence but the story had taken a decisive twist just before their departure with Nixon being forced to release the Oval Office tapes. In America, all hell broke loose. And elsewhere, too, apocalyptic events were jamming the news media: another Israeli war; Russia threatening to send troops to support the Arabs; Nixon placing American forces on standby alert; the oil crisis apparently heralding Western economic collapse. Muriel was fascinated and not at all alarmed. She had, she told Dorothy Olding, thought of another novel but would finish *The Takeover* first. Three weeks later she was writing one while researching the other.

Muriel worked over Christmas. At this rate she might have two books completed by springtime. Then in mid-January news arrived of a woman all but forgotten in the heat of composition. Her mother had been taken ill. Muriel put down her pen and flew to Edinburgh. Cissy stared up from her hospital bed, mind gone, barely able to recognise her daughter. Cancer of the bladder had been diagnosed. It could, the doctors said, take weeks or months: there was no point in waiting. So Muriel returned to Rome, knowing that Robin would telephone her every day with the latest bulletin. The final message came sooner than expected. Before the month was out, Cissy was dead.

CHAPTER 16

The Realm of Mythology

1974–1979

Muriel's brother learned of Cissy's death when he was on a business trip to Northern Ireland. As an ill-paid but successful 'value engineer' for the US Naval Air Systems Command, Philip rationalised military supplies – an unpopular, penny-pinching task that he enjoyed. In 1971 he had been awarded the Superior Civilian Service Award and mentioned in the Congressional Record for saving the North Island base $4.8m. He was a busy man, at the zenith of his career. Brother and sister spoke briefly by telephone. They had not seen, and had not tried to see, each other for nearly twelve years, since their father's last illness. Philip said that he had to be in Jacksonville the next day. It would be difficult for him to attend the funeral. Muriel told him to honour his commitments. A fortnight later he came over to help sort out the flat in Bruntsfield Place and his mother's will, returning to California with a few pieces of the family's best china as keepsakes in his baggage. All were smashed in transit.

It was a melancholy conclusion to the close household Muriel and Philip had known as children. Robin had signed the death certificate, arranged the ceremony, and Cissy was buried alongside her husband in the Jewish section of Piershill Cemetery. Muriel flew back for the burial in February 1974, content for Robin to interpret his grandmother's religion as he wished if that brought him greater comfort. She had already helped him to buy the flat, and they were on good terms again despite a certain incivility towards her that she had detected in the Rabbi conducting the funeral.[1]

For the last few years, Cissy had been housebound, dependent on a home help, still vigorous in gossip with her visitors. But beneath that ebullient exterior, neurosis had always seethed round the terror of isolation. Muriel had telephoned, paid the bills and sent a monthly allowance. The old way of doing things, however, Cissy's way with Adelaide, had collapsed with the Victorian extended family. Her children inhabited lives long estranged from hers. Even if they had offered her houseroom, she would not have wished to move. As wife and mother she had been a vivid hostess. As a widow she had been in poor health and often alone. In death, even her religious eclecticism, Muriel thought, had been smudged into an orthodoxy Cissy had never observed: a takeover, the complicated truth of lived experience airbrushed because one person's identity required the demolition of another's.

Muriel returned to Rome, and then moved quickly on to Geneva to consult an oculist. Brian de Breffny had booked her a room and was there to greet her. Given the oil crisis and currencies plummeting like Satan, she thought it best for the immediate future to be paid in Swiss francs. And, while in Switzerland, she came to another decision. *The Takeover* would be set aside for her shorter Watergate novel, *The Abbess of Crewe*, to complete the Viking three-book contract. There was a pragmatic element in this – the markets were rocking and she was looking sharp – but there was also a creative one. As the American scandal escalated, her imagination was constantly reshaping it into high theological comedy. It had to be written while it was hot in the mind.

The research for this was extensive. Muriel's files bulge with clippings. Books had accumulated: on politics, electronics, the Benedictine Order. But obstructing this work was a welter of business correspondence. She contemplated writing two biographies: of Bloody Mary and Noël Coward. A film and two play scripts of *Not to Disturb* were being negotiated, as were the dying throes of a futile deal to film *The Public Image*. The BBC were to televise *The Girls of Slender Means*, Mondadori to reprint *The Prime of Miss Jean Brodie* in Italy. Muriel's manuscripts had now been sorted and catalogued by the Gotham Book Mart in New York. In Rome, two more trunkfuls were ready to go. She was orchestrating complicated arrangements for their sale through her London lawyer (Michael Rubinstein), Alan Maclean, and Peter Shepherd of Ober. Maclean and Rubinstein, then her literary executors, were named as trustees. Every day, while burning to continue *Abbess*, she completed an exhausting quota of office work, trying to clear her desk. Amidst all this, David Lodge (a great admirer) came to see her in Rome, Muriel developed a hernia, and Harold Macmillan wrote to say that he would be visiting the city with his daughter, Carol Faber. A grand dinner party was arranged for 12 May, so grand that it exceeded even his expectations.

Everyone, of course, wanted Macmillan's views on the international chaos. In England, the miners' strike had defeated Edward Heath's Government and Harold Wilson was in power again. The whole world seemed to be blowing up. An IRA car bomb had killed twenty-three in Dublin; Patty Hearst had turned bank robber; India had detonated her first nuclear device; the Flixborough chemical plant had exploded. In Washington a federal grand jury had recently declared President Nixon an 'unindicted co-conspirator'. Impeachment loomed. Less than a week earlier, Willy Brandt had resigned as Chancellor of West Germany after an East German spy was discovered working in his office. Muriel approached the issue of espionage directly. Had Macmillan ever bugged anyone? That question he answered with his charming smile: 'Well, at least I was never such a damn fool as to bug myself.'[2] On a visit to Moscow, he said Krushchev had suggested that they walk in the garden to talk freely as the KGB had probably wired the office. They had walked and talked – but not freely. Macmillan knew that the trees concealed microphones – an idea soon planted in the opening pages of *Abbess*.

Muriel had planned to be in Monte Carlo and Nice a week later for the release of Rossellini's *The Driver's Seat*. It was a tempting excursion but she cancelled it in favour of total concentration on her novel. Just a fortnight after Macmillan's departure it was typed and ready for dispatch. To lesser mortals the near-permanent postal strike might have presented an obstacle. Muriel made other arrangements. David Watson of the English College couriered her parcels (for Macmillan, Viking, the *New Yorker*); Maclean picked them up from Gatwick airport. She tidied her study, set off for the Salvator Mundi with bronchitis, had her hernia operation, and by late June was clambering up hundreds of steps to Amalfi Cathedral. She was on holiday, difficult to trace. It was a day trip from her base in Naples with the Baron Langheim. Naples became important to her for a while.

*

As an adult, Muriel never kept a journal. But her appointments diaries tell their own story. Interspersed with her scribbled notation of dinner parties, flights, fittings, interviews, doctors, dentists (she had fragile teeth) and insurance agents, there are, from Rome onwards, other, tidier, entries made by her secretaries. These open books sat on her desk for business purposes. Appointments were duplicated in smaller diaries she kept in her handbag. On two occasions, a burst of anger intrudes but the rest is emotionally neutral. The function of these records was to act as aide-memoires, not merely for future events but also for past ones: a catalogue of expenses for income-tax returns. Details of clothes and travel sit alongside the mundanities of gas and electricity bills.

Penelope Jardine's entries are quite different from those of other secretaries. Her script is unmistakable: slanting, decisive strokes with a touch of italic, lucid and accurate. She had entered the documentation of Muriel's life in 1968, and from the outset brought precision to her work. The number of each cheque is noted, the monthly accounts for maid, car hire, secretary (herself), solicitors, furniture; in dollars, sterling or lire, all neatly totted up. She was a woman who could have succeeded as lawyer or literary agent, had she not been driven by her muse and a subversive sense of humour. Muriel had known her since Piazza di Tor Sanguigna. Jardine had worked at Palazzo Taverna and was now visiting the apartment overlooking the Tiber. At first she had come and gone with the other secretaries but, unlike most of them, she had her own creative life. She became a friend.

Alongside Jardine at this time, Muriel's second houseman, Leo

Coleman, helped out in the Trastevere flat, mainly as a cleaner. A benign and eccentric American, Coleman was approaching destitution when Muriel took him on. He had been a dancer, an icon of black male beauty, his lithe figure photographed by Jean Cocteau. Menotti had used him in *The Medium*. He was friends with, indeed revered, Francis Steegmuller, whom he had met while Steegmuller was preparing his biography of Cocteau. Coleman had many connections among Rome's gay artistic community. Vivacious and amusing, he was now part of its middle-aged flotsam. Muriel offered him work rather than charity. He was, she thought, an artist at heart. While she was in India, she had left him to keep house, and had returned with a lovely ring for him. But he was always in a muddle and perhaps mistook friendliness for intimacy. Jardine recalled his hanging out of those fourth-floor windows, trying (tediously) to scare her. Muriel's patience with clowning was limited. She was working on *Abbess* and *The Takeover* simultaneously, conducting complicated business transactions. On 8 January 1974, Coleman had drifted in late and, according to a letter he wrote to Steegmuller, found her standing there in a violet peignoir, waiting for him with prepared rage. In her hand was an envelope containing his wages. She threw it at him, threw him out, and with him went her last attempt at using a manservant to ease her life.

Jardine's father had been a Governor in Africa, Borneo and the Leeward Islands (Antigua). Her mother's family were Scottish and English gentry. Jardine was already much-travelled by the time she had come to Florence as an art student, moving on to Rome in 1964 to continue her studies, a beautiful bohemian who drew, painted, sculpted and made ceramics. In early 1974 she was forty-one, unattached, and living quietly on a small inheritance, with secretarial jobs and the sales of her work providing extra cash. Somehow she managed, determined to keep herself free as an artist. Resilient and amusing beneath a brusque British exterior, she was thoroughly integrated with expatriate Roman life, spoke fluent Italian, and was engagingly modest about her own considerable talent. She rented a dark, tumbledown flat in Vicolo del Gallo, a narrow commercial street between Campo dei Fiori and Piazza

Farnese, at the heart of Renaissance Rome. A short walk from there brought her to Muriel's place: past the Palazzo Farnese, down the Via Giulia, over the Ponte Sisto.

It was a period of anxiety in both women's lives. Muriel's fifty-sixth birthday had been clouded by preparations to leave for her mother's funeral. Briefly in London for an operation during February 1974, Jardine wrote to Muriel, trepidatious but devoid of self-pity, tender, funny, offering an avalanche of *joie de vivre* and concern for the progress of *Abbess*. The language is racy, as from one subversive free spirit to another. For all her friends, Muriel's attraction derived from the fun she could generate. She liked to entertain, to make people smile and, although she rarely laughed herself, she possessed the gift of making others want to please her. Jardine narrated whole jokes she had enjoyed, constructed elaborate fantasies from everything surrounding her. In mid-1974, however, there was no question of a shared household. Indeed, they seemed to be heading in opposite directions. Muriel was at last buying a flat: a studio apartment overlooking the lake at Nemi, the setting of *The Takeover*, some thirty miles south-east of Rome. Jardine had purchased a dilapidated priest's house with adjoining church in rural Tuscany and planned to live there. During July, Muriel flew to London to correct Macmillan's proofs of *Abbess* and to see Robin for his thirty-sixth birthday. The rest of the summer she spent touring Italy (Naples again) and resting, readying herself to resume *The Takeover*. When Alex Hamilton arrived in Rome that October for a pre-publication interview, she appeared poised and convivial, entirely independent – as she was, and remained.

*

Muriel's *Abbess*, like Jean Brodie, offered reviewers a clutch of quotable aphorisms, and one in particular: 'Here [...] we have discarded history. We have entered the sphere, dear Sisters, of mythology.'[3] Some critics drew parallels between this 'heroine' and her author. Was Mrs Spark not also entering this sphere? In fact, Muriel and Alexandra were quite different creatures, as Hamilton's interview made plain. Muriel comes over as funny, distracted, frank and both shocking and easily shocked.

She delighted in fantastical reconstructions of history. One of her favourites imagined Queen Victoria with an overpowering sex-drive: that she had, as Hamilton put it, 'screwed Albert to death' and spent her widowhood transmitting her guilt to the great British public. Had Maclean (who often warned interviewers of how 'difficult' Muriel could be) been consulted, he might have advised Hamilton to cut this. Surely Muriel would object to the vulgarity of the phrasing? And what of those other remarks: that as a nineteen-year-old she had rushed into marriage because it was then 'the only way to get sex'; that she was 'a Catholic *faute de mieux*', the present Pope and his predecessor a 'disaster'; that there ought to be three Popes; that she felt sorry for Nixon who 'had been carrying on according to the old Benedictine Rule, whereby what the superior had said is the justification for everything'; that she had been in a state of 'acute anxiety for months during Spider's [her cat's] last illness'?[4] In fact, she was pleased by his article.[5] With Hamilton she spoke freely, perhaps because of the company and his habit of listening to, rather than interrogating, her. She was among friends, the hostess.

On that first evening with Hamilton she invited de Breffny, Guy Strutt, George Mott and Jardine. Jardine appears as 'young, an occasional sculptress who gives occasional secretarial help'; Mott as 'a fine-art books photographer'; de Breffny as 'the Baron de Breffny'; Strutt as 'socially vigorous', a man who 'knows most people and is related to the rest'. Mott and Jardine soon dissolve out of focus. 'The Baron' is characterised as elegant, habitually late and habitually offering the same excuse (mislaid shoehorn), Strutt as always early, reliable, a useful researcher for Muriel and a good travelling companion. Off they walked to 'an expensive trattoria in the somewhat juiced-up poor quarter' where Muriel spent her time worrying about mistakes in the typescript of *Abbess*, eating almost nothing. At the end of the meal, she wrapped her calf's liver in a napkin to take home for the cats.[6]

That night she had worn a long black-and-white gown, her tawny hair loose about her shoulders. The next she altered 'her appearance entirely by wearing a close bottle-green dress and drawing back her hair severely, making it thereby much darker'. Hamilton was struck by the chameleon tendency of this quick-change artist. But the warmth was still there, the invitation. Over champagne she told him of the genesis of *Abbess* on the Sri Lanka beach, of her mother's death having obstructed *The Takeover*, of Macmillan's visit, of superstitions. She took him to 'her little workroom' and showed him part of the manuscript of *The Takeover* in 'a small school exercise book', written on every other line, on only one side of each page. Each notebook, she said, represented 10,000 words. 'The spread before us has a round smudge, as if splashed. A tear, she says.' She spoke of being offered her Stanford letters in New York and crying 'Blackmail', of the dirty tricks department in which she had worked during the war: 'the last of the morally justified liars. All this made her realise what secrets are. It had a profound effect on her. [...] Perhaps, she says, it goes back much earlier.'[7]

Betrayal, Hamilton suggested, figured throughout her work. Muriel agreed.

> 'Because betrayal is a funny thing. The girl in *Miss Brodie*, when she becomes a nun says, "It's only possible to betray where loyalty is due."' [... Spark] feels very strongly about this. It's demanding too much of any human to ask them to be loyal to a party, to a system or a person for the whole of their life. To say, 'You owe me loyalty' is a terrible thing.[8]

Hamilton pressed her on the question of secrets. Had she perhaps kept a diary as a girl, which her mother had read? Yes, she said, she had kept a diary then. She would also write shocking letters to herself from imaginary boyfriends and stuff them down the sofa for the inquisitive Cissy to find. (Four years later she recalled the opening lines of one of her fake replies: 'Dear Colin, You were wonderful last night.'[9]) Manipulating the truth in defence of a higher truth, in self-defence, in opposition to the world's legions of fact-mongers, was the artist's business.

*

On receiving the typescript of *Abbess*, Viking had been alarmed by its brevity. Was this, they wondered, adequate to fulfil that expensive three-book contract? In print it covered just 128 pages, many of which contained extensive quotation. There was also the question of its apparent object of attack. Nixon had resigned during the summer, Gerald Ford was, with moderate success, chewing gum while patrolling the Oval Office, and America wished to consign the last winter and spring to history. Watergate was 'over'. The novel was marketed as political satire. Cards were issued superimposing the faces of Nixon and his cronies upon four ill-drawn nuns. But the former President was now a broken man, confined to a wheelchair with phlebitis. Had the moment for such a book not passed? Any such doubts were soon dispelled. Muriel exempted *Abbess* from the contract, made a separate deal for it, and, with few exceptions, notices on both sides of the Atlantic were excellent. Updike broke his silence. Even Robert Nye became a fan.

Given the marketing and the fact that the novel concentrates on a bugging scandal, allusions to Watergate were inevitable. In a convent the old abbess is dying and her succession contentious. The favourite, Sister Alexandra, has a rival, Sister Felicity. Alexandra is stylish, Felicity vulgar. Alexandra represents centuries of aristocratic breeding, authority, hauteur; Felicity the bourgeois libertarianism in which all you need is love. Felicity is conducting an affair with a Jesuit, Thomas. She hides his love letters in her sewing box. The neatness of this box and its guilty secret become objects of Alexandra's contempt. Both are emblematic of narrowness of vision. Ladies, she declares, should place their '"love-letters in the casket provided for them in the main hall, to provide light entertainment for the community [...]."'[10] Determined to outwit her opponent, she bugs the nunnery and leaves her supporters to arrange a burglary. Two young Jesuits perform a reconnaissance break-in and remove Felicity's thimble as proof of their success. She, however, notices this loss and, ready for them when they return for the letters, alerts the authorities and elopes with Thomas to become an extramural revolutionary and media celebrity. In the proleptic opening scenes, the grounds are crawling with police and journalists. In the final pages, Alexandra, now Abbess, is aboard a ship, upright as though in a funeral gondola, triumphant. She is on her way to Rome, summoned there to explain why she replaced weaving in her nuns' practical training with surveillance electronics.

'Not wisely, perhaps, but very well,' *Time* magazine remarked,

Muriel Spark has written a take off on Old What's-His-Name. [...] Sister Walburga and Sister Mildred, the Lady Abbess's co-plotters and hatchet nuns, are obviously Haldeman and Ehrlichman. Peripatetic Sister Gertrude who phones in nightly from Reykjavik or Mombasa and, in a German accent, recommends the study of Machiavelli, is our very own Secretary of Snake. Sister Felicity seems to be an unstable amalgam of George McGovern and John Dean.[11]

Most saw Kissinger in Gertrude, and it was true that Muriel was fascinated by the man,[12] later recommending him for an Award for International Understanding for his work in the Middle East.[13] There were unambiguous Watergate allusions: the 'landslide victory', the 'third-rate burglary' and 'two of the finest nuns I have ever had the privilege to know'. But other attributions were less obvious. Alexandra's proud command of the situation bore small resemblance to Nixon's shifty burbling. (At a press conference he had declared that he considered Haldeman and Ehrlichman guilty until proven guilty.) As Frank Kermode suggested, 'If you impose [the novel] on Watergate you get not a simple transparency but a distortion: and it is in this distorted image that the real interest of the book resides.'[14]

For Kermode, *Abbess* was another version of Muriel's recurrent theme: 'the complex relationship between human plotting (or [...] "trying out scenarios"), which is dependent on lies and evasions, and that larger plot, true though virtually incredible, which is imposed on the world by its creator. [...] No-one has thought so brilliantly, so idiosyncratically about the relation of truth to lies, of life to fiction [...]'.[15] David Lodge suggested a parallel between *Abbess* and Carlyle's *Past and Present*, both of which compared a religious community to the body politic. But it was her Hamilton interview, he thought, which clarified the book's essential matter: her remark about the Superior's authority justifying everything under Benedictine rule, and the three-Popes joke. *Abbess* was, he concluded, 'a parable on the familiar theme that absolute power corrupts absolutely'.[16]

Many others agreed. The moral was seen as 'the folly of those in power who isolate themselves in myth [. . . ,] the historic tussle between liberation and modernism [. . .].'[17] 'The ideological difference between [Alexandra and Felicity]', Gabriele Annan noted, 'is that although the abbey is Benedictine, Felicity is [. . .] Franciscan. [. . .] One of [the novel's] main themes is paradox [. . .] the old paradox of freedom being inseparable from discipline.' If Alexandra's crew were entering the sphere of mythology, what 'Mrs Spark means by mythology seems to be closely akin to art, a thing which the Church with its *terre-à-terre* philistinism, cannot comprehend. [. . .] Perhaps the whole book is a parable about art and its incompatibility with religion.'[18] Or perhaps it was about the intense *compatibility* of theology with poetry which the Church has forgotten in its post-Vatican II craving to modernise? Alexandra is known to prefer the old Mass. It is assumed when she is mouthing words in chapel different from the newly imposed vernacular that she is reverting to Latin. In fact, she is chanting quotations from English metaphysical verse. Is she, then, a mystic and visionary akin to the early Jesuits?

For Updike, *Abbess* saw Muriel back in top form. 'Since the ambitious *Mandelbaum Gate*,' he wrote,

Spark's novels have been short, brusque, bleak, harsh and queer. They linger in the mind as brilliant shards, decisive as a smashed glass is decisive, evidence of unmistakable power casually applied [. . .] like letters from a daredevil friend abroad, they also had an unsettling air of concealing more than they told, and of having been posted in haste.[19]

All her fiction, he felt, possessed 'authority', but he was not alone in suggesting that her recent work had tested his loyalty. With *Abbess* she was 'back', and in a big way. Updike saw Muriel as ideologically on Felicity's side. 'But, confusingly, though the author cannot approve of [. . .] Alexandra, she does love her, love her as she hasn't loved a character in a decade.'[20] As other reviewers noted, Alexandra represents the paradox of Jean Brodie: the attraction of intelligence and imagination, of style in dress and discourse, which nevertheless steams off into lunatic egotism. Some also saw her as reflecting (what they guessed to be) Muriel's psyche. To what extent, they hinted, was Alexandra a self-portrait? Hamilton's interview – presenting her as a child of the gods: wise, mischievous, consorting only with artists and aristocrats – had an enduring effect on her public image.

In a radio discussion, Robert Kee, John Weightman, Marina Vaizey and Jonathan Raban struggled to attach the novel to this nebulous persona and to see the author behind it. *Abbess* was, in Weightman's view, 'a book that comes out of the centre of the writer [...] trying to deal with the problem of belief' (he thought that Muriel 'no longer believed in Christianity as such'). That Jerry Bauer photograph of the author on the back jacket, he continued, surely it represented Muriel Spark 'in the guise of [...] Alexandra with a white dress, the cross round her neck. The Church Militant in the form of a little metal statue with an armoured angel fighting the world. [...] I think this is obviously intentional.'[21] One of Alexandra's much-quoted dicta was: '"The ages of the Father and of the Son are past. We have entered the age of the Holy Ghost."'[22] What Mrs Spark means by 'the Holy Ghost', Weightman declared, 'is what Mrs Spark wants it to mean herself. Religion is uphold-ing the Catholic Church by the sheer force of your own belief and sublimity although you have no basis for your faith.' Pursuing this, Vaizey saw *Abbess* as 'amazingly snobbish [...], it's [...] really also about ladyship.' Kee detected 'Catholic camp', Raban a study of power when 'power is finally exercised by being stylish: very, very stylish, in the way that Mrs Spark herself as a novelist is stylish.'[23]

Interestingly, Weightman's description of the photograph was inaccurate. Although Muriel wore a white dress, there was no cross round her neck, the statue was Indian, and it was draped with a pagan necklace. For want of hard information about her, her critics were making her up. Everyone who knew Muriel could distinguish between that public image and her reality.[24] Indeed, other images were now beginning to appear in which operatic hauteur had entirely disappeared. For the first time she was pictured wearing glasses, slightly frazzled, staring quizzically over those spectacles into the faces of her inquisitors. Humour lights the eyes.

*

Muriel flew to England in December 1974 for publicity and to spend Christmas and New Year with Robin. Having inherited from Robert Doty (of *Time* magazine's Rome Bureau) several books on the First World War, she returned to Rome inspired by this legacy and wrote that quasi-autobiographical story discussed in the Preface, 'The First Year of My Life'. In London she had finally succumbed to appearing on a chat show, Russell Harty's, and had charmed both him and his audience. She seemed at ease, had even spent a delightful weekend with the Macleans.

This equanimity was in part due to recent success, and in part to Penelope Jardine. Often away from Rome now, Jardine was supervising the restoration of her Tuscan house. As *Abbess* was being published, she had been alone but for her dog, Pavoncino, in tempestuous weather with mice and snakes as house guests, filling her winter evenings by reading the biography of a Victorian prime minister. There was no telephone but occasionally she would motor down in her van to a local bar to ring Muriel and other friends. An artesian well was being dug, septic tank and bathroom installed. Her house, stone-built, thirteenth-century rustic, lay up a rugged track in the hills near Arezzo. The last priest had disappeared during the war after keeping a radio around which the villagers would gather to listen clandestinely to the BBC. Attached to the building, the deconsecrated church had been stripped out by local villains. The whole site was ruinous. But Jardine had plans for that church: it was to be her studio. And San Giovanni, as the house was known, was to be her home. Restoration, however, was a Herculean task. Six months later the place was barely habitable.

From this perspective, Muriel's metropolitan skirmishes seemed invigorating. During April 1975, she was visiting Edinburgh again, getting to know and like the eminent Jewish lawyer Lionel Daiches, brother of the literary critic David. When Jardine wrote to her there it was to a mythological creature. She now knew Muriel better than anyone, and knew her well enough to leave her alone, to be there only when wanted. They had been friends for seven years and had just taken their first working holiday together: a week in Venice where a future novel, *Territorial Rights*, was to be set. Muriel's work-in-progress, *The Takeover*, satirises a secretary, Miss Thin, who has ambitions to colonise her boss. Jardine had already typed the early sections and in letters would parody herself as this figure. Miss Thin, however, is a dreary parasite. Jardine would type but not copy her type. San Giovanni was *her* house and remained so throughout the thirty-odd years of the two women's time together there. Muriel never paid rent or contributed towards the costs of rebuilding. Instead, she supplied the means of escape: the cars, the holidays, the meals out, the business trips across Europe. Jardine always drove (she had a fear of flying). At home she cooked, washed up, catered for guests, and generally acted as personal assistant keeping the world at bay. In one respect, Muriel's life had always been like this. She was a cuckoo perching in others' nests, a go-away bird always ready to take flight. She disliked owning property, real estate seeming somehow unreal other than as an investment. In another respect, this relationship was becoming quite different from anything she had experienced. Slowly, almost reluctantly, she was learning to love again.

Muriel's new friendship with Lionel Daiches soon entered choppy waters. During her April visit, he had arranged a party for her in Edinburgh with two of his young colleagues, a man and a woman, and in March all three descended on her in Rome. Muriel met them at the airport and accompanied them to an hotel she had booked in haste, only to discover that it was unsuitable. This left her feeling obliged to accommodate them for a week in her own flat. Daiches's account of this visit is like a scene from *Not to Disturb*. Muriel, he recalled, had insisted that the woman have her hair restyled. When she returned looking (in his view) so ridiculous that the whole thing had to be redone, he became convinced that this had been a ploy to render the younger woman unattractive. More probably he was so far out of step with Roman high fashion that this coiffure was only explicable to him as an act of malice – and his reaction must have irritated Muriel. Nevertheless, she made great efforts to entertain her guests: threw a regal party in her apartment, invited them to another at de Breffny's, got Principessa Pallavicini to show them round her palace. She even took Daiches to her Nemi studio. Despite all this, however, he left unsatisfied, silently critical, regarding her as vain and egotistical. Uncomfortable in her social milieu, he found de Breffny precious and effeminate, the atmosphere 'overheated'.[25] There was something about Muriel which frightened him. When she telephoned him in Edinburgh, he secretly recorded their conversations and soon felt it necessary to terminate their association. Later he befriended Robin and held Muriel responsible for her son's problems. It seemed outrageous to Daiches (as usual wildly overstating the case) that a son should have to make an appointment to speak to his mother.

*

Muriel felt increasingly unsettled in her Roman life. Her landlady was proving troublesome, arriving unannounced and questioning the maid as to whether her mistress lived alone. It was this landlady's 'impudence' which had produced the first passionate diary entry about a year earlier.[26] She was also insisting on a substantial rent increase on pain of eviction and the installation of 'her daughter'. Déjà vu. This time Muriel resisted and the dispute was soon in the hands of her lawyer. When Strutt came over in August 1975, she asked him how she might convert her Nemi apartment to accommodate Jardine. Out of the question, he said: far too small. But by September, Muriel's life had changed. She was, she informed Dorothy Olding, going back and forth between Rome and Tuscany, finishing The Takeover – and on 2 October the novel was complete.

Muriel had always been a metropolitan animal and acclimatising herself to rustic life was not easy. Accommodation was rudimentary. At San Giovanni she was isolated from the variety which lent pace to social life. She had lived in a rougher terrain in Africa, and in the deep country at Allington Castle. But this was something else. It was silence and cohabitation. At a distance from her bolt-hole clinic, her business network and boyfriends, she found that getting things done in Arezzo was difficult. There was a fire in the photocopying shop that seemed to threaten The Takeover's typescript, hysterical behaviour on the part of the shop's owner. Two years later, still without a telephone, she remained uncertain about this alternative existence. Driving back and forth to Arezzo trying to call London, Paris and New York wasted whole days. The winters were cruel with no central heating, the summers oppressively hot, defeating creation.[27]

As usual, Muriel kept her options open. At first she would return to Rome every fortnight or so for her opera and dinners, to collect herself and her mail. Eugene Walter resurfaced as a peripheral figure in her chain of admirers alongside de Breffny, Rasponi, the Baron Langheim, Strutt, George Armstrong, George Mott and Zev. She continually made new friends, in particular Canon Bill Purdy, an English priest, later a Monsignor, and his cousin / housekeeper, Margaret Orrell; the Italian writer, Alberto Arbasino; John Cairncross – who, much to Muriel's alarm, was accused of being the Fifth Man. But where now was the centre of this life? Although Jardine would drive Muriel to Rome, she would often return and remain at San Giovanni. During 1976 this pattern changed. As publication of *The Takeover* approached that summer, she was usually with Muriel in Rome, would whisk her off to Tuscany for longer stretches. Although both still maintained independent lives, Jardine was becoming (almost) indispensable. She handled Muriel's work. They shared friends, appeared together at social engagements.

In June and July 1976, for instance, Jardine drove Muriel to London. From there, Strutt took her to Norwich and to Beaufront Castle (his childhood home in Northumberland), Jardine driving her on to Edinburgh and accompanying her back to Rome. The purpose of the trip was publicity, research and fun: to be in London for the publication of *The Takeover*, examine a Nemi archive Strutt had located, to meet Malcolm Bradbury in Norwich, to visit Roman sites in Northumberland and Strutt's people there, to attend Robin's birthday and to meet two of her old family friends, John and Jessie Rosenbloom. When they had set off, Muriel was uncertain whether she would continue to live in Italy. In an interview with Lorna Sage that May she had revealed that for some time she had been thinking of returning to England.[28] Writing ahead to

Souny de Tonnac-Villeneuve, she had enquired about Swiss pieds-à-terre, two or three rooms in Geneva.[29]

The Sage interview had rankled. It was a big piece, published to herald *The Takeover*. The article quoted Muriel quite fairly: about becoming more '"historically minded", more interested in roots' but loathing Scottish nationalism as sinister 'folklorism', despising any nationalism as ultimately fascist: '"out with the English, out with the Jews ..."'. She deplored 'the present Pope's lack of savvy, which she put down to the fact that he was born in Brescia "very correct and provincial. When he was young, nice people didn't go out after tea."' It was all one with that other provincial element in the Church and the world at large, the 'prurient old women' and their like: 'When two or three are gathered together – two or three of *anybody* – they're having sex, that's what they think.' It was the Church's 'sophistication' that she valued: 'those centuries of expertise in human failing, the sensible way it acknowledges that the unfathomable tangle of human motives *is* unfathomable, and concentrates on thoughts, words and deeds.' Sage was a distinguished critic, a colleague of Bradbury at the University of East Anglia, an Italophile with one foot in literary London. She had reviewed *Abbess* favourably, could quote great stretches of Muriel's work. She should have been ideal. What went wrong?

One cause of annoyance was the feisty tone of the printed text which attempted to sum her subject up:

> She has contrived an alarmingly smart reputation for herself [...]. It is difficult now to realise that back in 1960, she must have seemed one of the ruck of aspiring English writers, without any special brilliance or definition [...]. There was critical acclaim, certainly, but nothing out of the ordinary or un-English.[30]

'Contrived'? Nothing 'out of the ordinary' in *The Comforters*, *Robinson*, *Memento Mori*, *The Ballad of Peckham Rye*, *The Bachelors*? *Brodie* was described as Muriel's 'eighth' novel. It was her sixth. She was Scottish, not English. She was dubbed 'irretrievably grand', all 'style' and no 'moral earnestness'. The sketch, she thought, misrepresented her daily life. She was also unhappy at being associated with Donald Maclean, the spy, through the mention of his brother, Alan; felt that she was being taken over as a character in someone else's fiction. When she said that she hated 'being tied down by possessions – possessions, achievements of all kinds are changing their meaning utterly',[31] she was speaking the plain truth. Possession and dispossession were major themes in *The Takeover*. In Sage's story, however, in the 'grand' environment of that apartment depicted as humming with servants, these words were presented as at best self-deluding, at worst, hypocritical.

Sage had not read the new novel before the interview. Immediately afterwards, she did. 'I see what you mean about a revolution,' she wrote, '– the amazing way wealth circulates amongst your people makes the money system look Ptolemaic. And I especially enjoyed Berto, and Pauline, and the crook with ragout on his trousers.'[32] As the novel dealt with the despoliation of the rich by confidence tricksters, Sage had asked Muriel if she had ever been burgled. The report of this conversation enraged her. Sage had telephoned while Muriel was indeed investigating a burglary, and she had passed on the story as a scoop. Lawyers were in the house as she was speaking. The new maid, she explained, was suspected. The article, however, suggested that Muriel had accused Sage of the theft, that the day after her visit the table silver had gone missing: a dozen knives and forks and two antique spoons. In fact, Muriel and Jardine had travelled to Tuscany for a week after the interview and had only discovered the loss on their return. Sage, Muriel concluded, was a pathological liar.

Interview and review appeared just a week apart and were, to Muriel, of a piece in their negative inexactitude. Ostensibly talking her up, they seemed to talk her down. Mrs Spark, the review said, was 'full of surprises'. Her recent work had been 'nasty, allegorical and short'. Here we had something 'a lot more garrulous – as if she had some joke-phrase ("careless bravura"?) in her head while she was writing.' It was 'gossipy', larded with 'dollops of mythology', 'great fun' but 'What you're left with when the party's over [...] is not the teasingly complete and elegant structure she usually leaves shimmering in her wake but a lot of vivid fragments', 'weird glamour', lacking the 'hard stuff'.[33] No mention of the 'Ptolemaic' money system, of Berto or Pauline. The novel was, in short, a relative failure, skittish like its author, lacking seriousness, the product of 'careless bravura', amusing, slight.

Muriel, however, could afford to smile. Most of the other UK notices were raves. Kermode, Lodge and Auberon Waugh all trumpeted praise. The New English Fiction Society took it again. Joseph Losey was soon seeking film rights. And Muriel was there, in London, with the waves of celebrity lapping comfortably round her, lunching with Iris Murdoch at Strutt's Winchester Street house and looking forward to the trip north. On her return, she wrote again to Souny. Cancel that request for a Geneva pied-à-terre, she said. Italy would suffice for the immediate present.

*

The Takeover marked a turning point in Muriel's writing and in her life. It was her first long novel for eleven years, since *The Mandelbaum Gate.* After five abrupt works, all complex experiments often written in the present tense, she was spreading herself more comfortably in third-person narrative again. Mrs Spark, Kermode thought, could 'do any-thing'. Here she had dropped 'a whole chunk of Frazer almost *literatim* into the text [...] as if, but only as if, to make all plain [...].'[34] The novel had sent him to his books: to Sir James Frazer's *The Golden Bough;* to Suetonius, the Roman historian of Caligula, and to that emperor's connection with Diana and Nemi.

The novel opens in 1973 and is set at Nemi, the Roman focus of the cult of Diana. Its 'heroine', Maggie Radcliffe, is on her third husband, a cultured Italian aristocrat (Berto). Fabulously beautiful and rich, she seems to parallel Diana, the mythological goddess of the hunt and of the moon. Maggie owns three houses on the lake, one borrowed by an old friend, the English homosexual, Hubert Mallindaine; the second let to a respectable Italian family, the Bernadinis. The third she uses herself as one of her many pieds-à-terre. The thematic refrain is her attempt to reclaim the first house from Hubert. He refuses to move and under Italian law squatters have superior rights to owners. Meanwhile, he is steadily selling her antiques and replacing them with copies. Then suddenly, halfway through, the narrator introduces an epic theme:

> [...] 1973 [...] was in fact the beginning of something new in the world, a change in the meaning of property and money. [...] But it did not occur to those spirited and in various ways intelligent people that a complete mutation of our means of nourishment had already come into being where the concept of money and property were concerned, [...] not merely to be defined as a collapse of the capitalist system, or a global recession, but such a sea-change in the nature of reality as could not have been envisaged by Karl Marx or Sigmund Freud.[35]

Maggie first loses her furniture and paintings to Hubert, then her summer jewellery to burglars, then her entire fortune to the plausible financier Coco de Renault. Fighting liars with lying, she kidnaps Coco and, dressed as a peasant, holds him prisoner in a grove near the Temple of Diana. The ransom she demands is the return of her assets.

To Auberon Waugh, this was a cheap twist that marred an otherwise splendid reinforcement of his politics. *The Takeover*, he thought, represented 'the total and abject degradation at every level' of our civilisation, ruined by progressive legislation and the claims of the vulgar. Religion was personified by 'a pair of comic-opera Jesuits, and the working class represented by a walk-on cast of homosexual prostitutes, thieves, blackmailers and corrupt servants [...].' The 'degenerate parasite' is privileged 'at the expense of everyone else'. Maggie's becoming a crook herself seemed a cynical gesture in a novel whose 'message throughout [...] had been the inadequacy of the rich to protect their own interests, and their unworthiness to survive in any case'.[36] Was *The Takeover*, then, what another reviewer described as a 'seductive – rather than persuasive – piece of propaganda on behalf of the rich'?[37]

Nothing so simple. For Gabriel Pearson there was a recurrent question: what, if anything, could be saved? 'The answer seems to be "style", and beyond style, "myth".' The vague adversaries of the rich are known as 'They' ('*loro*'); the Italian manservant who sleeps with both Maggie and Berto, then marries a local girl whose family owns the land on which Maggie's houses are built and inherits the lot, is called 'Lauro'. Pearson therefore believed 'that that makes him the sexual and entrepreneurial embodiment of Loro: one of the takers-over'.[38] Kermode also noticed this link but interpreted it differently: 'Lauro, by the way, is an extremely unusual Christian name; perhaps he is all that's left of Frazer's tree-spirit, if we assume that the golden bough came from a laurel. Is he getting his own back?'[39] In one sense, of course, that is precisely what Lauro is doing. He is Italian, Maggie American, her houses built illegally, '*in abuso*'. On the other hand, she is the one who has invested in reconstruction of what otherwise would have remained ruins, and Lauro's fiancée's family have stood by, waiting to reclaim the improved property. The moral issue is thus perfectly balanced. There is no question of good or evil, merely one of intelligence and absurdity. Lauro is intelligent, a survivor, an attractive figure, and Maggie must copy him if she is to survive.

Muriel, it seems, was drawing deeply, if obliquely, on her Roman life here. Auberon Waugh might have been alarmed to learn that she was rather fond of people similar to those he took to be 'degenerate'. 'I am very unsure', Rasponi wrote to her, 'as to what happens to B.D.B. at the end of "the take over". Does he get away with it?',[40] and for those who knew Brian de Breffny this correspondence between him and Hubert seemed unmistakable. Just as 'Hubert's aunts [...] grew in the grace of his imagination', germinating ancestors 'springing from nowhere into the ever more present past, until [he] had a genealogy behind him',[41] so de Breffny had appropriated forebears from obscure genealogy. De Breffny and Mott were both keen votaries of the Charismatic Renewal, a Pentecostal movement in the Catholic Church which gathered at the Jesuits' Gregorian University in Rome. The place would be crowded with priests and nuns. 'It was about things like speaking in tongues and prophecy, spontaneous prayer and sharing. It had many American aspects [...]. Muriel came to a lot of meetings and she was amused by it, I think.'[42] Amused but distant. She attended, she said, only one meeting. In the novel, these passionate congregations become Hubert's pagan cult of Diana, a parody of Christianity in which 'she was flesh, miraculous flesh, be sure of that'.[43] His surname means 'malign Diana'; his 'genealogy' links him to her putative union with Caligula. He is, he insists, a direct descendant: 'I am the King of Nemi! It is my divine right!'[44] Hubert is both crazier and more self-aware than de Breffny, less handsome and amusing, equally ambitious. Shadows of his psychological features are detectable, particularly his pomposity and dandyism, but Hubert is rather a compound of all the fantastical gays she had known – Walter, Rasponi, Ambrosiani et al. – and the novel a mordantly tender valediction to them.

During September 1976 Muriel wrote to Strutt asking what had become of de Breffny.[45] Two months later she knew. De Breffny had at last found his heiress: a stunning Finnish beauty, widowed, wealthy, and apparently the owner of numerous houses and stretches of Barbados beach. Although there was perhaps a touch of jealousy in Muriel's reaction to the news and Jardine remembered someone saying at a party: 'Goodness, Muriel invented Maggie and Brian has married her', The Takeover is not an angry or embittered book. Maggie was the type of woman Muriel often admired: beautiful, stylish and free. The novel is relaxed, the product of an author confident of her powers and entering a new phase of her life. A transitional work, it was partly about a revolution in world affairs, partly about the ways in which 'fact' dissolves irretrievably into myth, partly a reflection of her changing state of mind, on ageing and the need to accommodate oneself to it with vigour. As an image of Italy in the early 1970s, Mott thought, it was exact. The confusion between the authentic and the fake was integral to its thrilling instability. In that sense Rome was oddly 'young' in the 1960s and 'grew up' in 1973 as the shades of the prison house closed in and it lost its narcissistic self-confidence and glamour.

'I have learned', Muriel wrote in 2001, 'that happiness or unhappiness in endings is irrelevant. The main thing about a book is that it should end well, and perhaps it is not too much to say that a book's ending casts its voice, colour, tone and shade over the whole work.'[46] The last words of The Takeover are:

> She said good night very sweetly [to Hubert] and, lifting her dingy skirts, picked her way along the leafy path, hardly needing her flashlamp, so bright was the moon, three-quarters full, illuminating the lush lakeside and, in the fields beyond, the kindly fruits of the earth.[47]

Maggie goes on her way, at one with the moon and her goddess, another woodland sprite, having liberated herself from Hubert's threat and made her peace with him. She disappears into a generative landscape 'lush' with 'kindly fruits'. The cult of Diana celebrated rebirth. Nemi is consistently described as green and fertile, like the 'umbrageous garden' of Abbess Alexandra's (and Marvell's and Muriel's) thoughts, with its Mirror of Diana, the tranquil, almost perfectly circular volcanic lake, as a still point in a turning world. And Muriel, too, was approaching another rebirth, leaving behind the energising fantasy of Rome and returning with Jardine's support to something more elemental. De Breffny had sometimes visited Muriel at Nemi. This casual affair had not worked out, as she knew it would not and had never wanted it to. Even her studio there had lost its romance, water leaking through the roof and damp-staining the rooms. De Breffny and Nemi were mythological constructs, aspects perhaps of mythological self-construction: amusing for a while but inevitably temporary. Like Maggie, Muriel was withdrawing into a simpler life.

*

If Muriel liked Hamilton's article because it allowed her voice, her possibilities, free rein, and disliked Sage's because it tried to sum her up, she provided a theological context for this discussion of how one's essential self is constructed by others in a 1987 interview. Consciousness of fundamental sin, she said, was integral to her art. This 'sin', however, was not one of the seven deadlies. It was 'the sin against the spirit, the sectarian sin, superstitious, this propensity of the human spirit for self-justification, thanks to which each diminishes himself, etiolates his intelligence, suffocates himself.' One French critic found this apt for *The Takeover* when it appeared in translation during 1988,[48] and it might be considered the great subject of her later years. It had always been there, of course, in some form: the hatred of provincialism, prurience, nationalism; the satire of vanity; the sense of alienation leavened by the spirit of mockery. 'I have inside me a laughter demon,' Hubert says, 'without which I would die.'⁴⁹ Muriel felt much the same. 'Everything is absurd', she told her French interviewer, 'without eternal life'.⁵⁰

'I bought San Giovanni', Jardine recalled, 'because I loved the birdsong in Tuscany and needed a studio that I wasn't turned out of by the landlord after I'd fixed it up (a common occurrence in Italy).'⁵¹ Muriel was in this position with her Roman landlady, fighting the *causa* through the courts and, eventually, losing. With *The Takeover* complete, the damp Nemi studio seemed uninhabitable. Jardine offered a welcoming home at a time when Muriel felt otherwise unsettled. American reviews had been another 'mixed bag', including a front-page attack in the *New York Times* by Margaret Drabble who saw the novel as unconsciously documenting a kind of stylistic crack-up:

> It is almost as though, midway through this novel, the author recognizes that all the trappings of her former style have, in the economic sea-change, lost their meaning and value, too. Will she shake off the confines of a public image and a public style that have at times looked like a *haute couture* straitjacket?⁵²

Here it was again, that ghostly public image suggesting that both Muriel and her work were glittering but insubstantial. 'It is easy to appear knowing', Drabble added, 'if one says little or one works, as she did in *The Abbess of Crewe*, on the level of tediously protracted fantasy. *The Takeover* exposes itself much more dangerously [...]. Those who aim at cleverness and elegance cannot afford to be careless.'⁵³

There were plenty of good notices: from the *Washington Post* ('chic, measured [...] a writer of hard-surfaced, high-polished prose'⁵⁴), from *Time* magazine, the *Chicago Daily News*, the *Chicago Tribune*, *Newsweek* and the *New York Review*.⁵⁵ But there was an alarming number of attacks. Anatole Broyard in the *New York Times* was vitriolic. *The Takeover*, he said, 'may be her worst novel'. It 'reaches out wildly toward anything and everything. The plot is so slovenly and improbable that even the barest summary would flatter it. [...] Her prose style, which has never been particularly distinguished, seems to have suffered something like a stroke.'[56] For the *Boston Globe*, the book outreached 'her limited talents' and offered a cast of 'Monty Python loonies'.[57] The *Chicago Sunday Times* thought it both essential and impossible to sympathise with Maggie.[58] Even Updike struggled. For him, the set-piece culminating riot merely 'fizzled': 'all the political, religious and sociological fuses threaded through the novel's crowded matter meet here but fail to be discharged. Instead an aerial scent of heretic-burning hovers in the grove.' There was, he agreed, much to admire but it was unsatisfying. The pyrotechnics didn't come off.[59]

Viking seem to have panicked and to have squandered their advertising budget on a large spread quoting innocuous phrases from Drabble and Susan Hill (in *The Times*[60]). Neither review had been strongly supportive. With another week's patience, Muriel's American publishers could have harvested a healthy crop of eulogy. But it was too late. Although the book was often recommended on Christmas lists, it was not selling vigorously. With other film and TV adaptations pending or released, however, she was financially secure and already busy with two other novels, relaxing into the stride of her new life: long stays in the country with Jardine to write, Rome for pleasure and business, trips to Venice, Naples, Florence and abroad. She was often on the move, and with Jardine now always at her side, relishing this new life. Over the next three years, the years of the Red Brigades' terrorism, which made Muriel feel distinctly uncomfortable, her Lungotevere apartment stood empty for longer and longer periods.

*

Muriel's letters during this time reflect both this sense of liberation and her anxiety about isolation and loss of independence. In her winter clothes on the first warm day of spring, she was enlivened. At other times, she felt claustrophobic. Not infrequently she presented herself as a refugee.[61] The theme of displacement recurs. Where should she go next? Geneva remained on the cards. England was impossibly dreary.[62] Italy was no longer an easy place in which to live.[63] 'I'm sure you don't regret leaving Rome,' she wrote to Ambrosiani,[64] adding that she, too, had had to escape. The place was chaotic.

'Funny,' Muriel wrote to Maclean in February 1977, 'I had already started writing about a boring dissenter from Bulgaria [...] when the dissenter problem blew up.'[65] This was a reference to *Territorial Rights*. The previous September she had sent the *New Yorker* a story under the same title. But writing was not proving as easy in her new life as it had in the past. The *New Yorker* rejected her story and, at that time, her main project had been another novel, *Watling Street*.[66] Neither was published. *Watling Street* was set in third-century Britain, the story of a Celt, servant of a centurion, who could foresee the future. She had begun it in November 1975 after dispatching *The Takeover*,[67] but had been thinking about it for a long time, reading volumes of history from the London Library, examining Roman censuses and slowly constructing a picture of daily life in the time of Constantine, as Evelyn Waugh had done with *Helena* (1950). Strutt had also been on the job, as had Jardine and John Rosenbloom in Edinburgh. It was background for this book with which she had been principally concerned during that 1976 tour with Jardine and Strutt. *Watling Street* was her only abandoned novel and it nagged her imagination for four more years. But her sense of artistic economy rarely wasted anything. Two decades later she spliced sections of this lost text into *Reality and Dreams* as Tom Richards's last film. In 1977 she had, for a change, to be patient with her muse.

'I'll be sixty next year,' she confided to Graham Greene during December, 'and am trying to shift my style of writing to the extent that I'm rewriting a book from the start. I was nearly through the first version when I realised it was awful.'[68] Rewriting was unusual for her. Shortly afterwards she fractured her toe and was laid up for fifteen days. But nothing, apparently, could disturb this peaceful reconsideration of her artistic practice. She had resumed a correspondence with Hugo Manning, her old friend from Kensington days, swapping books and reminiscences. Here was a man, a poet, devoid of resentment at her success, concerned only with the fulfilment of her vocation, anxious about her spiritual well-being. Sending *Conversations with Kafka*, he added:

> I think you'll like this [...]. To me he seems to be like some angel-being who strayed into the earth-dream as if by mistake. You've been on my mind a great deal recently. It is as if some force said, 'Muriel is in some sort of spiritual crisis. But all is well. It is like a period of spiritual reassessment for her. She will come out of it very well, will let go of some ideas to take on what is more vital [...].' Does this sound like a lot of nonsense to you?[69]

It did not. She shared that sense of the artist as other-worldly being exiled in the 'earth-dream'. Manning's letters returned her to a time when the purity of her vision had been uncluttered by fame and possessions. When he sent a book on the Brontës, she seized upon it. 'It takes me right back to my days of Brontë study,' she replied, 'with all the poverty, adventure and hope that went with them.'[70] It also set her imagination racing forward towards *Loitering with Intent* (1981) in which Manning was to feature as Solly Mendelsohn. Adventure had returned as she and Jardine wound their way across Europe and up and down Italy. Dangerous passes with night closing in and a sheer drop to one side merely raised their spirits.

Muriel wrote to Ambrosiani about her life at San Giovanni. She had, he recalled, 'found happiness [...]. Just a piece of Tuscan bread and a glass of wine made her feel well again.'[71] Simplicity had returned. Peace. Birdsong. Waking to innocence. When one looks at those desk diaries her existence seems as busy as ever – with one exception. She no longer needs sanctuary in the Salvator Mundi.

CHAPTER 17

Goodbye, Goodbye, Goodbye, Goodbye

1979–1982

'Now I'm eighty-one', Muriel remarked in 1999, 'and I think the happiest years of my life started between sixty and seventy. [...] For one thing, I can handle life. Up till the time I was sixty I was never very capable of saying "No", of really saying "This is the way I do it" and being absolutely firm.' Her interviewer, Janice Galloway, threw out a quotation, Jean Taylor's from *Memento Mori*: 'How nerve-racking it is to be growing old! How much better to be old!' Was it true? Muriel brightened. Yes, she said, 'That *is* true.' As an adult she had, eventually, said goodbye to anyone who infiltrated her artistic integrity. But she was making a clear distinction in that interview. Too often, she felt, she had wasted energy humouring those staking claims on her time. In the early 1970s her son and Macmillan remained on her loyalty list. By the end of the decade both were well on their way to becoming history.

Muriel had dutifully visited Robin in Edinburgh during 1974 and 1975, and had looked in again during that 1976 *Watling Street* tour when he had cooked a meal for her, Jardine, and a couple of his friends in an atmosphere of strained conviviality. *The Takeover* had just been published. Muriel was returning as the Queen of Scottish letters to her childhood home. But it was Robin's flat now (thanks to Muriel's assistance) and unequivocally that of an Orthodox Jew. She was perfectly content with this. All she wished for him was independence. Recently promoted, he had become Chief Clerk to the Scottish Law Commission. He had been sending her chatty epistles and she had replied in similar vein, apparently enclosing the odd cheque by way of a present. But there were two problems which obstructed familiarity: he insisted that Muriel was fully Jewish through the female line, and he had artistic ambitions of his own. There was, it seems, a question of territorial rights between mother and son. In London, just before this uncomfortable homecoming, she had changed her will, Penelope Jardine and Guy Strutt witnessing the document.

In July 1977, after paying her last visit to Robin for many years, Muriel bought a modest car (a Fiat 127) and, feeling liberated from family obligations, planned regular escape-travel.[2] The secret, she advised Strutt, was just to set out and to put up at whatever simple establishment one could find.[3] And so she and Jardine hit the road: France and Switzerland that summer, a trip to Gore Vidal's cliff-hanging villa at Ravello and dinner with Princess Margaret. Muriel was sixty on 1 February 1978. That autumn saw them in Baden-Baden with Jardine's dog, Pavoncino, in the back seat; in November they returned to Venice. Everything was exciting. Muriel was discovering France and Germany and, through Maclean again, preparing to buy a second racehorse. Should she ever return to live in England, she wrote to him, horse-purchase would probably take precedence over house-purchase.[4] The Black Forest was 'older than time',

> Baden-Baden is as it must have been in the early thirties. Elderly ladies all wearing pearls with their beige suits and elderly gents with their pale fawn felt hats. The faces were a general beige. Penelope drew much attention in a shop where she had to match a button. The entire emporium clucked.
>
> On the way back through Switzerland we had to cross a highly dangerous pass, the Furka [... ,] aware of our peril only when it was too late to turn back. Nothing but green-whiteness around us and night falling. At nine thousand feet we were euphorically consoled by the thought of

getting our name in the papers should we be found next spring, preserved and smiling, hugging the dog.[5]

There was nothing of 'general beige' about Muriel's entry into old age, and during April 1979 she was in England for the publication of *Territorial Rights*, leaving behind her a small symbolic moment: a farewell party for Ambrosiani on St Valentine's Day.

After a quarter of a century in Italy, Ambrosiani was returning to America. Eleven years earlier he had appeared in the BBC film to celebrate the Booker Prize nomination of *The Public Image*. A foot or more taller than Muriel, balding and built like a prize-fighter, he had escorted her gently round the damp cobbles of St Peter's, his arm in hers, umbrella aloft, posing for the cameras beneath the Pope on his balcony. Although their close friendship had long since evaporated, residual affection remained, and, as they would probably never see each other again, the themes of *Territorial Rights*, 'possessive love'[6] and 'impermanence as a state of mind',[7] perhaps seemed appropriate.

*

Territorial Rights, some critics thought, echoed motifs from Muriel's earlier work: the spies and snoopers of *The Comforters*, the 'old ghosts and guilts from World War II' of *Hothouse*.[8] But it offers much more than this. In the middle, the principal snooper and blackmailer, Robert Leaver, disappears à la Robinson, and his absence (like God's?) constitutes a presence for those left to decipher the mystery. At the heart of the book lies another puzzle and another disappearance. Victor Pancev vanished during the chaotic finale of World War II. Thirty-four years later his daughter, Lina, has come to Venice ostensibly to search for his grave but really to escape the rigours of Bulgarian communism. She is the 'boring dissenter' mentioned in that earlier letter: a painter of the social-realist school, good at beaming factory workers and the dignity of labour while she shirks, scrounges and demands her 'rights'. Thus a clash emerges between East and West with Byzantine Venice as an aqueous membrane between the two.

The novel opens with Leaver's arrival at the Pensione Sophia. He recalls the parting words of his American lover, Mark Curran: 'Goodbye, goodbye, goodbye, good*bye*. It was as if the older man had said, "You bore me. You can't even leave in good style. You haven't the slightest savvy about paintings. You've always bored me. Goodbye very much. *Goodbye*."'[9] Curran, at sixty-two, is a big-time art dealer, wealthy, stylish and used to power. He has followed Robert to Venice not to reclaim him but to ensure that he is gone from his life. And so another motif develops, echoing throughout in Robert's surname: partings, leaving with dignity.

Territorial Rights is a surreal compound of Muriel's early and late style, a mosaic. Stretching back from Leaver's life there is the strain of English satire typical of her early writing. His mother, Anthea (who remains throughout in Birmingham), click-clacks her vengeful way to a private detective, trying to get the dirt on her husband Arnold, a retired headmaster, who has decamped to Venice for a disappointingly clean weekend with the school's cookery teacher. The agency, interested more in blackmail than in assisting divorces, has vetted Arnold and found him too poor to be of interest. They have, says the mysterious Mr B, no territorial rights in Italy. Nothing to be done. But Anthea's equally judgemental friend, Grace Gregory, refusing to let it rest, flies out to nobble the villain. Each night Anthea induces sleep with a novel of the 'kitchen-sink' realist school, hilariously awful extracts from which structure the text and contrast unfavourably with the acerbic wit of Curran and Muriel's narrator. Stretching back from Curran, however, is another series of stories and characters linked by Pancev and more typical of Muriel's 'European' writing. Curran's oldest friend in Venice is Violet de Winter, the Italian widow of an English aristocrat. Curran and she have a history. They belong to the same operatic world, are like literary antiques from the world of Henry James. Venice is presented as an appropriate stage for their Machiavellian charm: a diaphanous creation, seeming effortlessly to float between sea and sky while also sinking and stinking, its fogs hiding malice and truth.

Muriel loved Venice, only visiting it in autumn and winter when most tourists stayed away. 'Any excuse to go to [it]', she informed Maclean, 'is a good one.'[10] Her first encounter with this 'compound of air, water, architecture, and [...] acoustics' had been with Jardine in February 1975 when they had briefly met Alan Bennett who was also staying at the Pensione Accademia. Three years later, the two women had arrived one stormy November midnight, all river traffic on strike, and negotiated their passage aboard a coal barge to the Accademia: black tempestuous water, shadowed palaces:

> the painted mooring poles gleaming suddenly in the light of our passing; the few lights from the windows were dim and greenish [...]. Nobody walked on the banks, and yet a strange effect that I can only describe as water voices came from those sidewalks and landing stages. Perhaps they were ghosts, wet and cold.[11]

The sounds of the city struck Muriel most forcibly: 'Like the effect of these elements on the ear, there are acoustics of the heart. [...] Voices, footsteps, bird cries, a cough from the window on the other side of the canal – all are different from the sounds of the land one has left. The traffic is entirely watery.'[12] That November her luggage had been heavy with reference books. She was there to correct the proofs of *Territorial Rights* in the place where 'apparently' seemed appropriate: 'Because, in Venice, anything can or might lie behind those high blank walls. It is well to say apparently. One never knows.'[13]

Throughout *Territorial Rights*, people construct stories about others in an attempt to nail them to the truth of their past. Self-definition for these 'authors' relies, as in bad fiction, on reductive characterisation. Was Grace a stripper? Was Curran a double agent and murderer? Leaver's blackmailing letters suggest parody of the worst kind of biography. He has spun a narrative about Pancev's disappearance which sometimes blunders upon the truth but as often invents malicious fictions. Ultimately we never know what 'really happened' other than that Pancev was probably murdered and that the two old ladies running the *pensione* had both been so in love with the man that after his death they had fought among the autumn leaves for the right to bury him. Each had one half of the garden, split lengthwise into discreet territory. The only solution had been to get a local butcher to hack the corpse in half. The body for which Lina is searching, then, is under her feet all the time and is, in any case, mutilated and distributed. One night, in an act of pure wickedness, the disguised Leaver forces her unwittingly to dance with his father on her father's graves. To Claire Tomalin, this suggested that the characters 'were dancing on the divided corpse of Europe itself'.[14] The job of a satirist, Muriel believed, was to isolate the object of attack and to dance on its grave.

This macabre comedy was more overtly symbolic than anything Muriel had written since *Robinson*, and, as with the island in that novel, as with London in *The Bachelors* and New York in *Hothouse*, Venice itself becomes the central character. David Lodge relished many of the tesserae, while feeling disappointed by the overall mosaic. The grave-dancing seemed contrived, Leaver's character too slight to bear the weight imposed upon it. Francis King suggested that the aquarelles of this novel contrasted 'interestingly' with the 'rich impasto' of another (rather similar?) Venetian story, 'Don't Look Now', producing 'airy impressionism' rather than Daphne du Maurier's 'meticulous attention to detail'.[15] Some American reviews agreed. Anatole Broyard liked the first fifty pages but found the rest 'whimsical'.[16] Anne Tyler, hugely supportive of the early work, could not tune in to these characters: 'mere personifications of superficiality: spiteful and quick-tempered, given to epigrammatic remarks, feverishly gay, gossipy, brittle [...] so empty that they're almost incorporeal.' Nevertheless: 'The whole novel glitters [...]. It's insubstantial, oddly hollow; but [...] it still gives off a fine, hard flash of light.'[17] With the diplomatic deletion of 'oddly hollow', this gave Coward, McCann & Geoghegan, Muriel's new American publishers, a splendid quotation for their advertisement. Alongside sat Edmund White's front-page *New York Times Book Review* eulogy: 'Once in a while a book comes along that is beautifully put together and effortlessly entertaining [...] the sort of elegant diversion we can enjoy and esteem.'[18] On the whole, Maclean, Joseph Kanon (her American editor) and Muriel were pleased by the reception: fifty-odd notices, eighty per cent of them favourable, and most of the big guns blazing for her.

In London during May 1979, when the novel was just out, Victoria

Glendinning had interviewed Muriel. A sense of permanent transition pervades this portrait: 'Success has not, for Muriel Spark, meant the acquisition of possessions. She doesn't like ownership [...].' Describing herself as 'a cuckoo in other people's nests', she seemed 'to have no need of the familiar domestic routines that spell security for most of us. "I draw the line," she said, "at 'forever'".' Depression was '"the enemy; but I just sit tight and wait." [...] Her depressions [...] are part of her unquestionable hopefulness.' Her working patterns were now 'fluid and unstructured', one week on, one week off. 'She works when she feels like it, and often does not feel like doing anything before six in the evening.' How, then, did she manage to produce so *much*? '"I've nothing else to do. I've put myself in that position."' There was steel, then, in this 'fragile, footloose woman'. Did the strong women of her fiction – Miss Brodie and Abbess Alexandra, for instance 'reflect something in herself'? 'I don't think of myself as dominant,' Muriel replied. 'But maybe one is; sooner or later I do what I want to do. By the wayside I do what others want me to do.'[19]

She was, at that very moment, doing what others wanted her to do. Scottish Television had produced a version of *The Prime of Miss Jean Brodie* and sold it to the American public service broadcasting networks. The first of six, hour-long episodes starring Geraldine McEwan was to be screened on 7 May, shortly before the launch of Coward, McCann's *Territorial Rights*, and Muriel had agreed for the first and last time to a promotional tour. So Jardine drove back to Italy and Muriel went on alone. In Washington, Philadelphia and New York she conducted numerous interviews, dispensing maxims and versions of auto-biography. The 'three deadly sins of the tongue', she said, were 'back-biting, murmuring and muttering'. All offended God and man. How was she at 'controlling her own tongue?' 'Well, I can always think of devastating things to say about someone but it's better to invent a character in a novel and say it there.' Libel? Offence to the original? 'Oh [...] the character isn't that person at all. You see, I have a strong sense that fiction is lies. It really is. Truth is truth. There never was a Miss Brodie, for instance.'[20]

Elsewhere she talked of 'the one particular teacher on which I based Miss Brodie'[21] and of writing six hours a day: 'My fingers ache by nightfall. That's what I mean by writer's cramp.'[22] It was pointless trying to explain apparent contradictions to the literal-minded: that although Miss Kay had prompted the idea of Miss Brodie, she was not *in fact* Miss Brodie (a far more conventional figure, indeed fearful of impurity); that sometimes Muriel worked during the day but *usually* at night, especially in the Tuscan heat. She was bored by these interrogators trying to fix her. 'Do not ask me who is the villain in my writing,' she responded wearily. 'My characters are not good and not bad.'[23] Photographs often show her holding a cigarette, staring askance as though wishing herself elsewhere. When asked why she lived in Italy, her reply was always the same. She lived in Italy because Italians knew how to treat writers. They left them alone. Catholicism? She thoroughly approved of Vatican II and had never had much time for all that incense-swinging. Her son? 'My mother sort of stole him from me. It was like her son all over again.'[24]

With a flood in her Philadelphia hotel suite after a bumpy commuter flight from Pittsburgh, with bad room service and an unpunctual sandwich, she was impatient to be gone. In New York, at the Algonquin, she was more relaxed and reflective. Asked about feminism she replied: 'I was brought up as an independent woman. [...] I'm in favour of women's liberation from the economic viewpoint, but I wouldn't want men's and women's roles reversed.' The Italian women's movement deterred her: 'no-one works hard at it except the Communists and they're so man-hating and fierce, they kick policemen and write ghastly obscenities on the walls. I think the war is pretty much won in most places – except in England where the women are a little masochistic, and really ought to wake up.'[25] Glendinning had also touched on this subject. Feminism, Muriel said, was a matter of 'equality in employment and pay, written into law. But castrating men is a bad idea [...]. I am an independent woman.' She had, she said, two new novels planned, 'one about the Romans in Britain; the other in the form of an autobiography [...] *Loitering with Intent* – which sort of sums up my life.'[26]

*

Just before her trip, Muriel had been told that she must vacate her Lungotevere flat by September. Back in Italy and greatly relieved to see Jardine again, she arranged, as an interim measure, to move to Tuscany. Three years earlier both had fled San Giovanni for an Arezzo hotel on discovering a snake in the house. But restoration was now further advanced. Amid workmen and rubble, Jardine was supervising the renovation of the top floor to accommodate Muriel: a bedroom, large workroom, and communal bathroom. A telephone was installed, electricity connected, and in good weather the place was paradisal. By October Muriel was telling everyone that she had moved to the country, although her furniture and archives remained in store for another six months. Meanwhile, she lived out of suitcases.

That summer of 1979 was a defining moment for her. In Tuscany, in her sixties, a more peacefully restless phase of her life was opening. She seems not to have minded a permanent shroud of dust, positively enjoyed candle-in-bottle dinners round a simple table. For a year she had been writing a screenplay of *The Takeover* for Joseph Losey, and was now busy with a requested alternative ending. When Losey invited her to Paris for a script conference she was flown first-class and given a suite at an expensive hotel. But she was growing tired of all this. She felt she had been cheated over the film of *Brodie* with a single, relatively small, payment; ripped off, too, over the latest TV adaptation through the carelessness of her agent. The films of *The Driver's Seat* and *Abbess* (*Nasty Habits*) had not been successes, the former, unknown to her then, produced shabbily to write off a tax debt, Elizabeth Taylor hopeless in the role of Lise. ('The producer [...] said, "Elizabeth, try to look as if you want to be killed", but she didn't at all. She looked as if she wanted a drink.')[27] Although the attraction of having Losey as director of her own words was strong, Muriel remained sceptical about other cinema people and disliked being addressed by them as 'Darling'.[28] As it turned out, Losey died and the film was never made. But Muriel did not react, as she might have done in the 1960s, with irritation at her lost work. She was retracting, slowing down a little. Guy Strutt had become an important figure, always welcome in Rome and at San Giovanni. She and Jardine wrote to him regularly, long affectionate letters with their news and troubles.

With Strutt they could be frank and funny, confidence assured. He was just himself: an independent gentleman with a taste for the arts. Like Muriel's maternal grandfather, he did nothing and did it perfectly, filling his life with the care of others and the pursuit of pleasure. Gentle, clever and practical, he would advise without being intrusive or judgemental. Lotus-eating trips abroad, odd bits of business for the family farming enterprise, inlaying ivory, historical research, kept Strutt busy. It had been difficult for him to watch Brian de Breffny flirting with other men and women. But he had said nothing, looked out for Sita, entertained the photographer George Mott and nurtured friendship wherever it was to be found. Muriel felt at home with him. He was the grandson of Lord Rayleigh (Nobel Prize-winner for Physics), son of another physicist, brother of Daphne, Lady Acton. As a child he had known Kipling; as a young man, Ronald Knox when he was staying as Daphne's guest, translating the Bible. It was true, Guy seemed to 'know everyone' and was 'related to the rest'. He was of the select band invited to lunch with the Queen Mother. But he was entirely unassuming and he also had that other life as buddleia to the butterflies of creative life, a host: William Walton, Tennessee Williams – and now Muriel who reciprocated by introducing Doris Lessing, Iris Murdoch, Angus Wilson, the Snows and Paul Scott.

In September 1979 Muriel revived a casual acquaintance with Sir Harold Acton. Again, there was instant attraction. Tall and languorous, Acton was charm personified. Half a century had passed since his undergraduate prancing with Evelyn Waugh. An outrageous figure then, advocate of modernism, seducer of oarsmen and friend of the Sitwells, he had, it seemed, a glittering literary future. Since then he had declined as poet and novelist, becoming a respected historian, memoirist, and translator of Chinese plays. He did not need to write to live. At his magnificent Florentine villa, La Pietra, he was a grand figure: more elegant than Strutt, whose clothes tended to rumple; a poised, cosmopolitan Roman Catholic, where Strutt was a shy, deeply English man who thought his sister's conversion to Catholicism unfortunate. Although in many respects dissimilar, to Muriel these two men were of a kind as hosts. Both effaced themselves to make others comfortable, were immune to social snobbery, and prized artists.

Jardine had numerous Tuscan friends. With these and Muriel's growing band, a social circuit was established. David Pryce-Jones inherited a villa outside Florence. A Roman acquaintance, the Australian painter Jeffrey Smart, had a country place near Arezzo. William Weaver, the translator and musicologist, was a neighbour; later, for summer visits, the playwright and novelist John Mortimer; the columnist Alexander Chancellor owned a house near by. Germaine Greer lived in Cortona for a while. From Rome and Florence, Arezzo was easily reached by road or rail. A few yards from the station stood the Hotel Continentale. Guests could be met there and quickly transported to San Giovanni. And plenty came: in 1979 Frank Tuohy and Tristram Cary from Muriel's past, Joe Kanon from her future.

In the early days Muriel and Jardine would go to the Continentale to make international telephone calls. Muriel remembered sitting there talking down the line to Dorothy Olding. Maclean, in New York for his annual visit, was sitting beside her. It was an important discussion: about Macmillan's contract for *Territorial Rights*. An offer was made. Jardine whispered: 'Tell them to double it.' 'I want double,' said Muriel. Dorothy, a grande dame herself, was momentarily dumbstruck. Then she explained that, honey, with the best will in the world ... Very well, then, said Muriel, she would put her novel away in a drawer. She had savings. She could live. There was a pause: they would see what they could do. Before long Macmillan doubled the advance – but issued it in two stages. Muriel came away from this feeling cross. If Macmillan could afford the higher figure, why had they tried to palm her off with half? It reminded her of earlier struggles: the undignified tussle for a living wage in 1960; the cheapskate advertising, the small printings, the typographical errors. If she rang up, the girl on the telephone would ask her to spell her name.[29]

When early copies of *Territorial Rights* arrived, Muriel immediately detected a misprint in the blurb. Maclean always composed jacket text,[30] clearing it with her before going to press. Proof-reading this – barely 170 words – she had left to him. But there, in the third line, 'countless' appeared as 'courtless', making nonsense of the sentence. Muriel rang London to discover that Maclean was on holiday. 'There's a mistake in the blurb,' she said. 'Yes, we know,' replied his secretary. 'We're going to leave it like that.' 'Put me through to Alexander Macmillan.' The secretary refused. Muriel rang again: 'I want to speak to Alexander Macmillan.' This time she was connected. He said, 'I can't read every comma...' 'Take it from me, it's wrong.' When Maclean returned, letters of abject apology were dispatched. But the books had already gone out and it was impossible to recall them without ruining the publishing schedule. All jackets of stock copies would be pulped and replaced. That was all he could do. 'I never went back to them after that,' she remarked. 'The girl was too rude.'[31]

*

Graham Greene sent Muriel two letters about *Territorial Rights*, the first on receipt, the second after reading it. They had only met twice, and then briefly at social functions, but for twenty-two years had exchanged books and letters. 'I took the almost unreadable *New Statesman* out to lunch,' he wrote on this occasion, '& saw that a woman called Elizabeth Berridge is advertised as saying of you "She's back in spanking form" – that's going to bring you quite a new class of reader.'[32] Ten days later came his verdict: 'It's your best, your very best. I thought you'd never top *Memento Mori*: but you have. I've been reading it all day in one gulp. Written with excitement at 9.35 p.m.'[33] Early in 1980 the novel was selected by the Arts Council as one of five contenders for the fiction section of the National Book Awards. With responses like this, and a choir of senior admirers on both sides of the Atlantic, Muriel felt she might have had a best-seller on her hands, possibly a film contract. But she didn't. So that, finally, was 'Goodbye' to Macmillan, and Greene offered her an escape route.

On 10 December Muriel recorded in her diary: 'Rang Bodley Head';[34]

in January 1980, Greene wrote, delighted by the prospect of her coming to his firm. From February to March, Muriel and Jardine were in England, staying with Strutt at his London house, 47 Winchester Street, Pimlico, while scouting the scenes of Muriel's life in the 1940s and 1950s for her next novel, *Loitering with Intent.* She rang Dr Lieber, the man who had treated her for 'anxiety neurosis', and discovered that he had died a decade earlier. She visited Vicarage Gate and sat in the graveyard of St Mary Abbots church where the opening scene of *Loitering* was already set. Jardine drove her down to Camberwell to see the irrepressible Mrs Lazzari: '92 & <u>lovely</u> and smart & alert. She is <u>leaving</u> <u>Baldwin Cres</u>[cent] and so was just in time to see every corner of my old flats upper & lower & the garden. Almost no furniture left. In Tiny no change. Deeply satisfying'[35] – as must have been the contemplation of her changed circumstances during the intervening quarter of a century. She attended BBC Radio's rehearsal of Russell Harty's adaptation of her story 'The Black Madonna', dined with him, Angus Wilson, Maria St Just (Tennessee Williams's friend) and Sita de Breffny at a chain of parties organised in her honour by Strutt; met Iris Murdoch again; went on to stay, cosseted and prized, with Strutt at Longwood, the Hampshire country house of his recently deceased mother.

Gossip seethed among publishers but still no one knew which way Muriel might jump. George Weidenfeld and André Deutsch were also angling for her work. Maclean, recently promoted to editor-in-chief and finding himself in an embarrassing position, tried to clear the air. How to phrase it, though, how to phrase it? 'I know that you are feeling that you may want to change publishers here for <u>Loitering with Intent</u>,' he wrote. 'If this happens I would v. much want you to go in peace and with all sorts of blessings. [...] This is <u>not</u> an evasive way of urging you out [...] and I hope you and Dorothy [Olding] will count us emphatically IN when the novel is finished and she's ready to deal.'[36] It was handwritten to 'Dearest Mu' but there was no avoiding the impression that he seemed less eager to keep her than his competitors were to poach.

Maclean was a Christian gentleman, half-Jewish, loved and respected by many in the trade. His friendship with Muriel went back to her origins as a novelist – the subject of her work in progress – and to his first faltering steps in publishing. Muriel did not take her decision lightly. She liked him as a man; as a businessman he made her impatient. 'Al' and 'Mu' remained on affectionate terms but since her removal to Italy, the relationship had steadily decayed. Over two excruciating years, his elder son, Daniel, had died from a form of Hodgkin's disease. Muriel had done her best to cheer Maclean but he remained saddened, and, in her view, distracted. She thought he ought to have pulled himself together. Her impression was that he had lost interest in his work and, indeed, before long he was writing to say that he planned to retire. Muriel planned never to retire. In September 1980, with *Loitering* complete, she had still not settled on a publisher. Of one thing, however, she was certain: it was not going to be Macmillan. When Olding suggested sending a courtesy typescript to Maclean, Muriel refused. Whatever anyone else offered, she said, Macmillan would only double it. No, not them; not at any price.

*

That April Muriel had set about reordering her life again. On her return from London she had begun negotiations to buy the Roman apartment which Jardine rented in Vicolo del Gallo, and to move the Lungotevere furniture, books and papers to the flat and to San Giovanni. An 'au pair', as Muriel termed him, flew in on the 10th: Peter Ginna, then a Harvard undergraduate studying history and literature, later a New York publishing executive. Looking to travel Europe, he had asked the advice of the alumni office. They had put him in touch with George Armstrong who had passed on the message. Jardine had interviewed Ginna and found him satisfactory. So he returned as she was loading the car and drove up the autostrada with them to San Giovanni.

It was a formative experience for this elegant young man. The weather was freezing and the house, apart from Muriel's upstairs quarters, rudimentary. During the day he could keep warm with movement. After dark the temperature crashed. All night in his bedroom a parabolic reflector flared, attached by a rubber tube to a gas cylinder ('alarming enough'). To heat the bed an oval wooden frame was supplied, from the middle of which hung a metal canister filled with hot embers. But overcoming his fear of setting the house ablaze, he soon settled to his three months as factotum. In the mornings he would light the kitchen fire, sometimes take Muriel her coffee in bed, then cut grass, chop wood, or drive off to Monte San Savino, the nearest serviceable town, to shop. Jardine would cook lunch, he wash up. After lunch he had two hours to himself. In the evenings they would all eat together again in the kitchen. His weekends were free. They rarely ate out or entertained. After a while, Muriel found him another job: unpacking and cataloguing her library, a collection which she thought revealed his ignorance because he found it oddly 'haphazard'.[37] She also believed (quite wrongly) that he had never heard of her or read any of her books.

Muriel was easy-going but she was usually upstairs writing *Loitering*. All day she would work, breaking only for lunch. Conversation was rarely literary. They listened to the BBC's World Service together and discussed the news. At first intimidated by the formidable Jardine, Ginna warmed towards her because 'we were both servants of Muriel's talent, people who were making it possible for the art to get created while the daily world was taken care of by us.' On his twenty-first birthday they threw a party for him attended by Frank Tuohy and the painter Jeffrey Smart. As a farewell thanks-offering, Jardine gave Ginna one of her paintings. He left regretfully, overwhelmed by their patience and generosity. They had paid him a small wage, encouraged him to explore Italy. In return, he had minded the house and waxed the tiles while they were off on their travels, often to Rome to arrange the purchase of Muriel's new flat.[38]

The Big Move finally took place in several stages in May 1980, and Muriel was no sooner reorganised than she began to fret. Her Vicolo del Gallo apartment was, she thought, uninhabitable as it stood: delightful period ceilings, rickety plumbing. In its narrow commercial street, between the Campo dei Fiori and the Piazza Farnese, she would have another base in the heart of Renaissance Rome; just four rooms and no view, 'a small but very exciting place just emerging from slumdom', but somewhere that could be transformed into a comfortable pied à terre once the builders had torn it apart and re-formed it to her taste. The flat was fifteenth century at the front, fourteenth century at the back. Originally it had formed part of an inn, La Vacca (The Cow), 'owned by La Vanozza, mistress of Pope Alexander Borgia and mother of Cesare Borgia. Her coat of arms, those of her husband and those of the Pope, all three joined, are set in the outside wall near my windows.'[39]

Renovation took a year and in the meantime Muriel remained at San Giovanni, anxious about her future. The August heatwave exhausted her. Unable to work, she was torn between loyalty to Jardine and the prospect of another winter in the country, wanting the freedom to roam but restricted by the need to find house-sitters. Reading Hans Kung, she found herself drawn to the theologian's notion of the dehumanising effect of a culture dominated by material success whose high achievers lost all sense of identity.[40] The cool spaces of England and the security of identity were much on her mind in the last stretch of *Loitering*, her autobiographical novel. It was a fresh start with a new British publisher, a product of that strength she felt in her sixties to simply say 'No'.

*

During 1980, Greene sent Muriel two books (later stolen by house guests at San Giovanni): *Dr Fischer of Geneva or The Bomb Party* and *Ways of Escape*. The first arrived in April at the beginning of the move, the second in November when the transfer to San Giovanni was complete and *Loitering* was (finally) with Bodley Head. Greene's literary methods intrigued her. *Dr Fischer* seemed unlike his usual work, the characters 'starkly themselves, predestined from beginning to end, which makes for an effect of moral shock'. He had, in other words, for the first time written something akin to her own fiction. *Ways of Escape* was autobiography, and discussed the problems of first-person narrative. Having just completed an I-novel, she had also found the perspective limiting but essential: '[...] I had to do an "I" because it's a fictional autobiography and treats of other autobiographies.'[41]

Loitering is about how Fleur Talbot becomes a writer. It is also about how Muriel became a writer and defined her identity. What happens in *Loitering* is not literally but metaphorically what happened to Muriel. Nevertheless, swathes of the narrator's commentary can be taken as the voice of the author, speaking from behind her mask. In her sixties Muriel became increasingly interested in her origins, in her own and her culture's mythology. Released from the cacophony of success, her reputation secure, she dedicated her future to examining her past. All her later novels centre on the notions epitomised by St Uncumber in her *Symposium* (1990). They are about freeing the spirit from encumbrance, and accommodation to fleshly ills. The relationship between reality and dream, as always, is fundamental: the reality of the dream which is artistic vision, the dream of reality which is self-justifying vanity. But to borrow the classification of Shakespeare's plays, it is as though she had done with comedy and tragedy and was now entering the final phase of her *oeuvre* with a form of romance. Restoration and regeneration become important. The joy of creation recurs as a theme, and of love not found where sought but arriving unbidden. In her old age she had scores to settle with those forces she saw as once ranged against her talent, and in *Loitering* for the first time she was using herself, directly, as a subject.

In order to do this, Muriel expunged any hint of suffering or complaint. It was important that Fleur should appear as no sort of victim. Reviewing 'a long life of change and infiltration',[42] Fleur adopts a tone of blithe fortitude rendering all her assailants absurd and transitory. They are pantaloons, these crooked publishers, English roses, *pisseurs de copie*, a mere blip in the graph of the heroine's inevitable rise and rise. Fleur writes poems, as Muriel had, in graveyards, and her autobiography is a graveyard of illusion. The reality, of course, had been otherwise. Muriel had suffered. She had been deserted by Sergeant and Stanford (who appear compounded in Leslie), wounded by her treatment at the Poetry Society (metamorphosed into the Autobiographical Association); she had taken Dexedrine and endured terrifying hallucinations. In the novel, the drug is administered by the slimy Sir Quentin Oliver, and Fleur never cries, as Muriel did, or wishes, as Muriel had, to marry. Fleur emerges, as Muriel wished to, not only unscathed but 'scatheless', having refashioned herself as the author of her destiny through her destiny as author.

The chronologies of the lives of heroine and author are thus quite different. *Loitering* opens on Friday 30 June, 1950, 'the last day of a whole chunk of my life',[43] on the eve of the publication of Fleur's first novel, *Warrender Chase*. It is a symbolic scene. The novel has been stolen and plagiarised by Sir Quentin, reclaimed by Fleur. She is reflecting on a period when 'I was thought rather mad, if not evil',[44] from a point at which, now self-evidently sane and talented, she can marvel at 'How wonderful it feels to be an artist and a woman in the twentieth century'.[45] Muriel's apprenticeship on the grubby fringe of literary life had lasted much longer: twelve years of hard labour. She had herself attempted a novel called *Warrender Chase* which had come to nothing. *Loitering* quickly flicks back to 4 October 1949 when Fleur begins her job at the Autobiographical Association. On that day Muriel had been in Vicarage Gate after being ejected by the Poetry Society. By August 1950 she had not even achieved her first triumph, winning the *Observer* short-story competition. *Loitering*, then, transforms the narrative of her own tortured life during these years into one celebrating triumph over adversity, self-belief justified. It was her revenge on all those who had thought her mad for wanting to be an artist: her brother, the snooty literary gentlemen, the dismissive lovers. It was a cathartic act, another goodbye as she entered her seventh decade.

Throughout *Loitering* we hear versions of statements made by Muriel in interview: that, when writing, she became a magnet for experiences relevant to her theme: 'My ears have a good memory';[46] that aural images preceded visual ones in the process of 'artistic apprehension';[47] that she conceived of 'everything poetically';[48] anything and everything feeding her 'poetic vigilance'.[49] 'The process by which I created my character', Fleur says, 'was instinctive, the sum of my whole experience of others and of my own potential self [...].'[50] 'All these years since, the critics have been asking whether Warrender was in love with his nephew. How do I know? Warrender Chase never existed, he is only some hundreds of words, some [. . .] marks on the page. If I had conceived [his] motives as a psychological study I would have said so. But I didn't go in for motives, I never have.'[51] Neither did Muriel. When Alan Jay Lerner wrote asking if she had anything for him to adapt as a musical, she replied sending *Loitering* and saying that 'It has the sort of "myth" which might be suitable [. . .].'[52] In the novel Fleur declares that Sir Quentin is

> using, stealing, my myth. Without a mythology, a novel is nothing. The true novelist, one who understands the work as a continuous poem, is a myth-maker, and the wonder of the art resides in the endless different ways of telling a story, and the methods are mythological by nature. [. . .] Never since have I shown my work to my friends or read it aloud to them before it has been published.[53]

After *The Comforters*, Muriel had also followed this practice.

What emerges more forcefully than in Muriel's public remarks, however, is the sense of passion and of possession. If possessive love and appropriation generally are anathema to Fleur, obsessive love for the work in hand is seen to be essential. Writing a novel is 'like being in love and better'.[54] Reclaiming her manuscript, she reacts as though to the return of a lost child or lover: '[. . .] my *Warrender Chase, mine.* I hugged it. I kissed it.'[55] But once this child is born and sent out into the world, the intensity of affection passes to the next in line. Two famous auto-biographers, Benvenuto Cellini and Cardinal Newman, act as spriritual companions. She appreciates Cellini not only because he is 'robust and full-blooded' with a 'touch of normality' (the man of the world, counterbalancing Newman's spirituality) but also for his 'long love-affair with his art', its adventure, his 'delight in every aspect of his craft'.[56] Newman is more neurotic but no less attractive for this, resisting '"the thousand whisperings against [him]"',[57] in honest, pellucid prose. '"I must [. . .] give the true key to my whole life"',[58] Newman wrote, and in her coded way Muriel was doing this in *Loitering*. The key to her life was the passion for her art.

This passion – the '*demon* inside me that rejoiced in seeing people as they were, and not only that, but more than ever as they were, and more, and more'[59] – isolates Fleur from the solace of conventional life, torments her with the clear vision of her persecutors' wickedness. Simultaneously, though, art saves her through its transforming power. As Masefield had told Muriel, nothing is wasted for the artist: 'When people say that nothing happens in their lives,' Fleur remarks, 'I believe them. But you must understand that everything happens to an artist; time is always redeemed, nothing is lost and wonders never cease.'[60] Sir Quentin, Dottie, Fleur's swinish landlord, and Beryl Tims, all infiltrate and attempt to burgle Fleur's talent. Yet all are indispensably perfect 'writing-meat'. Without them Fleur would have lacked self-definition and there would have been no novels or autobiography. The trustworthy and charming empower and enliven but make for social rather than creative life. The artist is thus in a paradoxical relationship with her comforters: she *needs* to be persecuted, for without the accommodation of that absence of good there can be no sense of virtue or identity. (Muriel once joked with the novelist Hugh Fleetwood that she was off to church to pray for her own virtue and others' sins.[61]) The ultimate paradox, and one to which Muriel's work always returns, is the Romantic one: that the 'insanity' of visionary perception locates a higher truth than the sanity of rationalism. Fleur quotes Cellini's 'I went on my way rejoicing' at seven crucial stages and these are also the last words of *Curriculum Vitae*. 'Finish. Cut it out.'[62] One of Muriel's favourite expressions, signing off letters to friends, was 'Looking forward'.

*

Muriel's last diary entry of 1980 was on 25 September, shortly after she had finished *Loitering*. Social life in the country had closed down for the autumn and would not revive until Easter. In one way this suited her seasonal temperament but in another it did not. She needed warmth and conversation, frequent change. '[...] *[P]eople* are what I write about,' she explained to Strutt the following April, '– not the actual people I meet – but my imagination only feeds on social life and on hearing the English tongue from time to time.'[63] Restoration of her Rome flat was now complete and she wanted to use it. Permanent rural cohabitation had never been her intention. During October, Jardine and she had toured Belgium and Holland. Now they were hunkered down, Muriel again contemplating the moribund *Watling Street*, Jardine picking olives, drawing, and, as they had no domestic help, cooking and cleaning when not occupied as Muriel's secretary. Both were attempting (again, and unsuccessfully) to give up cigarettes.

Muriel's life was better organised than it had been during 1979 (she now had two desks: one for business, one for creation). Nevertheless, she was anxious that Jardine's eagerness to help was distracting her from her own art. *Loitering* was due to appear simultaneously in England and America during May 1980. Bodley Head promised well with the scholarly James Michie as Muriel's editor. Jardine gladly took on the task of clearing the business desk, although Muriel dealt with a lot personally. Typically she would scribble a first-person reply on the original enquiry for Jardine to type. Sometimes she used her amanuensis to reply as ventriloquist's dummy. Muriel would compose these letters referring to herself in the third person and doubtless amusing herself with ingenious deflection. Keeping Macmillan sweet and simultaneously at bay was tricky. They were a useful resource for cut-price books (Muriel was reading her way though Henry James and rereading Newman's *Sermons*, ordering complete sets of both). But in abandoning the firm for Bodley Head she was in the position of a woman who had walked out of the family house, leaving her children and property behind. She wanted her rights back, wanted a clean break, and extricating herself proved complicated.

Macmillan naturally maintained their rights to the backlist but its sales were tiny. The previous October, on discovering that *The Public Image* was out of print, Muriel had tried to reclaim it and Macmillan had refused. Instead, they promised to reprint each novel in a small new hardback edition whenever stock was exhausted, thus technically keeping it in print while not being obliged to make any effort to sell it. Muriel knew the game exactly and for three years dealt diplomatically with the situation – until Jardine took those accounts apart.

When Strutt eventually found them some house-sitters during the latter part of July 1982, Muriel and Jardine drove to England, Muriel's spirits immediately levitating once she was on the road. As *Loitering* had been out for nearly two months, they avoided the publicity circus. Indeed, there was no need for one. American and British notices had roared approval and the book was selling fast. 'Of England's long-distance novelists [...],' said *Newsweek,* 'few have so unflaggingly sustained their wit and inventiveness as Muriel Spark.'[64] The *New York Times Book Review* raved at length: 'All [her] novels are, in one way or another, sly, frequently droll meditations on the Four Last Things [...]. She is a profoundly serious comic writer.'[65]

A. S. Byatt, Auberon Waugh,[66] A. N. Wilson, John Osborne and Malcolm Bradbury weighed in enthusiastically, each with a different interpretation. To Byatt, it was an accomplished study of 'the relation between truth and fiction, imagination [...] virtue [...] and the "possession" of other lives [...].'[67] Wilson saw it as an essay on 'Fiction and Autobiography':

> Are we imprisoned in our own egocentricity, or can we, on the viewless wings of art, 'go on our way rejoicing'? [...] [W]e are made to think about the very nature of perception itself, the illusions which enable us to claim knowledge of other minds. We can only see the world in our own way unless we see it through the eyes of great art.[68]

And he was adamant that this book *was* great art, as great as *Brodie,* 'one of the most perfect novels of the century'.[69] Osborne read this 'glorious new novel' as being about 'the common hatred of the solitary creative spirit, and written with the psalmist's lovely rage'.[70] Bradbury detected

> an awareness of the corruptions of those engaged in art; she has often, indeed, elevated them, as higher than the corruptions of life. Fleur is the wicked artist who is not quite as wicked as the ways of the world. [...] *Loitering* [...] is, therefore, an artist's criminal confession, a confession that leaves Fleur rejoicing. It is nasty, clever, good and great good fun.[71]

Forty-odd similar notices tripped over each other in their haste to genuflect. Bodley Head and Coward, McCann were overwhelmed, the latter running a huge advertisement plastered with eulogy in the *New York Times Book Review*. So rich was the crop that they could even afford to omit *The Times*'s: 'It has wit and grace. It is intelligent. It shimmers with love. [...] Britain's finest post-war novelist.'[72] Of the few with reservations – Jeremy Treglown, Martin Seymour-Smith, Anatole Broyard and William Boyd[73] – most expressed counterbalancing admiration. Biographers (Victoria Glendinning, Michael Holroyd)[74] saw it as a novel about life-writing, novelists saw it as about fiction, hacks as a comic romp.

By October 1981, Muriel was back in San Giovanni facing another winter. Jardine was installing central heating and, again, everything was in turmoil. Sheets shrouded furniture, rubble littered the floors; the air was heavy with brick dust. Jardine dashed around trying to maintain control while Muriel isolated herself with her next novel, *The Only Problem*. Amid this chaos the telephone rang. The single available extension was in the cellar. In her oldest clothes, groping down among the cobwebs, Muriel found herself speaking to Lord Snowdon. He was in Rome and wanted to come over to photograph her for *Vogue*. Perhaps later, she said. She could (just about) see the amusing side of it. Dislike of hotels and loyalty to Jardine kept her there. She bought a new car and looked forward. Although her independent life had suffered a hiatus, she anticipated soon settling back into its restless pattern, coming and going.

Everything seemed to be in place. In London Muriel could avoid hotels by staying at Strutt's Pimlico house. Sometimes he was there, sometimes not. She and Jardine were free to use it whenever necessary. Driving back to Italy, they would always choose a different route, surprises round every corner. Strutt had just moved his country home from Longwood to the Old Rectory in the village of Terling, Essex, and this comfortable Queen Anne structure became Muriel's principal English pied-à-terre for nearly twenty years. She often stayed there with Jardine. But as it turned out, Muriel made her first visit there alone during one of the less happy passages of their lives.

*

A certain tension seems to have been building between Muriel and Jardine during the autumn and winter of 1981/2. Muriel wanted more time in her new Rome flat; Jardine, having made huge efforts renovating San Giovanni to make Muriel comfortable there, not unnaturally wanted Tuscany to be their base. But living together in Rome was now a problem. The flat was small, Jardine had regularly to return to keep her house secure, and money that might have been spent on an au pair to allow them to escape would have to be used to pay a maid in Rome. It was a difficult period for both women. Muriel was on tranquillisers and seems to have been anxious about money. She now owned the Nemi studio and the Vicolo del Gallo apartment, paying for the upkeep of both in addition to settling bills for the car, au pairs, and gas at San Giovanni. Her dentist charged heavily for the repair of five deteriorating crowns; another large sum went on new furniture. When she checked her account she found that it contained very little. This was not a disaster. Her main income derived from spring and autumn royalties, advances and adaptations. She had begun to accept commissions for travel articles to raise extra cash and there was equity in her real estate. Money, however, was bleeding away at an alarming rate and, unable to attend to her novel, she was restive.

Jardine meanwhile suffered painful accidents at San Giovanni. Having broken two toes in August 1981, she was up a ladder in November when it slipped and she fell with it, fracturing her leg, her other foot and her wrist (which was also dislocated). The plumber drove her to Arezzo where her bones were set. Muriel hired a car and chauffeur, came down, drove her over to San Giovanni to shut up the house and to pick up the cat and dog, brought her back to Rome where Pavoncino was boarded at a kennel, installed Jardine for a week in the Salvator Mundi, paid all the hospital bills and finally took her to the flat to convalesce. A month later Jardine was out of plaster. The plan was that she should return to San Giovanni as soon as she could drive, while Muriel remained in Rome to pick up the threads of *The Only Problem*. By mid-January, however, she was herself in hospital with a slipped disc, the doctors (wrongly) telling her that the condition was irreversible as it involved the sciatic nerve and thus traction and surgery were to be avoided. In fact, she recovered just by lying flat. Muriel was stoical but the incident had drawn a line for her. She no longer thought it wise to be bumping around country roads or living in that chill stone house during the dead of winter. And the creative urge was on her. After twenty days on her back in the clinic she wanted to stay put in Rome: alone, warm and writing.

What happened next might have ended Muriel's and Jardine's time together and it says much for both that it did not. In the long perspective of their contented, if volatile, companionship, their argument in the Rome flat during April 1982 was a mere blip they wished to forget. But as it resulted in Muriel temporarily altering arrangements at San Giovanni, and as she recorded the events in her diary and deposited it in the National Library of Scotland, it must be discussed. This was the second, and final, occasion on which these otherwise anodyne documents evinced passion.

Since December 1981 it had seemed clear to Muriel that Jardine was suffering from depression and, on 7 April, finding herself under verbal attack, Muriel tried to arrange treatment with a London doctor who had helped Angus Wilson. When Jardine refused, Muriel lost patience and instituted her own, economic, therapy: the reconstitution of independent financial arrangements. Fifteen days later there was an almighty row. If Jardine rang, she brushed her off. A letter was dispatched, clarifying terms. Muriel would, she explained, no longer contribute to the expenses of San Giovanni. She telephoned Strutt who invited her to stay. The argument ran on by telephone through May while Muriel was trying to work on *The Only Problem*. Finding composition almost impossible, she finally retreated to the Salvator Mundi but when she emerged on 17 May only the first chapter was complete.

During August, with the heat removed from the discussion, the two women set off together at Muriel's expense for a restorative trip to the Austrian Tyrol, Munich and the Jura region. On their return, Muriel moved her books, best furniture, carpets and pictures from San Giovanni to the Vicolo del Gallo apartment. Archives were to be returned to store, and when this was done she planned to head off alone: to New York on business, to San Diego to see her brother. Adrift in the world again, she simply sought tranquillity, the time-space in which to write her novel about Job and the problem of suffering. She felt, she said, like the Wandering Jew.[75]

CHAPTER 18

A Speck in the Distance

1982–1988

Alone in her fastness, Jardine wrote to Muriel in New York, by turns elated and dispirited, longing for her friend's return. With only Pavoncino and Miss Fisher (the cat) for company, she felt isolated, unable to paint or sculpt as her fiftieth birthday approached.[1] She met Muriel from the airport, continued as secretary, invited her to stay at San Giovanni. For the next year Vicolo del Gallo was Muriel's principal address, San Giovanni a home always ready to welcome her. In a 1982 article, 'My Rome', written in Tuscany and typed by Jardine, no mention is made of Muriel's living part of her life there: 'Wherever I live I am in the writer's condition: work is pleasure and pleasure is work. I find Rome a good place to work.'[2] Nevertheless, for Muriel, too, the pleasure of work had temporarily fragmented. When she finished 'My Rome' in October 1982, she had hardly begun *The Only Problem*. Chapter 3 was not completed until March: less than 14,000 words in eighteen months. But she was patient. Short stories, she informed Strutt, could be written when the serenity necessary for a novel was obstructed.[3]

The American trip cheered her. In San Diego she had met for the first time her nephew and niece (David and Vivian, Phil and Sophie's children) and liked them. Back in Rome, there was a hiatus. Would the floors of Muriel's flat support the weight of her library? By Christmas, though, everything was packed in and she was turning out short work. When she had left for the States, she had ordered a gorgeous blue belt for Jardine's birthday. Muriel rang and wrote, tried to interest Maclean in using Jardine's illustrations for children's stories. Jardine was trying to secure a winter tenant so that she might share a flat with Muriel in Paris for a few months. Muriel's fiction was beginning to flourish there, published by Fayard, and although no tenant could be found and the Paris idea came to nothing, they began to travel extensively around Europe, Jardine quickly regaining her spirits, not least because of Muriel's evident concern for her.[4]

All the stories Muriel wrote during this distracting period – 'The Fortune Teller', 'The Executor', 'Another Pair of Hands' and 'The Dragon' – deal with the preservation of independence. In each, infiltration is rebuffed, identity re-established. The first two touch on the mystery of artistic transfiguration, the others on the relationship between master and servant, a subject which had long intrigued Muriel. We see it throughout her early work in the tension between employer and employee, teacher and pupil, nurse and patient, landlord and tenant. It appears more directly in a string of post-New York novels and was to recur in *Symposium*. With few exceptions, Muriel's fictional maids, butlers, houseboys, secretaries are fifth-columnists, salaried loyalty disguising resentment of their paymasters. Set against this, there was one story from her recent experience. During April 1983, Count Lanfranco Rasponi, her former admirer, had died of Aids in Brazil just four years after inheriting $35 million from his detested father. Everything was willed to his maid, Iride. A peasant girl who had been taken about to Florentine concerts and plays, she was to Muriel the epitome of natural gentility. Still living in Rasponi's elegant Roman apartment, she was inconsolable. The flat was unheated, the assets frozen. She had received no money. But this was not the source of her misery.[5] What struck Muriel most forcibly was this sixty-year-old woman's unconcern for material things. Given the choice, she would have preferred the Rasponis alive.

Servants had always been a problem for Muriel. She needed them but disliked both the word and the concept, preferring the idea of helpers whom she could treat as equals. Too often, they seemed to take advantage. The best model for 'dragon' gatekeeper had been Mrs Lazzari.

Hotels (the Beaux Arts in New York, the Raphael in Rome) had provided comprehensive service but at great cost and impersonally. In private apartments, her experience of manservants had been disastrous. Then had come Jardine, 'my pal Pen' as she termed her, not a servant at all but a fellow artist: independent, industrious, vivacious – but currently suffering a bad time.

*

Suffering was the subject of *The Only Problem*. It is set in the French countryside round Epinal, in the district of Meurthe, an area Muriel and Jardine had revisited during their Austria-Munich-Jura trip. Muriel had begun the book during this journey but under the circumstances (Jardine's condition worried her enormously) had not got far. The central character is a wealthy Canadian, Harvey Gotham, who has isolated himself in a cottage to write a monograph on the Book of Job. Throughout, various people from his previous life arrive to obstruct composition. First to visit is his brother-in-law, Edward Jansen, an unpleasant ex-curate-turned-actor, who is to be in a film, *The Love-Hate Relationship*. 'If there's anything I can't stand it's a love-hate relationship,' Gotham remarks:

> The element of love in such a relation simply isn't worthy of the name. It boils down to hatred pure and simple in the end. Love comprises among other things a desire for the well-being and spiritual freedom of the one who is loved. There's an objective quality about love. Love-hate is obsessive, it is possessive. It can be evil in effect.[6]

This was the problem of Job's relation to God, of Job's wife to her husband, and of all the narrators of all those new short stories. It was also, perhaps, the problem that had driven Muriel to re-establish her independence. The novel asks fundamental questions about love: how to define it, distinguish it from dependence, obsession, the desire to possess. Muriel always maintained that she loved her characters, especially the most offensive. Gotham wonders whether God treats Job so badly because the patriarch is so tediously *good*. Love was complicated. Maclean had once arranged a drink at the Ritz so that Iris Murdoch, a fan of Muriel's work, might meet her. 'What do you do when *they* come?' Murdoch had asked. They? Murdoch was speaking of the characters who begin to take over a novel. 'Well, mine don't,' replied Muriel. 'Mine do exactly what I tell them to.'[7] But it wasn't, she knew, that simple. As a poetic structure, *The Only Problem* remained earthbound and 'nothing seemed to square'.[8]

All this changed in April 1983 when Muriel and Jardine stopped off again in Epinal during a drive to London. Picking about among the tourist brochures in their hotel room, Jardine discovered that a local museum contained a Georges de La Tour painting, *Job visité par sa femme*. This became 'the turning point, providing all the impetus and logic I needed to continue with my story'.[9] Muriel had not known of the picture[10] yet suddenly here it was, glowing with wonderful ambiguities. By September the book was completed, to be published a year later. On the back jacket, de La Tour's painting was reproduced. In effect, she was completing her own abandoned monograph on Job by allowing Gotham to finish it. His debate exactly follows that of Muriel's 1955 review of Jung's *Answer to Job*. He is even given a quotation from it: Job 'not only argued the problem of suffering, he suffered the problem of argument',[11] echoing the novel's epigraph from *Job* 13.3: 'Surely I would speak to the Almighty, and I desire to reason with God.' This statement epitomised for Muriel the absurdity of the human condition, and her hero seems not only to be a modern-day Job but also Muriel. 'Harvey', we learn, 'believed in God, and this was what tormented him.'[12]

From Muriel's past life, shadows emerge of torments survived. Jansen asks Gotham if he is 'putting on an act' of being heartless;[13] Gotham is sceptical yet has 'abounding faith'.[14] Like Muriel, he is 'determined to be himself, thoughtfully in charge of his reasoning mind, not any sort of victim'.[15] And he resembles her in other ways: abhors linguistic redundancy, refuses to allow his own sufferings to become the subject for public discussion. 'To study, to think', he says, 'is to live and suffer painfully.'[16] To speak with the Almighty is impossible but art might approximate to this discourse. In Job, the anthropomorphic notion of God collapses because the link is broken between intention and action, justice and suffering; God's intentions remain obscure, as do those of Gotham's wife, Effie. And ultimately, perhaps, this was for Muriel the point of Job: 'Our limitations of knowledge make us puzzle over the cause of suffering, maybe it is the cause of suffering itself.'[17]

What, then, was it about that de La Tour painting which invigorated *The Only Problem*? Near the beginning of Part Two we find Gotham in the Musée d'Epinal, entranced by the image of

> Job's wife, tall, sweet-faced [...], bending, long-necked, solicitous over Job. In her hand is a lighted candle. It is night, it is winter [...]. Job sits on a plain cube-shaped block [...] naked except for a loin-cloth. He clasps his hands above his knees. His body seems to shrink, but it is the shrunkenness of pathos rather than want. Beside him is the piece of broken pottery that he has taken to scrape his wounds. His beard is thick. He is not an old man. Both are in their early prime, a couple in their thirties. [...] His face looks up at his wife, sensitive, imploring some favour, urging some cause. What is his wife trying to tell him [...]? What does he beg, this stricken man, so serene in his faith, so accomplished in argument?[18]

Gotham stands before the picture and finds more in its poetry to illuminate the mystery of Job's suffering than in all the scholarly commentaries. It is human, riddled with love's inarticulate complications. Job's wife appears only briefly in the Bible to say, 'Curse God and die.' Yet here she is tender. 'The text of the poem is full of impatience, anger; it is as if she is possessed by Satan.' Could her words have meant something else, something like, 'Are you still going to be so righteous? If you are going to die, curse God and get it off your chest first. It will do you good.' But no, this would not fit. De La Tour's was an idealised portrait of a couple 'deeply in love'.[19]

In one respect this is a strange interpretation. We do not know that it is winter and Job (if it is Job) in the picture is clearly an old man. Gotham nevertheless detects a resemblance between Job's wife and Effie. He has deserted her, just stepped out of the car at a service station during an Italian holiday, hitched a lift and never returned. She had stolen some chocolate, hypocritically presenting this as a political gesture against multinational companies. His friends are more shocked by his behaviour than by hers. He ignores her letters seeking a settlement. We soon discover, however, that she has been serially unfaithful – and she gets worse. While Gotham contemplates the painting, he notices strangers watching him and presumes them to be private detectives employed by Effie to trace him. In fact, the strangers are policemen. Effie has joined the Fronte de la Libération de l'Europe, a terrorist gang, and has come to the area to shoot up supermarkets, probably to implicate him.

Much of the rest of the book concerns Gotham's interrogation: by the police (who Muriel saw as representing the 'comforters'), by the press corps, and by himself. Before joining the FLE, Effie had had another affair and a baby, Clara, whom she left with her sister, Ruth. Ruth brings Clara to visit Gotham and stays as his lover. Ironically, he had taken to hanging baby clothes on the line to deter the attentions of local women. As a joke, he had told Jansen that if the police believed a house to contain a small child they would not attack with gunfire. It is this joke (betrayed by Jansen) to which the literal-minded police insistently return. They assume that Gotham must be funding Effie's activities. No explanation satisfies them. He should love Ruth and hate Effie but he doesn't. Against all the logic of self-preservation he loves Effie and is bored by Ruth. Effie is full of possibilities. Although she apparently cares nothing for him and, as the novel progresses, becomes an improbable object of veneration, his love for her increases. She is, then, not merely like Job's wife, but like Job's God. The suffering she creates helps him to define himself and to accommodate his own impatience and anger. It increases his capacity for love. Ultimately there is no resolution to these paradoxes, no happy ending. He loves Clara but can only have her with Ruth; he loves Effie who hates him and who is killed by the police. He ends up with Clara but also with Ruth, Auntie Pet and Jansen in the château he did not want to buy. Ruth is pregnant by Gotham. Asked what he will do now that he has finished his book, he says, 'Live another hundred and forty years. I'll have three daughters, Clara, Jemima and Eye-Paint.'[20] Ultimately it is a book about love's compromises.

*

Muriel continued to long for a large separate establishment almost anywhere in the world. She always wanted to be near water; her Rome flat felt cramped. Jardine drove her to Como to examine villas near by. The possibility of Muriel's departure from Tuscany was active for some years, and in the meantime both came and went from San Giovanni. As it happened, Muriel never moved out. Attached to the habitable section of San Giovanni, another part of the building, large and dilapidated, stretched out behind it. In early 1983, Jardine had had to decide whether to re-roof or to let it collapse – no easy choice. The structure was dangerous and renovation expensive. In the end, she gambled on repair, wisely in Muriel's view, and the restored section was to become essential to their coexistence.

Letters from both women at this time often spoke of chaos in the outside world: terrorism, political anarchy, wars, the deaths of friends. Rasponi was dead. Paul Scott was dead, also extinguished at his moment of triumph, only claiming the Booker Prize for *Staying On* when it was too late to enjoy it. Nineteen eighty-four had been a foul year for Italian weather: floods in the north and Tuscany awash. Strangers appeared at their gate with massive machinery to prospect for oil and natural gas. The idea of San Giovanni as a silent retreat often seemed hysterically inappropriate. Hunters surrounded them, apparently laying poison for others' dogs, shooting throughout the season. When the much-loved Pavoncino disappeared, the two women searched for him for months but ultimately had to give up, presuming him dead. The San Remo motor rally chose the dirt road outside the house for its route. The place was struck (as it often was) by lightning. And then there were the builders. When it all got too much – too cold, too hot, too noisy or too boring – Muriel and Jardine set off on their travels.

That autumn Jardine had sent Strutt a typed sheet, offering San Giovanni for low rent from January to March 1985. The new plan was to take a flat in London for those months. Again, this came to nothing. But 1984 saw many changes. Entries in Muriel's desk diary appear in Jardine's hand for the first time in four years. March and April were occupied with another drive to London and back, stays at Winchester Street, Terling and Edinburgh. In London there was pre-publication business for *The Only Problem*, more revisions to Muriel's will. In Edinburgh she was stepping further into the realm of mythology, having her portrait painted by Alexander ('Sandy') Moffat for the Scottish National Portrait Gallery. Legs crossed, in elegant black, her glasses held in both hands on her lap, she endured five sittings. The face is blank with a hint of vexation, the eyes expressionless. Moffat, she thought, was 'gloomy'. The red scarf had been her idea and it 'cheered the artist up' but one can sense irritation in his subject. When the picture was complete she cared little for it. It looked 'like a good poster [...]. I was just a model for "The Red Scarf" by Sandy Moffat. It isn't me; the author of my books is just not there.' Nobody, she said, recognised her.[21]

*

During that week in Edinburgh Muriel and Jardine had stayed at an hotel in Charlotte Square. Robin, a ten-minute walk away, was not contacted and he did not contact his mother. In May 1981 he had written a stiff letter stating that, since she continued to insist that her mother and grandmother were only half-Jews, he must break off relations.[22] She had replied, explaining that she and her brother Philip had attended the synagogue only rarely with their parents. Her father had always worked on Saturdays; ham, bacon and pork were eaten at home. There was an eclectic belief in 'the Almighty' but little more. It was an open-minded household. Robin was not there. Muriel and Philip were, and both were irritated by what they took to be Robin's attempt to reconstruct their cultural history.

This (largely silent) dispute rolled on for seventeen years at which point (1998), six years after Muriel had published *Curriculum Vitae*, Robin revealed to the press that he had his grandparents' *ketubah*, or marriage certificate, which stated that the ceremony had taken place at the East London Synagogue. Immediately, a raft of British papers pursued the story. The imputation was that Muriel had lied in her autobiography, concealing her Jewish origins. Finding herself accused of 'denial' and a form of anti-Semitism, she eventually responded. Her undiplomatic reply – '[My son] has got in on the act because he wants publicity [...]. He can't sell his lousy paintings and I have had a lot of success. [...] He's never done anything for me, except for being one big bore'[23] – merely fanned the flames.

All sorts of apocryphal data then flooded out. It was impossible, the Jewish authorities insisted, for anyone to be married in a synagogue without scrupulous examination of their credentials. Philip wrote to the papers confirming his sister's account in every detail. Professor David Daiches, Lionel's brother, said that as a child he had known the Camberg family and vaguely recalled Cissy's being converted to Judaism by his father (Rabbi Salis Daiches). The *ketubah* cited her surname as 'Uezzell-Hyams'. None of it hung together. Daiches and the authorities, after all, could not both be right (either Cissy was, or was not, Jewish through the female line and, if she was, she would not have needed conversion).

Daiches, it turned out, had not known the Cambergs. His father had only become Rabbi eight years after their marriage. The Chief Rabbi's Office admitted that between 1876 and 1940, 40,000 weddings had taken place at the East London Synagogue under a cheap marriages scheme, and that many of the families were immigrants with little or no documentation. Adelaide (Muriel's maternal grandmother) might well have been the child of immigrants. No birth certificate could be found for her. Was it impossible for her daughter, among this huge crowd, to have slipped through the net, marrying in a synagogue to please her husband? Muriel thought not. There was something, she felt, distinctly odd about that *ketubah*. To call Cissy (and her father) 'Uezzell-Hyams' was error or falsification. Cissy had produced no *ketubah* as evidence of her own parents' Jewish union – and the reason for this became plain with the discovery of Adelaide's marriage certificate. Adelaide was married to Tom Uezzell on 3 January 1886 in St Bartholomew's Parish Church, Bethnal Green, London. Banns were called. Muriel had always asserted that Adelaide, like all her children, was a Christian and here, at last, was evidence – or what looked like evidence.[24]

Some months later Muriel gave an interview in which she 'rather let

[herself] go – and did not regret it'.[25] This quoted from Robin's affectionate letters to her – 'like a good mother, I kept them' – but now, she
said, she was donating these to the National Library of Scotland to sit
with the rest of her personal archive 'as a point of historical fact'. It was
another valedictory gesture. 'He's made my life a misery. There's a long
history. Whenever I lift the phone, "snarl, snag, growl". I'm tired of it –
at my age I feel I can live without it.'[26] Philip had received anonymous
poison-pen letters, disgusting documents, abusing him and her as traitors to Judaism. Robin denied all connection with these but, in a futile
moment of rage, Philip had telephoned him in Edinburgh (during
the small hours to cause maximum disturbance) threatening to send
someone over to break his bones; then, thinking better of this, had
instead posted a parcel containing a joke-shop 'crying towel and
whoopee cushion'. On receiving this, Robin had apparently called the
bomb squad who evacuated his building. The whole scenario was
becoming horrifically comic – like a Muriel Spark novel – and when she
gave her interview he replied, indirectly, with an article in the *Edinburgh
Star*, writing her out of his life.

'Life with the Cambergs' offers his version, refusing to rise to her
insults and representing his lineage. 'Adelaide', he wrote, 'described
herself as a "Gentile Jewess", by which she meant that she was a Jew by
birth who lived with her Christian husband in a non Jewish environment. But she retained a loyalty to her Jewish roots and when her
daughter [...] reached her late teens, she sent her to live with her recently
widowed sister Sarah here in Edinburgh so that she might take her place
in a Jewish community.'[27] This seemed odd to Muriel, given that, thirty-
six years earlier, he had written to congratulate her on 'The Gentile
Jewesses', the autobiographical tale which offers a radically different
account of Adelaide. Robin, it seems, took what he wanted from this,
and ignored the rest. Because he had lived with Cissy for twenty-four
years, he implicitly claimed greater intimacy with her than could Muriel.
It was strangely reminiscent of the two old ladies in *Territorial Rights*
demanding that the corpse be hacked in half.

Muriel simply did not believe that Adelaide had sent Cissy to

Edinburgh to return to the fold. Where was the evidence? Robin described his father as a 'brilliant scholar', which also made her laugh.[28] No mention was made of Solly Spark's violent instability, or of his sister's threatening Barney and Cissy with a knife. To Muriel, the only explanations for Robin's scenario were profoundly insulting: that she and Philip were lying, or that both had been lied to by their mother who had somehow managed to disguise her orthodoxy from them. There was, however, a third possibility. One tiny, human detail emerged as a result of the investigations into birth, marriage and death records made necessary by this 'scandal': Adelaide was three months pregnant when she married.

Muriel was delighted by this news: 'It fits in somehow with her free and feminist character'[29] – and, although at the time she did not want the fact advertised, it is important now to discuss it because it might allow all parties to be, at least partially, right. For it is possible that Adelaide *was* Jewish through the female line. Her sister, after all, had married the son of the Jewish minister in Edinburgh, the senior religious figure in the city before there was a rabbi. Adelaide's maiden name was 'Hyams'. A Jewish girl falling pregnant by a Christian would not have been able to marry in a synagogue unless the father of her child converted. In the unlikely event of Tom's having agreed to this, he would have run the risk of being disinherited by his pious Anglican family, leaving him with no support in Watford where the young couple intended to set up home. But, in any case, there was no time. A wedding needed to be arranged and arranged quickly, before Adelaide's condition began to show.

Under these circumstances, it would have been easier to smuggle a Jewish bride into a church than a Christian groom into a synagogue and, given the stigma that then attached to pre-nuptial pregnancy, Adelaide might well have been reticent about her previous life, especially with her children. It is also possible that she had been thrown out by her own family, taken in by Tom's, and thus had turned her back on her parents' faith. But this seems unlikely. She had spoken affectionately of her parents, was proud of her Jewish forebears. Her sister, the daughter-in-law of the Jewish minister, was a witness at St Bartholomew's. Certainly Adelaide must have agreed to Cissy's going to Edinburgh to stay with this woman, Cissy's aunt, in her widowhood, and it was through the Jewish community that Cissy had met Barney. There is, though, a far simpler explanation than Robin's for this move: poverty. Adelaide and Tom lived in an overcrowded house on next to nothing. Her sister was more comfortably placed. Cissy could find work and a decent husband in Edinburgh, take a social step up from Watford. If Adelaide's prime motivation in consenting to this had been religious, as Robin says, why did she allow her two sons to 'follow the Christian tradition of their father'?[30] Why were they not packed off to return to the fold? Why did Adelaide attend the Watford church? Perhaps, having made her bed with Tom, she lay on it, somewhat uncomfortably, all her life. None of her children or grandchildren knew that she was pregnant at her wedding so why should they not believe that she was, as she insisted, half-Jewish?

*

In 1984 all this was a disaster waiting to burst upon Muriel's now well-regulated life with Jardine. 'Side Roads of Tuscany', another travel piece, offers a rare glimpse of this life. Muriel is seen to be often on the move, not just for the grander destinations but locally, too, eating out nearly every night. If 'My Rome' was a portrait of the metropolitan artist, 'Side Roads' presents the bucolic, rooted Muriel, depressed by the English voices of tourists. She avoids the poshocracy of Chiantishire, seeks the timeless: the resignation of the local people, the masterpiece murals in obscure churches, the peasant faces ghosting those of Renaissance painting. 'It was by chance, not choice, that I came to Tuscany five years ago [...],' she wrote, and it was by chance, not choice, that she had happened upon a capacity for love in herself. 'As with people, so with places: love is unforeseen, and we can all find ourselves affectionately attached to the minor and the less obvious.'[31]

Where Jardine was absent from 'My Rome', here she is mentioned briefly and anonymously as the friend in whose house Muriel stays on visits from her other home. The reader might be forgiven for thinking that Muriel was driving herself and her guests to all these places. Paintings are described, there is much about meals and where to eat cheaply. This was the itinerary the New York Times required but it got much more: a shard of autobiography concerned with the sources of spiritual peace. An English visitor had once asked her: 'Are you stationed out here?' 'Recalling this, I look out of the window and see Gino the horse farmer riding by proudly with his beasts; nobody has told him he lives "out here", and as for me, there's nothing in my life that corresponds to being stationed.'[32] The view from 'the heights of Camaldoli makes for a generous heart; it is one where mean thoughts are out of place, where the human spirit responds easily to the expansive benevolence of nature and its silence.' The benevolence of nature? This is not a concept Muriel had previously espoused but here, apparently, amid the 'cultivated plenty' of wild Romantic landscapes,[33] she felt at last free and integrated. Jardine's influence, although never mentioned, is everywhere apparent.

Joy, however, cannot have been unconfined when The Only Problem made its first appearance in America during June 1984. For 'those seeking richness of spirit in fiction', Vogue declared, 'there is not much sustenance here.'[34] Even A. N. Wilson had to confess that it 'does not, in honesty, hang together.' Such a book 'in which none of the characters [...] suffers seems superficial and pointless'.[35] Newsweek waited in vain for the trademark 'sleight of hand'. Time acknowledged 'bursts of wit and flashes of illumination' but ultimately saw the novel as 'a suite of lightweight sketches that aim at meaning and end as diversion'.[36] To the Los Angeles Times, 'the connection with Job is strenuously pressed [...] but the analogy continually recedes into absurdity.'[37] Plaudits rained down from the Sacramento Bee and a host of other provincial papers, but among the big-time notices, The Only Problem secured just one accolade: Anita Brookner's in the New York Times Book Review. The worst blow, perhaps, was Updike's 'A Romp with Job' in the New Yorker: '[Gotham] [...] is meant to be a modern Job, but he doesn't seem to suffer [...] somehow nothing builds [...] the author seems distracted and abrupt and to be gazing, often, at other problems.'[38] It was the old paradox, another version of Job's: to be condemned by one's own high standards. Muriel had a new editor (Ellis E. Amburn) because Coward, McCann had been subsumed into Putnam and the talented Mr Kanon had moved temporarily into management. A clutch of the early titles was reissued in paperback to coincide with the release of *The Only Problem*. The Franklin Library were to issue 22,000 copies of a signed, 'limited edition'. At the time, however, it must have distressed Putnam's to discover that an important work by a great writer could be appreciated by only one major American paper.

Brookner's analysis of the novel's 'existential distress', its 'seamless', 'unnerving' narrative, was more alert to the subtler touches: 'Finally Effie lies dead in a Paris morgue, her turbaned head lying bent at the same enquiring angle as that of Job's wife in the La Tour picture [...].' Attention is paid to the 'terrible reversals' of theology, 'terrible because it is God who asks the questions and Job who seems to have the answers'. To Brookner, Gotham was not impervious to suffering:

> In all her novels Muriel Spark gives the impression that although she has risen above the problem of evil, the struggle has been great; the effort has left her in possession of a high-spirited despair [...]. At times it has seemed as if the heart of the matter has been excised and only the nefarious transactions recorded. In *The Only Problem* this omission has been rectified. There is emotion here, despair and longing, kept in their place by precise and immediate writing. [...] It is Mrs Spark's best novel since *The Driver's Seat*, [...] again a disturbing and exhilarating experience.[39]

Both Brookner's and Updike's reviews suggest an uncanny perspicacity. For Muriel had indeed been distracted during composition – by personal troubles, by sciatica, removal, travel, schemes for alternative houses. She had been looking elsewhere, 'distracted and abrupt', 'gazing often at other problems', and the effort to overcome these difficulties had been great. 'Despair' is too strong a word for her response; rather it was high-spirited scepticism, a refusal to feel sorry for herself. But there remains much in what Brookner says to characterise Muriel's later life and work.

The heart of the matter has returned – on the wings of unbidden love and a greater openness to 'emotion, despair, and longing'.

The Only Problem, Muriel knew, was good. It would last – and she was right to look forward. The British (and Irish) reception three months later was distinctly warmer. Anthony Burgess and Frank Kermode gave it their imprimatur. To both, it was stimulating and profound. The book's allusiveness pleased the Joycean in Burgess: 'Heaven knows how many *sous-textes* the percipient critic will find here. Even odd throwaway lines have large resonance.'[40] Kermode, that pre-eminently percipient Spark critic, concentrated on one '*sous-texte*' in particular – the de La Tour painting – viewing it through the prism of biblical scholarship and, in a later essay, 'The Uses of Error', of art history. In the essay he explains that for centuries the subject of the painting had remained obscure. 'Some thought it represented the angel liberating St Peter from prison', others that it was an allegory, 'The Clothing of the Naked'. 'Only in 1935 did an art historian, taking account of the [...] potsherd, propose "Job Visited by his Wife".' Now the 'standard French study of de la Tour describes the woman's face as angry, her gesture as cruel; and the interaction of the glances is said to be one of conflict.'[41]

This visual image, then, is a perfect example of the 'nevertheless principle', of nothing ever being one thing, of meaning shifting inflexion through time, and Kermode touched on this in his review, linking Muriel's name with Henry James's. She was, he thought,

> [...] our best novelist. Although she is much admired and giggled at, I doubt if this estimate is widely shared. This may be because virtuosos, especially cold ones, aren't thought serious enough. Another reason is that although we have a special niche for certain religious novels, Mrs Spark's kind of religion seems bafflingly idiosyncratic. In fact she is a theological rather than a religious writer. [...] Treachery, adultery, even murder are aspects of the commonplace [...]. When somebody in *Territorial Rights* remarks, 'I don't know why the Catholic Church doesn't stick to politics, and keep its nose out of morals,' one can't

help feeling that part of the joke is that the author would, up to a point, agree.[42]

As a moralist, rather than as a moraliser, Muriel impressed her home-land with this book. Although Francis King found it 'unsatisfactory' and 'often slapdash',[43] Marghanita Laski thought it 'shapeless',[44] the *Jewish Chronicle* preferred the treatment of Job by a Jewish novelist (Edmund Season)[45] and the *London Magazine* pompously accused her of being 'strangely confused by the subjunctive',[46] elsewhere it was a triumph with both the intellectuals and the popular press, mentioned on numerous Christmas lists, and often selected as a 'Book of the Year'. Its omission from the Booker shortlist (Angela Carter's *Nights at the Circus* was another surprising casualty) prompted the *Guardian* to complain. Sales were satisfying but unspectacular. Her admirer, Anita Brookner, won the Booker with *Hotel du Lac*.

*

That July, between American and British publication, Hunter Davies interviewed Muriel in Italy for BBC Radio 4. It was like a regal audience offered to a republican. His sudden, sharp questions received oblique answers. Why had she come from Scotland to London? Why had she left England? Why had *The Only Problem* taken so long to write? ('I was interrupted [...] I think I was moving house.') One senses Davies's initial suspicion of her mythological status and his growing fascination. Discomfort, she said, was essential to development but

suffering is absolutely meaningless because [...] it retards us. There's nothing you can do when you have a God that comes blustering out of the whirlwind saying, 'I did this, I did that.' Well, I think that's comic, myself. [...] I think that absurdity might be a theme of the book. [...] It doesn't call for wit [...] the absurd situation that we're in as human beings.[47]

The state of exile was 'something one carries around with one' yet she did not consider herself an exile in Italy 'because I travel so much. I come and go whenever I want to.' Italy was a charming base, no more. She could be anonymous there. It 'offered more scope for meeting ordinary people if one is taken as an ordinary person'. That would be impossible in England. The conversation then took a turn which surprised Davies. One of the reasons for living in Italy, she stressed, was 'I have a job here. I'm a *New Yorker* correspondent. I write ... I've got a contract. It's a job. And the *New York Times* I write for. And that's a job.' 'But' Davies protested, 'your job is a writer, writing books. This is sort of secondary ...' 'No ... it's quite a good job to fall back on.' 'But you don't *need* to do it for the money, do you? 'I do.' 'You *don't*.' How could this be, he said, when *Brodie* was yet again being televised? At a few hundred dollars an episode, she explained, she would not get rich that way.[48]

Muriel was not joking about the need to seek other work. Davies was clearly under the impression that she was rich. In fact, she was not. The *New Yorker* took her stories and paid well but she had written nothing as their correspondent after they had rejected that Golda Meir piece. Nevertheless, the idea that it was a job she might 'fall back on' was important to her while she was looking to her next novel, *A Far Cry from Kensington*, to restore her popularity.[49] This it certainly did but in the meantime she needed to raise money in other ways, through journalism and a series of fierce enquiries about Macmillan's book-keeping. Having to instruct others in the proper conduct of their professions, Muriel wrote to Strutt, did rather waste one's time.[50]

This letter was written on 6 October 1984 when Strutt had just sent a press cutting about *Brodie* playing to packed houses in Manchester. No one else had thought to inform Muriel and she discovered that for ten years her share of the box-office receipts had been partly, and wrongly, paid to the original theatre, Wyndham's. This seems to have been the point at which she began to lose patience with her agent, Dorothy Olding. For some time, Muriel had been withdrawing her European business from Olding's firm, Harold Ober Associates. It was now Jardine who was hunting down rights and unpicking accounts. At this point, however, something extraordinary happened. After spending five days in her Roman hospital with bronchitis, Muriel had returned to San Giovanni at the end of October. She was in Rome again during

November when she suffered a serious accident. A card written to Ambrosiani in January explained that, while attempting to make her bed in the Vicolo del Gallo apartment, she had slipped, fracturing her entire ribcage on one side in fifteen places.

No sooner was Muriel out of hospital, then, than she was back in it and, recuperating in Vicolo del Gallo, felt trapped in Rome as blizzards swept Italy. The accident seems to have marked the point in her life beyond which the idea of an independent establishment faded. She had begun negotiations for a house in Como, but had been unable to agree a price. During 1984 she had sold the Nemi flat to two old ladies who had arrived with a large final payment in old banknotes smelling of mothballs,[51] and she was happy to be rid of the place. Her Rome flat seemed cramped. After her American trip that summer ('My brother has a lovely home: all push-button and gift-wrap'), she had been 'glad to get back to Tuscany and eat an egg from under the hen and a bit of ricotta warm from the goat'.[52] By May 1985, she was writing to Christine Brooke-Rose saying that she didn't know what she would do without Jardine,[53] and although Muriel continued to talk of moving back to England, it was during 1985 that San Giovanni really became home. Not that anyone would think so from her diary. The year 1985 saw them in Pisa, Portofino, La Spezia, Rome, Zurich, Essex, Paris, Florence, S. Margherita Ligure, Frankfurt, London; Essex twice, Rome and Florence several times – with San Giovanni only in between these constant flits, bowling along the roads of Europe in her Alfa Romeo. They were in Pisa and S. Margherita Ligure for a revision of Muriel's Mary Shelley book and an article Muriel was writing on Shelley's last house; in Paris being fêted by Fayard who had issued fifteen new contracts; in Rome to render unto Caesar; in Frankfurt and Zurich to meet her German publisher and for readings; in London for straight talks with Macmillan and to secure the Society of Authors' support. Essex was for relaxation with Strutt, Florence for dinner with the art historian John Pope-Hennessy. It was a formative year of endings and beginnings. Tiny Lazzari died on Christmas Eve; the blazing skirt of Halley's Comet raised Muriel's spirits.[54]

*

Mrs Lazzari was already in A *Far Cry from Kensington* as Milly Sanders, a direct, affectionate, portrait. (When the book was published in 1988 her family instantly identified her tricks of speech.) Muriel had last seen her in 1980. Now, here she was again, making an entrance with her exit, while another figure from that period had re-emerged. In Paris during April 1985, Muriel had found herself onstage at the British Council. Three French critics were discussing her work, the chairman sometimes turning his back to her. A member of the audience, irritated by this rudeness, stood up to ask the first question in an attempt to refocus attention on the guest of honour. Muriel's mask of polite boredom had instantly cracked as she recognised the voice: 'Christine!' – and so Brooke-Rose was invited to the dinner afterwards.[55]

Brooke-Rose was soon reading Muriel's Fayard translations ('I always feel the translations tend to "sweeten" my work'[56]), listing errors. But there was something else here beyond pragmatism and the pleasure of reclaiming a lost friend. Muriel enjoyed nothing better than to battle on behalf of neglected artists. Brooke-Rose was a professor at the University of Paris. As a critic she had a high reputation. As a novelist she had produced an impressive body of postmodern work, much of it then out of print. The clutter of academic life had dragged her away from creation. Her marriage had broken up. She longed to retire and to give her muse breathing space. In the meantime she was seeking a publisher to reissue her fiction. It was a subject close to Muriel's heart during her wrangles with Macmillan, and she not only encouraged Brooke-Rose to keep writing but also offered her somewhere to work.

Brooke-Rose had driven down to San Giovanni for a week under the blinding August sun and had left feeling – uncertain. In retrospect, she regarded her visit as a success. At the time, she was fearful that living alone might have rendered her fussy. Jardine had put her up in the guest room opposite the kitchen and their 'strange week together' evoked vivid memories for Brooke-Rose, 'locked away from the heat, writing under fans at different ends of the house, & going out to eat in the evening, or my preparing an over-rich salad dressing you didn't fancy, &

the bat, & the funny low bathroom [...].'⁵⁷ She was revising her new novel *Xorandor*, Muriel labouring at *Mary Shelley*.

Brooke-Rose had been taken about: to local restaurants, to Florence for dinner with David Pryce-Jones and to tea with Harold Acton. Both women cherished memories of shared hardships and support. Brooke-Rose recalled watching TV with Muriel when *Middlemen* was savaged by the pundits. Afterwards they had 'walked around Hyde Park [...], & you were almost more distressed than I was, & generally very nice about it. These flashes of memory about old friendships are very pleasant in one's old age.'⁵⁸ This was the spirit of their re-encounter; other, less enjoyable, Proustian moments were set aside. Muriel, for instance, had heard that information about her hallucinations had been supplied by Brooke-Rose to Maclean. Brooke-Rose believed that she and her ex-husband, Jerzy Peterkiewicz, had been summarily dropped once Muriel had become famous.

Both women, then, were simultaneously cautious of each other and delighted by this chance to start again. Sadly, the attempt foundered. Brooke-Rose had hoped to stay quietly at San Giovanni, talking, walking, catching up. But there seemed no way to engage with Muriel like this any more – and the smart Florentine life was Brooke-Rose's idea of hell. Walking in the garden of Acton's La Pietra, she had remarked, by way, she thought, of writer's fellowship, that she could never work in such a house. Muriel had replied with acid bonhomie: 'Thank heavens you don't have to' – and Jardine had found her guest equally difficult to please. '[Muriel] insisted on paying for everything,' Brooke-Rose recalled, 'treating me as a sort of poor relation, [...] it was generosity but it was also thoughtlessness. I mean [...] by then I was a full professor [...] it was all rather absurd. I should have contributed to expenses, and would have done.'⁵⁹ She felt uncomfortable about the way Muriel 'treated' Jardine, allowing her to do everything. Jardine saw it quite otherwise. Nevertheless, Muriel continued to write and to encourage. Unprompted, she approached the Hogarth Press on Brooke-Rose's behalf, vaunting her work. She admired her stamina as an artist.⁶⁰ If the friendship was dead, so be it.

*

Muriel wrote to Brooke-Rose in the spring of 1986 from that guest room opposite the kitchen. She had been working there all winter as it was the warmest place in the house, bored by the need to read through decades of scholarship to bring *Mary Shelley* up to date but nevertheless being meticulous.[61] It was March. Jardine was busy with the final checking. Betty T. Bennett, editor of Mary Shelley's *Letters*, had been employed as a scholarly authority. Muriel had only begun the project because the 1951 version, *Child of Light*, had never been published in America and had been pirated there as it had no Library of Congress registration. Mountainous correspondence had blocked most creative work and continued to do so for months. The revision was already a year late and did not appear until 1987, by which stage she had lost some of her affection for it. After all this labour, however, she did not expect her publishers to feel likewise. Dutton had offered enthusiasm, a decent advance and 15 per cent royalty. James Michie at Bodley Head was hesitant. The revisions, he suggested, were slight and the prospects for sales modest. He had greatly enjoyed the book but that was not the point. All he could offer was a more modest sum and 10 per cent. Muriel rejected this out of hand. She had met Michie the previous October and already had plans to replace him. Ten days later, Robin Baird-Smith had been invited to lunch at Terling where she was staying with Strutt.

Baird-Smith was Maclean's much-loved godson and Constable's bright young editorial director. Word had leaked out that Muriel was unhappy with Bodley Head. 'If you play your cards right,' Maclean had confided, 'you might get Muriel Spark.'[62] Baird-Smith was a Catholic. More importantly, though, he was a devoted admirer of her work. Nothing was arranged at that first meeting. Muriel kept him waiting until *A Far Cry* was complete and her agent could invite competitive bids. But Constable took a gamble, stumped up a large three-book advance and reeled in their big fish. Before long, Bodley Head was in trouble. Muriel had again jumped ship at precisely the right moment.

Dutton and Bodley Head published a collection of her stories in 1985 and 1987 respectively. Nineteen eighty-seven also saw Dutton offering

Mary Shelley. Reviews were good, often adulatory, the *Stories* meriting a front-page rave from David Lodge in the *New York Times Book Review*. This, it seems, was just the ammunition Muriel needed to continue her assault on Macmillan. The Bodley Head's *Collected Stories* contained only six previously uncollected pieces yet it was selling well. Why could Macmillan not reissue her novels and market them with equal energy? If they had no stomach for this, why could they not let them fall out of print and allow her to reclaim the rights? Into this three-year dispute Jardine entered with some vigour. At first she had corresponded as secretary – 'Muriel says', 'Muriel would be pleased'. Soon she began writing in her own voice, politely impatient and relentless. Dorothy Olding and Mary Pachnos (rights manager at Macmillan) must have dreaded her letters.

On the face of it, the accounts looked unfavourable to Muriel's case. Macmillan sent royalty statements which listed only unearned balances on post-*Mandelbaum* books. In 1983, for example, *The Takeover* and *Hothouse* had together sold only 334 copies in paperback, leaving a large debt. Penguin had sold 2,000 of *The Driver's Seat* and 1,500 of *Not to Disturb* but even more money was owing on them. It was the same story with *The Public Image* and *Territorial Rights*. On average, every year she sold 1,000–2,000 copies of every paperback novel and about 100 each of the hard-cover backlist. Up to and including *Mandelbaum*, these were 'paid out' and she received a small sum for each of these paperbacks, rather more for *Brodie*. There were other monies, of course, from spin-offs – audio-cassettes, translations, radio readings, adaptations (particularly Presson Allen's of *Brodie*), but by 1983 these did not amount to substantial sums. Fayard's fifteen contracts had helped considerably in this lean period. As for her later work, she was receiving nothing from Penguin, Granada or Macmillan, and with Losey's death in 1984, the screenplay of *The Takeover* had been killed. In her lifetime, there was never to be another film of her work: plenty of offers but no results. From her seventeen published novels she probably made little more than a middle-income professional salary each year. Driven by indignation on Muriel's behalf, Jardine demanded from Macmillan exact retail prices at time of sale, stock positions, accounts. Prices for the hardcover reprints arrived but the wrappers advertised them for sale at often double these figures, and misprints remained uncorrected.[63] Muriel asked Olding to renegotiate the contracts and was amazed when she saw no way to do this.

Olding and Macmillan were now alike in becoming the objects of Muriel's suspicion. During 1986 it emerged that for nine years 10 per cent of all her paperback income (including advances) had erroneously been sent to Ober. Muriel successfully billed Macmillan for this and 10 per cent compound interest, which heavily increased the repayment. With *Mary Shelley* about to appear in the States, and *Collected Stories* just out as her final book for Bodley Head, she went in for the kill. In February 1987 she wrote direct to Alexander Macmillan requesting reversion of rights.[64] Enclosed was a copy of a 1961 letter to her from Maurice Macmillan, Alexander's father, sent as a peace-offering when Muriel was threatening to leave them after *Brodie*. Maurice had stated that 'this firm has never [...] held an author to a contract [...] against that author's real interests or strongly held feelings.'[65] 'I do not think you personally would wish to challenge Maurice's promise to me,' she added. 'It dates back a long time [...] and I have been reasonable in considering it part of the contracts. Maurice [...] was head of the family publishing house, and I was right to trust his word.'[66]

Alexander (Viscount Stockton) took his time replying and, when he did, was amiable but resolute. It was impossible, he explained, to cancel contracts; she had misunderstood his father's letter, which referred to option clauses. He would be in Italy during August. Perhaps they could meet to discuss matters?[67] One might have expected a stiff response to this. But no: Muriel had another strategy. A delightful idea, she replied. She would be in England and Scotland from mid-July until about 10 August. After that she was free to welcome him and his family to lunch at Jardine's house. Her letter also contained some tough talking but between the invitation and the excoriation there nestled an olive branch: 'in the event of your surrendering the rights, one could arrange for compensation.'[68]

Compensation? Muriel must have swallowed hard before dictating that word but it was a wise move. Macmillan's agreed to talk terms. Clearly, she would never relent. Although Viscount Stockton failed to turn up in Tuscany, a process for final divorce was set in train. Muriel eventually handed over her spring royalties and some more, bought back the rights and a decree nisi was declared. It was money she could ill afford but it was soon earned back. For Muriel, though, the crucial matter was to be rid of this albatross. Macmillan represented an old life characterised in her view by their meanness and lack of belief in her. She was sixty-nine and had felt shackled to them for thirty years.

*

It was time for another massive restructuring. Paris with its enthusiasm for her work now attracted Muriel far more than London. During 1987 Jardine drove her there twice: once for Fayard interviews, once to pick up first prize for the Best Collection of Foreign Short Stories (Dutton edition). The Pompidou Centre delighted her. Nouvelle cuisine did not. Everything, though, seemed fresh. She now had an agent there, Michelle Lapautre, an elegant American. In June 1987 Bruce Hunter of David Higham Associates became her British agent and soon Muriel had a new American one, Georges Borchardt, whom she had met at Lapautre's Paris house. The deal with Constable was in place. Joe Kanon kept a watchful eye on her interests at Dutton where her literary editor was another intelligent and sensitive fan, William Abrahams. None of this charming crowd knew her well. They enjoyed her company and guarded her interests. That was enough. She flashed in and out of their lives. In England, there was Baird-Smith and Strutt; in America, Kanon; in Paris, Lapautre. And everywhere she travelled (usually excepting the States) Jardine accompanied her.

Muriel's phrase for San Giovanni was the 'work house', and they returned to it as to the still centre of a life otherwise in perpetual motion. Even when living there, they were frequently absent or entertaining: dashes to Florence for dinner with Acton, David and Clarissa Pryce-Jones, John Pope-Hennessy; eating out locally, alone together or visiting Jeffrey Smart or William Weaver; attending public functions in Florence, just eighty kilometres away. As ever, Muriel's diary appears to be solid with appointments – but it can be deceptive for, when busy on a book, she was rarely absent for more than two days. Work, as usual, came first. 'I'm just catching up with my letters after sitting at my desk some months without looking up,' she informed Brooke-Rose in June 1987. 'However the novel & Mary Shelley & several articles are all finished & I only have one little speech to write for Edinburgh before packing up for the summer.'[69]

The previous Christmas, Jardine had given Muriel a vast new desk in Tanganyika walnut. And Jardine, too, had updated her office: another new desk on which Muriel's 1960 Olivetti had been replaced by an IBM electric typewriter; a photocopier was installed. The earlier obstructions to travel (no regular house-sitters) had been removed by employing a cleaner and handyman, a local couple, Patrizia and Franco. By late 1987, Jardine was painting, Muriel correcting the proofs of *A Far Cry*, and both were running something like a family business, proud of their industry, rigorous over detail, long hours of labour balanced by sybaritic excursions. Had Muriel, then, at last settled? No. Nothing in her nature remotely approximated to being 'stationed' or even at rest. The dream of her own place with a mysterious garden remained, but she never had the time to search for it.[70]

Interviewers continued to try to box Muriel up – 'You are a Jew?' 'You are a feminist? – while Jardine left her free. Free to work. The back part of San Giovanni, being slowly restored by Jardine, a builder, and Franco as labourer, was approaching completion. Originally, Muriel had planned simply to move her books in there. They were still in Rome and she felt lonely without them. 'In the end, all one's books are reference books,'[71] she remarked rather sadly. But Jardine had infused life into the library idea, converting the new part of her house into a version of Muriel's dream: bedroom, bathroom, dining room, *salone* and two studies – all simply done but with immaculate taste. There was even a garden, practical rather than mysterious, but nevertheless beautiful, falling away beneath the windows towards the valley. Money was rolling in again, Muriel's reputation unassailable. She had no sooner returned from the prize-giving in Paris than she was informed that she had won the Saltire Society's Scottish Book of the Year Award for her short stories. This money, and that for the later T. S. Eliot Award in America, meant that she could buy a new car. Everything seemed set fair.

*

Baird-Smith was an excited young man. It would be helpful, he suggested, if she could come over for the launch of *A Far Cry* – and she agreed. January 1988 saw interviewers already arriving in Italy: John Mortimer for the *Sunday Telegraph*, Tim Parks for *Books & Bookmen*, Alan Jenkins for the *Sunday Times*. Baird-Smith dashed across to co-ordinate. By her seventieth birthday (1 February 1988), Muriel was exhausted. A new dress was ordered, new shoes. A raft of complex social and business arrangements in England was plotted in the diary. They were to leave on 8 March and to return around the 23rd. Muriel was to appear on Channel 4, BBC2, Radio 4 (twice) and Radio 3. Most important was the *Cover to Cover* TV programme to which A. J. Ayer, A. N. Wilson and Sebastian Faulks had been invited to discuss the novel with her. Ben Glazebrook, managing director of Constable, was to throw a party at the Garrick Club.

Muriel and Jardine were booked into the Stafford Hotel in London and planned to move on to Strutt's house at Terling. Off they set via Paris for business and for dinner with Lapautre. Between Paris and Boulogne, however, something happened. Baird-Smith arrived at the Stafford at 9.00 a.m. the next day to escort Muriel around the studios and was met by the hall porter who presented him with a telegram. It was brief and to the point. She had decided, she said, to cancel, due to circumstances beyond her control. He should not try to contact her. They had turned round and driven home. Viewers were told that ill-health had prevented her appearance but the guests knew this to be untrue. As usual with the mythological Spark, the truth was quite different and much simpler.

CHAPTER 19

Settling the Bill

1988–1992

Back at San Giovanni, Muriel wrote to Guy Strutt. To him alone she felt she owed an explanation. It saddened her, she said, that he was upset by her sudden change of plan. She had been travelling to England principally to see him. Blame was placed with Constable for their haggling over hotel expenses. In Paris she had received a telephone call from Baird-Smith urging yet another interview on her. It was all too oppressive. She felt she would not have been able to cope.[1] So she just went home.

Three months earlier, in the dining room of Arezzo's Hotel Continentale, Muriel had been in more convivial mood. Jardine had been beside her. Across the table sat John Mortimer and his sixteen-year-old daughter, Emily. Mortimer – later Sir John, the barrister, playwright and author of the Rumpole novels – knew how to conduct these interviews. It was like a family luncheon party rather than an interrogation. Had she ever been happy? he asked. 'Not for long. It's always been on, off, on, off. I mean, I sometimes think happiness is boring. Look at happy marriages, for instance. And I don't want to go to heaven if it means sitting looking at the Virgin Mary standing on a cloud for ever and ever. I may not have been happy but I've been very amused.'[2]

Mortimer's questions ranged casually across her entire life. Did she get on with her parents? 'Of course. They were my first audience.' Africa? 'I met the occasional chemist or priest or oddball I could talk to, but on the whole the white people were frightful. The black people weren't very nice either but I didn't blame them for that. I much preferred the birds, the beasts and the flowers.'[3] As a young writer, she said, her models had been Auden, Spender, MacNeice, Chaucer, Shakespeare and Marlowe. 'Milton's impossible. I can never get to the end of his sentences.' Virginia Woolf? 'A spoiled brat. All right, she committed suicide but she didn't have to take the dog with her.' 'But Muriel,' Jardine protested, 'how do you know [she] killed the dog?' On to Tiny Lazzari, presented in Mortimer's text as 'Milly', the name under which she appears in *A Far Cry from Kensington:* '[Tiny]'s husband was an organist at the Odeon. He sat at an organ which came up out of the ground all lit up, so [she] understood the life of an artist.' Religion? 'I joined the Church of England but I soon saw through *that:* it was so bounded by the British Empire. Then I became an Anglo-Catholic and went to a church in Queen's Gate all tricked out fit to dazzle the Pope. The vicar there preached this ridiculous sermon in which he said, "I am the Catholic authority in Queen's Gate!" I couldn't take that so I rang up a priest in Ealing. I go to church now but I leave before the sermon. I regard it as a mortal sin to listen to sermons.'[4]

Mortimer pressed her on her Catholicism. 'I noticed', she said, 'that you asked the two aunties, Runcie and Basil Hume, about the Holocaust [...]. Basil Hume should have said that it means God is: (a) good, or (b) evil, or (c) indifferent. But he didn't say that.' 'Which do you think He is?' 'I think He's a mystery. There's a passage by a mystic usually printed at the end of The Cloud of Unknowing which says that God is nothing that you think He is.' 'What do *you* think He is?' 'Sometimes I feel like agreeing with Dylan Thomas.' 'What did he say?' '"Oh God, thou art a bloody cat."'[5] 'Do you believe in hell?' 'I think hell is empty and all the devils are here. That's what it says in *The Tempest.* I believe in the spirit of life – that is really the Holy Ghost.'[6]

In retrospect, Edinburgh meant to her 'rationalism. Believing in a strong difference between right and wrong. Honesty of thought. The work ethic. [...] I went through all that.' 'The young', she remarked, looking at Mortimer's daughter, 'should sleep a lot and look beautiful.' Marriage? 'I might have made a good wife but not *very* good. I didn't have it in me to attract men for long.' Politics? 'Interest me, yes. But of course I'm an anarchist [...] all politicians simply want to manipulate people [...].'[7] Old age? Muriel had turned seventy the previous month and her response was to ignore it: 'It doesn't mean anything to me. It's just a number.'[8]

*

Muriel's failure to arrive in England did nothing to damage Constable's publicity campaign. True, her absence from the *Cover to Cover* programme probably released three of the contributors into franker commentary on A *Far Cry* than would otherwise have been possible. Only Sebastian Faulks was unequivocally in favour. Ruth Dudley Edwards found it 'delicious' but lacking 'moral point'. Polly Toynbee thought it good on the poverty of the 1950s' publishing world but something of a 'dim watercolour'. The '*pisseur de copie*' on whom the book hinged was only a minor Grub Street figure. Why expend so much energy on demolishing him? The philosopher Freddie Ayer agreed: 'I don't want to say it is a bad book, I want to say it is a slight book.'[9] Press reviews, however, were much more positive and, applauded as her funniest novel in years, A *Far Cry* shot into the best-seller lists. Reprinted even before release, it ultimately sold some 30,000 copies in the original hardback, and is still selling. Constable were jubilant.

Oddly (perhaps predictably) this success resulted from notices suggesting that A *Far Cry* was both hilarious and undemanding. It was, they said, a satire on publishers. Many concentrated on the advice dished out by the narrator, Mrs Nancy Hawkins. The best way to throw the income-tax authorities, we are instructed, is to send them a small, unexpected cheque for a precise amount. The best way to diet is to eat only half of each dish. The best way to write a novel is to imagine you are writing to a friend (Mortimer liked this one and often repeated it). For concentration one required a cat. For a successful relationship, it was wise to start severely and later ease off; for rheumatism, a banana a day (half a banana if you're following the diet). The women's magazine *She* was able to warn Spring Brides against marrying before seeing the fiancé drunk. The book was so full of Nancy's quotable bon mots ('I had a sense he was offering things abominable to me, like decaffeinated coffee or *coitus interruptus*')[10] that most reviewers simply laughed, listed them, and left it at that. Only five pieces – by Claire Tomalin, Alan Bold, Patricia Craig, Peter Kemp and Anita Brookner – attempted literary criticism.

'This is a novel about a hate affair,' Tomalin began. 'It is told with a sort of black good humour and a boldness approaching violence.'[11] 'For [Spark],' Bold wrote, 'nothing human is sacred: she confronts the reader with the sustained paradox that life is a ridiculous imitation of art. [...] Telling her tale in flashbacks [Nancy] reserves her passages of lyrical prose for the silence that sustained her through sleepless nights.'[12] Craig noted the pun of the title 'which is at the centre of her story: the cry of someone on the brink of suicide.'[13] Hatred and violence, then, controlled, distilled; insomnia, silence and reflection amid the world's noise; the self-conscious banality of Nancy's voice – casual, acerbic, disconcertingly amiable – begin to suggest the book's complications, and its relation to Muriel's own anxieties during the 1950s. As Kemp suggested: 'Larger than life, [Nancy] makes an apt narrator for [...] the second of Muriel Spark's instalments of autobiographical extravaganza.'[14]

Kemp was a seasoned Muriel-watcher. As the undergraduate living across the road from her in Baldwin Crescent, as the lecturer who had written a subtle critical book on her work, now as a senior reviewer for the *Sunday Times*, he had always seized upon her work, and the affinities between author and narrator immediately struck him: 'time spent in southern Africa, a brief marriage that has come to grief, resourceful potterings on the fringes of the literary world. Catholicism is an especially prominent and shared factor.'[15] In fact, the parallels are not exact. Nancy's religion is Anglo-Catholicism. *A Far Cry* is set in 1954–5 just after Muriel had abandoned St Augustine's, the Anglo-Catholic church in Queen's Gate, after her reception into the Roman Catholic Church and her hallucinations, while she was living in St Jude's Cottage and writing *The Comforters*. Because the reception and the crisis are omitted from the heroine's life, a gap opens between the author and her fictional alter ego. Nancy's experience is less intense than Muriel's. It has been transformed into another comedy in which the female lead is never damaged, only amused. Even so, Kemp was surely right: *A Far Cry* was, like *Loitering with Intent*, a form of autobiography.

Promoting *Loitering* in a rare TV interview five years earlier, Muriel had denied any connection between Fleur Talbot and herself. Frank Delaney, her questioner, was puzzled by this. 'But she did a lot of things which I suspect you must have done in your time.' 'Yes.' 'So therefore how is it not autobiographical?' 'It wasn't autobiographical because she didn't do the things, she did the *sort* of things.' Pause. Laughter from the audience. 'That's unfair.' 'It isn't really, because in a court of law [...], in fact, this character did not exist. [...] *I* did not do these things that I say she did in the book.' Delaney left it at that with, 'Yes, I'm surprised you didn't call it *Up the Garden Path*' – and passed on.[16] But it was an important exchange. For while it was true that literally the events of that novel were fictitious, it was also true that they accurately represented the spirit of crucial emotional events in Muriel's life.

The same thing applied to *A Far Cry*. 'Clearly', Brookner wrote, 'this is all based on personal reminiscence and may even constitute a true story, or rather reconstitute it.'[17] Milly's lodging house, supposedly in Kensington, is an image of Tiny Lazzari's house in Camberwell. The Ullswater Press is Peter Baker's Falcon Press. Mackintosh & Tooley resemble Macmillan & Co. Muriel, like Nancy, took control of her insomnia, indeed encouraged it with Dexedrine, and enjoyed the 'wide-eyed midnights' when the day's racket became a presence in its absence, 'auditory effects' tape-spooling in her 'mind's ear', 'noises off'. 'I kept my peace,'[18] Nancy says, and this simple statement encapsulates the novel's essential theme: how she extracted herself from chaos and tri-umphed over the white noise surrounding her, which comes in par-ticular from Hector Bartlett's continual disparagement.

Muriel's research for *A Far Cry* had been careful. Strutt had sent information on rationing and land girls, had found someone to scour newspapers for the rise and fall of the fraudulent Peter Baker. The novel is precisely dated with historical events: Roger Bannister's four-minute mile; *Lucky Jim;* the advent of espresso bars; the Sutherland portrait of

Churchill, later destroyed by his wife; Billy Graham; Nasser; London shows. These touches add an air of plausibility but also function as symbols. Bannister's run is set alongside Baker's speeding to self-immolation; the positioning of the book at the *end* of rationing reflects the transfiguration of Nancy's life from cramped austerity to spiritual freedom; the destruction of the portrait parallels the reinvention of her public image: fat and motherly to chic and sexy. The novel, Kemp thought, 'incorporates two versions of Muriel Spark [...]. Nancy, the robust, quirkily commonsensical Jill-of-all-trades, represents her earlier self. Emma Loy, a formidably poised and successful novelist [...] is her later avatar.'[19]

This was perceptive. For, although Muriel had never been as fat as Nancy, as a young woman she had been anxious about her weight. Nancy is at first called 'Mrs Hawkins', as Muriel was called 'Mrs Spark', and is regarded as a 'tower of strength' rather than as an attractive and talented woman. The change to the use of her first name (originally 'Agnes') comes with her svelte new figure. Details have been altered. Nancy is taller than Muriel; she is not an artist but an editor; Muriel had not been a strapping land girl; she had never married a medical student and lived happily ever after. Nancy's loathing of Bartlett, the *pisseur de copie*, does not correspond to Muriel's feelings about Stanford in 1954–5. At that time she was still considering marriage to him; he was her chief support and collaborator – or seemed to be.

Few of the London literati, however, can have doubted the object of Muriel's attack when she created the *pisseur*. Stanford's physical characteristics were reversed. He was short, thin, bald, wide-mouthed, where Bartlett is tall, chubby, wears his red hair *en brosse* and has a baby mouth. Bartlett's absurd books and articles were not Stanford's. The speech mannerisms and literary style, the yellow tie and check shirt, were. Stanford's unpublished autobiography was 'Goodbye Bohemia'. Bartlett entitles his memoirs *Farewell, Leicester Square*. Without replicating anything, she caught the tone of Stanford's literary work. 'His writings writhed and ached with twists and turns and tergiversations,' Nancy tells us, 'inept words, fanciful repetitions, far-fetched verbosity and long,

Latin-based words.'[20] She, conversely, pares back prose to its anorexic minimum: 'I worked on them meticulously; words, phrases, paragraphs, semi-colons.'[21] She removes exclamation marks and italics used for emphasis, excises sentimentality.

Character and prose style were often linked in Muriel's mind. 'Tergiversations' was a precise word with both stylistic and moral connotations: 'turning one's back on, forsaking [...]; abandonment, apostasy, renegation' and 'turning in a dishonourable manner from straightforward action or statement'.[22] Bartlett's prose reveals him not only as pompous but also as a traitor. Nancy feels claustrophobic in his presence, believes he is always trying to use her, senses 'a fear, a premonition, of the dangers of knowing him'.[23] He is locked in the material world, in mankind's time; she escapes him, evanescent in God's time, scatheless. All this corresponded exactly with Muriel's later feelings about Stanford, and was ingeniously worked into the novel's style. As Kemp puts it: 'Contemptuous of the chronological as obscuring the crucial fact of eternity, she curves and interlocks temporal perspectives through flashbacks, glances forward and unusual tenses into an entity. In the opening paragraphs of this novel Nancy's mind, alive with memories as she lies happily sleepless in the small hours of the 1980s, seems simultaneously to inhabit the past and the present.'[24]

The novel, then, is Proustian. It opens with the narrator, like Swann, in bed reflecting on the images flashed up on memory's screen, 'listening to the silence, prefiguring the future, picking out of the past the scraps I had overlooked, those rejected events which now came to the foreground, large and important, so that the weight of destiny no longer bore on the current problems of my life [...].'[25] For Nancy, this is not an artistic process. She does not, like Fleur, become a novelist. Nevertheless, these night-watches were the forge of her imagination, the autobiography we are reading is a work of art, and Peter Owen, who saw people he knew in this novel, recalled Muriel staying up all night writing *Robinson* when she was his editorial assistant in 1956–7, and coming in the next morning, dog-tired, to be 'the best bloody secretary' he had ever had.

Although *A Far Cry* does not draw directly on Muriel's 1954 hallucinations and religious conversion, both are there implicitly. Nancy is sad and 'touchy', depressed and in need of 'some compelling charm'.[26] In a magnificent lyrical passage we see her on the top decks of London buses feeling like Lucy Snow in *Villette* and sharing her 'state of hallucination'. Nancy is obsessively, aimlessly cruising the capital, listening in to the intimate conversations of other passengers as though trying, and failing, to make sense of the cacophony. She is between jobs, sacked for refusing to eat her words about Bartlett, experiences 'a throb and a choking hysteria in the London voices [...]'. Barmaids' lips appear too red. She is 'tempted to reflect that [her] diet had the same effect as a drug [...]'[27] but soon realises what is really wrong. It is not that she is too fat. It is not the diet. Indeed, it is the diet that changes her life, releases her. No, it is Hector Bartlett. It is the redundancy that he produces. Nancy hisses '*Pisseur de copie*' at him as Muriel did to Stanford throughout this novel. Students copied Stanford's remarks about her as though passing on a contagious disease. She saw him as a blight on her early life. Researching her autobiography, she discovered that he had been doing a regular small trade in her private papers. How had he got hold of them? There seemed to her to have been only one opportunity: when she had fallen ill, retired to St Jude's Cottage in 1954–5, and he had 'kindly' offered to clear her room.

The last scene of the novel is set thirty years later in a restaurant. Although unnamed, it resembles La Torre di Gargonza, where Muriel herself often dined, just outside the walls of the Castillo di Gargonza near Monte San Savino, overlooking the Val di Chiana: elegant and discreet, a far cry from bedsit Kensington. Nancy is now happily married to William and no longer subject to the snootiness of gentlemen publishers for being 'Ordinary Class',[28] no longer 'Mrs Hawkins'. She is on holiday, sitting on the terrace in warm sunshine, a woman who regularly travels to Italy, is integrated there and among friends. William has disappeared to make a telephone call and she goes in alone to pay the bill. As she turns to leave she hears an English voice hooting about 'a wealth of wild flowers': Bartlett, whey-faced, white-haired and still hectoring in clichés. They recognise each other. Surrounded by his travelling companions at the bar, he backs away. '*Pisseur de copie,*' she hisses – and walks out. 'Did you settle the bill?' William asks her. 'Yes,' she replies.[29] That was precisely it. Nancy's history is a revenge comedy, a 'novel about a hate affair'. Bartlett is misplaced here, out in the cold; she is at home, justified in the sunshine. She has settled the account, as Muriel had, and was soon to do more directly in *Curriculum Vitae*.

*

Just three months after Muriel's aborted publicity tour, she was buying a Manhattan apartment. It was a spur-of-the-moment decision. She still owned the Vicolo del Gallo flat in Rome but New York offered an altogether more exciting prospect for a pied-à-terre. William Weaver, the renowned musicologist and translator, a Tuscan neighbour and friend, had bought a studio apartment in a new six-storey building: Perry Street and Seventh, West Village, just round the corner from the Village Vanguard jazz club. The idea immediately appealed to Muriel. It was not only in the artists' quarter, it was also small, smart, secure and bare: one large room and a bathroom with a whirlpool bath.[30]

Why New York after Muriel had fled the place twenty years earlier, and when her life with Jardine had become so integrated? Certainly, with Weaver, William Shawn and Joe Kanon nearby, it promised pleasure. No publisher understood her better than Kanon. As a young man he had worked with Maclean in London. When Maclean was approaching retirement, Kanon sensed that he was being passed a jewel. She was *sui generis* to him, the best:

> [...] more pleasant to work with than any number of writers that I can think of, in some part because [she] is never insecure about the work. [...] She pleases herself. If she thinks it's good, it is good. [...] When you work with someone who is really wonderful it makes for an easier experience. [...] If you're her publisher, you're also in a position of trust because you're taking care of the thing that's most important.[31]

There was no interference on either side. She left publicity to him. He left the writing to her.

Kanon recalled their first meeting, again at the Hotel Continentale, sitting outside with his new wife, Jardine, Robin and Pavoncino, Muriel charming and unpretentious. When Robin declined her ice-cream, Muriel leaned forward: 'Well, if you're not going to eat it ...' The dog required a lot of attention. It was a family party again, as with Mortimer, who also became a friend. Kanon was struck by how closely she corresponded to his imagined image of her. It was the voice. 'If you've read the books, you've really met her. This is not a personality that's recessive in the work. [...] I know literally the sound of her voice. But I think people who have not met her have actually heard her without knowing it. It's a very clear-cut personality and it comes through in the prose.' Socially, there would be 'wonderful moments when if she sees that you have picked up on something she's noticed, there's almost a conspiratorial look that will pass between you. [...] She appreciates the fact that you've noticed and it's as if you share a secret. She's incredibly observant. [...] I've never had a dull moment with Muriel.'[32]

On his retirement from publishing, Kanon became a best-selling novelist. He also became one of Muriel's literary executors. Although he rarely saw her, he never felt that she was far away as she was often on the phone. He associated her both with jewels and asceticism. When she dressed up, he thought, she did so to please herself, yet she was not vain: 'truly an intellectual', someone constantly engaged in a supercharged mental process. Seeing her once at a party amid Tuscan expatriates, he wondered how she could bear the small talk. Somehow, though, she remained eternally separate, unique. Her proper habitat, he felt, was that Trastevere flat built for entertaining on the grand scale, overlooking the Tiber. It came as no surprise to him that she bought the Manhattan apartment. What did surprise him was that she never used it. It lay empty, like the Roman place, waiting.

Ten days in New York was all she needed to complete the deal, arrange for services, buy a telephone, furniture, blinds. Even then, she stayed in Weaver's flat and ate out every night, Kanon and Shawn separately in attendance. On 29 April she flew back to Italy: 'Economy,' Penelope had written in the diary, 'Ambassador' Muriel inserted, deleting the earlier entry. There was something about maintaining a Manhattan studio which was in keeping with her mythological status. It was a public ornament like her Cartier diamond wristwatch. But there was pragmatism too: an excellent investment for her old age. It did not matter if she never lived there. It did not matter that she had to pay monthly condominium fees. Its real-estate price escalated more rapidly than the outgoings and she could (and did) let it. All that mattered was that it was there: a bolt-hole should she need it, a source of possible future pleasure. 'Please don't talk of "a house to end your days",' she wrote to her old schoolfriend, Frances Cowell, three years later. 'How do you know? Every day brings new discoveries.'[33]

*

American reviews of *A Far Cry* were excellent and it sold there as well as in the UK. She could relax a little, settle to contemplating her infancy for *Curriculum Vitae*. The rest of 1988 was spent on that, hovering slowly into her past, piling up details. In October she put down her pen for a fortnight and went with Jardine for her first and last cruise (a *Sunday Times* commission) aboard a large ship, the *Orient Express:* Venice – Athens – Istanbul – Ephesus – Patmos – Olympia.[34] But she was soon back at work. Accumulating the fragments of her childhood was at this stage a distinct pleasure. It was the only period of her life about which she could feel intensely nostalgic. School. Holidays. Grandmother's caustic wit. Industry and security, protection, jokes, muddling through, looking forward, dreaming. 'He worked terribly hard, my father,' she recalled. 'And he did a lot of overtime [...]. He needed it for his family. He bought me a [...] fairy cycle. It was £3. He had to earn that money. Almost a week's pay. He had to save it up – for me.'[35] She was his pet. Such memories were precious. A picture of her, plump and happy aboard that bike appeared in the book. In *Curriculum Vitae* she played down the aspects of Edinburgh she had needed to escape: her mother, her brother, the Jewish community, provincialism, high teas, loveless alliances, and a kind of cautious, maidenly, one-track propriety. Her son, who still lived in the flat in which she was born, came to symbolise everything that had made her leave. Nothing much was said of him. He seemed to be in debt. She thought him feckless; his orthodoxy worried her. She had always tried to live within her means. It was this which had allowed her the freedom to be unorthodox.

Five years earlier, in 1983, Robin had thrown up his job in the Civil Service, taken private lessons in drawing and painting, attended evening classes at Edinburgh College of Art, and in 1984 had enrolled for a four-year full-time course. Graduating in 1987 with an Honours degree from Heriot-Watt University, he had won a scholarship and exhibited at the Royal Scottish Academy Summer Exhibition. The following year saw him exhibiting there again and in County Wexford and Aberdeen, winning another scholarship, and establishing a reputation as a portraitist of Jewish worthies.

Muriel usually applauded those who followed Gauguin's example. She had followed it herself. But her son, she felt, was not Gauguin and she suspected ulterior motives: a flavour of competition ('Anything you can do ... '), a desire to cash in on her fame. It seems not to have occurred to her that his desire to become an artist was a genuine passion perhaps connected with his craving for her approval. Instead, she saw the problem as twofold: he was fifty and lacked talent. In his alternative career she offered him no encouragement. It was difficult, she thought, to know how to help him. She could not afford the large sums it seemed to her he needed without endangering her own livelihood and independence.[36] And, as it happened, she was wise to be cautious about money. Over the next eighteen years she had to spend huge amounts on hospital bills.

*

After completing the first chapter of *Curriculum Vitae*, probably in early 1989, Muriel switched her attention to a new novel. Strutt had visited during May, comfortable and amusing as always, with his crossword puzzles and encyclopaedic knowledge. Muriel had just bought a shiny new Alfa ('Twin Spark'), her first air-conditioned car. Soon she was zooming to Paris in it for Fayard's launch of *A Far Cry* and queuing with Jardine for an hour in freezing rain for the Gauguin exhibition. The business side of the excursion entailed another round-table talk at the

British Council. She listened, one reporter noted, 'with her mouth drawn down at the corners like a clown's, while her *oeuvre* [was] explained to her [...].' Then came the questions.

Did she think of herself as a British writer? 'I am a Scottish writer,' she replied. 'I think one is what one is by formation. The point of view is Scottish, it is an Edinburgh point of view. And not only Edinburgh, it is Morningside.' Again, she insisted that she was a poet. 'Being a poet means looking at life as verbal art. "Naming a thing. Naming a thing precisely."' The supernatural in her work? She liked to include it 'as almost part of natural history, almost part of nature so there's no abrupt line between the natural and the supernatural. That's quite difficult. I haven't done it recently because normal life seems to me infinitely mysterious. Just every day is an infinitely mysterious affair.' Her current work? A novel on contemporary London, a frightening place, as unscrupulous as New York but more obscurely so. 'The whole general feeling is not on the surface where you can immediately pick out that's a crook and that's a cutthroat. No, these are people in ordinary society having a lovely dinner.'[37]

The novel was *Symposium*. Baird-Smith pleaded with her to change the title. Naturally, she refused. Naming things precisely was her business. There was magic in names, and everything sprang from the title where fiction was concerned. But this one was dragging. It was promised for 31 December 1989 and by the end of July she was getting nervous as its harmonies remained unsettled. After Paris in May, it had been London, Edinburgh and Terling in July. In London she had discussed *A Far Cry* on *Woman's Hour*. In Edinburgh she had unveiled a memorial to Robert Louis Stevenson. At Terling she had relaxed with Strutt. Back in Tuscany the heat had pushed all work into early mornings and evenings while during the day, both on diets, Muriel and Jardine wandered the house or just sat still, reading among the sleepy cats.[38]

Late August and September saw constant dramas: thunderstorms, snakes brought into the house by one of the cats; finally a hurricane with Penelope dashing from room to room slamming windows just in time against the torrent as though in mid-Atlantic. The stove caught fire, the fridge packed up, the car broke down and was then smashed about by hailstones. Tuscany's olive, wine and vegetable crop was badly damaged. Amid all this, Muriel bought six new champagne glasses and ignored the chaos. As the Berlin Wall came down in November, the first chapter of *Curriculum Vitae* was published in the *New Yorker*. She had never received such a fan mail for a short piece. Early December saw her in New York again for a fortnight. Christmas came and went, and missing *Symposium*'s deadline, she arranged a two-month extension.

In *Symposium*, everything centres on a dinner party given by an unmarried couple: Hurley Reed, an American Catholic painter, and Chris Donovan, a rich Australian widow. Most of the other characters are their guests or servants. Hurley and Chris have cohabited for years and this couple came as close to an image of a contented union as Muriel had so far dared venture. She had touched on it in *Mandelbaum* and *A Far Cry* but only distantly, offering parodic happy endings with sterilised gloves. Temperamentally she was herself a bachelor, sceptical of romantic love. But marriage was much on her mind as she contemplated her parents' relationship. They had married, she once remarked to me, because they found each other sexually attractive – which was healthy, good for the children, and infinitely preferable to the starched propriety of so many Edinburgh parents. On the other hand, as Hurley amusingly argues, '"[...] it is possible, and in fact 'imperative', for a Catholic [...] to believe in divorce between people who have been in love, the marriage vows being made in a state of mental imbalance [...]."' The 'vows of love-passion', he insists, '"are like confessions obtained under torture. Erotic love is a madness."'[39] Muriel's letters echo these views,[40] and *Symposium* is, like much of her later work, about love. Hurley and Chris love each other asexually and live together on the understanding that neither should compromise the other's freedom. But the Aids pandemic has rendered all partners suspicious of each other. Everyone is potentially infected by a chain of previous lovers: another twist in the problem of liberty / independence/ infiltration.

Although Muriel liked men in general, or could like them if they were charming – it boosted morale[41] – she could no longer love them. In her private life the necessary touches of charm were provided by Kanon, Strutt and Acton, each of whom she saw perhaps three times a year, and by her public life of interviews, business and parties. But she could put down her hand in that game whenever she wished and return to the 'work house', happiest at her desk with the exact manipulation of words, long periods of creation interspersed by simple meals and laughter round the kitchen table. Outdoor cats came and went through the window. She felt at home again with the birds, the beasts and the flowers, more easily touched by the death of an owlet falling from its nest than by her son's troubles.

*

Nineteen eighty-nine had seen two changes to improve conditions at San Giovanni. The renovation of the back part of the house was nearing completion and Muriel bought a fax machine. When the latter arrived, she stayed up all that night playing with it. It seemed miraculous: instant, accurate communication and the promise of huge savings on postage and time. It was also the perfect instrument of discrimination. There was only one number for both telephone and fax. She rarely heard anything beyond the ringing tone. None of these attempted communications was answered as telephone calls. Questions came through in writing, responses could be carefully considered, accurate records maintained. Muriel kept the valuable originals of her letters and kept herself to herself more effectively than ever. At the same time, it was like having a private telegraph service. For those with whom she wished to be in touch, replies would come back within minutes.

The two-month extension was all Muriel needed to complete *Symposium*, and by mid-February 1990 she was approaching the end of what had been an unusually difficult composition. Although most social life had been cancelled, the eighteen-year-old Frances Stonor-Saunders, later the historian of the Cold War, had been to stay and, by the end of May, after a quick tour of Spain and France, Muriel was back, reading proofs. Forest fires raged in the nearby countryside as she and Jardine waited for the book's launch in September and sweated to organise the huge library that had finally arrived from Rome. Gigantic packages littered the house, ready to be moved into Muriel's new quarters. In the car, being mended six feet up on a garage ramp in Monte San Savino, she sat beside Jardine sketching a play. Interviews were planned. The novel was being read on BBC radio to coincide with publication. Muriel's new lamps and a wool mattress were due for delivery. Heatwave. Exhaustion. Exhilaration. But Muriel did not stop. Pressing on with her autobiography, due the following July, she was chafing to escape. Not that she had any intention of being in England to assist Constable to sell her book. No, the necessary getaway was in October with Penelope's visiting cousins: Urbino, Ravenna (for the museums), and finally Venice for the Titian exhibition; then back to Florence for an exhibition of portraits at the Uffizi: 'I have a special interest in portrait-painting as touching almost on the novelist's activity. Penelope must see it, of course, as she has been doing portraits over the past years.'[42]

British reviews of *Symposium* were generally good. *The Times* had complaints: a book of two halves, it felt, the first superb, the second stirring no emotion, offering no insight, superficial.[43] But most were pleased and it entered the best-seller lists. 'The prevailing mood is urbane,' wrote Candia McWilliam. '[...] No living writer handles the tension between formality of expression and subversiveness of thought more elegantly.'[44] The theme of this 'extremely clever and highly entertaining novel', according to Penelope Lively, was 'wickedness'.[45] Even Francis King could say that although it was 'not great literature', it was 'great fun'[46] – which, if not good for reputation, was good for sales. There was a slight sense of disappointment after *A Far Cry*. Unequivocal 'raves' were rarer this time. It was again passed over for the Booker Prize and although shortlisted for the Scottish Saltire Prize, failed to win. Nevertheless, it was cruising nicely and the Americans liked it even better: excellent advance notices followed by plaudits in *Time* magazine, the *Washington Post*, *New York* and the *Los Angeles Times;* only one panning, by the *New York Times Book Review*.[47] Muriel now had her club of devoted British and American admirers who together would buy 40–60,000 hardbacks while thousands more waited for the softcover reprint. Her publishers would not make a fortune out of her but they could not lose. Why, then, does she appear somewhat gloomy in her correspondence at this time? There was illness and a nagging pain in her hip. There were annoying epistolary confrontations with Professor Norman Page and with Hilary Spurling's publishers, a falling out with George Armstrong, all of which we shall come to. But perhaps the inability of the critics to engage with the allusive structure of *Symposium* also had something to do with her mood. Scarcely anyone dealt with the title.

Plato's *Symposium* is a dialogue with Socrates about the nature of love and its delusions. Socrates relates what a wise woman, Diotima, has told him: that Love is 'neither beautiful nor good, for beauty and goodness are the things he lacks, and it is because he lacks them that he desires them. [...] Love [...] is really a demon or demigod, the mediator between gods and men [...].'[48] The dinner party in Muriel's *Symposium* parallels this dialogue. Lord Suzy (a loquacious bore) opens it by declaring that the recent burglary of his house is rape. It is not a rape, we learn, merely the loss of property. Thus we enter the discussion of spiritual good. 'According to some mystics,' says Margaret Damien, 'the supreme good is to divest yourself of all your best-loved possessions.'[49] As an ideal, this notion is given some weight in the novel. Hurley goes to great lengths to rid himself of a consignment of unwanted furniture, just as Muriel had gone to great lengths to pack and ship her literary manuscripts to the University of Tulsa. The freedom of the artistic mind is associated with isolation from worldly goods, the freedom of women connected to St Uncumber, and the problem of how to live independently without losing love focuses the whole debate.

Nevertheless, there is something fishy about Margaret, the initial proposer of this (Platonic and Christian) train of thought. She has no ideas beyond the mundane. Propelled by greed, she fakes up the good girl to seduce William while she plans to kill his mother, Hilda, to inherit her fortune. Living in the real world, the novel suggests, one must guard against despoliation by the envious and all those demons emptied out of hell (including Love). Margaret is perhaps the demon that is Love for there is also something fascinating about her. Although her allusion to the mystics may be hypocritical, she is more alive to paradox than Lord Suzy or even the kindly William. She is seen as a witch with her red hair, and indeed sticks pins in dolls. Her power alienates her from her family. She has an unnerving capacity for being close to serious accidents and she does not suffer from 'Stockholm syndrome': 'when you're so grateful to the man that's holding you prisoner just because he treats you better sometimes than the other times or than other people. Then you actually take an affection for the one that knocks you about least.'[50] She is in the driver's seat, an independent woman, another artist-figure, a creator of scenarios.

So, we have a problem. Plato's *Symposium* suggests that the search for truth is a form of love, for philosophers are lovers of wisdom. It is the desire to celebrate what is beautiful in body or soul. The quest for fame is a form of this in that it is a desire to live permanently as an immaculate image in the cultural memory. The love of art and of decent government are other forms. It is close to classical aesthetics: the disciplined contemplation of the beautiful draws the intellect upwards towards the conception of Absolute Good, and that supreme, ineffable beauty is, by implication, God. But while Muriel's *Symposium* discusses this, it is surely not, as many critics supposed, simply a satire on the rich. It is a contemplation of a paradox dear to her heart: that while the love of God in Christian teaching cultivates poverty, charity and obedience, the love of beauty is more easily pursued by the rich.

Looked at through the other end of the philosophical telescope, the love of beauty and possession per se is clearly madness. Sanity depends upon being able to cope with the inevitability of total loss ('Never own anything that you can't afford to lose'). There was no resolution to this conundrum as there was none to the nature of God. But perhaps this was the point of the novel. The admirable Hilda believes in destiny but cannot foresee her own. She is murdered randomly, outside the plot, as it were, of Margaret's or her own intentions, as the crème brulée is being served. Metaphorically, she is served up as another example of what cannot be known. The novel is prefaced by two quotations, one from Lucian's *Symposium*, one from Plato's. Plato's tells us that the geniuses of comedy and of tragedy are identical, Lucian's that 'the party was finally broken up by the shedding of blood.'[51] Both suggest that the search for truth is fraught with contradictions: comedic and tragic notions of integration and disintegration are relative to the point of view; harmonious discussion is never far from aggression. As a novelist Muriel could deal with these issues abstractly. As an autobiographer, she sometimes found them taking alarmingly concrete form.

*

'Truth', she wrote in *Curriculum Vitae*, 'by itself is neutral and has its own dear beauty',[52] and the protection of that beauty was closely allied in 1990 to the protection of her property – intellectual, psychological and material. Between the British and American publication of *Symposium* she wrote a letter to the press. Judy Sproxton had reviewed Norman Page's recent book on Muriel's fiction.[53] It was a favourable piece but Muriel wished to inform the public that while she 'naturally appreciate[d] all intelligent attention to [her] work', the book contained biographical errors. Page, she said, had never consulted her. Certain 'previous publications purporting to describe my early life are wildly and maliciously inaccurate'. In future, therefore, 'the interests of scholarship' would be best served if 'scholars and thesis writers simply applied to me for verification of biographical details (c/o Constable Publishers [. . .]).' She did not, of course, say that she rarely answered such questions. What she was prepared to offer, however, was the Authorised Version. 'My autobiography, at present in preparation, should amply put the record straight.'[54] The tone was mild and reasonable, revealing only a dash of indignation. The tone of her private letter to Page shocked him.

Poor Professor Page thought he had written a complimentary monograph. He was not noted as a controversialist. But he had said that she had owned Swedish furniture, that the phrase '*pisseur de copie*' 'appears not to exist in French' (an idea suggested by Freddie Ayer in the *Cover to Cover* programme), and worst of all, had referred to Stanford's *Inside the Forties* (1977). Page replied, courteous and apologetic. Muriel, however, had already faxed Macmillan's sister firm, St Martin's Press in New York, threatening court action should any American edition repeat the 'defamations'. Within two months Page and she were in correspondence and she was more amiable. Stanford was the problem, she explained, setting himself up as an authority on her and getting everything wrong. For her own memoirs she had resolved 'not to rely merely on my good memory, but to write nothing that cannot be proved by documentary evidence or by living witnesses'.[55]

Strutt was already on the job, checking the founders of Edinburgh schools, trying to trace Muriel's second cousin, Valerie Bradshaw. And Muriel, too, was busy compiling her 'autobiographical box', as she termed it. The daughter of the family's former lodger Professor Rule had made contact via the *New Yorker*. (Mrs Rule had taught Muriel to read.) Just before her first Exocet letter to Page, she had written speculatively to Frances Cowell, the girl who had shared those extra-curricular expeditions with Muriel and Miss Kay: Pavlova, Masefield, theatre, cinema. Cowell had left Gillespie's aged sixteen to attend secretarial college and had seen Muriel perhaps three times in the intervening fifty-six years. Muriel nevertheless had faith that this friend would still be there and still be her friend. Posting a letter to a thirty-year-old address, she found her.[56]

The correspondence that ensued reveals a quite different character from the tough-talking literary celebrity Page had encountered. To Cowell she was gentle and generous, at first swapping stories of their children's progress. Cowell, somewhat timid and conventional, was not to be troubled with the Robin saga – not yet at least. Chatter about Edinburgh was spiced with polite enquiries. Which school house was Frances in? How did the paraphrase of Psalm 121 in the Church of Scotland Bible ('I will lift up mine eyes to the hills') open? Frances had once written her a poem and had presented a 'tiny waxen laurel wreath' which Muriel still treasured. The poem read:

> Though on fame's dizzy heights you stand,
> Though you climb ladders without end,
> Please don't forget me for I am
> Your dear and most devoted friend.

'I must say,' Muriel added, 'I cherish this more than those doubtful honours. And I must also say that "fame's dizzy heights" are more often than not a great pain in the neck.'[57]

*

As the Gulf War raged, Muriel was now comfortably settled into her new rooms at the back of San Giovanni. Her books were in place, her two desks clear, and writing to Ambrosiani, she reviewed her Roman empire of the 1970s. What could she say? She scarcely went to Rome. Brian de Breffny had died in 1989. Lanfranco and Zev were also dead, leaving behind them contrasting legatees like characters from *Symposium*. The noble and grieving Iride with her thirty-five million was set against Zev's rapacious Trastevere street-boys who Muriel understood to be making claims on his estate. Muriel had introduced his widow to a lawyer and kept up with her but there was little to be done. Gore Vidal never wrote. George Armstrong she no longer counted a friend.[58]

To each of her correspondents she spoke in their voice – which was also an aspect of her voice. For Ambrosiani, a man obsessed with high fashion, she was the woman interested in good clothes; for Strutt, she was the working writer requesting information and a batch of Venus lead pencils. Frances Cowell had the early symptoms of Parkinson's disease. Muriel, herself in great pain, was sympathetic, never maudlin. There's always hope, she said. When Cowell's husband died Muriel offered brisk condolence: of course it was saddening to lose a life's companion. But men seemed more prone to melancholy with the onset of old age. Frances, she was sure, was a tough, independent Scot. She would survive. The main tenor of these letters was always encouragement: do not linger and languish, never cultivate victimhood. Fight to the last. For Cowell she was the Morningside lady, delighted to receive a lace hankie for her birthday and promising to have it peeping from her pocket. But to all, the message was the same: look forward. She had been reading an article recently, she told Cowell, in which the neurologist Oliver Sacks had distinguished between Parkinson's disease and 'Parkinsonianism'. This suggested to Muriel that the latter was not necessarily a neurological disease but depended upon the individual's will to confront it, to convert the inevitable into the possible.[59] Destination rather than destiny, then, was the order of the day. The Armstrong fiasco had been another case in point. An anonymous profile of Muriel (written by Lorna Sage) had appeared in the *Observer* to coincide with *Symposium*'s publication. In this, Armstrong had related some trivial, untrue gossip about Muriel and Penelope. More lies and invasion.

*

As she grew older, Muriel became ever more determined to resist misrepresentation, while her professional life took her off to a variety of engagements, some warm, some chilly. March 1991 had found her escaping the snow on the Tuscan hills for London, to receive the *Sunday Times* Award, staying with Strutt at Terling, ordering a shampoo and set in the village hairdresser's. Comfort, adulation, discreet and amusing company. The second instalment of her life had just appeared in the *New Yorker*. During May she was in Paris for another hectic week, this time to interview Marcello Mastroianni for the *New York Times* and to appear on TV with Françoise Sagan and an Austrian writer, Peter Handke. Handke, who had apparently criticised Sagan for being too '*legère*', she found a crashing bore. Mastroianni had kept Muriel and Jardine waiting for an hour and a half in a freezing park where he was filming, and had appeared unwelcoming until he discovered that they spoke Italian. The object was to ask him how he felt as an actor now that his youth and beauty had passed. He was, she thought, an exceptional performer but she was intrigued by a remark someone made about him: that as an artist he was like blotting paper, requiring total direction[60] – an image she harboured for a novel nine years hence.

Muriel was feeling the shivers. She had caught 'flu in that park. The journey back was bad – no antibiotics until the Val d'Aosta[61] – but she soon settled to *Curriculum Vitae* again, having just made a one-day flit to London to speak at Graham Greene's memorial requiem Mass, recalling a period about which she was soon to write: '[His] encouragement, his faith in my possibilities and his material support meant an enormous amount to my efforts to write a first novel.' The monthly cheque had often been accompanied by 'a few bottles of red wine to take the edge off cold charity'. The last time she had seen him (the second time) had been in Paris over luncheon with a friend. 'He lived to a good age,' she concluded. 'There is no tragedy in his dying. But certainly we will all miss him. We are aware of his absence.'[62] Perfectly judged, brief and unsentimental, this was a fine valediction, and she immediately flew back to life. Ahead lay a visit from Joan Winterkorn of Bernard Quaritch Ltd who was to examine Muriel's private archive for possible sale. Ahead also lay a three-week holiday on the German island of Sylt, just off the Danish coast. House-sitters had been arranged for July and August. Jardine loaded the car with books and she and Muriel set off to work in the bracing North Sea climate away from Italian heat.

The island was magical. Muriel sent postcards picturing a train rushing through the sea. Photographs capture her wind-blown and smiling. Usually, Muriel could never resist listening in to others' conversations. But as she did not speak German, the language merely hummed in the middle distance, leaving her isolated with her thoughts. She returned refreshed, a fourth chunk of autobiography written, only to find equanimity disturbed by another unreliable ghost. Spurling's *Paul Scott: A Life* had been published by Hutchinson during 1990 and contained an account of Scott meeting Tennessee Williams at Muriel's London flat. The inaccuracy of this story infuriated Muriel. She had met them – but at Strutt's house some twenty years later.

What had in fact happened was this. On 27 June 1977, Muriel had been staying with Strutt in Winchester Street. She had flashed over alone for ten days to discuss business and to visit Robin when she was in the middle of *Territorial Rights*. That evening Strutt had arranged a dinner. Muriel had asked him to invite Dorothy Olding, then on her annual British visit. Olding had brought Scott. Williams, for many years an admirer of Muriel's work, wanted to meet her and came, as usual, with Maria St Just. The remaining three comprised Angus Wilson, Alan Maclean and his wife, Robin. Already drunk and sensing from the conversation that the mysterious Mr Williams must be something in the theatre, Scott had finally asked his name. 'Tennessee.' 'No, not where you come from. I'm asking your first name.' 'Tennessee.' Only then, amid quiet laughter, did the penny crash.

Spurling's point was to draw out Scott's love of narrative: that he had told and retold this story of his embarrassment, honing it to a fine pitch of performance. Unfortunately, she used as her source one of Scott's Tulsa students, from the days when the novelist's memory was long soused. In this version Muriel was cooking supper and had supplied the surprise celebrity. All the other guests had evaporated. The scene was no longer Pimlico but Camberwell. Did it matter? Hutchinson apparently thought not. Muriel, however, saw this as presenting her in the role of vulgar hostess. She never cooked for her parties but bought in a catered buffet; she would never have left her guest alone and disappeared to the kitchen. At this gathering, *she* was the guest of honour. And, anyway, it was all *wrong*. With Spurling as with Page, just as she was trying to write her autobiography, she discovered others meddling with the record of her life. That this was a tiny detail in an otherwise brilliant book, that to make the corrections so late in the production process would have involved great expense and delay, were of no concern to Muriel. It was the Stanford theme again, the cancer of gossip. Her response – to Mary Cunnane of Norton who were to publish Spurling's American paperback – was blunt. If they did not remove the offending passage she would injunct.[63] Across the top, Cunnane scribbled a message to her legal department: 'A threat from Muriel Spark to sue. The relevant passage is on p. 405 & seems totally innocuous to me. Help.' As Bruce Hunter seemed unwilling to pursue the matter with the vigour Muriel sought, perhaps unsurprisingly as he was also Spurling's agent, Muriel took matters into her own hands, writing to Strutt and Maclean for corroboration, checking diaries, getting Jardine to scour the files, taking time off from *Curriculum Vitae* to construct a long, accurate account of the evening. The scenario was exact, even down to who was sitting next to whom – just as in *Symposium*. She was right and demanded justice.[64]

The dispute rumbled on from September to November 1991, with Jardine equally incensed, but with her sense of humour at least easing the tension. The idea of Muriel's cooking for a dinner party struck her as singularly amusing. Eventually the whole thing ran into the sand, although when Spurling spoke about the matter to the *Sunday Times*, Muriel won a published apology and costs from the newspaper. 'Lies', she wrote in the opening pages of *Curriculum Vitae*, 'are like fleas hopping from here to there, sucking the blood of the intellect.'

> One writer of a recent biography, having given a false account of me [...] expressed herself puzzled at my objection. Her scenario showed me in what she conceived a 'good' light. Be that as it might, it was all untrue. [...] What was damaging about the lie, the biographer wanted to know. Damaging! Slices of three people's biographies are falsified [...]. But far worse than personal damage is the damage done to truth and to scholarship.[65]

'Hilary Spurling', she remarked later, 'devoted her menopause to me.'[66] Victory – but Muriel already had other things to concern her. In the middle of this row she had returned to her Roman clinic because her hip had become increasingly painful. It was agony to climb stairs or to get in and out of the car. The diagnosis was unequivocal: arthritis and osteoporosis. An operation was advised but she shrugged off infirmity as another bore when she was otherwise fit. The BBC were planning to televise *Memento Mori* and she joked about applying for a part.

By November *Curriculum Vitae* was reaching the war, while the rain dripped through the roof and another war continued in nearby Yugoslavia. Under grey skies, with floods predicted in Florence, Jardine helped Muriel to concentrate entirely on her autobiography. Both women were on strict diets as the world beyond their windows grew ever bleaker. After Chernobyl had deposited clouds of radioactive dust across Europe, they thought they had better enjoy themselves while they could. There were a few elegant dinners in Florence. Another friend emerged, Andrew Porter, the music critic of the *New Yorker*. Jardine took Muriel to a twelfth-century abbey at Montalcino for her seventy-fourth birthday. But as 1992 began, the mood at San Giovanni was of intense and anxious concentration. The war chapter was the fifth of seven. Infant joy, Africa and marriage were behind her. The war was the transitional phase. Ahead lay Stanford. How to deal with *him?*

Muriel could hardly bear to touch the subject. Stanford's sale of her letters had been hurtful, an abuse of trust.[67] In her view, he was envious of her spiritual good.[68] By this she did not mean that she was spiritually good. Far from it. All Catholics had to live in this world and were therefore bad Catholics. No, envy of spiritual good was the desire to appropriate another's spiritual wealth, the desire, perhaps, for failure in another, the wishing to hurt or embarrass, emotional colonisation, being a leech, an incubus, a bum. Autobiography was an uneasy form for her.[69] Although the restraint she had placed on her memory and imagination was a challenge she had risen to and mastered, it had proved stressful.[70] But she was nearly there and determined to finish well. Because the first four chapters of *Curriculum Vitae* had appeared in the *New Yorker*, half the text was already polished and proof-read. Jardine had typed the rest as it came off Muriel's desk and the book appeared just three months after the last sentence was written. Muriel was due in London for Constable's launch. Excerpts were to appear in the *Sunday Times* and the *Scotsman*. The Royal Society of Literature, having awarded her its highest honour, a C.Litt. (Companion of Literature), had booked her for a reading, with John Mortimer as chairman. Her private archive had been sold to the National Library of Scotland, and she was invited to attend a ceremony to mark the deal. Before all this, however, and just after completing *Curriculum Vitae*, she had accepted a commission from the *Daily Mail* to review the second volume of a biography of Evelyn Waugh. Although she now rarely did such work, she remained intrigued by Waugh and his connection with her life.

The author of this biography was me. As she gave it a favourable notice, I sent a brief letter of thanks and was astonished to receive a reply. She hoped, she wrote, to have as good a biographer as me when her time came round. Was she serious? With little hope of success, I offered my services. This was, she thought, an interesting idea. If I was ever in Italy, we might discuss it. Later in the year would be best for her as she had promised to complete a novel. And so a date was set:

1 September 1992. I was to drop in while driving south for a holiday with my family and we would all stay for two nights.

That summer *Curriculum Vitae* was an instant best-seller. Column inches came by the yard; the C.Litt. and Edinburgh ceremonies were national news. The book was advertised as a 'first volume' and notices eagerly anticipated the next. Bruce Hunter was therefore puzzled to find Muriel making discreet enquiries about her prospective biographer. Indeed, when the news leaked out, everyone was surprised. 'I have to say I was amazed,' said Kanon. 'But also there's something so wonderfully funny because it is in fact *Loitering with Intent* all over again. The idea that Muriel is now actively participating in the creation of her own biography is like circles within circles.'[71] What was she up to?

If I was somewhat nervous when we met, my partner and our three-year-old daughter, Zuleika, saved the day. Zuli greeted Muriel with 'I can roar, you know', followed by her lion imitation. This seemed to go down well and, after Beerbohm's *Zuleika Dobson*, she was immediately dubbed 'Miss D'. Muriel and Jardine had just returned from three weeks in France, Le Fartoret in the Savoie, near that borderland country of the Jura again, where in an old village house on a plateau above the Rhône Muriel had started her next novel, *Reality and Dreams*. It dealt with redundancy, a theme much on her mind as the pain in her hip intensified. At home with her new guests, no hint of her suffering emerged. Within three months she was packing for hospital and an operation which almost killed her.

CHAPTER 20

Dark Music

1992–2006

Muriel's operation, a hip replacement, had originally been planned for September 1992, then deferred while she flew to Chicago to pick up the Ingersoll Foundation's T. S. Eliot Award. The prize money had already been spent on a new car. *Memento Mori* had recently been republished in Italy to great critical acclaim, and was now in its third edition. Fan mail was pouring in. All this was cheering. She could walk well enough, if stiffly. But the agony she suffered during the Chicago visit appears to have settled her mind. She would chance the Roman specialist. Jardine wrote vivaciously from the Salvator Mundi in late December. The operation, she said, had been a success. Under partial anaesthetic Muriel had been awake throughout as the surgeons cut her femur in two, mildly intrigued as they hammered and sawed like construction workers. She was keeping a notebook on the subject for me. In fact, Muriel endured a miserable time in hospital and her companion spent many anxious hours at her bedside. But the tone was positive. They were looking forward. Jardine was sketching Rome from the windows when she was sent from the room while medication was in progress, and had bought a bargain collection of one hundred classical CDs for Muriel to listen to through earphones in the middle of the night.[1] That music was never played there. Unknown to them then, this was the point at which Muriel began a life sentence of acute pain.

Six weeks later they were home, determined to resume their wandering lives with full vigour. A fortnight's fog cleared. The sun shone brightly. Muriel fought off her annual dose of influenza and returned to work. Proofs of a collection of her Brontë writings were due from Peter Owen. Constable and Houghton Mifflin were printing the first of four *Omnibus* volumes of seventeen of her novels and wanted introductions. In America a new batch of Avon reprints was shortly to be launched. Daily physiotherapy ate into Muriel's schedule but she remained optimistic. By Easter she expected to be fully recovered. Stephen Schiff was writing a 'landmark' article on her for the *New Yorker* to coincide with the American publication of *Curriculum Vitae*. When she made a ten-day flit to New York for this, however, with interviews and a reading at the 'Y' under the auspices of the Unterberg's Poetry Center, she found it difficult to walk.

Nine hundred people had attended the reading, an entranced Joe Kanon among them. When she spoke of her art, he said, she became immediately animated as though asking herself why she did it, what exactly it was that she did. It was a riveting performance with no sign of suffering. But she did not stay in her apartment, feeling unable to manage for herself there. Instead (all her expenses were paid) she took a luxurious room in the Carlyle, chauffeur-driven limousines smoothing her passage around the city. Schiff's piece was long and honorific, excellent publicity. Muriel was delighted by it – with the exception of Alan Maclean's stating that she was 'batty'[2] during her hallucinations, which might have been true but was to her another example of malicious false witness because she was cured by April 1954 and had not met him until 1955. Apparently he was recalling with misjudged levity what a friend had told him. She read his words to mean that she was mad when she was producing some of her finest work. He was, she thought, a traitor, possibly to his country, certainly to her.

There was much else in the article which might have irritated her, had it appeared anywhere other than in the *New Yorker* – that her 'demeanor is at once mandarin and schoolgirlish, her accent half Edinburgh and half Queen Elizabeth'; that 'the role of Famous Novelist has not been easy for her to adopt, [...] she's never been quite sure how to play it: should she be glamorous, provocative, slightly dotty, or all three?'; that *Curriculum Vitae* was painstakingly researched but 'something of a failure' because all we get is 'a series of surfaces'.[3] But no, if she did object to this portrait, she made no complaint. In essence it was positive. It took her work seriously. What she would not tolerate, however, was any intimation either that her writing was the product of madness or that she had lied in her autobiography. It was the latter suggestion which was to provoke the dispute about her Jewish origins four years later. Maclean had until recently been deemed a close friend. Now, suddenly, she saw him as a turncoat, an 'indescribably filthy liar (please quote)',[4] and she fought back in her New York interviews. Stanford? 'I hate the man's guts.' Maclean? 'I tried to be friends and I'm really sorry for him. Now he comes out with all this. I think he must be on the bottle again.'[5] Returned to San Giovanni, her mind seething around the insult, she set down a 'Memorandum' 'not for publication' but certainly for the record, and sent copies to me, to Robin Baird-Smith and to Maclean. It did not make comfortable reading.

Nineteen ninety-three was a year of great pleasure and great pain for Muriel. In New York she had suffered dreadfully from her hip and, although that June she became a Dame Commander of the British Empire and was delighted by the honour, the agony remained. When Joan Winterkorn arrived at San Giovanni to assess the next batch of private papers for sale, she was alarmed by the physical change in her client. Muriel had consulted Guy Strutt after her physiotherapist had finally refused to continue treatment, and soon she was booked into the Springfield Clinic in nearby Chelmsford to be examined by a British surgeon who discovered that horrific surgical mistakes had been made. The hip was ablaze with infection. This surgery put her back together again but during the Italian job the sciatic nerve had been sewn into the wound. It might take years, they said, to settle down. Muriel never relinquished the determination to live but over the next two years it required all of her monumental will to keep going. When I met her again that September at Strutt's Terling house, she was recovering, as ebullient as ever, hobbling with an orthopaedic stick and anticipating a prompt return to non-stick mobility. Back in Italy, Jardine was soon transporting her friend to boutiques in preparation for the investiture that December. But writing the novel was impossible. Instead, Muriel concentrated on a Walter Scott lecture she had agreed to give in Edinburgh during 1994. She had another appointment at the Springfield Clinic for an X-ray on 6 December, believing herself to be definitely on the mend, almost as though that would make it happen. Then, on the 8th, I heard from Jardine. They were in England again. Muriel was being operated on that day and would not be able to see me for some time.

*

By early 1994, Muriel was limping in great pain and soon to see a doctor in Florence, while Jardine was racked with viral arthritis. Harold Acton was dead, La Pietra willed to New York University and the whole estate subject to counter-litigation from one of his relatives. Italy was in political turmoil, Forza Italia ascendant, and from England came news of a terrible car crash. Robin Baird-Smith had barely survived it, but his wife and one of his children had not. In difficulties herself, Muriel was faultlessly generous of her time and sympathy for others' darknesses. She would ring Baird-Smith to raise his spirits, write to Frances Cowell, gentle and supportive, to Guy thanking him for obituaries of lost chums, anxious about his ailing relatives. It was a bad time, somehow epitomised by the poisoning of Algy, Penelope's third dog. The others had been killed in similar fashion. Muriel was convinced that responsibility lay with the local hunters, laying meat laced with strychnine to kill others' dogs. (According to the local priest, this was done by the *venatoria*, or game wardens, to control vermin.) Algy had expired, horribly, before her eyes: muscle contraction, asphyxiation. His brother, Mungo, now confined to a wire run, was taken out only on a lead. Later he, too, was poisoned while loose in the garden with Jardine.

Muriel and Jardine, both artists, both pragmatic, hated crowds, loved movement. In practical mode, Jardine had handrails erected on the stairs and Muriel sold her Rome flat, glad again to be rid of property. Now on two sticks, she was in severe and constant pain. She had planned to be in Edinburgh during May 1994 and to see me again at San Giovanni. Both visits were cancelled. That September, she and Jardine were installed in the Ivy Hill Hotel, Essex, awaiting another, and as it turned out, unnecessary, operation on Muriel's spine at the Springfield Clinic. By early October it was done and the news still bad. She had to try to walk but could not. Her pelvis was cracked. On the 13th she was to be transferred to a private hospital in Brentwood to use their heated therapy pool and, although she had never learned to swim, she remained upbeat. By 25 October, she had returned to the clinic to face further surgery. A fortnight later Jardine was in a London hotel opposite another hospital. Muriel was inside, in traction, after yet more operations. In a cat's cradle of antibiotic drips, stretched and subject to huge bolts of pain, she somehow maintained her sense of humour. Jardine was awed, as were the surgeons, by this small woman's strength. She was 'enormously plucky, brave & optimistic', saying that she was 'going to whack this infection'.[6] Her days were spent, as Jardine put it, 'reading Palgrave & the Bible to each other between Edith Wharton (Muriel) and Alan Sillitoe (me)'. They had no visitors. The nursing was intense.[7]

After five more months of treatment, Muriel was home again, driving back to Italy via the newly opened Channel Tunnel. In February 1995 she was hobbling on a crutch, her right leg one inch shorter and requiring a shoe-inset. The surgeons, she thought, were rather airy about this. The return journey had been through devastating French floods. But, re-routed up perilous mountain roads in the dark, snow and ice, Muriel, eyes intent upon the road ahead, was not to be deflected. Enough time had been wasted. At San Giovanni, Jardine struggled with the backlog of correspondence and by April, Muriel was free from acute pain for the first time in nearly two and a half years, furiously writing her novel and able to forget herself in it. She disliked being overweight as a result of the drugs. In London, the car had been hit by a lorry and the insurance wasn't paying up. But at least she had abandoned antibiotics and warfarin and, most importantly, she was practising her art again. For a year she was in moderately good health.

*

Shortly after her seventy-eighth birthday, in the last week of February 1996, Muriel could scarcely walk for pain and was taken by ambulance to a clinic in Florence where shingles was diagnosed. During Easter week of 1996 she nearly died. Before this, her walking had improved. Now both legs were affected with post-herpetic neuralgia. Even so, and with the help of vitamins and codeine, it was back to work. Penelope spent time in the garden repairing fallen walls and bought fifty file boxes for the next sale of papers. In agony again, Muriel reviewed a biography of Robert Burns and was particularly delighted by another honour: Commandeur de l'Ordre des Arts et des Lettres, the highest French literary award.

That June, Muriel did an extraordinary thing for so private a woman with a horror of computers as spreaders of verbal disease. At the request of Microsoft to be their first contributor, she wrote an Internet diary. 'It is terrible to be me,' she began. 'The shingles [...] have left me with burnt-out nerves in both legs. I walk with an elbow crutch, I shuffle. How long this will last I don't know. Three to nine months said the professor in Florence who gave me a lot of electric shocks in the legs to test the reactions.' Typically, though, this is not a record of self-pity but of a 'spirit of vast endurance', intrigued, even amused, by her own suffering. People wrote from England asking her to appear at charitable events such as egg-and-spoon races. Polite refusal usually met with further encouragement: how about the three-legged race? During recent gallery visits Jardine had manoeuvred her round the canvases in a wheelchair and Muriel had stocked up with silk scarves 'signed Mirò, Picasso, Kandinsky – quite a collection. I wear them sitting behind my desk where nobody new in my life can possibly guess that my walking is impaired.'[8] It had been her lifetime's work to secure her reputation among such names. Ironically, now that she was a DBE and Commandeur, now that she was showered with honorary degrees and prizes, she was immobile and took solace, like the hero of *Reality and Dreams*, in the spiritual company of fellow artists.

Muriel wrote this diary for ten days and another, in December, for five. In between, *Reality and Dreams* was published to trumpet blasts on both sides of the Atlantic. At home we see the writer at work, fishing out two incomplete short stories, struggling to reconcile them into one,[9] researching the literal truth of her novels' settings, puzzling over the upper-class use of 'one' (meaning 'we', excluding the lumpen proletariat) and finding it cold, elitist, pompous. Pomposity she saw as the enemy of good writing. There is a diary entry on this, as there is on a 'chilling and puzzling story' she had clipped from the Italian papers. A mother and her three sons had jumped to their deaths, hand-in-hand, from a viaduct. They had financial worries. Muriel thought that she might make something of it: a novel, a story. She never did. Perhaps the theme was too depressing. 'Suicide', she noted, 'is the fatal sickness of any hope, the death of any future. [...] On a beautiful day, amid beautiful scenery, they threw themselves in unison over a 100-metre bridge. What fools! What absolute fools!' [10]

*

With the publication of her twentieth novel, Muriel's Constable contract was complete and she was looking elsewhere. Reviews of *Reality and Dreams* had been good: a few carpers detecting failing powers, the rest delighted. Gore Vidal had chosen it as one of his 'Books of the Year', as had Frank Kermode, A. S. Byatt and John Mortimer. Amid the abundance of the olive harvest in December 1996, she was ready for new life and full of literary energy. Even her computer diary had produced fruit. Surfing the net in Alaska was the son of the chairman of the VZV Foundation for the study of post-herpetic neuralgia. His father, in California, contacted her New York agent, faxed her about a drug, Zostrix, unavailable in Italy, and then sent it to her by courier. It was a great help. The numbness in her legs was withdrawing. She was mobile again.

'A young woman reviewer of [...] *Reality and Dreams*', she recorded, 'complained that some of my characters are "nasty". I should have thought they were far worse than that; they are insufferable, even outrageous [...].' Her subject was corruption, the Fall, absurdity. No one was devoid of meanness: 'Who are these friends of the human race, and where?' In this entry she offered examples of shiftiness she had encountered and combated. One of her English editors had leaked discreet information to the press and denied the charge. She had trapped him with an old black propaganda trick: providing disinformation to him alone and watching it emerge like a stain on his character. Another (obviously Maclean) was 'distressingly alcoholic' and had given an interview 'full of wild and chronologically impossible inventions. Was his memory impaired by alcohol, or had he been harbouring some grudge for 35 years? Who cares?' Her best publisher had been Blanche Knopf ('I don't care', she had said, 'if people don't know [my clothes] are haute couture, so long as I know'). Blanche with her style and aesthetic passion, wearing her Legion d' Honneur rosette, putting 'all her heart and soul into the encouragement of my writing'[11] was exactly right: Blanche, dying bravely, listening on the phone to the sea.

Reality and dreams. Affectations (verbal and social), hypocrisy, the cowering behind euphemism: all irritated, stimulated. In a hotel lobby, a man had asked Muriel if her dog was 'dressed'. '"Is it what?" "Is it dressed?" "You don't mean *castrated*, do you?" "Well, yes," said the man, looking to right and left, terrified lest someone should have overheard.'[12] As Christmas approached, she was reading the Book of Ecclesiastes whose proverbs spoke 'right at the reader' of 'our everyday, unpredictable lives.' One of her favourite quotations (from Proverbs) was the catalogue of failings 'detestable to God' and to her:

> A proud look, a lying tongue, and hands that shed innocent blood. An heart that deviseth wicked imaginations, feet that are swift in running to mischief, a false witness that speaketh lies, and he that soweth discord among brethren.[13]

Throughout this diary, there is a sense of men, generally, being inadequate to the challenges of the living moment: men boring her with facts over lunch, leaking slander, threatening. 'He has a beard and a man-friend,' she wrote about an acquaintance in Italy. 'He is a painter. Sometimes they come to our house for dinner, sometimes we go to theirs. Both cases involve going downstairs to the dining room. Why do I always dislike descending in advance of the men? I have a fear of being pushed from behind. Why? In our friendship there is an unspoken hostility which perhaps only I feel. It could be imaginary but that is not the point. Going down to dinner, I cling to the handrail. I cling tight.'[14]

*

Reality and Dreams was as much concerned with the Book of Job as *The Comforters* had been. In many respects they parallel each other as accounts of suffering survived and made redundant. Redundancy, Muriel noted in interviews, was the 'subject' of her latest novel although, like her last, *The Finishing School*, it also investigates the mystery of the artistic process: its arbitrariness, its unteachable inspiration and the creator's love affair with the created. Tom Richards, an elderly film director, is the central character. 'How does one explain an act of art?' he asks, choosing his words carefully. An *act* of art involves, initially, a moment over which the imagination has no control. Richards's glimpse of a girl cooking hamburgers sparks an idea for a film but this epiphany cannot become art without subsequent acts of will, without the elimination of the inessential, the redundant, in a structure of interdependent images. When people ask him what his film is 'about', 'he simply laughed in their faces.' Art was about 'pictures inside frames'. About itself. His relationship to his work is obsessive until it is complete, at which point attention transfers to the next thing. Completion, paradoxically, engenders the work's redundancy.

Muriel had selected this theme before her first catastrophic operation, perhaps because it was part of the zeitgeist of the 1990s. The left-wing John Mortimer, now a dining companion on his Tuscan trips, was struck by how she

> bravely faces up to the exhaustion of England at the end of a millennium [...]. The last time we lived through the Nineties, they were called naughty. [She] sees our Nineties as tired and rather nasty [... and] rightly attributes the unhappiness [...] to redundancy, the euphemism for sacking vast numbers of people in order that a few [...] may become richer.[15]

Anti-Thatcher, he detected commentary on the machismo of a managerial culture disloyal to its workers. Certainly the novel touches on the collapse of trust (and Trusts: Barings Bank is mentioned), on things 'going out', but it is no political treatise. That is left to Tom's sour daughter, Marigold, with her idiotic books on the phenomenon of redundancy. Graceless and puritanical, she hates her father and what he represents, disguising this beneath insincere and greedy loyalty. For what he represents is what Muriel represented: the *auteur* tradition. He is the Father. Marigold desires her father's downfall, takes pleasure in his embarrassment and damage to his reputation. She is the enemy of art as Satan is God's enemy, subverting his creation.

Richards has literally fallen from a height. In a brilliant, surreal opening sequence his consciousness tunes in and out as he lies on his hospital bed, day and night, day-nurses and night-nurses merging. He has tumbled from a crane, an archaic item of cinematic equipment essential to his art. 'Yes,' he thinks to himself, 'I did feel like God up on that crane. It was wonderful to shout orders [...] and like God watch the team down there group and re-group as bidden. [...] What do they think a film set is? A democracy or, something?'[16] But ... twelve broken ribs and a fractured hip. He was lucky to survive. No more cranes, everyone insists, for him. He might never direct again. He is not, however, finished. It is the story of the recovery of his powers, his power of recovery.

For all its shapely abstraction, then, *Reality and Dreams* was an intensely personal book. Muriel was writing out of immediate and painful experience, writing her way out of it, in a fashion not attempted since *The Comforters*. By an ingenious double-take, it becomes another addition to her autobiographical writings: the story of her artistic spirit's resistance against infirmity and negativity. As an artist, Richards resembles her. He knows many of those Muriel has known (or met) – Greene, Auden, Tennessee Williams, Albee, Mary McCarthy. He does not believe in convictions (usually viewing them as hypocrisy), insists on plausibility in art, detects others' impatience with people like him who can just walk out; he owes no one any explanation, is immune to guilt. Almost everything he has to say about art, Muriel had also said in interview. He even takes on her abandoned novel, *Watling Street*, as his next film, and repeats an idea from *The Abbess of Crewe*: 'that the ages of the Father and the Son were over and we were approaching the age of the Holy Spirit, or as we used to say, Ghost.'[17] Like Muriel, he is a believer but no slave to dogma, a brooder and one who sees a parallel between his profession and God's. *Reality and Dreams*, the *TLS* thought, was 'a portrait of the artist as megalomaniac'.[18] Rather, it is a defence of the artist denigrated as megalomaniac and, by implication, of belief in a mysterious God who appears to act in this fashion. Ultimately, perhaps, it is 'about' mystery and the elimination of the 'non-necessary' people and things obstructing engagement with it. A ruthless book, it dismisses the worthy and the mundane as of no account. It is the opposite of George Eliot, literary realism, the ideology of meekness, equivalent centres of self, natural justice and the whole tradition of art as social conscience. It is a defence of (justified) arrogance, the necessary arrogance of the artist (and of God) if we are to have truth.

'He often wonders', the novel begins, 'if we are characters in God's dreams.' Richards finds it difficult to distinguish between life and art, for he is eternally transmuting the one into the other. To meet was to 'cast', and Muriel, it seems, experienced a similar sensation. She often spoke of others finding her only half there in conversation. A phrase, an image, the way someone sat, would catch her attention and she was off, dreaming fictions. She, too, was 'casting' all the time, 'her oracular eye', as Updike put it, '[...] always on the skull of damnation behind society's grinning face.'[19] 'Everything I do', Richards says, 'is basically connected with my work. Everything.'[20] All he wants is to resume his artistic life, to relieve himself of this feeling of drowning in redundancy, to get back on his crane. There were those, he knew, who would delight in his fall. Well, he was not going to give them that pleasure – and neither was Muriel.

*

In March 1997 she travelled to London to accept the David Cohen British Literature Prize. As it was for a 'lifetime's achievement' and an honour bestowed previously only on Naipaul and Pinter, she was thrilled, not least because at £30,000 it would easily pay for another car and offered an additional £10,000 for the cause of her choice. That cheque went to her old school, Gillespie's. Returned to San Giovanni, she heard that the

Arts Council of Scotland had awarded its Spring Book Prize to *Reality and Dreams*. Travels were planned, her reputation had never been higher. There was energy in her mental step again. On discovering that one of her great-grandmothers had died aged 105, she saw no reason why she should not emulate this longevity: twenty-six years of vigorous living still to be enjoyed.

After a lengthy European excursion that summer – London, Somerset, Liège, Dresden, Prague, Austria, Padua – Muriel settled to her next novel, *Aiding and Abetting*, another experiment, mixing the facts and fictions of Lord Lucan. When he had disappeared in 1974, she had collected cuttings, would telephone friends in London who had known him: 'I got as much as I could out of them [...] it was such a strange mixture of identities. It has been brooding in my mind ever since. I followed it always.' Recently she had approached Lady Annabel Goldsmith, widow of Sir James, one of Lucan's associates. Lady Annabel, who had not known Lucan well, thought him 'quite reasonable, a little shy'. This was of no interest. To Muriel, he was 'extremely stupid and dull, with a lot of pent-up resentment'.[21] A fellow Guards officer had told her of Lucan's unchanging dinner diet of first salmon, then lamb chops. This was more like it. He was to be another of her threatening males: pompous, violent, a bore, an iconic drone, an earl and a gambler looking for a quick return, incapable of an honest day's work. Opposing him would be a character from a parallel story of a fake stigmatic who would smear herself with menstrual blood. Back in her Camberwell days, Muriel had known Catholic nurses who would send this woman money.

It was a powerful scenario and Muriel must have felt that she was working on her best novel since *A Far Cry*, indeed one of her best ever. Its progress, though, was again obstructed, partly by her desire to enjoy herself, mainly by external factors. There was a September trip to Madrid for the British Council. Then Strutt visited, collapsed with a stroke, and was eventually rescued from hospital by his nephew. Her eightieth birthday – 1 February 1998 – was celebrated with eighteen guests for a champagne lunch. John and Thekla Clark, friends of Auden, were there, the art historians John Fleming and Hugh Honour, the painter Jeffrey Smart. Another *Brodie* play revival was in the offing, this time starring Fiona Shaw. Now that they had satellite TV, Muriel and Jardine watched Sky News each day, tracking the political instability of the Middle East and the Clinton / Lewinsky debacle or watching the soap opera *Beautiful*. Muriel used to watch the latter lying on her bed, sipping her coffee after lunch, and had scarcely returned to her desk before another soap opera, the 'racial origins dispute' (see Chapter 18), had erupted in the British press. Someone she had never heard of, Bryan Cheyette, was writing about her. The very idea was alarming – she thought him to be one source of the accusations of denial – but she was ready to sue should he slander her.[22]

Cheyette, it turned out, was a harmless academic writing a critical book on Muriel for the *Writers and Their Work* series. He had inadvertently generated this furore by giving a paper to the Edinburgh Jewish Literary Society in which he described Muriel as 'half-Jewish'. His subject had been her intense engagement with her Jewish origins. Afterwards, some members of the audience had buttonholed him. Did he realise, they said, that she was in fact a full Jew, that Robin had the *ketubah?* The *Jewish Chronicle*'s reporter pricked up his ears, an innocuous 'middle' was transferred to the front page and thus the 'scandal' began. A British journalist turned up uninvited at San Giovanni and returned three times trying to secure an interview. He did not get one, although eventually Muriel faxed a statement to him. Later, when she refused to comment further, the press feasted on her silence. That summer at the Hay-on-Wye Literary Festival she read 'The Gentile Jewesses' by way of response. She felt this matter keenly. Correspondence with me accelerated into an almost daily exchange, a lever arch file of papers over those twelve weeks. And it continued for many months afterwards. Hay was followed by another drive to England for a 'platform' at the National Theatre to launch *Brodie*. She was flying, triumphant, had rarely been so much in the news since the publication of that novel almost thirty years earlier. She even appeared in the *Guardian*'s 'Me and My Motor' column, commenting on her Twin-Spark.

Two three-thousand-mile round trips within two months, however, took their toll. In September she was supine again in excruciating pain, having fractured two vertebrae by stumbling over a carpet at home. Visitors still visited but excursions to Zurich and to Rome were cancelled. Her brother Phil turned up in October, the last time they were to see each other, another pause in her creative flow which tested her patience. As Franco dug out the cellars to lay terracotta floors, Muriel was glued to CNN news and the Clinton story, itching to resume her novel.

One of the honours which had come Muriel's way was election to an honorary Fellowship of the Royal Society of Edinburgh. In this capacity she was consulted on matters legal and moral relating to bills and government agency reports. Recently the topic had been posthumous insemination: the case of a young woman having a baby 'from her dead husband's sperm'. Such matters intrigued her (though not Strutt, to whom she wrote about them). What, she wondered, were the legal ramifications of inheritance? Suppose the father had left part of his estate to someone else? 'Suppose he is Lord Omnibus 4. His sperm is abstracted while he has been dying, without his consent since he is unconscious. His loving young widow waits for 10 years to inseminate herself and produces a son and heir, Lord Omnibus 5. However, in the meantime his nephew has successfully petitioned for the title [...]. Which of the two is Lord Omnibus?' No theological difficulty was raised. To Muriel it was merely a logical proposition about which the press had been 'far too sentimental'.[23]

*

Back on her feet again by early 1999, pain controlled with a daily injection from a nurse, Muriel attacked the new year with the vigour of an eighteen-year-old. In April there was a quick drive to Gloucestershire for a wedding, another to Oxford in June to receive an honorary D.Litt. alongside Sir Simon Rattle. Penelope's last dog, Shadow, had recently survived poisoning by herbicides and Muriel, for so long unwilling to interfere in local politics, at last used her name to support Alexander Chancellor's article exposing the 'pet killers'.[24] July found her in England again for the third time in six months. That was when Janice Galloway had interviewed her in London and she had talked of life beginning at sixty. It was early evening in a small, discreet hotel. Muriel was in sombre evening dress, ready for dinner elsewhere: 'a little [eye] liner: powder, pink lipstick', vivid.[25]

At Oxford, Muriel had been much fêted. John Bayley, whose *Iris* was selling briskly, had attended a dinner. Good manners were preserved but she hated the book as a betrayal of Murdoch's dignity: a form of disguised revenge, masquerading as praise and sympathy, by a weak man on a strong woman. October was for Spain and Portugal, contributing to a British Council 'Women Writers at the End of the Millennium' celebration in Madrid. Added to this, at her own expense, was the pleasure of touring five Spanish and Portuguese museums and galleries, the last being the new Guggenheim at Bilbao of which they only saw the foyer. For the use of a wheelchair, Muriel was asked to hand over her passport. She demanded a receipt. When this was refused, they returned to the car.

It was another year busy with excursions, while at home she was working on both *Aiding and Abetting* and a play, and being interviewed again. Priests? Narrow-minded dumbers-down. Film producers? Time-wasters. Family? Had to get away from them. Evil? It was 'just there [...] especially in this new book [...].' Job? Surprising that it was ever admitted to the canon: 'It questions everything [...] haunts my career. I read it all the time.' Her son? 'Nobody knows what to make of him. He's out of his depth, and there's nothing I can do about it [...].' Health? Sight fading, incipient glaucoma, having a cure.[26] The millennium cele-brations, she thought, were best ignored. Her first plan was to remain at home but in fact she saw in the next thousand years at a party, for there was plenty to celebrate. In January she completed *Aiding and Abetting* and sent it to Bruce Hunter to find a publisher. Interest was hot. For her birthday in February Penelope drove her to Turin to visit the gods, priests and emperors of the Egyptian Museum. April–May was booked for the *New Yorker*'s seventy-fifth anniversary bash, Alan Taylor, editor of the *Scotsman* and a supporter for many years, to accom-pany her.

That March, Muriel was corresponding with me on the question of intellectual property. *Hothouse*, she said, had been published in Italian in 1988. She had sent it out to film producers. The book contained 'an elaborate description of a stage production of *Peter Pan* in which all the actors are grown up. It is, and is meant to be, a satirical and grotesque comment on the "boy-who-never-grew-up" situation which I think is horrible.' During the 1990s, Spielberg's *Hook* had appeared 'in which all the [*Peter Pan*] characters are grown up, as in my book. Well, that ended any hope of mine for a film of "The Hothouse". I call it a coincidence.'[27] Muriel's sense of her originality was intense. If she felt she had invented a plot, a linguistic construction, coined a title, she was proprietary about it. When Peter O'Toole had entitled his memoirs *Loitering with Intent*, she had tried to get Macmillan to withdraw and rename the book. It was the theme of so many of her novels: the burglary of talent, blackmail, exploitation by the unoriginal. I replied saying that a related problem had arisen with the Internet. A Cambridge don had registered sites in the names of famous authors, offering to sell them back for a profit. Jeanette Winterson (whose work Muriel greatly admired) had successfully sued for the return of her territory. The Society of Authors was pursuing independent litigation, advising writers to purchase their own domain names. 'Muriel Spark.com' was still free. Was she interested? She certainly was, and within weeks her agent had created a site for her which revealed pirated editions.

Lightning was a powerful image for Muriel: the flash of inspiration, sudden death, creation. Jan Groth and Jardine had both researched the subject for her. An idea for *Hothouse*, later abandoned, had been to have someone electrocuted down a telephone line. Lovers are mortally shocked in *Not to Disturb*, sheltering beneath a tree. Jardine's house had been struck several times and, on 12 June 2000, it happened again, a thunderbolt sending parts of the small belfry crashing through the tiles into Muriel's bath. Had she been in it, she would have been killed. It was like a bomb dropping. Electricity entered the house down the external wires. She woke instantly at 2 a.m. as the current passed across her mouth, slightly burning her upper lip. Afterwards, she sometimes spoke of this, thankful to have escaped serious injury yet somehow intrigued by the experience.

The house itself had now become intensely interesting to Muriel. Local myth suggested that it had been built by the Lombards in the thirteenth century and she was convinced that there had been a tunnel running to it from their encampment further up the hill. She had found peace at San Giovanni although it was near two sites of suffering, a place of mystery and of paradox. During the war, the Villa Mazzi had, until May 1944, been a concentration camp for Jews. On 29 June 1944 almost the entire male population of Civitella della Chiana, a hilltop village a few miles away, had been executed by the Germans in reprisal for the killing of two German soldiers and the wounding of a third by Italian partisans. Troops had herded the men into the church square, emptied the church of those at 7 a.m. Mass, driven the women and children out, then lined the men up 'sideways in groups of five along the wall' and shot them in the back of the neck. The houses were then set ablaze. It was an infamous massacre, still a painful memory for the local people during Muriel's time at San Giovanni, only partially appeased two years after her death when an eighty-eight-year-old German sergeant was sentenced to life imprisonment. One hundred had died at Civitella. In all, there were 212 victims as the sweep continued through Burrone, Cornia, Gebbia, and San Pancrazzia.[28] In Civitella, only one young man, who later became the priest, had escaped by hopping over a wall. Muriel asked her own priest to find a civilised architect who would 'understand'[29] San Giovanni. On the top of the belfry there had been a small iron Holy Cross, lost after the storm, later found in the grass. The architect, Marcello Donati, remembered how delighted and grateful she was on hearing that this had been recovered. Repairs were begun, then suspended when Jardine and Muriel set off for London. During the night of the day they left, the house was burgled.

*

Between the thunderbolt and the burglary Muriel had dispensed her own lightning when *Aiding and Abetting* appeared to warm praise in September. Establishing shot: Paris consulting room of psychiatrist

Hildegard Wolf. It is not called a consulting room but a 'studio', for she is something of an artist. Before her sits a man who claims to be the missing Lord Lucan. At his feet a bulging briefcase supposedly contains the story most journalists would kill for: an account of his life on the run. She never asks to see this manuscript. Throughout, it remains (if it ever existed) obscure. Faced by this man, Hildegard is also confronted by a moral dilemma, for Lucan is blackmailing her. He knows that in a former life she was Beate Pappenheim, a fraudulent stigmatic. Thousands had sent her money. When exposed, she, like Lucan, had disappeared, only to re-enter public life as another form of mountebank. Lucan's problem, she tells him, is one of identity. It is her problem, too, although of a different order. She has no credentials as an analyst. He threatens to destroy her reputation. But is he Lucan? The previous week, another man, 'Robert Walker', had visited her, also claiming to be Lucan. Both men bear a striking resemblance to each other and to the 1974 photographs.

Cut to another set of characters, one of whom is not a fiction. Lady Lucan, described as 'unimaginative but honest', was apparently displeased by her walk-on part. Muriel had, as usual, researched the historical background thoroughly. To characterise 'Lucky' Lucan, she had isolated not only his diet and arrogant fecklessness but also his wife's evidence against him: that he took pleasure in caning her. The book, Spark says in her 'Note to Readers', is based on fact (including the stigmatic story) but metamorphosed into a 'hypothesis': that Lucan's chain of aristocratic aiders and abettors helped him escape.[30]

The daughter of one of these conspirators, Lacey Twickenham, focuses this scenario. Ashamed of her father's collusion, she determines to write a book exposing Lucan. Interviewing one of his former friends, Joe Murray, she persuades him to join her in the hunt. And so the chase is on. The novel has everything one could ask of a thriller: murder, blackmail, fraud, love interest, scandal, suspense. It leaps nimbly across the decades and between Paris, London, Scotland, Avila, Mexico and Africa. As usual, however, the plot is an irrelevance. Lucan is a man of no importance, a mere catalyst for the larger issues thrown up by his case. *Aiding and Abetting* is a metaphysical shocker about the nature of belief.

Muriel had always done a nice line in slimeball con artists who exploit our primitive urge to believe, to keep others believing in our public image. Her heroic figures deceive not to flatter but to fluster the hypocritical. Dougal Douglas in *The Ballad of Peckham Rye* lies throughout to tell the folk of Peckham the truth about themselves. Jean Brodie, a brilliant teacher, might nowadays be arrested for corrupting the youth of Edinburgh. These creatures are artists rather than con artists, and Hildegard belongs in this category. She heals. She is double, a walking non sequitur. In her role as Beate, she had performed miracles. Acting the psychiatrist, she stabilises mental illness. The distinction between her and the doppelgänger Lucans is that she is sane where they are not. They are stupid, cunning, have spent their lives 'attitudinising'. She is intensely private. As with all the strong women in Muriel's novels, she resists blackmail. To succumb would be to lose identity and a sense of moral cleanliness. Lucan is a cipher, 'could have been anybody', 'a perfect bore, a cut-to-measure gentleman'.[31]

Hildegard is not impressed. Lucan's identity problem is that he never had one. He is a dead soul. Hildegard, on the other hand, is simply (complicatedly) herself, controlling her artifice. Both have their 'believers' but the supporters of Lucan are as decadent as he. Her followers have a kind of faith, literally misplaced but actually regenerative. Her lover, Jean-Pierre Roget, has lived with her for five years, ignorant of her real name and past. When she tells him, he feels not betrayed but delighted. To him she is 'magic' in whatever guise. She '"wasn't a person to whom things happen. She did all the happenings."'[32] When she vanishes (as Muriel's characters often do), his faith in her remains undiminished. This, then, is love, and their love story runs parallel with that of Lacey and Joe. Lacey is in her thirties, Joe in his sixties. It is an unlikely liaison. Although they do not seek love, it arrives unbidden, as it frequently does in Muriel's later writing. Their relationship develops in proportion to their diminishing interest in their quarry. They never find him. She never writes her book. Lucan fades out, disintegrates again.

Instead, they discover something for which they were not searching.

Hildegard, then, bears a certain resemblance to Muriel, as do many Spark heroines, young or old. They resist. They disencumber themselves. They mock vanities and attempts to colonise them. They work, feed men at neither end, are 'free and full of enterprise, without any mess of impediments'.[33] The latter description, as it happens, is not of Hildegard but of Lacey embarking on her affair with Joe. But the words characterise Muriel's sceptical women equally well. It is this openness to experience which Muriel prized and which, ultimately, characterised her imagination. Boredom is seen as the litmus test of fakery. Art, good art, is the opposite of boredom. It takes us into the realm of the unknown, to places where the bearings of the rational world fail. The fear of the unknown, endemic to all fundamentalism, is the road to a hell of convention, paved with good, indifferent and plain evil intentions. There is no justice, no absolute truth on this earth. The search for absolute truth, however, through mysteries, signs and symbols, is as much the vocation of the artist as it is that of the priest, the theologian, the philosopher, the mystic. In her work, the dullards are chained in Plato's cave watching shadows cast by the light of reality dancing on the wall. Ghosts. It is the artist who walks out and returns to tell them of their illusion.

*

Muriel was halfway across France in October 2000 when her mobile phone rang to tell her that San Giovanni had been burgled. This trip had been to attend a colloquium including ex-President Gorbachev. Jardine turned round and drove home.

When they arrived, they discovered that the thieves had brought a lorry and quickly emptied the place of anything they thought valuable. Muriel lost many treasures. Furniture went, the refrigerator, an ormolu clock. It was the nightmare of the fake window cleaner in New York, of *Memento Mori*, of *The Takeover* and *Symposium* come true. Muriel's reaction, though, was to play it down. Property was just property, no matter how acute the sentimental attachment. Jardine's loss, she insisted, was by far the greater. Many of her paintings had gone, including two portraits of Muriel, and some of her sculptures. Muriel wrote a poem, 'The Empty Space', mourning the loss:

> A square space on the wall
> marks the memory of that picture
> painted at night, stolen at night,
> worked on at night, in Rome, from the artist's window.
> How I remember Castel St Angelo
> In her night picture, gleaming with
> history-in-darkness, guardian of old Rome,
> and the artist's home was full of midnight
> and the light of all Europe shone in her hands. [...]
> My honest close companion on the wall:
> It is all over now. The thieves came by night.[34]

'I mean, it's her *work*,' Muriel said to me, 'It would be like us having our manuscripts stolen.'[35]

But life went on going on. So long as there was creation there was hope. Burglary was an occupational hazard for those who wished to travel. Nobody could steal her imagination. By January, Muriel was working full-blast on her play and had signed up with Viking Penguin for her twenty-second novel, *The Finishing School*. Her brother, the last surviving member of her childhood family, had just died in America. Later in the year Hugh Honour's partner, John Fleming, also died. She attended the funeral of the latter, in Florence, not of the former, in Colorado. 'The success of my creative work was a great relief to me,' Muriel wrote at that time. 'I am reminded of [...] Leonardo Sciascia's advice to writers: "Want as much money as you like, but be careful not to need it"'[36] – another version of 'Never own anything that you can't afford to lose.' Although slowly, inevitably, she was losing many things – friends, property, family, mobility, even sight – and late in the year 2001 could work only for short stretches in bright light, each debilitation brought new experience. Three years later, talking to one rather shocked interviewer of her cataract operation in Zurich, it was as though she were intrigued by an event that had happened to someone else. '"They take your eyes out and hook these lenses on to them. It's all carried out under local anaesthetic," she explains with obvious relish. "You can still see but it's similar to when there is interference on the television."[37] Nothing was wasted on this artist. Her mind as sharp as ever, she took to wearing huge designer spectacles and often travelled back down the long escape road of her life, seeing it with fresh vision. No sentiment. No regrets. Memory touchstones, warmly fondled, still generated creative life and, like her God and her grandmother, like the Seraph of her first story, they sparkled with paradox.

*

The title of *The Finishing School* was typically slippery. Muriel did not know that this novel would complete her *oeuvre* but she wrote it as though it would, battling for four more years against acute pain. The final aria of the opera of her life, it orchestrates many tiny references to her earlier work around that perennial theme: the threat of the mundane to take over the original. In its way it is a contemplation of her life as an artist, as though asking herself why and how she did what she did, a celebration of the imagination, of youth, the Holy Spirit, another satire on the inauthentic. 'Finishing' here signifies several things: an education in manners; the final polish of a work of art, be it a book or a piece of furniture; and death, murder or 'polishing off'.

The setting is a lakeside house in Ouchy, Switzerland. There, College Sunrise, an unconventional finishing school, offers among its other classes tuition in creative writing by Roland Mahler. He and his shrewd wife, Nina Parker, run the place, although she does most of the work, allowing him time to write. *The Finishing School* documents the collapse of their marriage. She thought she had married a scholar and a playwright. But that husband no longer exists. Instead, she finds herself shackled to an obsessive who is trying hopelessly to compose a novel. One of his students, Chris Wiley, just seventeen years old, seems plainly more gifted than his tutor. Mahler comes to hate the boy, desire his death and the destruction of his work. A study of the jealousy of talent, ultimately it is another love story. Nina takes a lover, leaves the school and marries him. Mahler, after Wiley has tried to electrocute him in the bath, ends up running the school with him and becoming his sexual partner. There was, then, nothing demure about this book. Muriel was still asking awkward moral questions, and from the biographer's point of view, it offers an intriguing summation of her life. Wiley, like Tom Richards in *Reality and Dreams*, ventriloquises her views on art. If as a flesh-and-blood teenager he seems somewhat anaemic, just a voice, that is because he is possibly Muriel Spark in drag. He even has a conversation with Mahler which replicates the one she had had with Iris Murdoch about characters taking over the narrative. '"No,' says Wiley, "they live the lives I give them. [...] I'm in full control [...]."'[38]

Wiley's novel is an imaginative reconstruction of the story of Mary Queen of Scots, the mysterious murders of the young Italian courtier-musician, Rizzio, and of her husband, Lord Darnley. Wiley is thus completing another of Muriel's unfinished works: that surrealist play on Mary Queen of Scots abandoned when she was herself a struggling author in London during the late 1940s. At the time, and for many years afterwards, she had felt her own talent to be obstructed, just as Wiley's is, by dullards envious of her gifts. In retrospect, her own lovers, Howard Sergeant and Derek Stanford, epitomised this assault on her originality. She saw them as discouraging her, negative, feeding off her like leeches, trying to invade, steal the mystery of her genius. Her intense secrecy seems to be related to these experiences. Those terrifying hallucinations in 1954 had dramatised persecution mania in the form of a conviction that people were spying on, threatening her. To the end she was obsessive about anyone attempting to 'pry' into her private papers. When Wiley says of Mahler '"He wants my secrets"'[39] he echoes a recurrent theme in her fiction and her life. Just as Laurence Manders in *The Comforters* rifles though his grandmother's possessions seeking something that will reveal her essence, so Mahler empties out Wiley's bag, looking for the boy's novel.

'According to the catechism of the Roman Catholic faith, into which [Mahler] had been born,' Muriel wrote, 'six sins against the Holy Spirit are specified. The fourth is "Envy of Another's Spiritual Good", and that was the sin from which [Mahler] suffered.'[40] These were precisely the terms in which she had described Stanford in a letter to John Heath-Stubbs while writing *Curriculum Vitae*. Throughout *The Finishing School*, Mahler suffers a 'choking' sensation whenever he is gripped by envy of his pupil. Nine years earlier Muriel had used this word to describe Stanford's enraged jealousy of her work.[41] And this novel contains a message from the redeemed Mahler about vocation for those who thought she had at times been harsh. '"Art", he says, "is an act of daring."' If some tragedy obstructs composition:

> 'The average author can no doubt finish the book, but not well. However the dedicated author might seem callous, not easily shattered, tough. Hence the reputation of artists in all fields for ruthless, cold detachment. Too bad. [...] The true artist is almost unaware of other people's cares and distractions. [...] Once you have written The End to a book it is yours, not only till death do you part but for all eternity.'[42]

The Finishing School, however, is gentler with Stanford's ghost than *A Far Cry from Kensington* had been, and Muriel herself was gentler as death approached. Her last novel has a happy ending and, in her way, Muriel did, too.

*

After eight months of the 'racial origins dispute' with her son, on 1 December 1998, Muriel had registered her last will and testament. It was handwritten in sometimes erratic Italian on two sheets of yellow ruled paper, and it left everything, or rather all her physical, literary, and intellectual property in Italy, to Jardine 'my friend and collaborator for many years (since 1968)'. She also deposited a letter with her solicitor, Lorenzo Contri, specifically excluding her son, and she wrote to me saying that she was glad now to be free of Robin. He was another, she thought, who was jealous of her talent, and in the British press she was, indeed, presented as ruthless. At home in San Giovanni, she could be her more authentic self.

According to the local priest, Don Gualtiero Mazzeschi, Muriel, being Catholic, seemed close to the Italian way of life. Despite the fact that she spoke the language less well than her friend (somewhat stiffly to judge from a television recording, and with an impeccable Morningside accent), she tried, '*si capiva*', she could make herself understood. When he was walking a party of schoolchildren up the hill, she invited them into the garden and was photographed happily in their midst. For many years, the villagers had no idea that she was a celebrated author, and she liked it that way. It was only in 2004 that the young mayor of the *Comune* discovered her fame and arranged for her to be made an honorary citizen the following year. A ceremonial key was publicly presented at the Town Hall and it seems that of all the awards she had received, this one meant the most. Behind a bank of white roses, she radiated happiness. Don Gualtiero, unable to attend because a local child had been run over and killed by a school bus, went to San Giovanni to apologise for his absence. She explained how proud she was, showed him the key. At last, she said, she was free, a citizen and not a subject.[43]

Don Gualtiero did not see Muriel frequently yet he felt close to her through their theological conversations. He regarded Muriel as highly emotional, spiritual. She rarely attended church, usually only at Easter, when she would be driven the short distance from the house and enter through the sacristy side entrance, take communion and then disappear. She never confessed: a 'strange' Catholic, a convert who inhabited her own particular world and lived her religion 'personally'. But this world of hers was 'rich, profoundly cultured, philosophical'. Don Gualtiero had first met her when she was republishing *Memento Mori* in Italian. They spoke about this, about *The Only Problem*, about Job. 'She wanted to understand, was sensitively interested in understanding the problem of suffering.' She was, he said, profoundly religious, like a creature fallen from heaven. It was clear that she had been a fighter, remained a fighter, had endured a difficult life. But she had found peace. 'She faded out, just like a candle.'[44] Was this true? Jardine thought not. It was, she believed, a sentimental account by someone who had not known Muriel well.

*

On 29 November 2005 Muriel was admitted to Villa Donatello, a private hospital in Florence, where her right kidney was removed. Just before

Christmas, she returned to convalesce. To friends and business associates she wrote chirpily, hoping to be back to work within three months. But this time it was cancer and, as soon as she knew that she was dying, she called for Don Gualtiero. He found her sitting behind her desk, calm and very clear about what she wanted. She was, she told him, ready to die. She wished to leave this world simply, not dressed in her best clothes in the Italian funerary style but wrapped in a shroud, not in an ostentatious coffin but in one of '*legno fragile*', thin wood that decomposes easily, to be buried in the plain earth of the village cemetery. They agreed that he would administer last rites when the time came. In the event, he did not. As Easter approached, she was taken by ambulance, arranged several days earlier, to another hospital in Florence, Casa di Cura, Villa Cherubini, where she was attended by her private doctor. There a priest heard her confession and, at 10.40 on the night of Maundy Thursday, the first day of the Passover, 13 April 2006, she died aged eighty-eight. Jardine was with her to the end. The formalities took place in Florence on Good Friday and on Saturday she was taken to her local church for the funeral and burial. It was, Bruce Hunter remarked, a 'good death'.

Somehow Muriel remained young. She wrote young. Death was to her just a fact, another transition, a new beginning. It did not exist as an element of lived experience: rather disconcerting for the poor chap. Those early thoughts about whether she would rise again with missing teeth and appendix had always made her laugh. Death was a mystery, part of that cloud of unknowing, essential to creation, the same cloud that had gathered round her mind in Edinburgh's North British Hotel in 1962 and clarified the 'nevertheless principle'. She had been alone, expelled, she felt, from the family home, in a room meant for strangers to the city. The telephone rang. Her father was dead. From this point she knew she would be unprotected. It was the exact mid-point of her life, forty-four years after she was born, forty-four years before she would die, and she perhaps sensed the importance of the moment as the hinge of her earthly existence. The age of the Father was over. The age of the Son had never appealed. In the roles of daughter, mother, wife, she had felt misfitted. Her proper habitat, her art, lay in the age of the Holy Ghost. And there she remained, a ghost-writer for God whoever He may be, sending us disarming postcards from eternity. Dark music. Entering her realm you had to watch out, for you could be entering a fiction, visiting someone who was not there, a mistress of disguise and disappearances. Find the lady? A difficult proposition when she was in ceaseless movement.

EPILOGUE

The funeral on Holy Saturday was a quiet affair. It was Easter weekend, a hot, sunny day. The small church was full. About forty people, mostly local, attended a simple and dignified ceremony. Don Gualtiero, saddened that he had missed the opportunity to administer last rites, officiated. There was some urgency to arrange the burial as is customary in Italy but also because it was Easter and the priest busy. Jardine had spent most of Good Friday telephoning the bad news to friends. The international press heard on the day of the funeral through Reuters who sent a journalist from Italian Ansa, Paola Catani. Local TV recorded the event for the news, later scrapping its tape. The young mayor was there with his tricolour sash and the *Comune* gonfalon. It was he who made the public announcement. Inside the church a Dutch string trio played Schubert, Beethoven and Jacob while Jardine, dressed in white trousers and top, was supported by an elderly man none of the villagers recognised and whom she introduced as one of Muriel's cousins. He had come from London for his first visit. When Jardine emerged on his arm, it seemed that she could scarcely walk for grief. The coffin was loaded by six bearers into a hearse which headed an old-style cortège like those common in Italy until the late 1960s: the priest, the authorities, the men and, last, the women with children.

In the tiny walled cemetery, Muriel was buried beneath a simple grey stone slab inscribed: 'MURIEL SPARK / POETA / 1918–2006 / "NESSUN FOGLIA SI RIPETE / RIPETTIAMO SOLO LA PAROL"' ('Not a leaf repeats itself, we only repeat the word'). The quotation is from her poem, 'Canaan', one of her early religious verses, refused in 1953 by the *Tablet*, taken in 1966 by the *New Yorker*, and written when she was an Anglican soon to become a Catholic. The grave is surrounded by others with headstones bearing photographs of their incumbents. No headstone adorns Muriel's last resting-place, no photograph. It is modest, almost anonymous in its plainness. But one person there, oddly the priest, had been troubled by her self-effacement and hoped that she would forgive him for his interference. Believing that Muriel's body should be preserved for future generations, he had recommended a solid, zinc-lined coffin to be buried not directly in the earth but in a concrete niche. No matter how precisely she had tried to organise her death, others had intervened. In a strange way, it recalls the end of *The Driver's Seat*.

Jardine gave one interview, printed in *Scotland on Sunday*. In this she recalled Muriel giving a 'king's ransom' to a pianist at an hotel in the Italian Alps because she wanted to make someone happy: 'Muriel was just such an innocent person. That sounds bizarre, but that was what she was. She was so kind-hearted and generous and she helped out so many people with acts of kindness.' No one who had seen these two vivacious women in their daily domestic life could doubt that this was exactly how Jardine felt. They would disagree vigorously but they loved each other. Jardine was constantly protecting Muriel against her own impulsiveness. Whenever there was talk of a possible deal, Muriel would plunge in, explaining it hopefully while Jardine would hold back, ask her not to discuss it, suggesting that it was bad luck to count chickens. Reading that interview, I was reminded of Muriel's insistence on stopping the car when driving through the suburbs of Arezzo, to give money to a vagrant woman selling flowers. She understood poverty. There was a simplicity about her that would allow her to vent passionate feelings of love and hate. But this was not for public consumption. For if she was innocent, she was not naïve. This was a woman who could go white with rage. She would have been surprised neither by the glorious obituaries and the Internet being log-jammed with praise and grief at her death, nor by the journalists eager to muck-rake now that she could no longer sue them.

Some members of the press, it seems, could never forgive her for being a free woman. They concentrated on her relationship with her son. It was the human (the inhuman) angle. They doorstepped him and telephoned me. Did he receive cartloads of money from his mother? Did she lie about her grandmother being Jewish through the female

line? Was he a bad son? Was she a bad mother? A piece appeared in the
Daily Mail, 'The Crime of Miss Jean Brodie', implying that Muriel's
sending cheques to Robin might be construed as 'guilt money paid by a
mother who abandoned her child to fulfil her own dream of success'.
Her whole life was supposedly bottled up in this cod-Freudian scenario.
Robin was described as a 'troubled soul', his mother as someone who
'struggled to rid herself of her hated roots'.[1]

Robin, who was presenting a twenty-year retrospective of his paintings in Edinburgh, was interviewed at the gallery. 'She reinvented her
past,' he said, speaking of her attitude to her Jewish origins. 'She wouldn't
have liked to have admitted she was wrong. That was unfortunate. It
was a failing and it wasn't necessary because she was a very great writer.
We can all make mistakes. [...].' In a lecture he discussed 'several pictures
influenced by his difficult relationship with his mother. In one [...] titled
"The Illustrious Rabbi of Prague", two cats which in Jewish symbolism
represent the family, are painted turning their back to the Jewish holy
man. [...] The mother is a very important figure in the Jewish religion,'
he said. 'I suppose it makes it more poignant that my mother turned
away from her faith.'[2]

The story ran and ran, larded with inaccuracy. An inflated figure was
invented for the value of her estate – three million pounds – to establish
her meanness. Family 'friends' were found who testified to Muriel's
savage ambition and carelessness to Robin throughout his life. All lies,
damned lies, apparently manufactured from a desire to reduce her from
the complicated, unique artist that she was, determined to follow her
vocation, to a soap-opera stereotype. It was true that she could be harsh,
that she would rarely be corrected, and was remorselessly tough; the
image of a placable Morningside lady with a lace hankie up her sleeve
was something that belonged to her schoolgirl destination rather than
to her destiny as the expatriate writer who saw herself as Lucrezia Borgia
in trousers. She was a murderer of illusions, had a vision of hell on Earth
and had to live with it. This could lead her to overstate the villainy of
those she saw as betraying her. Sometimes she was unable to believe
that she had ever said or done things that contradicted what she wanted

to appear in the authorised version of her life. But she did not reinvent her past or turn away from her faith. Rather, she kept inventing her future. In one sense her life was a fiction, her public life, like that of all celebrities. In a more important sense, her fiction was her life. That was where she lived, tuning in to the absurdity of the human desire for absolute truth. The recording of her last major interview was delayed by the baying of her dog outside. 'Poor thing,' she said. 'It's howling for love.'[3]

NOTE ON REFERENCES

Quotations from Muriel Spark's novels are wherever possible taken from the latest edition overseen by her: the *Muriel Spark Omnibus*, volumes 1–4, published in the UK by Constable in 1993, 1994, 1996, and 1997 respectively, and in America by Houghton Mifflin. The pagination for both the UK and the US editions is identical. In the endnotes the title of each volume has been abbreviated to *MSO1, MSO2* etc. For those novels not included in the *Omnibus* volumes, the Penguin or first edition is cited. Reference to the short stories is to the collection *Open to the Public: New and Collected Stories* (New York: New Directions, 1997), abbreviated to *OTTP.* Reference to the poems is to Spark's final collection, *All the Poems* (Carcanet, 2004), abbreviated to *ATP.* In references to all books cited, place of publication is London unless otherwise stated.

ENDNOTE ABBREVIATIONS

ALI	Autograph letter, initialled
ALS, nd, np	Autograph letter, signed, no date, no place [i.e. no address]
AM	*Atlantic Monthly*
AMS	Autograph manuscript
AN	Autograph note
ANS	Autograph note, signed
APC, pm	Autograph postcard, post-marked
APCI	Autograph postcard, initialled
B&B	*Books & Bookmen*
BBCWAC	BBC Written Archives Centre
CEN	*Church of England Newspaper*
CH	*Catholic Herald*
CTBR	*Chicago Tribune Book Review*
CV	Muriel Spark, *Curriculum Vitae* (Constable, 1992)
DE	*Daily Express*
DM	*Daily Mail*
DT	*Daily Telegraph*
EN	*Evening News*
ES	*Evening Standard*

FT	*Financial Times*
GUL	Lauinger Library, Georgetown University, Washington DC
HRC	Harry Ransom Humanities Research Center, University of Texas at Austin
Interview with …	Martin Stannard's interview with …
JGHSM	*James Gillespie's High School Magazine*
LRB	*London Review of Books*
MS	Manuscript
NLS	National Library of Scotland
NS	*New Statesman*
NY	*New Yorker*
NYHT	*New York Herald Tribune*
NYHTBR	*New York Herald Tribune Book Review*
NYRB	*New York Review of Books*
NYT	*New York Times*
NYTBR	*New York Times Book Review*
PUL	Princeton University Libraries
SG	San Giovanni, Spark's home in Tuscany
ST	*Sunday Times*
S. Tel.	*Sunday Telegraph*
T & T	*Time & Tide*
TccL	Typed carbon copy of letter
TccLS	Typed carbon copy of letter, signed
THES	*Times Higher Education Supplement*
TLI	Typed letter, initialled
TLS	Typed letter, signed
TLS	*Times Literary Supplement*
TMS	Typed manuscript
TPCI	Typed postcard, initialled
TS	Typescript
Tulsa	McFarlin Library, University of Tulsa
UDL	University of Delaware Library, Special Collections
UVL	University of Victoria Library BC, Special Collection
WPBR	*Washington Post Book Review*
WPBW	*Washington Post Book World*
WUL	Washington University in St Louis Library

ENDNOTES

PREFACE

1 *CV*, p. 11.

2 *Ibid.*, p. 25.

3 *Ibid.*, p. 27.

4 *Ibid.*, p. 74.

5 *Ibid.*, p. 37.

6 *Ibid.*, pp. 21–22.

7 'Books', *Observer*, 19 July 1992, 59.

8 'She Who Can Do No Wrong', *LRB*, 6 August 1992, 8–9; 8.

9 'Rich Pickings', 'Life and Times', *The Times*, 23 July 1992.

10 'She Who Can Do No Wrong', *op. cit.*, 8.

11 Charles ['Chip'] McGrath, then fiction editor of the *NY*, later editor of the *NYTBR*, introduced Spark's readings from *CV* and *The Driver's Seat* at the 92nd Street Y's Unterberg Poetry Center, 22 May 1993.

12 *CV*, p. 11.

13 Interview with Spark, 1 September 1993.

14 *NY*, 2 June 1975; reprinted in *OTTP*, pp. 274–80.

15 *NY*, 22 June 1963; reprinted in *OTTP*, pp. 281–7. Spark stated that this 'story' was, in fact, autobiography.

16 'The First Year of My Life', *OTTP*, p. 274.

17 *Ibid.*, p. 274.

18 *Ibid.*, p. 275.

19 *Ibid.*, p. 276.

20 *Ibid.*, pp. 276–7.

21 *Ibid.*, p. 275.

22 *Ibid.*, p. 275.

23 *Ibid.*, p. 275.

24 *Ibid.*, p. 277.

25 *Ibid.*, p. 277.

26 *Ibid.*, p. 279.

27 *Ibid.*, p. 280.

28 *Ibid.*, p. 275.

29 Most of Spark's literary MSS are held by the McFarlin Library, University of Tulsa.

30 *Loitering with Intent* (Bodley Head, 1981); *MSO2*, p. 12.

CHAPTER 1: NIGHT AND DAY

1 2.30 p.m., 18 July 1912.

2 'Edinburgh-born', *NS*, 10 August 1962, 180; reprinted as 'What Images Return' in Karl Miller (ed.), *Memoirs of Modern Scotland* (Faber & Faber, 1970), pp. 151–3; 151.

3 'What Images Return', *op. cit.*, p. 151.

4 *Ibid.*, p. 151.

5 *Ibid.*, p. 152.

6 *CV*, p. 86.

7 Much of the information about Muriel's parents derives from two interviews with Philip Camberg: 16 July 1993 and 7 October 1993.

8 *CV*, p. 81.

9 Harry, Winifred, Phyllis, Hilda, Roger and Alec.

10 Interview with Roger Uezzell, 26 October 1993.

11 Interview with Phyllis Batchelor (née Uezzell), 1 December 1993. Much of the information about the Watford households and the Cambergs' visits derives from this and other interviews with Roger Uezzell (her brother), Philip Camberg and Muriel Spark.

12 Philip Camberg and Phyllis Batchelor thought Adelaide was Lady de Rothschild's companion. Spark doubted that Adelaide was quite so elevated.

13 Muriel Spark, 'The Gentile Jewesses', *op. cit., OTTP*, p. 284.

14 *Ibid.*, p. 285.

15 *Ibid.*, p. 285.

16 It was a fur muff in the version Muriel knew; in Philip's, it was a humbler pillow.

17 *CV*, p. 91.

18 *Ibid.*, p. 93.

19 *Ibid.*, p. 91.

20 *Loitering with Intent, MSO2*, p. 44.

21 *CV*, p. 95.

22 *Ibid.*, p. 96.

23 *Ibid.*, p. 88.

24 *Ibid.*, p. 89.

25 'Bluebell among the Sables', *ATP*, pp. 78–9.

26 *Loitering with Intent, MSO2*, pp. 73, 77.

CHAPTER 2: HOME AND AWAY

1 Interview with Philip Camberg, 7 October 1993.

2 *Ibid.*

3 *Evening Dispatch*, 28 September 1962, 2.

4 Higher National Diploma; not a degree but recognised as of degree standard.

5 Interview with Spark, 1 September 1993.

6 *CV*, p. 53.

7 Interview with Philip Camberg, 16 July 1993.

8   No. 40, South Richmond Street, Edinburgh in, respectively, 1876 and 1877.

9   *The Prime of Miss Jean Brodie* (Macmillan, 1961), *MSO1*, pp. 33–4.

10 Beatrice and Jacob in Canongate (1876, 1877); Rachel in Lawnmarket (1881).

11 15 February 1917.

12 10 August 1920. Her father is cited on the death certificate as Philip Radman, Baker, deceased; her mother as Pesha Radman, deceased.

13 Interview with Philip Camberg, 16 July 1993.

14 Charles, Ellis, Joel and Maurice. Charlie later emigrated to Canada; Ellis ran an erratic Edinburgh laundry; Joel, the eldest, left school at fourteen and ended up owning a large children's clothing factory; Maurice ('Mossie'), the youngest and cleverest, became a doctor and dentist, married the beautiful Rita Rosenbloom and died early.

15 There were three, in Rae's name: at 3 Comiston Road, 11 Haymarket Terrace, and 189 Morningside Road.

16 Interview with Philip Camberg, 16 July 1993.

17 *CV*, p. 22.

18 *Ibid.*, p. 23.

19 *Ibid.*, p. 96.

20 *Ibid.*, p. 24.

21 Frank Kermode, *Not Entitled: A Memoir* (New York: Farrar, Straus & Giroux, 1995), p. 15.

22 *CV*, p. 24.

23 *Ibid.*, p. 45.

24 'The Gentile Jewesses', *op. cit.*, *OTTP*, p. 287.

25 *CV*, p. 45.

26 *Ibid.*, p. 55.

27 *Ibid.*, pp. 56–7.

28 *Ibid.*, p. 64.

29 *Ibid.*, p. 96. Frances lived at No. 8, Stevenson at No. 10.

30 *Ibid.*, p. 96.

31 Elizabeth Vance, (née Murphy), quoted *CV*, pp. 58–9.

32 'On the Air', Win Fanning's interview with Muriel Spark, *Post-Gazette* (Pittsburgh), 7 May 1979, 28. Part of the publicity programme for the American TV screening of Scottish Television's adaptation, starring Geraldine McEwan.

33 *CV*, pp. 54 and 60.

34 *Ibid.*, pp. 62–3.

35 Interview with Shirley Hazzard, 21 September 1993.

36 'Today on TV [...]', Diane Mermigas's interview with Muriel Spark, *Daily Herald* (Illinois), 11 May 1979.

37 *JGHSM* (July 1936), 67.

38 *CV*, pp. 61–2.

39 Interview with Spark, 1 September 1993.

40 TLS (fax), 18 August 1995, Penelope Jardine to Stannard, from SG; © 2009 Penelope Jardine.

41 *Ibid.*

42 *The Prime of Miss Jean Brodie, MSO1*, p. 11.

43 *CV*, p. 46.

44 *Ibid.*, p. 79.

45 *Ibid.*, p. 100.

46 Interview with Spark, 1 September 1993.

47 Interview with Philip Camberg, 7 October 1993.

48 Interview with Spark, 1 September 1993.

49 *CV*, p. 115.

50 *Ibid.*, p. 63.

51 *Ibid.*, p. 115.

52 *JGHSM* (July 1933), pp. 86, 90–91.

53 *Ibid.* (July 1935), p. 73.

54 *CV*, p. 101.

55 *Ibid.*, p. 64.

56 *JGHSM* (July 1930), 40.

57 See 'The Door of Youth', *ibid.* (July 1931), 50.

58 *CV*, p. 68.

59 Interview with Spark, 1 September 1993.

60 See *CV*, p. 68.

61 *Ibid*, p. 68.

62 *JGHSM* (July 1934), 16.

63 *CV*, p. 101.

64 *Ibid.*, p. 103.

65 *Ibid.*, pp. 102–3.

66 *Ibid.*, p. 111.

67 *Ibid.*, p. 112.

68 *Ibid.*, p. 109.

69 *Loitering with Intent, MSO2*, p. 40.

70 *Ibid.*, p. 23.

71 Spark denied this stating that Philip never attended Jewish clubs. He was quite clear on the matter.

72 Interview with Spark, 2 August 1999.

73 Interview with Philip Camberg, 16 July 1993.

CHAPTER 3: OUT OF AFRICA

1 Interview with Spark, 14 July 1995.

2 *CV*, pp. 119–41.

3 Interview with Spark, 14 July 1995.

4 'The Curtain Blown by the Breeze', *OTTP*, p. 31.

5 *Ibid.*, p. 28.

6 'Bang-bang You're Dead', *OTTP*, p. 111.

7 *Ibid.*, p. 66.

8 *Ibid.*, p. 60.

9 *CV*, p. 122.

10 Interview with Spark, 14 July 1995.

11 *Ibid.*

12 *CV*, p. 125.

13 Interview with Spark, 14 July 1995.

14 *Ibid.*

15 *CV*, p. 130.

16 Deborah Ross, 'Dame Muriel Spark: The Brightest of Sparks [. . .]', *Independent*, 17 September 2001.

17 Interview with Spark, 14 July 1995.

18 *CV*, p. 128.

19 *Ibid.*, p. 129.

20 *Ibid.*, p. 128.

21 *Ibid.*, p. 128.

22 'The Seraph and the Zambesi', *OTTP*, p. 83.

23 'The Curtain Blown by the Breeze', *OTTP*, p. 27.

24 *CV*, p. 126.

25 'Bang-bang You're Dead', *OTTP*, p. 61.

26 *Ibid.*, p. 55.

27 *Ibid.*, p. 62.

28 *CV*, p. 127.

29 'Bang-bang You're Dead', *OTTP*, p. 59.

30 Interview with Spark, 18 December 1995.

31 *CV*, pp. 133–4.

32 *Ibid.*, p. 132.

33 *Ibid.*, p. 131.

34 *Ibid.*, p. 136.

35 *Ibid.*, p. 140.

36 'The Go-Away Bird', *OTTP*, p. 246.

37 *Ibid.*, pp. 249–50.

38 Telegram, 6 October 1942, from Cape Town, 6.17 p.m.; NLS.

39 *CV*, p. 137.

40 *Ibid.*, p. 139.

41 Interview with Spark, 14 July 1995.

42 *CV*, p. 138.

43 Interview with Spark, 14 July 1995.

44 *CV*, p. 135.

45 'The Pawnbroker's Wife', *OTTP*, p. 104.

46 'The First Year of My Life', *OTTP*, p. 277.

47 Sefton Delmer, *Black Boomerang: An Autobiography. Volume 2* (Secker & Warburg, 1962), p. 125.

48 *CV*, p. 147.

49 TLS, Spark to Sarah Camberg, 30 May 1944, from Box 2, W. Central District PO, New Oxford Street, London W1; NLS. Spark was uncertain whether she sent this letter.

50 See ALS [airgraph] from Sydney Spark, 20[?] May 1944, from Military Camp, Gwelo, S. Rhodesia, to Muriel Spark, c/o Rhodesia House, 429 Strand, London [address deleted]; NLS.

51 See ALS [airgraph], 27 August 1944, from Sgt. S. O. Spark, X 2869, Nervous Disorders Hospital, Bulawayo, S. Rhodesia, to Muriel Spark, c/o Box 3, W. Central District PO etc.; NLS.

52 *Black Boomerang, op. cit.*, p. 22.

53 Called 'Hans' in *CV*, p. 155; possibly Sgt. Sepp Obermeyer: see *Black Boomerang, op. cit.*, p. 87.

54 *Black Boomerang, op. cit.*, p. 148.

55 *Ibid.*, p. 151.

56 *CV*, p. 158.

57 *Ibid.*, pp. 154–5.

58 *Ibid.*, pp. 153 and 144.

59 Mary Steel, 'They're All Girls Together', *Illustrated*, 29 December 1951, 23–5.

60 Interview with Pamela Carrigan (née Flood), 14 October 1996.

61 *CV*, p. 144.

62 *The Hothouse by the East River* (Macmillan, 1973); *MSO4*, p. 203.

63 *Ibid.*, p. 201.

64 *CV*, p. 147.

65 *The Hothouse by the East River*, *MSO4*, p. 64.

66 *Black Boomerang, op. cit.*, p. 92.

67 *The Girls of Slender Means* (Macmillan, 1963); *MSO2*, p. 145.

68 *Ibid.*, p. 146.

69 *The Hothouse by the East River*, *MSO4*, p. 207.

70 See ALS [airgraph], 1 October 1944, Sgt. S. O. Spark, from Nervous Disorders Hospital, Bulawayo, S. Rhodesia, to Spark, c/o Rhodesia House, 429 Strand, WC2; NLS.

71 See ALS [airgraph], 25 October 1944, Sydney Oswald Spark, from Nervous Disorders Hospital, Bulawayo to Mrs S. Camberg at 160 Bruntsfield Place, Edinburgh; NLS.

72 ALS, 18 January 1945, from M. Benigna OP, Dominican Convent High School, Gwelo, to Spark c/o Rhodesia House etc., readdressed to 160 Bruntsfield Place, Edinburgh [London pm 15 March 1945]; NLS.

73 ALS, 9 September 1945, from Rotha Sanson, Gwelo, to Spark, c/o Rhodesia House etc.; NLS.

CHAPTER 4: FINDING A VOICE

1 ALS, 23 September 1945, Methven to Spark, from Baldowrie, Coupar Angus, Perthshire; NLS.

2 Interview with Spark, 14 July 1995.

3 *Ibid.*

4 TLS, October 1945, Office of the High Commissioner for S. Rhodesia to Spark, from Rhodesia House, 429 Strand, London WC2; NLS.

5 Son of Joe Shapiro / Jackson and Sarah Camberg, Barney's sister.

6 TLS, Office of the High Commissioner etc. to Spark c/o Helena Residential Club, 82 Lancaster Gate, London W2; NLS.

7 *Poetry Review New Verse Supplement* (Spring 1946), 81–2. The poem is dated 'October, 1943'.

8 ALS, 31 March 1946, Methven to Spark, from Baldowrie etc.; NLS.

9 *Poetry of To-day*, 3, 74 (1946), 10–11.

10 *Collected Poems 1* (Macmillan, 1969).

11 'They Sigh for Old Dreams', *Poetry of To-day, op. cit.*, 11.

12 TLS, 6 February [1949], Stanford to Spark, from 46 Lulworth Avenue, Osterley, Hounslow, Middx.; NLS.

13 See ALS, 20 May 1949, Spark to Stanford, np [Pearson Horder, London]; HRC.

14 Wrey Gardiner, *The Dark Thorn* (Grey Walls Press, 1946), p. 32.

15 Jon Wynne-Tyson's Centaur Press archive.

16 Dominic Hibberd, 'A Publisher of First World War Poetry: Galloway Kyle', *Notes & Queries*, 31, 2 (June 1986), 185–6; 185. The case came to court in March 1922.

17 See TLS, 7 August 1947, Spark to Seymour, from Poetry Society, 33 Portman Square, London W1; Tulsa. TS of poem enclosed with letter.

18 ALS, 21 July 1947, Spark to Seymour, from The Hind's Head Hotel, Bray, Berks.; Tulsa.

19 TLS, 21 September 1947, Spark to Seymour, from Poetry Society etc.; Tulsa.

20 Howard Sergeant, AMS diary, Saturday 20 September 1947; private collection.

21 *Ibid.*, Tuesday 23 September, 1947.

22 *Ibid.*, Saturday 11 October, 1947.

23 *Ibid.*, Monday 13 October, 1947.

24 *CV*, p. 176.

25 *Ibid.*, p. 175.

26 *Ibid.*, p. 176.

27 *Ibid.*, pp. 182–3.

28 ALS, 20 October 1947, Sergeant to Spark, from c/o The Chief Accountant, Messrs W. Macfarlane & Co. Ltd, Hawthorne St, Glasgow; NLS.

29 *Ibid.*

30 ALS, 8 April 1948, Sergeant to Spark, from Bonnybridge [nr. Glasgow]; NLS.

31 Howard Sergeant, AMS diary, Wednesday 15 October, 1947; private collection.

32 ALS, 11 November 1947, Sergeant to Spark, from c/o The Chief Accountant etc.; NLS.

33 *Ibid.*

34 *Ibid.*

35 *CV* notebook; SG.

36 See ALS, 12 November 1947, Sergeant to Spark, from c/o The Chief Accountant etc., NLS. The poem exists in two forms: '6 p.m. Blues' (TS, HRC) and in print (twice) as 'Standing in Dusk', *Variegation* (Summer 1948), 5, and 'Poem', *Prospect*, 2 (1948), 26.

37 ALS, 18 November 1947, Sergeant to Spark, from 'Glasgow'; NLS.

38 ALS, 12 November 1947, Sergeant to Spark, *op. cit.*, NLS.

39 Howard Sergeant, AMS diary, Saturday 15 November, 1947; private collection.

40 *Ibid.*, Wednesday 19 November, 1947.

41 See *ibid.* Tuesday 9 December, 1947.

42 *Ibid.*, Friday 12 December, 1947.

43 *Ibid.*, Wednesday 31 December, 1947.

44 TLS, 27 December 1947, from Furst & Furst enc. with TLS, 30 December 1947, to Spark at 160 Bruntsfield Place, Edinburgh, from MacKenzie & Black, Edinburgh; NLS.

45 See ALS, 3 February 1948, Spark to Seymour, from Poetry Society, etc.; Tulsa.

46 ALS, 5 February 1948, Sergeant to Spark, from Kelvin Bank Hotel, 32 Kelvin Drive, Glasgow N.W.

47 ALS, 6 February 1948, Sergeant to Spark, from Kelvin Bank Hotel etc.; NLS.

48 ALS, 26 February 1948, Sergeant to Spark, from Kelvin Bank Hotel etc.; NLS.

49 ALS, 27 February 1948, Sergeant to Spark, from co Messrs J. McQueen & Sons Ltd, Galashiels; NLS.

50 *Ibid.*

51 TLS [copy], 14 May 1948, Seymour to Spark, from [Crosslanes,] Peaslake [Surrey]; Tulsa.

52 See TLS, 17 May 1948, Spark to Seymour, from Poetry Society etc.; NLS.

53 TccLS, 18 May 1948, Seymour to Spark, from Peaslake etc.; Tulsa.

54 See TLS, 27 May 1948, Stopes to Spark, from Norbury Park, Dorking, Surrey; NLS.

55 TccL, 29 May 1949, Spark to Stopes, np [Poetry Society]; NLS.

56 ALS, 12 April 1948, Sergeant to Spark, from Bonnybridge etc., but as at Kelvin Bank Hotel etc.; NLS.

57 ALS, 15 June 1948, Sergeant to Spark, from 155 Croxted Road, West Dulwich, London SE21; NLS.

58 *Ibid.*

59 See ANS in Spark's hand, 'The Council of the Poetry Society (officially) told the Daily Express 19/11/48'; NLS.

60 Muriel Spark, Hugo Manning, Michael Redgrove, John Bayliss and Howard Sergeant.

CHAPTER 5: KENSINGTON

1 *Poetry Quarterly*, 10, 3 (Autumn 1948), 152–3.

2 'He is Like Africa', accepted for *New English Weekly*, 13 December 1948; NLS; reprinted as 'Like Africa', *ATP*, p. 71.

3 TLS, 6 February 1949, Spark to Stanford, from 1 Vicarage Gate, London W8.; HRC.

4 ALS, 6 April 1949, Sergeant to Spark, from Ministry of Supply; NLS.

5 See ALS, 20 April 1949, Spark to Stanford, from *Forum: Stories and Poems*, 1 Vicarage Gate etc.; WUL.

6 ALS, 21 April 1949, Sergeant to Spark, from 155 Croxted Road, West Dulwich, London SE21; NLS.

7 See ALS [copy], nd, Spark to Mr Armstrong [?], Forum blue notebook; HRC.

8 See ALS, 20 May 1949, Spark to Stanford, np [Pearson Horder]; NLS.

9 *Loitering with Intent, MSO2*, p. 52.

10 See ALS, 5 June 1995, Ian Savidge to Penelope Jardine.

11 *Loitering with Intent, MSO2*, p. 22.

12 *Ibid.*, p. 61.

13 *Ibid.*, pp. 37, 38.

14 *Ibid.*, p. 38.

15 ALS, 24 June 1949, Spark to Stanford, from 1 Vicarage Gate etc.; HRC.

16 See ALS, 1 August 1939 [*sic*; 1949], Spark to Stanford, from 1 Vicarage Gate etc.; HRC.

17 ALS, nd ['Monday at 11 p.m.'], pm 28 June 1949, Stanford to Spark, np [pm 'Hounslow']; NLS.

18 ALS, 11 July 1949, Spark to Stanford, from 1 Vicarage Gate etc.; HRC.

19 See AL [copy] in *AMS* notebook, nd [1949?]; HRC.

20 See ALS, 11 July 1949, Spark to Stanford, *op. cit.*, HRC.

21 ALS, pm 18[?] October[?] [1949], Stanford to Spark, from 1 Vicarage Gate etc.; NLS.

22 *Ibid.*

23 *Ibid.*

24 See ALS, 8 November 1949, Spark to Stanford, from 1 Vicarage Gate etc.; HRC.

25 Muriel described this as 'a magazine for women, covering all subjects of interest to women with the exception of household, beauty, fashion etc.', ALS to Iris Birtwistle, 'Good Friday' [25 April] 1949, from *Forum*, 1 Vicarage Gate etc.; private collection.

26 Stanford archive; HRC.

27 Spark and Stanford, 'Introduction', *Forum: Stories and Poems*, 1, 2, nd, 25.

28 Muriel Spark and Derek Stanford (eds.), *Tribute to Wordsworth* (Alan Wingate, 1950).

29 *Ibid.*, p. 131.

30 *Ibid.*, p. 134.

31 *Ibid.*, p. 130.

32 Quoted *ibid.*, p. 130.

33 ALS, 1 November 1950, Spark to Birtwistle, from 8 Sussex Mansions, 65 Old Brompton Road, SW7; private collection.

34 See *CV*, p. 65, and Chapter 2 above.

35 See ALS, 19 (?) [*sic*] July 1949, Spark to Stanford, from 1 Vicarage Gate etc.; HRC.

36 See ALS, 1 August 1949 [dated '1939'], Spark to Stanford from 1 Vicarage Gate etc.; HRC.

37 See ALS, nd, 'Wednesday night', probably May–June 1951, Spark to Stanford, from 8 Sussex Mansions etc.; HRC.

38 ALS, Stanford to Martin Stannard, 26 April 2003, from Hove, East Sussex; 'Silly bugger' was Ernest Dowson's description of Arthur Symons, a writer much admired by Stanford in his early days.

39 TLS [fax], 24 March 1997, Spark to Stannard, from SG.

40 Interview with Christopher Fry, 18 January 1997.

41 *The Lady's not for Burning:* Arts Theatre, Cambridge, 10 March 1948; Globe Theatre, London, 11 May 1949; *Venus Observed,* St James's Theatre, London, 28 January 1950.

42 TLS [fax], 24 March 1997, Spark to Stannard, *op. cit.*

43 Derek Stanford, *Inside the Forties: Literary Memoirs 1937–1957* (Sidgwick & Jackson, 1977).

44 TLS [fax], 24 March 1997, Spark to Stannard, *op. cit.*

45 ALS, 24 August 1950, Spark to Stanford from 'Morecambe', HRC.

46 See APC, nd [August 1950], 'Sarah' [Spark] to Stanford, np [Morecambe]; HRC.

47 Mary Wollstonecraft's A *Vindication of the Rights of Woman* (1792) was largely forgotten by the general reader until Germaine Greer drew heavily upon it in *The Female Eunuch* (1970).

48 Godwin's *Enquiry Concerning Political Justice* (1793), and his novels *The Adventures of Caleb Williams* (1794) and *St Leon* (1799), support French revolutionary ideas promoting liberation from all forms of slavery.

49 *Mary Shelley. A Biography* (Constable, 1988), p. 198; revised text of *Child of Light: A Reassessment of Mary Shelley* (Tower Bridge Publications, 1951).

50 *Ibid.,* p. 198.

51 *Ibid.,* p. 119.

52 *Ibid.,* pp. 52, 126, 7, 7, 159.

53 *Ibid.,* p. 153.

54 *Ibid.,* p. 33.

55 *Ibid.,* p. 122.

56 *Ibid.,* p. 123.

57 Muriel Spark, TS, nd, 'PROJECT I' [July 1949], p. 1; HRC. The book was to deal with Mrs Gaskell, George Eliot, Mary Wollstonecraft, Jane Austen, Mary Shelley, Dorothy Wordsworth, Charlotte and Emily Brontë, Elizabeth Barrett Browning, Christina Rossetti and Alice Meynell.

58 Authors to be included were Maria Edgeworth, Jane Austen, Mrs Gaskell, the three Brontës, George Eliot, Ouida, Mary Wollstonecraft, Mary Mitford, Fanny Burney, Mrs Clive, Mrs Marsh, Mrs Trollope, Charlotte Yonge, Mrs Oliphant and Mrs Lynn Lynton.

59 Muriel Spark, TS, nd, 'PROJECT I', *op cit.,* p. 4.

60 *Mary Shelley, op cit.,* p. 92.

61 Published in two instalments in the *Listener* as 'Mary Shelley – Wife to a Genius' and 'Mary Shelley: A Prophetic Novelist', 2 February and 22 February 1951, 26 and 305–6.

62 TLS, 11 July 1952, Spark to Gittings, from 8 Sussex Mansions etc., NLS.

63 See ALS [copy], 1 December 1950, Spark to Masefield, from 8 Sussex Mansions etc.; NLS; also TccL, 28 November 1950, Spark to Masefield from 8 Sussex Mansions etc.; NLS.

64 See TccL, 28 November 1950, *op. cit.*

65 TLS, 9 December 1950, Spark to Masefield, from 8 Sussex Mansions etc.; NLS.

66 ALS, nd, 'Wed. night' [possibly 24 January 1951], Spark to Stanford, from 8 Sussex Mansions etc.; HRC.

67 A selection of these in TccMSS is held in Stanford's archive at the HRC: 'Elegy for

the Tipsy Malingerers of Autumn'; 'Family Rose'; 'Invocation in a Churchyard on All-Hallows Eve', 'The Miners'; 'Air For Miss Bassano'; 'Ophelia Falls for the Wrong Sort'; 'Poem for a Kensington Churchyard'.

68 Foreword, *ATP*, p. xi.

69 *ATP*, p. 10.

70 *Ibid.*, p. 9.

71 See TccLS, 12 June 1951, Spark to Sergeant, from 8 Sussex Mansions etc.; NLS.

72 For detailed discussion, see Martin Stannard, 'Nativities: Muriel Spark, Baudelaire and the Quest for Religious Faith', *Review of English Studies*, New Series, 55, 218 (2003), 91–105.

73 See TccLS, 12 June 1951, Spark to Sergeant *op. cit.*, pp. 1–2.

74 ALS, Christmas Day 1951, Spark to Birtwistle, from 8 Sussex Mansions etc.; private collection.

CHAPTER 6: SACRAMENTAL

1 Marc T. Greene, 'Our Story Contest', *Observer*, 6 January 1952.

2 Muriel Spark, 'The Nativity', *Poetry Quarterly* (Winter 1951–1952), 158–62; reprinted *ATP*, pp. 84–9. For detailed discussion, see Martin Stannard, 'Nativities: Muriel Spark, Baudelaire and the Quest for Religious Faith', *op. cit.*

3 TccLS, 12 June 1951, Spark to Sergeant, *op. cit.*, NLS.

4 Spark's notebook, pp. 1–5; HRC.

5 'The Seraph and the Zambesi', *Observer*, 23 December 1951, 2; reprinted *OTTP*, pp. 77–84; 77, 79.

6 *Ibid.*, p. 80.

7 *Ibid.*, p. 81.

8 *Ibid.*, p. 81–2.

9 *Ibid.*, p. 83.

10 *Ibid.*, pp. 83–4.

11 'Evening With Muriel Spark', TS notes by Morton Cohen of talk given at the City College of New York, nd [1964?].

12 See Agius's reply, TLS, 29 January 1952, from Ealing Priory, Charlbury Grove, Ealing, London W5; NLS.

13 See ALS, nd [*c.* 29 February 1952], Spark to Stanford, from 160 Bruntsfield Place, Edinburgh; HRC.

14 See ALS, nd ['Sunday', *c.* 2 March 1952], Spark to Stanford, from 'Edinburgh'; HRC.

15 Muriel Spark, *John Masefield* (Peter Nevill, 1953; reprinted Hutchinson, 1991 and Pimlico p/b 1992), pp. 109, 134, 170.

16 *Ibid.*, pp. 24, 35, xiii, 39, 45, 51, 50.

17 *Ibid.*, pp. 60 and 168.

18 *Ibid.*, pp. 147–8.

19 *Ibid.*, p. 87.

20 *The Fanfarlo and Other Verse* (Aldington: Hand and Flower Press, 1952).

21 See Muriel Spark, ANS, 'My entrance into the C. of E.', p. 2; NLS, acc. 1067/104, no. 17.

22 *Ibid.*, p. 2.

23 Derek Stanford, *Inside the Forties: Literary Memoirs 1937–1957* (Sidgwick & Jackson, 1977), p. 185.

24 AMS, Derek Stanford, 'Gutch Book', p. 1; HRC.

25 *Ibid.*, pp. 2–3.

26 See ALS, Sunday 26 October, 1952, Spark to Stanford, from 8 Sussex Mansions etc.; HRC.

27 See ALS, 9 November 1952, Spark to Stanford, np [8 Sussex Mansions etc.], pp. 1–6; HRC.

28 'The House of the Famous Poet'; reprinted *OTTP*, pp. 192–9.

29 'Reflections on Mr Tate's Article', 'Letters and Points', *World Review* (New Series 47, January 1953), 2–3; a response to Allen Tate's 'The Man of Letters in the Modern World' in the October issue.

30 Muriel Spark, *The Brontë Letters* (Peter Nevill, 1954; Norman, Oklahoma: University of Oklahoma Press, 1954).

31 Muriel Spark and Derek Stanford (eds.), *My Best Mary: The Selected Letters of Mary Shelley* (Wingate, 1953).

32 ALS, 9 November 1952, Spark to Stanford, *op. cit.*, 'Postscript', pp. 3–4.

33 See ALS, 17 December 1952, Spark to Stanford, from 160 Bruntsfield Place etc.; HRC.

34 ALS, 9 November 1952, Spark to Stanford, *op. cit.*, 'Postscript', pp. 6–7.

35 *Masefield, op. cit.*, p. 132.

36 See ALS, 9 November 1952, Spark to Stanford, *op. cit.*, p. 8.

37 *Ibid.*, 'Postscript', p. 7.

38 *Selected Poems of Emily Brontë*, ed. Muriel Spark, Crown Classics series (Grey Walls Press, 1952). Although dated 1952, the book did not appear until 1953.

39 ALS, 5 March 1953, Ada Stanford to Spark, from 46 Lulworth Avenue, Lampton, Hounslow, Middx; NLS.

40 Derek Stanford, 'Poem in Separation', TS, nd [1952–3?]; HRC.

41 *ATP*, p. 64; first published in *TLS*, 6 July 1951, 419. The HRC TS, however, has the Sussex Mansions address deleted and replaced by '1 Queen's Gate Terrace', suggesting that the poem was still much on her mind in 1953 when she appears to have been seeking to publish it elsewhere.

42 Muriel Spark, Introduction, *Selected Poems of Emily Brontë, op. cit.*, pp. 9, 10, 11, 12, 14, 15 and 16–17.

43 Muriel Spark, Foreword, *The Essence of the Brontës* (Peter Owen, 1993), p. 7.

44 'Views and Reviews. The Poetry of Anne Brontë', *New English Weekly*, 26 May 1949, 79–80.

45 *ATP*, p. 27; dated '*c.* 1956' but the WUL MS has the address '1, Queen's Gate Terrace, S.W.7.', clearly dating it as 1953.

46 'Birthday Acrostic', *Poetry Quarterly* (Summer 1951), 68.

47 *The Colonies of Heaven. The Autobiography of a Poet* (1938), *The Once-loved God* (1943), *The Dark Thorn* (1946), *The Answer to Life Is No* (1960).

48 Moore had been a leading light at Cambridge; Marneau was a product of the Austro-Hungarian Empire and wrote in German; Sean Jeanette was a Czech symbolist.

49 Hilary Spurling, *Paul Scott: A Life* (Hutchinson, 1990), p. 176.

50 Derek Stanford, TS, p. 31, lent by Stanford via John Bayliss; private collection.

51 *Ibid.*, p. 26.

52 ALS, Stanford to Spark, 'Friday', pm 8 May 1953; HRC.

53 ALS, Stanford to Spark, nd, pm 10 June 1953, np; HRC. Toeman was another poet in their circle.

54 See Spark to Sheed, 28 June 1953, from 1 Queen's Gate Terrace etc.; property of Rosemary Middleton [the Sheeds' daughter]; private collection.

55 ALS, Sheed to Spark, 3 July 1953, from Sheed & Ward Ltd, 110–111 Fleet Street, London EC4; NLS.

56 ALS, Fr. Ambrose Agius OSB to Spark, 24 August 1953, from Ealing Priory etc.; NLS.

57 Muriel Spark, review of Michael Mason, *The Legacy* (Sheed & Ward, 1953), *Journal of the Scottish Secondary Teachers' Association* (October 1953), 8, 10, 12; 8.

58 *Ibid.*

59 Muriel Spark, 'Edinburgh Festival Diary. A Prophet's Married Life', *CEN*, 4 September 1953, 5. The 'prophet' of the title was Hoseah, the central figure of Norman Nicholson's verse play, *A Match for the Devil*.

60 Muriel Spark, 'Edinburgh Festival Diary. The Wisdom of Mr T. S. Eliot', *CEN*, 11 September 1953, 5.

61 TLS, T. S. Eliot to C. O. Rhodes, 30 September 1953, from Faber & Faber Ltd, 24 Russell Square, London WC1; NLS; © estate of T. S. Eliot. Rhodes had sent a copy of the review.

62 'The Wisdom of Mr T. S. Eliot', *op. cit.*, 5.

63 *Ibid.*, 5.

64 *CV*, p. 11.

65 Review of Mason's *The Legacy*, *op. cit.*, 10.

66 Muriel Spark, 'Karl Heim: Two Important Works', *Journal of the Scottish Secondary Teachers' Association* (February 1954), 53; review of Karl Heim, *The Transformation of the Scientific World View* and *Christian Faith and Natural Science* (SCM Press, 1953).

67 'Elementary', *ATP*, p. 56; dated '*c.* 1951'.

68 Review of Heim, *op. cit.*, p. 53.

69 Muriel Spark, 'The Religion of an Agnostic. A Sacramental View of the World in the Writings of Proust', *CEN*, 27 November 1953, 1.

70 *Ibid.*, 1.

71 *Ibid.*, 1. The divine quoted is Edward Reynolds.

72 See ALS, 20 September 1953, Spark to Sheed, from 1 Queen's Gate Terrace etc.; property of Rosemary Middleton; private collection.

73 ALS, 4 May 1954, Agius to Spark, from Ealing Priory etc.; NLS.

CHAPTER 7: CONVERSION

1 TccL, 21 May 1954, Spark to Ministry of National Insurance, from 8 Sussex Mansions, 65 Old Brompton Road, London SW7; NLS.

2 ALS, 10 January [1954], Foster to Spark, from 94 Warrender Park Road, Edinburgh 9; NLS. All quotations in this paragraph are from this letter.

3 'Copy of Medical Certificate' attached to TccL, 29 April 1954; NLS.

4 See ALS, 23 April 1954, Spark to Stanford, from 8 Sussex Mansions etc.; HRC.

5 Interview with June and Neville Braybrooke, 27 January 1994. The programme of *The Confidential Clerk*, the Braybrookes thought, had contained an additional printed slip, perhaps noting the replacement of one of the players by an understudy.

6 Interview with Peterkiewicz, 9 May 1994.

7 See P. H. Connell, *Amphetamine Psychosis*, Maudsley Monograph no. 5 (Oxford, 1958), the definitive work on this subject.

8 *That Angel Burning at My Left Side* (Macmillan, 1963).

9 Interview with Brooke-Rose, 13 March 1994.

10 *The Knotted Cord* (Heinemann, 1953).

11 Interview with Brooke-Rose, *op. cit.*

12 *Ibid.*

13 Interview with Peterkiewicz, *op. cit.*

14 APCS sent as letter nd [May 1954], Birtwistle to Spark, np [probably Crossways, Wroxton, Nr Banbury]; NLS.

15 Interview with June and Neville Braybrooke, *op. cit.*

16 TLS, 19 March 1954, Eliot to Stanford, from Faber & Faber Ltd, 24 Russell Square, London WC1; NLS; © the estate of T. S. Eliot 2009.

17 ALS, 26 March 1954, Spark to Stanford, from '150', presumably '50' [Old Brompton Road, SW7]; NLS.

18 TMS with A additions, 'Worksheet. Fri. 30 April–Sun. 2nd May' [1954]; NLS.

19 APCS as letter, 17 February 1999, Neville Braybrooke to Martin Stannard, np.

20 ALS, 31 May 1954, Spark to Stanford, from 8 Sussex Mansions, London SW7; HRC.

21 A citation from St Thomas, quoted earlier in this letter: 'Those who wish to discover the truth should previously, that is before they set to work, doubt well; that is to say, they should examine thoroughly what is to be doubted.'

22 ALS, 31 May 1954, Spark to Stanford, *op. cit.*

23 ALS, 'Thursday' [30 March 1954?], Stanford to Spark, np; NLS.

24 See TLS, 4 July 1954, Spark to Stanford, from The Hermitage, Callow End, Worcester; HRC.

25 ALS, 5 August [1954], Spark to Stanford, np; HRC.

26 TMS, 'Appeal or Reference to Local Tribunal', para. 2, 'Claimant's grounds of appeal dated 19.9.54'; NLS. The appeal was heard in the South Kensington office on 11 October 1954.

27 *Ibid.*

28 TLS, 7 October 1954, Lieber to Spark, from 59 Maida Vale, London W9; NLS.

29 Interview with June and Neville Braybrooke, *op. cit.*

30 *C.* 1165–1265, sixth Prior General of the Order.

31 ALS, 3 November 1954, Spark to Stanford, from The Friars, Aylesford, Kent; HRC.

32 See ALS, nd [January/February 1955?], Spark to Stanford, np [St Jude's Cottage, Allington Castle, Kent]; HRC.

33 TLS, 14 December 1954, Greene to Stanford, from C6 Albany, London W1; NLS; © Verdant 2009.

34 ALS, 31 January 1955, Spark to Maclean, from St Jude's Cottage etc.; NLS.

35 TLS, 4 February 1955, Maclean to Spark, from Macmillan & Co. Ltd, St Martin's Street, London WC2; NLS.

36 ALS, 5 February 1955, Spark to Maclean from St Jude's Cottage etc.; NLS.

37 Dust-jacket blurb of *The Ordeal of Gilbert Pinfold* (Chapman & Hall, 1957).

38 See ALS, 23 March 1955, Spark to Sheed, from St Jude's Cottage etc.; property of Rosemary Middleton.

39 C. G. Jung (trans. R. F. C. Hull), *Answer to Job* (1952); reprinted *Collected Works*, Vol. 11 (Routledge & Kegan Paul, 1958 and 1969). For detailed discussion of the work, see Kathleen Raine, 'Blake's Job and Jung's Job', in *The Human Face of God: William Blake and the Book of Job* (Thames & Hudson, 1982), pp. 267–98.

40 Muriel Spark, 'The Mystery of Job's Suffering: Jung's New Interpretation Examined', *CEN*, 15 April 1955, 7.

41 Louis de Bernières, Introduction: The Impatience of Job, *The Book of Job* (Edinburgh: Canongate Books Ltd., 1998); a volume in the Pocket Canons series, reprinting individual books from the Authorised King James Version of the Bible, pp. x, xi, xiii and xiv.

42 'The Mystery of Job's Suffering', *op. cit.*, 7.

43 *Ibid.*, 7.

44 See ALS [airletter], 23 March 1955, Spark to Frank Sheed, from St Jude's Cottage etc.; property of Rosemary Middleton. Sheed was in New York, at the offices of Sheed & Ward.

45 *Ibid.*, p. 2.

46 See ALS, 22 April 1955, Spark to Stanford, from St Jude's Cottage etc.; HRC.

47 ALS, 13 May 1955, Barnsley to Stanford, from 374 Loose Road, Maidstone, Kent [the Barnsleys' house]; HRC.

48 ALS, nd [May 1955], Spark to Stanford, from 374 Loose Road etc.; HRC. Read's poem was 'The Gold Disc. An Elegy', *Listener*, 5 May 1955, 797. The penultimate stanza begins: 'I believe in my unbelief – would not force / One fibre of my being to bend in the wind / Of determinate doctrine. In doubt there is stillness [...].'

49 ALS, nd [probably 9 June 1953: dated 'Thursday. Corpus Christi'], Spark to Stanford, np [St Jude's Cottage?]; HRC.

50 TLS, 28 June 1955, Maclean to Spark, from Macmillan & Co. etc.; NLS.

51 TccL, 1 July 1955, Spark to Maclean, from St Jude's Cottage etc.; NLS.

52 'A Letter at Christmas', *Outposts* 20 (1952), 5–6; 6.

53 TccLS, 22 April 1956, Spark to Maclean, from 13 Baldwin Crescent, Camberwell, London SE5; NLS.

54 ALS, 1 July 1955, Spark to Stanford, from St Jude's Cottage etc.; HRC.

55 ALS, 4 July 1955, Spark to Stanford, from St Jude's Cottage etc.; HRC.

56 'The Portobello Road', *OTTP*, pp. 1–20; pp. 1 and 20.

57 *Ibid.*, pp. 5 and 9.

58 *Ibid.*, pp. 5 and 17.

59 Spark also refers to these in an early poem, 'The Beads' [*Poetry Quarterly* (Autumn 1949), 144–5], describing her joy in the coloured glass and edible 'beads' as an image of her girlhood innocence.

60 'The Portobello Road', *op. cit.*, pp. 3–4.

61 *Ibid.*, pp. 19, 17 and 3.

62 TLS, 22 February 1956, Maclean to Spark, from Macmillan & Co. etc.; NLS.

63 TLS, 15 March 1956, Spark to Allen, from 13 Baldwin Crescent etc.; property of Paul Allen; private collection.

64 See *ibid.*

65 TccLS, 7 March 1956, Spark to Maclean, from 13 Baldwin Crescent etc.; NLS.

66 Muriel Spark, 'St Monica', *Month*, New Series, vol 17, no 5 (May 1957), 309–20; reprinted Philip Caraman (ed.), *Saints and Ourselves*, Third Series (Hollis & Carter, 1958), pp. 26–37; 26, 27, 28, 30, 31, 33, 35 and 37.

67 'Magdalen' [*sic*], *Gemini*, 1 (May 1949), 3.

68 'You, Dreamer', *Canadian Poetry Magazine* (March 1948), 23.

69 'Note by the Wayside', *ATP*, p. 40.

70 ALS, 29 October 1956, Evelyn Waugh to Spark, from Piers Court, Stinchcombe, Nr. Dursley, Gloucestershire; Tcc in NLS; see Mark Amory, ed., *The Letters of Evelyn Waugh* (Weidenfeld & Nicolson, 1980), p. 47.

71 TLS, 18 January 1957, Greene to Stanford, from C6 Albany etc.; NLS; © Verdant 2009. See also TLS, 5 February 1957, Maclean to Spark, from Macmillan & Co. etc.; NLS.

72 TLS, 27 November 1956, Maclean to Spark, from Macmillan & Co. etc.; NLS.

73 TccL, 22 April 1956, Spark to Maclean, *op. cit.;* NLS.

74 TMS, nd [1956], on compliments slip of Peter Owen Ltd, 50 Old Brompton Road, London SW7; property of Vicki Weissman; private collection.

CHAPTER 8: ACQUIRING LORGNETTES

1 TccLS, 20 January 1957, Spark to Major Norman Kark, from 13 Baldwin Crescent, Camberwell, London SE5; NLS.

2 'Questing Characters', *TLS*, 22 February 1957, 109.

3 See K. L., *Belfast Telegraph*, 25 March 1957, and John Foss, *B&B*, March 1957, 31.

4 Neville Braybrooke, *Aylesford Review* (Spring 1957), 155–6; Sir John McEwen, *Month*, 17, 6 (June 1957), 406.

5 Evelyn Waugh, 'Something Fresh', *Spectator*, 22 February 1957, 256.

6 *Ibid.*, 256.

7 See 22 April 1948, Howard Sergeant's 1948 diary; private collection.

8 TLS, 26 February 1957, Heppenstall to Spark, from BBC, Broadcasting House, London W1; NLS.

9 BBC Third Programme, broadcast *c.* 23 August 1957; reprinted *Voices at Play. Stories and Ear-Pieces* (Macmillan, 1961), pp. 229–48.

10 Muriel Spark and Derek Stanford (eds.), *The Letters of John Henry Newman* (Peter Owen, 1957); published *c.* 18 June.

11 Derek Stanford, *Western Review* (Summer 1957), 303–4.

12 See ALS, 6 June [1953], Spark to Stanford, from 1 Queen's Gate Terrace, London SW7; HRC. Oddly, she appears to date this letter '1957', but she only lived in Queen's Gate Terrace April–October 1953.

13 Muriel first met Paul Allen through Stanford in 1954, and through Allen others in a literary circle who would meet in the Star and Garter pub on Kew Bridge on Sunday mornings (Muriel never attended these gatherings as she slept late). Leonard Hill had a story published by the *New Yorker*, submitted radio plays unsuccessfully to Heppenstall, and returned to academic life in the English Department at Goldsmiths' College, London University. Geoffrey Tickell, elder brother of the novelist Gerard, lived with his mother at Strand on the Green: an obsessive theatregoer and literary scholar. Brian Parker was London correspondent of the *Belfast Newsletter*, later Deputy Secretary of the BBC, and often visited Muriel with Allen; Hugh Maguire was Leader of BBC Symphony Orchestra: a 'romantic' Pole in appearance (like Peterkiewicz), formerly at Jesuit Belvedere College, Dublin, with Allen. Igor de Chroustchoff was Allen's close friend, son of Baron de Chroustchoff.

14 Charles Wrey Gardiner, *The Answer to Life is No* (Rupert Hart-Davis, 1960), pp. 42–3.

15 See TLS, 21 August 1957, Spark to Stanford, from 13 Baldwin Crescent etc.; HRC.

16 TLS, 21 August 1957, Scott to Spark, from Pearn, Pollinger & Higham, 76 Dean Street, Soho, London Wl; NLS; © N.E. Avery Scott 2009.

17 Muriel Spark, 'A Drink With Dame Edith', *Literary Review* (February 1997), 31–2.

18 *Ibid.*, 32.

19 See ALS, 27 August 1957, Spark to Stanford, from 160 Bruntsfield Place, Edinburgh; HRC.

20 ALS, 2 September 1957, Spark to Stanford, from 160 Bruntsfield Place etc.; NLS.

21 ALS, nd[pm 3 July 1957], Sarah Camberg to Spark, from 160 Bruntsfield Place etc.; NLS.

22 TccLS, 13 October 1957, Spark to Scott, from 13 Baldwin Crescent etc.; NLS.

23 TLS, 15 October 1957, Scott to Spark, from Pearn, Pollinger & Higham etc.; NLS; © N.E. Avery Scott 2009.

24 See TLS, nd, 'Monday' [prob. 18 November 1957], Spark to Stanford, np [13 Baldwin Crescent etc.]; HRC.

25 See ALS, 28 November 1957, Spark to Stanford, np [13 Baldwin Crescent etc.]; HRC.

26 See TccLS, 4 February 1958, Spark to Scott, from 13 Baldwin Crescent etc.; NLS.

27 See TLI, 18 May 1958, Spark to Stanford, from 13 Baldwin Crescent etc.; UVL.

28 See ALS, nd, 'Friday' [*c.* 7 February 1958], Spark to Stanford, from 13 Baldwin Crescent etc.; HRC.

29 Muriel Spark, 'The Mystery of Job's Suffering', *op. cit.* (1955); quoted Chapter 7 above.

30 *Robinson* (Macmillan, 1958), *MSO4*, pp. 303, 314, 411.

31 See TLS, 19 November 1957, Spark to Stanford, np [13 Baldwin Crescent etc.]; WUL.

32 *Robinson, MSO4*, p. 372.

33 See TLS, nd, 'Tuesday' [November 1957], Muriel Spark to Derek Stanford, np; HRC.

34 *Robinson, MSO4*, p. 276.

35 *Ibid.*, p. 321.

36 See Chapter 5.

37 *Robinson, MSO4*, pp. 414–15.

38 *Ibid.*, pp. 415, 403, 415.

39 7 June 1958, 1941.

40 'Questions and Answers', *TLS*, 27 June 1958, 357.

41 Anonymous, 'Book Ends', *DM*, 12 July 1958; Geoffrey Nicholson, 'Somewhere in Europe', *Spectator*, 27 June 1958; Fred Urquhart, 'New Novels', *Time & Tide*, 28 June 1958, 805; Maurice Richardson, *NS*, 5 July 1958; Honor Tracey, *Listener*, 10 July 1958; Penelope Mortimer, 'New Novels: Masks and Faces', *ST*, 29 July 1958.

42 John Davenport, 'Courage and Cowardice', *Observer*, 29 June 1958, 17.

43 Donagh MacDonagh, Radio Eireann, Dublin, 15 September 1958.

44 Paul Ferris, 'World of Books', Network Three, 12 July 1958.

45 Anthony Bloomfield, *B&B*, August 1958, 27.

46 Interview with Frank Tuohy, 6 December 1993.

47 Alan Maclean, *No, I Tell a Lie, It Was the Tuesday ... A Trudge through his Life and Times* (Kyle Cathie, 1997), p. 139.

48 Stephen Schiff, 'Muriel Spark Between the Lines', *NY*, 24 May 1993, 36–43; 40.

49 See TLS, 1 June 1958, Spark to Stanford, from 13 Baldwin Crescent etc.; HRC.

50 ALS, nd [*c.* 2 June 1958], Stanford to Spark, np; NLS.

51 ALS, nd, 'Tuesday' [prob. 3 June 1958], Spark to Stanford, np; HRC.

52 AMS, 'Theodora. A Novel', Derek Stanford Collection, HRC.

53 Interview with Elizabeth Rosenberg, 21 October 1994.

54 See ALS, nd, 'Tuesday' [prob. 6 May 1958], Spark to Stanford, from 13 Baldwin Cresent etc.; HRC.

55 *Robinson, MSO4*, p. 292.

56 ALS, nd, 'Wednesday' [*c.* 15 May 1958], Stanford to Spark, from 46 Lulworth Avenue, Lampton, Hounslow, Middx; NLS.

57 ALS, nd [*c.* 16 May 1958], Spark to Stanford, from 13 Baldwin Crescent etc.; HRC.

58 See ALS, 22 May 1958, Spark to Stanford, from 13 Baldwin Crescent etc.; HRC.

59 Rosenberg went from MGM's London office to Romulus Films where he worked on *The Day of the Jackal;* later he became Head of Drama for Anglia TV. Despite producing five novels and a biography of Dorothy Richardson, he always felt frustrated as a writer.

60 See ALS, 17 May 1958, Spark to Stanford, from 13 Baldwin Crescent etc.; HRC.

61 See ALS, nd, 'Thurs. Corpus Christi, '58' [5 June], Spark to Stanford, from 13 Baldwin Crescent etc.; HRC.

62 ALS, 31 July 1958, Heppenstall to Spark, from Roamwood Farm, Debenham, Suffolk; NLS.

63 ALS, nd, 'Tuesday' [prob. 10 June, 1958], Stanford to Spark, np; NLS.

64 TccLS, 17 October 1957, Spark to Scott, from 13 Baldwin Crescent etc.; NLS.

65 See ALS, 12 June 1958, Spark to Stanford, from 13 Baldwin Crescent etc.; HRC.

66 ALS, 14 August 1958, 'Vigil of the Assumption', Spark to Edwina ['Dina'] Barnsley, from 13 Baldwin Crescent etc.; GUL.

67 Evelyn Cavallo [Muriel Spark], 'Ailourophilia', *Observer*, 15 December 1957, 12.

68 Muriel Spark, 'Top Cats on Show', *Observer*, 29 November 1959, 4.

69 See ALS, 14 August 1958, Spark to Barnsley, *op. cit.;* GUL.

70 ALS, nd, 'Tuesday' [pm 16 September 1958], Sarah Camberg to Spark, from 160 Bruntsfield Place etc.; NLS.

71 See ALS, nd [pm 21 September 1958], Stanford to Spark, np; NLS.

72 See ALS, nd, 'Sunday' [pm 21 September 1958], Stanford to Spark, np [pm South Kensington], NLS.

73 See ALS, 29 September 1958, Spark to Stanford, from 13 Baldwin Crescent etc.; WUL.

74 TLS, 17 October [1958], Heppenstall to Spark, from 14c Ladbroke Terrace, London W11; NLS.

75 ALS, 20 October 1958, Barnsley to Spark, from 374 Loose Road, Maidstone, Kent; NLS.

76 See TLS, nd [*c.* 6 November 1958], Spark to Stanford, from 13 Baldwin Crescent etc.; HRC.

77 TLS, 8 November 1958, Spark to Stanford, from 13 Baldwin Crescent etc.; HRC.

78 See Lettice Cooper, 'Short Stories', *Observer*, 23 November 1958; Elizabeth Hamilton, 'New Novels [. . .]. A Hurricane Comes to Barbados', *CH*, 19 December 1958; 'Colette without Enchantment', *DT*, 16 January 1959.

79 ALS, 14 October 1958, Spark to Stanford, from 13 Baldwin Crescent etc.; HRC.

80 TLS, 4 October 1958, Spark to June and Neville Braybrooke, from 13 Baldwin Crescent etc.; private collection.

81 ALS, nd, 'Sunday' [prob. 1 March 1959], Stanford to Spark, np; NLS.

82 ALS, nd, 'Monday' [prob. 2 March 1959], Spark to Stanford, np; HRC.

CHAPTER 9: EXPOSURE

1 TLS, nd [prob. late October 1957], Spark to Stanford, from 13 Baldwin Crescent, Camberwell, London SE5; HRC.

2 *Memento Mori* (Macmillan, 1959); *MSO1*, p. 496.

3 *Ibid.*, p. 500.

4 *Ibid.*, p. 501.

5 *Ibid.*, p. 501.

6 *Ibid.*, p. 644.

7 See preliminary papers to *The Prime of Miss Jean Brodie* file; Tulsa.

8 See 'My Conversion', *Twentieth Century*, 170 (Autumn 1961), 63.

9 The allusion is to Newman's *Life and Letters*, a passage quoted at length in Chapter 5 of the novel when it is read by Alec Warner. Newman ponders what the ancients

died of, feeling that it might be a comfort '"if we could associate ourselves with the great Confessor Saints in their illnesses and decline [...]"' (p. 539).

10 *Memento Mori, MSO1*, p. 671.

11 'Think about Death Says Muriel Spark', *B&B*, April 1959, 15.

12 TLS (fax), 20 October 1997, Spark to Stannard, from SG. Spark was commenting on her 1951 letter about 'The Ballad of the Fanfarlo'.

13 *NS*, 15 September 1934, 329.

14 *Memento Mori, MSO1, op. cit.*, p. 568.

15 *Ibid.*, p. 617.

16 V. S. Naipaul, 'Death on the Telephone', *NS*, 28 March 1959, 452; John Metcalf, *ST*, 22 March 1960; Goronwy Rees, *Listener*, 2 April 1959, 607; Elizabeth Jane Howard, *Queen*, 14 April 1959; John Davenport, *Observer*, 22 March 1959.

17 Advertisement, *NYTBR*, 17 May 1959.

18 'Think about Death [...]', *op. cit.*

19 See ALS, nd, 'Thurs.' [May–June 1959?], Spark to Scott, from 13 Baldwin Crescent etc.; HRC.

20 *Publishers' Circular*, 4 April 1959.

21 'Think about Death ..', *op. cit.*, 15.

22 St Mary's College, Tregyb, Llandilo, Carmarthenshire.

23 ALS, Spark to Allen, 21 August 1959, from Gasthof Antonitsch, Ferlach, S. Karnten, Austria; private collection.

24 See *ibid.*

25 See ALS, 27 August 1959, Spark to Allen, from Gasthof Antonitsch etc.; private collection.

26 TLS [email], 15 March 2003, Christine Brooke-Rose to Stannard.

27 See ALS, 21 August 1959, Spark to Allen, *op cit.*

28 'A Member of the Family' first published *Vogue;* reprinted *OTTP*, pp. 180–91.

29 *Ibid.*, p. 181.

30 'The Ormolu Clock', *NY*, 17 September 1960; reprinted *OTTP*, pp. 158–66.

31 'The Dark Glasses', *OTTP*, pp. 167–79.

32 'The Curtain Blown by the Breeze', *ibid.*, pp. 21–33.

33 See ALS, 27 August 1959, Spark to Allen, *op. cit.*; private collection.

34 ALS, 5 September 1959, Spark to Allen, from Strandhotel Obis, Seelach, Klopeiner See, S. Karnten; private collection.

35 Muriel Spark, 'A Drink with Dame Edith', *Literary Review* (February 1997), 31–2; 31.

36 See ALS, nd, 'Thurs.' [autumn 1959?], Spark to Scott, np; Tulsa.

37 'Keeping It Short – Muriel Spark Talks about Her Books to Ian Gillam', *Listener*, 24 September 1970, 411–13; 412.

38 See TccLS, 12 December 1959, Spark to Maclean from 13 Baldwin Crescent etc.; NLS.

39 George Millar, 'Women Write the Winners ... and No Punches Pulled', *DE*, 3 March 1960, 6.

40 Storm Jameson, 'Guest Critic', *Housewife*, April 1960.

41 Stevie Smith, 'A Gothic Comedy', *Observer*, 6 March 1960.

42 *The Ballad of Peckham Rye* (Macmillan, 1960), *MSO2*, p. 511.

43 Paul West, *NS*, 5 March 1960.

44 Christopher Derrick, 'Human Research', *Tablet*, 5 March 1960.

45 'Faith and Fancy', *TLS*, 4 March 1960.

46 See C. S. 'No Ring of Truth Here', *CH*, 11 March 1960; P. N. Furbank, 'New Novels', *Listener*, 3 March 1960; and Phyllis Young, 'Choice of Novels', *Yorkshire Post*, 10 March 1960.

47 Gerald Sykes, 'The Bewitching Ways of Dougal Douglas', *NYTBR*, 28 August 1960.

48 Robert Phelps, 'With a Happy Touch of the Brimstone', *NYHTBR*, 7 August 1960.

49 See ALS, 5 September 1959, Spark to Allen, *op. cit.*

50 See TccLS, Spark to Heppenstall, 4 July 1960, from 13 Baldwin Crescent etc.; NLS.

51 See ALS, 1 July 1960, Spark to Scott, from 13 Baldwin Crescent etc.; HRC.

52 See TLS, 16 July 1960, Spark to Scott, from 13 Baldwin Crescent etc.; HRC.

53 TLS, 20 September 1960, Heppenstall to Spark, from 14c Ladbroke Terrace, London W11; NLS.

54 See TccLS, 31 July 1960, Spark to Maclean, from 13 Baldwin Crescent etc.; NLS.

55 See TccLS, 28 July 1960, Spark to Maclean, from 13 Baldwin Crescent etc.; NLS.

56 TLS, 8 August 1960, Spark to Scott, from 13 Baldwin Crescent etc.; HRC. Higham's had sent Spark a small cheque for the Penguin *Ballad* on 21 April 1960.

57 Probably 'The Poet's House', which later formed the basis of her short story, 'The House of the Famous Poet'. See Chapter 14.

58 TLS with A addition, 13 July 1960, Scott to Spark, from 78 Addison Way, London N11; © N.E. Avery Scott 2009; NLS;.

59 J. W. M. Thomson, 'This Fascinating New Arrival in the World of Books', *ES*, 23 March 1960, 7.

60 See TLS, 5 July 1960, and TLS, 18 July 1960, Carrick to Spark, from J. B. Lippincott Company, 521 Fifth Avenue, New York; NLS.

61 George Millar, *DE*, 3 March 1960, 6.

62 *ES*, 23 March 1960, *op. cit.*

63 See TLS, 6 August 1960, Spark to Smith, from 13 Baldwin Crescent etc.; WUL.

64 See TccLS, 13 November 1960, Spark to Maclean, from 13 Baldwin Crescent etc.; NLS.

65 See TccLS, 13 November 1960, Spark to Smith, from 13 Baldwin Crescent etc.; WUL; covering letter to another copy of that to Maclean.

66 See ALS, 17 November 1960, Spark to Scott, from 13 Baldwin Crescent etc.; HRC.

67 See TccLS, 13 November 1960, Spark to Maclean, *op. cit.;* WUL.

CHAPTER 10: TRANSFIGURATION

1 See TccLS, 13 November 1960, Spark to Maclean, *op. cit.*, WUL.

2 Paul Scott, 'New Look at Bachelors [...]', *B&B*, October 1960, 14.

3 John Updike, 'Books. Creatures of the Air', *NY*, 30 September 1961, 161–2; 165–7; 165.

4 ALS, 11 October 1960, Waugh to Spark, from Combe Florey House, Nr. Taunton, Somerset; NLS; reprinted Mark Amory (ed.), *The Letters of Evelyn Waugh* (Weidenfeld & Nicolson, 1980), p. 55.

5 ALS, 10 September 1960, Spark to Mollie Lee [producer of *Woman's Hour*], from 13 Baldwin Crescent, Camberwell, London SE5.; BBCWAC.

6 'My Favourite Villain: Heathcliff in *Wuthering Heights*', BBC Light Programme, 12 October 1960; reprinted Muriel Spark, *The Essence of the Brontës* (Peter Owen, 1993), pp. 317–19.

7 Penelope Gilliatt, *Spectator*, 21 October 1960.

8 *The Bachelors* (Macmillan, 1960), *MSO2*, p. 327.

9 See Muriel Spark, AMS, 'Claiming Territory', nd [written on verso of TLS dated 'Milano, 11 November 1974']; Tulsa.

10 BBC Home Service, 26 April 1960, in 'Two of a Kind' series; reprinted *John O'London's Weekly*, December 1960, 683.

11 *Ibid.*, 683.

12 TccL, 4 November 1961, Spark to Smith, from 13 Baldwin Crescent etc.; NLS.

13 See ALS, 29 October 1960, Spark to Scott, from 13 Baldwin Crescent etc.; HRC.

14 See ALS, 15 November 1960, Dickson to Spark, from Macmillan & Co. Ltd., St Martin's Street, London WC2; NLS.

15 See ALS, 14 November 1960, Spark to Scott, from 13 Baldwin Crescent etc.; HRC.

16 ALS, 17 November 1960, Spark to Scott, *op. cit.*; HRC.

17 See *ibid.*

18 David Lodge, 'Various Vocations', *Tablet*, 17 December 1960.

19 See ALS, 18 March 1961, Spark to John Smith, from 13 Baldwin Crescent etc.; WUL.

20 *The Bachelors*, *MSO2*, pp. 403–4.

21 'I'm Very Fierce … when I Start. An Interview […] by […] Maurice Dolbier', *NYHT* (*Books* supplement), 11 February 1962, 7.

22 Muriel Spark, *The Mandelbaum Gate* (Macmillan, 1965); *MSO3*, p. 311.

23 See TccLI, 28 May 1961, Spark to Dickson, from 13 Baldwin Crescent etc., NLS.

24 See TLS, 28 May 1961, Spark to John Smith, from 13 Baldwin Crescent etc.; WUL.

25 See TccLI, 28 May 1961, Spark to Dickson, *op. cit.*, NLS.

26 See TccL, nd [*c.* 14 June 1961], Spark to Dickson, from 13 Baldwin Crescent etc.; NLS.

27 See TLS, 15 June 1961, Dickson to Spark, from Macmillan & Co. etc.; NLS.

28 See ALS, 3 July 1961, Spark to Smith, from Hotel Yarson [?], Tel Aviv; WUL.

29 See ALS, 25 July 1961, Spark to Braybrooke, from 13 Baldwin Crescent etc.; private collection.

30 ALS, 25 March 1961, Spark to Smith, from 13 Baldwin Crescent etc.; WUL.

31 See ALS, 3 July 1961, Spark to Smith, *op. cit.*; WUL.

32 See interview with Muriel Spark, 2 August 1999.

33 See TccLS, 20 March 1963, Spark to Robert Henderson, np [13 Baldwin Crescent etc.]; NLS.

34 Interview with Spark, 2 August 1999, *op. cit.*

35 See *ibid.*

36 See *ibid.*

37 *The Mandelbaum Gate*, *MSO3*, pp. 321–2.

38 Muriel Spark, *The Prime of Miss Jean Brodie* (Macmillan, 1961); *MSO1*, p.13.

39 *The Prime of Miss Jean Brodie*, *MSO1*, p. 98.

40 Interview with Muriel Spark, 3 August 1999.

41 The friends were the Chatterton-Henrys. He was a doctor who wrote novels for Heinemann under the name of L. Steni.

42 ALS, 25 July 1961, Spark to June Braybrooke, *op.cit.*

43 Interview with Muriel Spark, 3 August 1999.

44 *Ibid.*

45 *The Prime of Miss Jean Brodie, MSO1*, p. 51.

46 *Ibid.*, p. 68.

47 See MS p. 43 [Tulsa]; *The Prime of Miss Jean Brodie, MSO1*, p. 28.

48 *The Prime of Miss Jean Brodie, MSO1*, p. 111.

49 *Ibid.*, p. 77.

50 *Ibid.*, p. 105.

51 Interview with Muriel Spark, 2 August 1999.

52 Anthony Burgess, 'The Muse Steps In', *Yorkshire Post*, 2 November 1961.

53 Bamber Gascoigne, 'Quite a Few Cannibals', *S. Tel.*, 29 October 1961.

54 'New Fiction', *The Times*, 2 November 1961.

55 See TLS, 6 November 1961, Dickson to Spark, from Macmillan & Co. etc.; NLS.

56 *T&T*, 9 November 1961.

57 *T&T*, 23 November 1961; King's review, 16 November 1961; King's reply in *T&T*, 30 November 1961.

58 Arthur Calder-Marshall, 'Life and Art', *FT*, 9 November 1961.

59 APCI, nd [October 1961?], Waugh to Spark, from Combe Florey House etc.; NLS; © estate of Evelyn Waugh.

60 *The Prime of Miss Jean Brodie, MSO1*, pp. 66–7.

61 Evelyn Waugh, 'Threatened Genius: Difficult Saint', *Spectator*, 207 (7 July 1961), 28–9.

62 Evelyn Waugh, 'Love, Loyalty, and Little Girls', *Cosmopolitan* 152 (February 1962), 38. Waugh read the book as 'a parody of the cliques which formed around the famous English educators during the last hundred years'.

63 Brian Aldiss, 'Fiction of the Week [. . .]', *Oxford Mail*, 2 November 1961.

64 Peter Green, 'Men Remembered [. . .]', *DT*, 3 November 1961.

65 Malcolm Muggeridge, 'The Good Book & the Naughty Lady', *Daily Herald*, 11 December 1961.

66 Norman Shrapnel, 'The Great Divide', *Guardian*, 3 November 1961.

67 W. J. Igoe, 'Five Novels From Catholic Writers. Muriel Spark Looks Back', *CH*, 10 November 1961.

68 Christopher Derrick, '"Transfiguration of the Commonplace", The World of Muriel Spark', *CH*, 1 December 1961, 11, 8; David Lodge, 'Human Predicaments', *Tablet*, 11 November 1961. Derrick remarks on 'the mystery of derivative being itself, the relation between the creating mind and the thing it devises'; Lodge sees the book as a spider's web 'in which the spaces between the threads – the narrative unexplained, the descriptive detail withheld – are somehow as significant as the threads themselves'.

69 *TLS*, 'Mistress of Style', 3 November 1961, 785.

70 See TccL, 9 November 1961, Spark to Dickson, from 13 Baldwin Crescent etc.; NLS.

71 TccLS, 13 November 1961, Spark to Dickson, from 13 Baldwin Crescent etc.; NLS.

72 See TLS, 20 November 1961, Dickson to Spark, from Macmillan & Co. etc.; NLS.

73 TLS, 15 February 1962, Maurice Macmillan to Spark, from Macmillan & Co. etc.; NLS.

74 TccL, 16 February 1962, Spark to Maurice Macmillan, np [13 Baldwin Crescent etc.]; NLS.

75 Spark commented: 'On reading this record of my early transactions I am horrified that so much trivial and sordid business was loaded onto my shoulders, besides the responsibilities for my books. What were my agents of those days doing? They were receiving ten per cent of my literary earnings and I should not have had to wear out my strength and brains typing eight-page letters to publishers pointing out their plain duties. I knew that my work gave pleasure and had a strong natural desire to get it to the readers. It was certainly foolish of me to remain with Macmillan eighteen more years. But my English agents should have spared me much of the excessive trouble described above. In these days publishers have hugely improved in their efforts to market genuine works of literature. Agents, too, seem to have themselves far better organized. They now seem to realize that, as Graham Greene said, "Time is the most precious thing a writer has".'

76 Interview with Muriel Spark, 3 August 1999.

77 ALS, Tuesday morning [23] February 1962, Barnsley to Spark, from HM Prison, Maidstone; NLS.

78 See TccL, nd [prob. 24 February 1962], Spark to Barnsley, np [13 Baldwin Crescent etc.]; NLS.

79 ALS, 5 March 1962, Barnsley to Spark, from 374 Loose Road, Maidstone, Kent; NLS.

80 ALS, 1 January 1962, Barnsley to Spark, from 374 Loose Road etc.; NLS.

81 'Edinburgh-born', NS, 10 August 1962, 180; reprinted as 'What Images Return' in Karl Miller (ed.), Memoirs of Modern Scotland (Faber & Faber, 1970), pp. 151–3; p. 153.

82 TLS [fax], 6 May 1995, Spark to Stannard, from SG.

83 TLS, 14 February 1962, Spark to Shirley Hazzard from 13 Baldwin Crescent etc., private collection. 'Primordial' should read 'aboriginal'.

84 TPCS, 3 May 1962, Spark to O'Gorman, from 13 Baldwin Crescent etc.; St Michael's College, Vermont.

85 APCS, nd [pm 26 April 1962], Spark to Hazzard, np [Edinburgh]; private collection.

86 Interview with Muriel Spark, 2 August 1999.

CHAPTER 11: TIME / LIFE

1 TccL, 8 July 1962, Spark to Warne, np [13 Baldwin Crescent, Camberwell, London SE5]; NLS.

2 See ALS, 24 July 1962, Spark to Smith, from The Friars, Aylesford, Kent; WUL.

3 'Edinburgh-born', NS, 10 August 1962, 180; reprinted Karl Miller (ed.), Memoirs of Modern Scotland (Faber & Faber, 1970), pp. 151–3.

4 See TccL, 26 August 1962, Muriel Spark to Robert Yeatman from 13 Baldwin Crescent etc.; NLS.

5 Harold Hobson, 'An Ordinary Miracle', *ST*, 7 October 1962, 41.

6 T. C. Worsley, *FT*, 4 October 1962, p. 14.

7 *The Critics*, 14 October 1962, BBCWAC.

8 Interview with Alan Maclean, 6 December 1994.

9 *The Ballad of Peckham Rye, MSO2*, pp. 580–1.

10 See interview with Muriel Spark, 2 August 1999.

11 *Doctors of Philosophy* (Macmillan, 1963), I, ii, p. 35.

12 *Ibid.*, II, ii, p. 47.

13 *Ibid.*, II, ii, p. 67.

14 *Ibid.*, II, ii, p. 48.

15 *Ibid.*, II, ii, p. 63.

16 *Ibid.*, II, ii, p. 62.

17 *Ibid.*, II, ii, p. 65.

18 Interview with Shirley Hazzard, 21 August 1993.

19 *Ibid.*

20 AMS, 'Soviet Jews. Paris Conference', NLS, Acc.10989/120, Spark's notes on this congress.

21 Property of Shirley Hazzard, nd.

22 Interview with Ved Mehta, 9 July 1994.

23 TLS, 21 March 1962, Spark to O'Gorman, from 13 Baldwin Crescent etc.; St Michael's College, Vermont.

24 See TccL, 30 September 1963, Spark to Maclean, from Beaux Arts Hotel, 310 E. 44th Street, New York, 17; NLS.

25 Interview with Shirley Hazzard, 23 February 1994, and APCS, Hazzard to Martin Stannard, 14/15 November 1999, from 'Capri'.

26 Interview with Shirley Hazzard, *op. cit.*

27 Interview with Brendan Gill, 23 February 1994.

28 Brendan Gill, *Here at The New Yorker* (New York: Random House, 1975; reprinted p/b New York: Da Capo Press, 1997).

29 *Ibid.*, pp. 253–4. St Robert was a sixteenth-century Jesuit cardinal.

30 Interview with Brendan Gill, *op. cit.*

31 Interview with Shirley Hazzard, 23 February 1994.

32 Interview with William Maxwell, 24 February 1994.

33 A *New Yorker* writer, Ross eventually published her side of the story in *Here and Not Here* (New York: Random House, 1992).

34 TMS of telegram, 11 April 1965, Spark to John Hay Whitney of *NYHT*, from Beaux Arts Hotel etc. For Wolfe's account of his parody, see his *Hooking Up* (Farrar, Straus & Giroux, 2000).

35 *Ibid* (telegram).

36 Interview with Brendan Gill, *op. cit.*

37 See TccLS, 30 November 1962; NLS.

38 Interview with Shirley Hazzard, 21 August 1993.

39 *Ibid.*

40 Information on the MacKenzie episode derives from interviews with Shirley Hazzard, 21 August 1993; Brendan Gill, *op. cit.;* William Maxwell, *op. cit.;* Robert Henderson, 28 February 1994; and Ved Mehta, *op. cit.*

41 Interview with Alan Maclean, 6 December 1994.

42 Interview with Isabelle Holland, publicity director at Lippincott 1960–66, 8 July 1994.

43 See ALI, draft, nd [*c.* 23 November 1962], Spark to Carrick, np [New York]; NLS.

44 Interview with Muriel Spark, 3 August 1999.

45 Interview with Alan Maclean, *op. cit.*

46 'Blanche W. Knopf: July 30, 1884–June 4, 1966', *Borzoi Quarterly*, 15. 3 (1966), 13, 12.

47 Interview with Alan Maclean, *op. cit.*

48 *Ibid.*

49 Interview with Shirley Hazzard, 23 February 1994; private collection.

50 TLS, 23 November 1973, Spark to Susan Sheehan, from Lungotevere R. Sanzio 9, 00153–Roma; private collection.

51 TLS, Guest to Martin Stannard, 6 September 1994, from 26 Ecclestone Mews, Belgrave Place, London SW1.

52 See TccL, 30 September 1963, Spark to Maclean, from Beaux Arts Hotel etc.; NLS.

53 ALS, 6 August 1963, Spark to Hazzard, from 13 Baldwin Crescent etc.; private collection.

54 ALS, 26 December 1962, Spark to von Auw, from Beaux Arts Hotel etc.; PUL.

55 Interview with Morton Cohen, 28 September 1997.

56 See TLS, 30 May 1963, Spark to von Auw, from 13 Baldwin Crescent etc.; PUL.

57 See TLS, 9 March 1963, Spark to Hazzard, from 13 Baldwin Crescent etc.; private collection.

58 ALS, 5 April 1963, Spark to Hazzard, from Edinburgh [160 Bruntsfield Place]; private collection.

59 ALS, 6 February 1963, Spark to Hazzard, from 13 Baldwin Crescent etc.; private collection.

60 ALS, 3 December 1964, Spark to Hazzard, from Beaux Arts Hotel etc.; private collection.

61 See ALS, 6 February 1963, Spark to Hazzard, *op. cit.;* and ALS, 6 August 1963, Spark to Hazzard, *op. cit.*, private collection.

62 See ALS, 21 February 1963 [dated in error '1962'], Spark to Hazzard, *op. cit.*, private collection.

63 TLS, 9 March 1963, Spark to Hazzard, *op. cit.;* private collection.

64 ALS, 21 July 1963, Spark to Hazzard, from 13 Baldwin Crescent etc.; private collection.

65 See ALS, 6 August 1963, Spark to Hazzard, *op. cit.;* private collection.

66 See TLS, 23 June 1963, Spark to Hazzard, from 13 Baldwin Crescent etc; private collection.

67 ALS, 23 April 1963, Spark to von Auw from 13 Baldwin Crescent etc; private collection.

68 TLS, 23 June 1963, Spark to Hazzard, *op. cit.*

69 Muriel Spark, Foreword to Vincent Ferrer Blehl SJ, (ed.), *Realizations. Newman's*

Own Selection of His Sermons (Darton, Longman & Todd, 1964), pp. v–ix.

70 *Ibid.*, p. vii.

71 *Ibid.*, p. viii.

72 See TLS, 9 February 1963, Wynne-Tyson to Spark, as from Centaur Press Ltd, Fontwell, Sussex; NLS.

73 See ALS, 21 February 1963, Spark to Hazzard, *op. cit.*, private collection.

74 See TLS, 14 February 1963, Wynne-Tyson to Spark, from Centaur Press etc.; NLS.

75 See ALS, 9 August 1963, Muriel Spark to von Auw, from 13 Baldwin Crescent etc.; PUL.

76 See TLS, 13 July 1963, Spark to von Auw, from 13 Baldwin Crescent etc.; PUL.

77 See *Ibid.*, PUL.

78 See TLS, 24 July 1963, Spark to von Auw, from 13 Baldwin Crescent etc.; PUL.

79 ALS, 5 April 1963, Spark to Hazzard, *op. cit.*

80 See ALS, 21 July 1963, Spark to Hazzard, *op. cit.;* private collection.

81 See TLS, 29 June 1963, Spark to Hazzard, from 13 Baldwin Crescent etc.; private collection.

82 See ALS, 29 April 1963, Spark to Hazzard, from 13 Baldwin Crescent etc.; private collection.

83 TccL, 12 August 1963, Spark to Harding ('Pete') Lemay, np [London]; NLS.

84 Philip Hengist, *Punch*, 31 July 1962.

85 See TccL, 10 August 1963, Spark to Yeatman, from 'Number Thirteen' [Baldwin Crescent etc.]; NLS.

86 See ALS, 21 July 1963, Spark to Hazzard, *op. cit.*

CHAPTER 12: ARMOURS DE VOYAGE

1 See ALS, 28 August 1963, Waugh to Spark, from Combe Florey House, Combe Florey, Nr. Taunton, Somerset; NLS.

2 'Letters and Points. Reflections on Mr Tate's Article', *World Review* (New Series 47), January 1953, 2, responding to Tate's 'The Man of Letters in the Modern World' in the October 1952 issue.

3 Interview with Tristram Cary, 24 September 1996.

4 Interview with Gillon Aitken, 15 December, 2008, and with Harry McDowell, 19 June 1998.

5 ALS, 2 September 1963, Spark to Allen and Isabella Tate, from Cunard Line, RMS *Queen Mary*; PUL.

6 See APCS, pm 6 September 1963, Spark to Hazzard, from Barclay Hotel, 111 East 48th St, New York; private collection.

7 See TccLS, 12 August 1963, Spark to Lemay, *op. cit.*, NLS.

8 ALS, 21 July 1963, Spark to Hazzard, *op. cit.*, private collection.

9 See TLS, 30 September 1963, Spark to Maclean, from Beaux Arts Hotel etc.; private collection.

10 *Ibid.*

11 See TLS, 30 September, Spark to Maclean, *op. cit.;* private collection.

12 See interview with Muriel Spark, 2 August 1999.

13 See TccL, 26 April 1963, Spark to Yeatman, np [13 Baldwin Crescent, Camberwell, London SE5]; NLS.

14 See TccL, 26 June 1963, Spark to Yeatman, np [13 Baldwin Crescent etc.]; NLS.

15 See ALS, 22 May 1965, Spark to Maclean, from 1101-S, 310 E. 44th St, New York 17 [Beaux Arts Hotel]; private collection.

16 *The Girls of Slender Means* (Macmillan, 1963); *MSO2*, pp. 145, 145–6, 153 and 162.

17 Interview with Frank Kermode, 23 March 1993.

18 *The Girls of Slender Means, MSO2*, pp. 226–7.

19 *Ibid.*, pp. 228, 230.

20 John Henry Newman, *Parochial and Plain Sermons*, Vol. 8, 1878, pp. 217–29; quoted in TLS (fax), 19 May 2000, Spark to Stannard, from SG.

21 *The Girls of Slender Means, MSO2*, p. 237.

22 'Out of Eden', *Time*, 13 September 1963, 115–16.

23 'New Fiction', *The Times*, 19 September 1963.

24 'New Novels', *FT*, 26 September 1963.

25 Interview with Kermode, *op. cit.*

26 Frank Kermode, *NS*, 20 September 1963.

27 'Between a Wedding and a Funeral', *NY*, 15 September 1963, 192–3.

28 Simon Raven, 'Heavens Below', *Spectator*, 20 September 1963, 354.

29 John Davenport, 'Mrs Spark's Roses', *Observer*, 22 September 1963, 354.

30 Julian Jebb, 'Lonely Hearts', *ST*, 22 September 1963.

31 Alan Pryce-Jones, 'Doubts About the Human Race', *NYHT*, 'Daily Book Review', 5 October 1963.

32 *The Girls of Slender Means, MSO2*, p. 146.

33 ALS, 19 May [1963?], Una Pinder to Spark, from Barroby Court, Ridgeway North, Highlands, Salisbury, S. Rhodesia; NLS.

34 See TLS, 'Saturday' [pm 14 October 1963], Spark to Hazzard, from Beaux Arts Hotel etc.; private collection.

35 See TccLS, 7 March 1964, Spark to Alfred Knopf, np [Beaux Arts Hotel etc.]; NLS.

36 See ALS, 14 February 1964, Spark to Maclean from 310 E. 44 [Beaux Arts Hotel etc.]; private collection.

37 See ALS, 'New Year's Day' [1964], Spark to Maclean, from Beaux Arts Hotel etc; private collection.

38 TLI, Brinnin to Bill Read, 20 December 1963, np [St Thomas]; UDL.

39 TLI, Brinnin to Read, 26 December 1963, np [St Thomas]; UDL.

40 *Ibid.*

41 TLI, Brinnin to Read, 29 December 1963, np [St Thomas]; UDL.

42 See ALS, 'New Year's Day' [1964], Spark to Maclean, *op cit.*

43 TLS, 7 December 1963, Spark to von Auw, from Beaux Arts Hotel etc.; PU.

44 TLS, 13 October 1963, Spark to Maclean, from Beaux Arts Hotel etc.; PU.

45 Interview with Gillon Aitken, 19 November 1996.

46 See ALS, 9 July 1964, Spark to Maclean, from c/o *The New Yorker*, 25 West 43rd Street, New York 36, NY; private collection.

47 See ALS, 14 February 1964, Spark to Maclean, *op. cit.*

48 See ALS, nd, 'Saturday' [pm 13 September 1964], Spark to Hazzard, from Beaux Arts Hotel etc.; private collection.

49 *Ibid.*

50 ALS, nd [pm 5 October 1964], Spark to Maclean, from '1100-S' [Beaux Arts Hotel]; private collection.

51 ALS, 26 October 1964, Spark to Maclean, from the *New Yorker* etc.; private collection.

52 TLS [fax] and 'addenda', 17 May 2000, Spark to Stannard, from SG.

53 See ALS, 3 December 1964, Spark to Hazzard, from Beaux Arts Hotel etc.; private collection.

54 Interview with George Nicholson, 28 February 1994.

55 *Ibid.*

56 See ALS, 8 December 1964, Spark to Maclean, from the *New Yorker* etc.; private collection.

57 Interview with George Nicholson, *op. cit.*

58 *Ibid.*

59 *Ibid.*

60 Interview with Harding ('Pete') Lemay, 5 April 1995.

61 See TLS, 10 October 1964, Spark to von Auw, from the *New Yorker* etc.; PUL.

62 See ALS, 4 July 1964, Spark to Maclean, from c/o Sinkler, 112 W. 13th Street, NY 11; private collection.

63 See T memo with A additions, 31 March 1965 (received with Spark's comments 7 April 1965), von Auw to Spark, np [Harold Ober]; PUL.

64 See T memo with A additions, 10 March 1965 (received with Spark's comments 8 April 1965), von Auw to Spark, np [Harold Ober]; PUL.

65 See ALS, 9 April 1965, Spark to Maclean, from the *New Yorker* etc.; private collection.

66 See TccLS, 5 June 1965, Spark to von Auw, from Beaux Arts Hotel etc.; PUL.

67 Interview with Eugene Walter, 11 August 1994.

68 See ALS, 16 September 1964, Spark to Maclean, from Beaux Arts Hotel. etc.; PUL.

69 See ALS, 13 August 1965, Spark to von Auw, from 13 Baldwin Crescent etc.; PUL.

70 See ALS, 31 July 1965, Spark to von Auw, from 13 Baldwin Crescent etc.; PUL.

71 See ALS, 8 August 1965, Spark to von Auw, from 13 Baldwin Crescent etc.; PUL.

72 See ALS, 13 August 1965, Spark to von Auw, *op. cit.*; PUL.

73 See APCS, nd [mid-August 1965], Mr and Mrs Roy Grutman to von Auw, np [pm Hydra, Greece].

74 Frank Kermode, 'The Novel As Jerusalem', *AM* (October 1965), 92–8.

75 Interview with William Koshland, 25 February 1994.

76 *Borzoi Quarterly*, Third Quarter (1965), 3.

77 Interview with Sam Sachs, 24 September 1996.

78 *Muriel Spark* (Paul Elek, 1974); *Novelists and Their World* series, ed. Graham Hough.

79 Interview with Peter Kemp, 24 May 1998.

80 See TLS, 'Symposium – Amours de Voyage', Rutgers University; AMS notes, '542 George Street', 3 pp.; NLS.

81 See ALS, nd 'Saturday', [*c.* late April 1961], Spark to Brooke-Rose, from 'Camberwell' [13 Baldwin Crescent etc.); HRC.

82 See ALS, 25 March 1961, Spark to John Smith, from 13 Baldwin Crescent etc.; WUL.

83 Elizabeth Janeway, 'A Changing Spark', *Holiday*, September 1965, 126, 128; 126.

84 See TccLS, 22 August 1965, Spark to von Auw, from 13 Baldwin Crescent etc.; NLS.

85 Interview with Muriel Spark, 2 August 1999.

86 See TccLS, 26 September 1965, Muriel Spark to 'Tiny' Lazzari, np [Beaux Arts Hotel etc.); NLS.

CHAPTER 13: LOOKING ROUND

1 Interview with Nora Sayre, 2 April 1994.

2 John Gross, 'Passionate Pilgrimage', *NYRB*, 5, 6 (28 October 1965).

3 Alfred Kazin, 'Dispassionate Pilgrimage', *Sunday Herald Tribune, Book Week*, 17 October 1965, 2–3.

4 *Time*, 5 November 1965, 128.

5 'Scrolls and Sideburns', *Newsweek*, 18 October 1965.

6 Sybille Bedford, 'Frontier Regions', *Spectator*, 29 October 1965.

7 D. J. Enright, 'Public Doctrines – Private Judging', *NS*, 15 October 1965, 563, 566; 566.

8 Norman Shrapnel, 'Righteous Readability', *Guardian*, 15 October 1965.

9 'New Fiction', *The Times*, 14 October 1965.

10 Anthony Burgess, 'Talking About Jerusalem', *TLS*, 14 October 1965, 913.

11 Interview with Nora Sayre, *op. cit.*

12 See TccL, 23 October 1965, Spark to Signora Mostardi, from 1101-South [Beaux Arts Hotel]; NLS.

13 TLS, 8 October 1965, Mayer to Spark, from Avon Books, 9599 Eighth Avenue, New York, NY 10019; NLS.

14 See ANS [draft of telegram], nd [2 November? 1965], Spark to Moss, np [Beaux Arts Hotel?]; NLS.

15 TLS, 5 November 1965, Norman Roy Grutman to Spark, from 250 Broadway, New York 7; NLS.

16 *Ibid.*

17 Interview with Ved Mehta, 9 July 1994.

18 *The Letters of John Henry Newman. A Selection Edited and Introduced by Muriel Spark and Derek Stanford* (Peter Owen, 1957), Introduction to Part II, 'Newman as a Catholic by Muriel Spark', pp. 133–60.

19 'Minor Victorian', *Observer*, 19 February 1961, 29; review of Ronald Chapman, *Father Faber* (Burns & Oates, 1961).

20 See ALS, Spark to von Auw, 9 January 1966, from Stafford Hotel, St James's Place, London SW1; PUL.

21 See ALS, 13 January 1966 [wrongly dated '1965'], Spark to von Auw, from Stafford Hotel etc.; PUL.

22 See ALS, 23 January 1966, Spark to von Auw, from Stafford Hotel etc.; PUL.

23 See ALS, 13 May 1966, Spark to Maclean, from Beaux Arts Hotel etc.; private collection.

24 *Observer Review,* 12 October 2003, 2.

25 See TLS, 6 May 1966, Ramsay to von Auw, from 14A Goodwin's Court, St Martin's Lane, London WC2; PUL.

26 *Ibid.*

27 See ALS, 13 May 1966, Spark to von Auw, from Beaux Arts Hotel etc.; PUL.

28 See ALS, 31 January 1966, Spark to von Auw, from Stafford Hotel etc.; PUL.

29 See TccLs, 13 November 1965, Spark to Probert of Walter Herriot & Co. Ltd, from Beaux Arts Hotel etc.

30 TccLS, 1 June 1966, Maclean to Robin Spark, np [Macmillan & Co. Ltd.]; PUL.

31 Muriel Spark, 'My Rome', *New York Times Magazine,* 13 March 1983, 36, 39, 70, 72; 36, 39.

32 ALS, 24 August 1966, Spark to von Auw, from Hotel Raphael, Piazza di Tor Sanguigna, Rome; PUL.

33 TccLS, 21 October 1966, von Auw to Maclean, np [Ober]; PUL.

34 See ALS, 19 September 1966, Spark to von Auw, from Hotel Raphael etc.; PUL.

35 See ALS, 23 October 1966, Spark to Alan and Robin Maclean, from Beaux Arts Hotel etc.; private collection.

36 See ALS, 22 May 1965, Spark to Maclean, from 1101-S, 310 E. 44th St, New York 17 [Beaux Arts Hotel]; private collection.

37 See ALS, 23 October 1966, Spark to Macleans, *op. cit.;* private collection.

38 See ALS, 5 November 1966, Spark to Maclean, from Beaux Arts Hotel etc.; private collection.

39 See *Ibid.*

40 'NOTE FROM MURIEL SPARK' sent to Stannard, June 2004.

41 See TNI [Ober internal memo], 18 November 1966, von Auw to Claire Smith; PUL.

42 See ALS, 11 February 1967, Spark to von Auw, from Hotel Raphael [Piazza di Tor Sanguigna etc.]; PUL.

43 See ALS, 26 February 1967, Spark to Maclean, from Piazza di Tor Sanguigna etc.; private collection.

44 *Ibid.,* 26 February 1967, Spark to Maclean; private collection.

45 See ALS, 17 January 1967, Spark to Nicholson, from Salvator Mundi International Hospital, Viale Mura Gianicolensi 67, Rome; private collection.

46 See ALS, 11 February 1967, Spark to von Auw, *op. cit.;* PUL.

47 See ALS, 13 February 1967, Spark to von Auw, from Piazza di Tor Sanguigna etc.; PUL.

48 See ALS, 26 February 1967, Spark to Maclean, *op. cit.;* private collection.

49 See TLS, 18 June 1967, Spark to von Auw, from Hotel Raphael [Piazza di Tor Sanguigna etc.]; PUL.

50 TLS, 26 October 1967, Spark to von Auw, from Hotel Raphael [Piazza di Tor Sanguigna etc.]; PUL.

51 See ALS, 30 August 1967, Spark to von Auw, from Hotel Raphael [Piazza di Tor Sanguigna etc.]; PUL.

52 See ALS, 7 January 1967, Spark to von Auw, from Piazza di Tor Sanguigna etc.; PUL.

53 See TLS, 29 April 1967, Spark to von Auw, from Piazza di Tor Sanguigna etc.; PUL.

54 See TccLS, 30 May 1967, Spark to Robert F. Bonagura, np [Piazza di Tor Sanguigna etc.]; PUL.

55 See TLS, 2 July 1967, Spark to Olding, from Hotel Raphael [Piazza di Tor Sanguigna etc.]; PUL.

56 See ALS, 8 August 1967, Spark to von Auw, from Hotel Raphael [Piazza di Tor Sanguigna etc.]; PUL.

57 See *ibid.*

58 See TccLS, 2 January 1968, Spark to Lindey, np [Piazza di Tor Sanguigna etc.]; PUL.

59 See TLS, 16 December 1967, Spark to von Auw, from Piazza di Tor Sanguigna etc.; PUL.

60 See TLS, 16 January 1968, Spark to von Auw, np [Rome]; PUL.

61 TccLS, 3 January 1968, Spark to Lindey, np [Piazza di Tor Sanguigna etc.]; PUL.

62 See TccLS, 2 January 1968, Spark to Lindey, *op. cit.*, PUL.

63 TccLS, 6 February 1968, Faye Podell [Muriel Spark] to secretary to Lindey, np [Piazza di Tor Sanguigna etc.]; PUL.

64 See TLS, 6 April 1965, Spark to von Auw, from Palazzo Taverna, Via di Monte Giordano 36, 00188 Roma; PUL.

CHAPTER 14: IN THE DRIVER'S SEAT

1 See TLS, 26 May 1968, Spark to von Auw, from Palazzo Taverna, Via di Monte Giordano 36, 00188 Roma; PUL.

2 Interview with Muriel Spark, 19 December 1995.

3 Muriel Spark, 'My Rome', *New York Times Magazine*, 13 March 1983, 36, 39, 70, 72; 39.

4 Interview with Brendan Gill, 23 February 1994.

5 Interview with Ned O'Gorman, 9 July 1994.

6 See TLS, 13 April 1970, Spark to von Auw, from Palazzo Taverna etc.; PUL.

7 See TccMS, 'List of Guests' etc., 26 May 1968, Box 83, 22; Tulsa.

8 See TccMS, 'Dinner given by Sir Eugen [...] in honour of Lady Gurney [...]' etc., 9 October 1968, Box 83, 22; Tulsa.

9 'My Rome' *op. cit.*, 39.

10 *Ibid.*, 39.

11 *Ibid.*, 39.

12 'The Poet's House', *The Critic* (Chicago), 19, 4 (February–March 1961); reprinted in *Encounter* 30 (May 1968), 48–50; 49.

13 *Harper's Bazaar* (November 1968), 159.

14 Martin Green, 'Fictions', *Month*, (November 1968), 286.

15 Saul Maloff, 'Lady-Tiger', *Newsweek*, 21 October 1968, 108, 110; 108.

16 R. G. G. Price, 'New Novels', *Punch*, 12 June 1968, 864.

17 William Hogan, *San Francisco Chronicle*, 4 October 1968; Jilly Cooper, 'The Public Image', *Penguiners*, June 1968.

18 Joyce Carol Oates, 'Press Agents' "Hot Stuff" Just a Cold Potato', *Detroit News*, 24 November 1968.

19 Charles Moore, 'Books of the Times. Wars between Sexes', *NYT*, 24 October 1968.

20 'Shallowness Everywhere', *TLS*, 13 June 1968, 612.

21 Rebecca West, 'High Roman Fashion', *S. Tel.*, 16 June 1968.

22 Auberon Waugh, 'Private Answer', *Spectator*, 7 June 1968.

23 William Trevor, 'Discipline From Within', *Guardian*, 14 June 1968.

24 A. S. Byatt, 'Empty Shell', *NS*, 14 June 1968, 807–8; 807.

25 Anne Fremantle, 'In Its Brief, Spare Way, It Packs a Wallop', *Sunday Herald Traveler*, 1 December 1968, 4.

26 Frank Kermode, 'Antimartyr', *Listener*, 13 June 1968.

27 Richard Holmes, 'Fiction: Into a Limbo of Poise', *The Times Saturday Review*, 15 June 1968, 21.

28 *Ibid.*

29 *Ibid.*

30 'Portrait of a [Man] Woman Reading. xxiii. Muriel Spark [. . .] Interviewed by Israel Shenker', *Book World*, 29 September 1968, 2.

31 Melvin Maddocks, 'The Spark Flair for Well-bred Demonology', *Life* (unattributed clipping; September 1968?).

32 *The Public Image* (Macmillan, 1968); *MSO4*, p. 440.

33 *Ibid.*, p.435.

34 TLS, 25 April 1968, Whitehead to Spark, from 1545 Broadway, New York, NY 10036; PUL.

35 See TLS, 2 May 1968, Spark to von Auw, from Palazzo Taverna etc.; PUL.

36 *The Public Image, MSO4*, p. 477.

37 *Ibid.*, p. 443.

38 *Ibid.*, p. 442.

39 See TccLS, 2 January 1968, Spark to Lindey, *op. cit.*; PUL.

40 Edwin Morgan, 'Public Faces, Private Faces', *ST*, 16 June 1968.

41 *The Public Image, MSO4*, pp. 441–2.

42 Hugh Herbert, 'Six Under Starter's Orders for the £5,000 Literary Stakes', *Guardian*, 28 March 1969.

43 See TLS, 1 March 1969, Spark to von Auw, from Palazzo Taverna etc.; PUL.

44 *Ibid.* The BBC film was in the 'Release' series.

45 See TLS, 29 November 1968, Spark to von Auw, from Salvator Mundi etc.; PUL.

46 See *ibid.*

47 See ALS, 14 October 1969, Spark to von Auw, from Salvator Mundi etc.; PUL.

48 Spark believed this to be inaccurate, and that she first met Ambrosiani when Armstrong brought him to see her in hospital.

49 Interview with Dario Ambrosiani, 18 December 1994.

50 *Ibid.*

51 *Ibid.*

52 Interview with Margaret Sachs (née Aubrey-Smith), 18 October 1996.

53 *Ibid.*

54 Interview with Muriel Spark, 17 December 1995.

55 Interview with George Mott, 9 July 1994.

56 Interview with George Mott, 4 May 1994.

57 See TLS, 21 January 1969, Spark to von Auw, from Palazzo Taverna etc.; PUL.

58 See TLS, 28 July 1969, Spark to von Auw, from Palazzo Taverna etc.; PUL.

59 See TLS, 4 September 1969, Spark to von Auw, from Palazzo Taverna etc.; PUL.

60 *The Driver's Seat*, AMS; Tulsa.

61 *The Driver's Seat* (Macmillan, 1970); *MSO1*, 1995, p. 437.

62 *Ibid.*, pp. 452, 448, 436, 453, 484.

63 *Ibid.*, pp. 430, 432, 466.

64 *Kirkus Reviews*, 15 July 1970.

65 *Publisher's Weekly*, 27 July 1970.

66 Robert Cogsell, 'Treacherous Double-Dealing [...]', *Western Mail*, 26 September 1970. See also 'Meal for a Masochist', *TLS*, 25 September 1970, 1074; and Mary Conroy, *ST*, 27 September 1970.

67 Derek Stanford, 'Back to the Batty Woman', *Scotsman*, 26 September 1970.

68 See D.T., *Washington D.C. Star*, 4 October 1970; Elizabeth Easton, *The Saturday Review*, 10 October 1970, 34, 65; and Mary Ellin Barrett, *Cosmopolitan* (October 1970), 6.

69 Muriel Spark, 'The Desegregation of Art', *Proceedings of the American Academy of Arts and Letters and the National Institute of Arts and Letters*, Second Series, 21 (New York, 1971), pp. 21–7.

CHAPTER 15: LUCREZIA BORGIA IN TROUSERS

1 Interview with Joseph Kanon, 24 February 1994.

2 Interview with Margaret Sachs, 18 October 1996.

3 See ALS, 18 September 1970, Spark to Shirley Hazzard and Francis Steegmuller, from Palazzo Taverna, Via di Monte Giordano 36, 00188 Rome; private collection.

4 Interview with Margaret Sachs, *op. cit.*

5 *Not to Disturb* (Macmillan, 1971); *MSO3*, p. 255.

6 Interview with Margaret Sachs, *op. cit.*

7 Beryl Hartland, 'Step Into Muriel Spark's Palazzo, and You're in Velvet', *DT*, 24 March 1971, 15.

8 *Ibid.*, 15.

9 Interview with Margaret Sachs, *op. cit.*

10 *NY*, 5 June 2000, 78–80.

11 Interview with Dario Ambrosiani, 18 November 1994.

12 Muriel Spark, *Reality and Dreams* (Constable, 1996), pp. 45–6.

13 See TLS, 1 October 1971, Spark to von Auw, from Lungotevere Raffaello Sanzio 9 etc. ; PUL.

14 See TLS, 27 August 1970, Spark to von Auw, from Palazzo Taverna etc.; PUL.

15 'Observer Art Offer. Muriel Spark Limited Edition', *Observer* (Colour Supplement), 7 November 1971, 73–4; 73.

16 See ALS, 10 April 1972, Spark to von Auw, np [Lungotevere Raffaello Sanzio 9 etc.]; PUL.

17 'Observer Art Offer', *op. cit.*, p. 73.

18 *Ibid.*, p. 74

19 See ALS, 18 October 1971, Spark to von Auw, np [Lungotever Raffaello Sanzio 9 etc.]; PUL.

20 TLS, 13 October 1971, Maclean to von Auw, from Macmillan & Co. Ltd., Little Essex Street, London WC2R 3LF; PUL.

21 TLS, 26 November 1971, Spark to von Auw, np [Lungotevere Raffaello Sanzio 9 etc.]; PUL.

22 'George Armstrong Talks to Muriel Spark at her Home in Rome', *Guardian*, 30 September 1970, 8.

23 See ALS, 12 March 1972, Spark to von Auw, from 'Rome' [Lungotevere Raffaello Sanzio 9 etc.]; PUL.

24 Bruce Williams, 'A Beautiful Night's Work', *FT*, 13 November 1971.

25 Frank Kermode, 'Foreseeing the Unforeseen', *Listener*, 11 November 1971, 657–8.

26 Claire Tomalin, 'The Servants' Revenge', *Observer Review*, 14 November 1971.

27 A. S. Byatt, 'Life, Death and the Media', *The Times*, 11 November 1971, 10.

28 Isobel Quigley, *FT*, 11 November 1971.

29 Robert Nye, *Guardian*, 11 November 1971.

30 Derek Stanford, *Scotsman*, 13 November 1971.

31 Francis King, *S. Tel.*, 14 November 1971.

32 *TLS*, 12 November 1971.

33 Nina Bawden, *DT*, 11 November 1971, 10.

34 Alexander Walker, 'Slender Means or Thin Stuff?', *Birmingham Post*, 13 November 1971.

35 Jonathan Raban, 'Vague Scriptures', *NS*, 12 November 1971, 657–8.

36 At FAO, the Food and Agricultural Organisation of the United Nations, based in Rome.

37 Interview with Dario Ambrosiani, 18 November 1994.

38 Interview with George Mott, 4 May 1994.

39 *Ibid.*

40 Interview with Hon. Guy Strutt, 15 January 2001.

41 *Ibid.*

42 *Ibid.*

43 See TLS, 21 January 1973, Spark to Dorothy Olding, from Lungotevere Raffaello Sanzio 9 etc.; Tulsa.

44 Interview with Dario Ambrosiani, 18 November 1994.

45 Muriel Spark, 'When Israel Went to the Vatican', *Tablet*, 24 March 1973, 277–8; 278.

46 *Ibid.*, 278.

47 *Ibid.*, 278.

48 See TLS, 29 December 1973, Spark to Olding, from Lungotevere Raffaello Sanzio 9 etc.; PUL.

49 Calder-Marshall, 'Penthouse Puzzles', *S. Tel.*, 4 March 1973; Bawden, 'Recent Fiction', *DT*, 1 March 1973; Pearson, 'Dry Gothic', *Guardian*, 1 March 1973, 20; May, 'Holy

Outrage', *Listener*, 1 March 1973, 283–4; Ellmann, 'The Problem of Elsa', *NS*, 2 March 1973, 308; Ratcliffe, 'Hell and Chaos as Farce', *The Times*, 1 March 1973, 14; Dick, 'Their Slow Dance of Death', *Weekend Scotsman*, 3 March 1973, 3; Seymour-Smith, 'Raising the Temperature', *FT*, 1 March 1973, 29.

50 Auberon Waugh, 'Spark Plug', *Spectator*, 17 March 1973.

51 Timothy Foote, 'Ars Moriendi', *Time*, 23 April 1973, 100.

52 John Barkham, 'The Literary Scene', *New York Post*, 30 April 1973.

53 Richard P. Brickner, 'Three Novels: Nightmares, Conspirators and Maniacs', *NYTBR*, 29 April 1973.

54 Diane Johnson, 'Books', *Washington Post*, 11 May 1973.

55 Florence Rome, 'New York's Nice to Visit, but is Anyone Living There?', *Chicago Tribune Book World*, 29 April 1973.

56 Muriel Spark, *The Hothouse by the East River* (Macmillan 1973); *MSO4*, pp. 163, 212, 241. The last is not an exact repetition, 'right' being omitted.

57 *Ibid.*, p. 271.

58 *Ibid.*, p. 271.

59 *Ibid.*, pp. 245–6.

60 *Ibid.*, p. 167.

61 *Ibid.*, p. 215.

62 *Ibid.*, p. 187.

63 *Ibid.*, p. 165.

64 *Ibid.*, p. 189.

65 *Ibid.*, p. 198.

66 *Ibid.*, p. 172.

67 'British Author Writes Best in N.Y.', *Books*, January 1965, 3.

68 *The Hothouse by the East River*, *MSO4*, pp. 184, 181, 180, 226.

69 See ALS, 1 September 1973, Muriel Spark to Shirley Hazzard, from Lungotevere Raffaelo Sanzio 9 etc.; private collection.

70 'Alex Hamilton Interviews Muriel Spark.', *Guardian (Arts Guardian* section), 8 November 1974, 10.

71 Interview with George Mott, 4 May 1994.

CHAPTER 16: THE REALM OF MYTHOLOGY

1 See TLS (fax), 12 January 2001, Jardine (quoting Spark) to Stannard, from SG.

2 'Alex Hamilton Interviews Muriel Spark', *Guardian (Arts Guardian* section), 8 November 1974, 10.

3 Muriel Spark, *The Abbess of Crewe* (Macmillan, 1974); *MSO2*, p. 251.

4 'Alex Hamilton Interviews Muriel Spark', *op. cit.*, 10.

5 See TLS, 25 November 1974, Spark to Hamilton, from Lungotevere Raffaello Sanzio 9, Rome; NLS.

6 'Alex Hamilton Interviews Muriel Spark', *op. cit.*, 10.

7 *Ibid.*, 10.

8 *Ibid.*, 10.

9 Nan Robertson, 'The Prime Time of Muriel Spark', *NYT*, 14 May 1979, A16.

10 *The Abbess of Crewe, MSO2*, p. 291.

11 *Time*, 11 November 1974, E12, CM7.

12 'Bugs and Mybug', *Listener*, 28 November 1974, 706.

13 See TccLS, 11 March 1975, Spark to Mrs S. Kochar, Secretary of the Jury, Jawaharlal Nehru Award for International Understanding, from Lungotevere Raffaello Sanzio 9 etc.; NLS.

14 Frank Kermode, *New Fiction Society, December Choice*, December 1974.

15 *Ibid.*

16 David Lodge, 'Prime Spark', *Tablet*, 7 December 1974, 1185.

17 Mary S. Pinkham, 'The Wicked Ways of a Convent Run Watergate Style', *Boston Sunday Globe*, 27 October 1974.

18 Gabriele Annan, 'Holy Watergate', *TLS*, 15 November 1974.

19 John Updike, 'Topnotch Witcheries', *NY*, 6 January 1975, 76–8; 76–7.

20 *Ibid.*, 77.

21 *Critics' Forum*, BBC Third Programme, 28 November 1974; BBCWAC.

22 *The Abbess of Crewe, MSO2*, p. 247.

23 *Critics' Forum, op. cit.*

24 See APCS, nd, pm blurred [1976?], Sean O'Faolain to Spark, from 17 Rosmeen Park, Dun Laoghaire, Dublin; NLS: 'The photograph of you would not deceive a bee. But henceforth you shall be to me dear Alexa – a lovely portrait of the artist.'

25 Interview with Lionel Daiches, 26 September 1994.

26 See desk diary, 17 December 1974; NLS.

27 See ALS, 27 July 1977, Spark to Guy Strutt, from 'at [SG]', Lungotevere Raffaello Sanzio 9 etc; private collection.

28 'The Prime of Muriel Spark', *Observer*, 30 May 1976, 81.

29 See TccLS, 17 May 1976, Spark to Comtesse de Tonnac-Villeneuve, from c/o Jardine, SG; NLS.

30 'The Prime of Muriel Spark', *op. cit.*

31 *Ibid.*

32 TLS, Sage to Spark, 6 May 1976, from Pensione Attica, Via Pandolfini 27, Florence; NLS.

33 Lorna Sage, 'Roman Scandals', *Observer Review*, 6 June 1976, 29.

34 Frank Kermode, 'Diana of the Crossroads', *NS*, 4 June 1976, 746–7.

35 Muriel Spark, *The Takeover* (Macmillan, 1976); *MSO3*, pp. 96–7.

36 Auberon Waugh, 'Room With A View', *ES*, 8 June 1976.

37 Derwent May, 'Maggie's Money', *Listener*, 3 June 1976, 718.

38 Gabriel Pearson, 'Loro', *Guardian*, 3 June 1976.

39 Frank Kermode, 'Diana of the Crossroads', *op. cit.* 'Lauro', Muriel insisted, is not an unusual name in Italy.

40 APC in letter, nd, pm 13 July [1976?], from 70 Via della Frezza, Rome; NLS.

41 *The Takeover, MSO3*, pp. 73–4.

42 Interview with George Mott, 4 May 1994.

43 *The Takeover, MSO3*, p. 71.

44 *Ibid.*, p. 48.

45 See APCS as letter, 15 September 1976, Spark to Strutt, from SG; private collection.

46 Muriel Spark, 'The Writing Life', *WPBW*, 11 March 2001, 6.

47 *The Takeover, MSO3*, p. 197.

48 *Le Croix*, 21 May 1987; quoting Josyane Savigneau, 'Affreux, Riches et Méchants' [review of *The Takeover (L'Appropriation)* on publication (Fayard, 1988) of French translation by P. Miriam], 6 May 1988.

49 *The Takeover, MSO3*, p.19.

50 Josyane Savigneau, *op. cit.*

51 TLS (fax), 8 March 2001, Jardine to Stannard, from SG; © Penelope Jardine.

52 Margaret Drabble, *NYTBR*, 3 October 1976, 1–2.

53 *Ibid.*, 2.

54 William McPherson, *WPBW*, 3 October 1976, F1, F2.

55 Paul Gray, 'Decline & Fall?', *Time*, 18 October 1976; Hoke Norris, 'Mrs Spark's Elegant Follies', *Chicago Daily News*, 10 October 1976; Susan Fromberg Schaeffer, *CTBR*, 17 October 1976; Walter Clemons, 'Funny Money', *Newsweek*, 25 October 1976, 53; Michael Wood, 'Endangered Species', *NYRB*, 11 November 1976, 30–32.

56 Anatole Broyard, 'Money Can't Buy Personality', *NYT*, 7 October 1976.

57 Shawn O'Connoll, 'All Values Vulnerable', *Boston Globe*, 17 October 1976.

58 Susan Philipson, 'Earning the Last Laugh', *Chicago Sunday Times*, 31 October 1976.

59 John Updike, 'Seeresses', *NY*, 29 November 1976, 164–74.

60 Susan Hill, 'Fiction', *The Times* (*Reviews* section), 3 June 1976, 10.

61 See TLS, 6 September 1976, Spark to Hazzard, from Lungotevere Raffaello Sanzio 9 etc.; private collection.

62 See ALS, 22 September 1976, Spark to Manning, from Lungotevere Raffaello Sanzio 9 etc.; NLS.

63 See ALS, 31 March 1977, Spark to Tristram Cary, from Lungotevere Raffaello Sanzio 9 etc.; private collection.

64 ALS, 2 May 1977, Spark to Ambrosiani, from c/o Jardine, SG; private collection.

65 ALS, 25 February 1977, Spark to Maclean, from 'Naples'; private collection.

66 See TLS, 10 October 1976, Spark to Isobel Poole, from Lungotevere Raffaello Sanzio 9 etc.; NLS.

67 See TLS with A addition, 18 November 1975, Spark to Dorothy Olding [of Ober], from Lungotevere Raffaello Sanzio 9 etc.; PUL.

68 TccLS, 28 December 1977, Spark to Greene, from Lungotevere Raffaello Sanzio 9 etc.; NLS.

69 ALS, 17 November 1975, Manning to Spark, from 46 Belsize Park, London NW3; NLS.

70 TLS, 10 October 1976, Spark to Manning, from Lungotevere Raffaello Sanzio 9 etc.; NLS.

71 Interview with Dario Ambrosiani, 31 March 1995.

CHAPTER 17: GOODBYE, GOODBYE, GOODBYE, GOOD*BYE*

1 Janice Galloway, 'The Vital Spark', *Sunday Herald*, 11 July 1999.

2 See ALS, 27 July 1977, Spark to Strutt, '(at [SG])', Lungotevere Raffaello Sanzio 9, Rome; private collection.

3 See ALS, 7 September [1978, misdated 1979], Spark to Strutt, '(At [SG])', Lungotevere Raffaello Sanzio 9 etc.; private collection.

4 See TccLS, 20 October 1978, Spark to Maclean, 'as from Lungotevere Raffaello Sanzio 9' etc., 'at' SG; NLS.

5 TccLS, 15 October 1978, Spark to Maclean, 'as from Lungotevere Raffaello Sanzio 9' etc., 'at' SG; NLS.

6 *Kirkus Reviews*, 1 March 1979.

7 Alexander Walker, *Birmingham Post*, 26 April 1979.

8 David Lodge, 'Prime Cut', *NS*, 27 April 1979, 597.

9 *Territorial Rights* (Macmillan, 1979); *MSO4*, 9.

10 TccLS, 20 October 1978, Spark to Maclean, *op. cit.* NLS.

11 'Venice in Fall and Winter', in Susan Cahill (ed.), *Desiring Italy* (New York: Fawcett Columbine, 1977), pp. 69–75; 70, 72–3.

12 *Ibid.*, p. 70.

13 *Ibid.*, p. 74.

14 Claire Tomalin, 'Growing Pains', *Punch*, 25 April 1979, 56.

15 Francis King, 'Venetian Lark', *Spectator*, 28 April 1979, 28–9.

16 Anatole Broyard, 'Thinking A Novel in Venice', *NYT*, 19 May 1979.

17 Anne Tyler, *New Republic*, 26 May 1979.

18 Edmund White, 'Fun in Venice', *NYTBR*, 20 May 1979, 1, 46.

19 Victoria Glendinning, 'Talk With Muriel Spark', *NYTBR*, 20 May 1979, 47–8.

20 Colman McCarthy, 'That Spark of Satire', *Washington Post*, 4 May 1979, F1, F10.

21 Barbara Holsopple, 'TV Version Best "Jean Brodie", Author Says', *Pittsburgh Press*, 4 May 1979, B-22.

22 Toby Kahn, *People Weekly*, 21 May 1979, vol. 11, 20, 145.

23 Nan Robertson, 'The Prime Time of Muriel Spark', *NYT*, 14 May 1979, A16.

24 Barbara Kantrowitz, 'The Prime of Muriel Spark,' *Philadelphia Enquirer*, 8 May 1979, 1E, 5E; 1E.

25 Joan Hanauer, 'Everyone Has Had a Miss Jean Brodie', *Madisonville Ky Messenger*, 7 May 1979, D9.

26 Glendinning, *op. cit.*

27 From Muriel Spark's reading and 'audience' at Edinburgh International Book Festival, 22 April 2003, chaired by Alan Taylor.

28 See TLS, 10 July 1979, Spark to Strutt, from c/o Jardine, SG; private collection.

29 Interview with Muriel Spark, 17 December 1995.

30 See TccLS, 15 October 1978, Spark to Maclean, *op. cit.*, NLS.

31 Interview with Muriel Spark, 17 December 1995.

32 ALS, 26 May 1979, Greene to Spark, from La Résidence des Fleurs, Avenue Pasteur, 06600 Antibes; NLS; © Verdant 2009. The Berridge review was 'Recent Fiction', *DT*, 26 April 1979, 14.

33 ALS, 5 June 1979, Greene to Spark, from La Résidence des Fleurs etc.; NLS; © Verdant 2009.

34 AMS diary, 10 December 1979; NLS.

35 *Ibid.*, 13 February 1980; NLS.

36 ALS, 3 March 1980, Maclean to Spark, from 21 Abingdon Court, Abingdon Villas, London W8; NLS.

37 Interview with Peter Ginna, 17 February 1994.

38 *Ibid.*

39 Muriel Spark, 'My Rome', *New York Times Magazine*, 13 March 1983, 70.

40 See ALS, 1 August 1980, Spark to Strutt, from c/o Jardine, SG; private collection.

41 See TccLS, 11 November 1980, Spark to Greene, from SG; NLS.

42 Muriel Spark, *Loitering with Intent* (Macmillan, 1981); *MSO2*, p. 12.

43 *Ibid.*, p. 11.

44 *Ibid.*, p. 12.

45 *Ibid.*, p. 22.

46 *Ibid.*, p. 17.

47 *Ibid.*, p 16.

48 *Ibid.*, p. 23.

49 *Ibid.*, p. 22.

50 *Ibid.*, p. 21.

51 *Ibid.*, p. 57.

52 TccLS, 9 September 1980, Spark to Lerner, from c/o Jardine, SG; NLS.

53 *Loitering with Intent*, *MSO2*, p. 91.

54 *Ibid.*, p. 42.

55 *Ibid.*, p. 108.

56 *Ibid.*, pp. 70, 81–2.

57 Quoted *ibid.*, p. 98.

58 Quoted *ibid.*, p. 126.

59 *Ibid.*, p. 12.

60 *Ibid.*, p. 77.

61 Interview with Hugh Fleetwood, 2 April 1998.

62 *Loitering with Intent*, *MSO2*, p. 98.

63 ALS, 16 March 1981, Spark to Strutt, from c/o Jardine, SG; private collection.

64 Peter S. Prescott, 'Writer's Nightmare', *Newsweek*, 18 May 1981, 11.

65 Barbara Grizzuti Harrison, 'To Be an Artist and a Woman', *NYTBR*, 31 May 1981, 11, 48.

66 Auberon Waugh, 'What Just One Spark Can Set Alight', *DM*, 21 May 1981.

67 A. S. Byatt, 'Truth, Lies, Fiction', *Guardian*, 21 May 1981, 16.

68 A. N. Wilson, 'Cause for Rejoicing', *Spectator*, 23 May 1981, 20–21.

69 *Ibid.*, 20.

70 John Osborne, 'The Vital Spark', *NS*, 26 May 1981.

71 Malcolm Bradbury, *Vogue*, May 1981.

72 Peter Tinniswood, 'Fiction', *The Times*, 21 May 1981, 16.

73 Jeremy Treglown, 'A Literary Life', *TLS*, 22 May 1981, 561; Martin Seymour-Smith, 'Loiterer's Luck', *FT*, 23 May 1981, 10; Anatole Broyard, 'Lightness with Shading', *NYT*, 23 May 1981; William Boyd, *ST*, 24 May 1981, 42.

74 Victoria Glendinning, *Book World*, 24 May 1981, 4, 14; Michael Holroyd, 'Suspicious Characters', *New York*, 25 May 1981, 99.

75 See ALS, nd [pm 3 August 1982], Spark to Strutt, from 9 Vicolo del Gallo, Rome 00186; private collection.

CHAPTER 18: A SPECK IN THE DISTANCE

1 See ALS, 30 August [1982], Jardine to Spark, from SG; NLS.

2 'My Rome', *New York Times Magazine*, 13 March 1983, 72.

3 See ALS, 26 December 1982, Spark to Strutt, from 9 Vicolo del Gallo, Rome 00186; private collection.

4 See *ibid.*

5 See ALS, 13 January 1984, Spark to Strutt, from SG; private collection.

6 Muriel Spark, *The Only Problem* (Bodley Head, 1984); *MSO1*, p. 303.

7 Interview with Alan Maclean, 6 December 1994.

8 Muriel Spark, 'The Writing Life', *WPBW*, 11 March 2001, 6.

9 *Ibid.*

10 See ALS, 28 May 1983, Spark to Strutt, from 9 Vicolo del Gallo etc.; private collection.

11 *The Only Problem, MSO1*, p. 310; 'The Mystery of Job's Suffering: Jung's New Interpretation Examined', *CEN*, 15 April 1955, 7. In the essay, the verbs are in the present tense.

12 *The Only Problem, MSO1*, p. 303.

13 *Ibid.*, p. 310.

14 *Ibid.*, p. 383.

15 *Ibid.*, p. 387.

16 *Ibid.*, p. 395.

17 *Ibid.*, p. 366.

18 *Ibid.*, p. 343.

19 *Ibid.*, p. 344.

20 *Ibid.*, p. 419.

21 'The Sitter's Tale' (interview with Chloe Walker), *Independent on Sunday*, 22 August 1999, 14.

22 See TLS, 12 May 1981, Robin Spark to Muriel Spark, from 160 Bruntsfield Place, Edinburgh; NLS.

23 Dean Nelson, 'Spark and Son in Feud over Jewish Origins', *Observer*, 29 March 1998, 15.

24 See Martin Stannard, 'The Letter Killeth', *Spectator*, 6 June 1998, 36–7.

25 TLS (fax), 27 May 1999, Spark to Stannard, from SG.

26 Interview with Dean Nelson, *Observer Review*, 14 March 1999.

27 Robin Spark, 'Life with the Cambergs', *Edinburgh Star*, 32 (February 1999), 13–17.

28 See TLS (fax), 27 May 1999, Spark to Stannard, from SG.

29 ALS (fax), nd [9 May 1998], Spark to Stannard, from SG.

30 *Ibid.*

31 Muriel Spark, 'Side Roads of Tuscany', *New York Times Magazine*, 7 October 1984, 28–9, 72, 74, 76, 79; 28.

32 *Ibid.*, 74.

33 *Ibid.*, 77.

34 Cathleen Medwick, 'Books in Vogue', *Vogue* (July 1984), 120.

35 A. N. Wilson, 'Suffering, Salvation and Sex', *WPBW*, 1 July 1984.

36 Stefan Kanfer, 'Job Hunting in the Eternal City', *Time*, 16 July 1984.

37 Elaine Kendall, 'The Story of Job with Modern Twists', *Los Angeles Times*, 26 July 1984, 18, 20.

38 John Updike, 'Books. A Romp with Job', *New Yorker*, 23 July 1984, 104–7.

39 Anita Brookner, 'How Effie Made Him Suffer', *NYTBR*, 15 July 1984, 1, 26.

40 Anthony Burgess, 'Yellow Eyeballs', *Observer Review*, 9 September 1984.

41 Frank Kermode, 'The Uses of Error: Sermon before the University, King's College Chapel, 11 May 1986'; reprinted in Kermode, *The Uses of Error* (Collins, 1990), pp. 425–32; 427.

42 Frank Kermode, 'Old Testament Capers', *LRB*, 20 September–3 October 1984, 10–11; 10.

43 Francis King, 'Job Updated', *Spectator*, 8 September 1984, 27.

44 Margharita Laski, 'Insufficient Reasons', *Country Life*, September 1984, 647.

45 Clive Sinclair, 'Book Reviews', *Jewish Chronicle*, 28 September 1984.

46 David Taylor, 'Two By Two', *London Magazine*, October 1984, 91–2; 92.

47 Interview with Hunter Davies, Radio 4 *Bookshelf*, 4 November 1984 (recorded 3 July 1984).

48 *Ibid.*

49 See ALS, 6 October 1984, Spark to Strutt, from SG; private collection.

50 *Ibid.*

51 See ALS, 27 October 1984, Spark to Maclean, from SG; private collection.

52 ALS, 5 August 1984, Spark to Ambrosiani, from SG; private collection.

53 See ALS, 12 May 1985, Spark to Brooke-Rose, from c/o Jardine [SG]; HRC.

54 See diary, 19 and 26 December 1985; NLS.

55 Interview with Christine Brooke-Rose, 13 March 1994.

56 ALS, 12 May 1985, Spark to Brooke-Rose, *op. cit.*

57 ALS, 15 June 1986, Brooke-Rose to Spark, from 'Paris'; NLS; © Christine Brooke-Rose.

58 ALS, 3 February 1986, Brooke-Rose to Spark, from 16 rue St Victor, 75005 Paris; NLS; © Christine Brooke-Rose.

59 Interview with Christine Brooke-Rose, 27 January 1994.

60 See ALS, 7 December 1985, Spark to Brooke-Rose, from c/o Jardine, Tuscany; NLS.

61 *Ibid.*

62 Interview with Robin Baird-Smith, 2 April 2001.

63 See TccLS, 16 May 1985, Spark to Olding, from SG; NLS.

64 See ALS, 22 February 1987, Spark to Viscount Stockton (Alexander Macmillan) from SG; NLS.

65 TccL, 20 December 1961, Maurice Macmillan to Spark, from Macmillan & Co. Ltd, St Martin's Street, London WC2; NLS.

66 TccL, 22 February 1987, Spark to Viscount Stockton, *op. cit.*

67 See TLS, 6 May 1987, Viscount Stockton to Spark, from Macmillan Publishers Ltd, Little Essex Street, London WC2R 3LF.
68 TccLS, 21 May 1987, Spark to Viscount Stockton, from SG; NLS.
69 ALS, 15 June 1987, Spark to Brooke-Rose, from SG. The speech was to be given at her old school, Gillespie's, to inaugurate a series of 'Muriel Spark Lectures' sponsored by the Post Office. The articles were 'Echoes of Shelley in Italy', *Architectural Digest* 43 (1986), 262, 266; and 'Gardens: Plotting an Alpine Cliffhanger – The Baggatti-Valsecchi Villa above Lake Como', *Architectural Digest* (February 1987), 124–7.
70 See ALS, 15 June 1987, Spark to Brooke-Rose, *op. cit.*
71 ALS, 12 May 1985, Spark to Brooke-Rose, *op. cit.*

CHAPTER 19: SETTLING THE BILL

1   See ALS, 22 March 1988, Spark to Strutt, from SG; private collection.
2   'The Culture of an Anarchist [. . .]', *DT Sunday Magazine*, 20 March 1988, 16–18, 20; 16. The interview took place on 6 January 1988.
3   *Ibid.*, 16.
4   *Ibid.*, 18.
5   Misprinted as 'cad' in the original.
6   'The Culture of an Anarchist', *op. cit.*, 18.
7   *Ibid.*, 20.
8   *Ibid.*, 20.
9   A. J. Ayer, *Cover to Cover*, BBC TV, 17 March 1988.
10 Muriel Spark, A *Far Cry From Kensington* (Constable, 1988; reprinted Penguin Books, 1989), p. 101.
11 Claire Tomalin, 'Joys of a Fat Useful Person', *Independent*, 24 March 1988, 21.
12 Alan Bold, 'Single Cream', *NS*, 25 March 1988, 21–2.
13 Patricia Craig, 'Taking a Stand with Aplomb', *TLS*, 18–24 March 1988, 301.
14 Peter Kemp, 'Loitering with Intent in Literary London', *ST*, 30 March 1988.
15 *Ibid.*
16 *Frank Delaney*, 21 November 1983, BBC2.
17 Anita Brookner, 'Memory Speak, but Do Not Condemn', *Spectator*, 20 March 1988, 31.
18 *A Far Cry from Kensington*, *op.cit.*, pp. 79, 68, 9, 18, 13.
19 Kemp, *op. cit.*
20 *A Far Cry from Kensington*, *op. cit.*, p. 46.
21 *Ibid.*, p. 22.
22 *Shorter Oxford English Dictionary*, p. 2265.
23 *A Far Cry from Kensington*, *op. cit.*, p. 140.
24 Kemp, *op. cit.*
25 *A Far Cry from Kensington*, *op. cit.*, p. 5.
26 *Ibid.*, pp. 87, 90, 120.
27 *Ibid.*, p. 114.
28 *Ibid.*, pp. 44–5, 95.

29 *Ibid.*, p. 189.

30 See ALS, 22 March 1988, Spark to Strutt, from SG; private collection.

31 Interview with Joseph Kanon, 24 February 1994.

32 *Ibid.*

33 TLS, 1 June 1991, Spark to Cowell, from SG; private collection.

34 See ALS, 16 November 1988, Spark to Strutt, from SG; private collection.

35 Interview with Muriel Spark, 17 December 1995.

36 *Ibid.*

37 Mary Blume, 'Muriel Spark: The Infinitely Mysterious', *International Herald Tribune*, 8 May 1989, 16.

38 See ALS, 26 July 1989, Spark to Strutt, from SG; private collection.

39 *Symposium* (Constable, 1990; reprinted Penguin Books 1991), p. 44.

40 See TLS, 30 August 1990 and TLS, 22 September 1992, Spark to Strutt, from SG; private collection.

41 See ALS, 25 October 1992, Spark to Cowell, from SG; private collection.

42 TLS, 14 October 1990, Spark to Strutt, from SG; private collection.

43 Frances Hill, 'The Cracks in the Dinner Table', *The Times*, 27 September 1990, 19.

44 Candia McWilliam, 'Rich Pickings at the Dining Table', *Independent on Sunday, (Arts Supplement)*, 23 September 1990, 31.

45 Penelope Lively, 'Turning the Fables', *ES*, 20 September 1990, 37.

46 Francis King, 'Sex, Robbery and Murder before the Coffee', *Spectator*, 22 September 1990, 43.

47 Margaret Carlson, 'Death Comes with Dessert', *Time*, 25 November 1990; Nina King, 'Speaking of Love and Death', *WPBW*, 20, 47 (25 November 1990); Rhoda Koewig, 'Supper Club', *New York*, 3 December 1990, 174; Richard Eder, 'Memento Muriel', *Los Angeles Times Book Review*, 2 December 1990; Judith Martin, 'The Action is not at the Table', *NYTBR*, 25 November 1990.

48 P. B. Shelley's translation, *Prose Works*, ed. Buxton Forman, Vol. 3. (Reeves and Turner, 1880), pp. 209–10.

49 *Symposium*, *op cit.*, p. 15.

50 *Ibid.*, p. 127.

51 *Ibid.*, p. 5.

52 *CV*, p. 11.

53 Norman Page, *Muriel Spark* (Macmillan, 1990).

54 'Spark of Scholarship' (letter to the editor), *THES*, 23 November 1990.

55 TLS, 11 January 1991, Spark to Page, from SG; private collection.

56 See ALS, 27 October 1990, Spark to Cowell, from SG; private collection.

57 TLS, 15 November 1990, Spark to Cowell, from SG; private collection.

58 See TLS, 27 January 1991, Muriel Spark to Dario Ambrosiani, from SG; private collection.

59 See TLS, 23 December 1990, Spark to Cowell, from SG; private collection.

60 See ALS, nd [pm 12 June 1990], Spark to Strutt, from 'Tuscany' [SG]; private collection.

61 See *ibid.*

62 'Muriel Spark, O.B.E.' in *Tributes to Graham Greene, O.M., C.H., 1904–1991, at the Memorial Requiem Mass at Westminster Cathedral* (Reinhardt Books, 1991), pp. 15–16.

63 See TccLS, 12 September 1991, Spark to Cunnane, from SG; NLS.

64 See TccLS (fax), 30 September 1991, Spark to Hunter, from SG; NLS.

65 *CV*, pp. 11–12.

66 Alan Taylor, 'Morningside', *Scotsman*, 29 April 1995, 'Weekend' section, 7–8; 7.

67 See TLS, 1 June 1991, Spark to Cowell, from SG; private collection.

68 See TLS, 14 August 1989, Spark to John Heath-Stubbs, from SG; private collection.

69 See ALS, 7 February 1992, Spark to Strutt, from SG; private collection.

70 See TLS, 5 April 1992, Spark to Cowell, from SG; private collection.

71 Interview with Joseph Kanon, 24 February 1994.

CHAPTER 20: DARK MUSIC

1 See ALS, 29 December 1992, Jardine to Stannard, from Salvator Mundi International Hospital, Viale Mura Gianicolensi 67, Rome, private collection.

2 Stephen Schiff, 'Muriel Spark between the Lines', *NY*, 24 May 1993, 36–43; 40.

3 *Ibid.*, 36, 37, 38.

4 TLS (fax), 6 April 1995, Spark to Stannard, from SG.

5 'Muriel Spark Fired Up', interview with David Straitfeld, *WP*, 12 August 1993, C1, C6.

6 ALS, 10 November 1994, Jardine to Stannard, from Hotel La Place, 17 Nottingham Place, London W1M 3FB; © Penelope Jardine.

7 See ALS, 19 November 1994, Jardine to Stannard, np [Hotel La Place].

8 'Slate Diary, Slate Archives http://slate.msn.com, 'Day One. Posted Wednesday, June 5 1996, at 3.01 p.m. PT'.

9 'The Young Man Who Discovered the Secret of Life' and 'The Ghost That Was a Terrible Snob' (ultimately 'The Snob') eventually appeared in Alexander Waugh's *Travelman* pamphlet series alongside 'The Pearly Shadow' (1999).

10 'Slate Diary', *op. cit.* 'Day Nine. Posted: Thursday, June 13 1996, at 9.51 a.m. PT'.

11 *Ibid.*, 'Posted: Wednesday, December 11 1996, at 4.30 p.m. PT'.

12 *Ibid.*, 'Posted: Thursday, December 12 1996, at 4.30 p.m. PT'.

13 *Ibid.*, 'Posted: Friday, December 13 1996, at 4.30 p.m. PT'; Proverbs 6:16.

14 *Ibid.*, 'Posted: Thursday, December 10 1996, at 4.30 p.m. PT'.

15 John Mortimer, 'Naughty Nineties? Not a Chance in a Millennium', *Observer Review*, 15 September 1996, 17.

16 *Reality and Dreams* (Constable, 1996), p. 14.

17 *Ibid.*, p. 59.

18 Shena Mackay, 'The Olympian View', *TLS*, 20 September 1996.

19 John Updike, 'Muriel Goes to the Movies', *NY*, 26 May 1997, 76–8, 77.

20 *Reality and Dreams, op. cit.*, p. 65.

21 Jan Moir, 'Dame With an Eye for Danger', *DT* (*Arts and Books*), 9 September 2005.

22 See TLS (fax), 16 March 1998, Spark to Stannard, from SG.

23 ALS, 4 February 1999, Spark to Strutt, from SG; private collection.

24 Alexander Chancellor, 'Hunting Down the Pet Killers', *DT*, 'Weekend' section, 20 March 1999, 1–2.

25 Janice Galloway, 'The Vital Spark', *Sunday Herald*, 11 July 1999.

26 Lewis Jones, 'Divine Spark', *S. Tel.*, 19 December 1999, 16–18, 20.

27 TLS (fax), 27 March 2000, Spark to Stannard, from SG.

28 See Michael Geyer, 'Civitella della Chiana on 29 June 1944: The Reconstruction of a German "Measure"', in Hannes Heer and Klaus Naumann (eds.), *War of Extermination: The German Military in World War II, 1941–1945* (New York: Berghahn Books, 2004), pp. 175–216; 175–6. See also Alexander Chancellor, 'Britain in the 1950s was not perfect. [. . .]', *Guardian, G2* section, 28 November 2008, 9.

29 Interview with Don Gualtiero Mazzeschi, 7 April 2008.

30 Muriel Spark, *Aiding and Abetting* (Viking, 2000), pp. v–vi.

31 *Ibid.*, pp. 171, 125.

32 *Ibid.*, pp. 32, 110.

33 *Ibid.*, p. 91.

34 'The Empty Space', *ATP*, p. 44.

35 Telephone call, 1 December 2000, Spark to Stannard.

36 Muriel Spark, 'The Writing Life', *Washington Post*, 11 March 2001, 6.

37 Kenny Farquharson, 'Ecosse: the Vital Spark', *ST*, 17 October 2004.

38 Muriel Spark, *The Finishing School* (Viking, 2004), pp. 48–9.

39 *Ibid.*, p. 28.

40 *Ibid.*, p. 80.

41 See interview with Muriel Spark, 17–18 December, 1995.

42 *The Finishing School, op. cit.*, p. 147.

43 Interview with Don Gualtiero Mazzeschi, 7 April 2008.

44 *Ibid.*

EPILOGUE

1 Danielle Gusmaroli, *DM*, 22 April 2006, 34–5.

2 Karin Goodwin, *ST*, 21 May 2006, 7.

3 Mark Lawson, 'Dame Muriel Spark', *Guardian*, 17 April 2006, 6.

SELECT BIBLIOGRAPHY

[Place of publication London unless otherwise stated]

1. WORKS BY MURIEL SPARK

Novels

The Comforters (Macmillan, 1957; Philadelphia: Lippincott, 1957).
Robinson (Macmillan, 1958; Philadelphia: Lippincott, 1958).
Memento Mori (Macmillan, 1959; Philadelphia: Lippincott, 1959).
The Ballad of Peckham Rye (Macmillan, 1960; Philadelphia: Lippincott, 1960).
The Bachelors (Macmillan, 1960; Philadelphia: Lippincott, 1961).
The Prime of Miss Jean Brodie (Macmillan, 1961; Philadelphia: Lippincott, 1962).
The Girls of Slender Means (Macmillan, 1963; New York: Knopf, 1963).
The Mandelbaum Gate (Macmillan, 1965; New York: Knopf, 1965).
The Public Image (Macmillan, 1968; New York: Knopf, 1968).
The Driver's Seat (Macmillan, 1970; New York: Knopf, 1970).
Not to Disturb (Macmillan, 1971; New York: Viking, 1972).
The Hothouse by the East River (Macmillan, 1973; New York: Viking, 1973).
The Abbess of Crewe (Macmillan, 1974; New York: Viking, 1974).
The Takeover (Macmillan, 1976; New York: Viking, 1976).
Territorial Rights (Macmillan, 1979; New York: Coward, McCann & Geoghegan, 1979).
Loitering with Intent (Bodley Head, 1981; New York: Coward, McCann & Geoghegan, 1981).
The Only Problem (Bodley Head, 1984; New York: Putnam, 1984).
A Far Cry from Kensington (Constable, 1988; Boston: Houghton Mifflin, 1988).
Symposium (Constable, 1990; Boston: Houghton Mifflin, 1990).
Reality and Dreams (Constable, 1996; Boston: Houghton Mifflin, 1997).
Aiding and Abetting (Viking, 2000; New York: Doubleday, 2001).
The Finishing School (Viking, 2004; New York: Doubleday, 2004).

Collected Short Stories

The Go-Away Bird and Other Stories (Macmillan, 1958; Philadelphia: Lippincott, 1960).
Collected Stories I (Macmillan, 1967; New York: Knopf, 1968).
Bang-bang You're Dead and Other Stories (Granada, 1982).
The Stories of Muriel Spark (New York: Dutton, 1985; Bodley Head, 1987).
Open to the Public: New and Collected Stories (New York: New Directions, 1997).
The Complete Short Stories (Viking, 2001); *All the Stories of Muriel Spark* (New York: New Directions, 2001).

Children's Stories

The Very Fine Clock (New York: Knopf, 1968; Macmillan, 1969).
The Small Telephone (Colophon Press, 1983).
The French Window (Colophon Press, 1993).

Collected Poetry

The Fanfarlo, and Other Verse (Aldington: Hand and Flower Press, 1952).
Collected Poems I (Macmillan, 1967; New York: Knopf, 1968).
Going Up to Sotheby's and Other Poems (St Albans: Granada, 1982).
All the Poems (Manchester: Carcanet, 2004).

Uncollected Poetry

Juvenilia, AMS notebook, University of Victoria, BC Special Collections.

AMS notebook (1931–2), Harry Ransom Humanities Research Center, University of Texas at Austin.

AMS notebook, 'The Ides of March. To Francis. 15 March, 1932. Muriel Camberg'; estate of Francis Cowell.

'The Idiot', *School: the Annual of the Rhodesia Teachers Association*, 2 (1941), 39. Winning entry of Open Verse Section of Rhodesian Eisteddfod, 1941.

'Frantic a Child Ran' and 'Three Thoughts in Africa' (latter dated October 1943), *Poetry of To-day. Poetry Review New Verse Supplement*, 1, 72 (Spring 1946), 80–82.

'Poem for a Pianist', 'They Sigh for Old Dreams', and 'I Have a Lovely Meadow Land', *Poetry of To-day. Poetry Review New Verse Supplement*, 3, 74 (1946), 10–12.

'The Victoria Falls', *Poetry Review*, 37, 4 (August–September 1946), 285.

'The Well', *Poetry Review*, 38, 1 (January–February 1947), 82–6.

'Leaning Over an Old Wall' and 'Autumn' [a trio of sonnets], *Poetry Review*, 38, 2 (March–April 1947), 106, 155–6.

'The Robe and the Song', *Poetry Review*, 38, 3 (May–June 1947), 192–3; reprinted Christmas Humphreys (ed.), *Poems I Remember* (Michael Joseph, 1960), p. 52.

'Birthday', *Poetry Review*, 38, 4 (July–August 1947), 270.

'The Bells at Bray' and 'Cadmus', *Poetry Review*, 38, 5 (September–October 1947), 353, 379.

'Omega (For E. V. F.)', *Poetry Review*, 38, 6 (December 1947), 519.

'Song', *Outposts*, 9 (Winter 1947), 10.

'You, Dreamer', *Canadian Poetry Magazine*, 11, 3 (March 1948), 23.

'Invocation to a Child. For Robin', *Poetry Quarterly*, 10, 1 (Spring 1948), 22.

'Song of the Divided Lover', *Poetry Commonwealth*, 1 (Summer 1948), 5.

'Standing in Dusk', *Variegation. Free Verse Quarterly* [Los Angeles], 3, 3 (Summer 1948), 5; reprinted as 'Poem', *Prospect*, 2 (Summer 1948), 26.

'Sin', *Punch*, 215 (27 October 1948), 395.

'Anniversary', *Variegation. Free Verse Quarterly* [Los Angeles], 3, 4 (Autumn 1948), 17.

'A Letter to Howard', *Poetry Quarterly*, 10, 3 (Autumn 1948), 152–3.

'Lost Lover', *Outposts*, 11 (Autumn 1948), 3.

'Tracing the Landscape . . . ', *Poetry Commonwealth*, 2 (Autumn 1948), 5.

'She Wore His Luck on Her Breast', *Outposts*, 12 (Winter 1948), 10–11.

'Magdalen', *Gemini*, 1 (May 1949), 3.

'This Plato', *Arena* [New Zealand], 21 (June 1949), 12–13.

'The Beads', *Poetry Quarterly*, 11, 3 (Autumn 1949), 144–5.

'Indian Feathers (For Robin)', *Variegation. Free Verse Quarterly* [Los Angeles], 4, 4 (Autumn 1949), 4.

'The Voice of One Lost Sings Its Gain', *Poetry Quarterly*, 11, 4 (Winter 1949–1950), 221. Used in revised form in *Loitering with Intent* (1981).

With Derek Stanford, 'Invocation in a Churchyard on All Hallows Eve', *Gemini*, 3 (January 1950), 2.

—— 'Guillaume Apollinaire, "Poem XVII from *Shadows of my Love*"', trans. Muriel Spark and Derek Stanford, *Poetry Quarterly*, 12, 3 (Autumn 1950).

'The Dancers', *World Review*, 12 (1950), 30.

'Kindness or Weakness?', *Public Opinion*, 17 November 1950, 24.

'Snow-Fall', *Public Opinion*, 16 March 1951, 28.

'No Need For Shouting (for D.S.)', *Poetry Quarterly*, 13, 1 (Spring 1951), 24.

'Birthday Acrostic', *Poetry Quarterly*, 13, 2 (Summer 1951), 68.

'Portrait', *Recurrence*, 2, 2 (Autumn 1951), 7.

'Conundrum' and 'The Miners', *Chanticleer*, 1, 1 (1952), 10.

'A Letter at Christmas', *Outposts*, 20 (1952), 5–6.

'Pearl Miners', *Poetry* (Chicago), September 1953.

'A Sleep of Prisoners', *Spectator*, 25 May 1951, 688.

'Domestic Dawn', *Saturday Review*, 13 April 1957, 30.

Plays

Voices at Play: Stories and Ear-Pieces (Macmillan, 1961; Philadelphia: Lippincott, 1961) [contains the radio plays *The Party through the Wall* (1957), *The Interview* (1958), *The Dry River Bed* (1959), and *The Danger Zone* (1961)].

Doctors of Philosophy (Macmillan, 1963; New York: Knopf, 1966).

Biography

Child of Light. A Reassessment of Mary Wollstonecraft Shelley (Hadleigh: Tower Bridge Publications, 1951); revised as *Mary Shelley* (New York: Dutton, 1987; Constable, 1988; reprinted as New American Library paperback, New York: Meridan, 1987).

John Masefield (Peter Nevill, 1953; New York: Coward, McCann, 1966).

Autobiography

'How I Became a Novelist', *John O'London's Weekly*, 1 December 1960, 683.

'The Poet's House', *The Critic* (Chicago), 19, 4 (February–March 1961); reprinted *Encounter*, 30 (May 1965), 48–50.

'Edinburgh-born', *New Statesman*, 10 August 1962, 180; reprinted as 'What Images Return', in Karl Miller (ed.), *Memoirs of Modern Scotland* (Faber & Faber, 1970), pp. 151–3.

'Exotic Departures', *New Yorker*, 28 January 1967, 31–2.

'The Books That Made Writers. Muriel Spark', *New York Times Book Review*, 25 November 1979, 7.

'My Rome', *New York Times Magazine*, 13 March 1983, 36, 39, 70, 72.

'Guest Speaker: Muriel Spark. Footnote to a Poet's House', *Architectural Digest*, 42 (1985), 38, 44, 48.

'Personal History: The School on the Links', *New Yorker*, 25 March 1991, 75–85; excerpt from *Curriculum Vitae*.

'Personal History: Visiting the Laureate', *New Yorker*, 26 August 1991, 63–4, 66–7; excerpt from *Curriculum Vitae*.

'Personal History: Venture into Africa', *New Yorker*, 2 March 1992, 73–80; excerpt from *Curriculum Vitae*.

Curriculum Vitae (Constable, 1992; Boston: Houghton Mifflin, 1993).

'Slate Diary', Slate Archives http://slate.msn.com, 'Day One. Posted Wednesday June 5, 1996, at 3.01 p.m. PT'.

'Slate Diary', 'Posted: Thursday, June 13 1996, at 9.51 a.m. PT'.

'Slate Diary', 'Posted: Thursday, December 10 1996, at 4.30 p.m. PT'.

'Slate Diary', 'Posted: Wednesday, December 11 1996, at 4.30 p.m. PT'.

'Slate Diary', 'Posted: Thursday, December 12 1996, at 4.30 p.m. PT'.

'Slate Diary', 'Posted: Friday, December 13 1996, at 4.30 p.m. PT'.

'Harold Macmillan: A Memoir', *Literary Review* (January 1997), 20.

'A Drink with Dame Edith', *Literary Review* (February 1997), 31–2.

'The Best Part of a Lifetime. Muriel Spark on her Place in English Letters', *The Times*, 20 March 1997, 24. Acceptance speech at David Cohen British Literature Prize ceremony, 19 March 1997.

'Death in Tuscany', *Guardian* (*G2* section), 18 March 1999, 2–3.

'My Madeleine', *New Yorker*, 25 December 2000 and 1 January 2001, 105.

'The Writing Life', *Washington Post Book World*, 11 March 2001, 6.

Edited Volumes

With Derek Stanford, *Tribute to Wordsworth* (Wingate, 1950).

Selected Poems of Emily Brontë (Grey Walls Press, 1952).

With Derek Stanford, *My Best Mary: The Selected Letters of Mary Wollstonecraft Shelley* (Wingate, 1953).

With Derek Stanford, *Emily Brontë: Her Life and Work* (Peter Owen, 1953; New York: Coward, McCann, 1966).

The Brontë Letters (Peter Nevill, 1954; Norman: University of Oklahoma Press, 1954).

With Derek Stanford, *Letters of John Henry Newman* (Peter Owen, 1957).

The Essence of the Brontës (Peter Owen, 1993).

Essays, Articles and Reviews

'Editorial: The Catholic View', *Poetry Review*, 38, 6 (December 1947), 402–5.

'Editorial: Criticism, Effect and Morals', *Poetry Review*, 39, 1 (January–February 1948), 3–6.

'Poetry and Politics', *Parliamentary Affairs. Journal of the Hansard Society*, 1 (1948), 5.

'The Golden Fleece', *Argentor: The Journal of the National Jewellers' Association* (March 1948), 29–32, 70.

'Editorial: Reassessment', *Poetry Review*, 39, 2 (April–May 1948), 103–4.

'[Editorial] Reassessment – II', *Poetry Review*, 39, 3 (August–September 1948), 234–6.

'[Editorial] A Pamphlet From the U.S.', *Poetry Review*, 39, 4 (October–November 1948), 318.

'[Editorial] Poetry and the Other Arts', *Poetry Review*, 39, 5 (December 1948–January 1949), 390.

Review of C. M. Bowra, *Edith Sitwell* (Anglo-French Library Services through the Lyrebird Press) and James Kirkup, *The Drowned Sailor* (Grey Walls Press), *Outposts*, 12 (Winter 1948), 19–20.

'Reassessment', *Women's Review*, 4 (January 1949), 18–19.

'The Dramatic Works of T. S. Eliot', *Women's Review*, 5 (March–April 1949), 2–4.

'African Handouts', *New English Weekly*, 35, 8 (28 April 1949), 32–3.

'Views and Reviews. The Poetry of Anne Brontë', *New English Weekly*, 26 May 1949, 79–80.

'Introduction', *Forum: Stories and Poems*, 1, 1 (Summer 1949), 1.

'The Poet in Mr Eliot's Ideal State', *Outposts*, 14 (Summer 1949), 26–8.

'Cecil Day Lewis', *Poetry Quarterly*, 11, 3 (Autumn 1949), 162–8.

Review of Jack Lindsay's translation of *Catullus* (Sylvan Press), *Outposts*, 15 (Winter 1949), 31.

'Poetry and the American Government', *Parliamentary Affairs*, 3, 1 (1949), 260–72.

With Derek Stanford, 'Introduction', *Forum: Stories and Poems*, 1, 2, nd [early 1950?], 25.

'Mary Shelley – Wife to a Genius', *Listener*, 2 February 1951, 26.

'Mary Shelley: A Prophetic Novelist', *Listener*, 22 February 1951, 305–6.

'Passionate Humbugs', review of Alan Walbank, *Queens of the Circulating Library* (Evans) and Eileen Bigland, *Ouida* (Jarrolds), *Public Opinion*, 23 February 1951, 20.

'The Complete Frost', review of *The Complete Poems of Robert Frost* (Jonathan Cape), *Public Opinion*, 30 March 1951, 21.

'Two-way', *Church of England Newspaper*, 25 May 1951, 5.

'Psychology and Criticism', *Times Literary Supplement*, 25 May 1951, 325.

'In Defence of the Highbrow', *Public Opinion*, 8 June 1951, 28.

'Does Celibacy Affect Judgement?', *Church of England Newspaper*, 16 November 1951, 10.

'Talks in Moscow', *Church of England Newspaper*, 31 October 1952, 10.

'Civilised Humour', review of Max Beerbohm, *Works and More* (John Lane), Stephan Themerson, *Woof Woof, or Who Killed Richard Wagner?* (Gaberbocchus Press), and Amos Tutuola, *The Palm-Wine Drinkard* (Faber), *Journal of the Scottish Secondary Teachers' Association* (October 1952), 30, 32.

'Ex-pagan Reader', *Church of England Newspaper*, 19 December 1952, 10.

'Eyes and Noses', *Observer*, 18 January 1953, 6.

'Reflections on Mr Tate's Article', 'Letters and Points', *World Review* (New Series 47, January 1953), 2–3.

'All Laugh Together?', *The English-Speaking World*, 35, 2 (March 1953), 32, 34, 36.

'New Pamphlet Verse', review of Raymond Garlick (ed.), *Poetry from Wales* (Poetry Book Magazine), Christine Brooke-Rose, *Gold* (Hand and Flower Press), *Hispania*, trans. Maria F. de Laguna (Ranking Bros.), and Bernard Bergonzi, *Descartes and the Animals* (Platform), *Tablet*, 18 June 1953, 598–9.

'If I were "Punch" . . . ', *The English-Speaking World*, 35, 4 (June 1953), 23–5.

'Edinburgh Festival Diary. A Prophet's Married Life', *Church of England Newspaper*, 4 September 1953, 5.

'Edinburgh Festival Diary. The Wisdom of Mr T. S. Eliot', *Church of England Newspaper*, 11 September 1953, 5.

'Awkward Saint', review of J. B. Perrin and G. Thibon, trans. Emma Craufurd, *Simone Weil as We Knew Her* (Routledge), *Observer*, 20 September 1953, 10.

'A New Voice on an Old Theme', review of Michael Mason, *The Legacy* (Sheed & Ward), *Journal of the Scottish Secondary Teachers' Association* (October 1953), 8, 10, 12.

'The Religion of an Agnostic: A Sacramental View of the World in the Writings of Proust', *Church of England Newspaper*, 27 November 1953, 1.

'Karl Heim: Two Important Works', review of Karl Heim, *The Transformation of the Scientific World View* and *Christian Faith and Natural Science* (both SCM Press), *Journal of the Scottish Secondary Teachers' Association* (February 1954), 53.

'In Kent and Christendom' [anon.], *Tablet*, 12 February 1955, 154.

'The Mystery of Job's Suffering. Jung's New Interpretation Examined', review of C. J. Jung, *Answer to Job*, trans. R. C. Hull, *Church of England Newspaper*, 15 April 1955, 7.

'Priest of the Plague', review of Philip Caraman, *Henry Morse: Priest of the Plague* (Longmans), *Observer*, 12 May 1957, 16.

'St Monica', *Month*, New Series, 17, 5 (May 1957), 309–20; reprinted Philip Caraman (ed.), *Saints and Ourselves*, Third Series (Hollis & Carter, 1958), pp. 26–37.

'Shorter Notices. Psychic Searchlight' [signed 'M.S.'], review of D. J. West, *Psychical Research To-day* (Duckworth), *Observer*, 1 August 1957, 7.

'Light Fantastic' [anon.], review of Stevie Smith, *Not Waving but Drowning* (André Deutsch), *Times Literary Supplement*, 4 October 1957, 588.

'Short Stories', review of Frank O'Connor, *Domestic Relations* (Hamish Hamilton), Irwin Shaw, *Tip on a Dead Jockey* (Cape), and Mavis Gallant, *The Other Paris* (André Deutsch), *Observer*, 6 October 1957, 14.

'Remembrance of Things Past', review of Ursula Bloom, *The Elegant Edwardian* (Hutchinson), Ernest H. Shepard, *Drawn From Memory* (Methuen), Peter Bull, *Bulls in the Meadows* (Peter Davies), and G. D. Roberts, *Without My Wig* (Macmillan), *Time & Tide*, 19 October 1957, 1306–7.

Evelyn Cavallo [Muriel Spark], 'Ailourophilia' (review), *Observer*, 15 December 1957, 12.

'New Short Stories', review of *Winter's Tales 3* (Macmillan), Doris Lessing, *The Habit of Loving* (MacGibbon & Kee), William Saroyan, *The Whole Voyald*, and Sarah Gertrude Millin, *Two Bucks without Hair* (Faber), *Observer*, 15 December 1957, 12.

'All by Themselves', review of Ernest W. D. Tennant, *True Account* (Max Parrish), John O'Donoghue, *In a Quiet Land* (Batsford), Vera Dean, *Three Steps Forward* (Faber), and Ram Gopal, *Rhythm in the Heavens* (Secker & Warburg), *Time & Tide*, 1 February 1958, 136.

'Worlds Within a World', review of Peter Fletcher, *The Long Sunday* (Faber) and Dominic Reeve, *Smoke in the Lanes* (Constable), *Time & Tide*, 1 March 1958, 266.

'The Little Flower', review of *Autobiography of a Saint*, trans. Ronald Knox (Harvill Press), *Observer*, 25 May 1958, 17.

'Thérèse of Lisieux', review of Ida Gorrës, *The Hidden Face* (Burns & Oates), *Observer*, 18 January 1959, 20.

'Top Cats on Show', review of Stevie Smith *Cats in Colour* (Batsford), Paul Dehn etc., *Cat's Cradle* (Longmans), Dorothy Margaret Stuart, *A Book of Cats* (Methuen), Frank Crew, *All These and Kittens, Too* (Herbert Jenkins), Warren Chetham-Strode, *Top Off the Milk*, and Doreen Tovey, *Cats in May* (Elek), *Observer*, 29 November 1959, 4.

Review of Evelyn Waugh's *Ronald Knox, Twentieth Century* (January 1960), 83–5.

'Minor Victorian', review of Ronald Chapman, *Father Faber* (Burns & Oates), *Observer*, 19 February 1961, 29.

'On the Lack of Sleep', *New Yorker*, 7 December 1963, 58.

Foreword to Vincent Ferrer Blehl SJ, (ed.), *Realizations. Newman's Own Selection of His Sermons* (Darton, Longman & Todd, 1964), v–ix; reprinted as 'The Sermons of Newman', *The Critic*, 22, 6 (June–July 1964), 27–9.

'The Brontës as Teachers', *New Yorker*, 22 January 1966; reprinted in Spark, *The Essence of the Brontës*, pp. 13–20.

'The Desegregation of Art', in *Proceedings of the American Academy of Arts and Letters, 1971* (New York: Spiral Press), pp. 21–7. Blashfield Foundation Address. Reprinted *Month*, 5 (1972), 152–3.

'When Israel Went to the Vatican', *Tablet*, 24 March 1973, 277–8.

'Three Champagnes', *Tablet*, 11 January 1975, 40.

'Heinrich Boll', *New York Times Book Review*, 4 December 1977, 66, 70.

'Created and Abandoned', *New Yorker*, 12 November 1979, 60.

'Venice in Fall and Winter', *New York Times*, 25 October 1981; reprinted in Susan Cahill (ed.), *Desiring Italy* (New York: Fawcett Columbine, 1997), pp. 69–75.

'Conversation Piece', *New Yorker*, 23 November 1981, 54.

'I Would Like to have Written', *New York Times Book Review*, 87, 35 (1982), 7.

'My Most Obnoxious Writer', *New York Times Book Review*, 87, 35 (1982), 7.

'The Pleasures of Rereading', *New York Times Book Review*, 88, 24 (1983), 14.

'Breaking Up With Jake', review of Renata Adler, *Pitch Dark*, *New York Times*, 88, 51 (18 December 1983), 1.

'On Love', *Partisan Review*, 51, 4 (1984), 780–83.

'Side Roads of Tuscany', *New York Times Magazine*, 7 October 1984, 28–9, 72, 74, 76, 79.

'Spirit and Substance', *Vanity Fair*, 12, 47 (December 1984), 28–9, 72–9.

'Echoes of Shelley in Italy', *Architectural Digest*, 43, 6 (1986), 262, 266.

'Gardens: Plotting an Alpine Cliffhanger – The Baggatti-Valsecchi Villa above Lake Como', *Architectural Digest*, 44, 2 (February 1987), 124–7.

'Ravenna's Jewelled Churches', *New York Times Magazine*, 4 October 1987, 50–51, 68–71.

'A Winterson Tale', review of Jeanette Winterson, *The Passion*, *Vanity Fair*, May 1988.

'Manzu Giacomo: Triumphs of Matter and Spirit in Bronze', *Architectural Digest*, 45, 5 (1988), 40.

'Whose Europe is it Anyway?', *New Statesman*, 22 June 1990, 12.

'Home Thoughts. Muriel Spark on How to Write a Letter', *Independent Magazine*, 18 August 1990, 16.

'The Ravenna Mosaics', *Antique and New Art* (Winter 1990), 122–5.

'Soldier and Saint', review of Philip Caraman, *Ignatius Loyola* (Collins, 1990), *Month*, 24, 7 (July 1991), 301–2.

'Muriel Spark, O.B.E.' in *Tributes to Graham Greene, O.M., C.H., 1904–1991, at the Memorial Requiem Mass at Westminster Cathedral* (Reinhardt Books, 1991), pp. 15–16.

'The Truth About "Snooty" Waugh', review of Martin Stannard, *Evelyn Waugh: The Later Years: 1939–1966* (Dent), *Daily Mail*, 23 April 1992, 40.

'Highland Flings', *Sunday Times* (Section 7, *Books*), 23 June 1996, 1.

'International Books of the Year and the Millennium. Muriel Spark', *Times Literary Supplement*, 3 December 1999, 10.

2. INTERVIEWS WITH MURIEL SPARK

(in chronological order)

Venetia Murray, 'Think About Death Says Muriel Spark', *Books & Bookmen*, April 1959, 15.

J. M. W. Thompson, 'This Fascinating New Arrival in the World of Books', *Evening Standard*, 23 March 1960, 7.

Malcolm Muggeridge, 'Appointment with Muriel Spark', Granada Television, 2 June 1961. Unpublished.

Anthony Hern, 'Why Miss Spark Went Back to the Forgotten Days', *Scottish Daily Express*, 3 June 1961.

Elizabeth Jane Howard, 'Writers in the Present Tense', *Queen*, 219 (August 1961), 137, 139.

'My Conversion', *Twentieth Century*, 170, 1011 (Autumn 1961), 58–63. [In later life, Spark denied that this text, presented as a report of her conversation with W. J. Weatherby, recorded her statements accurately.]

Maurice Dolbier, 'I'm Very Fierce ... when I Start', *New York Herald Tribune* (*Books* supplement), 11 February 1962, 7.

Joyce Emerson, 'The Mental Squint of Muriel Spark', *Sunday Times*, 30 September 1962, 14.

Frank Kermode, 'The House of Fiction: Interviews with Seven English Novelists', *Partisan Review* 30, 1 (Spring 1963), 61–82; 79–82; reprinted Malcolm Bradbury (ed.), *The Novel Today: Contemporary Writers on Modern Fiction* (Fontana/Collins paperback, 1977), pp. 111–35; 131–5.

'British Author Writes Best in N.Y.', *Books* (New York), January 1965, 3.

Mary Holland, 'The Prime of Muriel Spark', *Observer* (Colour Supplement), 17 October 1965, 8, 10.

Israel Shenker, 'Portrait of a [Man] Woman Reading. xxiii. Muriel Spark [. . .]', *Book World*, 29 September 1968, 2.

Peter Grosvenor, 'In Search of Her Own Killer!', *Daily Express*, 24 September 1970, 12.

'Keeping It Short – Muriel Spark talks about her books to Ian Gillam', *Listener*, 24 September 1970, 411–13.

Jean Scroggie, 'Mementos for Muriel Spark', *Daily Telegraph*, 25 September 1970, 15.

'George Armstrong Talks to Muriel Spark at her Home in Rome', *Guardian*, 30 September 1970, 8.

Beryl Hartland, 'Step Into Muriel Spark's Palazzo, and You're in Velvet', *Daily Telegraph*, 24 March 1971, 15.

Philip Toynbee, 'Observer Art Offer. Muriel Spark Limited Edition', *Observer* (Colour Supplement), 7 November 1971, 73–4.

Graham Lord, 'The Love Letters that Muriel Spark Refused to Buy', *Sunday Express*, 4 March 1973, 6.

'Alex Hamilton Interviews Muriel Spark', *Guardian* (*Arts Guardian* section), 8 November 1974, 10.

'Bugs and Mybug', *Listener*, 28 November 1974, 706.

Hugh Mulligan, 'Muriel Spark's "Naughty" Watergate Satire', *Daily American* [Rome], 11 February 1975, 5.

Lorna Sage, 'The Prime of Muriel Spark', *Observer*, 30 May 1976, 81.

Barbara Holsopple, 'TV Version Best, "Jean Brodie" Author Says', *Pittsburgh Press*, 4 May 1979, B-22.

Colman McCarthy, 'That Spark of Satire', *Washington Post*, 4 May 1979, F1, F10.

Judy Flander, '"Miss Brodie's" Longevity Is No Surprise to her Creator', *Washington Star*, 6 May 1979, C1, C4.

Win Fanning, 'On the Air. TV's "Jean Brodie" Star Lived Part On, Off Screen', *Post-Gazette* (Pittsburgh), 7 May 1979, 28.

Joan Hanauer, 'Everyone Has Had a Miss Jean Brodie', *Madisonville Ky Messenger*, 7 May 1979.

Barbara Kantrowitz, 'The Prime of Muriel Spark', *Philadelphia Enquirer*, 8 May 1979, 1E, 5E.

Diane Mermigas, 'Today on TV', *Daily Herald* (Illinois), 11 May 1979.

Nan Robertson, 'The Prime Time of Muriel Spark', *New York Times*, 14 May 1979, A-16.

Toby Kahn, 'Now It's really Prime Time for Miss Jean Brodie and her Creator, Muriel Spark', *People Weekly*, 11, 20 (21 May 1979), 142, 145.

Victoria Glendinning, 'Talk with Muriel Spark', *New York Times Book Review*, 20 May 1979, 47–8.

Frank Delaney, BBC2 TV, 21 November 1983. Unpublished.

Nicholas Shakespeare, 'Suffering and the Vital Spark', *The Times*, 21 November 1983, 8.

Hunter Davies, BBC Radio 4 *Bookshelf*, 4 November 1984. Unpublished.

Sarah Frankel, 'An Interview with Muriel Spark', *Partisan Review*, 54 (Summer 1987), 443–57.

John Mortimer, 'The Culture of an Anarchist', *Telegraph Sunday Magazine*, 20 March 1988, 16–18, 20.

Josyane Savigneau, 'Affreux, Riches et Méchants', *Le Monde*, 6 May 1988, 17.

Mary Blume, 'Muriel Spark: The Infinitely Mysterious', *International Herald Tribune*, 8 May 1989, 16.

J. Devoize and P. Valette, 'An Interview with Muriel Spark', *Journal of the Short Story in English*, 13 (Autumn 1989), 11–22.

Lynn Barber, 'The Elusive Magician', *Independent on Sunday*, 23 September 1990, 8–10.

'A Sinister Affair. Books and Arts. Muriel Spark in Conversation' [Paris], *Economist*, 23 November 1991, 158.

Stephen Schiff, 'Muriel Spark Between the Lines', *New Yorker*, 24 May 1993, 36–43.

David Streitfeld, 'Muriel Spark Fired Up', *Washington Post*, 12 August 1993, C1, C6.

John Cornwell, 'Publish and be Damed', *Sunday Times Magazine*, 15 May 1994, 18–19, 21, 23, 25.

Alan Taylor, 'Morningside', *Scotsman*, *Week-End* section, 29 April 1995, 7–8.

Helena de Bertodano, 'Muriel's Coming of Age', *Sunday Telegraph*, 23 March 1997, 6.

Alan Franks, 'Igniting the Spark', *The Times Magazine*, 13 June 1998, 19–22.

Martin McQuillan, '"The Same Informed Air": An Interview with Muriel Spark', November 1998, in McQuillan (ed.), *Theorising Muriel Spark: Gender, Race, Deconstruction* (Basingstoke and New York: Palgrave, 2002), pp. 210–29.

Dean Nelson, 'Mother's Pride and Prejudice', *Observer Review*, 14 March 1999, 4.

Janice Galloway, 'The Vital Spark', *Sunday Herald*, 11 July 1999.

Chloe Walker, 'The Sitter's Tale', *Independent on Sunday*, 23 August 1999, 14.

Lewis Jones, 'Divine Spark', *Sunday Telegraph Magazine*, 19 December 1999, 16–18, 20.

Emma Brockes, 'The Genteel Assassin', *Guardian Saturday Review*, 27 May 2000, 6–7.

Jan Moir, 'Dame With an Eye for Danger', *Daily Telegraph* (*Arts and Books* supplement), 9 September 2000, 5.

Stephanie Merritt, '"Weak Men Can't Cope With Women Who Are Successful"', *Observer Review*, 10 September 2000, 15.

Deborah Ross, 'Dame Muriel Spark: the Brightest of Sparks (and Still in Her Prime)', *Independent*, 17 September, 2001.

Valerie Grove, 'The People-watcher', *The Times*, 19 September 2001, 8.

James Brooker and Margarita Estévez Saá, 'Interview with Dame Muriel Spark', *Women's Studies* 33 (2004), 1035–46.

Kenny Farquharson, 'Ecosse: The Vital Spark', *Sunday Times*, 17 October 2004.

Mark Lawson, 'Dame Muriel Spark', *Guardian*, 17 April 2006, 6.

3. MURIEL SPARK ARCHIVES

Harry Ransom Humanities Research Center, University of Texas at Austin

Lauinger Library Special Collections, Georgetown University, Washington DC

McFarlin Library, Special Collections, University of Tulsa (literary manuscripts)

National Library of Scotland (personal archive), Edinburgh

Princeton University Libraries (Harold Ober archive)

Robert Woodruff Library for Advanced Studies, Emory University, Atlanta
St Michael's College, Vermont
University of Victoria Library Special Collection, Canada
Washington University in St Louis Library, Special Collections (John Smith archive)

4. SECONDARY SOURCES

Books and Monographs

Auerbach, Nina, *Communities of Women: An Idea in Fiction* (Cambridge, Mass.: Harvard University Press, 1978).

Bold, Alan, *Muriel Spark.* Contemporary Writers series (Methuen, 1986).

—— (ed.) *Muriel Spark: An Odd Capacity for Vision.* Critical Studies series (Vision Press, 1984; Totowa, NJ: Barnes & Noble, 1984).

Cheyette, Bryan, *Muriel Spark.* Writers and Their Work series (Horndon, Tavistock: Northcote House, 2000).

Edgecombe, Rodney Stenning, *Vocation and Identity in the Fiction of Muriel Spark* (Columbia, Miss.: University of Missouri Press, 1990).

Hynes, Joseph, *The Art of the Real: Muriel Spark's Novels* (Rutherford, NJ: Fairleigh Dickinson University Press / Associated University Presses, 1988).

—— (ed.) *Critical Essays on Muriel Spark* (New York: G. K. Hall, 1992).

Kane, Richard C., *Iris Murdoch, Muriel Spark and John Fowles: Didactic Demons in Modern Fiction* (Rutherford, NJ: Fairleigh Dickinson University Press / Associated University Presses, 1988).

Kemp, Peter, *Muriel Spark.* Novelists and Their World series (Paul Elek, 1974).

Little, Judy, *Comedy and the Woman Writer: Woolf, Spark, and Feminism* (Lincoln: University of Nebraska Press, 1983).

McQuillan, Martin (ed.), *Theorising Muriel Spark: Gender, Race, Deconstruction* (Basingstoke and New York: Palgrave, 2002)

Malkoff, Karl, *Muriel Spark.* Columbia Essays on Modern Writers series (Columbia University Press, 1968).

Massie, Allan, *Muriel Spark* (Edinburgh: Ramsey Head Press, 1979).

Meaney, Gerardine, *(Un)Like Subjects: Women, Theory, Fiction* (Routledge, 1993).

Page, Norman, *Muriel Spark.* Macmillan Modern Novelists series (Macmillan, 1990).

Pearlman, Mickey, *Re-inventing Reality: Patterns and Characters in the Novels of Muriel Spark.* Studies in Romantic and Modern Literature (New York: P. Lang, 1989).

Randsi, J. L., *On Her Way Rejoicing: the Fiction of Muriel Spark* (Washington DC: The Catholic University of America Press, 1991).

Richmond, Velma Bourgeois, *Muriel Spark* (New York: Frederick Ungar, 1984).

Sproxton, Judy, *The Women of Muriel Spark* (Constable, 1992).

Stanford, Derek, *Muriel Spark: A Biographical and Critical Study* (Fontwell: Centaur Press, 1963).

Stubbs, Patricia, *Muriel Spark.* Writers and Their Work Series (Harlow: Longman for the British Council, 1973).

Walker, Dorothea, *Muriel Spark* (Boston: Twayne Publishers, 1988).

Waugh, Patricia, *Feminine Fictions: Revisiting the Postmodern* (Routledge, 1988).

—— *Metafiction: The Theory and Practice of Self-Conscious Fiction* (Methuen, 1984).

Whittaker, Ruth, *The Faith and Fiction of Muriel Spark* (New York: St Martin's Press, 1982).

Articles and Chapters on Muriel Spark

Apostolou, Fotini. 'Seduction, Simulacra and the Feminine: Spectacles and Images in Muriel Spark's *The Public Image*', *Journal of Gender Studies*, 9, 3 (2000), 281–97.

Baldanza, Frank, 'Muriel Spark and the Occult', *Wisconsin Studies in Contemporary Literature*, 6 (Summer 1965), 190–203.

Blodgett, Harriet, 'Desegregated Art by Muriel Spark', *International Fiction Review*, 3 (January 1976), 25–9.

Bower, Anne L., 'The Narrative Structure of Muriel Spark's *The Prime of Miss Jean Brodie*', *Midwest Quarterly*, 31 (Summer 1990), 488–98.

Bradbury, Malcolm, 'Muriel Spark's Fingernails', *Critical Quarterly*, 14 (Autumn 1972), 241–50. Reprinted in Bradbury, *Possibilities: Essays on the State of the Novel* (Oxford: Oxford University Press, 1973), pp. 247–55.

Brooke-Rose, Christine, 'Le Roman Experimental en Angleterre', *Les Langues Modernes*, 63 (1969), 158–68.

Calder, A., 'Miss Jean Brodie and the Kaledonian Klan', in *Revolving Culture: Notes from the Scottish Republic* (I. B. Tauris, 1994).

Casson, Allan, 'Muriel Spark's *The Girls of Slender Means*', *Critique*, 7 (Spring–Summer 1965), 94–6.

Cixous, Hélène, 'La Farce Macabre de Muriel Spark: Un Catholicisme Grimaçant', *Le Monde*, 17 January 1968, viia.

—— 'Le Dernier Roman de Muriel Spark: L'Image Publique', *Le Monde*, 9 November 1968, viiia.

Dobie, Ann B., 'Muriel Spark's Definition of Reality', *Critique*, 12, 1 (1970), 20–27.

—— '*The Prime of Miss Jean Brodie*: Muriel Spark Bridges the Credibility Gap', *Arizona Quarterly*, 25 (Autumn 1969), 217–28

—— and Carl Wooton, 'Spark and Waugh: Similarities by Coincidence', *Midwest Quarterly*, 13 (July 1972) 423–34.

Edgecombe, Rodney Stenning, 'Muriel Spark, Cardinal Newman and an Aphorism in *Memento Mori*', *Notes on Contemporary Literature*, 24, 1 (January 1994), 12.

Feinstein, Elaine, 'Loneliness is Cold', *London Magazine* (February–March 1972), 177–80.

Galvin, J., 'Muriel Spark's Unknowing Fiction', *Women's Studies: An Interdisciplinary Journal*, 15, 1–3 (1988), 221–41.

Gilliatt, Penelope, 'The Dashing Novellas of Muriel Spark', *Grand Street*, 8 (Summer 1989), 139–46.

Halio, Jay L., 'Muriel Spark: The Novelist's Sense of Wonder', in Jack I. Biles (ed.), *British Novelists Since 1900* (New York: AMS, 1987), pp. 267–77.

Harrison, Bernard, 'Muriel Spark and Jane Austen' in Gabriel Josipovici (ed.), *The Modern English Novel: The Reader, the Writer, and the Work* (Open Books, 1976; New York: Barnes & Noble, 1976), pp. 225–51.

Hendry, D., 'Spooky Spark: On Muriel Spark and the Post-war Poetry Society', *Poetry Review*, 823 (1992), 70–71.

Holloway, John, 'Narrative Structure and Text Structure: Isherwood's *A Meeting by the River* and Muriel Spark's *The Prime of Miss Jean Brodie*', *Critical Inquiry*, 1 (March 1975), 581–604.

Hosmer, Robert E., Jr, 'The Book of Job: The Novel of Harvey', *Renascence*, 39 (Spring 1987), 442–9.

Hoyt, Charles Alva, 'Muriel Spark: The Surrealist Jane Austen', in Charles Shapiro (ed.), *Contemporary British Novelists* (Carbondale and Edwardsville: Southern Illinois University Press, 1965), pp. 125–43.

Hynes, Joseph, 'After Marabar: Reading Forster, Robbe-Grillet, Spark', *Iowa Review*, 5 (Winter 1974), 120–26.

Jacobsen, Josephine, 'A Catholic Quartet', *Christian Scholar*, 47 (Summer 1964), 139–54.

Kimball, R., 'The First Half of Muriel Spark', *New Criterion*, 11, 8 (April 1993), 9–16.

Kelleher, V. M. K., 'The Religious Artistry of Muriel Spark', *Critical Review* (Melbourne), 18 (1976), 79–92.

Kennedy, Alan, 'Cannibals, Okapis, and Self-Slaughter in the Fiction of Muriel Spark', in *The Protean Self: Dramatic Action in Contemporary Fiction* (New York: Columbia University Press, 1974), pp. 151–211.

Keyser, Barbara Y., 'Muriel Spark, Watergate, and the Mass Media', *Arizona Quarterly*, 32 (Summer 1976), 146–53.

Laffin, Garry S., 'Muriel Spark's Portrait of the Artist as a Young Girl', *Renascence*, 24 (Summer 1972), 213–23.

Leonard, Joan, 'Muriel Spark's Parables: The Religious Limits of Her Art', in John V. Apczynski (ed.), *Foundations of Religious Literacy* (Chico, Calif.: Scholars' Press, 1982), pp. 153–64.

Little, Judy, 'Endless Different Ways: Muriel Spark's Re-Visions of the Spinster' in L. L. Doan (ed.), *Old Maids to Radical Spinsters: Unmarried Women in the Twentieth-Century Novel* (Urbana: University of Illinois Press, 1991), pp. 19–35.

Litvack, L. B., 'The Road to Rome: Muriel Spark, Newman and the "Nevertheless Principle"', in David Bevan (ed.), *Literature and the Bible* (Amsterdam: Rodopi, 1993), pp. 29–46.

Lodge, David, 'The Uses and Abuses of Omniscience: Method and Meaning in Muriel Spark's *The Prime of Miss Jean Brodie*', *Critical Quarterly*, 12 (Autumn 1970), 235–57. Reprinted in Lodge, *The Novelist at the Crossroads and Other Essays on Fiction and Criticism* (Routledge & Kegan Paul, 1971), pp. 119–44.

—— *The Art of Fiction* (Secker & Warburg, 1992; Penguin Books, 1992), pp. 74–7.

McBrien, William, 'Muriel Spark: The Novelist as Dandy', in Thomas F. Staley (ed.), *Twentieth-Century Women Novelists* (Totowa, NJ: Barnes & Noble, 1982), pp. 153–78.

MacLachlan, C., 'Muriel Spark and Gothic', in S. Hagemann (ed.), *Studies in Scottish Fiction: 1945 to the Present* (Frankfurt: Peter Lang, 1996), pp. 125–44.

Malin, Irving, 'The Deceptions of Muriel Spark', in Melvin J. Friedman (ed.), *The Vision Obscured: Perceptions of Some Twentieth-Century Catholic Novelists* (New York: Fordham University Press, 1970), pp. 95–107.

Malkoff, Karl, 'Demonology and Dualism: The Supernatural in Isaac Singer and Muriel Spark', in Irving Malin (ed.), *Critical Views of Isaac Bashevis Singer* (New York: New York University Press, 1969), pp. 149–68.

Mengham, Rod, '1973: The End of History: Cultural Change According to Muriel Spark,' in Mengham (ed.), *An Introduction to Contemporary Fiction: International Writing in English since 1970* (Cambridge: Polity, 1999).

Metzger, Linda, 'Muriel Spark' in *Contemporary Authors*, new rev. series, 12 (Detroit: Gale Research, 1984), pp. 450–7.

Montgomery, B., 'Spark and Newman: Jean Brodie Reconsidered', *Twentieth-Century Literature*, 43, 1 (Spring 1997), 94–106.

Nelson, Dean, 'Spark and Son in Feud Over Jewish Origins', *Observer*, 29 March 1998, 15.

Ohmann, Carol B., 'Muriel Spark's *Robinson*', *Critique*, 8, 1 (1965), 70–84.

Parrinder, Patrick, 'Muriel Spark and her Critics', *Critical Quarterly*, 25 (Summer 1983), 23–31.

Pearlman, M., 'The Element of the Fantastic and the Artist Figure in the Novels of Muriel Spark', in M. K. Langford (ed.), *Contours of the Fantastic: Selected Essays from the Eighth International Conference on the Fantastic in the Arts* (New York: Greenwood, 1994), pp. 149–61.

Pyper, H., 'The Reader in Pain: Job as Text and Pretext', *Literature and Theology: An International Journal of Theory, Criticism and Culture*, 7, 2 (June 1993), 111–29.

Raban, Jonathan, 'On Losing the Rabbit', *Encounter* (May 1973), 80–85.

Rankin, Ian, 'Surface and Structure: Reading Muriel Spark's *The Driver's Seat*', *Journal of Narrative Technique*, 15 (Spring 1985), 146–55.

Richmond, Velma Bourgeois, 'The Darkening Vision of Muriel Spark', *Critique*, 15, 1 (1973), 71–85.

Rowe, Margaret Moan, 'Muriel Spark and the Angel of the Body', *Critique*, 28 (Spring 1987), 167–76.

Sage, Lorna, 'Female Fictions' in Malcolm Bradbury and David Palmer (eds.), *The Contemporary English Novel*, Stratford-upon-Avon Studies series, 18 (Edward Arnold, 1979), pp. 77–9.

Sears, Sallie, 'Too Many Voices', *Partisan Review*, 31 (Summer 1964), 471–5.

Shaw, Valerie, 'Muriel Spark' in Cairns Craig (ed.), *The History of Scottish Literature, IV: Twentieth Century* (Aberdeen: Aberdeen University Press, 1987), pp. 277–90.

Spark, Robin, 'Life with the Cambergs', *Edinburgh Star*, 32 (February 1999), 13–17.

Stanford, Derek, 'The Work of Muriel Spark: An Essay on Her Fictional Method', *Month* 28 (August 1962), 92–9. Revised in Stanford, *Muriel Spark*.

Stannard, Martin, 'The Letter Killeth', *Spectator*, 6 June 1998, 36–7.

—— 'Nativities: Muriel Spark, Baudelaire and the Quest for Religious Faith', *Review of English Studies*, New Series, 55, 218 (2003), 91–105.

Stevenson, S., '"Poetry Deleted": Parody Added: Watergate, Spark's Style, and Bakhtin's Stylistics', *ARIEL*, 24, 4 (1993), 71–85.

Stonebridge, Lyndsey, 'Hearing Them Speak: Voices in Wilfred Bion, Muriel Spark and Penelope Fitzgerald', *Textual Practice*, 19, 4 (2005), 445–65.

Stubbs, Patricia, 'Two Contemporary Views on Fiction: Iris Murdoch and Muriel Spark', *English*, 23 (Autumn 1974), 102–10.

Wallace, G., 'The Deliberate Cunning of Muriel Spark', in G. Wallace and R. Stevenson (eds.), *The Scottish Novel since the Seventies: New Visions, Old Dreams* (Edinburgh: Edinburgh University Press, 1993), pp. 41–53.

Whittaker, Ruth, '"Angels Dining at the Ritz": The Faith and Fiction of Muriel Spark', in Malcolm Bradbury and David Palmer (eds.), *The Contemporary English Novel*, Stratford-upon-Avon Studies series, 18 (Edward Arnold, 1979), pp. 157–79.

Memoirs, Biography and History

'Blanche W. Knopf: July 30 1884–June 4, 1966', *Borzoi Quarterly*, 15, 3 (1966), 13, 12.

Daiches, David, *Edinburgh* (Hamish Hamilton, 1978).

Delmer, Sefton, *Black Boomerang: An Autobiography*. Vol. 2 (Secker & Warburg, 1962).

Dick, Kay, *Friends and Friendship: Conversations and Reflections* (Sidgwick & Jackson, 1974).

Dickson, Lovat, *The House of Words* (Macmillan, 1963).

Donleavy, J. P., *The History of the Ginger Man: An Autobiography* (Viking, 1994).

Geyer, Michael, 'Civitella della Chiana on 29 June 1944: The Reconstruction of a German "Measure"', in Hannes Heer and Klaus Naumann (eds.), *War of Extermination: The German Military in World War II, 1941–1945* (New York: Berghahn Books, 2004), pp. 175–216; 175–6.

Fraser, G. S., *A Stranger and Afraid: Autobiography of an Intellectual* (Manchester: Carcanet New Press, 1983).

Gardiner, Wrey, *The Dark Thorn* (Grey Walls Press, 1946).

—— *The Answer To Life Is No* (Rupert Hart-Davis, 1960).

Gill, Brendan, *Here at The New Yorker* (New York: Random House, 1975).

Greacen, Robert, *Even Without Irene: An Autobiography* (Dublin: The Dolmen Press, 1969).

Heath-Stubbs, John, *Hindsights: An Autobiography* (Sevenoaks: Hodder & Stoughton, 1993).

Heppenstall, Rayner, *The Intellectual Part: An Autobiography* (Barrie & Rockliff, 1963).

—— *Portrait of the Artist as a Professional Man* (Peter Owen, 1969).

—— Jonathan Goodman (ed.), *The Master Eccentric: The Journals of Rayner Heppenstall 1969–1981* (Allison & Busby, 1986).

Hibberd, Dominic, 'A Publisher of First World War Poetry: Galloway Kyle', *Notes & Queries*, 231, 2 (June 1986), 185–6; 185.

Kermode, Frank, 'The Uses of Error: Sermon Before the University, King's College Chapel, 11 May 1986'; reprinted in Kermode, *The Uses of Error* (Collins, 1990), pp. 425–32.

—— *Not Entitled: A Memoir* (New York: Farrar, Straus & Giroux, 1995).

Maclean, Alan, *No, I Tell a Lie, It Was the Tuesday: A Trudge Through His Life and Times* (Kyle Cathie, 1997).

Ross, Lillian, *Here and Not Here* (New York: Random House, 1992).

Smith, Charles J., *Historic South Edinburgh*. Vol. 1 (Edinburgh: Charles Skilton, 1978).

Spurling, Hilary, *Paul Scott: A Life* (Hutchinson, 1990).

Stallworthy, Jon, *Louis MacNeice* (Faber & Faber, 1995).

Stanford, Derek, *Inside the Forties: Literary Memoirs, 1937–57* (Sidgwick & Jackson, 1977).

Wynne-Tyson, Jon, *Finding the Words: A Publishing Life* (Norwich: Michael Russell, 2004).

Bibliographies

Rees, D., *Muriel Spark, William Trevor, Ian McEwan: A Bibliography of their First Editions* (Colophon Press, 1992).

Schwartz, Narda Lacy (ed.), *Articles on Women Writers: A Bibliography* (Oxford and Santa Barbara, Calif.: Clio Press, 1977).

Tominaga, Thomas T., and Wilma Schneidermeyer (eds.), *Iris Murdoch and Muriel Spark: A Bibliography.* Scarecrow Author Bibliographies, 27 (Metuchen, NJ: Scarecrow Press, 1976).

INDEX

NOTE: Works by Muriel Spark (MS) appear directly under title;
works by others under author's name

Abbess of Crewe, The (MS): based on press report, 364, 407; writing, 401–2, 404–5; proofs, 405; reception and interpretation, 405–6, 408–11; brevity, 407–8; plot, 408–9; publication and marketing, 408; film version (*Nasty Habits*), 435; and *Reality and Dreams*, 515

Aberfan disaster (1966), 331

Abrahams, William, 476

Abse, Dannie, 153

Acton, Daphne (née Strutt), 388

Acton, Sir Harold: in Italy, 436–7, 472, 476, 493; death, 509

Ader, Mr (US businessman in Rome), 347

Africa: MS's life in, 44–8, 50–3, 56, 70, 479–80; MS leaves, 58–9; in MS's later poetry, 100

Agius, Dom Ambrose, 129, 139, 143–4, 150

Aiding and Abetting (MS), 517, 520, 522–5

Aitken, Gillon, 250, 291–2, 301, 345

Albery, Donald, 230, 325

Aldiss, Brian, 254

Allen, Jay Presson, 309, 325–6, 331, 354, 474

Allen, Paul, 178, 181, 210, 216, 240

Allington Castle, Kent, 161, 172

Amalfi Cathedral, 403

Ambrosiani, Dario: friendship with MS, 357–62, 365, 385, 421; *The Driver's Seat* dedicated to, 357, 370; background and character, 361; estrangement from MS, 370, 375–6; meets Auden with MS, 376–7; and de Breffny, 385–6; meets Najar, 390; and MS's move to San Giovanni, 425–6; returns to USA, 429; told of MS's fractured ribs, 470; letter from MS on life in Italy, 499

Amburn, Ellis E., 466

American Academy of Arts and Letters, 360, 369

Amico, Masolino d', 390

Amis, (Sir) Kingsley, 378

Amman, 244

Andipatan, Mr & Mrs (landlords), 114, 129, 139

Annan, Gabriele, Lady, 410

Anne Brontë (MS), 160

Annikin, Ken, 230

'Another Pair of Hands' (MS; story), 454

anti-Semitism, 245–6

Antigonish Review, 162

Arbasino, Alberto, 415

Are You Being Served? (TV sitcom), 40

Arezzo *see* San Giovanni

Argentor (journal), 82

Arlen, Michael, 384

Armstrong, George, 358–9, 363, 381, 415, 440, 495, 499–500

Armstrong, Robert, 80, 81

Arnold, Matthew, 115

Arts Council of Scotland: awards Spring Book Prize to MS, 517

Asquith, Herbert Henry, 1st Earl, xx–xxi, 16

Astor, David, 123–4, 161

Attlee, Clement (*later* 1st Earl), 295

Aubrey-Smith, Margaret, 357–60, 373–6

Auden, W. H., 83, 142, 256, 273, 359, 376–7, 385; 'Every eye shall weep alone', 157

Austen, Jane: MS proposes edition of letters, 106, 160

Austria: MS visits with Brooke-Rose and Peterkiewicz, 212–16

Auw, Ivan von: as MS's US agent, 182, 227, 260, 279, 282–4; friendship with MS, 283, 285, 289, 293, 300; private life, 283; and Stanford's sale of MS letters, 288; and MS's difficulties with *Mandelbaum*, 301, 304; MS's fondness for, 301–2, 308, 330, 360; granted power of attorney for MS, 311, 317, 324, 328; and Knopf's request for publicity material from MS, 311; sends review of *Mandelbaum* to MS, 316; proposes spreading payments to MS, 318; disputes with MS, 319, 322, 328, 359; and success of *Mandelbaum*, 320; traces MS's published magazine work, 324; and London success of stage production of *Brodie*, 326; and MS in Rome, 329, 340; refuses to continue as MS's agent, 332; revises business arrangements with MS, 332–4; retirement, 334, 385; MS invites to Buckingham Palace ceremony, 336; and MS's tax and accountancy problems, 341–2; MS invites to Palazzo Taverna, 345, 365; and printing of stage version of *Brodie*, 354; informed of MS's hysterectomy, 357; and MS's relations with Ambrosiani, 358; praises *The Driver's Seat*, 364; and writing of *Hothouse*, 364; and MS's leaving Knopf, 372; and MS's dealings with Maclean, 379–80

Avon (paperback publishers), 321, 507

Ayer, (Sir) A. J. ('Freddie'), 478, 481, 497

Aylesford Priory, Kent, 161–2, 165, 199, 256, 265

Aylesford Review, 162

Ayrton, Michael, 378

Bachelors, The (MS): writing, 171, 212; publication, 225, 227; success and reception, 230, 232–3, 238, 240, 297; plot and themes, 234–6, 240, 252–3, 432;

publicised, 237; class bore in, 241

Baird-Smith, Robin, 473, 476, 478–9, 508–9

Baker, Captain Peter, 140–2, 483

Baker, Reginald, 142

Baldwin Crescent *see* Camberwell

Baldwin, James, 273

'Ballad of the Fanfarlo, The' (MS; poem), 121–2, 124–6, 131, 137, 139, 149

Ballad of Peckham Rye, The (MS): writing, 171, 199, 201; published in USA, 209, 223–4; royalties, 210; Paul Allen's PR experience depicted in, 216; published by Penguin, 220; reception and success, 221–3; themes and plot, 221–2, 524; musical version, 224, 226, 233, 266, 292, 309, 311; film rights, 230; stage version, 240; lampoons Pamela Hansford Johnson, 267; film version, 343

'Bang-bang You're Dead' (MS; story), 45–6, 52–3

Bannister, (Sir) Roger, 483–4

Barnsley, Alan ('Gabriel Fielding'): friendship with MS, 163, 167, 198; sends *The Comforters* to Waugh, 176, 178; MS dedicates *The Comforters* to, 178; marriage difficulties, 197; and Heppenstall, 200–1; MS's quarrel with, 238, 260–1, 266; attends to MS's cut knee, 256; Stanford writes article on, 287; *The Birthday King*, 260; *In the Time of Greenbloom*, 163, 168

Barnsley, Edwina ('Dina'), 162–3, 178

Barrie, Sir James Matthew: *Peter Pan*, 394

Bassett, Woody, 328, 332–3

Batchelor, Rosamund, 143, 156

Baudelaire, Charles: 'The Fanfarlo', 121–2, 124–5

Bauer, Jerry, 329, 331, 346, 355, 411

Bawden, Nina, 384, 392

Bayley, John, 520

Bayliss, John, 97, 100

Beaux Arts Hotel, New York, 269, 278, 293, 300, 307–8, 310, 323, 326–7, 335, 455

Beck, Bert, 292–3
Becker, Renée de, Baronne, 347, 363
Beckett, Samuel, 268, 353, 378
Bedford, Sybille, 319
Beerbohm, Max: 'A Defence of
    Cosmetics', 353
Bellow, Saul, 353
'Bells at Bray, The' (MS; poem), 81
Bennett, Alan, 431
Bergman, Ingmar, 303, 309
Bernières, Louis de, 166
Berridge, Elizabeth, 351, 438
Best Plays of 1968, The, 354
'Birthday Acrostic' (MS; for Gardiner),
    141
Birtwistle, Damien, 156
Birtwistle, Iris: published in Forum, 103;
    view of Stanford, 108; and Fraser's
    description of MS, 110; supplies
    theological books to MS, 122; and
    MS's winning Observer prize, 123;
    dines with MS and Stanford, 134;
    introduces MS to Sheed, 143; and MS's
    conversion to Catholicism, 150;
    fondness for Sheed, 156; domestic
    obligations, 197
'Black Madonna, The' (MS; story), 180,
    187; TV adaptation, 439
Black, Susan (later Sheehan), 302
Blashfield Foundation Address
    (American Academy of Arts and
    Letters, 1970), 360, 369–70
Blehl, Father Vincent, 285
Bloomfield, Anthony, 192
'Bluebell among the Sables' (MS; poem),
    18
Bodley Head (publishing house): MS
    moves to, 379–80, 438–9, 442, 447–8;
    and revisions to MS's Child of Light,
    473
Bold, Alan, 482
Bonagura, Robert, 326, 338–42
Bonaparte, Marie (Princess Marie of
    Greece), 58

Booker Prize: The Public Image
    nominated for, 356–7, 429
Books & Bookmen (magazine): prints
    MS's 'How I Became a Novelist', 237
Borchardt, Georges, 476
Boston, Mass.: Brodie staged in, 341
Botteghe Oscura (magazine), 249
Bowen, Arnold Vincent, 82–3, 86
Boyd, William, 449
Bradbury, (Sir) Malcolm, 368, 415–16, 448
Bradshaw, Valerie, 498
Brandt, Willy, 402
Bransten (US publisher), 106
Bray, Berkshire, 81
Braybrooke, June ('Isobel English'):
    friendship with MS, 107–8, 143, 150,
    153, 156–7, 219; view of Alan Barnsley,
    168; and MS's return from Israel, 245;
    confides in MS, 250; MS sends money
    to Kay Dick through, 289; Every Eye,
    157; Four Voices, 157
Braybrooke, Neville: friendship with MS,
    107–8, 143, 150, 153, 156–7, 219; view of
    Alan Barnsley, 168; MS visits in south
    of France, 249
Braybrooke, Victoria (Neville's
    stepdaughter), 158
Breffny, 'Baron' Brian de: Ambrosiani
    dislikes, 376, 386; friendship with MS,
    376, 386, 414–15; in MS story, 376;
    introduces Strutt to MS, 385;
    background and character, 386–8, 420;
    marriage to Jytsna, 388; tours India
    with MS, 397; in Geneva, 401; in Abbess,
    406; in Takeover, 420–2; marries
    heiress, 421; Strutt's unease over, 436;
    death, 499; My First Naked Lady, 389
Breffny, Jytsna de, 388–9
Breffny, Sita-Maria de, 388–9, 436, 439
Brennan, Maeve, 303
Brinnin, John, 300–1
British Broadcasting Corporation
    (BBC), 279–80, 401, 468
British Council, 471, 491, 517, 520
British Institute of Political Research, 98

Brontë family: MS writes on, 105, 143, 507; effect on MS, 138; MS reads book on, 426

Brontë, Anne: MS proposes editing complete works, 102, 105; Charlotte's attitude to, 138; MS's biography of, 158, 160

Brontë, Charlotte, 120, 138

Brontë, Emily: MS proposes book with Stanford, 136, 140, 150; Charlotte's attitude to, 138; Peter Owen contracts book from MS, 160; *Selected Poems*, 136, 138

Brontë Letters, The (ed. MS), 112, 135, 136

Brooke-Rose, Christine: friendship with MS, 143, 195, 219, 270, 315, 352, 471; and MS's hallucinations, 155–6; in Austria with MS, 212–14; as 'academic type', 267; visits MS in Rome, 345; and MS's attachment to Jardine, 470; stays with MS and Jardine at San Giovanni, 471–2; and MS's work load, 477; *The Dear Deceit*, 212; *The Grammar of Metaphor*, 213; *The Middlemen*, 315, 472; *Xorandor*, 472

Brookner, Anita: xvii, xxii, 465–6, 482–3; *Hotel du Lac*, 168

Broyard, Anatole, 423, 432, 449

Bruntsfield Place, Edinburgh, 1, 4–5, 19, 42, 400

Burdwan, Maharaja of, 388

Burgess, Anthony, 253–4, 320, 467

Burgess, Guy, 174

Bennett, Betty T., 473

Burney, Christopher: *Solitary Confinement*, 306

Burton, Richard, 397

Bush House, London, 60

Butcher, Maryvonne, 156

Buzzard, Mrs, 347

Byatt, (Dame) A. S., 351, 368, 383, 448, 512

Cabrini, Mother, 258

Carcaci, Marie, Duchessa di, 347

Caetani, Princess, 249

Cairncross, John, 415

Calder-Marshall, Arthur, 254, 298, 368, 392

Caldwell, Zoe, 341, 354

Camberg, Bernard (MS's father; 'Barney'): death, 1, 3–4, 14, 18, 261–4, 531; Jewishness, 2–3, 247; marriage, 2, 11–12, 464; career, 5–6, 40; social life and entertaining, 6, 42; marriage relations, 7, 11; manner, 12; takes in mother-in-law Adelaide, 13; claims Uezzell goods, 14; singing, 19; temper, 20; and lodgers, 21; sends children to fee-paying schools, 23; family background, 24–5; MS's fondness for, 35, 251, 263; influence on children, 40; cares for Robin, 75, 77, 185; Ossie stays with, 75; MS withholds news of baptism from, 135; retirement, 250; MS's final Christmas with, 256; in *Curriculum Vitae*, 489

Camberg, David (Philip's son): birth, 61, 327; MS meets in San Diego, 453

Camberg, Gertie (MS's aunt), 26–7

Camberg, Louis and Henrietta (MS's paternal grandparents), 24–5

Camberg, Muriel Sarah *see* Spark, Dame Muriel

Camberg, Philip (MS's brother): birth, 1; relations with MS, 1, 20, 43, 400; sense of alienation, 5; on mother's appearance, 6; on family life, 7–8, 20–1; in Watford with Uezzell relations, 12; nearly suffocates infant MS, 14; character and manner, 21–2; engineering career, 21–3, 400; schooling, 22–3; on Camberg family relations, 25–6; on unmentioned sex, 35; influenced by father, 40; social life, 42; meets Sophie, 43; birth of son David, 61; arranges father's funeral, 263; temporary posting to England, 324, 327; and mother's death, 400; MS visits in San Diego, 452–3, 470; on

Jewish inheritance, 461–3; last visit to MS, 519; death, 526

Camberg, Sarah (née Uezzell; MS's mother; 'Cissy'): marriage, 2, 11–12, 464; at home in Edinburgh, 4–5, 19, 23; background, 5; social life and entertaining, 6, 19–20, 42; drinking, 7, 263–4; generosity, 7–8; and brother Phil, 9–10; takes in and nurses mother, 13, 15; piano playing, 19; and MS's upbringing, 20, 23; and religion, 25, 27; superstitions, 27; and MS's return from Africa, 60; Ossie stays with, 72, 75; cares for Robin, 75, 77; meets Sergeant, 90; meets Stanford, 111; MS's exasperation with, 129, 145, 251, 288–90, 327; not told of MS's baptism, 135; Robin's apparent resentment towards, 185; Stanford informs of MS's hallucinations, 199; in Curriculum Vitae, 249–50; MS settles debts and provides capital sum, 251, 264; in widowhood, 263; seventy-fifth birthday, 286; finds new boyfriend, 288, 328; breaks leg, 303–4; letters to MS in New York, 327; cancer of bladder and death, 398–400; life in later years, 401; Robin and Judaism, 461

Camberg, Sophie (Philip's wife), 43, 327, 453

Camberg, Vivian (Philip/Sophie's daughter), 327, 453

Camberwell (Baldwin Crescent): MS lives in, 171–3, 228; MS expands space, 240; MS returns to from New York, 284; MS decides to leave, 304, 309–10, 317; MS revisits, 439

Campbell, Roy, 142

'Canaan' (MS; poem), 533

Cape, Jonathan (publishers), 257, 265

Cape Town, 57–8

Caraman, Father Philip, 156, 174

Carrick, Lynn, 186, 209–10, 278–9, 282

Carrick, Virginia, 278, 282

Carrigan, Pamela (née Flood), 87

Carter, Angela, xix; Nights at the Circus, 468

Cary, Tristram, 226, 266, 292, 437

Catani, Paola, 533

Cecil, Lord David, 97

Cellini, Benvenuto, 445–6; La Vita, 103

Centaur Press, 286

Chancellor, Alexander, 437, 519

Chandler, Robert, 342–3

Charismatic Renewal, 420

Cheyette, Bryan, 518

Chicago, 506

Chicago Tribune, 393

Child of Light: A Reassessment of Mary Wollstonecraft Shelley (MS), 112, 115–20, 267, 309–10; revised, 470, 472–4, 477; published in USA, 475

Christian, Princess, 66

Christie, Bill, 328

Christy & Moore (literary agents), 163, 226, 279

Chroustchoff, Igor de, 181

'Chrysalis' (MS; poem), 137

Church of England Newspaper, 132, 144–5, 148, 158

Churchill, (Sir) Winston, 295

Civitella della Chiana, Italy: wartime massacre, 522

Clark, John and Thekla, 517

Clayton, Jack, 326

Cochor, René de, 342

Cockerill, Sir George, 97–9

Cocktail's not for Drinking, The (MS; satirical drama), 136

Cocteau, Jean, 378, 404

Codron, Michael, 265–6, 282

Cohen, Morton, 276–7, 284, 287–8, 300, 302

Coleman, Leo, 397, 403–4

Coleridge, Samuel Taylor, 117

Collected Poems 1 (MS), 76, 121

Collected Stories (MS), 473–5

Comfort, Alex, 142

Comforters, The (MS): as self-revelation, xix, 165, 515; eccentric old lady in, 16;

Comforters, The (MS):—*contd*
  influence of Mary Shelley on, 117;
  writing, 161, 164, 167, 171; plot and
  characters, 164–5, 168–9, 175, 368, 528;
  belief and unbelief in, 168; title, 168–9;
  published, 176; read and praised by
  Greene and Waugh, 176; dedicated to
  the Barnsleys, 178; reception, 178–9;
  Stanford reviews, 181–2; US
  publication and reception, 181–2, 186,
  209; radio adaptation, 201; paperback
  edition, 321; and Book of Job, 514
Como, Lake, 459, 470
Compton-Burnett, Dame Ivy, 60, 379
Connolly, Cyril: founds and edits
  Horizon, 79; *Enemies of Promise*, 77
Conrad, Joseph, xx; *Heart of Darkness*,
  45
Constable (publishers), 473, 476, 479, 481,
  494, 507, 512
Constantine, King of Greece, 58, 348
Contri, Lorenzo, 529
Cork, Edmund, 283
Couling, Arthur, 32
Cover to Cover (TV programme), 478,
  481, 497
Coward, McCann & Geoghegan (US
  publishers), 432–3, 448
Cowell, Frances, 111, 489, 498–9, 509
Craig, Patricia, 482
Cronin, A. J.: contributes to MS plight
  fund, 161
Crossman, R. H. S., 69
Cunnane, Mary, 502
Curriculum Vitae (MS): publication,
  xv–xix; chapters published in *New
  Yorker*, xvii, 492, 500, 504; and MS's
  roots, xxi, 249; time-span, xxiii; and
  MS's exploring systems, 35; and
  feminism, 41; on Africa and marriage,
  45, 128; on Sergeant, 102; ending, 446;
  writing, 489–90, 494, 500, 503; on truth
  and lies, 497, 503; and Stanford, 504,
  529; success, 505; US publication, 507;
  in *New Yorker* article on MS, 508

'Curtain Blown by the Breeze, The' (MS;
  story), 45, 49, 215, 217

D-Day (6 June 1944), 63
Daiches, David, 461
Daiches, Lionel, 412–14
Daiches, Rabbi Salis, 461
Daily Express: and MS's dismissal from
  Poetry Society, 97; reviews *Hothouse*,
  393
Daily Mail: reviews *Hothouse*, 393; MS
  reviews Waugh biography for, 504; on
  MS's relations with Robin, 535
Daily Mirror's *Public Opinion* magazine,
  120
Daily Telegraph, 374
Danger Zone, The (MS; radio play),
  224–6, 233
'Dark Glasses, The' (MS; story), 215, 217
Davenport, John, 191, 209, 254, 298
David Cohen British Literature Prize, 516
David, King of Israel, 247
Davies, Hunter, 468–9
Delaney, Frank, 483
Delmer, Sefton: runs wartime 'black
  propaganda', 60, 62–5, 68–9
Dent, Dr John, 192
Derrick, Christopher, 254
'Desegregation of Art, The' (MS;
  Blashfield Address), 369
Deutsch, André, 439
Dick, Kay, 157, 195, 250, 289, 393, 396;
  Solitaire, 201
Dickson, Rache Lovat: as MS's editor at
  Macmillan, 224–6, 239–40, 255–6; and
  MS's trip to Holy Land, 242–4; and
  MS's response to critics of *Brodie*, 253;
  correspondence with disgruntled MS,
  255–6; offends MS with joke, 255; in
  New York for MS's visit, 257–8;
  fondness for MS, 259; relations with
  MS, 265, 310; and production of
  Doctors of Philosophy, 266; Shirley
  Hazzard and, 270; drives MS to
  Waterloo for travel to New York, 291

Doctors of Philosophy (MS; play), 240, 256, 260, 265–9, 282, 303, 309; MS seeks publication by Knopf, 308–9, 326

Dolce Vita, La (film), 311, 363

Donleavy, J.P., 306

Door of Youth, The (school poems), 38

Doty, Robert, 412

Doubleday (US publishers) xv

Drabble, (Dame) Margaret, 423–4

'Dragon, The' (MS; story), 454

Driver's Seat, The (MS): avant-garde nature, 316; dedicated to Ambrosiani, 357; qualities, 358; as *Identikit* in Italian, 363; based on press report, 364; writing, 364; plot and themes, 365–6, 368; narrative style, 366–7, 379; publication and reception, 368–70, 377, 383; publicity campaign, 374; film version, 390, 397, 402, 436; sales, 474

Drummond, Lindsay, 102, 105–6

Druten, John van, 182, 194

Dry River Bed, The (MS; radio play), 45, 212

Du Maurier, Daphne, 432

Durrell, Lawrence, 265; *Alexandria Quartet*, 378

Dutton (publishers), 473, 476

Edinburgh: MS's birth and upbringing in, xvi, xxi, xxiv, 1–5, 19; MS's personal archive in National Library of Scotland, xxi–xxii; cosmopolitanism, 24; Jewish immigrants and inhabitants, 24–5, 34, 43, 251; portrayed in *Miss Jean Brodie*, 31; social deprivation, 34; MS revisits on return from Africa, 59–60, 74; MS uncomfortable in, 126, 129, 288; MS spends Christmases in, 135–6, 256; Festival, 144–5; MS visits for mother's 75th birthday, 286; MS visits before departure for Rome, 324; MS meets Lionel Daiches in, 412–13; MS visits Robin in, 427; MS visits with Jardine, 460; MS's views on, 480; in *Curriculum Vitae*, 489

Edinburgh Jewish Literary Society, 518

Edinburgh Star, 462

'Edinburgh Villanelle' (MS; poem), 121

Edward VIII, King (*later* Duke of Windsor): abdication, 43

Edwards, Ruth Dudley, 481

Eichmann, Adolf, 244–6

'Elementary' (MS; poem), 147, 351

Eliot, T. S.: MS writes on, 101, 139, 145, 153, 160; and MS's wariness of psychoanalysis, 110; influence on MS, 116; MS parodies, 136; MS hallucinates over encrypted 'messages', 151, 153–4, 157; *The Confidential Clerk*, 144–6, 150, 153, 157; *Four Quartets*, 149

Elizabeth the Queen Mother, 361

Ellmann, Mary, 392

Emily Brontë (MS), 143, 150, 160

'Empty Space, The' (MS; poem), 526

Encounter (magazine), 349

English, Isobel *see* Braybrooke, June

Enright, D. J., 319

Epinal, France, 455–6

European Affairs (magazine), 98, 108

Evening Standard, 228–9

'Executor, The' (MS; story), 454

Faber, Carol, 402

Falcon Press, 140–1, 158, 483

Fanfarlo, The, and Other Verse, (MS), 132, 136

Far Cry from Kensington, A (MS): autobiographical content, xix, 483–6; on Owen's office, 173; writing, 469, 473; Mrs Lazzari in, 471; proofs, 477; publication and reception, 478, 481–2, 489; historical research for, 483–4; Stanford portrayed in, 484–7, 529; style, 484–5; publication in France, 490

Farrell, Kathleen, 157

Faulks, Sebastian, 478

Fayard (French publishers), 454, 470–1, 474, 476, 490

Feldman, Lew, 287–8

Fellini, Federico, 311
feminism: MS's view of, 3, 41, 116, 118, 434
ffolliott, Rosemary, 386
Fielding, Fenella, 265
Fiennes family, 198
Finishing School, The (MS), 514, 526–9
Firbank, Ronald, 379
'First Year of My Life, The' (MS; story):
    autobiographical elements, xix, xxi;
    MS's uncle Harry in, 10; and effect of
    Great War, 33; on wartime action, 59;
    and anti-Semitism, 245–6; writing, 412
Fitz, Mr (Linder's partner), 342
Fleetwood, Hugh, 446
Fleming, John, 518, 526
Flood, Pamela *see* Carrigan, Pamela
Florence, Italy, 363
Flower into Animal (MS; poems), 121
Foch, Marshal Ferdinand, xx
Ford, Gerald, 408
Forde, Florrie, 27, 29
Fort Victoria (Masvingo), Southern
    Rhodesia, 48–9
'Fortune Teller, The' (MS; story), 454
Forum: Stories and Poems (magazine), 99,
    101, 103–4, 107–9, 119
Foster, Alison, 33–4, 38, 150, 152
Foster, Revd Roy, 150
Franco (San Giovanni handyman), 477,
    519
'Frantic a Child Ran' (MS; poem), 76
Frazer, Sir James: *The Golden Bough*, 418,
    420
Frederica, Queen (*earlier* Princess) of
    Greece, 58, 348, 386
Fremantle, Anne, 351
Freud, Sigmund, 377
Frost, Basil, 54–5
Fry, Christopher, 112–14, 119, 136, 195

Galloway, Janice, 427, 520
Gant, Roland, 141
Gardiner, Charles Wrey: edits *Poetry
    Quarterly*, 76, 79; friendship with MS,
    79–80; character and lifestyle, 85, 108,

141–2, 197; and Gawsworth, 97;
    supports MS and Stanford, 100, 140–1;
    and MS's proposal to edit Brontë
    letters, 106; as literary editor of *Daily
    Mirror*'s *Public Opinion* magazine,
    119–20; publishes MS's *Selected Poems
    of Emily Brontë*, 136; autobiography, 182
Gardiner, Cynthia, 141
Gascoigne, Bamber, 253
Gascoigne, David, 107
Gawsworth, John, 97, 109
Geneva, 401
'Gentile Jewesses, The' (MS), xix, 269,
    275, 316, 462, 518
Gerson, Mark, 233, 257, 274
Gill, Brendan, 273, 274–5, 302, 345
Gillespie's (Edinburgh school): MS
    attends, 22–5, 28, 31, 33, 37, 39; Robin
    enrolled at, 75; MS gives £10,000 from
    David Cohen Prize, 516
Ginna, Peter, 440–1
Girls of Slender Means, The (MS): depicts
    Helena Club, 68, 70, 293–4; on wartime
    London, 70; on victory celebrations in
    London, 74; on friends in poverty, 157;
    publication and reception, 265, 287,
    292–3, 297–8; writing, 265, 270, 282;
    Waugh praises, 291; Macmillan's
    publicity for, 294; MS's self-portrayal
    in, 294–5, 299; plot and themes, 294–7;
    and historical events, 295–6; MS tries
    to remove typographical errors, 308;
    Auden praises, 377; TV film of, 401
Gittings, Robert, 119
Glazebrook, Ben, 478
Glendinning, Victoria, 432–3, 449
Go-Away Bird and Other Stories, The
    (MS), 173, 176, 198–9, 201, 209
'Go-Away Bird, The' (MS; story), 45–6,
    57, 59, 182, 198
Godwin, Tony, 220
Godwin, William, 115, 117
Goldfar, Esther (née Camberg; MS's
    aunt), 25–8
Goldfar, Isador, 26

Goldsmith, Lady Annabel, 517

Gotham Book Mart, New York, 402

Granada (publishers), 474

Greacen, Robert, 142

Green, Henry, 379

Green, Martin, 350

Green, Peter, 254

Greene, Graham: as Catholic writer, xv, 179; need for isolation, 126; contributes to MS plight fund, 161–2, 300; praises MS's stories, 163; praises *The Comforters*, 176, 178; MS sends 'The Black Madonna' to read, 187; praises *Memento Mori*, 209; on the devil, 235; on guilt and failure, 381; and MS's approaching sixty, 425; praises *Territorial Rights*, 438; and MS's move to Bodley Head, 439; sends books to MS, 442; MS speaks at memorial requiem mass, 500–1; *Dr Fischer of Geneva or The Bomb Party*, 442; *A Sort of Life*, xvi; *Ways of Escape*, 442

Greenstein, Milton, 276, 278, 293, 302, 304, 334, 341–2

Greer, Germaine, 437

Grey Walls Press, 136, 140–2

Gross, John, 319

Groth, Janet, 302, 333–4, 336, 341–2, 345, 521

Grutman, Roy, 312, 319, 321

Guest, John, 282

Gwelo, Southern Rhodesia, 54, 57

Hamilton, Alex, 405–7, 409, 422

Hand and Flower Press, 122

Handke, Peter, 500

Harding, H. W., 82–3

Hardy, Laurence, 265

Harold Ober Associates (US literary agents), 182, 227, 469, 475

'Harper and Wilton' (MS; story), 137

Harper's Bazaar (magazine), 180

Harris, Daniel ('Zev'), 338, 358, 362, 390, 415, 499

Hartland, Beryl, 374

Harty, Russell, 412, 437

Hay-on-Wye Literary Festival, 518

Hazzard, Kit (Shirley's mother), 314

Hazzard, Shirley: asks about Sandy's small eyes, 31; on MS's spiritual quality, 36; friendship and correspondence with MS, 257, 263, 270–4, 276, 284–5, 299, 396; and MS's move to New York, 269–70; courtship and marriage to Steegmuller, 271–2, 284, 302; on atmosphere at *New Yorker*, 275; and Rachel MacKenzie, 277–8, 284–5; MS gives copy of Stanford's biography to, 287; and MS's relations with mother and son, 289; sends gifts to MS, 289; and Bert Beck, 293; relationship with MS cools, 302; MS turns against, 322; present at MS's Blashfield Address, 370

'He is Like Africa' (MS; poem), 100

Hearst, Patty, 402

Heath, (Sir) Edward, 402

Heath-Stubbs, John, 142, 529

Heim, Karl, 144, 146–7

Helena Club, Lancaster Gate, London, 60, 66–8, 70–1, 74, 80, 86, 97, 294

Hemingway, Ernest, 378

Henderson, Robert, 278, 282

Heppenstall, Rayner: relations with MS, 180, 182, 193–4, 198, 200–1, 270; relationship with MS ends, 224–6, 277; *Blaze of Noon*, 193; *The Greater Infortune* (earlier *Saturnine*): dedicated to MS, 219, 224

Heriot-Watt College, Edinburgh, 23, 40

Hesketh, Phoebe, 110

Heygate, May, 54–5

Higham, David: as MS's agent, 218–19, 224; MS leaves, 226–7

Highsmith, Patricia, 343

Hill, Leonard, 181

Hill, Susan, 424

Hobson, (Sir) Harold, 266

Hogarth Press, 472

Holme, Christopher, 224–6, 266

Holmes, Richard, 351–2

Holroyd, (Sir) Michael, 449

Holy Land *see* Israel

Honour, Hugh, 518

Hopkins, Gerard Manley: 'The Wreck of the *Deutschland*', 297

Horder, Pearson, 101–3, 120, 158, 222

Horizon (magazine), 79

Hothouse by the East River, The (MS): Milton Bryan POW compound in, 68–9; on solitude, 71; avant-garde nature, 316; MS plans, 318; Macmillan's payment for, 324; writing, 324, 326, 331–2, 334–7, 341, 344, 364, 370, 385; contract with Knopf, 339; proofs corrected, 390; reception, 392–4, 397; narrative structure, 394–5; and *Peter Pan*, 394, 521; plot and themes, 394, 396–7, 432; autobiographical content, 396; paperback sales, 474; lightning in, 521

Houghton Mifflin (US publishers), 507

'House of the Famous Poet, The' (MS; story), 135, 350

'How I Became a Novelist' (MS; radio talk and article), 237

Howard, Elizabeth Jane, 209

Howell, Ursula, 265

Hughes Massie (literary agents), 283

Hume, Cardinal Basil, Archbishop of Westminster, 480

Humphreys, Christmas ('Toby'), 95–7

'Hundred and Eleven Years Without a Chauffeur, A' (MS; story), 376

Hunter, Bruce, 475, 502, 505, 520, 531

Hutchens, Patricia, 142

Hutchinson (publishers), 501–2

Hyams, Philip (Adelaide Uezzell's father), 10–11

Igoe, W. J., 254

India: MS visits with de Breffny and Strutt, 397–8, 404

Ingersoll Foundation: T. S. Eliot Award, 506

International Writers' Festival, Edinburgh (1962), 264

Ireland: MS visits with de Breffny and Mott, 386–7

Iride (Rasponi's maid), 454, 499

Irish Arts Review, 389

Israel: MS plans trip to, 228, 242–3; MS in, 244–8; in *The Mandelbaum Gate*, 319; relations with Vatican, 390–2

Italia Prize, 240, 266, 292

Italy: MS's love for, 30, 249, 341, 468–9; taxes, 340; *see also* Rome; San Giovanni

Jackson, Edgar, 76

James, Henry, 447, 467

Jameson, Storm, 221, 227

Jardine, Penelope: MS meets, 343; told of MS's hysterectomy, 357; friendship with MS, 376, 403–5, 455, 470; character and background, 403–4; keeps MS's diaries, 403; secretarial work for MS, 406, 447, 453; improves San Giovanni, 412, 449–50, 477; pet dogs and cats, 412, 453, 459, 488, 509, 519; travels with MS, 413, 415, 426, 428, 431, 446–7, 451, 454–6, 459, 470, 476, 478, 488, 490, 501, 505; MS stays with at San Giovanni, 414–15, 424; home burgled, 417, 525–6; home in San Giovanni, 423, 491; witnesses MS's will, 428; writes to Strutt, 436; social circle, 437; in London with MS, 439; and Peter Ginna, 440–1; breaks bones, 450; tension and argument with MS, 450–1; and MS's absence in USA, 453; illustrations for children's books, 454; suffering, 455; mentioned in 'Side Roads of Tuscany', 464; investigates and negotiates MS's publishing rights, 469, 474; Brooke-Rose stays with, 471–2; gives new desk to MS, 477; replaces office equipment, 477; sketching, 494; and MS's dispute over Tennessee Williams–Paul Scott meeting, 502; helps MS with autobiography, 503; on MS's hip operation, 506; and MS's physical decline after operation, 509–10; viral arthritis, 509; returns to San Giovanni with MS in old age, 510–11; researches lightning for MS, 521; inheritance from MS, 529; at MS's funeral, 533; memorial interview for MS, 534

Jaysingh (cook), 397

Jeanette, Sean, 141

Jebb, Julian, 298, 351

Jenkins, Alan, 478

Jerusalem, 246–7

Jews: in Edinburgh, 24–5, 34, 43, 251

Job (Biblical figure), 139, 143–4, 150, 158, 160, 165–7, 170, 188, 368, 455–7, 465–6, 514

John Masefield (MS), 119, 121, 129–30, 135–7

Johnson, Pamela Hansford (Lady Snow), 255, 266–7, 436

Jordan, 244–5

Joyce, James, 2

Jung, Carl Gustav: *Answer to Job*, 165, 456

Kallman, Chester, 376

Kanon, Joseph, 432, 437, 466, 476, 487–8, 493, 505, 506

Kay, Christina: portrayed in *Miss Jean Brodie*, 28, 31–2, 251; teaches and influences MS, 28–32, 35–6, 38–9, 41, 111, 119

Kazin, Alfred, 319, 379

Keane, Molly, 386

Keats, John: grave, 312

Kee, Robert, 411

Kemp, Peter, 314, 482–5

Kennedy, John F., 296

Kermode, Sir Frank: sees Florrie Forde perform, 27; reviews *Girls of Slender Means*, 248; mistakes von Auw for MS's boyfriend, 283; introduces MS to Tates, 291; and assassination of President Kennedy, 296; in USA, 302; MS tells of intention to settle in Paris, 310; writes on *Mandelbaum*, 313, 319; on

The Public Image, 351; serves as Booker judge, 356; on *The Driver's Seat*, 368; on *Not to Disturb*, 382–3; on *Abbess* and Watergate scandal, 409; praises *The Takeover*, 418, 420; reviews *The Only Problem*, 467; chooses *Reality and Dreams* as Book of the Year, 512

Khrushchev, Nikita S., 296, 402

Kierkegaard, Søren: *Diaries*, 157

Kilmartin, Terence, 124, 195, 379

King, Francis, 157, 253–5, 383, 432, 468, 494

Kingsley, Charles, 286

Kissinger, Henry, 409

Knopf, Alfred, 279–81, 300, 313, 332

Knopf, Blanche, 227, 279–81, 292, 300, 309–10, 312, 326, 334, 513

Knopf (New York publishing house): takes over MS from Lippincott, 279, 282; launches *Girls of Slender Means*, 292; MS's irritation with, 304, 307; MS dismisses Lemay, 309; publishes *Doctors of Philosophy*, 308–9, 326; requests publicity material from MS, 311–12; MS leaves, 313, 370, 372–3; and publicity for *The Mandelbaum Gate*, 320; reservations over *The Public Image*, 356; inadequate sales of *The Driver's Seat*, 370

Koshland, William, 280, 309, 313, 336, 345, 370

Kung, Hans, 442

Kyle, Chevalier Galloway, 78, 80, 94–5

Labour Party: 1966 election victory, 331

'Ladies and Gentlemen' (MS; story), 136

Laffont (French publishers), 286

Langheim, Baron, 403, 415

Lapautre, Michelle, 476, 478

Lash, Jini, 197

Laski, Marghanita, 468

La Tour, Georges de: *Job visité par sa femme* (painting), 456–7, 466–7

Lawrence, D.H., xx

Lazzari, Bunny, 261

Lazzari, Mrs ('Tiny'): as MS's landlady, 172–3, 190, 194, 215, 238, 240, 284, 299–300, 313, 454, 483; understanding of MS, 225; and Barnsley's visit to Baldwin Crescent, 260–1; deters MS's mother, 264; MS accompanies to Paris and Ireland, 286; and MS's trips to New York, 303; and MS's leaving Baldwin Crescent, 304, 309–10, 317; leaving gifts from MS, 323; MS revisits, 439; death, 470; portrayed in *A Far Cry from Kensington*, 471, 480, 483

Lee, Harper: *To Kill a Mocking Bird*, 279

Legouis, Emile, 109–6

Lemay, Harding ('Pete'), 280–1, 289, 302, 304, 308–9, 319

Lerner, Alan Jay, 445

Lessing, Doris, 436

'Letter to Howard' (MS; poem), 100

Levenson, Miriam, 43

Lieber, Dr, 153–4, 161, 245, 312, 439

Liebling, A. J., 276

Lifeboat (MS's racehorse), 317, 324, 331

Linder, Erich, 340, 342

Lindey, Alexander, 340–2

Lippincott, Sarah, 302, 324

Lippincott (US publisher): publishes MS, 176, 181, 186, 209, 227, 253, 256–7; MS leaves, 278–9, 282

Lively, Penelope, 494

Lodge, David, 240, 254, 402, 409, 418, 432, 474

Loitering with Intent (MS): autobiographical content, xix, 103, 130, 133–4, 443, 483; hoarding in, xxii; eccentric old lady in, 16; and sexuality, 41–2; Manning portrayed in, 103, 426; portrays Stanford, 104, 211, 443; opening set in St Mary Abbots churchyard, 134, 439; writing, 439–42; plot and themes, 442–6; MS sends to Alan Jay Lerner for musical adaptation, 445; publication and reception, 447–9

London: MS moves to (1944), 60; MS's life in, 66–8, 70–1, 74, 77; MS visits from Italy, 439, 460, 500, 519–20

London Library, 425

London Mystery Magazine, 178

Losey, Joseph, 418, 435, 474

Lowell, Robert, 273

Lucan, Richard John Bingham, 7th Earl of, 517, 523–4

Lucian: *Symposium*, 496–7

Lungotevere Raffaello Sanzio 9, Rome, 372, 424, 435

Macaulay, (Dame): *The Towers of Trebizond*, 320

McCarthy, Mary: *The Group*, 298

McCrindle, Joe, 293, 345

McCrum, Robert, 325

McCullers, Carson, 364

Macdonald, Dwight, 257, 273, 276

Macdonald, Gloria, 273

McEwan, Geraldine: plays Miss Jean Brodie, 31, 433

McEwan, Nita, 50, 52

McGrath, Charles, xvii

Macken, Walter, 255

MacKenzie, Rachel, 180, 182, 218, 257, 269, 277–8, 284–5

Maclean, Alan: as MS's editor at Macmillan, 163–4, 168, 173–4, 176, 178, 183, 186, 210, 219–20, 226–7; alcoholism, 192–3, 198, 513; relations with MS, 193, 220, 224–6, 231, 234, 265, 285, 303–4, 310, 322, 417, 440; and John Rosenberg, 195; MS reprimands, 230–1, 236, 239; replaced as MS's editor, 239, 255; and MS's trip to Israel, 243; mother's illness, 265; MS dedicates *Girls of Slender Means* to, 265; and production of *Doctors of Philosophy*, 266; and Snows, 267; friendship with Shirley Hazzard, 270; on Blanche Knopf, 280–1, 284; in USA, 302; and MS's relations with her mother, 303–4; sees MS off to New York, 303; and Nora Sayre, 306; accompanies MS to race meetings, 312; gifts from MS on leaving Camberwell, 323; and payment for *Hothouse*, 324; marriage, 332; MS invites to Buckingham Palace ceremony, 336; visits MS in Rome, 345; on *The Driver's Seat*, 364; MS requests von Auw to communicate with, 379; and MS's rejection of 'madness', 381, 507–8; and sale of MS's manuscripts, 402; collects MS's post from Italy, 403; and Hamilton's interview with MS, 406; and MS's writing of *Territorial Rights*, 425; and MS's purchase of racehorse, 428; and success of *Territorial Rights*, 432; discusses contract for *Territorial Rights*, 437; and misprint in blurb for *Territorial Rights*, 438; and MS's changing publishers, 439; death of son Daniel, 440; MS attempts to persuade to use Jardine's illustrations, 453–4; arranges meeting between MS and Iris Murdoch, 455; and MS's leaving Bodley Head, 473; at Strutt's party for Tennessee Williams and MS, 501–2; MS turns against as traitor, 508

Maclean, Daniel (Alan/Robin's son), 336, 440

Maclean, Donald, 174, 192, 417

Maclean, Robin (Alan's wife), 332, 336, 345

Macmillan, Alexander (Viscount Stockton), 438, 475–6

Macmillan, Harold (*later* 1st Earl of Stockton), 174, 176, 222, 260, 317, 331, 402

Macmillan, Maurice (*later* Viscount), 239, 243, 259, 266, 317, 475

Macmillan (publishers): publish MS, 163–4, 173–4, 178, 180, 183, 186, 191–2, 210, 227; MS's disputes and dissatisfaction with, 218, 220, 229, 231, 234, 238, 242–3, 255–6, 265, 370; publish MS's radio plays and stories, 226; launch party for *The Bachelors*, 233; send MS's 'How I Became a Novelist'

to *Books & Bookmen*, 237; MS rejects financial offer, 239–40, 250; support MS's trip to Holy Land, 242–3; and publicity for *Brodie*, 243; publication party for *Brodie*, 254; MS negotiates with, 259, 372, 469, 470, 474–6; remain MS's publisher, 259–60; publish Shirley Hazzard, 270; and launch of *Girls of Slender Means*, 292, 294; contracts for *Child of Light*, 310; publicise MS's purchase of racehorse, 317; move premises in London, 332; choose publicity photograph of MS, 356; publish *Not to Disturb*, 377, 380; claim to MS's British rights, 380; advance for *Territorial Rights*, 437; MS leaves, 438–40; MS maintains relations with, 447; reprint MS's books, 447; portrayed in *A Far Cry*, 483

MacNeice, Louis, 349, 378

McWhinnie, Donald, 265–6

McWilliam, Candia, 494

Madrid: MS visits, 517

'Magdalen' (MS; poem), 175

Maguire, Hugh, 181

Mailer, Norman, 265, 273, 353, 378

Malamud, Bernard, 353

Maloff, Saul, 350

Mameli, Count, 347

Mandelbaum Gate, The (MS): autobiographical elements, xix, 301, 315; themes, 228, 255, 285, 320; religious content, 242, 247, 285, 307; and MS's visit to Holy Land, 245; on life in Israel, 247; slow writing, 264–5, 284–6, 289, 291, 300–4, 306, 308, 312; academic woman in, 267; *New Yorker* publishes sections, 282, 306, 316; importance to MS, 285, 293, 312; publication, 310, 313; advance notices, 313; structure, 316; mixed reception, 319–20; film companies refuse, 334

Manning, Hugo, 103, 157, 180–1, 425–6; *Conversations with Kafka*, 426

Margaret, Princess, 428

Maria (Italian maid), 345

Marneau, Frederic, 141

Martin, Miss ('Martie'), 163

Marwick, Rachel (née Camberg; MS's aunt; Rae), 25–6

Marwick, Stuart, 26

Marx, Erica, 122

Mary, Blessed Virgin, 191

Mary Magdalene, 175

Mary Queen of Scots: MS writes verse play on, 74, 528; in *The Finishing School*, 528

Maschler, Tom, 257, 265

Masefield, John: MS hears reading, 30, 119; MS admires, 37, 119, 131; MS writes on, 112, 118, 119, 121, 129–30, 134; MS visits, 130

Mason, Michael, 156; *The Legacy*, 144, 146–7

Mastroianni, Marcello, 363, 500

Maxwell, William, 271, 273, 278, 369

May, Derwent, 392

Mayer, Peter, 306, 319, 321

Mazzeschi, Don Gualtiero, 529–31, 533–4

'Meditation on Disaffection' (MS), 126

Mehta, Ved, 257, 272, 275–6, 322

Meir, Golda, 390–2

'Member of the Family, A' (MS; story), 214–16

Memento Mori: and MS's grandmother Adelaide, 16; writing, 171, 186, 196, 198; publication, 186, 201; plot and themes, 204–9, 212; reception and success, 209, 220, 254; stage adaptation, 326; on growing old, 427; TV version, 503; republished in Italy, 506

Menotti, Gian-Carlo, 404

Methven, Colin: background and character, 65, 81; on Robin Spark's return to England, 74; MS sends poems to, 76; friendship with MS, 87; provides household goods and furniture for MS, 89–90, 97; and MS's position at Poetry Society, 96

Methven, Deirdre (Colin's daughter), 65, 74

Mexico City: MS visits, 299, 305

Meynell, Alice, 118

Michie, James, 447, 473

Millais, Sir John Everett, 149

Miller, Jonathan, 343

Millington-Drake, Sir Eugen, 82, 346, 360

Millington-Drake, Teddy, 346

Mills, George, 220

Milton Bryan, Bedfordshire, 61–2, 65, 68–9

Mitchell, Joseph, 276

Moffat, Alexander ('Sandy'), 460

Mondadori (Italian publishers), 311, 401

Monica, St, 174–5, 177, 183

Monteluce, Contessa di, 347

Moore, Nicholas, 141

Mortimer, Emily, 479–80

Mortimer, Sir John, 437, 478–81, 488, 504, 512, 514

Mortimer, Penelope, 191

Mosley, Sir Oswald, 25, 245

Moss, Howard, 276, 292–3, 302, 319, 321

Mott, George: and MS in Rome, 362–3, 415; in Ireland with MS and de Breffny, 385; on de Breffny, 386–7, 389; on MS's concealing problems, 396; on Indian tour with MS, 397–8; meets Hamilton, 406; and Charismatic Renewal, 420; Strutt entertains, 436

Muggeridge, Malcolm, 254

Munroe, Anna, 33–4

Murdoch, (Dame) Iris, 353, 378, 418, 436, 455–6, 520, 528; *The Black Prince*, 392

Murray, Venetia: interviews MS, 210–11, 220, 238

Mussolini, Benito, 30–1

My Best Mary: Selected Letters of Mary Shelley (ed. MS and Stanford), 112, 114, 135, 136

'My Kingdom for a Horse' (MS; poem), 139

'My Rome' (MS; article), 453, 464

Naipaul, (Sir) Vidya S., 209, 516
Najar, Amiel E., 390–1
Najar, Vida, 390
Naples, 403, 405
National Insurance, Ministry of: MS appeals to, 152, 161
National Library of Scotland, 462, 504
National Theatre: stages *Brodie*, 518
'Nativity, The' (MS; poem), 124, 131
Nemi, Italy, 405, 414, 418, 421–3, 450, 470
Neo-Romanticism, 83, 140–2, 145, 150
Nevill, Peter (publisher), 106, 114, 120, 135, 136, 139–40, 160–1
New Arts Theatre Club, London, 265
New English Fiction Society, 418
New York: MS first visits, 172, 256–8; MS revisits and works in, 263, 269–79, 282–3, 291–2, 300, 303, 310, 324, 331, 340, 452–3, 492, 507; MS's social circles in, 302, 313; MS turns against, 318–23, 396; *Brodie* staged in, 341, 354; in *Hothouse*, 395–6; MS buys Manhattan apartment, 487–9
New York Times, 500
New York Times Book Review, 393
New Yorker (magazine): prints version of *Brodie*, xv, 249, 253; publishes chapters of *Curriculum Vitae*, xvii, 492, 500, 504; invites contribution from MS, 180; praises *Memento Mori*, 209; publishes MS's stories, 217–18; Updike praises MS in, 232; celebrates MS's visit to New York, 257; provides room for MS, 269–70, 274, 276, 331; publishes 'The Gentile Jewesses', 269; Gill on atmosphere at, 275; organisation and staff, 276; publishes sections of *The Mandelbaum Gate*, 282, 306, 317; payments and offers to MS, 310–11; MS acts as Rome correspondent, 348, 390–2, 469; publishes MS's story 'The House of the Famous Poet', 350; publishes *The Driver's Seat* in entirety, 364, 368; ignores *Hothouse*, 393; rejects MS's story version of *Territorial*

Rights, 425; Stephen Schiff article on MS in, 507; seventy-fifth anniversary celebration, 520
Newman by his Contemporaries (MS and Stanford), 186
Newman, John Henry, Cardinal: on fall of man, 70; MS reads and admires, 144, 262, 295–6; MS and Stanford plan book on, 174, 181, 198; and *The Mandelbaum Gate*, 285–6; on conversion, 297; MS's affinity with over sense of persecution, 322–3; spirituality, 445; *Apologia Pro Vita Sua*, 103, 445; *Sermons*, 447
Newsweek (magazine): reviews *The Mandelbaum Gate*, 319
Nice: MS visits with Robin, 204, 226
Nicholson, George, 305–7, 313, 320, 322, 332
Nine (magazine), 109
Niven, Frances, 29–30, 43
Nixon, Richard M., 398, 402, 406, 408
Norseman (magazine), 135
Norton (US publishers), 502
Not to Disturb (MS): Clovis in, 35; qualities, 316, 379; writing, 357, 370, 373–4; based on press report, 364, 373; themes and plot, 372, 381–2, 397; publication and reception, 377, 380, 382–5; literary quotations in, 382–3; film and play scripts, 401; sales, 474; lightning in, 521
Notaristefani, Contessa de, 347
'Note by the Wayside' (MS; poem), 175
Nussey, Ellen, 120
Nye, Robert, 383, 408

Oates, Joyce Carol, 350
Observer (newspaper): MS wins story competition, 122–4, 136, 444; MS reviews for, 135, 158; Toynbee interviews MS for, 378–9
O'Connor, Frank, 353
O'Gorman, Ned, 262, 272, 276, 345–6
Olding, Dorothy: visits London, 283; and MS's tax bill, 339; succeeds von Auw as

Olding, Dorothy—*contd*
  MS's agent, 385; and MS's life in Italy,
    414; MS telephones from Italy, 437; and
    MS's changing London publisher,
    439–40; MS turns against, 469, 474–5;
    Strutt invites to dinner, 501
O'Malley, Father, 154, 161–2, 165, 172, 182,
  194
Omnibus edition (MS works), 507
'On Music for Statues' (MS; poem), 94
Onassis, Jacqueline Kennedy, xv
Only Problem, The (MS): on Job, 166;
  writing, 449–51, 453; themes and plot,
  455–8; publication and reception, 460,
  465–8; qualities, 467
Orient Express (cruise ship), 489
'Ormolu Clock, The' (MS; story),
  215–18
Orrell, Margaret, 415
Orton, Joe: *Loot*, 282
Osborne, John, 448
Oswald, Lee Harvey, 296
O'Toole, Peter: *Loitering with Intent*, 521
Outposts (magazine), 79
Overseas Club, Edinburgh, 43
Owen, Peter (publisher), 136, 150, 160,
  173–4, 176, 180, 485, 507
Oxford University: awards honorary
  D.Litt. to MS, 519–20

Pachnos, Mary, 474
Pagano, Mark, 276
Page, Norman, 495, 497–8
Palazzi, Carlo, 362
Palazzo Taverna, Rome: MS occupies,
  344–7, 358, 360; MS leaves, 371–2, 374
Pallavicini, Principessa, 414
Palmer, Herbert, 97, 100, 103, 110, 133
Paramount film corporation, 343
Paris: MS visits, 476, 477–8, 490–1
Parker, Brian, 181
Parks, Tim, 478
'Party through the Wall, The' (MS; radio
  play), 180
Patrizia (San Giovanni cleaner), 477

Paul VI, Pope, 390–2
'Pauline Privilege' (in canon law), 143–4
Pavlova, Anna, 29
'Pawnbroker's Wife, The' (MS; story), 45,
  58, 136–7
'Pearly Shadow, The' (MS; story), 136
Pearn, Pollinger & Higham (literary
  agents), 142, 181
Pearson, Gabriel, 392, 419
Penguin Books: publish MS, 212, 220, 226,
  230, 330, 474
Peregrine Press, 140, 142
Perry, Eleanor, 326
Peterkiewicz, Jerzy: friendship with MS,
  143, 156, 315; and MS's Eliot obsession,
  153; novel on angels, 155; relations with
  Brooke-Rose, 155; and Elizabeth
  Rosenberg, 195; in Austria with MS and
  Brooke-Rose, 212–14, 216; on MS's
  uplifting qualities, 219; visits MS in
  Rome, 345; divorce from Brooke-Rose,
  472
Peters, Paul, 283–4, 385
Phelps, Robert, 223
Piazza di Tor Sanguigna, Rome: MS's
  apartment in, 329, 335, 337–8, 343
Pinder, Una (née Brighten), 299
Pinter, Harold, 516; *The Homecoming*, 268
Plato: *Symposium*, 496
Podell, Faye, 339, 341
Poetry London (magazine), 79
Poetry Quarterly, 76, 80, 140–2
Poetry Review, 78–83, 102, 109
Poetry Society: MS as secretary, 42,
  78–82, 86, 92, 95; MS joins, 76;
  Portman Square flat, 78–9, 89; internal
  conflicts and intrigues, 79–83, 86,
  89–90, 92–6, 156; Council resignations,
  90; dismisses MS, 97, 443–4
Poetry of Today (supplement to *Poetry
  Review*), 76
'Poet's House, The' (MS; radio broadcast
  and essay), 349, 355
Pope-Hennessy, Sir John, 470, 476
Porter, Andrew, 503

Porter, Daphne, 29

'Portobello Road, The' (MS; story), 45, 169–73, 180, 249

Potter, Dennis: *The Glittering Coffin*, 223

Powell, Barbara, 385

Powys, John Cowper, 82

Prime of Miss Jean Brodie, The (MS): *New Yorker* issue devoted to, xv, 249, 253; on Edinburgh slums, 25; Christina Kay portrayed in, 28, 31–2, 37; influenced by Gillespie's school, 28; TV versions, 31, 433, 469; on female adolescence, 34; betrayal in, 206, 250, 252, 407; and art of fiction, 207; success and earnings, 230, 325, 340, 360; publicity for, 237, 243, 255; writing, 238–9, 246; character of Brodie in, 248, 251–2, 267, 524; narrative structure, 248; Edinburgh Calvinism in, 251–2; themes, 252–3, 293; publication and reception, 253–4; US publication and reception, 256–8; and *Girls of Slender Means*, 293–4; stage adaptation and productions, 309–10, 324, 325–6, 331, 341, 354, 469, 474, 518; MS reads proofs, 315; film version, 331, 333–4, 339–40, 354, 364; film selected for Royal Command Performance, 357; reprinted in Italy, 401

Probert, Beryl, 327

Profumo, John, 162

Proust, Marcel: MS writes on, 144, 146, 148–9; *À La Recherche du Temps Perdu*, 129

Pryce-Jones, Alan, 298

Pryce-Jones, Clarissa, 476

Pryce-Jones, David, 351, 437, 472, 476

Public Image, The (MS): writing, 18, 332, 337–8; avant-garde nature, 316, 352–3; plot and themes, 337, 350, 353–6, 365, 397; proposed film version, 343, 360, 401; publication and reception, 350–2; nominated for Booker Prize, 356–7, 429; success in USA, 356; and identity, 363; out of print, 447; sales, 474

Punch (magazine), 289

Purdy, Canon Bill, 415

Putnam (US publishers), 466

Quant, Mary, 332

Queen Mary, RMS, 291

Queen's Gate Terrace, London, 137, 139, 150

Quennell, Marcelle, 65, 69, 71

Quennell, (Sir) Peter, 208

'Quest for Lavishes Ghast, The' (MS; story), 137

Quigly, Isobel, 383

Raban, Jonathan, 384, 411

Radziwill, Princess Lee (née Bouvier), 347

Radziwill, Prince Stanislaus, 347

Ramsay, Peggy, 265, 325–6

Ramsey, Weston, 90, 93

Raphael Hotel, Rome, 320, 328–9, 334–5, 340, 455

Rasponi, Count Lanfranco, 376, 386, 415, 420–1, 454, 459; death, 499

Ratcliffe, Michael, 392

Rattle, Sir Simon, 519

Raven, Simon, 298

Read, Bill, 300–1

Read, (Sir) Herbert, 107, 109, 142, 168, 273

Reality and Dreams (MS), 377, 425, 505, 511–12, 514–17, 528

Redgrave, Vanessa, 325, 331

Reid, Alastair, 273

Rhodes, Clifford, 132–3

Rhodesia *see* Southern Rhodesia

Rhodesian Eisteddfod Society, 54

Richards, Tom, 425

Rilke, Rainer Maria, 116

Robbe-Grillet, Alain, xviii, 316, 352–3, 378

Robinson (MS): as self-revelation, xix, 189–90; writing, 171, 173, 176, 182, 485; publication and reception, 180, 186–7, 191–3, 198; Paul Scott on, 183–4, 225; plot and themes, 187–91, 193, 432

Roebuck (publishing house), 136

Rome: MS moves to, 172, 317, 320, 326, 328–31; MS visits, 249, 299, 311–12; character, 311–12, 329, 338, 361–3; MS's discomfort in, 335–6; MS settles in (Palazzo Taverna), 343–5, 360–1; MS's social life in, 345–8; MS seeks seclusion in, 367; MS writes on for *New Yorker*, 390–1; MS's disenchantment with, 390, 414; MS's article on, 453

Romulus Films, 343

Rosenberg, Elizabeth, 195–7

Rosenberg, John, 195–7, 343; *The _Desperate Art*, 194

Rosenbloom, Jessie, 303, 415

Rosenbloom, John, 415, 425

Rospigliosi, Princess Margherita, 346

Ross, Lillian, 275

Rossellini, Franco, 397, 402

Rossini, Gioacchino Antonio: *La Cenerentola*, 187

Royal Literary Fund: award to Stanford, 113

Royal Society of Edinburgh: MS elected to honorary Fellowship, 519

Royal Society of Literature: awards Companionship to MS, 504

Rubinstein, Hilary, 257

Rubinstein, Michael, 287, 333, 402

Rule, Professor and Mrs, xvi, 5–6, 498

Runcie, Robert, Archbishop of Canterbury, 480

Russell, Peter, 109

Rutger's University: MS's post as Writer in Residence, 310, 313–15

Sachs, Sam, 314

Sacks, Oliver, 499

Sagan, Françoise, 500

Sage, Lorna, 415–17, 422, 500

St Albans, Hertfordshire, 133, 186–7

St Just, Maria, 439, 501

St Martin's Press (New York publishers), 497

St Mary Abbots church, Kensington, 134, 439

Saints and Ourselves (publisher's series), 174

Salvator Mundi (hospital), Rome, 357–9, 370, 403, 426, 450–1, 506

Salzburg Festival, 309, 311

San Diego, California, 452–3

San Giovanni (house), near Arezzo: Jardine renovates, 412, 435, 449–50, 459, 477, 593; as Jardine's home, 412–13, 423, 453; MS stays in, 414–15, 426, 435, 440–2, 449, 453, 459; social life at, 437; MS threatens to withhold contributions to, 451; MS settles in, 470, 476, 493–4, 499; MS returns to after operations, 510; burgled, 522, 525; MS investigates history, 522

Sanson, Rotha, 72

Sayre, Nora, 305–7, 313, 318, 322

Schiff, Stephen, 193, 507

Sciascia, Leonardo, 526

Scotland on Sunday (newspaper), 534

Scotsman (newspaper): publishes extracts from *Curriculum Vitae*, 504

Scott, Paul: as MS's agent, 141, 142, 181, 183–4, 186, 195, 198–9, 210, 218, 227; marriage relations, 197; view of MS, 219; friendship with MS, 225, 228; praises *The Bachelors*, 232; and MS's view of Macmillan's, 239; alcoholism and depression, 250; MS introduces Strutt to, 436; death, 459; meets Tennessee Williams at Strutt's, 501–2; Spurling's biography of, 501; *The Chinese Love Pavilion*, 225, 228

Scott, Sir Walter: MS lectures on, 509

Scottish Television, 433

Season, Edmund, 468

Selected Poems of Emily Brontë (ed. MS), 136, 138

Selincourt, Ernest de, 109

'Seraph and the Zambesi, The' (MS; story), 45, 51, 123–9, 131, 155, 378

Sergeant, Deirdre (Howard's daughter), 85, 88–9, 91

Sergeant, Dorothy (Howard's wife), 85, 88–9, 91, 93

Sergeant, Howard: ends relationship with MS, 42, 98; at Poetry Society, 79, 82–4, 86; affair with MS, 84–91, 93–4, 96–7, 111, 180, 273; qualities, 84, 100; relations with wife, 88, 91, 93; visits Edinburgh, 90; resigns from Poetry Society, 97; resumes relationship with MS, 99, 101–2; portrayed in Loitering, 104, 443; Stanford discusses MS with, 111; writes on Wordsworth, 112; MS sends poem to, 121–2, 137; and Heppenstall, 180; reprints MS's poem 'Sin', 331; effect on MS, 528

Sesame Club, London, 183

Sewell, Father Brocard, 162, 212, 245

Seymour, William Kean, 80–4, 87, 92–5, 97

Seymour-Smith, Martin, 393, 449

Shankman, Dr (of Southern Rhodesia), 55–6

Shaw, George Bernard, xx

Shawn, William, 257, 269, 275–6, 278, 390–1, 487–8

She (magazine), 481

Sheed & Ward (publishers), 143, 150

Sheed, Frank, 143–4, 153, 156, 165, 167

Sheehan, Neil, 302

Shelley, Mary: letters, 112, 114, 135; MS writes on, 112, 115–18, 126, 267, 470, 472–3, 477; Frankenstein, 117; The Last Man, 142, 158; Letters (ed. Burnett), 473

Shelley, Percy Bysshe, 115–17, 470

Shepherd, Peter, 402

Shrapnel, Norman, 24, 319

Side Effects, The (MS): writing, 341

'Side Roads of Tuscany' (MS; travel piece), 464–5

'Sin' (MS; poem), 331

Singer, Isaac Bashevis, 277

Sitwell, Dame Edith, 183–4

Small Telephone, The (MS; children's story), 324, 328, 332

Small, William & Sons (department store), 40

Smart, Jeffrey, 437, 476, 518

Smith, Corlies ('Cork'), 257–8, 278–9, 282

Smith, John (literary agent): as MS's agent, 163; MS and Stanford leave, 181; MS returns to, 226–7, 239; and MS's trip to Israel, 244, 246; sells Brodie to New Yorker, 249; and MS's answer to critics of Brodie, 253; and MS's retreat to Aylesford Priory, 256; deters MS's mother, 264; researches for MS, 265

Smith, (Dame) Maggie: in film of Miss Jean Brodie, 31

Smith, Stevie, 221

Smith, William G., 237

Snow, C. P. (later Baron), 230, 267, 378, 436

Society of Authors: dispute with Kyle, 80; MS joins, 101; and MS's negotiations with Macmillan, 470; on intellectual property, 521

Socrates, 495

'Song of the Divided Lover' (MS; poem), 100

Sonkin, Robert, 273, 276

Southern Rhodesia (later Zimbabwe): MS in, xxiv; conditions, 48–9; in Second World War, 57

Spark, Louis (MS's brother–in–law), 47

Spark, Dame Muriel
  HEALTH: hallucinations and paranoia, xxiii–xxiv, 151–7, 193, 396, 443; appendectomy, 76; takes Dexedrine, 150, 153–4; depressions and nervous exhaustion, 245, 336, 433; delicate health, 302, 312, 335, 357, 370; hysterectomy, 357, 361; hernia, 402–3; dental problems, 403, 450; fractures toe, 425; slipped disc, 450–1; breaks ribs in serious accident, 470; hospital bills, 490; suffers acute pain from surgical mistakes, 499, 506, 508–11; hip problem, 503; operation for hip

Spark, Dame Muriel—*contd*

HEALTH—*contd*

replacement, 505–6; enters Springfield Clinic, Chelmsford, 508; further operation on spine, 510; problems in old age, 511; cataract operation, 526–7; kidney removed for cancer, 530–1

HONOURS & AWARDS: literary prizes as schoolgirl, 38; wins Italia Prize, 240, 266, 292; OBE, 334–6; French short story prize, 476, 478; wins Saltire Society's Scottish Book of Year Award, 478; made Companion of Literature by Royal Society of Literature, 504; wins T. S. Eliot Award (1992), 506; appointed DBE, 508; France makes Commandeur de l'Ordre des Arts et des Lettres, 511; David Cohen British Literature Prize, 516; wins Arts Council of Scotland Spring Book Prize, 517; honorary D.Litt. at Oxford, 519; honorary Fellowship of Royal Society of Edinburgh, 519; made honorary citizen of *comune* in Italy, 530

INTERESTS & ACTIVITIES: studies Catholic teaching, 139, 144; acquires Persian kitten ('Bluebell'), 163; and death of pet cat ('Bluebell'), 199; interest in developing theatrical career, 309; attends race meetings, 312; buys painting, 312; buys racehorses, 317, 324, 331, 428; buys motor cars, 428, 449, 478, 490, 506

LITERARY LIFE: reputation and success, xv, 180–2, 201, 229, 232–3; autobiographical elements in fiction, xix, 53, 103, 130, 133–4, 165, 170, 189, 214–16, 221, 267, 294, 299, 301, 315, 396, 443, 515, 525, 483–6; personal archive, xxi–xxiii, 334; reading, 37, 129, 144, 447; juvenile poetry, 38–9; as General Secretary of Poetry Society and editor of *Poetry Review*, 42, 78–82, 86, 92, 95; short story writing on Africa, 45–6, 49, 51–3, 217; amorality in writings, 70; poetry, 76, 110; dismissed from Poetry Society, 97; writes on Wordsworth, 109–10; on origin of inspiration and creation, 110, 125, 128, 169; collaborations with Stanford, 112; literary earnings, 112, 160, 165, 168, 187, 210, 229–30, 474; on Mary Shelley, 112, 115–18; portrayed in Stanford's 'Goodbye Bohemia', 113–14; poetic influences on, 116; radio and TV broadcasts, 118, 233, 237, 379–80, 412, 478, 483, 491; reviews and journalistic essays, 120, 134, 144–5, 148; wins *Observer* Christmas short-story competition, 122–3; Memorandum Book, 130; publications and literary successes, 136–7; reports on Edinburgh Festival, 144–5; working methods, 158, 168–9, 171–2; Maclean commissions short story from, 168; radio plays and adaptations, 180, 212; stimulated by writing, 218–19; independence in literary business management, 219–20; firm dealings with agents and publishers, 225–7, 230–2, 234, 237–8, 259, 278–9, 309, 437–8, 469, 474–6; declines Macmillan's financial package, 239–40, 250–1, 255–6; international celebrity, 247, 253, 257, 266; transfers to Knopf in New York, 279–81; refuses to read Stanford's biography, 287; letters and papers valued for sale, 288; as Writer in Residence at Rutger's University, 310, 313–15; on construction in writing, 315–16; threatens to sue Mayer over paperback edition of *The Comforters*, 321; demands on style and printing of works, 330; loses von

Auw as agent, 332; revises business arrangements with von Auw, 333; delivers Blashfield Address in New York, 360, 369–70; narrative voice, 366–7; interviewed by Toynbee for *Observer*, 378–9; manuscripts sorted and catalogued by Gotham Book Mart, 402; leaves Macmillan, 438–40; stories published by Dutton and Bodley Head, 473–4; cancels launch trip to London, 479, 481; sales of books, 494; dispute with Hilary Spurling over Paul Scott story, 501–2; gives reading in New York, 507; *New Yorker* article on, 507–8; writes internet diary for Microsoft, 511–13; and questions of intellectual property, 521

PERSONAL LIFE: family background and upbringing, xvi–xvii, xix–xxi, 1–3, 7–9, 20, 35; privacy, xvi, xxiii; complex character, xxiv–xxv, 21–2; birth, 1; relations with brother Philip, 1, 20–2, 43; in Watford with Uezzell relations, 11–12; relations with grandmother Adelaide, 13–15, 26; and word 'Bluebell', 18; schooling, 22–4, 28–30, 33, 35, 37–9; relations with men, 26–7, 33, 66, 77–8, 81, 137, 273–4, 292–3, 492, 513; appearance, 34, 38, 210, 257, 356, 362, 406; attitude to sex, 34–5, 41; fondness for father, 35; early religious experience, 36; imaginative and spiritual nature, 36; secretarial work, 40–2, 54; teaching, 40; Sergeant ends relationship, 42, 98–9; adolescent romances and boyfriends, 43; engagement and marriage to Ossie Spark, 43–4, 47, 445; life in Africa, 44–8, 50–3, 56, 70; unhappy marriage, 45, 47, 50–1, 53–4; pregnancy and birth of son, 49–50; sexuality, 53; divorce, 56, 144; moves to London (1944), 60;

wartime work with Sefton Delmer, 60–5, 68–9; relations with Colin Methven, 65–6, 74; social life in London, 65–7, 70–1, 74, 77, 250; solitary and private nature, 71, 126, 189–90, 201–2, 218–19, 238, 308, 311, 327, 344, 357; temporary jobs in London, 71; and Robin's arrival from Africa, 74–5; and care of Robin, 77; earnings, 79, 87, 173; affair with Sergeant, 84–91, 93–4, 96–7, 99, 101–2; relations with Stanford, 92, 94, 99–100, 102–8, 110–15, 117, 119–20, 126, 135, 140, 142–3, 150–1, 157–9, 161–2, 181–2, 186–7, 196–8, 202–4; hopes for reunion with son Robin, 98; moves to Vicarage Gate, 98; part-time employment, 98, 101, 103, 114, 120, 139, 160, 173; edits magazine *Forum*, 99, 101, 103–4, 107–9; post-war poverty, 103–4; conversion to Catholicism, 109–10, 150, 156, 297; protective feelings for Robin, 129–30; partings from Stanford, 132, 162, 171, 185–6; baptised into Anglican Church and confirmed, 133, 137; commitment to celibacy, 133–4; takes first Anglo-Catholic communion, 143; appeals to National Insurance tribunal, 152, 161; in Catholic social circle, 156–7; considers becoming nun, 160; financial difficulties, 160–1; retreats to Aylesford Priory, Kent, 161–5, 172, 199, 256, 265; Robin describes, 163; cuts up grandmother's bluebell dress, 167; recovery from delusions, 167; moves to Camberwell, 171–3; and Stanford's new love, 196–7; on prospect of death, 208; interviews and publicity, 210–12, 220, 228–9, 237–8, 326–7, 405–7, 415–17, 427, 433, 468, 478–80, 520, 536; public image, 228–9, 302, 322, 347, 375, 411; expands home in Camberwell flat, 240–1;

Spark, Dame Muriel—*contd*

PERSONAL LIFE—*contd*

Jewish lineage and inheritance, 241–3, 245, 379, 382, 460, 518, 535; as confidante, 250; and father's death, 261–2, 531; breaks contact with Edinburgh family, 264; financial means, 264, 317, 325, 469, 477; financial support for mother, 264; power of foresight, 271; power over friends, 272; defends Shawn, 276; alienated by Rachel MacKenzie, 277–8; later relations with mother and Robin, 288–90, 327; and practice of virtue, 291–2; social circle in New York, 302; prepares to leave London, 304, 309; relations with George Nicholson, 307–8, 322; outspokenness, 308, 322; burgled, 310, 417, 522, 525; drinking, 314, 322; income tax and accountancy concerns, 318, 339–41; quarrels with and casts off friends and acquaintances, 321–2; sells off Camberwell possessions, 323; resident alien status in USA, 324, 326; granted UK tax exemption, 326; liaison with Bassett, 328, 332–3; photographed by Bauer, 331; handwriting, 337; pet cats in Rome, 338, 343, 397, 406; social life in Rome, 338, 345–8, 365, 415; dispute with Bonagura over tax affairs, 339; settles in Palazzo Taverna, Rome, 343–5, 355, 360–1; relations with Ambrosiani, 357–62, 365, 376–7; self-doubts, 360–1; moves to new Rome apartment, 372–4; Italian manservant, 373–4; home life in Rome, 374–5; sued by butler for unfair dismissal, 374, 385; friendship with Strutt, 385; attends mother's funeral, 400, 405; appointments diaries, 403; buys flat at Nemi, 405, 450; relations with Jardine, 412–15,

423–4, 426, 428, 434–5, 450–1, 459, 470; entertains Lionel Daiches in Rome, 413–14; contentment in old age, 427, 429; changes will, 428, 460; sixtieth birthday, 428; moves into Jardine's San Giovanni house, 435; buys and occupies Vicolo del Gallo apartment, 440–2, 450–1, 453; engages Ginna as 'au pair', 440–1; tension and argument with Jardine, 450–1; denies Robin's claims to Jewish forebears, 460–3; Moffat portrait, 460; sells Nemi flat, 470; re-encounters Brooke-Rose, 471–3; buys Manhattan apartment, 487–9; acquires fax machine, 493; dispute with Norman Page, 497–8; sells Rome flat, 509; struck by lightning, 521; spoken Italian, 529–30; limited religious observance, 530; death and funeral, 531–3; generosity, 534

TRAVELS: to Africa, 44, 47; makes way back to England via Cape Town, 57–9; moves to Rome, 172, 317, 320, 326, 328–9, 335–6; first trip to Europe, 212–16; plans trip to Holy Land, 228, 242; in Israel and Middle East, 244–7; visits USA, 256–8, 299, 310, 313, 452–3; revisits and works in New York, 263, 269–79, 282–3, 291, 303, 310, 324–5, 331, 452–3; in Europe, 299–300, 376–7, 428, 430–1, 446–7, 451, 454–6, 459, 470, 476, 478, 490, 493, 501, 505, 517, 518–20; in Virgin Islands, 299–300; visits Mexico, 299, 305; visits Florence, 363; trip to Ireland with de Breffny and Mott, 386–7; to India, 397–8; restlessness in Italy, 424–5; revisits England with Jardine, 447, 449, 460; Mediterranean cruise, 489; holiday on Sylt, 501

VIEWS & OPINIONS: intellectual ambitions, 78; disparages psychoanalysis, 110; move towards

Christian faith, 122, 125, 130–2, 134–6, 145–50; on disaffection, 126, 131, 171; shift towards Catholicism, 143; Catholic view of marital status after divorce, 144; on sacramental, 148–9; on Time, 148–9; attitude to Catholic faith and practices, 158–9, 162, 307, 381; on acceptance of matter as fact, 207; on evil, 235; rejects class feelings, 241; and anti-Semitism, 245–6; on transfiguration, 247–8; on academic women, 267; and contemporary world events, 296; opposes censorship, 380; on freeing spirit from material concerns, 442–3; attitude to servants, 454–5; on religion, 480

Spark, Rebecca (Ossie's sister), 62

Spark, Robin (MS's son; 'Sonny'): birth, 49–50; childhood in Africa, 54, 61–2, 71–2; custody after parents' divorce, 56–7, 75–6, 87, 89, 92; travels to England, 72–5; in Edinburgh with grandparents, 75, 77, 90–2, 96, 135, 250; MS's attitude to care of, 77, 160; and MS's relations with Sergeant, 88; proposed move to Reigate school abandoned, 92, 96; Morecambe holiday with MS and family, 115; MS's protective feelings for, 129–30; celebrates bar mitzvah, 130; and MS's baptism, 135; and MS's relations with Stanford, 135; and MS's prospective taking the veil, 160; not told of MS's hallucinations, 167; MS's relations with as adult, 201, 204, 226, 256, 288, 400–1, 405, 412, 415, 427, 490, 501, 534–5; National Service, 204; *The Ballad of Peckham Rye* dedicated to, 204; MS proposes buying sports car for, 210; holiday in Wales with MS, 212; works in jeweller's shop, 250; apparent dependency on grandparents and MS, 251; and grandfather's death, 263; antique dealing, 288–9; and Cissy's

broken leg, 303; engagement, 327; takes Civil Service job, 327; drawing and illustrating, 328; and Cissy's illness and death, 398, 400; Lionel Daiches befriends, 414; as Chief Clerk to Scottish Law Commission, 428; asks MS to acknowledge Jewish lineage, 460–4; cuts out MS from life, 462; in *Curriculum Vitae*, 489–90; career as portrait artist, 490, 535; emphasises Jewishness, 518, 535; excluded from MS's will, 529

Spark, Sydney Oswald (Solly; Ossie): mental instability, 39, 46–7, 49–50, 56, 62, 71, 75, 144; background and character, 43, 47; engagement and marriage to MS, 44, 47; marriage relations, 45, 47, 50–1, 54–5, 111, 144; life in Africa, 49; army service, 54–5; harasses MS, 55; and custody of son Robin, 56–7, 89, 92; divorce from MS, 56, 72, 144; expected return from Africa, 61–2; letters from MS, 62; and MS's writing, 71; travels back to England, 72–3, 275; in Edinburgh, 75; disgraced over assault on pupil, 92; effect on MS's later life, 273

Spender, (Sir) Stephen, 273

Spielberg, Stephen: *Hook* (film), 521

Springfield Clinic, Chelmsford, 508–10

Sproxton, Judy, 497

Spurling, Hilary, 142, 495, 503; *Paul Scott: A Life*, 501–2

Sri Lanka, 398

Stafford Hotel, London, 323

Stanbrook Abbey, Worcestershire, 160, 189

'Standing in Dusk' (MS; poem), 89

Stanford, Derek: literary criticism of MS's work, xxii; and MS's early sexual experience with brother, 35; on autobiographical elements in MS's works, 53; on own thinking, 78; relations with MS, 92, 94, 100, 102–8, 110–15, 117, 119–20, 126, 135, 140, 142–3,

Stanford, Derek—*contd*
150–1, 157–9, 161–2, 167, 181–2, 186–7, 196–8, 202–4, 273, 528; aesthetic discussions with MS, 96; resigns from Poetry Society, 97; character and appearance, 99–100, 107–8, 114; co-edits *Forum* with MS, 99, 107–9; literary activities and ambitions, 104–8, 112–13, 140; portrayed in *Loitering*, 104, 211, 443; co-edits *Tribute to Wordsworth* and *My Best Mary* with MS, 109, 112; and Christopher Fry, 112–14, 119; grant from Royal Literary Fund, 113; literary decline, 119; and MS's winning *Observer* short-story competition, 123; and MS's move to church, 131–2, 143, 145; and MS's insistence on chastity, 132–3, 144; hesitancy over marriage to MS, 134, 136; and proposed book on Emily Brontë with MS, 136, 140; mother's correspondence with MS, 137; partings from MS, 137, 162, 167, 171, 185–6; in Old Brompton Road flat, 139; and MS's hallucinations, 153, 167, 190; and MS's religious doubts and commitment, 158–60; submits MS's appeal to National Insurance tribunal, 161; runs MS's business affairs, 163; co-edits Newman letters with MS, 174, 181, 202; secures Greene's recommendation of *The Comforters*, 176, 178; reviews *The Comforters*, 181–2; intervenes to support Robin, 185; finds new love, 194–7, 201; on Heppenstall's attempted seduction of MS, 194; psychological problems, 194; disappears, 199–200; reveals MS's breakdown to her parents, 199, 201; and MS's sense of isolation, 201–2; marriage, 202; operation for gallstones, 202; in MS's fiction, 214; writes on MS's life and work, 287; sells letters from MS, 288, 337, 407, 504; and MS's *The Public Image*, 332, 336–7, 352; on *The Driver's Seat*, 368; reviews *Not to Disturb*, 383; and MS's *Hothouse*, 396; portrayed in *A Far Cry*, 484–7, 529; in Norman Page's study, 497–8; in *Curriculum Vitae*, 504, 529; registers last will and testament, 529; 'The Dug–Out' (story), 194; *Fénelon's Spiritual Letters*, 181; *The Freedom of Poetry*, 107; 'Goodbye Bohemia: An Idyll' (unfinished novel), 113–14, 181, 194; *Inside the Forties*, 114, 133, 497; 'A Mug's Game' (unpublished autobiography), 142; *Muriel Spark: A Biographical and Critical Study*, 287; *Music for Statues*, 92, 107; 'Poem in Separation', 137

Stannard, Martin: MS accepts as biographer, 504–5; receives copy of MS's 'Memorandum', 508; correspondence with MS, 518, 521

Steegmuller, Francis, 271–2, 274, 276, 284, 299, 404

Stein, Beatrice, 271

Steinberg, Saul, 273

Stevens, George, 278

Stockholm: MS visits, 299, 303

Stone, Grace Zaring ('Ethel Vance'), 363

Stonor-Saunders, Frances, 493

Stopes, Marie, 82, 87, 95

Storey, David: *Radcliffe*, 298; *This Sporting Life*, 223

Storrs, Sir Ronald, 94

Strachan, Tony, 163, 220

Straneo, Contessa, 347

Strutt, Guy: and de Breffny, 385, 387–8; MS meets, 385; on tour of India with MS, 397; researches for MS, 406, 425, 483, 498–9; and MS at Nemi, 414; MS visits in England, 415, 418, 439, 449, 470, 473, 478, 500, 501; witnesses MS's will, 428; friendship and support for MS, 435, 493; qualities, 436–7; and MS's writing about people, 446; finds house-sitters for MS, 447; and MS's differences with Jardine, 451; and MS's writing stories, 453; and MS's dealings with publishers, 469, 476; and MS's cancelled trip to England, 479; and MS's meeting with Tennessee Williams and Paul Scott, 502; and MS's deteriorating physical condition, 508; letters from MS, 509, 519; suffers stroke on visit to MS, 517

Sugarman, Dr Rose, 56

Sunday Times: commissions Mediterranean cruise for MS, 489; award to MS, 500; MS wins costs from over Paul Scott story, 503; publishes extracts from *Curriculum Vitae*, 504

Sussex Mansions, Old Brompton Road, London, 112–14, 137, 150, 162

Swan, Michael, 200

Swift, Richard, 276–7, 287, 300, 302

Swinburne, Algernon Charles, 138

Switzerland, 401

Sylt (island), 501

Symons, Arthur, 138

Symons, Julian, 392

Symposium (MS): on freeing the spirit, 443; on master–servant relationships, 454; writing, 491, 493; plot and themes, 492, 495–7; publication and reception, 494–5; read on BBC radio, 494

Tablet (journal), 158, 391

Takeover, The (MS): writing, 385, 387, 397–8, 401, 404–5, 407, 414; plot and themes, 413, 417–22; publication, 415–16, 426; reception, 418, 420, 423–4, 474; in USA, 423–4; screenplay, 435; paperback sales, 474

Tambimuttu, Meary James, 79, 82

Tate, Allen, 291–2

Tate, Isabella, 291–2

Taylor, Alan, 520

Taylor, Elizabeth, 397, 435

Tennyson, Sir Charles, 94

Terling, Essex, 449, 473, 500, 508

Territorial Rights (MS): writing, 413, 425, 501; plot, 429–32, 462; publication and reception, 429, 432, 438; proofs, 431;

MS negotiates advance, 437; misprint in blurb, 438; sales, 474

Texas, University of, 288

'They Sigh for Old Dreams' (MS; poem), 76

Thomas, Dylan, 140, 480

Thomson, J. W. M., 228

'Three Thoughts in Africa' (MS; poem), 76

Tickell, Geoffrey, 181

Time magazine, 319, 393, 409

Times, The: reviews *The Mandelbaum Gate*, 319

Tomalin, Claire, 368, 383, 432, 482

Tonnac-Villeneuve, Souny, Contesse G. de, 397, 416, 418

Tower Bridge Publications, 120, 140

Toynbee, Philip, 123–4, 378–9

Toynbee, Polly, 481

Tracy, Honor, 191

Transatlantic Review, 311

'Transfiguration of the Commonplace, The' (Sandy Stranger's treatise in *Brodie*), 248

Treece, Henry, 83

Treglown, Jeremy, 449

Trevor, William, 351

Tribute to Wordsworth (ed. MS and Stanford), 109, 112, 119

Trilling, Diana, 271, 273–4

Trilling, Lionel, 256–7, 270–1, 273–4

T. S. Eliot Award: MS wins, 478, 506

Tulsa, University of, 288, 495

Tuohy, Frank, 192, 437, 441

Twentieth-Century Fox film corporation, 331, 333, 364

Uezzell, Adelaide (MS's maternal grandmother): moves to MS's Edinburgh home, 5, 13–14; life in Watford, 8–10, 13; character, 10–13, 15, 175; as 'Gentile Jewess', 11, 242; incapacitated, 15; influence on MS, 16, 26, 242; death, 17, 37; disputed Jewish origins and lineage, 461–4

Uezzell, Alice (MS's aunt), 9

Uezzell, Bessie (Harry's wife), 10

Uezzell, Harry (MS's uncle), 10, 33

Uezzell, Hilda (MS's cousin), 12

Uezzell, John (Tom's father), 11

Uezzell, Phil (MS's uncle), 9–10, 12–14

Uezzell, Phyllis (MS's cousin), 9–10, 12, 14, 19

Uezzell, Roger (MS's cousin), 9, 12, 19

Uezzell, Tom (MS's maternal grandfather), 5, 8, 11–14, 461, 463

United States of America: MS published in, 181–2, 186, 209, 223, 232, 249, 255, 282, 382, 423, 448, 489, 494; MS visits, 256–7, 299, 310, 313, 452–3; MS applies for and receives resident alien status, 324–5; MS's tax dues, 339–40; and Watergate scandal, 398, 401, 408; MS's promotional tour for TV version of *Brodie*, 433–4; *see also* New York

Unterberg's Poetry Center, New York, 507

Updike, John: praises MS in *New Yorker*, 232; meets MS in New York, 256, 273; on *The Bachelors*, 297; praises *Girls of Slender Means*, 298; silence over *Hothouse*, 393; reviews *Abbess*, 408, 410; reviews *The Takeover*, 424; criticises *The Only Problem*, 465–6; on *Reality and Dreams*, 516

Ustinov, (Sir) Peter, 91

V-1 flying bombs, 63

Vaizey, Marina, 411

Vallon, Annette, 109

Vance, Ethel *see* Stone, Grace Zaring

Vatican: relations with Israel, 390–2

Venice, 430–2

Verlaine, Paul, 116

'Verlaine Villanelle' (MS; poem), 121

Vestley, Mrs William, 99

Vicarage Gate, Kensington: MS's flat in, 98, 101

Vicolo del Gallo: MS buys Jardine's apartment in, 440–2, 446, 450–1, 453, 487

Victoria Falls, 50–1, 128

Victoria, Queen, 406

Vidal, Gore, 364–5, 428, 499

Viking Penguin (publishers), 401, 407, 424, 526; *see also* Penguin Books

Villa Donatello (hospital), Florence, 530

Virgin Islands: MS visits, 299–300

Visconti, Luchino, 390

Voices at Play (MS; collection), 240, 249, 254, 309, 330

VZV Foundation, 512

Wade, Rosalind (Mrs W.K. Seymour), 84

Wain, John, 232, 255, 378

Walker, Alexander, 384

Waller, John, 100, 142

Walshe, Teresa, 172, 198

Walter, Eugene: in Rome, 249, 311–12, 328, 330–1, 335, 341, 343, 347, 358, 421; friendship with MS, 338, 346, 361, 415; falls out with MS, 358–9

Walton, Sir William and Susana, Lady, 388, 436

Ward, Maisie, 143

Ward, Stephen, 162

Warhol, Andy, 397

Warne, Arthur, 264, 309, 317, 334, 342

Warrender Chase (MS; unfinished novel), 444

Washington Post, 393

Watergate scandal, 398, 401, 408–9

Watford, 7–12, 14–15

Watling Street (MS; unpublished), 425, 447, 515

Watson, David, 403

Watson, Sheila, 218

Waugh, Auberon, 250, 351, 393, 418–20, 448

Waugh, Evelyn: as Catholic writer, xv, 179; on MS's saintliness, 36; schoolboy writings, 38; mental problems, 152–3, 164; advises MS to move from Camberwell, 172; praises *The Comforters*, 176, 178–9; use of dialogue, 206; praises *Memento Mori*, 209; black comedy, 222; praises *The Bachelors*, 233; admires *Brodie*, 254; and Acton, 436; MS reviews Stannard biography, 504; *Brideshead Revisited*, 285; *A Handful of Dust*, 208; *Helena*, 425; *The Ordeal of Gilbert Pinfold*, 164–5; *Unconditional Surrender*, 254; *Vile Bodies*, 127

Wavell, Field Marshal Archibald, 1st Earl, 83–4, 86, 94

Weaver, William, 437, 476, 487–8

Weidenfeld, George, Baron, 439

Weightman, John, 411

Weil, Simone, 155

Wells, Father, 132

West, Dame Rebecca, 350–1, 356

White, Edmund, 432

Whitehall News (journal), 98

Whitehead, Robert, 354

Wilde, Oscar: 'The Decay of Lying', 353–4

Williams, Bruce, 382

Williams, Tennessee, 436, 501–2

Wilson, A. N., 448, 465, 478

Wilson, (Sir) Angus, 265, 378, 436, 439, 451, 501

Wilson, Edmund, 274, 302

Wilson, Harold (*later* Baron), 331, 402

Wingate, Alan, 106, 140

Winter, Fred, 281, 317, 324

Winterkorn, Joan, 501, 508

Winter's Tales (Macmillan series), 168–9

Winterson, Jeannette, 521

Wittgenstein, Ludwig, 131

Woburn Abbey, 61

Wolfe, Tom, 276

Wollstonecraft, Mary, 115

Woman's Hour (radio programme), 491

Women's Review, 101, 108

Wood, Peter, 325

Woodcock, George, 142

Woolf, Virginia: MS on, xx, 480

Wordsworth, Dorothy, 106

Wordsworth, William, MS edits centenary volume on, 106, 109–10

World Review, 135

World War I: effects, 10, 33

World War II: outbreak, 50, 54

Worsley, T. C., 266

Wright, Billy, 20

Wyndham's Theatre, London, 469

Wynne-Tyson, John, 286–7, 292

Yeatman, Robert, 265–6, 289, 310

Yeats, William Butler, 116, 159, 377

'You, Dreamer' (MS; poem), 175

Young, Phyllis, 223

Zambesi river, 50–1, 128

'Zev' *see* Harris, Daniel

Zimbabwe ruins, 48